CRITICAL THINKING, READING, and WRITING

A Brief Guide to Argument

EIGHTH EDITION

CRITICAL THINKING, READING, and WRITING

A Brief Guide to Argument

SYLVAN BARNET
Professor of English, Tufts University

HUGO BEDAU
Professor of Philosophy, Tufts University

Bedford/St. Martin's   BOSTON ◆ NEW YORK

For Bedford / St. Martin's

Senior Developmental Editor: Adam Whitehurst
Senior Production Editor: Harold Chester
Senior Production Supervisor: Jennifer Peterson
Marketing Manager: Emily Rowin
Copy Editor: Virginia Perrin
Indexer: Melanie Belkin
Photo Researcher: Connie Gardner
Art Director: Lucy Krikorian
Text Design: Linda M. Robertson
Cover Design: Donna Dennison
Cover Photo: Igloo with Electricity © Thomas Roepke/Corbis
Composition: Cenveo
Printing and Binding: RR Donnelley-Crawfordsville

President, Bedford/St. Martin's: Denise B. Wydra
Editor in Chief: Karen S. Henry
Director of Development: Erica T. Appel
Director of Marketing: Karen R. Soeltz
Production Director: Susan W. Brown
Director of Rights and Permissions: Hilary Newman

Manufactured in the United States of America.

8 7 6 5 4 3
f e d c b a

For information, write: Bedford/St. Martin's, 75 Arlington Street, Boston, MA 02116 (617-399-4000)

ISBN: 978-1-4576-4997-4

Acknowledgments

Preface

This book is a text—a book about reading other people's arguments and writing your own arguments—and it is also an anthology—a collection of more than a hundred selections, ranging from Plato to the present, with a strong emphasis on contemporary arguments and, in this edition, new modes of argument, from documentary film trailers to political speeches to infographics. Before we describe these selections further, we'd like to describe our chief assumptions about the aims of a course that might use *Critical Thinking, Reading, and Writing: A Brief Guide to Argument.*

Probably most students and instructors would agree that, as *critical readers,* students should be able to

- Summarize accurately an argument they have read;
- Locate the thesis (the claim) of an argument;
- Locate the assumptions, stated and unstated, of an argument;
- Analyze and evaluate the strength of the evidence and the soundness of the reasoning offered in support of the thesis; and
- Analyze, evaluate, and account for discrepancies among various readings on a topic (for example, explain why certain facts are used, why probable consequences of a proposed action are examined or are ignored, or why two sources might interpret the same facts differently).

Probably, too, students and instructors would agree that, as *thoughtful writers,* students should be able to

- Imagine an audience and write effectively for it (for instance, by using the appropriate tone and providing the appropriate amount of detail);

- Present information in an orderly and coherent way;
- Be aware of their own assumptions;
- Locate sources and incorporate them into their own writing, not simply by quoting extensively or by paraphrasing but also by having digested material so that they can present it in their own words;
- Properly document all borrowings—not merely quotations and paraphrases but also borrowed ideas; and
- Do all these things in the course of developing a thoughtful argument of their own.

In the first edition of this book we quoted Edmund Burke and John Stuart Mill. Burke said,

> He that wrestles with us strengthens our nerves, and sharpens our skill. Our antagonist is our helper.

Mill said,

> He who knows only his own side of the cause knows little.

These two quotations continue to reflect the view of argument that underlies this text: In writing an essay one is engaging in a serious effort to know what one's own ideas are and, having found them, to contribute to a multisided conversation. One is not setting out to trounce an opponent, and that is partly why such expressions as "marshaling evidence," "attacking an opponent," and "defending a thesis" are misleading. True, on television talk shows we see right-wingers and left-wingers who have made up their minds and who are concerned only with pushing their own views and brushing aside all others. But in an academic community, and indeed in our daily lives, we learn by listening to others and also by listening to ourselves.

We draft a response to something we have read, and in the very act of drafting we may find—if we think critically about the words we are putting down on paper—we are changing (perhaps slightly, perhaps radically) our own position. In short, one reason that we write is so that we can improve our ideas. And even if we do not drastically change our views, we and our readers at least come to a better understanding of why we hold the views we do.

FEATURES

The Text

Parts One and Two   Critical Thinking and Reading (Chapters 1–4) and Critical Writing (Chapters 5–7), together offer a short course in methods of thinking about and writing arguments. By "thinking" we mean serious analytic thought, including analysis of one's own assumptions (Chapter 1); by "writing" we mean the use of effective, respectable techniques, not gimmicks (such as the notorious note a politician scribbled in the margin of the text of his speech: "Argument weak; shout here"). For a delightfully wry account of the use of gimmicks, we recommend that you consult "The Art of Controversy" in *The Will to Live* by the nineteenth-century German philosopher Arthur Schopenhauer. Schopenhauer reminds readers that a Greek or Latin quotation (however irrelevant) can be impressive to the uninformed and that one can knock down almost any proposition by loftily saying, "That's all very well in theory, but it won't do in practice."

We offer lots of advice about how to set forth an argument, but we do not offer instruction in one-upmanship. Rather, we discuss responsible ways of arguing persuasively. We know, however, that before one can write a persuasive argument, one must clarify one's own ideas—a process that includes arguing with oneself—to find out what one really thinks about a problem. Therefore, we devote Chapter 1 to critical thinking, Chapters 2, 3, and 4 to critical reading (Chapter 4 is about reading images), and Chapters 5, 6, and 7 to critical writing.

Parts One and Two together contain thirty-four readings (six are student papers) for analysis and discussion. Some of these essays originated as op-ed newspaper pieces, and we reprint some of the letters to the editor that they generated, so students can easily see several sides to a given issue. In this way students can, in their own responses, join the conversation, so to speak. (We have found, by the way, that using the format of a letter helps students to frame their ideas, and therefore in later chapters we occasionally suggest writing assignments in the form of a letter to the editor. In an e-Pages section on ethical arguments, we reprint three letters written by Randy Cohen of the *New York Times Magazine,* and we invite students to write their own responses.)

All of the essays in the book are accompanied by a list of Topics for Critical Thinking and Writing.[1] This is not surprising, given the emphasis we place on asking questions in order to come up with ideas for writing. Among the chief questions that writers should ask, we suggest, are "What is *X*?" and "What is the value of *X*?" (pp. 232–33). By asking such questions—for instance (to look only at these two types of questions), "Is the fetus a person?" or "Is Arthur Miller a better playwright than Tennessee Williams?"—a writer probably will find ideas coming, at least after a few moments of head scratching. The device of developing an argument by identifying issues is, of course, nothing new. Indeed, it goes back to an ancient method of argument used by classical rhetoricians, who identified a stasis (an issue) and then asked questions about it: Did

---

[1]With a few exceptions, the paragraphs in the essays are, for ease of reference, numbered in increments of five (5, 10, 15, and so on). The exceptions involve essays in which paragraphs are uncommonly long; in such cases, every paragraph is numbered.

X do such and such? If so, was the action bad? If bad, how bad? (Finding an issue or stasis—a position where one stands—by asking questions is discussed in Chapter 6.)

In keeping with our emphasis on writing as well as reading, we raise issues not only of what can roughly be called the "content" of the essays but also of what can (equally roughly) be called the "style"—that is, the *ways* in which the arguments are set forth. Content and style, of course, cannot finally be kept apart. As Cardinal Newman said, "Thought and meaning are inseparable from each other. . . . *Style is thinking out into language.*" In our Topics for Critical Thinking and Writing we sometimes ask the student

- To evaluate the effectiveness of an essay's opening paragraph,
- To explain a shift in tone from one paragraph to the next, or
- To characterize the persona of the author as revealed in the whole essay.

In short, the book is not designed as an introduction to some powerful ideas (though in fact it is that, too); it is designed as an aid to *writing* thoughtful, effective arguments on important political, social, scientific, ethical, legal, and religious issues.

The essays reprinted in this book also illustrate different styles of argument that arise, at least in part, from the different disciplinary backgrounds of the various authors. Essays by journalists, lawyers, judges, social scientists, policy analysts, philosophers, critics, activists, and other writers—including first-year undergraduates—will be found in these pages. The authors develop and present their views in arguments that have distinctive features reflecting their special training and concerns. The differences in argumentative styles found in these essays foreshadow the differences students will encounter in the readings assigned in many of their other courses.

Parts One and Two, then, offer a preliminary (but we hope substantial) discussion of such topics as

- Identifying assumptions;
- Getting ideas by means of invention strategies;
- Finding, evaluating, and citing printed and electronic sources;
- Interpreting visual sources;
- Evaluating kinds of evidence; and
- Organizing material

as well as an introduction to some ways of thinking.

Part Three Further Views on Argument consists of Chapters 8 through 13.

- Chapter 8, A Philosopher's View: The Toulmin Model, is a summary of the philosopher Stephen Toulmin's method for analyzing arguments. This summary will assist those who wish to apply Toulmin's methods to the readings in our book.

- Chapter 9, A Logician's View: Deduction, Induction, Fallacies, offers a more rigorous analysis of these topics than is usually found in composition courses and reexamines from a logician's point of view material already treated briefly in Chapter 3.

- Chapter 10, A Psychologist's View: Rogerian Argument, with an essay by psychotherapist Carl R. Rogers and an essay by a student, complements the discussion of audience, organization, and tone in Chapter 6.

- Chapter 11, A Rhetorician's View: Rhetorical Analysis of Nontraditional Texts, offers students strategies for analyzing and writing about artifacts of popular culture, from public service announcements to reality television.

- Chapter 12, A Literary Critic's View: Arguing about Literature, should help students to see the things literary critics argue about and *how* they argue. Students can apply what they learn not only to the literary readings that appear in the chapter (poems by Robert Frost and Andrew Marvell and a story by Kate Chopin) but also to the readings that appear in Part Six, Enduring Questions: Essays, a Story, Poems, and a Play. Finally, Part Three concludes with

- Chapter 13, A Debater's View: Individual Oral Presentations and Debate, which introduces students to standard presentation strategies and debate format.

- In e-Pages, A Moralist's View: Ways of Thinking Ethically consists of a discussion of amoral, immoral, and moral reasoning; A Checklist for Moral Reasoning; two challenging essays; and three short responses to highly specific moral questions.

- Also in e-Pages, A Lawyer's View: Steps toward Civic Literacy introduces students to some basic legal concepts, such as the distinction between civil and criminal cases, and then gives majority and minority opinions in two cases: burning the flag and establishing the right to an abortion. We accompany these judicial opinions with questions that invite the student to participate in these exercises in democracy.

Part Four   Finally, Part Four is a casebook on the state and the individual, consisting of Chapter 14, which asks the question, What Is the Ideal Society? The voices here include Thomas More, Niccolò Machiavelli, Thomas Jefferson, Elizabeth Cady Stanton, Martin Luther King Jr., and Ursula K. Le Guin.

WHAT'S NEW IN THE EIGHTH EDITION

We have made some significant changes in the eighth edition that we believe enrich the book and make the content more accessible.

Fresh and timely new readings. One-third of readings are new, as are a dozen topics such as student loan debt, locavorism, social media dependency, women in combat, the regulation of firearms, and online privacy. (In fact, the number of new readings is more than than one-third because some of these new essays were editorials and op-ed pieces that generated letters, some of which we have reprinted.)

A new chapter on rhetorical analysis of popular culture gives students a framework for making arguments about popular culture, from public service announcements to *Here Comes Honey Boo Boo*.

More help for research. This edition includes a new MLA research paper on corporate social responsibility and additional material about working with sources, including a heavily revised section on summary, paraphrase, and patchwriting (the practice of copying and pasting material from sources without appropriate integration or attribution).

More help with writing strategies. Three new Idea Prompts, or templates, offer strategies for establishing *ethos*, varying tone, and constructing Toulmin arguments. Three new checklists break down strategies for considering audience and conducting sound rhetorical analysis.

e-Pages for *Critical Thinking, Reading, and Writing* take advantage of what the Web can do with coverage of ethical and legal arguments as well as additional multimodal readings, from speeches to documentary film trailers. For example, students can watch a speech by President Obama on the death of Osama bin Laden and then answer questions about how such a speech seeks to connect with both Americans and a broader world audience. For a complete list of e-Pages, see the table of contents. Instructors can also use the free tools accompanying the e-Pages to download a syllabus, readings, and assignments to share with the class.

You and your students can access the e-Pages at **bedfordstmartins .com/barnetbedau**, the media page for *Crtical Thinking, Reading, and Writing*. Students receive access automatically with the purchase of a new book. If the activation code printed on the inside back cover of the student edition doesn't work, it might have expired. Students can purchase access at **bedfordstmartins.com/barnetbedau**. To get instructor access, register as an instructor at this site.

ACKNOWLEDGMENTS

Finally, it is our pleasant duty to thank those who have strengthened this book by their comments and advice on the seventh edition: Isabel Anderson, College of San Mateo; Kathryn Bartle Angus, California

State University, Fullerton; Larry Beason, University of South Alabama; Safet Dabovic, Stony Brook University; Daniel DeRoulet, Irvine Valley College; Helen Duclos, Arkansas State University; Scott Goldstone, Foothill College; Catherine Gorman, ECPI University; Melissa Heidari, Columbia College; Judy Joshua, Irvine Valley College; Meredith Love-Steinmetz, Francis Marion University; Rhea Mendoza, Hartnell College; Pamela Meyers, University of South Alabama; Coretta Pittman, Baylor University; Celeste Sonnier, Morton College; Peter Tatiner, Pace University; Mark Taylor, Berry College; and Mary Waguespack, Loyola University–New Orleans.

We would also like to thank Anthony Atkins, who graciously provided his feedback on the text and contributed a new chapter on rhetorical analysis and popular culture, and Martha Friedman, Connie Gardner, Linda Winters, and Margaret Gorenstein, who adeptly managed art research and text permissions.

We are also deeply indebted to the people at Bedford/St. Martin's, especially to our editor, Adam Whitehurst, who is wise, patient, supportive, and unfailingly helpful. Steve Scipione, Maura Shea, and John Sullivan, our editors for all of the preceding editions, have left a lasting impression on us and on the book; without their work on the first seven editions, there probably would not be a eighth. Others at Bedford/St. Martin's to whom we are deeply indebted include Charles H. Christensen, Joan E. Feinberg, Denise Wydra, Shuli Traub, and Harold Chester, all of whom have offered countless valuable (and invaluable) suggestions. Intelligent, informed, firm yet courteous, persuasive—all of these folks know how to think and how to argue.

YOU GET MORE DIGITAL CHOICES FOR *CRITICAL THINKING, READING, AND WRITING*

Critical Thinking, Reading, and Writing doesn't stop with a book. Online, you'll find both free and affordable premium resources to help students get even more out of the book and your course. You'll also find convenient instructor resources, such as downloadable sample syllabi, classroom activities, and even a nationwide community of teachers. To learn more about or order any of the products below, contact your Bedford/St. Martin's sales representative, e-mail sales support (sales_support@bedfordstmartins.com), or visit the Web site at **bedfordstmartins.com**.

Student Resources

ReWriting **3.0, bedfordstmartins.com/rewriting.** The best collection of open writing resources on the Web, *Re:Writing* 3.0 gives you and your students even more ways to think, watch, practice, and learn about writing concepts. Listen to Nancy Sommers on using a teacher's comments to revise. Try a logic puzzle. Consult our resources for writing centers. Send your students to free and open resources, choose flexible premium resources to supplement your print text, or upgrade to an expanding collection of innovative digital content.

Bedford e-Book to Go for *Critical Thinking, Reading, and Writing*. Students can purchase *Critical Thinking, Reading, and Writing* in downloadable e-book formats for computers, tablets, and e-readers. For more details, visit **bedfordstmartins.com/ctrw/formats**.

VideoCentral is a growing collection of videos for the writing class that captures real-world, academic, and student writers talking about how and why they write. VideoCentral can be packaged for free with *Critical Thinking, Reading, and Writing*. An activation code is required. To order VideoCentral packaged with the print book, use **ISBN 978-1-4576-7683-3**.

i-series

Add more value to your text by choosing one of the following tutorial series, free when packaged with *Critical Thinking, Reading, and Writing*. This popular series presents multimedia tutorials in a flexible format—because there are things you can't do in a book. To learn more about package options or any of the products below, contact your Bedford/St. Martin's sales representative or visit **bedfordstmartins.com**.

ix visualizing composition 2.0. (available online) helps students put into practice key rhetorical and visual concepts. To order *ix visualizing composition* packaged with the print book, use **ISBN 978-1-4576-7686-9**.

i-claim: visualizing argument 2.0. (available online) shows students how to analyze and compose arguments in words, images, and sounds with six tutorials, an illustrated glossary, and over seventy multimedia arguments. To order *i-claim: visualizing argument* packaged with the print book, use **ISBN 978-1-4576-7684-0**.

Instructor Resources

You have a lot to do in your course. Bedford/St. Martin's wants to make it easy for you to find the support you need—and to get it quickly.

Resources for Teaching Critical Thinking, Reading, and Writing is available in a PDF file that can be downloaded from **bedfordstmartins.com/barnetbedau/catalog**. In addition to chapter overviews and discussion prompts, *Resources for Teaching* includes suggested answers to the questions in the text.

TeachingCentral (**bedfordstmartins.com/teachingcentral**) offers the entire list of Bedford/St. Martin's print and online professional resources in one place. You'll find landmark reference works, sourcebooks on pedagogical issues, award-winning collections, and practical advice for the classroom—all free for instructors.

Bits **(bedfordbits.com)** collects creative ideas for teaching a range of composition topics in an easily searchable blog. A community of teachers—leading scholars, authors, and editors—discusses revision, research, grammar and style, technology, peer review, and much more. Take, use, adapt, and pass the ideas around. Then, come back to the site to comment or share your own suggestions.

Brief Contents

Contents

For readings that go beyond the printed page, see **bedfordstmartins.com/barnetbedau**.

PART TWO   CRITICAL WRITING   177

5 Writing an Analysis of an Argument   179

PART THREE   FURTHER VIEWS ON ARGUMENT   335

:e bedfordstmartins.com/barnetbedau

CRITICAL THINKING, READING, and WRITING

A Brief Guide to Argument

PART ONE

CRITICAL THINKING
and READING

Critical Thinking

What is the hardest task in the world? To think.

—RALPH WALDO EMERSON

I write entirely to find out what I'm thinking, what I'm looking at, what I see and what it means. What I want and what I fear.

—JOAN DIDION

In all affairs it's a healthy thing now and then to hang a question mark on the things you have long taken for granted.

—BERTRAND RUSSELL

Although Emerson said simply "to think," he clearly was using the word *think* in the sense of *critical thinking*. By itself, *thinking* can mean almost any sort of mental activity, from idle daydreaming ("During the chemistry lecture I kept thinking about how I'd like to go camping") to careful analysis ("I'm thinking about whether I can afford more than one week—say two weeks—of camping in the Rockies," or even "I'm thinking about whether Emerson's comment is true").

In short, when we add the adjective *critical* to the noun *thinking*, we eliminate reveries, just as we also eliminate snap judgments. We are talking about searching for hidden assumptions, noticing various facets, unraveling different strands, and evaluating what is most significant. The word *critical* comes from a Greek word, *krinein*, meaning "to separate," "to choose"; it implies conscious, deliberate inquiry, and especially it implies adopting a skeptical state of mind. To say that it implies a skeptical state of mind is by no means to say that it implies a self-satisfied faultfinding state of mind. Quite the reverse: Because critical thinkers seek to draw intelligent conclusions, they are sufficiently open-minded that they can adopt a skeptical attitude

- Toward *their own* ideas,
- Toward *their own* assumptions, and
- Toward the evidence *they themselves* tentatively offer,

"He saves all his critical thinking for my behavior."

as well as toward the assumptions and evidence offered by others. When they reread a draft they have written, they read it with a skeptical frame of mind, seeking to improve the thinking that has gone into it.

THINKING ABOUT DRIVERS' LICENSES AND PHOTOGRAPHIC IDENTIFICATION

By way of illustration, let's think about a case that was in the news in 2003. When Sultaana Freeman, an American Muslim woman in Florida, first applied for a driver's license, she refused on religious grounds to unveil her face for the photograph that Florida requires. She was allowed to remain veiled for the photo, with only her eyes showing. Probably in a response to the terrorist attacks of September 11, 2001, she was informed in 2002 that her license would be revoked if she refused to allow the Department of Motor Vehicles to photograph her face. She sued the state of Florida, saying that unveiling would violate her Islamic beliefs. "I'm fighting for the principle and the religious freedom of all people in the country," she said. "It's not about me."

Well, let's think about this—let's think critically, and, to do this, we will use a simple aid that is equal to the best word processor, a pencil. Your own experience has already taught you that thinking is largely a matter of association; one thought leads to another, as when you jot down "peanut butter" on a shopping list and then add "bread," and "bread" somehow reminds you—you don't know why—that you also need paper napkins. As the humorist Finley Peter Dunne observed, philosophers and cows have the gift of meditation, but "others don't begin to think till they begin to talk or write." So what are some thoughts that come to mind when we begin to talk or write about this Florida case?

Critical thinking means questioning not only the assumptions of others but also questioning *your own* assumptions. We will discuss this point at some length later in this chapter, but here we want to say only that when you write an argument, you ought to be *thinking*, evaluating evidence and assumptions, not merely collecting evidence to support a preestablished conclusion.

Back to the Florida case: Here is what we came up with in a few minutes, using a process called *clustering*. (We illustrate clustering again on page 230.)

In the center of a sheet of paper, we jotted down a phrase summarizing the basic issue, and then we began jotting down what must be the most obvious justification for demanding the picture—national

4. Not the point: She believes her face ought not to be seen by a cop who might ask for her license.

3. Compromise: Maybe have a woman photographer take the picture in private.

1. National security is more important than private beliefs.

2. Infringement on one's religious beliefs.

5. She is *not* being discriminated against, as a Muslim. All people who want a Florida license need a photo.

6. Not quite true. Temporary licenses are issued without a photo.

safety. (We might equally well have begun with the most obvious justifications for refusing to be photographed—religious belief and perhaps privacy, to think of arguments that Sultaana Freeman—or, more likely, her lawyer—might set forth.) Then we let our minds work, and one thought led to another. Sometimes almost as soon as we jotted down an idea we saw that it wasn't very good, but we made considerable progress.

In the illustration, we have added numbers to the ideas, simply so that you can see how our minds worked, which is to say how we jumped around. Notice, for instance, that our fifth point—our fifth idea—is connected to our first point. When we were rereading our first four jottings, the fifth idea—that she is not being discriminated against as a Muslim—came to mind, and we saw that it should be linked with the first point. Our sixth point—a modification of our fifth, occurred to us even before we finished writing the fifth. The sixth point, that temporary licenses in Florida are issued without photographs, prompted us to start thinking more vigorously about the arguments that Ms. Freeman, or her lawyer, might offer.

A very brief digression: A legal case is usually a matter of guilty or not guilty, right or wrong, yes or no. Of course in some trials a defendant can be found guilty of certain charges and innocent of others, but, again, it is usually an either/or situation: The prosecution wins, or the defense wins. But in many other aspects of life, there is room for compromise, and it may well be that *both* sides win—by seeing what ground they share and by developing additional common ground. We go into this topic at greater length on p. 392, where we discuss Rogerian argument (named for Carl Rogers, a psychotherapist) and in our introduction to several chapters that offer pairs of debates.

Now back to *Freeman v. State of Florida, Department of Highway Safety and Motor Vehicles*, where we began by trying to list arguments on one side versus arguments on the other.

- After making our seventh note, which goes back to the issue of religious liberty (hence we connected it with a line to the central issue) and which turned out to be an argument that the government rather than the plaintiff might make, we decided to keep thinking about government positions and wrote the eighth note—that some states do not require pictures on drivers' licenses.

- The ninth note—that the government is prohibiting a belief, not a harmful action—in some degree refutes our seventh note, so we connected it to the seventh.

Again, if you think with a pencil and a sheet of paper and let your mind make associations, you will find, perhaps to your surprise, that you have plenty of interesting ideas. Doubtless you will also have some not-so-interesting ones. We confess that we have slightly edited our

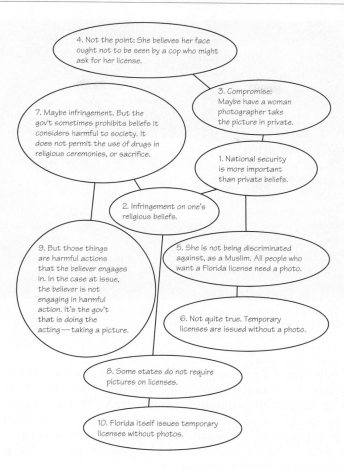

4. Not the point: She believes her face ought not to be seen by a cop who might ask for her license.

3. Compromise: Maybe have a woman photographer take the picture in private.

7. Maybe infringement. But the gov't sometimes prohibits beliefs it considers harmful to society. It does not permit the use of drugs in religious ceremonies, or sacrifice.

1. National security is more important than private beliefs.

2. Infringement on one's religious beliefs.

9. But those things are harmful actions that the believer engages in. In the case at issue, the believer is not engaging in harmful action. It's the gov't that is doing the acting—taking a picture.

5. She is not being discriminated against, as a Muslim. All people who want a Florida license need a photo.

6. Not quite true. Temporary licenses are issued without a photo.

8. Some states do not require pictures on licenses.

10. Florida itself issues temporary licenses without photos.

notes; originally they included two points that we are ashamed we thought of:

- "What is she complaining about? In some strict Islamic countries they don't even let women drive, period."
- "Being deprived of a license isn't a big deal. She can take the bus."

It will take only a moment of reflection to decide that these thoughts can scarcely be offered as serious arguments: What people do in strict Islamic countries has nothing to do with what we should do in ours, and that bus service is available is utterly irrelevant to the issue of whether this woman's rights are being infringed. Still, if a fear of making fools of ourselves had prevented us from jotting down ideas, we would not have jotted down any decent ideas, and the page would not have gotten written.

Plaintiff in *Freeman v. State of Florida, Department of Highway Safety and Motor Vehicles.*
(Peter Cosgrove/© AP/Worldwide Photos.)

The outcome of the driver's license photo case? Judge Janet C. Thorpe ruled against the plaintiff, explaining that "the State has always had a compelling interest in promoting public safety. That interest is served by having the means to accurately and swiftly determine identities in given circumstances." (You can read Judge Thorpe's entire decision online—sixteen highly readable double-spaced pages—by going to Google and typing in "Sultaana Lakiana.")

> **A RULE FOR WRITERS:** One good way to start writing an essay is to start generating ideas—and at this point don't worry that some of them may be nonsense. Just get ideas down on paper, and evaluate them later.

TOPICS FOR CRITICAL THINKING AND WRITING

1. Think about Judge Thorpe's comment, quoted in the preceding paragraph. Even if we agree that a photograph establishes identity—itself a debatable point—one might raise a question: Given the fact that Florida has not passed a law requiring a photo ID, why should it say that the driver of a vehicle must provide a photo ID? Isn't a driver's license a mere certification of permission to drive?

2. Judge Thorpe wrote the following as part of her explanation for her decision:

> Although the Court acknowledges that Plaintiff herself most likely poses no threat to national security, there likely are people who would be willing to use a ruling permitting the wearing of fullface cloaks in driver's license photos by pretending to ascribe to religious beliefs in order to carry out activities that would threaten lives.

Is the judge in effect saying that we should infringe on Sultaana Freeman's religious beliefs because someone else might do something wicked?

3. In England in 2006 a Muslim woman—a British citizen—was removed from her job as a schoolteacher because she wore a veil. The stated reason was that the veil prevented her from effectively communicating with children. What do you think of the view that a woman has a right to wear a veil, but when she enters the marketplace she may rightly be denied certain jobs? What are your reasons?

THINKING ABOUT ANOTHER ISSUE CONCERNING DRIVERS' LICENSES: ANALYZING AND EVALUATING MULTIPLE PERSPECTIVES

Let's think critically about a law passed in West Virginia in 1989. The law provides that although students may drop out of school at the age of sixteen, no dropout younger than eighteen can hold a driver's license. (Several states now have comparable laws.)

What ought we to think of such a law?

- Is it fair?
- What is its purpose?
- Is it likely to accomplish its purpose?
- Might it unintentionally cause some harm?
- If so, can we weigh the potential harm against the potential good? Who gains something and who loses something?

Suppose you had been a member of the West Virginia state legislature in 1989: How would you have voted? Why?

In thinking critically about a topic, we try to see it from all sides before we come to our conclusion. We conduct an argument with ourselves, advancing and then questioning opinions:

- What can be said *for* the proposition, and
- What can be said *against* it?

Our first reaction may be quite uncritical, quite unthinking: "What a good idea!" or "That's outrageous!" But critical thinking requires us to reflect further, trying to support our position *and also* trying to see the other side. One can almost say that the heart of critical thinking is a *willingness to face objections to one's own beliefs*, a willingness to adopt a skeptical attitude not only toward authority and toward views opposed to our own but also toward common sense—that is, toward the views that seem obviously right to us. If we assume we have a monopoly on the truth and we dismiss as bigots those who oppose us, or if we say our opponents are acting merely out of self-interest and we do not in fact analyze their views, we are being critical but we are not engaged in critical thinking.

> **A RULE FOR WRITERS:** Early in the process of jotting down your ideas on a topic, stop to ask yourself, "What might reasonably be offered as an *objection* to my view?"

In short, as we will say several times (because we think the point is basic, *argument is an instrument of learning* as well as of persuasion.

Critical thinking requires us to see things from perspectives other than our own and to envision the likely consequences of our positions. (This sort of imaginative thinking—grasping a perspective other than our own and considering the possible consequences of positions—is imperative if we want others to take our positions seriously.)

Thinking critically involves a twofold activity:

analysis, finding the parts of the problem and then separating them, trying to see how things fit together; and

evaluation, judging the merit of our claims and assumptions and the weight of the evidence in their favor.

If we engage in imaginative, analytic, and evaluative thought, we will have second and third ideas; almost to our surprise we may find ourselves adopting a position that we initially couldn't imagine we would hold. As we think about the West Virginia law, we might find ourselves coming up with a fairly wide variety of ideas, each triggered by the preceding idea but not necessarily carrying it a step further. For instance, we may think *X* and then immediately think, "No, that's not quite right. In fact, come to think of it, the opposite of *X* is probably true." We haven't carried *X* further, but we have progressed in our thinking.

Critical Thinking at Work: From Jottings to a Short Essay

We have already seen examples of **clustering** or **mapping** on pages 5 and 7, which is to say we have seen examples of *thinking* or, more specifically, generating ideas by imagining responses—counterthoughts—to first thoughts. Here is another example, this time showing a student's thoughts about the issue of whether homeschooled students should be permitted to participate in extracurricular activities, especially varsity sports, in public schools.

A first reaction might be, "Yes, of course. Their parents pay taxes, so the schools should be available, even if the parents have chosen not to make full use of them," or, on the other hand, a first reaction might be, "Certainly not. The parents have opted out of the system. School is not a cafeteria where one chooses the things one likes, and rejects the rest."

One of our students, Steve Jeffries, began by jotting down his first thoughts—and also the counterresponses that he himself generated. He numbered his notes so that we could easily see their sequence.

IDEA PROMPT 1.1 MAPPING PROS AND CONS

Should homeschooled students be allowed to play on public school sports teams?

Yes	No
1. Parents of homeschoolers pay taxes that support public schools.	2. But so what? They have chosen homeschooling. They have rejected the ideas of the public school.
3. Homeschooling is <u>officially</u> approved. These aren't truant students. It's just that they or their parents think they can do a better job on <u>some</u> things—not all things—than the public schools.	4. But it is unfair to deprive a public school student of the shot to play on the high school football team because an outside kid gets the spot.
5. Speaking of unfairness, is it fair to deprive a talented homeschooler of the possibility of an athletic scholarship? Or of participating in a National Academy of Science project?	6. Yes, it <u>is</u> fair. The public school students get the opportunity because they have competed under conditions that are monitored. They have their coursework standardized and their grades are monitored according to the same criteria as other students.
	7. By the way, I have learned that some homeschool proponents <u>oppose</u> the idea of kids participating in public school activities. They say it <u>weakens</u> the homeschool program.

A STUDENT'S ESSAY, DEVELOPED FROM
A CLUSTER AND A LIST

Steve Jeffries, the student who submitted the cluster or preliminary map of ideas concerning homeschooling, transformed the material into a list and ultimately wrote a short essay (the assigned essay was to be "250–500 words") on the topic. Notice that in the essay—the product of several revised drafts—the student introduced points he had *not* thought of when he was mapping, notably the material about the football player Tim Tebow. The cluster, in short, was a *first* step, not a road map of the final essay.

Play Ball! Why Homeschoolers Should Be Allowed to Play on Public School Teams

Perhaps the most famous homeschooler is Tim Tebow, now a star quarterback with the New York Jets, but how can a homeschooler have much chance to play high school football? How can a young person, however talented in a sport that is a team sport, further develop this talent if there is no team on which he or she can play? Fortunately for Tebow—and for football fans throughout the country—Tebow was raised in Florida, a state that allows homeschoolers to play on teams in their school districts. Most states are not so enlightened.

The chief arguments against homeschoolers playing on public school teams seem to be three: First, they (or their parents) have chosen *not* to participate in the public school system; second, if they do get on the team, they may deprive a public school student of his or her place on the team; and, third, public school students are eligible to play on a team only if they meet certain standards concerning grades and the number of courses they are taking, but homeschoolers sometimes are not evaluated in this way. A fourth argument comes, surprisingly, from some home-school parents themselves: Some of these parents say they do *not* want their children to participate in the extracurricular activities of the public school because such participation undermines the very idea of home-schooling. We do not need to consider this last objection, since if the parents don't want their children to participate in any of the activities, there is no problem for the public school, no question about whether the students are eligible.

The first argument is correct in saying that the parents have chosen to homeschool the children, but this does not mean, or should not mean, that the parents have also chosen to prevent the children from participating in extracurricular activities. It merely means that for various reasons the parents think they can do a better job of *teaching* their children than the public school system does—and the plan of the parents has been officially approved by the local school board. The plan concerns reading, writing, and 'rithmetic, not sports, or, for that matter, the chess team or the band. The second argument, about depriving a public school student of a place on the team, perhaps has some merit, but surely all members of a team want—for their *own* sake—all of the players to be the best available players, and if a homeschooler is (say) a better quarterback than any present student in the public school, almost surely the members of the team want the homeschooler. Chess players and musicians similarly want to play with the best players, knowing that their own skills are improved when they are teamed with superior players. Third, although homeschoolers are not always evaluated in terms of numbers of courses they are taking, everyone knows that homeschoolers (or at least their parents!) are very serious, and that homeschooled children are being well-educated.

Not every homeschooler is a Tim Tebow, who brought fame to his Florida high school, but every talented homeschooler ought to be given the opportunity to participate in extracurricular affairs in the local school if their parents are willing to let them. It's good for *all* of the people concerned and, what's more, it is fair, and fairness is part of what American education is about.

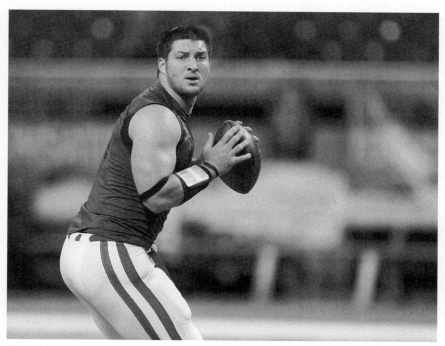

Tim Tebow

The Essay Analyzed

The title, by its first two words, immediately engages a reader's attention, and the subtitle states the thesis. This introductory material—a paper begins with its title, not with its first paragraph—lets the readers know where they will be going.

The first paragraph mentions a name familiar to many—probably to most—readers, and reminds them that Tebow was a homeschooler who was allowed to play on the team of a public high school. The writer's implication presumably is this: If Tebow, an American hero, did it, it must be OK.

The second paragraph draws heavily on the student's preliminary map. It sets forth pretty much all of the objections, and, at the end of this paragraph, the writer explains to the readers why only three of the four points will be discussed. Again, the writer is keeping the readers informed of where they are going. And presumably the readers are interested in hearing more from this thoughtful writer.

The third paragraph fulfills the expectations that the second paragraph set up. Ordinarily a writer would not attempt to cover three objections in one paragraph—probably each objection would get a paragraph to itself—but the assignment limited the student to 250–500 words. The second and third paragraphs are in effect the central body of this essay. By the end of the third paragraph the author has argued his case—offered his evidence in support of his thesis—and now the writer merely has to wrap things up, to make an effective exit.

The fourth paragraph employs a time-tested formula for ending: It returns to a point made at the beginning—Tebow—and thus the wheel comes full circle. This paragraph, in addition to providing a sense of completeness or finality, also appeals to the reader's sense of fairness—normally an effective gesture, though in this instance a reader may wonder if the writer has convincingly demonstrated that fairness requires public schools to admit homeschoolers to extracurricular activities. Are *you* convinced that it is *unfair* to deny homeschoolers access to a public school's extracurricular activities? Why, or why not?

WRITING AS A WAY OF THINKING

We have already seen, in the clusters that students have written, concise examples of how the act of writing helps thinkers to think. "To learn to write," Robert Frost said, "is to learn to have ideas." But how do you "learn to have ideas"? Often we discover ideas while we are in the process of talking with others. A friend says X about some issue, and we—who have never really thought much about the matter—say,

- "Well, yes, I see what you are saying, but, come to think of it, I'm not of your opinion. I see it differently—*not* X *but* Y." Or maybe we say,
- "*Yes*, X, *sure, and also* a bit of *Y*, too."

Mere chance—the comment of a friend—has led us to an idea that we didn't know we had. This sort of discovery may at first seem something like the discovery we make when we reach under the couch to retrieve a ball that the dog has pushed and we find a ten-dollar bill instead. "How it got there, I'll never know, but I'm glad I found it."

In fact, learning to have ideas is not largely a matter of chance. Or if chance *is* involved, well, as Louis Pasteur put it, "Chance favors the prepared mind." What does this mean? It means that somehow, lurking in the mind, are some bits of information or hints or maybe hunches that in the unexpected circumstance—when talking, or when listening to a lecture or a classroom discussion, or especially when reading—are triggered and result in useful thoughts. A sort of seat-of-the-pants knowledge that, when brought to the surface, when worked on, when thought about, produces good results.

Consider the famous episode of Archimedes, the ancient Greek mathematician, who discovered a method to determine the volume of an irregularly shaped object. The problem: A king gave a goldsmith a specific weight of gold with which to make a crown in the shape of laurel leaves. When the job was finished the king weighed the crown, found that it was the weight of the gold he had provided, but he nevertheless suspected that the goldsmith might have substituted some silver for the gold. How could Archimedes find out (without melting or in any other way damaging the crown) if the crown was pure gold? Meditating produced no ideas, but when he entered a bathtub Archimedes noticed that the level of water rose as he immersed his body. He suddenly realized that he could thus determine the volume of the crown—by measuring the amount of displaced water. Since silver is less dense than gold, it takes a greater volume of silver to equal a given weight of gold. That is, a given weight of gold will displace less water than the same weight of silver. Archimedes then immersed the given weight of gold, measured the water it displaced, and found that indeed the crown displaced more water than the gold did. In his excitement at hitting upon his idea, Archimedes is said to have leaped out of the tub and run naked through the street, shouting "Eureka" (Greek for "I have found [it]").

Getting Ideas

Why do we tell this story? Partly because we like it, but chiefly because the word *eureka* comes from the same Greek word that has given our language the word **heuristic** (pronounced hyooRIStik), a method or process of discovering ideas, in short, of thinking. In this method, one thing triggers another. (Note: In computer science *heuristic* has a more special-ized meaning.) Now, one of the best ways of getting ideas is to hear what is going on around you—and what is going on around you is talk, in and out of the classroom, and talk in the world of books. You will find, as we said at the beginning of this discussion, that your response may be, "Well, yes, I see what you are saying, but, come to think of it, I don't see it quite that way. I see it differently—not *X* but *Y*." As we said earlier, argument is an instrument of learning as well as of persuasion. For instance,

> *Yes*, solar power is a way of conserving energy, *but* do we need to de-spoil the Mojave Desert and endanger desert life with—literally—fifty thousand solar mirrors, so that folks in Los Angeles can heat their pools? Doesn't it make sense to reduce our use of energy, rather than merely to develop sources of renewable energy that violate the environ-ment? Some sites should be off-limits.

Or maybe your response to the proposal (now at least ten years old) that wind turbines be placed in Cape Cod, Massachusetts, is,

> *Given our need* for wind power, *how can a reasonable person object* to the proposal that we put 130 wind turbines in Cape Cod, Massachusetts? *Yes*, the view will be changed, *but* in fact the turbines are quite attrac-tive. No one thinks that windmills in Holland spoil the landscape. So the view will be changed, but not spoiled, *and furthermore* wind turbines do not endanger birds or aquatic life.

When you are asked to write about something you have read in this book, if your first response is that you have no ideas, remember the re-sponses that we have mentioned—"No, I don't see it that way," or "Yes, but," or "Yes, and moreover"—and see if one of them helps you to re-spond to the work—helps you, in short, to get ideas.

A related way of getting ideas practiced by the ancient Greeks and Romans and still regarded as among the best ways, is to consider what the ancients called **topics,** from the Greek word *topos*, meaning "place," as in our word *topography* (a description or representation of a place). For the ancients, certain topics, put into the form of questions, were in ef-fect places where one went to find ideas. Among the classical topics were definition, comparison, relationship, and testimony. By prompting one-self with questions about these topics, one finds oneself moving toward answers (see Idea Prompt 1.2).

If you think you are at a loss for ideas when confronted with an issue (and when confronted with an assignment to write about it), you probably will find ideas coming to you if you turn to the relevant classical topics and begin jotting down your responses. (In classical terminology, you are en-gaged in the process of invention, from the Latin *invenire*, "to come upon," "to find.") Seeing your ideas on paper—even in the briefest form—will help bring other ideas to mind and will also help you to evaluate them. For instance, after jotting down ideas as they come and responses to them,

IDEA PROMPT 1.2 UNDERSTANDING CLASSICAL TOPICS

Definition	*What is it?*	"The West Virginia law defines a high school dropout as . . ."
Comparison	*What is it like or unlike?*	"Compared with the national rate of teenagers involved in fatal accidents, teenagers from West Virginia . . ."
Relationship	*What caused it, and what will it cause?*	"The chief cause of teenage fatal driving accidents is alcohol. Admittedly, there are no statistics on whether high school dropouts have a higher rate of alcoholism than teenagers who remain in school, but nevertheless . . ."
Testimony	*What is said about it, for instance, by experts?*	"Judge Smith, in sentencing the youth, said that in all of his long experience . . ."

1. You might go on to organize them into two lists, pro and con;
2. Next, you might delete ideas that, when you come to think about them, strike you as simply wrong or irrelevant; and
3. Then you might develop those ideas that strike you as pretty good.

You probably won't know where you stand until you have gone through some such process. It would be nice if we could make a quick decision, immediately justify it with three excellent reasons, and then give three further reasons showing why the opposing view is inadequate. In fact, however, we almost never can come to a reasoned decision without a good deal of preliminary thinking.

Consider again the West Virginia law we discussed earlier in this chapter. Here is a kind of inner dialogue that you might engage in as you think critically about it:

The purpose is to give students an incentive to stay in school by making them pay a price if they choose to drop out.

Adolescents will get the message that education really is important.

But come to think of it, *will* they? Maybe they will see this as just another example of adults bullying young people.

According to a newspaper article, the dropout rate in West Virginia decreased by 30 percent in the year after the bill was passed.

Well, that sounds good, but is there any reason to think that kids who are pressured into staying really learn anything? The *assumption* behind the bill is that if would-be dropouts stay in school, they—and society—will gain. But is the assumption sound? Maybe such students will become resentful, will not learn anything, and may even be so disruptive that they will interfere with the learning of other students.

Notice how part of the job is *analytic,* recognizing the elements or complexities of the whole, and part is *evaluative,* judging the adequacy of all of these ideas, one by one. Both tasks require critical thinking in the form of analyzing and evaluating, and those processes themselves require a disciplined *imagination.*

So far we have jotted down a few thoughts and then immediately given some second thoughts contrary to the first. Of course, the counterthoughts might not immediately come to mind. For instance, they might not occur until we reread our notes or try to explain the law to a friend, or until we sit down and begin drafting an essay aimed at supporting or undermining the law. Most likely, in fact, some good ideas won't occur until a second or third or fourth draft.

Here are some further thoughts on the West Virginia law. We list them more or less as they arose and as we typed them into a computer—not sorted out neatly into two groups, pro and con, or evaluated as you would want to do in further critical thinking of your own. And, of course, a later step would be to organize the material into some useful pattern. As you read, you might write your own responses in the margin.

Education is *not* optional, something left for the individual to take or not to take—like going to a concert, jogging, getting annual health checkups, or getting eight hours of sleep each night. Society has determined that it is *for the public good* that citizens have a substantial education, so we require education up to a certain age.

Come to think about it, maybe the criterion of age doesn't make much sense. If we want an educated citizenry, it would make more sense to require people to attend school until they demonstrated competence in certain matters rather than until they reached a certain age. Exceptions, of course, would be made for mentally challenged persons and perhaps for certain other groups with special needs.

What is needed is not legal pressure to keep teenagers in school but schools that hold the interest of teenagers.

A sixteen-year-old usually is not mature enough to make a decision of this importance.

Still, a sixteen-year-old who finds school unsatisfying and who therefore drops out may become a perfectly useful citizen.

Denying a sixteen-year-old a driver's license may work in West Virginia, but it would scarcely work in a state with great urban areas, where most high school students rely on public transportation.

We earn a driver's license by demonstrating certain skills. The state has no right to take away such a license unless we have demonstrated that we are unsafe drivers.

To prevent a person of sixteen from having a driver's license prevents that person from holding certain kinds of jobs, and that's unfair.

A law of this sort deceives adults into thinking that they have really done something constructive for teenage education, but it may work *against* improving the schools. It may be *counterproductive:* If we are really serious about educating youngsters, we have to examine the curriculum and the quality of our teachers.

Doubtless there is much that we haven't said, on both sides, but we hope you will agree that the issue deserves thought. In fact, several states now revoke the driver's license of a teenager who drops out of school, and four of these states go even further and revoke the licenses of students whose academic work does not reach a given standard. On the other hand, Louisiana, which for a while had a law like West Virginia's, dropped it in 1997.

If you were a member of a state legislature voting on this proposal, you would *have* to think about the issue. But just as a thought experiment, try to put into writing your tentative views.

✓ A CHECKLIST FOR CRITICAL THINKING

Attitudes

☐ Does my thinking show imaginative open-mindedness and intellectual curiosity?

  ☐ Am I willing to examine my assumptions?

  ☐ Am I willing to entertain new ideas—both those that I encounter while reading and those that come to mind while writing?

  ☐ Am I willing to exert myself—for instance, to do research—to acquire information and to evaluate evidence?

Skills

☐ Can I summarize an argument accurately?

☐ Can I evaluate assumptions, evidence, and inferences?

☐ Can I present my ideas effectively—for instance, by organizing and by writing in a manner appropriate to my imagined audience?

One other point about this issue. If you had to think about the matter *today*, you might also want to know whether the West Virginia legislation of 1989 is considered a success and on what basis. That is, you would want to get answers to such questions as the following:

- What sort of evidence tends to support the law or tends to suggest that the law is a poor idea?
- Did the reduction in the dropout rate continue, or did the reduction occur only in the first year following the passage of the law?
- If indeed students who wanted to drop out did not, was their presence in school a good thing, both for them and for their classmates?
- Have some people emerged as authorities on this topic? What makes them authorities, and what do they have to say?
- Has the constitutionality of the bill been tested? With what results?

Some of these questions require you to do **research** on the topic. The questions raise issues of fact, and some relevant evidence probably is available. If you are to arrive at a conclusion in which you can have confidence, you will have to do some research to find out what the facts—the objective data—are. Merely explaining your position, without giving the evidence, will not be very convincing.

Even without doing any research, however, you might want to look over the ideas, pro and con, perhaps adding some totally new thoughts or perhaps modifying or even rejecting (for reasons that you can specify) some of those already given. If you do think a bit further about this issue, and we hope that you will, notice an interesting point about *your own* thinking: It probably is not *linear* (moving in a straight line from *A* to *B* to *C*) but *recursive*, moving from *A* to *C* and back to *B* or starting over at *C* and then back to *A* and *B*. By zigging and zagging almost despite yourself, you'll get to a conclusion that may finally seem correct. In retrospect it seems obvious; *now* you can chart a nice line from *A* to *B* to *C*—but that was not at all evident to you at the start.

A SHORT ESSAY ILLUSTRATING
CRITICAL THINKING

When we read an essay, we expect the writer to have thought things through, at least to a considerable degree. We do not want to read every false start, every fuzzy thought, every ill-organized paragraph that the writer knocked off. Yes, writers make false starts, put down fuzzy thoughts, write ill-organized paragraphs, but then they revise and revise yet again, and they end by giving us a readable essay that seems effortlessly written. Still—and here we get to our real point—in argumentative essays, writers need to show their readers that they have made some effort; they need to show us *how* they got to their final (for the moment) views. It is not enough for the writer to say, "I believe *X*"; rather, the writer must in effect say, "I believe *X*—and I hope you will believe it also—because *Y* and *Z*, though attractive, just don't stand up to inquiry as well as *X* does. *Y* is superficially plausible, but..., and *Z*, which is an attractive alternative to *Y*, nevertheless fails because..."

Notice in the following short essay—on parents putting spyware into the computers of their children—that Harlan Coben frequently brings up objections to his own position; that is, he shows his awareness of other views and then tries to show why he thinks his position is preferable. Presumably he thus communicates to his readers a sense that he is thoughtful, well-informed, and fair-minded.

Harlan Coben

Harlan Coben (b. 1962) is the author of Hold Tight *(2009). Reprinted here is an essay published in the* New York Times *on March 16, 2008. Following is a letter that was written in response and was later published in the* Times.

The Undercover Parent

Not long ago, friends of mine confessed over dinner that they had put spyware on their fifteen-year-old son's computer so they could monitor all he did online. At first I was repelled at this invasion of privacy. Now, after doing a fair amount of research, I get it.

Make no mistake: If you put spyware on your computer, you have the ability to log every keystroke your child makes and thus a good portion of his or her private world. That's what spyware is—at least the parental monitoring kind. You don't have to be an expert to put it on your computer. You just download the software from a vendor and you will receive reports—weekly, daily, whatever—showing you everything your child is doing on the machine.

Scary. But a good idea. Most parents won't even consider it.

Maybe it's the word: spyware. It brings up associations of Dick Cheney sitting in a dark room, rubbing his hands together and reading your most private thoughts. But this isn't the government we are talking about—this is your family. It's a mistake to confuse the two. Loving parents are doing the surveillance here, not faceless bureaucrats. And most parents already monitor their children, watching over their home environment, their school.

Today's overprotective parents fight their kids' battles on the play- 5 ground, berate coaches about playing time and fill out college applications— yet when it comes to chatting with pedophiles or watching beheadings or gambling away their entire life savings, then . . . then their children deserve independence?

Some will say that you should simply trust your child, that if he is old enough to go on the Internet he is old enough to know the dangers. Trust is one thing, but surrendering parental responsibility to a machine that allows the entire world access to your home borders on negligence.

Some will say that it's better just to use parental blocks that deny access to risky sites. I have found that they don't work. Children know how to get around them. But more than that—and this is where it gets tough—I want to know what's being said in e-mail and instant messages and in chat rooms.

There are two reasons for this. First, we've all read about the young boy unknowingly conversing with a pedophile or the girl who was cyberbullied to the point where she committed suicide. Would a watchful eye have helped? We rely in the real world on teachers and parents to guard against bullies—do we just dismiss bullying on the Internet and all it entails because we are entering difficult ethical ground?

Second, everything your child types can already be seen by the world—teachers, potential employers, friends, neighbors, future dates. Shouldn't he learn now that the Internet is not a haven of privacy?

One of the most popular arguments against spyware is the claim that you are reading your teenager's every thought, that in today's world, a computer is the little key-locked diary of the past. But posting thoughts on the Internet isn't the same thing as hiding them under your mattress. Maybe you should buy your children one of those little key-locked diaries so that they too can understand the difference. 10

Am I suggesting eavesdropping on every conversation? No. With new technology comes new responsibility. That works both ways. There is a fine line between being responsibly protective and irresponsibly nosy. You shouldn't monitor to find out if your daughter's friend has a crush on Kevin next door or that Mrs. Peterson gives too much homework or what schoolmate snubbed your son. You are there to start conversations and to be a safety net. To borrow from the national intelligence lexicon—and yes, that's uncomfortable—you're listening for dangerous chatter.

Will your teenagers find other ways of communicating to their friends when they realize you may be watching? Yes. But text messages and cell phones don't offer the anonymity and danger of the Internet. They are usually one-on-one with someone you know. It is far easier for a predator to troll chat rooms and MySpace and Facebook.

There will be tough calls. If your sixteen-year-old son, for example, is visiting hardcore pornography sites, what do you do? When I was sixteen, we looked at *Playboy* centerfolds and read *Penthouse Forum*. You may argue that's not the same thing, that Internet pornography makes that stuff seem about as harmful as "SpongeBob."

And you're probably right. But in my day, that's all you could get. If something more graphic had been out there, we probably would have gone for it. Interest in those, um, topics is natural. So start a dialogue based on that knowledge. You should have that talk anyway, but now you can have it with some kind of context.

Parenting has never been for the faint of heart. One friend of mine, using spyware to monitor his college-bound, straight-A daughter, found out that not only was she using drugs but she was sleeping with her 15 dealer. He wisely took a deep breath before confronting her. Then he de-cided to come clean, to let her know how he had found out, to speak with her about the dangers inherent in her behavior. He'd had these conversa-tions before, of course, but this time he had context. She listened. There was no anger. Things seem better now.

Our knee-jerk reaction as freedom-loving Americans is to be suspi-cious of anything that hints at invasion of privacy. That's a good and noble thing. But it's not an absolute, particularly in the face of the new and evolving challenges presented by the Internet. And particularly when it comes to our children.

Do you tell your children that the spyware is on the computer? I side with yes, but it might be enough to show them this article, have a discus-sion about your concerns and let them know the possibility is there.

Overall View of the Essay

Before we comment in some detail on Coben's essay, we need to say that in terms of the length of its paragraphs, this essay is not a model for you to imitate. Material in newspapers customarily is given in very short paragraphs, partly because readers are reading it while eating breakfast or while commuting to work, and partly because the columns are nar-row; a paragraph of only two or three sentences may still be an inch or two deep.

The title, "The Undercover Parent" is provocative, attention-getting.

Paragraph 1 contains cues that telegraph the reader that there will be a change ("Not long ago," "At first," and "Now"). These cues set up expec-tations, and then Coben to some degree fulfills the expectations. We say "to some degree" because the essay still has a number of paragraphs to go.

Paragraph 2 presses the point, almost aggressively ("Make no mistake").

Paragraph 3 pretty much does the same. The writer is clearly reas-suring the readers that he knows how most of them feel. The idea is "scary," yes—and then comes a crucial word, "but," signaling to the reader that Coben takes a different view. We then expect him to tell us why. And—who knows?—he may even convince us.

Paragraph 4 reassures us that Coben does have some idea of why the idea is "scary," and it goes on—with another "but"—to clarify the point. We may not agree with Coben, but it is evident that he is *thinking*, inch-ing along from one idea to the next, frequently to an opposing idea.

Paragraph 5 shows that again Coben has a sense of what is going on in the world ("Today's overprotective parents"), or, rather, he has two senses, because he adds "yet," equivalent to "but." In effect he says, "Yes *A*, but also *B*."

Paragraph 6 begins "Some will say," another indication that the writer knows what is going on. And we can expect that "some will say" will, sooner or later, lead into another "but" (or other comparable word), indicating that although some say *X*, he says *Y*.

Paragraph 7 again begins "Some will say." *We* will say that again the reader knows Coben's report of what "some" say will lead to a report that what *Coben* says (i.e., thought) is different.

Paragraph 8 begins, "There are two reasons." OK, we as readers know where we will be going: We will hear two reasons. Now, when Coben drafted this paragraph he may — who knows? — have first written "There are three reasons," or "There is one reason." Whatever he wrote as a prompt, it got him moving, got him thinking, and then, in the course of writing, of finding ideas, he revised when he found out exactly how many reasons he could offer. In any case, in the paragraph as we have it, he promises to give two reasons, and in this paragraph he gives the first, nicely labeled "First." Notice too, that he provides *evidence*, and he draws in the reader: "we've all read." In short, he establishes a cozy relationship with his reader.

Paragraph 9 begins, helpfully, "Second." Fine, we know exactly where Coben is taking us: He is giving us the second of the two reasons that he discovered, and that he implicitly promised to give when in the previous paragraph he said, "There are two reasons."

Paragraph 10 begins, "One of the most popular arguments against spying is," and so we know, again, where Coben will be taking us: He will, in effect, be telling us what some folks — but not Coben — say. Very simple, very obvious — Coben will be summarizing one of the most popular arguments against spying — and we are grateful to him for letting us know at the beginning of the paragraph what his intentions are.

Paragraph 11 continues his intimate relation with the reader ("Am I suggesting eavesdropping . . . ?") He thus lets us know that he has a good sense of how the reader probably is responding. As we will say several times in this book, good writers are able to put themselves into their readers' shoes. Because they have a sense of how the reader is responding, they offer whatever the reader needs at the moment, for instance a definition, or an example.

Paragraph 12 begins with a question ("Will your teenagers find other ways of communicating . . . ?"), and this question again indicates that Coben is walking in the shoes of his readers; he knows that this question is on their minds. His answer is twofold, "Yes," and "But." Again the "but" is a sign of critical thinking, a sign that Coben has a clear sense of position *A* but wants to move his reader from *A* to *B*.

Paragraph 13, beginning "There will be tough calls," is yet another example of Coben's demonstration to his readers that he is aware of their doubts, aware that they may be thinking Coben has simplified things.

Paragraph 14 (beginning "And you're probably right") continues his demonstration that he is aware of how his readers may respond — but it is immediately followed with a "But." Again, he is nudging us from position *A* to his position, position *B*.

Paragraph 15, like several of the earlier paragraphs, shows Coben is sympathetic to the real-world problems of his readers ("Parenting has never been for the faint of heart"), and it also shows that he is a person of experience. In this paragraph, where he refers to the problem of a friend, he tells us of the happy solution. In short, he tells us that life is tough, but experience shows that there is hope. (The letter-writer, Carol Weston, strongly implies that this bit of experience Coben offers in this paragraph is *not* at all typical.)

Paragraph 16 again indicates the writer's sense of the reader ("Our knee-jerk reaction"), and it again evokes a "But."

Paragraph 17, the final paragraph, pretty directly addresses the reader ("Do you tell your children that the spyware is on the computer?"), and it offers a mixed answer: "I side with yes, but . . . ." Again Coben is showing not only his awareness of the reader but also his awareness that the problem is complicated: There is something to be said for *A* but also something to be said for *B*. He ends by suggesting that indeed this article might be discussed by parents with their children, thereby conveying to his readers the suggestion that he is a fair-minded guy, willing to have his ideas put up for discussion.

Since this essay was published, smartphones have become increasingly popular, complicating Coben's point that "text messages and cell phones don't offer the anonymity and danger of the Internet." Many students' phones are now their primary means of accessing the Internet. How does this trend invite you to reconsider Coben's argument?

Following is Carol Weston's response to Coben's essay that the *Times* later published (March 23, 2008).

Letter of Response by Carol Weston

To the Editor:

In "The Undercover Parent" (Op-Ed, March 16), the novelist Harlan Coben writes that putting spyware on a child's computer is a "good idea."

As a mother and advice columnist for girls, I disagree. For most families, spyware is not only unnecessary, but it also sends the unfortunate message, "I don't trust you."

Mr. Coben said a friend of his "using spyware to monitor his college-bound, straight-A daughter, found out that not only was she using drugs but she was sleeping with her dealer." He confronted her about her behavior. "She listened. There was no anger. Things seem better now."

Huh?! No anger? No tears or shouting or slammed doors? C'mon. If only raising teenagers were that simple.

Parenting is both a job and a joy. It does not require spyware, but it does require love, respect, time, trust, money, and being as available as possible 24/7. Luck helps, too.

Carol Weston
New York, March 16, 2008

The writer is an advice columnist for Girls' Life *magazine.*

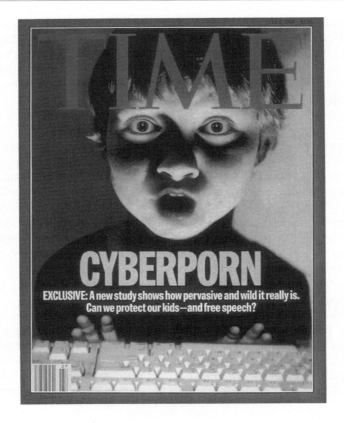

Topics for Critical Thinking and Writing

1. How important is the distinction (para. 4) between government invasion of privacy and parental invasion of privacy?

2. Complete the following sentence: An invasion of privacy is permissible if and only if . . .

3. Identify the constructive steps a normal parent might consider taking before going so far as to install spyware.

4. Do you agree with Weston's statement that installing spyware translates to "I don't trust you"? Would you feel differently (or not) if you were a parent?

5. How does Weston effectively use her audience when responding to Coben?

6. Write your own letter to the editor, indicating your reasons for supporting or rejecting Coben's argument.

✓ A CHECKLIST FOR EVALUATING LETTERS OF RESPONSE

After reading the letters responding to an editorial or to a previous letter, go back and read each letter. Have you asked yourself the following questions?

☐ What assumption(s) does the letter-writer make? Do you share the assumption(s)?

☐ What is the writer's claim?

☐ In what ways does the writer consider the audience?

☐ What evidence, if any, does the writer offer to support the claim?

☐ Is there anything about the style of the letter—the distinctive use of language, the tone—that makes the letter especially engaging or especially annoying?

EXAMINING ASSUMPTIONS

In Chapter 3 we will discuss **assumptions** in some detail, but here we want to introduce the topic by emphasizing the importance of *identifying* and *examining* assumptions—the assumptions you will encounter in the writings of others and the assumptions you will rely on in your own essays.

With this in mind, let's return again to considering the West Virginia driver's license law. What assumptions did the legislature make in enacting this statute? We mentioned earlier one such assumption: If the law helped to keep teenagers from dropping out of school, then that was a good thing for them and for society in general. For all we know, the advocates of this legislation may have made this assumption *explicit* in the course of their argument in favor of the statute. Perhaps they left this assumption *tacit*, believing that the point was obvious and that everyone shared this assumption. The assumption may be obvious, but it was not universally shared; the many teenagers who wanted to drop out of school at sixteen and keep their drivers' licenses did not share it.

Another assumption that the advocates of this legislation may have made is this:

> The provisions of this statute are the most efficient way to keep teenagers in high school.

Defending such an assumption is no easy task because it requires identifying other possible legislative strategies and evaluating their merits against those of the proposed legislation.

✓ A CHECKLIST FOR EXAMINING ASSUMPTIONS

☐ What assumptions does the writer's argument presuppose?

☐ Are these assumptions explicit or implicit?

☐ Are these assumptions important to the author's argument or only incidental?

☐ Does the author give any evidence of being aware of the hidden assumptions in her or his argument?

☐ Would a critic be likely to share these assumptions, or are they exactly what a critic would challenge?

☐ What sort of evidence would be relevant to supporting or rejecting these assumptions?

☐ Am I willing to grant the author's assumptions? Would most readers grant them?

  ☐ If not, why not?

Consider now two of the assumptions involved in the Sultaana Freeman case. Thanks to the "clustering" exercise (pp. 4–8), these and other assumptions are already on display. Perhaps the most important and fundamental assumption Ms. Freeman made is this:

> Where private religious beliefs conflict with duly enacted laws, the former should prevail.

This assumption is widely shared in our society and is by no means unique to Muslim women seeking drivers' licenses in Florida after September 11, 2001. Freeman's opponents, however, probably assumed a very different but equally fundamental proposition:

> Private religious practices and beliefs must yield to the demands of national security.

Obviously these two assumptions were on a collision course and neither side could hope to prevail so long as the key assumptions of the other side were ignored.

Jena McGregor

Jena McGregor, a graduate of the University of Georgia, writes a daily blog for the Washington Post. We reprint a piece that she published on May 25, 2012, when women in the military forces were still prohibited from serving in combat positions. On January 24, 2013, Defense Secretary Leon Panetta, acting on a recommendation from the Joint Chiefs of Staff, lifted the ban on women in combat roles, but opposition remains. For example, a group called Concerned Women for America immediately protested that "our military cannot continue to choose social experimentation and political correctness over combat readiness." Other topics for discussion are printed below, after the essay.

Military Women in Combat: Why Making It Official Matters

It's been a big couple of weeks for women in the military.

Last week, female soldiers began formally moving into jobs in previously all-male battalions, a program that will later go Army-wide. The move is a result of rule changes following a February report that opened some 14,000 new positions to women in critical jobs much closer to the front lines. However, some 250,000 combat jobs still remain officially closed to them.

The same week, Rep. Loretta Sanchez (D, Calif.) and Sen. Kirsten Gillibrand (D, N.Y.) introduced legislation in both houses of Congress that would encourage the "repeal of the Ground Combat Exclusion policy" for women in the armed forces. Then this Wednesday, two female U.S. Army reservists filed a lawsuit that seeks to overturn the remaining restrictions on women in combat, saying they limit "their current and future earnings, their potential for promotion and advancement, and their future retirement benefits." (A Pentagon spokesperson told Bloomberg News that Defense Secretary Leon Panetta "is strongly committed to examining the expansion of roles for women in the U.S. military, as evidenced by the recent step of opening up thousands of more assignments to women.")

One of the arguments behind both the lawsuit and the new legislation is that the remaining restrictions hurt women's opportunities for advancement. Advocates for women in the military say that even if women like Gen. Ann Dunwoody have reached four-star general status, she and women like her without official frontline combat experience apparently haven't been considered for the military's very highest posts. "If women remain restricted to combat service and combat service support specialties, we will not see a woman as Commandant of the Marine Corps, or CENTCOM commander, or Chairman of the Joint Chiefs of Staff," writes Greg Jacob, policy director for the Service Women's Action Network. "Thus women in the military are being held back simply because they are women. Such an idea is not only completely at odds with military ethics, but is distinctly un-American."

Women have been temporarily "attached" to battalions for the last 5 decade; still, allowing women to formally serve in combat operations could help to break down the so-called brass ceiling.

Another way to break down the ceiling would be to consider talented women for top military leadership positions, whether or not they've officially held certain combat posts. Presidents have chosen less-senior officers for Joint Chiefs roles, which are technically staff jobs, wrote Laura Conley and Lawrence Korb, a former assistant defense secretary in the Reagan administration and a senior fellow at the Center for American Progress, in the *Armed Forces Journal* last year. They argue that putting a woman on the Joint Chiefs would help the military grapple with rising sexual harassment issues, bring nontraditional expertise (which women have developed because of some of their role exclusions) at a time when that's increasingly critical, and send the signal that the military is not only open to women, but puts no barriers in their way.

Yes, putting women in combat roles beyond those that have been recently formalized would require many adjustments, both logistical and psychological, for the military and for its male troops. There are plenty of women who may not be interested in these jobs, or who do not meet the physical demands required of them. And gradual change may be prudent. The recent openings are a start; Army Chief of Staff Ray Odierno's acknowledgment last week that if women are allowed into infantry, they will at some point probably go through Ranger School, is encouraging.

But at a time when experience like the infantry is reportedly crucial for getting top posts, it's easy to see how official and sizable policy changes are needed in order to create a system that lets talented women advance to the military's highest echelons. In any field where there are real or perceived limitations for women's advancement, it's that much harder to attract the best and brightest. Indeed, the Military Leadership Diversity Commission recommended last March that the services end combat exclusion policies for women, along with other "barriers and inconsistencies, to create a level playing field for all qualified service members." As the commission chairman, Retired Air Force Gen. Lester L. Lyles, told the American Forces Press Service at the time, "we know that [the exclusion] hinders women from promotion."

For the military to achieve the diverse workforce it seeks, interested and capable women should either not face exclusions, or the culture of the armed forces needs to change so that women without that particular experience can still reach the very top. Both changes may be difficult, but the latter is extraordinarily so. Ending the restrictions is the shortest route to giving the military the best pool of talent possible and the most diverse viewpoints for leading it.

TOPICS FOR CRITICAL THINKING AND WRITING

1. How would you characterize McGregor's tone (her manner)? Thoughtful? Pushy? Point to passages that support your view.

2. Explain the term *brass ceiling* (para. 5).

3. One argument *against* sending women onto an actual battlefield, as infantry or as members of a tank crew, is that if they are captured they might be gang-raped. In your view, how significant is this as an argument?

4. Here is a second argument that has been made against sending women into direct combat: Speaking generally, women do not have the upper-body strength that men have, and a female soldier (again, we are speaking generally, not about a particular individual) would thus be less able to pull a wounded companion out of a burning tank or off a battlefield. To put the matter strongly: Male soldiers might feel that they could not count on their female comrades in a time of need. What is your reply?

5. In her final paragraph, McGregor suggests that if the armed forces changed their policy and did not in effect require battlefield experience for the very highest jobs, the military thus would achieve diversity at the top and women would have an opportunity for top pay. What are your thoughts? For instance, is the idea that the top officers should have experienced hand-to-hand combat out of date, romantic, hopelessly *macho*, or irrelevant to modern warfare? Explain.

6. What do you make of the following argument? If women in the military should be treated exactly the way men are, why, if there is a national draft, should the draft be limited to males? If a national emergency requires conscription, why shouldn't women be drafted, just like men?

Five Exercises in Critical Thinking

As you are drafting your essays for one or more of the assignments, consider typing your notes in a Google document and writing your essay in a blog so that you can easily share your thoughts on your topic. As always, submit and complete assignments the way that your teacher directs. However, free online venues can serve as good places for you to maintain copies of your notes and essays for later consultation.

1. Think further about the 1989 West Virginia law that prohibits high school dropouts younger than eighteen from holding a driver's license. Jot down pros and cons, and then write a balanced dialogue between two imagined speakers who hold opposing views on the merits of the law. You'll doubtless have to revise your dialogue several times, and in revising your drafts you will find that further ideas come to you. Present *both* sides as strongly as possible. (You may want to give the two speakers distinct characters; for instance, one may be a student who has dropped out and the other a concerned teacher, or one a parent—who perhaps argues that he or she needs the youngster to work full-time driving a delivery truck—and one a legislator. But do not write as if the speakers must present the arguments they might be expected to hold. A student might argue *for* the law, and a teacher *against* it.)

2. Take one of the following topics and write down all the pro and con arguments you can think of in, say, ten minutes. Then, at least an hour

or two later, return to your notes and see whether you can add to them. Finally, as in Exercise 1, write a balanced dialogue, presenting each idea as strongly as possible. (If none of these topics interests you, talk with your instructor about the possibility of choosing a topic of your own.) Suggested topics:

a. Colleges should not award athletic scholarships.
b. Bicyclists and motorcyclists should be required by law to wear helmets.
c. High school teachers should have the right to search students for drugs on school grounds.
d. Smoking should be prohibited in all parts of all college buildings.
e. College administrators should take no punitive action against students who use racist language or language that offends any minority.
f. Students should have the right to drop out of school at any age.
g. In rape trials, the names of the alleged victims should not be released to the public.
h. The United States ought to require a national identity card.

3. On the evening of July 31, 2001, after court employees had left the Alabama Judicial Building in Montgomery, Chief Justice Roy S. Moore of the Alabama Supreme Court and his supporters installed in the lobby of the courthouse a four-foot-high, 5,200-pound granite block bearing the text of the Ten Commandments. Moore had not discussed his plan with other justices. Civil liberties groups complained that the monument was an unconstitutional attempt to endorse a specific religion (the First Amendment to the U.S. Constitution says, "Congress shall make no law respecting an establishment of religion"), and in 2002 a federal judge ordered Moore to remove the monument. He refused, saying that the monument is a symbol of the roots of American law. He also said, "To do my duty, I must obey God." His supporters have offered several arguments on his behalf, notably that (a) the Founding Fathers often spoke of God; (b) every courtroom has a Bible to swear in witnesses and jurors; (c) the U.S. Supreme Court has a frieze of lawgivers, including Moses with the Ten Commandments, Hammurabi, Confucius, and Muhammad. In August 2003, Moore was suspended from his position on the court, and the monument was removed from view. Your views?

4. Since 1937, when San Francisco's Golden Gate Bridge opened, some 1,200 people have leaped from it to their deaths. The board of the Golden Gate Bridge, Highway and Transportation District periodically contemplates plans to make it suicide-proof. It discusses the kinds of devices proposed (railings, nets, or a combination), the cost (an estimated $15.25 million, which could be used for other civic purposes), the aesthetic factor (the devices may spoil the appearance of this renowned art deco work), and the engineering uncertainties (some engineers express reservations about the aerodynamic drag the barrier may create). And now consider these additional arguments against altering the bridge: (a) the government has no business paternalistically interfering with the free will of persons who wish to commit suicide; (b) if the Golden Gate Bridge is made suicide-proof, persons who wish to commit suicide will easily find some other site, such as the nearby Bay Bridge; (c) only 3 percent

of the persons who commit suicide in the Bay Area do so by leaping from the bridge.

The assignment: You are on the board of the Golden Gate Bridge. Suicides on the bridge are now averaging two a month, and a proposal to make the bridge suicide-proof has come up. Taking account of the arguments just mentioned, and any others—pro and con—that you can think of, what is your well-reasoned 500-word response?

5. In September 2004, the year of a presidential election, the Bush-Cheney campaign approached Allegheny College (in northwest Pennsylvania), asking to rent for October 13 the college's gymnasium, the largest enclosed space in the area. Because the electoral votes of Pennsylvania were uncertain, Vice President Cheney's appearance at Allegheny was likely to get national attention, at least briefly. The college did *not* have in place a policy against renting space to a political organization, so refusal to rent the gymnasium might seem like discrimination against the Republican Party. Further, the college faculty and administrators involved in making the decision concluded that the event would strengthen town–gown relationships and energize the students to participate in the political process. The gymnasium was therefore rented to the Bush-Cheney campaign, so that the vice president could appear.

   The event was a sort of town-hall-style presentation, but tickets were limited: The campaign personnel distributed most of the six hundred tickets to local Republican activists; forty tickets were given to a group called College Republicans, who could distribute the tickets as they saw fit. Obviously the idea was to keep out hecklers and demonstrators, an entirely reasonable plan from the Republican point of view. Why should Republicans rent a hall and stage an event that might get national coverage if the opposing party could use it to get TV attention?

   The issue: Should a college—supposedly a site where inquiry is open, where ideas are exchanged freely in robust debate—allow its facilities to be used by those who would stifle debate? Professor Daniel M. Shea, who initially favored the decision to rent the gymnasium, ultimately concluded that he was mistaken. In an essay in the *Chronicle of Higher Education* (August 4, 2006), Shea discusses the affair, and he suggests that colleges and universities ought to band together to "form an open-event alliance." Candidates might have at their disposal half of the available seats, but the other half would be for the college to distribute through some sort of open procedure, perhaps a lottery.

   The assignment: Assume that a political party wanted to rent your institution's gymnasium or a large lecture hall. What would your position be? Why? In a letter of about 500 words addressed to the college paper, set forth your views.

 For additional arguments online, visit the e-Pages at
bedfordstmartins.com/barnetbedau.

2

Critical Reading: Getting Started

Some books are to be tasted, others to be swallowed, and some few to be chewed and digested.

—FRANCIS BACON

ACTIVE READING

In the passage that we quote at the top of this page, Bacon makes at least two good points. One is that books are of varying worth; the second is that a taste of some books may be enough.

But even a book (or an essay) that you will chew and digest is one that you first may want to taste. How can you get a taste—that is, how can you get some sense of a piece of writing *before* you sit down to read it carefully?

Previewing

Even before you read a work, you may have some ideas about it, perhaps because you already know something about the **author.** You know, for example, that a work by Martin Luther King Jr. will probably deal with civil rights. You know, too, that it will be serious and eloquent. On the other hand, if you pick up an essay by Woody Allen, you will probably expect it to be amusing. It may be serious—Allen has written earnestly about many topics, especially those concerned with the media—but it's your hunch that the essay will be at least somewhat entertaining and probably will not be terribly difficult to understand. In short, a reader who has some knowledge of the author probably has some idea of what the writing will be like, and so the reader reads it in a certain mood. Admittedly, most of the authors represented in this book are not widely known, but we give biographical notes that may provide you with some sense of what to expect.

The **place of publication** may also tell you something about the essay. For instance, the *National Review* is a conservative journal. If you notice that an essay on affirmative action was published in the *National Review,* you are probably safe in tentatively assuming that the essay will not endorse affirmative action. On the other hand, *Ms. Magazine* is a liberal publication, and an essay on affirmative action published in *Ms.* will probably be an endorsement. You often can learn a good deal about a journal or magazine simply by flipping through it and looking at the kinds of advertisements in it.

The **title** of an essay, too, may give you an idea of what to expect. Of course, a title may announce only the subject and not the author's thesis or point of view ("On Gun Control," "Should Drugs Be Legal?"), but fairly often it will indicate the thesis too, as in "Give Children the Vote" and "Gay Marriages: Make Them Legal." Knowing more or less what to expect, you can probably take in some of the major points even on a quick reading.

Skimming: Finding the Thesis

Although most of the material in this book is too closely argued to be fully understood by merely skimming, still, skimming can tell you a good deal. Read the first paragraph of an essay carefully because it may announce the author's **thesis** (chief point, major claim), and it may give you some sense of how the argument for that thesis will be conducted. (What we call the *thesis* can also be called the *main idea,* the *point,* or even the *argument,* but in this book we use *argument* to refer not only to the thesis statement but also to the entire development of the thesis in the essay.) Run your eye over the rest, looking for key expressions that indicate the author's conclusions, such as "It follows, then, that . . ." Passages of this sort often occur as the first or last sentence in a paragraph. And of course, pay attention to any headings within the text. Finally, pay special attention to the last paragraph because it probably will offer a summary and a brief restatement of the writer's thesis.

Having skimmed the work, you probably know the author's thesis, and you may detect the author's methods—for instance, whether the author supports the thesis chiefly by personal experience, by statistics, or by ridiculing the opposition. You also have a clear idea of the length and some idea of the difficulty of the piece. You know, then, whether you can read it carefully now before dinner or whether you had better put off a careful reading until you have more time.

Reading with a Careful Eye: Underlining, Highlighting, Annotating

Once you have a general idea of the work—not only an idea of its topic and thesis but also a sense of the way in which the thesis is argued—you can then go back and start reading it carefully.

As you read, **underline** or **highlight** key passages, and make **annotations** in the margins. Because you are reading actively, or interacting with the text, you will not simply let your eye rove across the page.

- You will highlight what seem to be the chief points, so that later when you review the essay you can easily locate the main passages.

- But don't overdo a good thing. If you find yourself highlighting most of a page, you are probably not thinking carefully enough about what the key points are.

- Similarly, your marginal annotations should be brief and selective. They will probably consist of hints or clues, things like "really?" "doesn't follow," "good," "compare with Jones," and "check this."

- In short, in a paragraph you might highlight a key definition, and in the margin you might write "good," or "on the other hand," or "?" if you think the definition is fuzzy or wrong.

- With many electronic formats you can use tools to highlight or annotate. Also consider copying and pasting passages you would normally highlight in a Google document. Include a link to the piece and create an RSS feed to the journal's Web site. Having your notes in an electronic format makes it easy to access and use them later.

You are interacting with the text and laying the groundwork for eventually writing your own essay on what you have read.

What you annotate will depend largely on your **purpose.** If you are reading an essay in order to see the ways in which the writer organizes an argument, you will annotate one sort of thing. If you are reading in order to challenge the thesis, you will annotate other things. Here is a passage from an essay entitled "On Racist Speech," with a student's rather skeptical, even aggressive annotations. But notice that at least one of the annotations—"Definition of 'fighting words'"—apparently was made chiefly in order to remind the reader of where an important term appears in the essay. The essay, printed in full on page 64, is by Charles R. Lawrence III, a professor of law at Georgetown University. It originally appeared in the *Chronicle of Higher Education* (October 25, 1989), a publication read chiefly by college and university faculty members and administrators.

Example of such a policy?

University officials who have formulated <u>policies</u> to respond to incidents of racial harassment have been <u>characterized</u> in the press as "thought police," but such policies generally do nothing more than ⟨?⟩ impose ⟨<u>sanctions</u>⟩ against intentional face-to-face insults. When *What about* racist speech takes the form of <u>face-to-face insults</u>, catcalls, or other *sexist speec* assaultive speech aimed at an <u>individual or small</u> group of persons, *Example?* it falls directly within the <u>"fighting words"</u> exception to First *Definition of* Amendment protection. The <u>Supreme Court</u> has held that <u>words</u> *"fighting* which <u>"by their very utterance inflict</u> injury or tend to <u>incite</u> *words"* an immediate breach of the peace" are not protected by the First Amendment.

If the purpose of the First Amendment is to foster the great- *Really? Prob* est amount of speech, racial insults disserve that purpose. Assaul- *ably depend* tive racist speech functions as a preemptive strike. The <u>invective is</u> *on the indi-* <u>experienced as a blow, not as a proffered idea</u>, and once the blow *vidual.*

is struck, it is unlikely that a dialogue will follow. Racial insults are particularly undeserving of First Amendment protection because the perpetrator's <u>intention is not to discover truth</u> or initiate dialogue but to injure the victim. <u>In most situations</u>, members of minority groups realize that they <u>are likely to lose</u> if they respond to epithets by fighting and are forced to remain silent and submissive.

Why must speech always seek "to discover truth"?

How does he know?

"This; Therefore, That"

To arrive at a coherent thought or a coherent series of thoughts that will lead to a reasonable conclusion, a writer has to go through a good deal of preliminary effort. On page 14 we talked about patterns of thought that stimulate the generation of specific ideas. The path to sound conclusions involves similar thought patterns that carry forward the arguments presented in the essay:

- While these arguments are convincing, they fail to consider . . .
- While these arguments are convincing, they must also consider . . .
- These arguments, rather than being convincing, instead prove . . .
- While these authors agree, in my opinion . . .
- Although it is often true that . . .

And consider also

- What sort of audience would agree with such an argument?
- What sort of audience would be opposed?
- What are the differences in values between these two kinds of audiences?

All of these patterns can serve as heuristics or prompts—that is, they can stimulate the creation of ideas.

And if the writer is to convince the reader that the conclusion is sound, the reasoning that led to the conclusion must be set forth in detail, with a good deal of "This; therefore, that"; "If this, then that"; and "It might be objected at this point that . . ." The arguments in this book require more comment than President Calvin Coolidge provided when his wife, who hadn't been able to go to church on a Sunday, asked him what the preacher's sermon was about. "Sin," he said. His wife persisted: "What did the preacher say about it?" Coolidge's response: "He was against it."

But, again, when we say that most of the arguments in this book are presented at length and require careful reading, we do not mean that they are obscure; we mean, rather, that the reader has to take the sentences thoughtfully, one by one. And speaking of one by one, we are reminded of an episode in Lewis Carroll's *Through the Looking-Glass:*

"Can you do Addition?" the White Queen asked. "What's one and one and one and one and one and one and one and one and one and one?"

"I don't know," said Alice. "I lost count."

"She can't do Addition," the Red Queen said.

It's easy enough to add one and one and one and so on, and Alice can, of course, do addition, but not at the pace that the White Queen sets. Fortunately, you can set your own pace in reading the cumulative thinking set forth in the essays we reprint. Skimming won't work, but slow reading—and thinking about what you are reading—will.

When you first pick up an essay, you may indeed want to skim it, for some of the reasons mentioned on page 35, but sooner or later you have to settle down to read it and to think about it. The effort will be worthwhile. John Locke, the seventeenth-century English philosopher, said,

> *Reading* furnishes the mind with materials of knowledge; it is *thinking* [that] makes what we read ours. We are of the ruminating kind, and it is not enough to cram ourselves with a great load of collections; unless we chew them over again they will not give us strength and nourishment.

First, Second, and Third Thoughts

Suppose you are reading an argument about pornographic pictures. For the present purpose, it doesn't matter whether the argument favors or opposes censorship. As you read the argument, ask yourself whether *pornography* has been adequately defined. Has the writer taken the trouble to make sure that the reader and the writer are thinking about the same thing? If not, the very topic under discussion has not been adequately fixed; and therefore further debate over the issue may well be so unclear as to be futile. How, then, ought a topic such as this be defined for effective critical thinking?

It goes without saying that pornography can't be defined simply as pictures of nude figures or even of nude figures copulating, for such a definition would include not only photographs taken for medical, sociological, and scientific purposes but also some of the world's great art. Nobody seriously thinks that such images should be called pornography.

Is it enough, then, to say that pornography "stirs lustful thoughts" or "appeals to prurient interests"? No, because pictures of shoes probably stir lustful thoughts in shoe fetishists, and pictures of children in ads for underwear probably stir lustful thoughts in pedophiles. Perhaps, then, the definition must be amended to "material that stirs lustful thoughts in the average person." But will this restatement do? First, it may be hard to agree on the characteristics of "the average person." In other matters, the law often does assume that there is such a creature as "the reasonable person," and most people would agree that in a given situation there might be a reasonable response—for almost everyone. But we cannot be so sure that the same is true about the emotional responses of this "average person." In any case, far from stimulating sexual impulses, sadomasochistic pictures of booted men wielding whips on naked women probably turn off "the average person," yet this is the sort of material that most people would agree is pornographic.

Something must be wrong, then, with the definition that pornography is material that "stirs lustful thoughts in the average person." We began with a definition that was too broad ("pictures of nude figures"), but now we have a definition that is too narrow. We must go back to the drawing board. This is not nitpicking. The label "average person" was found to be inadequate in a pornography case argued before the Supreme Court; because the materials in question were aimed at a homosexual audience, it was agreed that the average person would not find them sexually stimulating.

One difficulty has been that pornography is often defined according to its effect on the viewer ("genital commotion," Father Harold Gardiner, S.J., called it, in *Catholic Viewpoint on Censorship*), but different people, we know, may respond differently. In the first half of the twentieth century, in an effort to distinguish between pornography and art—after all, most people don't want to regard Botticelli's *Venus* or Michelangelo's *David* as "dirty"—it was commonly said that a true work of art does not stimulate in the spectator ideas or desires that the real object might stimulate. But in 1956, Kenneth Clark, probably the most influential English-speaking art critic of the twentieth century, changed all that; in a book called *The Nude* he announced that "no nude, however abstract, should fail to arouse in the spectator some vestige of erotic feeling."

SUMMARIZING AND PARAPHRASING

Perhaps the best approach to a fairly difficult essay is, after first reading, to reread it and simultaneously to take notes on a sheet of paper, perhaps summarizing each paragraph in a sentence or two. Writing a summary will help you to

- understand the contents and
- see the strengths and weaknesses of the piece.

Don't confuse a summary with a paraphrase. A paraphrase is a word-by-word or phrase-by-phrase rewording of a text, a sort of translation of the author's language into your own. A paraphrase is therefore as long as the original or even longer; a summary is much shorter. A book may be summarized in a page, or even in a paragraph or a sentence. Obviously the summary will leave out all detail, but—if the summary is a true summary—it accurately states the gist, the essential thesis or claim or point of the original.

Why would anyone ever summarize, and why would anyone ever paraphrase? Because, as we have already said, these two activities—in different ways—help readers follow the original author's ideas. But, again, summarizing and paraphrasing are not the same.

- **When you summarize,** you are standing back, saying very briefly what the whole adds up to; you are seeing the forest, not the individual trees.

- **When you paraphrase,** you are inching through the forest, scrutinizing each tree—that is, finding a synonym for almost every word in the original, in an effort to make sure that you know exactly what you are dealing with. (*Caution:* Do not incorporate a summary or a paraphrase into your own essay without acknowledging your source and stating that you are summarizing or paraphrasing.)

Let's examine the distinction between summary and paraphrase in connection with the first two paragraphs of Paul Goodman's essay, "A Proposal to Abolish Grading," which is excerpted from Goodman's book, *Compulsory Miseducation and the Community of Scholars* (1966). The two paragraphs run thus:

> Let half a dozen of the prestigious universities—Chicago, Stanford, the Ivy League—abolish grading, and use testing only and entirely for pedagogic purposes as teachers see fit.
>
> Anyone who knows the frantic temper of the present schools will understand the transvaluation of values that would be effected by this modest innovation. For most of the students, the competitive grade has come to be the essence. The naive teacher points to the beauty of the subject and the ingenuity of the research; the shrewd student asks if he is responsible for that on the final exam.

A **summary** of these two paragraphs might run thus:

> If some top universities used tests only to help students to learn, students would stop worrying about grades and might share the teacher's interest in the beauty of the subject.

We hope we have accurately summarized Goodman's point, though we know we have lost his flavor, his style—for instance, the wry tone in his pointed contrast between "the naive teacher" and "the shrewd student."

Now for a **paraphrase**. Suppose you are not quite sure what Goodman is getting at, maybe because you are uncertain about the meanings of some words (perhaps *pedagogic* and *transvaluation*?), or maybe just because the whole passage is making such a startling point that you want to make sure that you have understood it. In such a case, you may want to move slowly through the sentences, translating them (so to speak) into your own English. For instance, you might turn Goodman's "pedagogic purposes" into "goals in teaching" or "attempts to help students to learn" or something else. Here is a paraphrase—not a summary but an extensive rewording—of Goodman's paragraphs:

Suppose some of the top universities—such as Chicago, Stanford, Harvard, and Yale, and whatever other schools are in the Ivy
League—stopped using grades and used tests only in order to help students to learn.

Everyone who is aware of the hysterical mood in schools today
will understand the enormous change in views of what is good and bad
that would come about by this small change. At present, instructors,
unworldly folk, talk about how beautiful their subjects are, but smart
students know that grades are what count, so they listen to instructors
only if they know that the material the instructor is talking about will
be on the exam.

In short, you may want to paraphrase an important text that your imagined reader may find obscure because it is written in specialized, technical language, for instance, the language of psychiatry or of sociology.
You want the reader to see the passage itself—you don't want to give
just the gist, just a summary—but you know that the full passage will
puzzle the reader, so you offer help, giving a paraphrase before going on
to make your own point about the author's point.

A second good reason to offer a paraphrase is if there is substantial
disagreement about what the text says. The Second Amendment to the
U.S. Constitution is a good example of this sort of text:

> A well regulated Militia being necessary to the security of a free
> State, the right of the people to keep and bear Arms shall not be
> infringed.

Exactly what, one might ask, is a "Militia"? And what does it mean
for a militia to be "well regulated"? And does "the people" mean each
individual, or does it mean—something very different—the citizenry as
some sort of unified group? After all, elsewhere in the document, when
the Constitution speaks of individuals, it speaks of a "man" or a "person," not "the people." To speak of "the people" is to use a term (some
argue) that sounds like a reference to a unified group—perhaps the citizens of each of the thirteen states?—rather than a reference to individuals. On the other hand, if Congress did mean a unified group rather than
individuals, why didn't it say "Congress shall not prohibit the states from
organizing militias"?

In fact, thousands of pages have been written about this sentence,
and if you are going to talk about it, you certainly have to let your
reader know exactly what you make out of each word. In short, you
almost surely will paraphrase it, going word by word, giving your
reader your sense of what each word or phrase says. Here is one
paraphrase:

> Because an independent society needs the protection of an armed force
> if it is to remain free, the government may not limit the right of the
> individuals (who may some day form the militia needed to keep the
> society free) to possess weapons.

In this interpretation, the Constitution grants individuals the right to possess weapons, and that is that. Other students of the Constitution, however, offer very different paraphrases, usually along these lines:

> Because each state that is now part of the United States may need to protect its freedom [from the new national government], the national government may not infringe on the right of each state to form its own disciplined militia.

This second paraphrase says that the federal government may not prevent each state from having a militia; it says nothing about every individual person having a right to possess weapons. The first of these two paraphrases, or something like it, is one that might be offered by the National Rifle Association or any other group that interprets the Constitution as guaranteeing individuals the right to own guns. The second paraphrase, or something like it, might be offered by groups that seek to limit the ownership of guns.

Why paraphrase? Here are two reasons (perhaps the *only* two reasons) why you might paraphrase a passage:

- To help yourself to understand it. In this case, the paraphrase does not appear in your essay.
- To help your reader to understand a passage that is especially important but that for one reason or another is not immediately clear. In this case, you paraphrase the passage to let the reader know exactly what it means. This paraphrase, of course, does appear in your essay.

PARAPHRASE, PATCHWRITING, AND PLAGIARISM

We have indicated that only on rare occasions will you have a reason to introduce a paraphrase into your essays, but in your preliminary work, when you take notes, you may find yourself sometimes copying word for word, sometime paraphrasing (usually in an effort to get the author's idea clearly into your mind), sometimes summarizing, and—here we get to patchwriting—sometimes producing a medley of borrowed words and original words that, if submitted in the final essay, opens you to the charge of **plagiarism** *even if you have rearranged the phrases and clauses, and even if you have cited your source.*

Here is an example. First, we give the source, a paragraph from Jena McGregor's essay on whether women serving in the armed forces should be allowed to participate directly in combat. (The entire essay is printed on pages 28–30.)

> Last week, female soldiers began formally moving into jobs in previously all-male battalions, a program that later will go Army-wide. The move

is a result of rule changes following a February report that opened some 14,000 new positions to women in critical jobs much closer to the front lines. However, some 250,000 jobs still remain officially closed to them.

Now for a student's patchwriting version:

> Women in the army recently began to formally move into jobs in bat-
> talions that previously were all-male. This program later will go through-
> out the Army. According to author Jena McGregor, the move comes
> from changes in the rules following a February report that opened
> about 14,000 new jobs to women in critical jobs that are much closer
> to the front lines. About 250,000 jobs, however — as McGregor points
> out — continue to be officially closed to women.

As you can see, the writer has followed the source, pretty much phrase by phrase — certainly sentence by sentence — making small verbal changes, such as substituting

> Women in the army recently

for McGregor's

> Last week, female soldiers

and substituting

> the move comes from changes in the rules

for McGregor's

> The move is a result of rule changes. . . .

What the student should have done is either (a) *quote the passage exactly,* setting it off to indicate that it is a quotation and indicating the source, or (b) *summarize it briefly* and give credit to the source — maybe in a sentence such as

> Jena McGregor points out that although a recent change in army rules
> has resulted in new jobs being opened for women in the military, some
> 250,000 jobs "continue to be officially closed."

We think you will agree that patchwriting — as opposed to this ex-ample of a sentence frankly summarizing a source — is *not* essentially the student's writing but, rather, is the source material thinly disguised: In a given paragraph of patchwriting, usually some of the words are copied from the source, and all or almost all of the rest consists of synonyms substituted for the words of the source, sometimes with minor rear-rangement of phrases and clauses. That is, the sequence of ideas and their arrangement, as well as most of the language, are entirely or almost entirely derived from the source, even if some of the words are different. **The fact that you may cite a source is not enough to protect you from the charge of plagiarism.** The citation of a source tells a reader that some fact or some idea—or some groups of words enclosed within quotation marks or set off by indentation—is derived from the named source; it does *not* tell the reader that almost everything in the paragraph is, in effect, the writing of someone else with a few words changed, a few words added, and a few phrases moved around.

The best way to prevent yourself from introducing patchwriting into your final essay is to make certain that when you take notes you indicate, *in the notes themselves,* what sorts of notes they are. For example:

- When you are quoting word for word, put the passage within quotation marks, and cite the page number(s) of the source.

- When you are paraphrasing—perhaps in an effort to make certain that you understand the writer's idea, or perhaps because the original uses highly technical language and you know that your reader will not understand the idea unless you put it into somewhat simpler nontechnical language—use some sign, perhaps *(par)*, to remind yourself later that this passage is a paraphrase and thus is not really *your* writing.

- When you are summarizing, again use some key, such as *(sum)*, and cite the page(s) of the source.

Make certain that in your notes you indicate the degree of indebtedness to your source, and, again, do *not* think that in a paraphrase if you name a source you are not plagiarizing. The reader assumes the name indicates the source of a fact or an idea—not that it indicates that the paragraph is essentially a rewriting of the original with perhaps an occasional original phrase inserted here and there.

If you have taken notes properly, with indications of the sort we have mentioned, when you write your paper you can say things like

> *X*'s first reason is simple. He says, " . . ." (and here you quote *X*'s words, putting them within quotation marks).

or

> *X*'s point can be summarized thus . . . . (and here too you will cite the page).

or

> *X*, writing for lawyers, not surprisingly uses some technical language, but we can paraphrase her conclusion thus: . . . . (here you give the citation).

In short,

- Avoid patchwriting; it is *not* acceptable.
- Enclose direct quotations within quotation marks, or, if the quotations are long, set them off.
- If you offer a paraphrase, tell your readers that you are paraphrasing and tell them *why* you are paraphrasing rather than quoting directly or summarizing.

For additional information about plagiarism, see page 283.

✓ **A CHECKLIST FOR A PARAPHRASE**

☐ Do I have a good reason offering a paraphrase rather than a summary?

☐ Is the paraphrase entirely in my own words—a sort of word-by-word translation—rather than a patchwork of the source's words and my own words with some of my own rearrangement of phrases and clauses?

☐ Do I not only cite the source but also explicitly say that the entire passage is a paraphrase?

A RULE FOR WRITERS: Your essay is *likely to include brief summaries* of points of view that you are agreeing or disagreeing with, but it will *rarely include a paraphrase* unless the original is obscure and you think you need to present a passage at length but in words that are clearer than those of the original. If you do paraphrase, explicitly identify the material as a paraphrase. Never submit patchwriting.

Last Words (Almost) about Summarizing

Summarizing each paragraph or each group of closely related paragraphs will help you to follow the thread of the discourse and, when you are finished, will provide you with a useful map of the essay. Then, when you reread the essay yet again, you may want to underline passages that you now understand are the author's key ideas—for instance, definitions, generalizations, summaries—and you may want to jot notes in the margins, questioning the logic, expressing your uncertainty, or calling attention to other writers who see the matter differently. Here is a paragraph from a 1973 decision of the U.S. Supreme Court, written by Chief Justice Warren Burger, setting forth reasons that the government may censor obscene material. We follow it with a sample summary.

If we accept the unprovable assumption that a complete education requires the reading of certain books, and the well-nigh universal belief that good books, plays, and art lift the spirit, improve the mind, enrich the human personality, and develop character, can we then say that a state legislature may not act on the corollary assumption that commerce in obscene books, or public exhibitions focused on obscene conduct, have a tendency to exert a corrupting and debasing impact leading to antisocial behavior? The sum of experience, including that of the past two decades, affords an ample basis for legislatures to conclude that a sensitive, key relationship of human existence, central to family life, community welfare, and the development of human personality, can be debased and distorted by crass commercial exploitation of sex. Nothing in the Constitution prohibits a State from reaching such a conclusion and acting on it legislatively simply because there is no conclusive empirical data.

Now for a student's summary. Notice that the summary does not include the reader's evaluation or any other sort of comment on the original; it is simply an attempt to condense the original. Notice too that, because its purpose is merely to assist the reader to grasp the ideas of the original by focusing on them, it is written in a sort of shorthand (not every sentence is a complete sentence), though, of course, if this summary were being presented in an essay, it would have to be grammatical.

Unprovable but acceptable assumption that good books etc. shape character, so that legislature can assume obscene works debase character. Experience lets one conclude that exploitation of sex debases the individual, family, and community. Though "there is no conclusive empirical data" for this view, the Constitution lets states act on it legislatively.

Notice that

- A few words (in the last sentence of the summary) are quoted exactly as in the original. They are enclosed within quotation marks.
- For the most part, the original material is drastically reduced. The first sentence of the original, some eighty words, is reduced in the summary to nineteen words.

Of course, the summary loses much of the detail and flavor of the original: "Good books etc." is not the same as "good books, plays, and art"; and "shape character" is not the same as "lift the spirit, improve the mind, enrich the human personality, and develop character." But the statement in the summary will do as a rough approximation, useful for a quick review. More important, the act of writing a summary forces the reader to go slowly and to think about each sentence of the original. Such thinking may help the reader–writer to see the complexity—or the hollowness—of the original.

The sample summary in the preceding paragraph was just that, a summary; but when writing your own summaries, you will often find it useful to inject your own thoughts ("seems far-fetched," "strong point," "I don't get it"), enclosing them within square brackets or in some other way to keep these responses distinct from your summary of the writer's argument.

Review: If your instructor asks you to hand in a summary,

- It should not contain ideas other than those found in the original piece.
- You can rearrange these, add transitions as needed, and so forth, but the summary should give the reader nothing but a sense of the original piece.
- If the summary includes any of the original wording, these words should be enclosed within quotation marks.
- In your notes, keep a clear distinction between *your* writing and the writing of your *source*. For the most part you will summarize, but if you paraphrase, indicate that the words are a paraphrase, and if you quote directly, indicate that you are quoting.

We don't want to nag you, but we do want to emphasize the need to read with a close eye, taking notes as you go along using a pen or pencil or highlighter or a computer program, blog, or Google document. If you read slowly and take notes, you will find that what you read will give you the "strength and nourishment" that John Locke spoke of.

> **A RULE FOR WRITERS:** Remember that when you write a summary, you are putting yourself into the author's shoes.

Having insisted that the essays in this book need to be read slowly because the writers build one reason on another, we will now seem to contradict ourselves by presenting an essay that can almost be skimmed. Susan Jacoby's essay originally appeared in the *New York Times*, a thoroughly respectable newspaper but not one that requires its readers to linger over every sentence. Still, compared with most of the news accounts, Jacoby's essay requires close reading. When you read the essay, you will notice that it zigs and zags, not because Jacoby is careless or wants to befuddle her readers but because she wants to build a strong case to support her point of view and must therefore look at some widely held views that she does *not* accept; she must set these forth and then give her reasons for rejecting them.

Susan Jacoby

Susan Jacoby (b. 1946), a journalist since the age of seventeen, is well known for her feminist writings. "A First Amendment Junkie" (our title) appeared in the Hers column in the New York Times *in 1978.*

A First Amendment Junkie

It is no news that many women are defecting from the ranks of civil libertarians on the issue of obscenity. The conviction of Larry Flynt, publisher of *Hustler* magazine—before his metamorphosis into a born-again Christian—was greeted with unabashed feminist approval. Harry Reems, the unknown actor who was convicted by a Memphis jury for conspiring to distribute the movie *Deep Throat,* has carried on his legal battles with almost no support from women who ordinarily regard themselves as supporters of the First Amendment. Feminist writers and scholars have even discussed the possibility of making common cause against pornography with adversaries of the women's movement—including opponents of the equal rights amendment and "right-to-life" forces.

All of this is deeply disturbing to a woman writer who believes, as I always have and still do, in an absolute interpretation of the First Amendment. Nothing in Larry Flynt's garbage convinces me that the late Justice Hugo L. Black was wrong in his opinion that "the Federal Government is without any power whatsoever under the Constitution to put any type of burden on free speech and expression of ideas of any kind (as distinguished from conduct)." Many women I like and respect tell me I am wrong; I cannot remember having become involved in so many heated discussions of a public issue since the end of the Vietnam War. A feminist writer described my views as those of a "First Amendment junkie."

Many feminist arguments for controls on pornography carry the implicit conviction that porn books, magazines, and movies pose a greater threat to women than similarly repulsive exercises of free speech pose to other offended groups. This conviction has, of course, been shared by everyone—regardless of race, creed, or sex—who has ever argued in favor of abridging the First Amendment. It is the argument used by some Jews who have withdrawn their support from the American Civil Liberties Union because it has defended the right of American Nazis to march through a community inhabited by survivors of Hitler's concentration camps.

If feminists want to argue that the protection of the Constitution should not be extended to *any* particularly odious or threatening form of speech, they have a reasonable argument (although I don't agree with it). But it is ridiculous to suggest that the porn shops on 42nd Street are more disgusting to women than a march of neo-Nazis is to survivors of the extermination camps.

The arguments over pornography also blur the vital distinction be- 5 tween expression of ideas and conduct. When I say I believe unreservedly in the First Amendment, someone always comes back at me with the issue of "kiddie porn." But kiddie porn is not a First Amendment issue. It is an issue of the abuse of power—the power adults have over children—and not of obscenity. Parents and promoters have no more right to use their children to make porn movies than they do to send them to work in coal mines. The responsible adults should be prosecuted, just as adults who use children for back-breaking farm labor should be prosecuted.

Susan Brownmiller, in *Against Our Will: Men, Women, and Rape*, has described pornography as "the undiluted essence of antifemale propaganda." I think this is a fair description of some types of pornography, especially of the brutish subspecies that equates sex with death and portrays women primarily as objects of violence.

The equation of sex and violence, personified by some glossy rock record album covers as well as by *Hustler*, has fed the illusion that censorship of pornography can be conducted on a more rational basis than other types of censorship. Are all pictures of naked women obscene? Clearly not, says a friend. A Renoir nude is art, she says, and *Hustler* is trash. "Any reasonable person" knows that.

But what about something between art and trash—something, say, along the lines of *Playboy* or *Penthouse* magazines? I asked five women for their reactions to one picture in *Penthouse* and got responses that ranged from "lovely" and "sensuous" to "revolting" and "demeaning." Feminists, like everyone else, seldom have rational reasons for their preferences in erotica. Like members of juries, they tend to disagree when confronted with something that falls short of 100 percent vulgarity.

In any case, feminists will not be the arbiters of good taste if it becomes easier to harass, prosecute, and convict people on obscenity charges. Most of the people who want to censor girlie magazines are equally opposed to open discussion of issues that are of vital concern to women: rape, abortion, menstruation, contraception, lesbianism—in fact, the entire range of sexual experience from a women's viewpoint.

Feminist writers and editors and filmmakers have limited finan- 10 cial resources: Confronted by a determined prosecutor, Hugh Hefner[1] will fare better than Susan Brownmiller. Would the Memphis jurors who convicted Harry Reems for his role in *Deep Throat* be inclined to take a more positive view of paintings of the female genitalia done by sensitive feminist artists? *Ms.* magazine has printed color reproductions of some of those art works; *Ms.* is already banned from a number of high school libraries because someone considers it threatening and/or obscene.

Feminists who want to censor what they regard as harmful pornography have essentially the same motivation as other would-be censors: They want to use the power of the state to accomplish what they have been unable to achieve in the marketplace of ideas and images. The impulse to censor places no faith in the possibilities of democratic persuasion.

It isn't easy to persuade certain men that they have better uses for $1.95 each month than to spend it on a copy of *Hustler*? Well, then, give the men no choice in the matter.

[1]**Hugh Hefner** Founder and longtime publisher of *Playboy* magazine. [Editors' note.]

I believe there is also a connection between the impulse toward censorship on the part of people who used to consider themselves civil libertarians and a more general desire to shift responsibility from individuals to institutions. When I saw the movie *Looking for Mr. Goodbar*, I was stunned by its series of visual images equating sex and violence, coupled with what seems to me the mindless message (a distortion of the fine Judith Rossner novel) that casual sex equals death. When I came out of the movie, I was even more shocked to see parents standing in line with children between the ages of ten and fourteen.

I simply don't know why a parent would take a child to see such a movie, any more than I understand why people feel they can't turn off a television set their child is watching. Whenever I say that, my friends tell me I don't know how it is because I don't have children. True, but I do have parents. When I was a child, they did turn off the TV. They didn't expect the Federal Communications Commission to do their job for them.

I am a First Amendment junkie. You can't OD on the First Amend-   15
ment, because free speech is its own best antidote.

Summarizing Jacoby, Paragraph by Paragraph

Suppose we want to make a rough summary, more or less paragraph by paragraph, of Jacoby's essay. Such a summary might look something like this (the numbers refer to Jacoby's paragraphs):

1. Although feminists usually support the First Amendment, when it comes to pornography, many feminists take pretty much the position of those who oppose ERA and abortion and other causes of the women's movement.

2. Larry Flynt produces garbage, but I think his conviction represents an unconstitutional limitation of freedom of speech.

3, 4. Feminists who want to control (censor) pornography argue that it poses a greater threat to women than similar repulsive speech poses to other groups. If feminists want to say that all offensive speech should be restricted, they can make a case, but it is absurd to say that pornography is a "greater threat" to women than a march of neo-Nazis is to survivors of concentration camps.

5. Trust in the First Amendment is not refuted by kiddie porn; kiddie porn is not a First Amendment issue but an issue of child abuse.

6, 7, 8. Some feminists think censorship of pornography can be more "rational" than other kinds of censorship, but a picture of a nude woman strikes some women as base and others as "lovely." There is no unanimity.

9, 10. If feminists censor girlie magazines, they will find that they are unwittingly helping opponents of the women's movement to censor discussions of rape, abortion, and so on. Some of the art in the feminist magazine *Ms.* would doubtless be censored.

11, 12. Like other would-be censors, feminists want to use the power of the state to achieve what they have not achieved in "the marketplace of ideas." They display a lack of faith in "democratic persuasion."

13, 14. This attempt at censorship reveals a desire to "shift responsibility from individuals to institutions." The responsibility—for instance, to keep young people from equating sex with violence—is properly the parents'.

15. We can't have too much of the First Amendment.

Jacoby's **thesis**, or major claim, or chief proposition—that any form of censorship of pornography is wrong—is clear enough, even as early as the end of her first paragraph, but it gets its life or its force from the **reasons** offered throughout the essay. If we want to reduce our summary even further, we might say that Jacoby supports her thesis by arguing several subsidiary points. We will merely assert them briefly, but Jacoby **argues** them—that is, she gives reasons:

a. Pornography can scarcely be thought of as more offensive than Nazism.

b. Women disagree about which pictures are pornographic.

c. Feminists who want to censor pornography will find that they help antifeminists to censor discussions of issues advocated by the women's movement.

d. Feminists who favor censorship are in effect turning to the government to achieve what they haven't achieved in the free marketplace.

e. One sees this abdication of responsibility in the fact that parents allow their children to watch unsuitable movies and television programs.

If we want to present a brief summary in the form of one coherent paragraph—perhaps as part of our own essay to show the view we are arguing in behalf of or against—we might write something like this summary. (The summary would, of course, be prefaced by a **lead-in** along these lines: "Susan Jacoby, writing in the *New York Times,* offers a forceful argument against censorship of pornography. Jacoby's view, briefly, is . . .".)

> When it comes to censorship of pornography, some feminists take a position shared by opponents of the feminist movement. They argue that pornography poses a greater threat to women than other forms of offensive speech offer to other groups, but this interpretation is simply a mistake. Pointing to kiddie porn is also a mistake, for kiddie porn is an issue involving not the First Amendment but child abuse. Feminists who support censorship of pornography will inadvertently aid those who wish to censor discussions of abortion and rape or censor art that is published in magazines such as *Ms.* The solution is not for individuals to turn to

institutions (that is, for the government to limit the First Amendment)
but for individuals to accept the responsibility for teaching young people
not to equate sex with violence.

Whether we agree or disagree with Jacoby's thesis, we must admit
that the reasons she sets forth to support it are worth thinking about. Only
a reader who closely follows the reasoning with which Jacoby buttresses
her thesis is in a position to accept or reject it. Indeed, one might want to
do research on some of her points to see if her interpretation is satisfactory.

TOPICS FOR CRITICAL THINKING AND WRITING

1. What does Jacoby mean when she says she is a "First Amendment junkie"
   (para. 15)?

2. The essay is primarily an argument against the desire of some feminists
   to try to censor pornography of the sort that appeals to some heterosexual adult males, but the next-to-last paragraph is about television and
   children. Is the paragraph connected to Jacoby's overall argument? If so,
   how?

3. Evaluate the final paragraph as a final paragraph. (Effective final paragraphs are not, of course, all of one sort. Some, for example, round off
   the essay by echoing something from the opening; others suggest that
   the reader, having now seen the problem, should think further about
   it or even act on it. But a good final paragraph, whatever else it does,
   should make the reader feel that the essay has come to an end, not just
   broken off.)

4. This essay originally appeared in the *New York Times.* If you are unfamiliar with this newspaper, consult an issue or two in your library. Next,
   in a paragraph, try to characterize the readers of the paper—that is,
   Jacoby's audience.

5. Jacoby claims in paragraph 2 that she "believes . . . in an absolute interpretation of the First Amendment." What does such an interpretation involve? Would it permit shouting "Fire!" in a crowded theater
   even though the shouter knows there is no fire? Would it permit shouting racist insults at blacks or immigrant Vietnamese? Spreading un-
   truths about someone's past? If the "absolutist" interpretation of the
   First Amendment does permit these statements, does that argument
   show that nothing is morally wrong with uttering them? (*Does* the First
   Amendment, as actually interpreted by the Supreme Court today, permit any or all of these claims? Consult your reference librarian for help
   in answering this question.)

6. Jacoby implies that permitting prosecution of persons on obscenity charges
   will lead eventually to censorship of "open discussion" of important issues such as "rape, abortion, menstruation, contraception, lesbianism"
   (para. 9). Do you find her fears convincing? Does she give any evidence
   to support her claim?

> ✓ A CHECKLIST FOR GETTING STARTED
>
> ☐ Have I adequately previewed the work?
> ☐ Can I state the thesis?
> ☐ If I have written a summary,
>   ☐ Is the summary accurate?
>   ☐ Does the summary mention all the chief points?
>   ☐ If there are inconsistencies, are they in the summary or the original selection?
>   ☐ Will the summary be clear and helpful?
>   ☐ Have I considered the audience for whom the author is writing?

ESSAYS FOR ANALYSIS

Zachary Shemtob and David Lat

Zachary Shemtob teaches criminal justice at Central Connecticut State University; David Lat is a former federal prosecutor. We reprint an essay that originally appeared in the New York Times *in 2011.*

Executions Should Be Televised

Earlier this month, Georgia conducted its third execution this year. This would have passed relatively unnoticed if not for a controversy surrounding its videotaping. Lawyers for the condemned inmate, Andrew Grant DeYoung, had persuaded a judge to allow the recording of his last moments as part of an effort to obtain evidence on whether lethal injection caused unnecessary suffering.

Though he argued for videotaping, one of Mr. DeYoung's defense lawyers, Brian Kammer, spoke out against releasing the footage to the public. "It's a horrible thing that Andrew DeYoung had to go through," Mr. Kammer said, "and it's not for the public to see that."

We respectfully disagree. Executions in the United States ought to be made public.

Right now, executions are generally open only to the press and a few select witnesses. For the rest of us, the vague contours are provided in the morning paper. Yet a functioning democracy demands maximum accountability and transparency. As long as executions remain behind closed doors, those are impossible. The people should have the right to see what is being done in their name and with their tax dollars.

This is particularly relevant given the current debate on whether ⁵ specific methods of lethal injection constitute cruel and unusual punishment and therefore violate the Constitution.

There is a dramatic difference between reading or hearing of such an event and observing it through image and sound. (This is obvious to those who saw the footage of Saddam Hussein's hanging in 2006 or the death of Neda Agha-Soltan during the protests in Iran in 2009.) We are not calling for opening executions completely to the public—conducting them before a live crowd—but rather for broadcasting them live or recording them for future release, on the Web or TV.

When another Georgia inmate, Roy Blankenship, was executed in June, the prisoner jerked his head, grimaced, gasped, and lurched, according to a medical expert's affidavit. The *Atlanta Journal-Constitution* reported that Mr. DeYoung, executed in the same manner, "showed no violent signs in death." Voters should not have to rely on media accounts to understand what takes place when a man is put to death.

Cameras record legislative sessions and presidential debates, and courtrooms are allowing greater television access. When he was an Illinois state senator, President Obama successfully pressed for the videotaping of homicide interrogations and confessions. The most serious penalty of all surely demands equal if not greater scrutiny.

Opponents of our proposal offer many objections. State lawyers argued that making Mr. DeYoung's execution public raised safety concerns. While rioting and pickpocketing occasionally marred executions in the public square in the eighteenth and nineteenth centuries, modern security and technology obviate this concern. Little would change in the death chamber; the faces of witnesses and executioners could be edited out, for privacy reasons, before a video was released.

Of greater concern is the possibility that broadcasting executions ¹⁰ could have a numbing effect. Douglas A. Berman, a law professor, fears that people might come to equate human executions with putting pets to sleep. Yet this seems overstated. While public indifference might result over time, the initial broadcasts would undoubtedly get attention and stir debate.

Still others say that broadcasting an execution would offer an unbalanced picture—making the condemned seem helpless and sympathetic, while keeping the victims of the crime out of the picture. But this is beside the point: the defendant is being executed precisely because a jury found that his crimes were so heinous that he deserved to die.

Ultimately the main opposition to our idea seems to flow from an unthinking disgust—a sense that public executions are archaic, noxious, even barbarous. Albert Camus related in his essay "Reflections on the Guillotine" that viewing executions turned him against capital punishment. The legal scholar John D. Bessler suggests that public executions might have the same effect on the public today; Sister Helen Prejean, the death penalty abolitionist, has urged just such a strategy.

That is not our view. We leave open the possibility that making executions public could strengthen support for them; undecided viewers might find them less disturbing than anticipated.

Like many of our fellow citizens, we are deeply conflicted about the death penalty and how it has been administered. Our focus is on accountability and openness. As Justice John Paul Stevens wrote in *Baze v. Rees*, a 2008 case involving a challenge to lethal injection, capital punishment is too often "the product of habit and inattention rather than an acceptable deliberative process that weighs the costs and risks of administering that penalty against its identifiable benefits."

A democracy demands a citizenry as informed as possible about the   15 costs and benefits of society's ultimate punishment.

Topics for Critical Thinking and Writing

1. In paragraphs 9–13 the authors discuss objections to their position. Are you satisfied with their responses to the objections, or do you think the authors do not satisfactorily dispose of one or more of the objections. Explain.

2. In paragraph 4 the authors say that "the people should have the right to see what is being done in their name and with their tax dollars." But while we are on the subject of *rights*, might the person who is being executed not have a right to die in privacy? Articulate your view.

"And now let's welcome, for the first and last time . . ."

3. In their concluding paragraph the authors imply that their proposal, if enacted, will help to inform citizens "about the costs and benefits of society's ultimate punishment." Do you agree? What reasons do they offer to support their proposal?

4. In your view, what is the strongest argument the authors give on behalf of their proposal? What is the weakest? Explain why you made these choices.

Gwen Wilde

This essay was written for a composition course at Tufts University.

Why the Pledge of Allegiance Should Be Revised

(Student Essay)

All Americans are familiar with the Pledge of Allegiance, even if they cannot always recite it perfectly, but probably relatively few know that the *original* Pledge did *not* include the words "under God." The original Pledge of Allegiance, published in the September 8, 1892, issue of the *Youth's Companion*, ran thus:

> I pledge allegiance to my flag, and to the Republic for which it stands:
> one Nation indivisible, with Liberty and justice for all. (Djupe 329)

In 1923, at the first National Flag Conference in Washington, D.C., it was argued that immigrants might be confused by the words "my Flag," and it was proposed that the words be changed to "the Flag of the United States." The following year it was changed again, to "the Flag of the United States of America," and this wording became the official—or, rather, unofficial—wording, unofficial because no wording had ever been nationally adopted (Djupe 329).

In 1942, the United States Congress included the Pledge in the United States Flag Code (4 USC 4, 2006), thus for the first time officially sanctioning the Pledge. In 1954, President Dwight D. Eisenhower approved adding the words "under God." Thus, since 1954 the Pledge reads:

> I pledge allegiance to the flag of the United States of America, and to
> the Republic for which it stands: one nation under God, indivisible, with
> Liberty and Justice for all. (Djupe 329)

In my view, the addition of the words "under God" is inappropriate, and they are needlessly divisive—an odd addition indeed to a Nation that is said to be "indivisible."

Very simply put, the Pledge in its latest form requires all Americans to say something that some Americans do not believe. I say "requires" because although the courts have ruled that students may not be compelled to recite the Pledge, in effect peer pressure does compel all but the bravest to join in the recitation. When President Eisenhower authorized the change, he said,

> In this way we are reaffirming the transcendence of religious faith in America's heritage and future; in this way we shall constantly strengthen those spiritual weapons which forever will be our country's most powerful resource in peace and war. (Sterner)

Exactly what did Eisenhower mean when he spoke of "the transcendence of faith in America's heritage," and when he spoke of "spiritual weapons"? I am not sure what "the transcendence of faith in America's heritage" means. Of course many Americans have been and are deeply religious—no one doubts it—but the phrase certainly goes far beyond saying that many Americans have been devout. In any case, many Americans have *not* been devout, and many Americans have *not* believed in "spiritual weapons," but they have nevertheless been patriotic Americans. Some of them have fought and died to keep America free.

In short, the words "under God" cannot be uttered in good faith by many Americans. True, something like 70 or even 80% of Americans say they are affiliated with some form of Christianity, and approximately another 3% say they are Jewish. I don't have the figures for persons of other faiths, but in any case we can surely all agree that although a majority of Americans say they have a religious affiliation, nevertheless several million Americans do *not* believe in God.

If one remains silent while others are reciting the Pledge, or even if   5 one remains silent only while others are speaking the words "under God," one is open to the charge that one is unpatriotic, is "unwilling to recite the Pledge of Allegiance." In the Pledge, patriotism is connected with religious belief, and it is this connection that makes it divisive and (to be blunt) un-American. Admittedly the belief is not very specific: one is not required to say that one believes in the divinity of Jesus, or in the power of Jehovah, but the fact remains, one is required to express belief in a divine power, and if one doesn't express this belief one is—according to the Pledge—somehow not fully an American, maybe even un-American.

Please notice that I am not arguing that the Pledge is unconstitutional. I understand that the First Amendment to the Constitution says that "Congress shall make no law respecting an establishment of religion, or prohibiting the free exercise thereof." I am not arguing that the words "under God" in the Pledge add up to the "establishment of religion," but they certainly do assert a religious doctrine. Like the words "In God we trust," found on all American money, the words "under God" express an idea that many Americans do not hold, and there is no reason why these Americans—loyal people who may be called upon to defend the country with their lives—should be required to say that America is a nation "under God."

It has been argued, even by members of the Supreme Court, that the words "under God" are not to be taken terribly seriously, not to be taken to say what they seem to say. For instance, Chief Justice Rehnquist wrote,

> To give the parent of such a child a sort of "heckler's veto" over a patriotic ceremony willingly participated in by other students, simply because the Pledge of Allegiance contains the descriptive phrase "under God," is an unwarranted extension of the establishment clause, an extension which would have the unfortunate effect of prohibiting a commendable patriotic observance. (qtd. in Mears)

Chief Justice Rehnquist here calls "under God" a "descriptive phrase," but descriptive of *what*? If a phrase is a "descriptive phrase," it describes something, real or imagined. For many Americans, this phrase does *not* describe a reality. These Americans may perhaps be mistaken—if so, they may learn of their error at Judgment Day—but the fact is, millions of intelligent Americans do not believe in God.

Notice, too, that Chief Justice Rehnquist goes on to say that reciting the Pledge is "a commendable patriotic observance." Exactly. That is my point. It is a *patriotic* observance, and it should not be connected with religion. When we announce that we respect the flag—that we are loyal Americans—we should not also have to announce that we hold a particular religious belief, in this case a belief in monotheism, a belief that there is a God and that God rules.

One other argument defending the words "under God" is often heard: The words "In God We Trust" appear on our money. It is claimed that these words on American money are analogous to the words "under God" in the Pledge. But the situation really is very different. When we hand some coins over, or some paper money, we are concentrating on the business transaction, and we are not making any affirmation about God or our country. But when we recite the Pledge—even if we remain silent at the point when we are supposed to say "under God"—we are very conscious that we are supposed to make this affirmation, an affirmation that many Americans cannot in good faith make, even though they certainly can unthinkingly hand over (or accept) money with the words "In God We Trust."

Because I believe that *reciting* the Pledge is to be taken seriously,   10 with a full awareness of the words that is quite different from when we hand over some money, I cannot understand the recent comment of Supreme Court Justice Souter, who in a case said that the phrase "under God" is "so tepid, so diluted, so far from compulsory prayer, that it should, in effect, be beneath the constitutional radar" (qtd. in "Guide"). I don't follow his reasoning that the phrase should be "beneath the constitutional radar," but in any case I am willing to put aside the issue of constitutionality. I am willing to grant that this phrase does not in any significant sense signify the "establishment of religion" (prohibited by the First Amendment) in the United States. I insist, nevertheless, that the phrase is neither "tepid" nor "diluted." It means what it says—it *must* and *should* mean what it says, to everyone who utters it—and, since millions of loyal Americans cannot say it, it should not be included in a statement in which Americans affirm their loyalty to our great country.

In short, the Pledge, which ought to unite all of us, is divisive; it includes a phrase that many patriotic Americans cannot bring themselves to utter. Yes, they can remain silent when others recite these two words, but, again, why should they have to remain silent? The Pledge of Allegiance should be something that *everyone* can say, say out loud, and say with pride. We hear much talk of returning to the ideas of the Founding Fathers. The Founding Fathers did not create the Pledge of Allegiance, but we do know that they never mentioned God in the Constitution. Indeed the only reference to religion, in the so-called establishment clause of the First Amendment, says, again, that "Congress shall make no law respecting an establishment of religion, or prohibiting the free exercise thereof." Those who wish to exercise religion are indeed free to do so, but the place to do so is not in a pledge that is required of all schoolchildren and of all new citizens.

WORKS CITED

Djupe, Paul A. "Pledge of Allegiance." *Encyclopedia of American Religion and Politics.* Ed. Paul A. Djupe and Laura R. Olson. New York: Facts on File, 2003. Print.
"Guide to Covering 'Under God' Pledge Decision." *ReligionLink.* Religion Newswriters Foundation, 17 Sept. 2005. Web. 9 Feb. 2007.
Mears, Bill. "Court Dismisses Pledge Case." *CNN.com* Cable News Network 15 June 2004. Web. 9 Feb. 2007.
Sterner, Doug. "The Pledge of Allegiance." *Home of Heroes.* N.p., n.d. Web. 9 Feb. 2007.

TOPICS FOR CRITICAL THINKING AND WRITING

1. Summarize the essay in a paragraph.

2. Does the background material about the history of the pledge serve a useful purpose? Should it be deleted? Why, or why not?

3. Does the writer give enough weight to the fact that no one is compelled to recite the pledge? Explain your answer.

4. What arguments does the writer offer in support of her position?

5. Does the writer show an adequate awareness of other counterarguments?

6. Which is the writer's strongest argument? Is any argument notably weak, and, if so, how could it be strengthened?

7. What assumptions—tacit or explicit—does the author make? Do you agree or disagree with them? Please explain.

8. What do you take the words "under God" to mean? Do they mean "under God's special protection"? Or "acting in accordance with God's rules"? Or "accountable to God"?

9. Chief Justice Rehnquist wrote that the words "under God" are a "descriptive phrase." What do you think he meant by this?

10. What is the purpose of the Pledge of Allegiance? Does the phrase "under God" promote or defeat that purpose? Explain your answer.

11. What do you think about substituting "with religious freedom" for "under God"? Set forth your response, supported by reasons, in about 250 words.

12. Wilde makes a distinction between the reference to God on U.S. money and the reference to God in the Pledge. Do you agree with her that the two cases are not analogous? Explain.

13. What readers might *not* agree with Wilde's arguments? What values do they hold? How might you try to persuade an audience who disagrees with her to consider her proposal?

14. Putting aside your own views on the issue, what grade would you give this essay as a work of argumentative writing? Support your evaluation with reasons.

A CASEBOOK FOR CRITICAL READING:
Should Some Kinds of Speech Be Censored?

Now we present a series of essays that we think are somewhat more difficult than Jacoby's, Shemtob and Lat's, and Wilde's but that address in more detail some of the issues of free speech that they raise. We suggest you read each one through to get its gist and then read it a second time, writing down after each paragraph a sentence or two summarizing the paragraph. Keep in mind the First Amendment to the Constitution, which reads, in its entirety,

> Congress shall make no law respecting an establishment of religion, or prohibiting the free exercise thereof; or abridging the freedom of speech, or of the press; or the right of the people peaceably to assemble, and to petition the government for a redress of grievances.

For links related to free speech, see the companion Web site
bedfordstmartins.com/barnetbedau.

Susan Brownmiller

Susan Brownmiller (b. 1935), a graduate of Cornell University, is the founder of Women against Pornography and the author of several books, including Against Our Will: Men, Women, and Rape *(1975). The essay reprinted here is from* Take Back the Night *(1980), a collection of essays edited by Laura Lederer. The book has been called "the manifesto of antipornography feminism."*

Let's Put Pornography Back in the Closet

Free speech is one of the great foundations on which our democracy rests. I am old enough to remember the Hollywood Ten, the screenwriters who went to jail in the late 1940s because they refused to testify before a congressional committee about their political affiliations. They tried to use the First Amendment as a defense, but they went to jail because in those days there were few civil liberties lawyers around who cared to champion the First Amendment right to free speech, when the speech concerned the Communist party.

The Hollywood Ten were correct in claiming the First Amendment. Its high purpose is the protection of unpopular ideas and political dissent. In the dark, cold days of the 1950s, few civil libertarians were willing to declare themselves First Amendment absolutists. But in the brighter, though frantic, days of the 1960s, the principle of protecting unpopular political speech was gradually strengthened.

It is fair to say now that the battle has largely been won. Even the American Nazi party has found itself the beneficiary of the dedicated, tireless work of the American Civil Liberties Union. But—and please notice the quotation marks coming up—"To equate the free and robust exchange of ideas and political debate with commercial exploitation of obscene material demeans the grand conception of the First Amendment and its high purposes in the historic struggle for freedom. It is a misuse of the great guarantees of free speech and free press."

I didn't say that, although I wish I had, for I think the words are thrilling. Chief Justice Warren Burger said it in 1973, in the United States Supreme Court's majority opinion in *Miller v. California*. During the same decades that the right to political free speech was being strengthened in the courts, the nation's obscenity laws also were undergoing extensive revision.

It's amazing to recall that in 1934 the question of whether James 5 Joyce's *Ulysses* should be banned as pornographic actually went before the Court. The battle to protect *Ulysses* as a work of literature with redeeming social value was won. In later decades, Henry Miller's *Tropic* books, *Lady Chatterley's Lover,* and the *Memoirs of Fanny Hill* also were adjudged not obscene. These decisions have been important to me. As the author of *Against Our Will*, a study of the history of rape that does contain explicit sexual material, I shudder to think how my book would have fared if James Joyce, D. H. Lawrence, and Henry Miller hadn't gone before me.

I am not a fan of *Chatterley* or the *Tropic* books, I should quickly mention. They are not to my literary taste, nor do I think they represent female sexuality with any degree of accuracy. But I would hardly suggest that we ban them. Such a suggestion wouldn't get very far anyway. The battle to protect these books is ancient history. Time does march on, quite methodically. What, then, is unlawfully obscene, and what does the First Amendment have to do with it?

In the *Miller* case of 1973 (not Henry Miller, by the way, but a porn distributor who sent unsolicited stuff through the mails), the Court came up with new guidelines that it hoped would strengthen obscenity laws by giving more power to the states. What it did in actuality was throw everything into confusion. It set up a three-part test by which materials can be adjudged obscene. The materials are obscene if they depict patently offensive, hard-core sexual conduct; lack serious scientific, literary, artistic, or political value; and appeal to the prurient interest of an average person—as measured by contemporary community standards.

"Patently offensive," "prurient interest," and "hard-core" are indeed words to conjure with. "Contemporary community standards" are what we're trying to redefine. The feminist objection to pornography is not based on prurience, which the dictionary defines as lustful, itching desire. We are not opposed to sex and desire, with or without the itch, and we certainly believe that explicit sexual material has its place in literature, art, science, and education. Here we part company rather swiftly with old-line conservatives who don't want sex education in the high schools, for example.

No, the feminist objection to pornography is based on our belief that pornography represents hatred of women, that pornography's intent is to humiliate, degrade, and dehumanize the female body for the purpose of erotic stimulation and pleasure. We are unalterably opposed to the presentation of the female body being stripped, bound, raped, tortured, mutilated, and murdered in the name of commercial entertainment and free speech.

These images, which are standard pornographic fare, have nothing 10 to do with the hallowed right of political dissent. They have everything to do with the creation of a cultural climate in which a rapist feels he is merely giving in to a normal urge and a woman is encouraged to believe that sexual masochism is healthy, liberated fun. Justice Potter Stewart once said about hard-core pornography, "You know it when you see it," and that certainly used to be true. In the good old days, pornography looked awful. It was cheap and sleazy, and there was no mistaking it for art.

Nowadays, since the porn industry has become a multimillion dollar business, visual technology has been employed in its service. Pornographic movies are skillfully filmed and edited, pornographic still shots using the newest tenets of good design artfully grace the covers of *Hustler, Penthouse,* and *Playboy,* and the public—and the courts—are sadly confused.

The Supreme Court neglected to define "hard-core" in the *Miller* decision. This was a mistake. If "hard-core" refers only to explicit sexual intercourse, then that isn't good enough. When women or children or men—no matter how artfully—are shown tortured or terrorized in the service of sex, that's obscene. And "patently offensive," I would hope, to our "contemporary community standards."

Justice William O. Douglas wrote in his dissent to the *Miller* case that no one is "compelled to look." This is hardly true. To buy a paper at the corner newsstand is to subject oneself to a forcible immersion in pornography, to be demeaned by an array of dehumanized, chopped-up parts of the female anatomy, packaged like cuts of meat at the supermarket. I happen to like my body and I work hard at the gym to keep it in good shape, but I am embarrassed for my body and for the bodies of all women when I see the fragmented parts of us so frivolously, and so flagrantly, displayed.

Some constitutional theorists (Justice Douglas was one) have maintained that any obscenity law is a serious abridgement of free speech. Others (and Justice Earl Warren was one) have maintained that the First Amendment was never intended to protect obscenity. We live quite compatibly with a host of free-speech abridgements. There are restraints against false and misleading advertising or statements—shouting "fire" without cause in a crowded movie theater, etc.—that do not threaten, but strengthen, our societal values. Restrictions on the public display of pornography belong in this category.

The distinction between permission to publish and permission to display publicly is an essential one and one which I think consonant with First Amendment principles. Justice Burger's words which I quoted above support this without question. We are not saying "Smash the presses" or "Ban the bad ones," but simply "Get the stuff out of our sight." Let the legislatures decide—using realistic and humane contemporary community standards—what can be displayed and what cannot. The courts, after all, will be the final arbiters.

15

Topics for Critical Thinking and Writing

1. Objecting to Justice Douglas's remark that no one is "'compelled to look'" (para. 13), Brownmiller says, "This is hardly true. To buy a paper at the corner newsstand is to subject oneself to a forcible immersion in pornography, to be demeaned by an array of dehumanized, chopped-up parts of the female anatomy, packaged like cuts of meat at the supermarket." Is this true at your local newsstand, or are the sex magazines kept in one place, relatively remote from the newspapers?

2. Who is Brownmiller talking to—that is, who is her audience? Do you think she holds the attention of her intended audience?

3. When Brownmiller attempts to restate the "three-part test" for obscenity established by the Supreme Court in *Miller v. California,* she writes (para. 7): "The materials are obscene if they depict . . ." and so on. She should have written: "The materials are obscene if and only if they depict . . ." and so on. Explain what is wrong here with her "if," and why "if and only if" is needed.

4. In her next-to-last paragraph, Brownmiller reminds us that we already live quite comfortably with some "free-speech abridgements." The examples she gives are that we may not falsely shout "fire" in a crowded theater and may not issue misleading advertisements. Do you think that these widely accepted restrictions are valid evidence in arguing on behalf of limiting the display of what Brownmiller considers pornography? Why, or why not?

5. Brownmiller insists that defenders of the First Amendment, who will surely oppose laws that interfere with the freedom to publish, need not go on to condemn laws that regulate the freedom to publicly display pornographic publications. Do you agree? Suppose a publisher insists that he cannot sell his product at a profit unless he is permitted to display it to advantage and that restriction on the latter amounts to interference with his freedom to publish. How might Brownmiller reply?

6. In her last paragraph Brownmiller says that "contemporary community standards" should be decisive. Can it be argued that because standards vary from one community to another and from time to time even in the same place, her recommendation subjects the rights of a minority to the whims of a majority? (The Bill of Rights, after all, was supposed to safeguard the constitutional rights of the minority from the possible tyranny of the majority.) How is "contemporary community standards" defined in the essay? How do you define the term?

7. When Brownmiller accuses "the public . . . and the courts" of being "sadly confused" (para. 11), what does she think they are confused about? The definition of *pornography* or *obscenity*? The effects of such literature on men and women? Or is it something else?

Charles R. Lawrence III

Charles R. Lawrence III (b. 1943), author of numerous articles in law journals and coauthor of We Won't Go Back: Making the Case for Affirmative Action *(1997), teaches law at Georgetown University. This essay originally appeared in the* Chronicle of Higher Education *(October 25, 1989), a publication read chiefly by faculty and administrators at colleges and universities. An amplified version of the essay appeared in* Duke Law Journal *(February 1990).*

On Racist Speech

I have spent the better part of my life as a dissenter. As a high school student, I was threatened with suspension for my refusal to participate in a civil defense drill, and I have been a conspicuous consumer of my First Amendment liberties ever since. There are very strong reasons for protecting even racist speech. Perhaps the most important of these is that such protection reinforces our society's commitment to tolerance as a value, and that by protecting bad speech from government regulation, we will be forced to combat it as a community.

But I also have a deeply felt apprehension about the resurgence of racial violence and the corresponding rise in the incidence of verbal and symbolic assault and harassment to which blacks and other traditionally subjugated and excluded groups are subjected. I am troubled by the way the debate has been framed in response to the recent surge of racist incidents on college and university campuses and in response to some universities' attempts to regulate harassing speech. The problem has been framed as one in which the liberty of free speech is in conflict with the elimination of racism. I believe this has placed the bigot on the moral high ground and fanned the rising flames of racism.

Above all, I am troubled that we have not listened to the real victims, that we have shown so little understanding of their injury, and that we have abandoned those whose race, gender, or sexual preference continues to make them second-class citizens. It seems to me a very sad irony that the first instinct of civil libertarians has been to challenge even the smallest, most narrowly framed efforts by universities to provide black and other minority students with the protection the Constitution guarantees them.

The landmark case of *Brown v. Board of Education* is not a case that we normally think of as a case about speech. But *Brown* can be broadly read as articulating the principle of equal citizenship. *Brown* held that segregated schools were inherently unequal because of the *message* that segregation conveyed—that black children were an untouchable caste, unfit to go to school with white children. If we understand the necessity of eliminating the system of signs and symbols that signal the inferiority of blacks, then we should hesitate before proclaiming that all racist speech that stops short of physical violence must be defended.

University officials who have formulated policies to respond to in- 5 cidents of racial harassment have been characterized in the press as "thought police," but such policies generally do nothing more than impose sanctions against intentional face-to-face insults. When racist speech takes the form of face-to-face insults, catcalls, or other assaultive speech aimed at an individual or small group of persons, it falls directly within the "fighting words" exception to First Amendment protection. The Supreme Court has held that words which "by their very utterance inflict injury or tend to incite an immediate breach of the peace" are not protected by the First Amendment.

If the purpose of the First Amendment is to foster the greatest amount of speech, racial insults disserve that purpose. Assaultive racist speech functions as a preemptive strike. The invective is experienced as a blow, not as a proffered idea, and once the blow is struck, it is unlikely that a dialogue will follow. Racial insults are particularly undeserving of First Amendment protection because the perpetrator's intention is not to discover truth or initiate dialogue but to injure the victim. In most situations, members of minority groups realize that they are likely to lose if they respond to epithets by fighting and are forced to remain silent and submissive.

Courts have held that offensive speech may not be regulated in public forums such as streets where the listener may avoid the speech by moving on, but the regulation of otherwise protected speech has been permitted when the speech invades the privacy of the unwilling listener's home or when the unwilling listener cannot avoid the speech. Racist posters, fliers, and graffiti in dormitories, bathrooms, and other common living spaces would seem to clearly fall within the reasoning of these cases. Minority students should not be required to remain in their rooms in order to avoid racial assault. Minimally, they should find a safe haven in their dorms and in all other common rooms that are a part of their daily routine.

I would also argue that the university's responsibility for ensuring that these students receive an equal educational opportunity provides a compelling justification for regulations that ensure them safe passage in all common areas. A minority student should not have to risk becoming the target of racially assaulting speech every time he or she chooses to walk across campus. Regulating vilifying speech that cannot be anticipated or avoided would not preclude announced speeches and rallies—situations that would give minority-group members and their allies the chance to organize counterdemonstrations or avoid the speech altogether.

The most commonly advanced argument against the regulation of racist speech proceeds something like this: We recognize that minority groups suffer pain and injury as the result of racist speech, but we must allow this hate mongering for the benefit of society as a whole. Freedom of speech is the lifeblood of our democratic system. It is especially important for minorities because often it is their only vehicle for rallying support for the redress of their grievances. It will be impossible to formulate a prohibition so precise that it will prevent the racist speech you want to suppress without catching in the same net all kinds of speech that it would be unconscionable for a democratic society to suppress.

Whenever we make such arguments, we are striking a balance on 10 the one hand between our concern for the continued free flow of ideas and the democratic process dependent on that flow, and, on the other, our desire to further the cause of equality. There can be no meaningful discussion of how we should reconcile our commitment to equality and our commitment to free speech until it is acknowledged that there is real harm inflicted by racist speech and that this harm is far from trivial.

To engage in a debate about the First Amendment and racist speech without a full understanding of the nature and extent of that harm is to

risk making the First Amendment an instrument of domination rather than a vehicle of liberation. We have not known the experience of victimization by racist, misogynist, and homophobic speech, nor do we equally share the burden of the societal harm it inflicts. We are often quick to say that we have heard the cry of the victims when we have not.

The *Brown* case is again instructive because it speaks directly to the psychic injury inflicted by racist speech by noting that the symbolic message of segregation affected "the hearts and minds" of Negro children "in a way unlikely ever to be undone." Racial epithets and harassment often cause deep emotional scarring and feelings of anxiety and fear that pervade every aspect of a victim's life.

Brown also recognized that black children did not have an equal opportunity to learn and participate in the school community if they bore the additional burden of being subjected to the humiliation and psychic assault contained in the message of segregation. University students bear an analogous burden when they are forced to live and work in an environment where at any moment they may be subjected to denigrating verbal harassment and assault. The same injury was addressed by the Supreme Court when it held that sexual harassment that creates a hostile or abusive work environment violates the ban on sex discrimination in employment of Title VII of the Civil Rights Act of 1964.

Carefully drafted university regulations would bar the use of words as assault weapons and leave unregulated even the most heinous of ideas when those ideas are presented at times and places and in manners that provide an opportunity for reasoned rebuttal or escape from immediate injury. The history of the development of the right to free speech has been one of carefully evaluating the importance of free expression and its effects on other important societal interests. We have drawn the line between protected and unprotected speech before without dire results. (Courts have, for example, exempted from the protection of the First Amendment obscene speech and speech that disseminates official secrets, that defames or libels another person, or that is used to form a conspiracy or monopoly.)

Blacks and other people of color are skeptical about the argument 15 that even the most injurious speech must remain unregulated because, in an unregulated marketplace of ideas, the best ones will rise to the top and gain acceptance. Our experience tells us quite the opposite. We have seen too many good liberal politicians shy away from the issues that might brand them as being too closely allied with us.

Whenever we decide that racist speech must be tolerated because of the importance of maintaining societal tolerance for all unpopular speech, we are asking blacks and other subordinated groups to bear the burden for the good of all. We must be careful that the ease with which we strike the balance against the regulation of racist speech is in no way influenced by the fact that the cost will be borne by others. We must be

certain that those who will pay that price are fairly represented in our deliberations and that they are heard.

At the core of the argument that we should resist all government regulation of speech is the ideal that the best cure for bad speech is good, that ideas that affirm equality and the worth of all individuals will ultimately prevail. This is an empty ideal unless those of us who would fight racism are vigilant and unequivocal in that fight. We must look for ways to offer assistance and support to students whose speech and political participation are chilled in a climate of racial harassment.

Civil rights lawyers might consider suing on behalf of blacks whose right to an equal education is denied by a university's failure to ensure a nondiscriminatory educational climate or conditions of employment. We must embark upon the development of a First Amendment jurisprudence grounded in the reality of our history and our contemporary experience. We must think hard about how best to launch legal attacks against the most indefensible forms of hate speech. Good lawyers can create exceptions and narrow interpretations that limit the harm of hate speech without opening the floodgates of censorship.

Everyone concerned with these issues must find ways to engage actively in actions that resist and counter the racist ideas that we would have the First Amendment protect. If we fail in this, the victims of hate speech must rightly assume that we are on the oppressors' side.

Topics for Critical Thinking and Writing

1. Summarize Lawrence's essay in a paragraph. (You may find it useful first to summarize each paragraph in a sentence and then to revise these summary sentences into a paragraph.)

2. In a sentence state Lawrence's thesis (his main point).

3. Why do you suppose Lawrence included his first paragraph? What does it contribute to his argument?

4. In paragraph 8 Lawrence speaks of "racially assaulting speech" and of "vilifying speech." It is easy to think of words that fit these descriptions, but what about other words? Is *Uncle Tom,* used by an African American about another African American who is eager to please whites, an example of "racially assaulting speech"? Or take the word *gay.* Surely this word is acceptable because it is widely used by homosexuals, but what about *queer* (used by some homosexuals but usually derogatory when used by heterosexuals)? What might makes these words seem "assaulting" or "vilifying"?

5. Think about those provisions in the Code of Conduct of Shippensburg University in Pennsylvania: The code says that each student has a "primary" right to be free from harassment, intimidation, physical harm, and emotional abuse, and has a "secondary" right to express personal beliefs in a manner that does not "provoke, harass, demean, intimidate,

or harm" another. The code prohibits conduct that "annoys, threatens, or alarms a person or group," such as sexual harassment, "innuendo," "comments, insults," "propositions," "humor/jokes about sex or gender-specific traits," and "suggestive or insulting sounds, leering, whistling, [and] obscene gestures." The president of the university has said (according to the *New York Times,* April 24, 2003, p. A23) that the university encourages free speech as a means to examine ideas and that the university is "committed to the principle that this discussion be conducted appropriately. We do have expectations that our students will conduct themselves in a civil manner that allows them to express their opinions without interfering with the rights of others." Use this material to help you generate your own thoughts about speech on college campuses.

6. Find out if your college or university has a code — perhaps online — governing hate speech. If it does, evaluate it. If your college has no such code, make a case for why such a policy should be readily available to students and faculty. Compose a blog entry evaluating your current code, or draft your own code.

Derek Bok

Derek Bok was born in 1930 in Bryn Mawr, Pennsylvania, and educated at Stanford University and Harvard University, where he received a law degree. From 1971 to 1991 he served as president of Harvard University. The following essay, first published in the Boston Globe *in 1991, was prompted by the display of Confederate flags hung from a window of a Harvard dormitory.*

Protecting Freedom of Expression on the Campus

For several years, universities have been struggling with the problem of trying to reconcile the rights of free speech with the desire to avoid racial tension. In recent weeks, such a controversy has sprung up at Harvard. Two students hung Confederate flags in public view, upsetting students who equate the Confederacy with slavery. A third student tried to protest the flags by displaying a swastika.

These incidents have provoked much discussion and disagreement. Some students have urged that Harvard require the removal of symbols that offend many members of the community. Others reply that such symbols are a form of free speech and should be protected.

Different universities have resolved similar conflicts in different ways. Some have enacted codes to protect their communities from forms of speech that are deemed to be insensitive to the feelings of other groups. Some have refused to impose such restrictions.

It is important to distinguish between the appropriateness of such communications and their status under the First Amendment. The fact that speech is protected by the First Amendment does not necessarily

mean that it is right, proper, or civil. I am sure that the vast majority of Harvard students believe that hanging a Confederate flag in public view—or displaying a swastika in response—is insensitive and unwise because any satisfaction it gives to the students who display these symbols is far outweighed by the discomfort it causes to many others.

I share this view and regret that the students involved saw fit to behave in this fashion. Whether or not they merely wished to manifest their pride in the South—or to demonstrate the insensitivity of hanging Confederate flags, by mounting another offensive symbol in return—they must have known that they would upset many fellow students and ignore the decent regard for the feelings of others so essential to building and preserving a strong and harmonious community.

To disapprove of a particular form of communication, however, is not enough to justify prohibiting it. We are faced with a clear example of the conflict between our commitment to free speech and our desire to foster a community founded on mutual respect. Our society has wrestled with this problem for many years. Interpreting the First Amendment, the Supreme Court has clearly struck the balance in favor of free speech.

While communities do have the right to regulate speech in order to uphold aesthetic standards (avoiding defacement of buildings) or to protect the public from disturbing noise, rules of this kind must be applied across the board and cannot be enforced selectively to prohibit certain kinds of messages but not others.

Under the Supreme Court's rulings, as I read them, the display of swastikas or Confederate flags clearly falls within the protection of the free-speech clause of the First Amendment and cannot be forbidden simply because it offends the feelings of many members of the community. These rulings apply to all agencies of government, including public universities.

Although it is unclear to what extent the First Amendment is enforceable against private institutions, I have difficulty understanding why a university such as Harvard should have less free speech than the surrounding society—or than a public university.

One reason why the power of censorship is so dangerous is that it is extremely difficult to decide when a particular communication is offensive enough to warrant prohibition or to weigh the degree of offensiveness against the potential value of the communication. If we begin to forbid flags, it is only a short step to prohibiting offensive speakers.

I suspect that no community will become humane and caring by restricting what its members can say. The worst offenders will simply find other ways to irritate and insult.

In addition, once we start to declare certain things "offensive," with all the excitement and attention that will follow, I fear that much ingenuity will be exerted trying to test the limits, much time will be expended trying to draw tenuous distinctions, and the resulting publicity will eventually attract more attention to the offensive material than would ever have occurred otherwise.

his solutions:

(1) Rather than prohibit such communications, with all the resulting risks, it would be better to ignore them, since students would then have little reason to create such displays and would soon abandon them. If this response is not possible—and one can understand why—the wisest course is to speak with those who perform insensitive acts and try to help them understand the effects of their actions on others.

13

(2) Appropriate officials and faculty members should take the lead, as the Harvard House Masters have already done in this case. In talking with students, they should seek to educate and persuade, rather than resort to ridicule or intimidation, recognizing that only persuasion is likely to produce a lasting, beneficial effect. Through such effects, I believe that we act in the manner most consistent with our ideals as an educational institution and most calculated to help us create a truly understanding, supportive community.

14

Topics for Critical Thinking and Writing

1. Bok sketches the following argument (paras. 8 and 9): The First Amendment protects free speech in public universities and colleges; Harvard is not a public university; therefore, Harvard does not enjoy the protection of the First Amendment. Bok finds this argument plainly invalid. He clearly rejects the conclusion. "I have difficulty understanding why . . . Harvard should have less free speech . . . than a public university." What would need to be revised in the premises to make the argument valid? Do you think Bok would accept or reject such a revision?

2. Bok objects to censorship that simply prevents students from being "offended." He would not object to the campus police preventing students from being harmed. In an essay of 100 words, explain the difference between conduct that is *harmful* and conduct that is (merely?) *offensive*. (If you think that such a distinction cannot be made, explain why.)

3. Bok advises campus officials (and students) simply to "ignore" offensive words, flags, and so forth (para. 13). Do you agree with this advice? Or do you favor a different kind of response? Write a 250-word essay on the theme "How We Ought to Respond to the Offensive Misconduct of Others."

Thinking Further about Freedom of Expression and Facebook

On February 8, 2009, the *New York Times* reported that a high school senior, Katherine Evans, believed that her English teacher, Sarah Phelps, behaved offensively in two ways: Evans said that the teacher ignored her requests for help with assignments and, further, that Phelps brusquely reproached her when Evans missed a class because she attended a blood drive. Evans, an honor student, logged into Facebook and wrote about her teacher:

> To those select students who have had the displeasure of having Ms. Sarah Phelps, or simply knowing her and her insane antics: Here is the place to express your feelings of hatred.

The posting drew several responses, including some that criticized the student and supported the teacher. Here is one, written by a former student of Ms. Phelps, quoted by the *Times*:

> Whatever your reasons for hating her are, they're probably very immature.

Ms. Evans removed the posting a few days later but subsequently she was nevertheless reprimanded by the principal and was given a three-day suspension for "cyberbullying." Ms. Evans sued the principal of the high school. She was not asking for money other than legal fees: She wanted the suspension removed from her record. (She eventually settled the suit, and the suspension was wiped from her record.)

The issue to think about: Was the suspension an attack on Ms. Evans's right to free speech? Or did her comment and her invitation to "express feelings of hatred" constitute a verbal assault that crossed the line of freedom of expression? Howard Simon, executive director of the American Civil Liberties Union of Florida, takes the first position. The *Times* quotes him as saying, "Since when did criticism of a teacher morph into assault? If Katie Evans said what she said over burgers with her friends at the mall, there is no question it would be protected by free speech."

Two Writing Assignments

1. Construct a definition (perhaps two or three sentences) of *cyberbullying*. (If you draw on any sources be sure to cite them.)

2. Given the admittedly scanty information that we have on the Evans case, do you think a suspension was reasonable? If you think it was reasonable, explain why. If you think it was unreasonable, explain why, and indicate whether you think some other (lesser) punishment might have been appropriate. Your essay should be about 250 to 300 words long.

Exercise: Letter to the Editor

Your college newspaper has published a letter that links a hateful attribute to a group and that clearly displays hate for the entire group. (For instance, the letter charges that interracial marriages should be made illegal because "African Americans contain a criminal gene," or that "Jews should not be elected to office because their loyalty is to Israel, not the United States," or that "Muslims should not be allowed to enter the country because they are intent on destroying America.") The letter generates many letters of response; some responses, supporting the editor's decision to publish the letter, make these points:

- The writer of the offending letter is a student in the college, and she has a right to express her views.
- The point of view expressed is probably held only by a few persons, but conceivably it expresses a view held by a significant number of students.
- Editors should not act as censors.
- The First Amendment guarantees freedom of speech.
- Freedom of expression is healthy, i.e., society gains.

On the other hand, among the letters opposing the editor's decision to publish, some make points along these lines:

- Not every view of every nutty student can be printed; editors must make responsible choices.
- The First Amendment, which prohibits the government from controlling the press, has nothing to do with a college newspaper.
- Letters of this sort do not foster healthy discussion; they merely heat things up.

Write a 250- to 500-word letter to the editor, expressing your view of the editor's decision to publish the first letter. (If you wish, you can assume that the letter was on one of the topics we specify in the second sentence of this exercise. But in any case, address the general issue of the editor's decision, not only the specific issue of the charge or charges made in the first letter.)

Critical Reading:
Getting Deeper into Arguments

He that wrestles with us strengthens our nerves, and sharpens our skill.
Our antagonist is our helper.

— EDMUND BURKE

PERSUASION, ARGUMENT, DISPUTE

When we think seriously about an argument (not name calling or mere rationalization), not only do we hear ideas that may be unfamiliar, but we are also forced to examine closely our own cherished opinions, and perhaps for the first time really come to see the strengths and weaknesses of what we believe. As John Stuart Mill put it, "He who knows only his own side of the case knows little."

It is customary, and useful, to distinguish between **persuasion** and **argument**. Persuasion has the broader meaning. To **persuade** is to win over — whether

- by giving reasons (that is, by argument, by logic),
- by appealing to the emotions, or, for that matter,
- by using torture.

Argument, one form of persuasion, relies on reason; *it offers statements as reasons for other statements*. Rhetoricians often use the Greek word *logos*, which merely means "word" or "reason," to denote this aspect of persuasive writing — the appeal to reason. An appeal to reason may by supported by

- physical evidence;
- the testimony of experts;
- common sense; and
- probability.

We can put it this way: The goal of *argument* is to convince by demonstrating the truth (or probable truth) of an assertion, whereas the goal of *persuasion* is to conquer, by one means or another.

The appeal to the emotions is known as **pathos.** Strictly speaking, *pathos* is Greek for "feeling," and especially for "suffering," but it now covers all sorts of emotional appeals — for instance, to one's sense of pity or sympathy (Greek for "feeling with") or one's sense of patriotism.

Notice that an argument, in the sense of statements that are offered as reasons for other statements, does not require two speakers or writers who represent opposed positions. The Declaration of Independence is an argument, setting forth the colonists' reasons for declaring their independence. In practice, of course, someone's argument usually advances reasons for a claim in opposition to someone else's position or belief. But even if one is writing only for oneself, trying to clarify one's thinking by setting forth reasons, the result is an argument. **Dispute,** however, is a special kind of argument in which two or more people express views that are at odds.

Most of this book is about argument in the sense of the presentation of reasons in support of claims, but of course, reason is not the whole story. If an argument is to be effective, it must be presented persuasively. For instance, the writer's **tone** (attitude toward self, topic, and audience) must be appropriate if the discourse is to persuade the reader. The careful presentation of the self is not something disreputable, nor is it something that publicity agents or advertising agencies invented. Aristotle (384–322 B.C.) emphasized the importance of impressing on the audience that the speaker is a person of good sense and high moral character. (He called this aspect of persuasion *ethos,* the Greek word for "character," a basis of persuasion different from *logos,* which we have noted is the word for persuasion by appealing to reason.)

Writers convey their trustworthiness by

- using language appropriate to the setting, avoiding vulgar language;
- showing an awareness of the complexity of the issue (for instance, by granting the goodwill of those offering other points of view and by recognizing that there may be some merit to contrary points of view); and
- showing attention to detail (for instance, by citing relevant statistics).

In short, writers who are concerned with *ethos* — and all writers should be — employ devices that persuade readers that the writers are trustworthy, are fair-minded, intelligent persons in whom the reader can have confidence.

We talk at length about tone, along with other matters such as the organization of an argument, in Chapter 5, Writing an Analysis of an Argument, but here we deal with some of the chief devices used in reasoning, and we glance at emotional appeals.

We should note at once, however, that an argument presupposes a fixed **topic.** Suppose we are arguing about Thomas Jefferson's assertion, in the Declaration of Independence, that "all men are created equal." Jones subscribes to this statement, but Smith says it is nonsense and argues that one has only to look around to see that some people are brighter than others, or healthier, or better coordinated, or whatever. Jones and Smith, if they intend to argue the point, will do well to examine what Jefferson actually wrote:

> We hold these truths to be self-evident, that all men are created equal: that they are endowed by their Creator with certain unalienable rights; and that among these are life, liberty, and the pursuit of happiness.

There is room for debate over what Jefferson really meant and about whether he is right, but clearly he was talking about *equality of rights.* If Smith and Jones wish to argue about Jefferson's view of equality—that is, if they wish to offer their reasons for accepting, rejecting, or modifying it—they will do well first to agree on what Jefferson said or what he probably meant to say. Jones and Smith may still hold different views; they may continue to disagree on whether Jefferson was right and proceed to offer arguments and counterarguments to settle the point. But only if they can agree on *what* they disagree about will their dispute get somewhere.

IDEA PROMPT 3.1 ESTABLISHING TRUSTWORTHINESS AND CREDIBILITY

Acknowledge weaknesses, exceptions, and complexities.	"Although the unemployment rate continues to decline, further investigation into underemployment and the loss of jobless benefits is necessary in order to truly understand the unemployment crisis in the United States."
Use personal experience when appropriate.	"As a student who works and attends school full time, I can speak firsthand about the importance of increased availability of financial aid."
Use a tone that respects your audience.	When appropriate, use humor to connect to your readers. Avoid vulgarity or incendiary language that might alienate an audience.
Mention the qualifications of any sources as a way to boost your own credibility.	"According to Deborah Tannen, author and noted professor of linguistics at Georgetown University . . ."

REASON VERSUS RATIONALIZATION

Reason may not be our only way of finding the truth, but it is a way we often rely on. The subway ran yesterday at 6:00 A.M. and the day before at 6:00 A.M. and the day before, and so I infer from this evidence that it will also run today at 6:00 A.M. (a form of reasoning known as **induction**). Bus drivers require would-be passengers to present the exact change; I do not have the exact change; therefore, I infer I cannot ride on the bus (**deduction**). (The terms *deduction* and *induction* are discussed in more detail on pages 55–86 and 90–91.)

We also know that, if we set our minds to a problem, we can often find reasons (not necessarily sound ones but reasons nevertheless) for almost anything we want to justify. Here is an entertaining example from Benjamin Franklin's *Autobiography:*

> I believe I have omitted mentioning that in my first voyage from Boston, being becalmed off Block Island, our people set about catching cod and hauled up a great many. Hitherto I had stuck to my resolution of not eating animal food, and on this occasion, I considered with my master Tryon the taking of every fish as a kind of unprovoked murder, since none of them had or ever could do us any injury that might justify the slaughter. All this seemed very reasonable. But I had formerly been a great lover of fish, and when this came hot out of the frying pan, it smelt admirably well. I balanced some time between principle and inclination, till I recollected that when the fish were opened I saw smaller fish taken out of their stomachs. Then thought I, if you eat one another, I don't see why we mayn't eat you. So I dined upon cod very heartily and continued to eat with other people, returning only now and then occasionally to a vegetable diet. So convenient a thing it is to be a *reasonable creature,* since it enables one to find or make a reason for everything one has a mind to do.

Franklin is being playful; he is *not* engaging in critical thinking. He tells us that he loved fish, that this fish "smelt admirably well," and so we are prepared for him to find a reason (here one as weak as "Fish eat fish, therefore people may eat fish") to abandon his vegetarianism. (But think: Fish also eat their own young. May we therefore eat ours?)

Still, Franklin touches on a truth: If necessary, we can find reasons to justify whatever we want. That is, instead of reasoning we may *rationalize* (devise a self-serving but dishonest reason), like the fox in Aesop's fables who, finding the grapes he desired were out of his reach, consoled himself with the thought that they were probably sour.

Perhaps we can never be certain that we are not rationalizing, except when, like Franklin, we are being playful—but we can seek to think critically about our own beliefs, scrutinizing our assumptions, looking for counterevidence, and wondering if different conclusions can reasonably be drawn.

SOME PROCEDURES IN ARGUMENT

Definition

Definition, we mentioned in our first chapter, is one of the classical topics, a "place" to which one goes with questions; in answering the questions, one finds ideas. When we define, we are answering the question "What is it?" and in answering this question as precisely as we can, we will find, clarify, and develop ideas.

We have already glanced at an argument over the proposition that "all men are created equal," and we saw that the words needed clarification. *Equal* meant, in the context, not physically or mentally equal but something like "equal in rights," equal politically and legally. (And of course, *men* meant "white men and women.") Words do not always mean exactly what they seem to: There is no lead in a lead pencil, and a standard 2-by-4 is currently $1^5/_8$ inches in thickness and $3^3/_8$ inches in width.

Definition by Synonym   Let's return, for a moment, to *pornography,* a word that, we saw, is not easily defined. One way to define a word is to offer a **synonym.** Thus, pornography can be defined, at least roughly, as "obscenity" (something indecent). But definition by synonym is usually only a start because we find that we will have to define the synonym and, besides, that very few words have exact synonyms. (In fact, *pornography* and *obscenity* are not exact synonyms.)

"It all depends on how you define 'chop.'"

Definition by Example   A second way to define something is to point to an example (this is often called **ostensive definition,** from the Latin *ostendere,* "to show"). This method can be very helpful, ensuring that both writer and reader are talking about the same thing, but it also has its limitations. A few decades ago many people pointed to James Joyce's *Ulysses* and D. H. Lawrence's *Lady Chatterley's Lover* as examples of obscene novels, but today these books are regarded as literary masterpieces. Possibly they can be obscene and also be literary masterpieces. (Joyce's wife is reported to have said of her husband, "He may have been a great writer, but . . . he had a very dirty mind.")

One of the difficulties of using an example, however, is that the example is richer and more complex than the term it is being used to define, and this richness and complexity get in the way of achieving a clear definition. Thus, if one cites Lawrence's *Lady Chatterley's Lover* as an example of pornography, a reader may erroneously think that pornography has something to do with British novels or with heterosexual relationships outside of marriage. Yet neither of these ideas is part of the concept of pornography.

We are not trying here to formulate a satisfactory definition of *pornography.* Our object is to show that:

- An argument will be most fruitful if the participants first agree on what they are talking about.

- One way to secure such agreement is to define the topic ostensively.

- Choosing the right example, one that has all the central or typical characteristics, can make a topic not only clear but also vivid.

Definition by Stipulation   Arguments frequently involve matters of definition: In a discussion of gun control, for instance, you probably will hear one side speak of *assault weapons* and the other side reject the term and speak of *so-called assault weapons.* In arguing, you can hope to get agreement—at least on what the topic of argument is—by offering a **stipulative definition** (from a Latin verb, "to bargain"). You and a representative of the other side can agree, for instance, that by *assault weapon* you both mean (and this was the meaning of the term in the ban approved by Congress in 1994, which expired in 2004, and which President Obama in 2013 asked Congress to renew) a semiautomatic firearm (the spent cartridge case is automatically extracted and a new round is automatically reloaded into the chamber but is not fired until the trigger is pulled again) with a detachable magazine *and at least two of the following five characteristics:*

- collapsible or folding stock

- pistol grip (thus allowing the weapon to be fired from the hip)

- bayonet mount
- grenade launcher
- flash suppressor (to keep the shooter from being blinded by muzzle flashes).

Again, this is an agreed-upon definition. Congress put *fully* automatic weapons into an entirely different category, and the legislatures of California and of New York each agreed on a stipulation different from that of Congress: In these two states, an assault weapon is a semiautomatic firearm with a detachable magazine and with any *one* (not two) of the five bulleted items.

Let's now look at stipulative definitions in other contexts. Who is a *Native American*? In discussing this issue, you might stipulate that by *Native American* you mean any person with any Native American blood; or you might say, "For the purpose of the present discussion, I mean by a *Native American* any person who has at least one grandparent of pure Native American blood." A stipulative definition is appropriate where

- no fixed or standard definition is available, and
- some arbitrary specification is necessary to fix the meaning of a key term in the argument.

Not everyone may be willing to accept your stipulative definition, and alternatives can probably be defended. In any case, when you stipulate a definition, your audience knows what *you* mean by the term thus defined.

It would *not* be reasonable, of course, to stipulate that by *Native American* you mean anyone with a deep interest in North American aborigines. That's just too idiosyncratic to be useful. Similarly, an essay on Jews in America will have to rely on some definition of the key idea. Perhaps the writer will stipulate the definition used in Israel: A Jew is a person who has a Jewish mother or, if not born of a Jewish mother, a person who has formally adopted the Jewish faith. Or perhaps the writer will stipulate another meaning: Jews are people who consider themselves to be Jews. Some sort of reasonable definition must be offered.

To stipulate, however, that by *Jews* you mean "persons who believe that the area formerly called Palestine rightfully belongs to the Jews" would hopelessly confuse matters. Remember the old riddle and the answer: If you call a dog's tail a leg, how many legs does a dog have? Answer: Four. Calling a tail a leg doesn't make it a leg.

Later in this chapter you will see, in an essay called "When 'Identity' Politics Is Rational," Stanley Fish begin by stipulating a definition. His first paragraph begins thus:

> If there's anything everyone is against in these election times, it's "identity politics," a phrase that covers a multitude of sins. Let me start with a definition. (It may not be yours, but it will at least allow the discussion

to be framed.) You're practicing identity politics when you vote for or against someone because of his or her skin color, ethnicity, religion, gender, sexual orientation, or any other marker that leads you to say yes or no independently of a candidates' ideas or policies.

Fish will go on to argue, in later paragraphs, that sometimes identity politics makes very good sense, that it is *not* irrational, is *not* logically indefensible, but here we simply want to make two points—one about how a definition helps the writer, the second about how it helps the reader:

- A definition is a good way to get yourself started when you are drafting an essay, a useful stimulus (idea prompt, pattern, template, heuristic) that will help *you* to think about the issue, a device that will stimulate your further thinking.

- A definition lets readers be certain that they are clear about what the author means by a crucial word.

Readers may disagree with Fish, but at least they know what he means when he speaks of identity politics.

A stipulation may be helpful and legitimate. Here is the opening paragraph of an essay by Richard B. Brandt titled "The Morality and Rationality of Suicide" (from *A Handbook for the Study of Suicide,* edited by Seymour Perlin). Notice that

- the author first stipulates a definition, and

- then, aware that the definition may strike some readers as too broad and therefore unreasonable or odd, he offers a reason on behalf of his definition.

"Suicide" is conveniently defined, for our purposes, as doing something which results in one's death, either from the intention of ending one's life or the intention to bring about some other state of affairs (such as relief from pain) which one thinks it certain or highly probable can be achieved only by means of death or will produce death. It may seem odd to classify an act of heroic self-sacrifice on the part of a soldier as suicide. It is simpler, however, not to try to define "suicide" so that an act of suicide is always irrational or immoral in some way; if we adopt a neutral definition like the above we can still proceed to ask when an act of suicide in that sense is rational, morally justifiable, and so on, so that all evaluations anyone might wish to make can still be made.

Sometimes a definition that at first seems extremely odd can be made acceptable, if strong reasons are offered in its support. Sometimes, in fact, an odd definition marks a great intellectual step forward. For instance, in 1990 the U.S. Supreme Court recognized that *speech* includes symbolic nonverbal expression such as protesting against a war by wearing armbands or by flying the American flag upside down. Such actions, because they express ideas or emotions, are now protected by the First

Amendment. Few people today would disagree that *speech* should include symbolic gestures. (We include an example of controversy over precisely this issue, in Derek Bok's "Protecting Freedom of Expression on the Campus," in Chapter 2, Critical Reading: Getting Started.)

A definition that seems notably eccentric to many readers and thus far has not gained much support is from page 94 of Peter Singer's *Practical Ethics,* in which the author suggests that a nonhuman being can be a *person.* He admits that "it sounds odd to call an animal a person" but says that it seems so only because of our bad habit of sharply separating ourselves from other species. For Singer, *persons* are "rational and self-conscious beings, aware of themselves as distinct entities with a past and a future." Thus, although a newborn infant is a human being, it is not a person; on the other hand, an adult chimpanzee is not a human being but probably is a person. You don't have to agree with Singer to know exactly what he means and where he stands. Moreover, if you read his essay, you may even find that his reasons are plausible and that by means of his unusual definition he has enlarged your thinking.

The Importance of Definitions   Trying to decide on the best way to define a key idea or a central concept is often difficult as well as controversial. *Death,* for example, has been redefined in recent years. Traditionally, a person was dead when there was no longer any heartbeat. But with advancing medical technology, the medical profession has persuaded legislatures to redefine death as cessation of cerebral and cortical functions—so-called brain death.

Some scholars have hoped to bring clarity into the abortion debate by redefining *life.* Traditionally, human life begins at birth or perhaps at viability (the capacity of a fetus to live independently of the uterine environment). However, some have proposed a *brain birth* definition, in the hope of resolving the abortion controversy. Some thinkers want abortion to be prohibited by law at the point where "integrated brain functioning begins to emerge," allegedly about seventy days after conception. Whatever the merits of such a redefinition, the debate is convincing evidence of just how important the definition of certain terms can be.

Last Words about Definition   Since Plato's time, in the fourth century B.C., it has often been argued that the best way to give a definition is to state the *essence* of the thing being defined. Thus, the classic example defines *man* as "a rational animal." (Today, to avoid sexist implications, instead of *man* we would say *human being* or *person.*) That is, the property of *rational animality* is taken to be the essence of every human creature, and so it must be mentioned in the definition of *man.* This statement guarantees that the definition is neither too broad nor too narrow. But philosophers have long criticized this alleged ideal type of definition, on several grounds, one of which is that no one can propose such definitions without assuming that the thing being defined has an essence in the first place—an assumption that is not necessary. Thus, we may want to define *causality,* or *explanation,* or even *definition* itself, but it is doubtful whether it is sound to assume that any of these things has an essence.

A much better way to provide a definition is to offer a set of **sufficient and necessary conditions.** Suppose we want to define the word *circle* and are conscious of the need to keep circles distinct from other geometrical figures such as rectangles and spheres. We might express our definition by citing sufficient and necessary conditions as follows: "Anything is a circle *if and only if* it is a closed plane figure and all points on the circumference are equidistant from the center." Using the connective "if and only if" (called the *biconditional*) between the definition and what is being defined helps to force into our consciousness the need to make the definition neither too exclusive (too narrow) nor too inclusive (too broad). Of course, for most ordinary purposes we don't require such a formally precise and explicit definition. Nevertheless, perhaps the best criterion to keep in mind when assessing a proposed definition is whether it can be stated in the "if and only if" form, and whether, if it is so stated, it is true; that is, if it truly specifies *all and only* the things covered by the word being defined. Idea Prompt 3.2 provides examples.

We are not saying that the four sentences in the table are incontestable. They are arguable. We offer them merely to show ways of defining, and the act of defining is one way of helping you to get your own thoughts going. Notice, too, that the fourth of these examples, a "statement of necessary and sufficient conditions" (indicated by "if and only if") is a bit stiff for ordinary writing. An informal prompt along this line might begin, "Essentially, something can be called *pornography* if it presents. . . ."

IDEA PROMPT 3.2 WAYS TO GIVE DEFINITIONS

Synonym	"Pornography, simply stated, is obscenity."
Example	"Pornography is easily seen in D. H. Lawrence's *Lady Chatterley's Lover* in the scene where . . ."
Stipulation	"For the purposes of this essay, *pornography* refers to . . ."
Statement of necessary and sufficient conditions	"Something can be called pornography if and only if it presents sexually stimulating material without offering anything of redeeming social value."

Assumptions

In Chapter 1, Critical Thinking, we discussed the **assumptions** made by the authors of two essays on campus discipline. But we have more to say about assumptions. We have already said that in the form of discourse known as argument certain statements are offered as reasons for other statements. But even the longest and most complex chain of reasoning or proof is fastened to assumptions—one or more *unexamined beliefs*. (Even if such a belief is shared by writer and reader, it is no less an assumption.) Benjamin Franklin argued against paying salaries to the holders of executive offices in the federal government on the grounds that men are moved by ambition (love of power) and by avarice (love of money) and that powerful positions conferring wealth incite men to do their worst. These assumptions he stated, though he felt no need to argue them at length because he assumed that his readers shared them.

An assumption may be unstated. A writer, painstakingly arguing specific points, may choose to keep one or more of the argument's assumptions tacit. Or the writer may be as unaware of some underlying assumption as of the surrounding air. For example, Franklin didn't even bother to state another assumption. He must have assumed that persons of wealth who accept an unpaying job (after all, only persons of wealth could afford to hold unpaid government jobs) will have at heart the interests of all classes of people, not only the interests of their own class. Probably Franklin did not state this assumption because he thought it was perfectly obvious, but if you think critically about the assumption, you may find reasons to doubt it. Surely one reason we pay our legislators is to make certain that the legislature does not consist only of people whose incomes may give them an inadequate view of the needs of others.

An Example: Assumptions in the Argument Permitting Abortion

1. Ours is a pluralistic society, in which we believe that the religious beliefs of one group should not be imposed on others.
2. Personal privacy is a right, and a woman's body is hers, not to be violated by laws that tell her she may not do certain things to her body.

But these (and other) arguments *assume* that a fetus is not—or not yet—a person and therefore is not entitled to the same protection against assaults that we are. Virtually all of us assume that it is usually wrong to kill a human being. Granted, we may find instances in which we believe it is acceptable to take a human life, such as self-defense against a would-be murderer. But even here we find a shared assumption that persons are ordinarily entitled not to be killed.

The argument about abortion, then, usually depends on opposed assumptions: For one group, the fetus is a human being and a potential person—and this potentiality is decisive. But for the other group it is not. Persons arguing one side or the other of the abortion issue ought to be aware that opponents may not share their assumptions.

Premises and Syllogisms

Premises are stated assumptions used as reasons in an argument. (The word comes from a Latin word meaning "to send before" or "to set in front.") A premise thus is a statement set down—assumed—before the argument is begun. The joining of two premises—two statements taken to be true—to produce a conclusion, a third statement, is called a **syllogism** (Greek for "a reckoning together"). The classic example is this:

Major premise: All human beings are mortal.
Minor premise: Socrates is a human being.
Conclusion: Socrates is mortal.

Deduction

The mental process of moving from one statement ("All human beings are mortal") through another ("Socrates is a human being") to yet a further statement ("Socrates is mortal") is called **deduction,** from Latin for "lead down from." In this sense, deductive reasoning does not give us any new knowledge, although it is easy to construct examples that have so many premises, or premises that are so complex, that the conclusion really does come as news to most who examine the argument. Thus, the great detective Sherlock Holmes was credited by his admiring colleague, Dr. Watson, with unusual powers of deduction. Watson meant in part that Holmes could see the logical consequences of apparently disconnected reasons, the number and complexity of which left others at a loss. What is common in all cases of deduction is that the reasons or premises offered are supposed to contain within themselves, so to speak, the conclusion extracted from them.

Often a syllogism is abbreviated. Martin Luther King Jr., defending a protest march, wrote in "Letter from Birmingham Jail":

You assert that our actions, even though peaceful, must be condemned because they precipitate violence.

Fully expressed, the argument that King attributes to his critics would be stated thus:

Society must condemn actions (even if peaceful) that precipitate violence.

This action (though peaceful) will precipitate violence.

Therefore, society must condemn this action.

An incomplete or abbreviated syllogism in which one of the premises is left unstated, of the sort found in King's original quotation, is called an **enthymeme** (Greek for "in the mind").

Here is another, more whimsical example of an enthymeme, in which both a premise and the conclusion are left implicit. Henry David Thoreau remarked that "circumstantial evidence can be very strong, as when you find a trout in the milk." The joke, perhaps intelligible only to people born before 1930 or so, depends on the fact that milk used to be sold "in bulk"—that is, ladled out of a big can directly to the customer by the farmer or grocer. This practice was finally prohibited in the 1930s because for centuries the sellers, in order to increase their profit, were diluting the milk with water. Thoreau's enthymeme can be fully expressed thus:

Trout live only in water.

This milk has a trout in it.

Therefore, this milk has water in it.

These enthymemes have three important properties: Their premises are *true*, the form of their argument is *valid*, and they leave *implicit* either the conclusion or one of the premises.

Sound Arguments

The purpose of a syllogism is to present reasons that establish its conclusion. This is done by making sure that the argument satisfies both of two independent criteria:

- First, all of the premises must be *true.*
- Second, the syllogism must be *valid.*

Once these criteria are satisfied, the conclusion of the syllogism is guaranteed. Any such argument is said to establish or to prove its conclusion, or to use another term, it is said to be **sound.** Here's an example of a sound argument, a syllogism that proves its conclusion:

Extracting oil from the Arctic Wildlife Refuge would adversely affect the local ecology.

Adversely affecting the local ecology is undesirable, unless there is no better alternative fuel source.

Therefore, extracting oil from the Arctic Wildlife Refuge is undesirable, unless there is no better alternative fuel source.

Each premise is **true,** and the syllogism is **valid,** so it establishes its conclusion.

But how do we tell in any given case that an argument is sound? We perform two different tests, one for the truth of each of the premises and another for the validity of the argument.

The basic test for the **truth** of a premise is to determine whether what it asserts corresponds with reality; if it does, then it is true, and if it doesn't, then it is false. Everything depends on the content of the premise—what it asserts—and the evidence for it. (In the preceding syllogism, the truth of the premises can be tested by checking the views of experts and interested parties, such as policymakers, environmental groups, and experts on energy.)

The test for **validity** is quite different. We define a valid argument as one in which the conclusion follows from the premises, so that if all the premises are true then the conclusion *must* be true, too. The general test for validity, then, is this: If one grants the premises, one must also grant the conclusion. Or to put it another way, if one grants the premises but denies the conclusion, is one caught in a self-contradiction? If so, the argument is valid; if not, the argument is invalid.

The preceding syllogism passes this test. If you grant the information given in the premises but deny the conclusion, you have contradicted yourself. Even if the information were in error, the conclusion in this syllogism would still follow from the premises—the hallmark of a valid argument! The conclusion follows because the validity of an argument is a purely formal matter concerning the *relation* between premises and conclusion based on what they mean.

This relationship can be seen more clearly by examining an argument that is valid but that, because one or both of the premises are false, does *not* establish its conclusion. Here is an example of such a syllogism:

The whale is a large fish.

All large fish have scales.

Therefore, whales have scales.

We know that the premises and the conclusion are false: Whales are mammals, not fish, and not all large fish have scales (sharks have no scales, for instance). But when the validity of the argument is being determined, the truth of the premises and the conclusion is beside the point. Just a little reflection assures us that *if* both of these premises were true, then the conclusion would have to be true as well. That is, anyone who grants the premises of this syllogism and yet denies the conclusion has contradicted herself. So the validity of an argument does not in any way depend on the truth of the premises or the conclusion.

A sound argument, as we said, is an argument that passes both the test of true premises and the test of valid inference. To put it another way, a sound argument

- passes the test of content (the premises are true, as a matter of fact) and it
- passes the test of form (its premises and conclusion, by virtue of their very meanings, are so related that it is impossible for the premises to be true and the conclusion false).

Accordingly, an unsound argument, an argument that fails to prove its conclusion, suffers from one or both of two defects.

- First, not all of the premises are true.
- Second, the argument is invalid.

Usually, we have in mind one or both of these defects when we object to someone's argument as "illogical." In evaluating someone's deductive argument, therefore, you must always ask: Is it vulnerable to criticism on the ground that one (or more) of its premises is false? Or is the inference itself vulnerable because even if all the premises are all true, the conclusion still wouldn't follow?

A deductive argument *proves* its conclusion if and only if *two conditions* are satisfied: (1) All the premises are *true,* and (2) it would be *inconsistent to assert the premises and deny the conclusions.*

A Word about False Premises   Suppose that one or more of the premises of a syllogism are false but the syllogism itself is valid. What does that tell us about the truth of the conclusion? Consider this example:

All Americans prefer vanilla ice cream to other flavors.

Tiger Woods is an American.

Therefore, Tiger Woods prefers vanilla ice cream to other flavors.

The first (or major) premise in this syllogism is false. Yet the argument passes our formal test for validity; it is clear that if one grants both premises, then one must accept the conclusion. So we can say that the conclusion *follows from* its premises, even though the premises *do not prove* the conclusion. This is not as paradoxical as it may sound. For all we know, the conclusion of this argument may in fact be true; Tiger Woods may indeed prefer vanilla ice cream, and the odds are that he does because consumption statistics show that a majority of Americans prefer vanilla. Nevertheless, if the conclusion in this syllogism is true, it is not because this argument proved it.

A Word about Invalid Syllogisms   Usually, one can detect a false premise in an argument, especially when the suspect premise appears in someone else's argument. A trickier business is the invalid syllogism. Consider this argument:

All terrorists seek publicity for their violent acts.

John Doe seeks publicity for his violent acts.

Therefore, John Doe is a terrorist.

In the preceding syllogism, let us grant that the first (major) premise is true. Let us also grant that the conclusion may well be true. Finally, the person mentioned in the second (minor) premise could indeed be a terrorist. But it is also possible that the conclusion is false; terrorists are not the only ones who seek publicity for their violent acts; think, for example, of the violence committed against doctors, clinic workers, and patients at clinics where abortions are performed. In short, the truth of the two premises is no guarantee that the conclusion is also true. It is possible to assert both premises and deny the conclusion without self-contradiction.

How do we tell, in general and in particular cases, whether a syllogism is valid? Chemists use litmus paper to enable them to tell instantly whether the liquid in a test tube is an acid or a base. Unfortunately, logic has no litmus test to tell us instantly whether an argument is valid or invalid. Logicians beginning with Aristotle have developed techniques that enable them to test any given argument, no matter how complex or subtle, to determine its validity. But the results of their labors cannot be expressed in a paragraph or even a few pages; not for nothing are semester-long courses devoted to teaching formal deductive logic. Apart from advising you to consult Chapter 9, A Logician's View: Deduction, Induction, Fallacies, all we can do here is repeat two basic points.

First, validity of deductive arguments is a matter of their *form* or *structure*. Even syllogisms like the one on the Arctic Wildlife Refuge on page 87 come in a large variety of forms (256 different ones, to be precise), and only some of these forms are valid. Second, all valid deductive arguments (and only such arguments) pass this test: If one accepts all the premises, then one must accept the conclusion as well. Hence, if it is possible to accept the premises but reject the conclusion (without self-contradiction, of course), then the argument is invalid.

Let us exit from further discussion of this important but difficult subject on a lighter note. Many illogical arguments masquerade as logical. Consider this example: If it takes a horse and carriage four hours to go from Pinsk to Chelm, does it follow that a carriage with two horses will get there in two hours?

Note: In Chapter 9, we discuss at some length other kinds of deductive arguments, as well as **fallacies,** which are kinds of invalid reasoning.

Induction

Whereas deduction takes our beliefs and assumptions and extracts their hidden consequences, **induction** uses information about observed cases to reach a conclusion about unobserved cases. (The word comes from the Latin *in ducere,* "to lead into" or "to lead up to.") If we observe that the bite of a certain snake is poisonous, we may conclude on this evidence that another snake of the same general type is also poisonous. Our inference might be even broader. If we observe that snake after snake of a certain type has a poisonous bite and that these snakes are all rattlesnakes, we are tempted to **generalize** that all rattlesnakes are poisonous.

By far the most common way to test the adequacy of a generalization is to confront it with one or more **counterexamples.** If the counterexamples are genuine and reliable, then the generalization must be false. For example, Ronald Takaki's essay on the "myth" of Asian racial superiority (p. 123) is full of examples that contradict the alleged superiority of Asians; they are counterexamples to that thesis, and they help to expose it as a "myth." What is true of Takaki's reasoning is true generally in argumentative writing. We are constantly testing our generalizations against actual or possible counterexamples, or by doing research on the issue.

Unlike deduction, induction gives us conclusions that go beyond the information contained in the premises used in their support. Not surprisingly, the conclusions of inductive reasoning are not always true, even when all the premises are true. On page 77, we gave as an example our observation that on previous days a subway has run at 6:00 A.M. and that therefore we believe that it runs at 6:00 A.M. every day. Suppose, following this reasoning, we arrive at the subway platform just before 6:00 A.M. on a given day and wait an hour without a train. What inference should we draw to explain this? Possibly today is Sunday, and the subway doesn't run before 7:00 A.M. Or possibly there was a breakdown earlier this morning. Whatever the explanation, we relied on a sample that was not large enough (a larger sample might have included some early morning breakdowns) or not representative enough (a more representative sample would have included the later starts on holidays).

A Word about Samples   When we reason inductively, much depends on the size and the quality of the sample—"sample" because a writer probably cannot examine every instance. If, for example, we are offering an argument concerning the politics of members of sororities and fraternities, we probably cannot interview *every* member. Rather, we select a sample. But is the sample a fair sample? Is it representative of the larger group? We may interview five members of Alpha Tau Omega and find that all five are Republicans, yet we cannot legitimately conclude that all members of ATO are Republicans. The problem is not always one of failing to interview large numbers. A poll of ten thousand college students tells us very little about "college students" if all ten thousand are white males at the University of Texas. Such a sample, because it leaves out women and minority males, obviously is not sufficiently *representative* of "college students" as a group. Further, though not all of the students at the University of Texas are from Texas or even from the Southwest, it is quite likely that the student body is not fully representative (for instance, in race and in income) of American college students. If this conjecture is correct, even a truly representative sample of University of Texas students would not allow one to draw firm conclusions about American college students.

In short: An argument that uses samples ought to tell the reader how the samples were chosen. If it does not provide this information, the argument may rightly be treated with suspicion.

Evidence: Experimentation, Examples, Authoritative Testimony, Statistics

Different disciplines use different kinds of evidence:

- In literary studies, the texts are usually the chief evidence.
- In the social sciences, field research (interviews, surveys) usually provides evidence.

In the sciences, reports of experiments are the usual evidence; if an assertion cannot be tested—if an assertion is not capable of being shown to be false—it is a *belief*, an *opinion*, not a scientific hypothesis.

Experimentation   Induction is obviously useful in arguing. If, for example, one is arguing that handguns should be controlled, one will point to specific cases in which handguns caused accidents or were used to commit crimes. If one is arguing that abortion has a traumatic effect on women, one will point to women who testify to that effect. Each instance constitutes **evidence** for the relevant generalization.

In a courtroom, evidence bearing on the guilt of the accused is introduced by the prosecution, and evidence to the contrary is introduced by the defense. Not all evidence is admissible (hearsay, for example, is not, even if it is true), and the law of evidence is a highly developed subject in jurisprudence. In the forum of daily life, the sources of evidence are less disciplined. Daily experience, a particularly memorable observation, an unusual event we witnessed—any or all of these may be used as evidence for (or against) some belief, theory, hypothesis, or explanation. The systematic study of what experience can yield is what science does, and one of the most distinctive features of the evidence that scientists can marshal on behalf of their claims is that it is the result of **experimentation.** Experiments are deliberately contrived situations that are often complex in their technology and designed to yield particular observations. What the ordinary person does with unaided eye and ear, the scientist does, much more carefully and thoroughly, with the help of laboratory instruments.

The variety, extent, and reliability of the evidence obtained in daily life and in the laboratory are quite different. It is hardly a surprise that in our civilization much more weight is attached to the "findings" of scientists than to the corroborative (much less the contrary) experiences of the ordinary person. No one today would seriously argue that the sun really does go around the earth just because it looks that way; nor would we argue that because viruses are invisible to the naked eye they cannot cause symptoms such as swellings and fevers, which are quite plainly visible.

Examples One form of evidence is the **example.** Suppose that we argue that a candidate is untrustworthy and should not be elected to public office. We point to episodes in his career—his misuse of funds in 1998 and the false charges he made against an opponent in 2002—as examples of his untrustworthiness. Or if we are arguing that President Truman ordered the atom bomb dropped to save American (and, for that matter, Japanese) lives that otherwise would have been lost in a hard-fought invasion of Japan, we point to the stubbornness of the Japanese defenders in battles on the islands of Saipan, Iwo Jima, and Okinawa, where Japanese soldiers fought to the death rather than surrender.

These examples, we say, show us that the Japanese defenders of the main islands would have fought to their deaths without surrendering, even though they knew they would be defeated. Or if we argue that the war was nearly won when Truman dropped the bomb, we can cite secret peace feelers as examples of the Japanese willingness to end the war.

An example is a sample; these two words come from the same Old French word, *essample,* from the Latin *exemplum,* which means "something taken out"—that is, a selection from the group. A Yiddish proverb shrewdly says that "'For example' is no proof," but the evidence of well-chosen examples can go a long way toward helping a writer to convince an audience.

In arguments, three sorts of examples are especially common:

- real events,
- invented instances (artificial or hypothetical cases), and
- analogies.

We will treat each of these briefly.

REAL EVENTS   In referring to Truman's decision to drop the atom bomb, we have already touched on examples drawn from real events—the battles at Saipan and elsewhere. And we have also seen Ben Franklin pointing to an allegedly real happening, a fish that had consumed a smaller fish. The advantage of an example drawn from real life, whether a great historical event or a local incident, is that its reality gives it weight. It can't simply be brushed off.

On the other hand, an example drawn from reality may not provide as clear-cut an instance as could be wished for. Suppose, for instance, that someone cites the Japanese army's behavior on Saipan and on Iwo Jima as evidence that the Japanese later would have fought to the death in an American invasion of Japan and would therefore have inflicted terrible losses on themselves and on the Americans. This example is open to the response that in June and July 1945, Japanese diplomats sent out secret peace feelers, so that in August 1945, when Truman authorized dropping the bomb, the situation was very different.

Similarly, in support of the argument that nations will no longer resort to atomic weapons, some people have offered as evidence the fact that since World War I the great powers have not used poison gas. But the argument needs more support than this fact provides. Poison gas was not decisive or even highly effective in World War I. Moreover, the invention of gas masks made it obsolete.

In short, any *real* event is so entangled in its historical circumstances that it might not be adequate or even relevant evidence in the case being argued. In using a real event as an example (and real events certainly can be used), the writer ordinarily must demonstrate that the event can be taken out of its historical context and be used in the new context of argument. Thus, in an argument against using atomic weapons in warfare, the many deaths and horrible injuries inflicted on the Japanese at Hiroshima and Nagasaki can be cited as effects of nuclear weapons that would invariably occur and did not depend on any special circumstances of their use in Japan in 1945.

INVENTED INSTANCES   **Artificial** or **hypothetical cases—invented instances**—have the great advantage of being protected from objections of the sort just given. Recall Thoreau's trout in the milk; that was a colorful hypothetical case that nicely illustrated his point. An invented instance ("Let's assume that a burglar promises not to shoot a householder if the householder swears not to identify him. Is the householder bound by the oath?") is something like a drawing of a flower in a botany textbook or a diagram of the folds of a mountain in a geology textbook. It is admittedly false, but by virtue of its simplifications it sets forth the relevant details very clearly. Thus, in a discussion of rights, the philosopher Charles Frankel says,

> Strictly speaking, when we assert a right for X, we assert that Y has a duty. Strictly speaking, that Y has such a duty presupposes that Y has the capacity to perform this duty. It would be nonsense to say, for example, that a nonswimmer has a moral duty to swim to the help of a drowning man.

This invented example is admirably clear, and it is immune to charges that might muddy the issue if Frankel, instead of referring to a wholly abstract person, Y, talked about some real person, Jones, who did not rescue a drowning man. For then he would get bogged down over arguing about whether Jones *really* couldn't swim well enough to help, and so on.

Yet invented cases have their drawbacks. First and foremost, they cannot be used as evidence. A purely hypothetical example can illustrate a point or provoke reconsideration of a generalization, but it cannot substitute for actual events as evidence supporting an inductive inference. Sometimes such examples are so fanciful, so remote from life that they fail to carry conviction with the reader. Thus the philosopher Judith Jarvis Thomson, in the course of her argument entitled "A Defense of Abortion," asks you to imagine that you wake up one day and find that against your will a celebrated violinist whose body is not adequately functioning has been hooked up into your body for life support. Do you have the right to unplug the violinist? Readers of the essays in this book will have to decide for themselves whether the invented cases proposed by various authors are helpful or whether they are so remote that they hinder thought. Readers will have to decide, too, about when they can use invented cases to advance their own arguments.

But we add one point: Even a highly fanciful invented case can have the valuable effect of forcing us to see where we stand. We may say that we are, in all circumstances, against vivisection—the practice of performing operations on live animals for the purpose of research. But what would we say if we thought that an experiment on one mouse would save the life of someone we love? Or conversely, if one approves of vivisection, would one also approve of sacrificing the last giant panda to save the life of a senile stranger, a person who in any case probably would not live longer than another year? Artificial cases of this sort can help us to see that, well, no, we didn't really mean to say such-and-such when we said so-and-so.

ANALOGIES   The third sort of example, **analogy,** is a kind of comparison. An analogy asserts that things that are alike in some ways are alike in yet another way. Example: "Before the Roman Empire declined as a world power, it exhibited a decline in morals and in physical stamina; our culture today shows a decline in morals (look at the high divorce rate, and look at the crime rate) and we also show a decline in physical culture (just read about obesity in children). America, like Rome, will decline as a world power."

Strictly, an analogy is an extended comparison in which different things are shown to be similar in several ways. Thus, if one wants to argue that a head of state should have extraordinary power during wartime, one can argue that the state at such a time is like a ship in a storm: The crew is needed to lend its help, but the decisions are best left to the captain. (Notice that an analogy compares things that are relatively *un*like. Comparing the plight of one ship to another or of one government to another is not an analogy; it is an inductive inference from one case of the same sort to another such case.)

Or take another analogy: We have already glanced at Judith Thomson's hypothetical case in which the reader wakes up to find himself or herself hooked up to a violinist. Thomson uses this situation as an analogy in an argument about abortion. The reader stands for the mother, the violinist for the unwanted fetus. Whether this analogy is close enough to pregnancy to help illuminate our thinking about abortion is something that you may want to think about.

The problem with argument by analogy is this: Two admittedly different things are agreed to be similar in several ways, and the arguer goes on to assert or imply that they are also similar in another way—the point that is being argued. (That is why Thomson argues that if something is true of the reader-hooked-up-to-a-violinist, it is also true of the pregnant mother-hooked-up-to-a-fetus.) But the two things that are said to be analogous and that are indeed similar in characteristics A, B, and C are also different—let's say in characteristics D and E. As Bishop Butler is said to have remarked in the early eighteenth century, "Everything is what it is, and not another thing."

Analogies can be convincing, especially because they can make complex issues simple. "Don't change horses in midstream," of course, is not a statement about riding horses across a river but about choosing leaders in critical times. Still, in the end, analogies do not necessarily prove anything. What may be true about riding horses across a stream may not be true about choosing leaders in troubled times or about deciding on a given change of leadership. Riding horses across a stream and choosing leaders are, at bottom, different things, and however much these activities may be said to resemble one another, they remain different, and what is true for one need not be true for the other.

Analogies can be helpful in developing our thoughts and in helping listeners or readers to understand a point we are trying to make. It is sometimes argued, for instance—on the analogy of the doctor–patient or the lawyer–client or the priest–penitent relationship—that newspaper and television reporters should not be required to reveal their confidential sources. That is worth thinking about: Do the similarities run deep enough, or are there fundamental differences? Or take another example: Some writers who support abortion argue that the fetus is not a person any more than the acorn is an oak. That is also worth thinking about. But one should also think about this response: A fetus is not a person, just as an acorn is not an oak, but an acorn is a potential oak, and a fetus is a potential person, a potential adult human being. Children, even newborn infants, have rights, and one way to explain this claim is to call attention to their potentiality to become mature adults. And so some people argue that the fetus, by analogy, has the rights of an infant, for the fetus, like the infant, is a potential adult.

Three analogies for consideration: First, let's examine a brief comparison made by Jill Knight, a member of the British Parliament, speaking about abortion:

Babies are not like bad teeth, to be jerked out because they cause suffering.

Her point is effectively put; it remains for the reader to decide whether or not fetuses are *babies* and if a fetus is not a baby, *why* it can or can't be treated like a bad tooth.

Now, a second bit of analogical reasoning, again about abortion: Thomas Sowell, an economist at the Hoover Institute, grants that women have a legal right to abortion, but he objects to a requirement that the government pay for abortions:

Because the courts have ruled that women have a legal right to an abortion, some people have jumped to the conclusion that the government has to pay for it. You have a constitutional right to privacy, but the government has no obligation to pay for your window shades. (*Pink and Brown People*, 1981, p. 57)

We leave it to the reader to decide whether the analogy is compelling— that is, if the points of resemblance are sufficiently significant to allow one to conclude that what is true of people wanting window shades should be true of people wanting abortions.

And one more: A common argument on behalf of legalizing gay marriage draws an analogy between gay marriage and interracial marriage, a practice that was banned in sixteen states until 1967, when the Supreme Court declared miscegenation statutes unconstitutional. The gist of the analogy is this: Racism and discrimination against gay and lesbian people are the same. If marriage is a fundamental right—as the Supreme Court held in its 1967 decision when it struck down bans on miscegenation—then it is a fundamental right for gay people as well as heterosexual people.

Authoritative Testimony   Another form of evidence is **testimony,** the citation or quotation of authorities. In daily life we rely heavily on authorities of all sorts: We get a doctor's opinion about our health, we read a book because an intelligent friend recommends it, we see a movie because a critic gave it a good review, and we pay at least a little attention to the weather forecaster.

In setting forth an argument, one often tries to show that one's view is supported by notable figures, perhaps Jefferson, Lincoln, Martin Luther King Jr., or scientists who won the Nobel Prize. You may recall that in the second chapter, in talking about definitions of pornography, we referred to Kenneth Clark. To make certain that you were impressed by his testimony even if you had never heard of him, we described him as "probably the most influential English-speaking art critic of the twentieth century." But heed some words of caution:

- Be sure that the authority, however notable, is an authority on the topic in question (a well-known biologist might be an authority on vitamins but not on the justice of a war).

- Be sure that the authority is not biased. A chemist employed by the tobacco industry isn't likely to admit that smoking may be harmful, and a "director of publications" (that means a press agent) for a hockey team isn't likely to admit that watching or even playing ice hockey stimulates violence.

- Beware of nameless authorities: "a thousand doctors," "leading educators," "researchers at a major medical school."

- Be careful when using authorities who indeed were great authorities in their day but who now may be out of date (Adam Smith on economics, Julius Caesar on the art of war, Louis Pasteur on medicine).

- Cite authorities whose opinions your readers will value. William F. Buckley Jr.'s conservative/libertarian opinions mean a good deal to readers of the magazine that he founded, the *National Review*, but probably not to most liberal thinkers. Gloria Steinem's liberal/feminist opinions carry weight with the readers of the magazines that she cofounded, *New York* and *Ms.* magazine, but probably not to most conservative thinkers. If you are writing for the general reader, your usual audience, cite authorities who are likely to be accepted by the general reader.

One other point: *You* may be an authority. You probably aren't nationally known, but on some topics you perhaps can speak with the authority of personal experience. You may have been injured on a motorcycle while riding without wearing a helmet, or you may have escaped injury because you wore a helmet; you may have dropped out of school and then returned; you may have tutored a student whose native language is not English, or you may be such a student and you may have received tutoring. You may have attended a school with a bilingual education program. In short, your personal testimony on topics relating to these issues may be invaluable, and a reader will probably consider it seriously.

Statistics   The last sort of evidence we discuss here is quantitative or statistical. The maxim "More is better" captures a basic idea of quantitative evidence. Because we know that 90 percent is greater than 75 percent, we are usually ready to grant that any claim supported by experience in 90 percent of the cases is more likely to be true than an alternative claim supported by experience only 75 percent of the time. The greater the difference, the greater our confidence. Consider an example. Honors at graduation from college are often computed on a student's cumulative grade-point average (GPA). The undisputed assumption is that the nearer a student's GPA is to a perfect record (4.0), the better scholar he or she is and therefore the more deserving of highest honors. Consequently, a student with a GPA of 3.9 at the end of her senior year is a stronger candidate for graduating summa cum laude than another student with a GPA of 3.6. When faculty members on the honors committee argue over the relative academic merits of graduating seniors, we know that these quantitative, statistical differences in student GPAs will be the basic (even if not the only) kind of evidence under discussion.

GRAPHS, TABLES, NUMBERS   Statistical information can be marshaled and presented in many forms, but it tends to fall into two main types: the graphic and the numerical. Graphs, tables, and pie charts are familiar ways of presenting quantitative data in an eye-catching manner. (See pages 163–65.) To prepare the graphics, however, one first has to get the numbers themselves under control, and for some purposes it may be acceptable simply to stick with the numbers themselves.

But should the numbers be presented in percentages or in fractions? Should one report, say, that the federal budget underwent a two-fold increase over the decade, that it increased by 100 percent, that it doubled, or that the budget at the beginning of the decade was one-half what it was at the end? Taken strictly, these are equivalent ways of saying the same thing. Choice among them, therefore, in an example like this perhaps will rest on whether one's aim is to dramatize the increase (a 100 percent increase looks larger than a doubling) or to play down the size of the increase.

THINKING ABOUT STATISTICAL EVIDENCE   Statistics often get a bad name because it is so easy to misuse them, unintentionally or not, and so difficult to be sure that they have been correctly gathered in the first place. (We remind you of the old saw "There are lies, damned lies, and statistics.") Every branch of social science and natural science needs statistical information, and countless decisions in public and private life are based on quantitative data in statistical form. It is important, therefore, to be sensitive to the sources and reliability of the statistics and to develop a healthy skepticism when confronted with statistics whose parentage is not fully explained.

Consider, for instance, statistics that kept popping up during the baseball strike of 1994. The owners of the clubs said that the average salary of a major-league player was $1.2 million. (The **average** in this case — technically the **mean** — is the result of dividing the total number of salary dollars by the number of players.) The players' union, however, did not talk about the average; rather, the union talked about the **median,** which was less than half of the average, a mere $500,000. (The *median* is the middle value in a distribution. Thus, of the 746 players, 363 earned less than $500,000, 361 earned more, and 22 earned exactly $500,000.) The union said, correctly, that *most* players earned a good deal less than the $1.2 million figure that the owners kept citing; but the $1.2 million average sounded more impressive to the general public, and that is the figure that the guy in the street mentioned when asked for an opinion about the strike.

Consider this statistic: In Smithville in 2011, 1 percent of the victims in fatal automobile accidents were bicyclists. In 2012 the percentage of bicyclists killed in automobile accidents was 2 percent. Was the increase 1 percent (not an alarming figure), or was it 100 percent (a staggering figure)? The answer is both, depending on whether we are comparing (a) bicycle deaths in automobile accidents with *all* deaths in automobile accidents (that's an increase of 1 percent), or (b) bicycle deaths in automobile accidents *only with other bicycle deaths* in automobile accidents (an increase of 100 percent). An honest statement would say that bicycle deaths due to automobile accidents doubled in 2012, increasing from 1 to 2 percent. But here's another point: Although every such death is lamentable, if there was one such death in 2009 and two in 2010, the increase from one death to two (an increase of 100 percent!) hardly suggests that there is a growing problem that needs attention. No one would be surprised to learn that in the next year there were no deaths, or only one or even two.

If it is sometimes difficult to interpret statistics, it is often at least equally difficult to establish accurate statistics. Consider this example:

Advertisements are the most prevalent and toxic of the mental pollutants. From the moment your radio alarm sounds in the morning to the wee hours of late-night TV, microjolts of commercial pollution flood into your brain at the rate of about three thousand marketing messages per day. (Kalle Lasn, *Culture Jam,* 1999, pp. 18–19)

Lasn's book includes endnotes as documentation, so, curious about the statistics, we turn to the appropriate page and we find this information concerning the source of his data:

"three thousand marketing messages per day." Mark Landler, Walecia Konrad, Zachary Schiller, and Lois Therrien, "What Happened to Advertising?" *BusinessWeek,* September 23, 1991, page 66. Leslie Savan in *The Sponsored Life* (Temple University Press, 1994), page 1, estimated that "16,000 ads flicker across an individual's consciousness daily." I did an informal survey in March 1995 and found the number to be closer to 1,500 (this included all marketing messages, corporate images, logos, ads, brand names, on TV, radio, billboards, buildings, signs, clothing, appliances, in cyberspace, etc., over a typical twenty-four hour period in my life). (219)

Well, this endnote is odd. In the earlier passage, you will recall, the author asserted that "about three thousand marketing messages per day" flood into a person's brain. Now, in the documentation, he helpfully cites a source for that statistic, from *BusinessWeek*—though we have not the faintest idea of how the authors of the article in *BusinessWeek* came up with that figure. Oddly, he goes on to offer a very different figure (16,000 ads), and then, to our utter confusion, he offers yet a third figure, 1,500, based on his own "informal survey."

Probably the one thing we can safely say about all three figures is that none of them means very much. Even if the compilers of the statistics told us exactly how they counted—let's say that among countless other criteria they assumed that the average person reads one magazine per day and that the average magazine contains 124 advertisements—it would be hard to take them seriously. After all, in leafing through a magazine, some people may read many ads, some·may read none. Some people may read some ads carefully—but perhaps to enjoy their absurdity. Our point: Although the author in his text said, without implying any uncertainty, that "about three thousand marketing messages per day" reach an individual, it is evident (if one checks the endnote) that even he is confused about the figure he gives.

Some last words about the unreliability of some statistical information, stuff that looks impressive but that is, in fact, insubstantial. Marilyn Jager Adams studied the number of hours that families read to their children in the five or so years before the children go to school. In her book on the topic, *Beginning to Read: Thinking and Learning about Print,* she pointed out that in all those preschool years, poor families read to their children only twenty-five hours, whereas in the same period middle-income families read 1,000 to 1,700 hours. The figures were much

✓ A CHECKLIST FOR EVALUATING STATISTICAL EVIDENCE

Regard statistical evidence (like all other evidence) cautiously, and don't accept it until you have thought about these questions:

☐ Was it compiled by a disinterested (impartial) source? Of course, the name of the source does not always reveal its particular angle (for example, People for the American Way), but sometimes the name lets you know what to expect (National Rifle Association, American Civil Liberties Union).

☐ Is it based on an adequate sample? (A study pointed out that criminals have an average IQ of 91 to 93, whereas the general population has an IQ of 100. The conclusion drawn was that criminals have a lower IQ than the general population. This reading may be accurate, but some doubts have been expressed. For instance, because the entire sample of criminals consisted only of convicted criminals, this sample may be biased; possibly the criminals with higher IQs have enough intelligence not to get caught. Or if they are caught, perhaps they are smart enough to hire better lawyers.)

☐ Is the statistical evidence recent enough to be relevant?

☐ How many of the factors likely to be relevant were identified and measured?

☐ Are the figures open to a different and equally plausible interpretation?

☐ If a percentage is cited, is it the average (or *mean*), or is it the median?

quoted in newspapers and by children's advocacy groups. Dr. Adams could not, of course, interview every family in these two groups; she had to rely on samples. What were her samples? For poor families, she selected twenty-four children in twenty families, all in Southern California. One might wonder if families from only one geographic area can provide an adequate sample, but let's think about Dr. Adams's sample of middle-class families. How many families constituted the sample? Exactly one, her own. We leave it to you to decide how much value her findings—again, they were much cited—have.

We are not suggesting that everyone who uses statistics is trying to deceive or even that many who use statistics are unconsciously deceived by them. We mean to suggest only that statistics are open to widely different interpretations and that often those columns of numbers, so precise with their decimal points, are in fact imprecise and possibly even worthless because they may be based on insufficient or biased samples.

Quiz

What is wrong with the following statistical proof that children do not have time for school?

One-third of the time they are sleeping (about 122 days);

One-eighth of the time they are eating (three hours a day, totaling 45 days);

One-fourth of the time is taken up by summer and other vacations (91 days);

Two-sevenths of the year is weekends (104 days).

Total: 362 days—so how can a kid have time for school?

NONRATIONAL APPEALS

Satire, Irony, Sarcasm, Humor

In talking about definition, deduction, and evidence, we have been talking about means of rational persuasion. But as mentioned earlier, there are also other means of persuasion. Take force, for example. If X kicks Y, threatens to destroy Y's means of livelihood, or threatens Y's life, X may persuade Y to cooperate. One form of irrational but sometimes highly effective persuasion is **satire**—that is, witty ridicule. A cartoonist may persuade viewers that a politician's views are unsound by caricaturing (and thus ridiculing) the politician's appearance or by presenting a grotesquely distorted (funny, but unfair) picture of the issue.

Satiric artists often use caricature; satiric writers, also seeking to persuade by means of ridicule, often use **verbal irony.** Irony of this sort contrasts what is said and what is meant. For instance, words of praise may be meant to imply blame (when Shakespeare's Cassius says, "Brutus is an honorable man," he means his hearers to think that Brutus is dishonorable), and words of modesty may be meant to imply superiority ("Of course, I'm too dumb to understand this problem"). Such language, when heavy-handed, is called **sarcasm** ("You're a great guy," said to someone who will not lend the speaker ten dollars). If it is witty—if the jeering is in some degree clever—it is called irony rather than sarcasm.

Although ridicule is not a form of argument (because it is not a form of reasoning), passages of ridicule, especially verbal irony, sometimes appear in essays that are arguments. These passages, like reasons, or for that matter like appeals to the emotions, are efforts to persuade the hearer to accept the speaker's point of view. The great trick in using humor in an argument is, on the one hand, to avoid mere wisecracking, which makes the writer seem like a smart aleck, and, on the other hand, to avoid mere clownishness, which makes the writer seem like a fool. Later in this chapter (p. 107) we print an essay by George F. Will that is (or seeks to be?) humorous in places. You be the judge.

Emotional Appeals

It is sometimes said that good argumentative writing appeals only to reason, never to emotion, and that any sort of emotional appeal is illegitimate, irrelevant. "Tears are not arguments," the Brazilian writer Machado de Assis said. Logic textbooks may even stigmatize with Latin labels the various sorts of emotional appeal—for instance, *argumentum ad populam* (appeal to the prejudices of the mob, as in "Come on, we all know that schools don't teach anything anymore") and *argumentum ad misericordiam* (appeal to pity, as in "No one ought to blame this poor kid for stabbing a classmate because his mother was often institutionalized for alcoholism and his father beat him").

True, appeals to emotion may get in the way of the facts of the case; they may blind the audience by, in effect, throwing dust in its eyes or by stimulating tears.

Learning from Shakespeare   A classic example is found in Shakespeare's *Julius Caesar*, when Marc Antony addresses the Roman populace after Brutus, Cassius, and others have assassinated Caesar. The real issue is whether Caesar was becoming tyrannical (as the assassins claim) and would therefore curtail the freedom of the people. Antony turns from the evidence and stirs the mob against the assassins by appealing to its emotions. In the ancient Roman biographical writing that Shakespeare drew on, Sir Thomas North's translation of Plutarch's *Lives of the Noble Grecians and Romans*, Plutarch says that Antony,

> perceiving that his words moved the common people to compassion, . . . framed his eloquence to make their hearts yearn [that is, grieve] the more, and, taking Caesar's gown all bloody in his hand, he laid it open to the sight of them all, showing what a number of cuts and holes it had upon it. Therewithal the people fell presently into such a rage and mutiny that there was no more order kept.

Here are a few extracts from Antony's speeches in Shakespeare's play. Antony begins by asserting that he will speak only briefly:

> Friends, Romans, countrymen, lend me your ears;
> I come to bury Caesar, not to praise him.

After briefly offering some rather insubstantial evidence that Caesar gave no signs of behaving tyrannically (for example, "When that the poor have cried, Caesar hath wept"), Antony begins to play directly on the emotions of his hearers. Descending from the platform so that he may be in closer contact with his audience (like a modern politician, he wants to work the crowd), he calls attention to Caesar's bloody toga:

> If you have tears, prepare to shed them now.
> You all do know this mantle; I remember

> The first time ever Caesar put it on:
> 'Twas on a summer's evening, in his tent,
> That day he overcame the Nervii.
> Look, in this place ran Cassius' dagger through;
> See what a rent the envious Casca made;
> Through this, the well-belovèd Brutus stabbed. . . .

In these few lines Antony

- first prepares the audience by suggesting to them how they should respond ("If you have tears, prepare to shed them now"),

- then flatters them by implying that they, like Antony, were intimates of Caesar (he credits them with being familiar with Caesar's garment),

- then evokes a personal memory of a specific time ("a summer's evening")—not just any old specific time but a very important one, the day that Caesar won a battle against the Nervii (a particularly fierce tribe in what is now France).

In fact, Antony was not at the battle, and he did not join Caesar until three years later.

Antony does not mind being free with the facts; his point here is not to set the record straight but to stir the mob against the assassins. He goes on, daringly but successfully, to identify one particular slit in the garment with Cassius's dagger, another with Casca's, and a third with Brutus's. Antony cannot know which slit was made by which dagger, but his rhetorical trick works.

Notice, too, that Antony arranges the three assassins in climactic order, since Brutus (Antony claims) was especially beloved by Caesar:

> Judge, O you gods, how dearly Caesar loved him!
> This was the most unkindest cut of all;
> For when the noble Caesar saw him stab,
> Ingratitude, more strong than traitor's arms,
> Quite vanquished him. Then burst his mighty heart. . . .

Nice. According to Antony, the noble-minded Caesar—Antony's words have erased all thought of the tyrannical Caesar—died not from the wounds inflicted by daggers but from the heartbreaking perception of Brutus's ingratitude. Doubtless there was not a dry eye in the house. We can all hope that if we are ever put on trial, we have a lawyer as skilled in evoking sympathy as Antony.

Are Emotional Appeals Fallacious?   The oration is obviously successful in the play and apparently was successful in real life, but it is the sort of speech that prompts logicians to write disapprovingly of attempts to stir feeling in an audience. (As mentioned earlier in this chapter, the evocation of emotion in an audience is called **pathos,** from the Greek word for "emotion" or "suffering.") There is nothing inherently wrong in stimulating our audience's emotions when attempting to establish a claim, but when an emotional appeal confuses the issue that is being argued about or shifts the attention away from the facts of the issue, we can reasonably speak of the fallacy of emotional appeal.

No fallacy is involved, however, when an emotional appeal heightens the facts, bringing them home to the audience rather than masking them. If we are talking about legislation that would govern police actions, it is legitimate to show a photograph of the battered, bloodied face of an alleged victim of police brutality. True, such a photograph cannot tell the whole truth; it cannot tell us if the subject threatened the officer with a gun or repeatedly resisted an order to surrender. But it can tell us that the victim was severely beaten and (like a comparable description in words) evoke in us emotions that may properly enter into our decision about the permissible use of police evidence. Similarly, an animal rights activist who is arguing that calves are cruelly confined might reasonably tell us about the size of the pen in which the beast—unable to turn around or even to lie down—is kept. Others may argue that calves don't much care about turning around or have no right to turn around, but the verbal description, which unquestionably makes an emotional appeal, can hardly be called fallacious or irrelevant.

In appealing to emotions then, the important things are

- not to falsify (especially by oversimplifying) the issue,
- not to distract attention from the facts of the case,
- to think ethically about how emotions may affect the audience.

Focus on the facts and concentrate on offering reasons (essentially, statements linked with "because"), but you may also legitimately bring the facts home to your readers by seeking to induce in them the appropriate emotions. Your words will be fallacious only if you stimulate emotions that are not rightly connected with the facts of the case.

DOES ALL WRITING CONTAIN ARGUMENTS?

Our answer to the question we have just posed is no—but probably *most* writing *does* contain an argument of sorts. Or put it this way: The writer wants to persuade the reader to see things the way the writer sees them—at least until the end of the essay. After all, even a recipe for a cherry pie in a food magazine—a piece of writing that is primarily expository (how to do it) rather than argumentative (how a reasonable person ought to think about this topic)—probably includes, near the beginning, a sentence with a hint of an argument in it, such as "*Because* [a sign that a *reason* will be offered] this pie can be made quickly and with ingredients (canned cherries) that are always available, give it a try, and it will surely become one of your favorites." Clearly, such a statement cannot stand as a formal argument—a discussion that takes account of possible counterarguments, that relies chiefly on logic and little if at all on emotional appeal, and that draws a conclusion that seems irrefutable.

Still, the statement is something of an argument on behalf of making a pie with canned cherries. In this case, a claim is made (the pie will become a favorite), and two *reasons* are offered in support of this claim:

- It can be made quickly, and
- the chief ingredient—because it is canned—can always be at hand.

The underlying *assumptions* are

- You don't have a great deal of time to waste in the kitchen.
- Canned cherries are just as tasty as fresh cherries—and even if they aren't, well, you wouldn't know the difference.

✔ A CHECKLIST FOR ANALYZING AN ARGUMENT

NOTE: See also Chapter 11, A Rhetorician's View, pages 404–19.

☐ What is the writer's claim or thesis? Ask yourself:
  ☐ What claim is being asserted?
  ☐ What evidence is imagined?
  ☐ What assumptions are being made—and are they acceptable?
  ☐ Are important terms satisfactorily defined?

☐ What support (evidence) is offered on behalf of the claim? Ask yourself:
  ☐ Are the examples relevant, and are they convincing?
  ☐ Are the statistics (if any) relevant, accurate, and complete? Do they allow only the interpretation that is offered in the argument?
  ☐ If authorities are cited, are they indeed authorities on this topic, and can they be regarded as impartial?
  ☐ Is the logic—deductive and inductive—valid?
  ☐ If there is an appeal to emotion—for instance, if satire is used to ridicule the opposing view—is this appeal acceptable?

☐ Does the writer seem to you to be fair? Ask yourself:
  ☐ Are counterarguments adequately considered?
  ☐ Is there any evidence of dishonesty or of a discreditable attempt to manipulate the reader?
  ☐ How does the writer establish the image of himself or herself that we sense in the essay? What is the writer's tone, and is it appropriate?

When we read a lead-in to a recipe, then, we won't find a formal argument, but we probably will get a few words that seek to persuade us to keep reading. And most writing does contain such material— sentences that give us a reason to keep reading, that engage our interests, and that make us want to stay with the writer for at least a little longer. If the recipe happens to be difficult and time-consuming, the lead-in may say,

> Although this recipe for a cherry pie, using fresh cherries that you will have to pit, is a bit more time-consuming than the usual recipe that calls for canned cherries, once you have tasted it you will never go back to canned cherries.

Again, although the logic is scarcely compelling, the persuasive element is evident. The assumption here is that you have a discriminating palate; once you have tasted a pie made with fresh cherries, you will never again enjoy the canned stuff. The writer is not giving us a formal argument, with abundant evidence and with a detailed refutation of counterarguments, but we do know where the writer stands and how the writer wishes us to respond.

In short, almost all writers are trying to persuade readers to see things *their* way.

AN EXAMPLE: AN ARGUMENT AND A LOOK AT THE WRITER'S STRATEGIES

This essay concerns President George W. Bush's proposal that drilling be allowed in part of the Arctic National Wildlife Refuge (ANWR, pronounced "An-war"). The section of the ANWR that is proposed for drilling is called the "1002 area," as defined by Section 1002 of the Alaska National Interest Lands Conservation Act of 1980. In March 2003, the Senate rejected the Bush proposal, but the issue remains alive.

We follow George F. Will's essay with some comments about the ways in which he constructs his argument.

George F. Will

George F. Will (b. 1941), a syndicated columnist whose writing appears in 460 newspapers, was born in Champaign, Illinois, and educated at Trinity College (Hartford), Oxford University, and Princeton University. Will has served as the Washington, D.C., editor of the National Review *and now writes a regular column for* Newsweek. *His essays have been collected in several books.*

This essay was originally published in 2002, and therefore it is in some respects dated—for instance in its reference to the price of gasoline—but we think you can still learn from it a great deal about certain ways to argue.

Being Green at Ben and Jerry's

Some Environmental Policies Are Feel-Good Indulgences for an Era of Energy Abundance

If you have an average-size dinner table, four feet by six feet, put a dime on the edge of it. Think of the surface of the table as the Arctic National Wildlife Refuge in Alaska. The dime is larger than the piece of the coastal plain that would have been opened to drilling for oil and natural gas. The House of Representatives voted for drilling, but the Senate voted against access to what Sen. John Kerry, Massachusetts Democrat and presidential aspirant, calls "a few drops of oil." ANWR could produce, for twenty-five years, at least as much oil as America currently imports from Saudi Arabia.

Six weeks of desultory Senate debate about the energy bill reached an almost comic culmination in . . . yet another agriculture subsidy. The subsidy is a requirement that will triple the amount of ethanol, which is made from corn, that must be put in gasoline, ostensibly to clean America's air, actually to buy farmers' votes.

Over the last three decades, energy use has risen about 30 percent. But so has population, which means per capita energy use is unchanged. And per capita GDP has risen substantially, so we are using 40 percent less energy per dollar output. Which is one reason there is no energy crisis, at least none as most Americans understand such things—a shortage of, and therefore high prices of, gasoline for cars, heating oil for furnaces and electricity for air conditioners.

In the absence of a crisis to concentrate the attention of the inattentive American majority, an intense faction—full-time environmentalists—goes to work. Spencer Abraham, the secretary of Energy, says "the previous administration . . . simply drew up a list of fuels it *didn't* like—nuclear energy, coal, hydropower, and oil—which together account for 73 percent of America's energy supply." Well, there are always windmills.

Sometimes lofty environmentalism is a cover for crude politics. The 5 United States has the world's largest proven reserves of coal. But Mike Oliver, a retired physicist and engineer, and John Hospers, professor emeritus of philosophy at USC, note that in 1996 President Clinton put 68 billion tons of America's cleanest-burning coal, located in Utah, off-limits for mining, ostensibly for environmental reasons. If every existing U.S. electric power plant burned coal, the 68 billion tons could fuel them for forty-five years at the current rate of consumption. Now power companies must import clean-burning coal, some from mines owned by Indonesia's Lippo Group, the heavy contributor to Clinton, whose decision about Utah's coal vastly increased the value of Lippo's coal.

The United States has just 2.14 percent of the world's proven reserves of oil, so some people say it is pointless to drill in places like ANWR because "energy independence" is a chimera. Indeed it is. But domestic supplies can provide important insurance against uncertain foreign supplies. And domestic supplies can mean exporting hundreds of billions of dollars less to oil-producing nations, such as Iraq.

Besides, when considering proven reserves, note the adjective. In 1930 the United States had proven reserves of 13 billion barrels. We then fought the Second World War and fueled the most fabulous economic expansion in human history, including the electricity-driven "New Economy." (Manufacturing and running computers consume 15 percent of U.S. electricity. Internet use alone accounts for half of the growth in demand for electricity.) So by 1990 proven reserves were . . . 17 billion barrels, not counting any in Alaska or Hawaii.

In 1975 proven reserves in the Persian Gulf were 74 billion barrels. In 1993 they were 663 billion, a ninefold increase. At the current rate of consumption, today's proven reserves would last 150 years. New discoveries will be made, some by vastly improved techniques of deep-water drilling. But environmental policies will define opportunities. The government estimates that beneath the U.S. outer continental shelf, which the government owns, there are at least 46 billion barrels of oil. But only 2 percent of the shelf has been leased for energy development.

Opponents of increased energy production usually argue for decreased consumption. But they flinch from conservation measures. A new $1 gasoline tax would dampen demand for gasoline, but it would stimulate demands for the heads of the tax increasers. After all, Americans get irritable when impersonal market forces add 25 cents to the cost of a gallon. Tougher fuel-efficiency requirements for vehicles would save a lot of energy. But who would save the legislators who passed those requirements? Beware the wrath of Americans who like to drive, and autoworkers who like to make cars that are large, heavy, and safer than the gasoline-sippers that environmentalists prefer.

Some environmentalism is a feel-good indulgence for an era of 10 energy abundance, which means an era of avoided choices. Or ignored choices—ignored because if acknowledged, they would not make the choosers feel good. Karl Zinsmeister, editor in chief of the *American Enterprise* magazine, imagines an oh-so-green environmentalist enjoying the most politically correct product on the planet—Ben & Jerry's ice cream. Made in a factory that depends on electricity-guzzling refrigeration, a gallon of ice cream requires four gallons of milk. While making that much milk, a cow produces eight gallons of manure, and flatulence with another eight gallons of methane, a potent "greenhouse" gas. And the cow consumes lots of water plus three pounds of grain and hay, which is produced with tractor fuel, chemical fertilizers, herbicides and insecticides, and is transported with truck or train fuel:

"So every time he digs into his Cherry Garcia, the conscientious environmentalist should visualize (in addition to world peace) a pile of grain, water, farm chemicals, and energy inputs much bigger than his ice cream bowl on one side of the table, and, on the other side of the table, a mound of manure eight times the size of his bowl, plus a balloon of methane that would barely fit under the dining room table."

Cherry Garcia. It's a choice. *Bon appétit.*

George F. Will's Strategies

Now let's look at Will's essay, to see some of the techniques that he uses, techniques that enable him to engage a reader's interest and perhaps enable him to convince the reader, or at least make the reader think, that Will probably is on to something.

We need hardly add that if you think some or all of his techniques—his methods, his strategies—are effective, you will consider adapting them for use in your own essays.

The title, "Being Green at Ben and Jerry's," does not at all prepare the reader for an argument about drilling in the National Arctic Wildlife Refuge, but if you have read any of Will's other columns in *Newsweek,* you probably know that he is conservative and that he will be poking some fun at the green folk—the environmentalists. Will can get away with using a title that is not focused because he has a body of loyal readers— people who will read him because they want to read him, whatever the topic is—but the rest of us writers have to give our readers some idea of what we will be talking about. In short, let your readers know early, perhaps in the title, where you will be taking them.

The subtitle, "Some Environmental Policies Are Feel-Good Indulgences for an Era of Energy Abundance," perhaps added by an editor of the magazine, does suggest that the piece will concern energy, and the words "feel-good indulgence" pretty clearly tell readers that Will believes the environmentalists are indulging themselves.

Paragraph 1 offers a striking comparison. Will wants us to believe that the area proposed for drilling is tiny, so he says that if we imagine the entire Arctic National Wildlife Refuge as a dinner table, the area proposed for drilling is the size of a dime. We think you will agree that this opening seizes a reader's attention. Assuming the truth of the figure—but there seems to be some dispute, since opponents have said that the area would be more like the size of a dinner plate—the image is highly effective. A dime is so small! And is worth so little! Still, one might ask (but probably one doesn't, because Will's figure is so striking) if the tininess of the area really is decisive. One might easily, and apparently with reason, dismiss as absurd the idea that a minuscule tsetse fly could kill a human being, or that the plague is spread by fleas that have bitten rats, because these proposals sound ridiculous—but they are true.

One other point about the first paragraph: Will's voice sounds like a voice you might hear in your living room: "If you have an average-size dinner table," "the dime is larger," "at least as much oil." Don't think that in your own essays you need to adopt a highly formal style. Your reader should think of you as serious but not solemn.

Will goes on to say that Senator John Kerry, an opponent of drilling and therefore on the side that Will opposes, dismisses the oil in the refuge as "a few drops." Will replies that it "could produce, for twenty-five years, at least as much oil as America currently imports from Saudi Arabia." Kerry's "a few drops" is, of course, not to be taken literally; he means, in effect, that the oil is a drop in the bucket. But when one looks into the issue, one finds that estimates by responsible sources vary considerably, from 3.2 billion barrels to 11.5 billion barrels.

Paragraph 2 dismisses the Senate's debate ("almost comic . . . actually to buy farmers' votes").

Paragraph 3 offers statistics to make the point that "there is no energy crisis." Here, as in the first paragraph (where he showed his awareness of Kerry's view), Will indicates that he is familiar with views other than his own. In arguing a case, it is important for the writer to let readers know that indeed there are other views—which the writer then goes on to show are less substantial than the writer's. Will is correct in saying that "per capita energy use is unchanged," but those on the other side might say, "Yes, per capita consumption has not increased, but given the population increase, the annual amount has vastly increased, which means that resources are being depleted and that pollution is increasing."

Paragraph 4 asserts again that there is no energy crisis, pokes fun at "fulltime environmentalists" (perhaps there is a suggestion that such people really ought to get a respectable job), and ends with a bit of whimsy: These folks probably think we should go back to using windmills.

Paragraph 5, in support of the assertion that "Sometimes lofty environmentalism is a cover for crude politics," cites an authority (often an effective technique), and, since readers are not likely to recognize the name, it also identifies him ("professor emeritus of philosophy at USC"), and it then offers further statistics (again effective). The paragraph begins by talking about "crude politics" and ends with the assertion that "Now power companies must import clean-burning coal, some from mines owned by Indonesia's Lippo Group, the heavy contributor to Clinton." In short, Will does what he can to suggest that the views of at least some environmentalists are rooted in money and politics.

Paragraph 6 offers another statistic ("The United States has just 2.14 percent of the world's proven reserves of oil"), and he turns it against those who argue that therefore it is pointless for us to drill in Alaska. In effect, Will is replying to people like Senator Kerry who say that the Arctic refuge provides only "a few drops of oil." The point, Will suggests, is not that we can't achieve independence; the point is that "domestic supplies can provide important insurance against uncertain foreign supplies."

Paragraph 7 begins nicely with a transition, "Besides," and then offers additional statistics concerning the large amount of oil that we have. It was, for instance, enough to fuel "the most fabulous economic expansion in human history."

Paragraph 8 offers additional statistics, first about "proven reserves" in the Persian Gulf and then about an estimate—but it is only an estimate—of oil "beneath the U.S. outer continental shelf." We are not certain of Will's point, but in any case the statistics suggest to a reader that the author has done his homework.

Paragraph 9 summarizes the chief position (as Will sees it) of those on the other side: They usually argue for decreased consumption, but they are afraid to argue for the sort of tax on gasoline that might indeed decrease consumption because they know that many Americans want to drive large, heavy cars. Further, the larger, heavier cars that the environmentalists object to are in fact "safer than the gasoline-sippers that environmentalists prefer."

Paragraph 10 uses the term "feel-good indulgence," which is also found in the subtitle of the essay, and now, in the third sentence of the paragraph, we hear again of Ben and Jerry, who have not been in our minds since the title of the essay, "Being Green at Ben and Jerry's." Perhaps we have been wondering all this while why Ben and Jerry are in the title. Almost surely the reader knows that Ben and Jerry are associated with ice cream and therefore with cows and meadows, and probably many readers know, at least vaguely, that Ben and Jerry are somehow associated with environmentalism and with other causes often thought to be on the left. Will (drawing on an article by Karl Zinsmeister, editor of the *American Enterprise*) writes what we consider an extremely amusing paragraph in which he points out that the process of making ice cream "depends on electricity-guzzling refrigeration" and that the cows are, so to speak, supported by fuel that transports fertilizers, herbicides, and insecticides. Further, in the course of producing the four gallons of milk that are required for one gallon of ice cream, the cows themselves—those darlings of environmentalists—contribute "eight gallons of manure, and flatulence with another eight gallons of methane, a potent 'greenhouse' gas." As we see when we read Will's next paragraph, the present paragraph is in large measure a lead-in for the following quotation. Will knows it is is not enough to give a quotation; a writer has to make use of the quotation—has to lead in to it or, after quoting, has to comment on it, or do both.

Paragraph 11 is entirely devoted to quoting Zinsmeister, who imagines an environmentalist digging into a dish of one of Ben and Jerry's most popular flavors, Cherry Garcia. We are invited to see the bowl of ice cream on one side of the table—here Will effectively evokes the table of his first paragraph—and a pile of manure on the other side, "plus a balloon of methane that would barely fit under the dining room table." Vulgar, no doubt, but funny too. George Will knows that humor as well as logic (and statistics and other kinds of evidence) can be among the tools a writer uses in getting an audience to accept or at least to consider an argument.

Paragraph 12 consists of three short sentences, adding up to less than a single line of type: "Cherry Garcia. It's a choice. *Bon appétit.*" None of the sentences mentions oil or the Arctic Refuge or statistics, and therefore this ending might seem utterly irrelevant to the topic, but we think Will is very effectively saying, "Sure, you have a choice about drilling in the Arctic Refuge; any sensible person will choose the ice cream (drilling) rather than the manure and the gas (not drilling)."

TOPICS FOR CRITICAL THINKING AND WRITING

1. What, if anything, makes Will's essay interesting? What, if anything, makes it highly persuasive? How might it be made more persuasive?

2. In paragraph 10, Will clowns a bit about the gas that cows emit, but apparently this gas, which contributes to global warming, is no laughing matter. The government of New Zealand, in an effort to reduce livestock emissions of methane and nitrous oxide, proposed a tax that would subsidize future research on the emissions. The tax would cost the average farmer $300 a year. Imagine that you are a New Zealand farmer. Write a letter to your representative, arguing for or against the tax.

3. Senator Barbara Boxer, campaigning against the proposal to drill in ANWR, spoke of the refuge as "God's gift to us" (*New York Times,* March 20, 2002). How strong an argument is she offering? Some opponents of drilling have said that drilling in ANWR is as unthinkable as drilling in Yosemite or the Grand Canyon. Again, how strong is this argument? Can you imagine circumstances in which you would support drilling in these places? Do we have a moral duty to preserve certain unspoiled areas?

4. The Inupiat (Eskimo) who live in and near ANWR by a large majority favor drilling, seeing it as a source of jobs and a source of funding for schools, hospitals, and police. But the Ketchikan Indians, who speak of themselves as the "Caribou People," see drilling as a threat to the herds that they depend on for food and hides. How does one balance the conflicting needs of these two groups?

5. Opponents of drilling in ANWR argue that over its lifetime of fifty years, the area would produce less than 1 percent of the fuel we need during the period and that therefore we should not risk disturbing the area. Further, they argue that drilling in ANWR is an attempt at a quick fix to U.S. energy needs, whereas what is needed are sustainable solutions, such as the development of renewable energy sources (e.g., wind and sun) and fuel-efficient automobiles. How convincing do you find these arguments?

6. Proponents of drilling include a large majority—something like 75 percent—of the people of Alaska, including its governor and its two senators. How much attention should be paid to their voices?

7. Analyze the essay in terms of its use of *ethos*, *pathos*, and *logos*.

8. What sort of audience do you think Will is addressing? What values do his readers probably share? What makes you think so?

ARGUMENTS FOR ANALYSIS

Stanley Fish

Stanley Fish (b. 1938) established his reputation as a student of English litera-ture—he has taught literature at the University of California, Berkeley, Johns Hopkins University, and Duke University—but he has also published on legal issues. He now teaches at Florida International University's College of Law. This essay was published in 2008, when Hillary Clinton and Barack Obama were candidates for the Democratic Party's nomination for president, and inevitably there was much talk about the candidacy of a woman and an African American.

When "Identity Politics" Is Rational

If there's anything everyone is against in these election times, it's "identity politics," a phrase that covers a multitude of sins. Let me start with a definition. (It may not be yours, but it will at least allow the dis-cussion to be framed.) You're practicing identity politics when you vote for or against someone because of his or her skin color, ethnicity, religion, gender, sexual orientation, or any other marker that leads you to say yes or no independently of a candidate's ideas or policies. In essence identity politics is an affirmation of the tribe against the claims of ideology, and by ideology I do not mean something bad (a mistake frequently made), but any agenda informed by a vision of what the world should be like.

An identity politics voter says, in effect, I don't care what views he holds, or even what bad things he may have done, or what lack of ability he may display; he's my brother, or he's my kinsman, or he's my lands-man, or he comes from the neighborhood, or he's a Southerner, or (and here the tribe is really big) my country right or wrong. "My country right or wrong" is particularly useful in making clear how identity politics dif-fers from politics as many Americans would prefer to see it practiced. Rather than saying she's right on immigration or he's wrong on the war, the identity-politics voter says he looks like me or she and I belong to the same church.

Identity politics is illiberal. That is, it is particularist whereas liberalism is universalist. The history of liberalism is a history of extending the fran-chise to those who were once excluded from it by their race, gender, or national origin. Although these marks of identification were retained (by the census and other forms of governmental classification) and could still be celebrated in private associations like the church and the social club, they were not supposed to be the basis of decisions one might make "as a citizen," decisions about who might best lead the country or what laws should be enacted or voted down. Deciding as a citizen means deciding not as a man or a woman or a Jew or an African American or a Caucasian or a heterosexual, but as a human being.

Stanley Crouch believes that the project of liberal universalizing is now pretty much complete and that "elements of distinction"—his phrase for the thinking that was fashionable in "the era of 'identity politics'"—"have become secondary to the power of human qualities with which anyone can identify or reject" (*Daily News,* Feb. 11). But his judgment is belied by almost everything that is going on in this campaign. As I write this I am watching the returns from the "Potomac Primary" and the news is being presented entirely in racial, ethnic, and gender terms. Every newspaper or magazine article I read does the same thing. The Obama and Clinton campaigns accuse each other of playing the race card or the gender card. An Hispanic superdelegate warns that by replacing her Latino campaign manager with a black one, Senator Clinton risks losing his vote and the vote of other Hispanic delegates he is in the process of contacting.

Christopher Hitchens looks at the scene and is disgusted by behavior that, in his view, "keeps us anchored in the past" (*Wall Street Journal,* Jan. 18). He will not, he tells us, vote for Clinton just so that we can have the "'first woman president'" (I don't remember that one from the past); and he won't vote for Obama who, he says, "wants us to transcend something at the same time he implicitly asks us to give that same something as a reason to vote for him." It would seem that we are far from realizing Ken Connor's dream that we might judge "all of the presidential hopefuls on the basis of the content of their character and their qualifications to serve" (Townhall.com, Jan. 20). 5

But is it as bad as all that? Is it so irrational and retrograde to base one's vote on the gender or race or religion or ethnicity of a candidate? Not necessarily. If the vote is given (or withheld) only because the candidate looks like you or has the same religion, it does seem a shallow and meretricious act, for it is an act unsupported by reasons. "Because she is a woman as I am" is of course a reason, but it is not a reason of the relevant kind, a reason that cites goals and programs, and argues for them. But suppose what was said was something like this: "As a woman I find government sponsored research skewed in the direction of diseases that afflict men and inattentive to the medical problems faced by women, and it is my belief that a woman president will devote resources to the solution of those problems." That's an identity politics argument which is thick, not thin; the she's-like-me point is not invoked as sufficient unto itself, but as it relates to a matter of policy. The calculation may or may not pan out (successful candidates both disappoint and surprise), but it is a calculation of the right kind.

One objection to identity politics (Crouch makes it in the same column) is that groups and populations are not monolithic, but display a diversity of attitudes and positions. Yes they do, but members of a group who might disagree with each other on any number of things could nevertheless come together on a matter of shared concern. American Jews, for example, have widely varying views on many important issues — tax cuts, tort reform, gay marriage, the Iraq war. Still, the vast majority believes that it is important to defend the security of Israel. This is a belief shared even by those American Jews who are strongly critical of Israel's treatment of the Palestinians. They may deplore Israel's actions and agree with Jimmy Carter when he likens them to apartheid, but if the choice is between a politician who pledges to support Israel and a politician who would withdraw support and leave the Jewish state to fend for itself, most of them would vote for the first candidate every time.

African Americans are no less heterogeneous in their views than Jewish Americans. Yet every African American — conservative or liberal, rich or poor, barely educated or highly educated — meets with obstacles to his or her success and mobility that are all the more frustrating because they are structural (built into the culture's ways of perceiving) rather than official. To the non–African American these obstacles will be more or less invisible, especially in a country where access to opportunity is guaranteed by law. It makes sense, therefore, that an African American voter could come to the conclusion that an African American candidate would be likely to fight for changes that could remove barriers a white candidate might not even see. A vote given for that reason would be a vote based on identity, but it would be more than a mere affirmation of fellowship (he's one of mine and I have to support him); it would be a considered political judgment as to which candidate will move the country in a preferred direction. Identity might be the trigger of the vote, but it would not be the whole of its content.

We should distinguish, I think, between two forms of identity politics. The first I have already named "tribal"; it is the politics based on who a candidate is rather than on what he or she believes or argues for. And that, I agree, is usually a bad idea. (I say "usually" because it is possible to argue that the election of a black or female president, no matter what his or positions happen to be, will be more than a symbolic correction of the errors that have marred the country's history, and an important international statement as well.) The second form of identity politics is what I call "interest" identity politics. It is based on the assumption (itself resting on history and observation) that because of his or her race or ethnicity or gender a candidate might pursue an agenda that would advance the interests a voter is committed to. Not only is there nothing wrong with such a calculation — it is both rational and considered — I don't see that there is an alternative to voting on the basis of interest.

The alternative usually put forward is Crouch's: Vote "for human 10 qualities" rather than sectarian qualities. That is, vote on the basis of reasons everyone, no matter what his or her identity, will acknowledge as worthy. But there are no such reasons and no such human qualities. To be sure, there are words often attached to this chimera—integrity, dedication, honesty, intellect, to name a few. But these qualities, even when they are found, will always be in the service of some set of policies you either favor or reject. It is those policies, not the probity of their proposer, that you will be voting for. (If your candidate is also a good person, that's a nice bonus, but it isn't the essential thing.) You will be voting, in short, for interests, and those who do not have an investment in those interests will be voting for someone else.

What this means is that the ritual deprecation of "special interests" makes no sense. All interests are special interests—proceed from some contestable point of view—and none is "generally human." And that is why identity interests, as long as they are ideological and not merely tribal, constitute a perfectly respectable reason for awarding your vote.

Topics for Critical Thinking and Writing

1. Fish starts out his essay with a formal and explicit definition of "identity politics." What do you think of that definition? Is it too broad? Too narrow? Too vague? Can you think of any ways to improve it?

2. What is the origin of the epigram, "My country right or wrong"? Does Fish endorse it? Do you? Why is it offered as an example of identity politics? Explain your views.

3. Suppose someone said that it is naïve to advocate deciding issues of public concern by appeal to one's status as "a human being" (para. 3). How would you reply? Do so in an essay of 300 words.

4. Fish speaks of two different practices under the rubric of "identity politics." What are they? Which, if either, does Fish prefer, and why? Is either of these related to what Fish in the title of his essay refers to as "rational" politics?

5. Is the appeal at Fish's essay all *logos* and *ethos*, or do you also find some humor and some *pathos*? If so, cite passages.

Gloria Jiménez

Gloria Jiménez married immediately after she graduated from high school, worked briefly, had two children, and then, after her younger child started school, continued her own formal education. This essay, written for a composition course at Tufts University in 2003, is her first publication.

Against the Odds, and against the Common Good

(Student Essay)

State-run lotteries are now so common—thirty-nine states and Washington, D.C., operate lotteries—that the states probably will never get out of the lottery business. Still, when all is said and done about lotteries bringing a bit of excitement into the lives of many people and bringing a vast amount of money into the lives of a few, the states should not be in the business of urging people to gamble.

And they *do* urge people. Consider a slogan used in Maryland, "Play Today. Cash Tomorrow." If the statement were, "Get a job today and you will have cash tomorrow," it would be true; it would make sense, however small the earnings might be. But "Play Today. Cash Tomorrow" falsely suggests that the way to have money tomorrow is to buy a ticket today. In fact, buying a ticket is an almost sure-fire way of getting nothing for something.

Maryland is not the only state that uses a clever slogan to get its citizens to part with hard-earned money. New York's ads say, "You Can't Win If You Don't Play," and Oregon's ads say, "There Is No Such Thing as a Losing Ticket." This last slogan—which at first glance seems to say that every ticket will benefit the purchaser—is built on the idea that the state's share of the money goes to a worthy cause, usually education or some social service. But no matter how you look at it, this slogan, like the others, urges people to buy a product—a jackpot—that they have almost no chance of receiving.

The chief arguments *in favor* of state-run lotteries seem to be these: (1) people freely choose to participate; (2) funds are used for education or for other important services; (3) if this source of funding disappears, the states will have to compensate by imposing taxes of one sort or another; (4) operation by the government ensures that the lotteries are run honestly; and (5) lotteries create jobs. We can respond briefly to the last two points, and then concentrate on the first three.

So not a reason

It probably is true that the lotteries are run honestly (though I 5 seem to recall reading in the newspaper about one state in which corruption was found in administering the lottery), but that is not the point. If it is wrong to encourage people to gamble, it is hardly relevant to say that the game is run honestly. The other point that can be dismissed briefly is that lotteries create jobs. This argument is usually advanced in connection with the creation of casinos, which surely do create jobs, not only in the casinos but also in nearby restaurants, parking lots, movie theaters, and so forth. But lottery tickets are sold in places where the clerks are already employed. Presumably the only new jobs created by the lottery are the relatively few jobs of the people who dream up the slogans or who are in charge of collecting and processing the receipts.

opposition

so not a reason

The three other claims require more attention. The first, that people freely choose to participate, probably is largely true. Although some buyers are compulsive gamblers, people who are addicted and therefore cannot really be said to choose freely, I grant that most people do have a free choice—although, as I have already said, I think that some of the slogans that states use are deceptive, and if this is the case, purchasers who are misled by the ads are not entirely free. Consider a slogan that Illinois used on billboards, especially in poor neighborhoods: "This Could Be Your Ticket Out." Yes, a person might hit the jackpot and get out of poverty, but the chances are one in several million, and to imply that the lottery is a reasonable option to get out of present poverty is to be deceptive. Further, the message is essentially unwholesome. It implies that the way out is luck, rather than education and hard work. Of course, luck plays a part in life, but 99.99 percent of the people who rely on the ticket as the "ticket out" of poverty are going to be terribly disappointed. But again, we can grant that except for gambling addicts, people who buy lottery tickets are freely doing so.

Probably the strongest claim is that the funds are used for important purposes, usually education. This claim apparently is true: The legislators are smart enough to package the lottery bills this way. And the revenue gained seems enormous—$20 billion in 2002, according to the *New York Times* (May 18, 2003, sec. 4, p. 1). On the other hand, this amount is only about 4 percent of the total revenue of the states. That is, this amount could be raised by other means, specifically by taxation, but legislators understandably do not want to be associated with increasing taxes. And so, again, advocates of state lotteries emphasize the voluntary nature of the lottery: By buying lottery tickets, they say, people are in effect volunteering to give money to the states, in exchange for the chance (however remote) of getting a ticket out. Buying a ticket, in this view, is paying an optional tax; if you don't want to pay the tax, don't buy the ticket.

I now get to the point in my argument where I may sound condescending, where I may offend decent people. The point is this: Studies show that most of the tickets are bought by people who don't have much money, people who are near the bottom of the economic scale. According to one study, adults whose income was under $10,000 spent nearly three times as much buying lottery tickets as did adults who earned $50,000 or more.[1] I say that this argument is delicate because anyone who advances it is liable to be accused of being snobbish and paternalistic, of saying, in effect, "Poor people don't know how to manage their money, so we ought to remove temptation from their eyes." But such a reply does not get to the central issues: The central issues are (1) that the state should not tempt people, rich or poor, with dreams of an easy buck

---

[1] Verna V. Gehring, "The American State Lottery: Sale or Swindle?" *Report from the Institute for Philosophy and Public Policy 20* (Winter/Spring 2000): 15.

b.

and (2) that education and social services are immensely important to the whole of society, so they should not be disproportionately financed by the poor and the addicted.

Let me end a bit indirectly. Surely everyone will grant that tobacco is a harmful product. Yes, it is legal, but everyone knows it is harmful. The state puts very heavy taxes on it, presumably not to raise revenue but to discourage the use of tobacco. We agree, surely, that it would be almost criminal if, in an effort to increase its revenues, the state *enticed* people to smoke — for example, by posting billboards showing attractive people smoking or cartoon characters that appealed to children. Would we say, "Oh, well, we need the revenue (from the taxes) to provide services, so let's make smoking as attractive as we can to get people to buy cigarettes"? No, we would say, "People should not smoke, but if they will, well, let's use the revenue from the taxes for two chief purposes: *to dissuade* people from smoking and *to treat* people who have become ill from smoking."

State legislators who genuinely have the interests of their constituents at heart will not pass bills that put the state into the lottery business and that cause the state to engage in an activity that is close to pickpocketing. Rather, they will recognize that, however unpopular taxes are, taxes may have to be raised to support education and social services that the people rightly expect the state to provide. It's against the odds to expect politicians to act this way, but let's hope that some politicians will do the right thing and will vote for the common good.

Topics for Critical Thinking and Writing

1. Jiménez omits at least one important argument that advocates of state-run lotteries sometimes offer: If our state doesn't run a lottery, residents will simply go to nearby states to buy tickets, so we will just be losing revenue that other states pick up; poor people will still be spending money that they can't afford, and our state will in no way benefit. What do you suppose Jiménez might say in reply? And what is your own view of this argument?

2. A bit of humor appears at the end of Jiménez's second paragraph. Is it appropriate? Or is the essay too solemn, too preachy? If you think it is too preachy, cite some sentences, and then revise them to make them more acceptable.

3. What would you say are the strengths and the weaknesses of this essay? What grade would you give it, and why? If you were the instructor in this first-year composition course, what comment (three or four sentences) would you write at the end of the essay?

4. The essay was written in a composition course. If you were the editor of your college's newspaper, might you run it as an op-ed piece? Why or why not?

Anna Lisa Raya

Daughter of a second-generation Mexican American father and a Puerto Rican mother, Anna Lisa Raya grew up in Los Angeles. While an undergraduate at Columbia University in New York, she wrote and published this essay on identity.

It's Hard Enough Being Me

(Student Essay)

When I entered college, I *discovered* I was Latina. Until then, I had never questioned who I was or where I was from: My father is a second-generation Mexican American, born and raised in Los Angeles, and my mother was born in Puerto Rico and raised in Compton, California. My home is El Sereno, a predominantly Mexican neighborhood in L.A. Every close friend I have back home is Mexican. So I was always just Mexican. Though sometimes I was just Puerto Rican—like when we would visit Mamo (my grandma) or hang out with my Aunt Titi.

Upon arriving in New York as a first-year student, 3,000 miles from home, I not only experienced extreme culture shock, but for the first time I had to define myself according to the broad term "Latina." Although culture shock and identity crisis are common for the newly minted collegian who goes away to school, my experience as a newly minted Latina was, and still is, even more complicating. In El Sereno, I felt like I was part of a majority, whereas at the College I am a minority.

I've discovered that many Latinos like myself have undergone similar experiences. We face discrimination for being a minority in this country while also facing criticism for being "whitewashed" or "sellouts" in the countries of our heritage. But as an ethnic group in college, we are forced to define ourselves according to some vague, generalized Latino experience. This requires us to know our history, our language, our music, and our religion. I can't even be a content "Puerto Mexican" because I have to be a politically-and-socially-aware-Latina-with-a-chip-on-my-shoulder-because-of-how-repressed-I-am-in-this-country.

I am none of the above. I am the quintessential imperfect Latina. I can't dance salsa to save my life, I learned about Montezuma and the Aztecs in sixth grade, and I haven't prayed to the *Virgen de Guadalupe* in years.

Apparently I don't even look Latina. I can't count how many times 5 people have just assumed that I'm white or asked me if I'm Asian. True, my friends back home call me *güera* ("whitey") because I have green eyes and pale skin, but that was as bad as it got. I never thought I would wish my skin were a darker shade or my hair a curlier texture, but since I've been in college, I have—many times.

Another thing: My Spanish is terrible. Every time I call home, I berate my mama for not teaching me Spanish when I was a child. In fact, not knowing how to speak the language of my home countries is the biggest problem that I have encountered, as have many Latinos. In Mexico there is a term, *pocha,* which is used by native Mexicans to ridicule Mexican Americans. It expresses a deep-rooted antagonism and dislike for those of us who were raised on the other side of the border. Our failed attempts to speak pure, Mexican Spanish are largely responsible for the dislike. Other Latin American natives have this same attitude. No matter how well a Latino speaks Spanish, it can never be good enough.

Yet Latinos can't even speak Spanish in the U.S. without running the risk of being called "spic" or "wetback." That is precisely why my mother refused to teach me Spanish when I was a child. The fact that she spoke Spanish was constantly used against her: It prevented her from getting good jobs, and it would have placed me in bilingual education—a construct of the Los Angeles public school system that has proved to be more of a hindrance to intellectual development than a help.

To be fully Latina in college, however, I *must* know Spanish. I must satisfy the equation: Latina [equals] Spanish-speaking.

So I'm stuck in this black hole of an identity crisis, and college isn't making my life any easier, as I thought it would. In high school, I was being prepared for an adulthood in which I would be an individual, in which I wouldn't have to wear a Catholic school uniform anymore. But though I led an anonymous adolescence, I knew who I was. I knew I was different from white, black, or Asian people. I knew there was a language other than English that I could call my own if I only knew how to speak it better. I knew there were historical reasons why I was in this country, distinct reasons that make my existence here easier or more difficult than other people's existence. Ultimately, I was content.

Now I feel pushed into a corner, always defining, defending, and 10 proving myself to classmates, professors, or employers. Trying to understand who and why I am, while understanding Plato or Homer, is a lot to ask of myself.

A month ago, I heard three Nuyorican (Puerto Ricans born and raised in New York) writers discuss how New York City has influenced their writing. One problem I have faced as a young writer is finding a voice that is true to my community. I was surprised and reassured to discover that as Latinos, these writers had faced similar pressures and conflicts as myself; some weren't even taught Spanish in childhood. I will never forget the advice that one of them gave me that evening: She said that I need to be true to myself. "Because people will always complain about what you are doing—you're a 'gringa' or a 'spic' no matter what," she explained. "So you might as well do things for yourself and not for them."

I don't know why it has taken 20 years to hear this advice, but I'm going to give it a try. *Soy yo* and no one else. *Punto.*[1]

---

[1]**Soy yo . . . Punto.** I'm me . . . Period (Spanish). [Editors' note.]

Topics for Critical Thinking and Writing

1. When Raya says she "discovered" she was Latina (para. 1), to what kind of event is she referring? Was she coerced or persuaded to declare herself as Latina, or did it come about in some other way?

2. Is Raya on balance glad or sorry that she did not learn Spanish as a child? What evidence can you point to in her essay one way or the other?

3. What is an "identity crisis" (para. 9)? Does everyone go through such a crisis about the time one enters college? Did you? Or is this an experience that only racial minorities in predominantly white American colleges undergo?

Ronald Takaki

Ronald Takaki (1939–2009), the grandson of agricultural laborers who had come from Japan, was a professor of ethnic studies at the University of California at Berkeley. He edited From Different Shores: Perspectives on Race and Ethnicity in America *(1987) and wrote (among other writings)* Strangers from a Different Shore: A History of Asian-Americans *(1989). The essay that we reprint appeared originally in the* New York Times *on June 16, 1990.*

The Harmful Myth of Asian Superiority

Asian Americans have increasingly come to be viewed as a "model minority." But are they as successful as claimed? And for whom are they supposed to be a model?

Asian Americans have been described in the media as "excessively, even provocatively" successful in gaining admission to universities. Asian American shopkeepers have been congratulated, as well as criticized, for their ubiquity and entrepreneurial effectiveness.

If Asian Americans can make it, many politicians and pundits ask, why can't African Americans? Such comparisons pit minorities against each other and generate African American resentment toward Asian Americans. The victims are blamed for their plight, rather than racism and an economy that has made many young African American workers superfluous.

The celebration of Asian Americans has obscured reality. For example, figures on the high earnings of Asian Americans relative to Caucasians are misleading. Most Asian Americans live in California, Hawaii, and New York—states with higher incomes and higher costs of living than the national average.

 Even Japanese Americans, often touted for their upward mobility, 5 have not reached equality. While Japanese American men in California earned an average income comparable to Caucasian men in 1980, they did so only by acquiring more education and working more hours.

Comparing family incomes is even more deceptive. Some Asian American groups do have higher family incomes than Caucasians. But they have more workers per family.

The "model minority" image homogenizes Asian Americans and hides their differences. For example, while thousands of Vietnamese American young people attend universities, others are on the streets. They live in motels and hang out in pool halls in places like East Los Angeles; some join gangs.

Twenty-five percent of the people in New York City's Chinatown lived below the poverty level in 1980, compared with 17 percent of the city's population. Some 60 percent of the workers in the Chinatowns of Los Angeles and San Francisco are crowded into low-paying jobs in garment factories and restaurants.

"Most immigrants coming into Chinatown with a language barrier cannot go outside this confined area into the mainstream of American industry," a Chinese immigrant said. "Before, I was a painter in Hong Kong, but I can't do it here. I got no license, no education. I want a living; so it's dishwasher, janitor, or cook."

Hmong and Mien refugees from Laos have unemployment rates that reach as high as 80 percent. A 1987 California study showed that three out of ten Southeast Asian refugee families had been on welfare for four to ten years.

Although college-educated Asian Americans are entering the professions and earning good salaries, many hit the "glass ceiling"—the barrier through which high management positions can be seen but not reached. In 1988, only 8 percent of Asian Americans were "officials" and "managers," compared with 12 percent for all groups.

Finally, the triumph of Korean immigrants has been exaggerated. In 1988, Koreans in the New York metropolitan area earned only 68 percent of the median income of non-Asians. More than three-quarters of Korean greengrocers, those so-called paragons of bootstrap entrepreneurialism, came to America with a college education. Engineers, teachers, or administrators while in Korea, they became shopkeepers after their arrival. For many of them, the greengrocery represents dashed dreams, a step downward in status.

For all their hard work and long hours, most Korean shopkeepers do not actually earn very much: $17,000 to $35,000 a year, usually representing the income from the labor of an entire family.

But most Korean immigrants do not become shopkeepers. Instead, many find themselves trapped as clerks in grocery stores, service workers in restaurants, seamstresses in garment factories, and janitors in hotels.

Most Asian Americans know their "success" is largely a myth. They also see how the celebration of Asian Americans as a "model minority" perpetuates their inequality and exacerbates relations between them and African Americans.

Topics for Critical Thinking and Writing

1. What is the thesis of Takaki's essay? What is the evidence he offers for its truth? Do you find his argument convincing? Explain your answers to these questions in an essay of 500 words. Alternatively, write a 500-word blog post that responds to this essay.

2. Takaki several times uses statistics to make a point. What effect do the statistics have on the reader? Do some of the statistics seem more convincing than others? Explain.

3. Consider Takaki's title. To what group(s) is the myth of Asian superiority harmful?

4. Suppose you believed that Asian Americans are economically more successful in America today, relative to white Americans, than African Americans are. Does Takaki agree or disagree with you? What evidence, if any, does he cite to support or reject the belief?

5. Takaki attacks the "myth" of Asian American success and thus rejects the idea that they are a "model minority" (recall the opening and closing paragraphs). What do you think a genuine model minority would be like? Can you think of any racial or ethnic minority in the United States that can serve as a model? Explain why or why not in an essay of 500 words.

James Q. Wilson

James Q. Wilson (1931–2012) was Collins Professor of Management and Public Policy at the University of California at Los Angeles. Among his books are Thinking about Crime *(1975),* Bureaucracy *(1989),* The Moral Sense *(1993), and* Moral Judgment *(1997). The essay that we reprint appeared originally in the* New York Times Magazine *on March 20, 1994.*

Just Take Away Their Guns

The president wants still tougher gun control legislation and thinks it will work. The public supports more gun control laws but suspects they won't work. The public is right.

Legal restraints on the lawful purchase of guns will have little effect on the illegal use of guns. There are some 200 million guns in private ownership, about one-third of them handguns. Only about 2 percent of the latter are employed to commit crimes. It would take a Draconian, and politically impossible, confiscation of legally purchased guns to make much of a difference in the number used by criminals. Moreover, only about one-sixth of the handguns used by serious criminals are purchased from a gun shop or pawnshop. Most of these handguns are stolen, borrowed, or obtained through private purchases that wouldn't be affected by gun laws.

What is worse, any successful effort to shrink the stock of legally purchased guns (or of ammunition) would reduce the capacity of law-abiding people to defend themselves. Gun control advocates scoff at the importance of self-defense, but they are wrong to do so. Based on a household survey, Gary Kleck, a criminologist at Florida State University, has estimated that every year, guns are used—that is, displayed or fired—for defensive purposes more than a million times, not counting their use by the police. If his estimate is correct, this means that the number of people who defend themselves with a gun exceeds the number of arrests for violent crimes and burglaries.

Our goal should not be the disarming of law-abiding citizens. It should be to reduce the number of people who carry guns unlawfully, especially in places—on streets, in taverns—where the mere presence of a gun can increase the hazards we all face. The most effective way to reduce illegal gun-carrying is to encourage the police to take guns away from people who carry them without a permit. This means encouraging the police to make street frisks.

The Fourth Amendment to the Constitution bans "unreasonable   5 searches and seizures." In 1968 the Supreme Court decided (*Terry v. Ohio*) that a frisk—patting down a person's outer clothing—is proper if the officer has a "reasonable suspicion" that the person is armed and dangerous. If a pat-down reveals an object that might be a gun, the officer can enter the suspect's pocket to remove it. If the gun is being carried illegally, the suspect can be arrested.

The reasonable-suspicion test is much less stringent than the probable-cause standard the police must meet in order to make an arrest. A reasonable suspicion, however, is more than just a hunch; it must be supported by specific facts. The courts have held, not always consistently, that these facts include someone acting in a way that leads an experienced officer to conclude criminal activity may be afoot; someone fleeing at the approach of an officer; a person who fits a drug courier profile; a motorist stopped for a traffic violation who has a suspicious bulge in his pocket; a suspect identified by a reliable informant as carrying a gun. The Supreme Court has also upheld frisking people on probation or parole.

Some police departments frisk a lot of people, but usually the police frisk rather few, at least for the purpose of detecting illegal guns. In 1992 the police arrested about 240,000 people for illegally possessing or carrying a weapon. This is only about one-fourth as many as were arrested for public drunkenness. The average police officer will make *no* weapons arrests and confiscate *no* guns during any given year. Mark Moore, a professor of public policy at Harvard University, found that most weapons arrests were made because a citizen complained, not because the police were out looking for guns.

It is easy to see why. Many cities suffer from a shortage of officers, and even those with ample law-enforcement personnel worry about having their cases thrown out for constitutional reasons or being accused of police harassment. But the risk of violating the Constitution or engaging in actual, as opposed to perceived, harassment can be substantially reduced.

Each patrol officer can be given a list of people on probation or parole who live on that officer's beat and be rewarded for making frequent stops to insure that they are not carrying guns. Officers can be trained to recognize the kinds of actions that the Court will accept as providing the "reasonable suspicion" necessary for a stop and frisk. Membership in a gang known for assaults and drug dealing could be made the basis, by statute or Court precedent, for gun frisks.

The available evidence supports the claim that self-defense is a legitimate form of deterrence. People who report to the National Crime Survey that they defended themselves with a weapon were less likely to lose property in a robbery or be injured in an assault than those who did not defend themselves. Statistics have shown that would-be burglars are threatened by gun-wielding victims about as many times a year as they are arrested (and much more often than they are sent to prison) and that the chances of a burglar being shot are about the same as his chances of going to jail. Criminals know these facts even if gun control advocates do not and so are less likely to burgle occupied homes in America than occupied ones in Europe, where the residents rarely have guns.

Some gun control advocates may concede these points but rejoin that the cost of self-defense is self-injury: Handgun owners are more likely to shoot themselves or their loved ones than a criminal. Not quite. Most gun accidents involve rifles and shotguns, not handguns. Moreover, the rate of fatal gun accidents has been declining while the level of gun ownership has been rising. There are fatal gun accidents just as there are fatal car accidents, but in fewer than 2 percent of the gun fatalities was the victim someone mistaken for an intruder.

Those who urge us to forbid or severely restrict the sale of guns ignore these facts. Worse, they adopt a position that is politically absurd. In effect, they say, "Your government, having failed to protect your person and your property from criminal assault, now intends to deprive you of the opportunity to protect yourself."

Opponents of gun control make a different mistake. The National Rifle Association and its allies tell us that "guns don't kill, people kill" and urge the Government to punish more severely people who use guns to commit crimes. Locking up criminals does protect society from future crimes, and the prospect of being locked up may deter criminals. But our experience with meting out tougher sentences is mixed. The tougher the prospective sentence the less likely it is to be imposed, or at least to be imposed swiftly. If the Legislature adds on time for crimes committed with a gun, prosecutors often bargain away the add-ons; even when they do not, the judges in many states are reluctant to impose add-ons.

Worse, the presence of a gun can contribute to the magnitude of the crime even on the part of those who worry about serving a long

prison sentence. Many criminals carry guns not to rob stores but to protect themselves from other armed criminals. Gang violence has become
more threatening to bystanders as gang members have begun to arm
themselves. People may commit crimes, but guns make some crimes
worse. Guns often convert spontaneous outbursts of anger into fatal encounters. When some people carry them on the streets, others will want
to carry them to protect themselves, and an urban arms race will be un-
derway.

And modern science can be enlisted to help. Metal detectors at air-   15
ports have reduced the number of airplane bombings and skyjackings
to nearly zero. But these detectors only work at very close range. What
is needed is a device that will enable the police to detect the presence
of a large lump of metal in someone's pocket from a distance of ten or
fifteen feet. Receiving such a signal could supply the officer with reasonable grounds for a pat-down. Underemployed nuclear physicists and
electronics engineers in the post-cold-war era surely have the talents for
designing a better gun detector.

Even if we do all these things, there will still be complaints. Innocent people will be stopped. Young black and Hispanic men will probably be stopped more often than older white Anglo males or women of
any race. But if we are serious about reducing drive-by shootings, fatal
gang wars and lethal quarrels in public places, we must get illegal guns
off the street. We cannot do this by multiplying the forms one fills out at
gun shops or by pretending that guns are not a problem until a criminal
uses one.

TOPICS FOR CRITICAL THINKING AND WRITING

1. If you had to single out one sentence in Wilson's essay as coming close
   to stating his thesis, what sentence would that be? Why do you think it
   states, better than any other sentence, the thesis of the essay?

2. In his third paragraph Wilson reviews some research by a criminologist
   purporting to show that guns are important for self-defense in American households. Does the research as reported show that displaying
   or firing guns in self-defense actually prevented crimes? Or wounded
   aggressors? Suppose you were also told that in households where guns
   may be used defensively, thousands of innocent people are injured,
   and hundreds are killed — for instance, children who find a loaded gun
   and play with it. Would you regard these injuries and deaths as a fair
   trade-off? Explain. What does the research presented by Wilson really
   show?

3. In paragraph 12 Wilson says that people who want to severely restrict
   the ownership of guns are in effect saying, "'Your government, having
   failed to protect your person and your property from criminal assault,

now intends to deprive you of the opportunity to protect yourself.'" What reply might an advocate of severe restrictions make? (Even if you strongly believe Wilson's summary is accurate, try to put yourself in the shoes of an advocate of gun control, and come up with the best reply that you can.)

4. Wilson reports in paragraph 7 that the police arrest four times as many drunks on the streets as they do people carrying unlicensed firearms. Does this strike you as absurd, reasonable, or mysterious? Does Wilson explain it to your satisfaction?

5. In his final paragraph Wilson grants that his proposal entails a difficulty: "Innocent people will be stopped. Young black and Hispanic men will probably be stopped more often than older white Anglo males or women of any race." Assuming that his predictions are accurate, is Wilson's proposal therefore fatally flawed and worth no further thought, or (to take the other extreme view) do you think that innocent people who fall into certain classifications will just have to put up with frisking for the public good?

6. In an essay of no more than 100 words, explain the difference between the "reasonable-suspicion" test (para. 5) and the "probable-cause standard" (para. 6) that the courts use in deciding whether a street frisk is lawful. (You may want to organize your essay into two paragraphs, one on each topic, or perhaps into three if you want to use a brief introductory paragraph.)

7. Wilson criticizes both gun control advocates and the National Rifle Association for their ill-advised views. In an essay of 500 words, state his criticisms of each side, and explain whether and to what extent you agree.

Kayla Webley

Kayla Webley, the education correspondent for Time *magazine, did her undergraduate work at the University of Washington, concentrating on journalism and political science, and her graduate work at Northwestern University, specializing in new media. The essay that we reprint originally appeared in* Time *magazine on April 20, 2012.*

Is Forgiving Student Loan Debt a Good Idea?

Every few weeks now a petition pops up in my Facebook newsfeed urging the government to forgive all student debt. The comment from the person posting the petition usually goes something like this, "Guessing this will never happen, but can't hurt to sign on!"

The petition now has nearly 670,000 signatures. Scrolling through the stories posted on the petition (and similar stories told on the related

Occupy Student Debt site) can be a heart-wrenching experience. Former students tell stories of unemployment, worthless majors, low-paying jobs and resulting six-figure debt, insurmountable interest, forbearance and default. From a human standpoint, it's easy to see why forgiving student debt holds some appeal. But many have questioned not only the enormous and economically unfeasible cost, but the purported benefits and fairness of a one-time student loan bailout.

Feeling shackled by an estimated $88,000 in student loan debt, Robert Applebaum started the petition in 2009 and has seen its popularity skyrocket since last fall as some members of the Occupy Wall Street movement adopted the battle cry. His proposal is simple: Provide a one-time bailout of student loan debt—currently valued at $1 trillion—as a way to stimulate the still-limping economy. After all, college graduates are the type of people society needs to do things like start businesses, buy homes and cars, invent things, and make babies—and people burdened with debt are less likely to make those kinds of decisions. Unburden them and the housing market might improve, along with the overall economy. "With the stroke of the President's pen, millions of Americans would suddenly have hundreds, or in some cases, thousands of extra dollars in their pockets each and every month with which to spend on ailing sectors of the economy," Applebaum writes in the petition.

That sounds like a very expensive proposition, of course. But so were the bank and auto bailouts—and, the thinking goes, if "fat cat" bankers and auto makers got a bailout, why not college graduates?

Well, as Justin Wolfers writes on the Freakonomics blog, one rea-   5
son why not is that such a scheme wouldn't be a particularly efficient fiscal stimulus. Someone who has $50,000 in debt forgiven isn't likely to pump all those dollars back into the economy in a short amount of time. A much more effective stimulus, Wolfers says, would be to give fifty poor people $1,000 each because that money would almost immediately be spent.

Another problem with such a plan is that most borrowers actually can afford to pay off their student loan debt. There are some borrowers who desperately need relief, but there are many others who would just rather not have to fork over a certain percentage of their income each month to pay for the education they received years ago. But if forgiveness was offered, who wouldn't take the handout?

As it turns out, the six-figure debts that we keep hearing about in the media are actually pretty unusual. By most estimates, only a tiny minority of student loan borrowers—as little as 1 percent—graduate with more than $100,000 in debt. Mark Kantrowitz of FinAid.org and FastWeb.com says that only a few thousand students out of the several million who finish college each year graduate with that much debt. The average debt total at graduation is a much more reasonable—yet still significant—$27,500.

What's more, even borrowers who can't afford the standard repayment plan have existing alternatives if the loan is from the government. There are already programs in place that offer forgiveness, not to mention the government's effective and underutilized Income Based Repayment program. What might be a more politically viable approach to student debt — although it would provide less fiscal stimulus — would be for the government and loan providers to have a better way of distinguishing between those borrowers who really need help and those who don't. But of course that's no easy task.

Many of the concerns surrounding Applebaum's plan involve the idea of fairness. Why should current debt holders be forgiven when for years people have paid their debts? Why should taxpayers — especially those who never attended college in the first place — foot the bill for the borrowers' education? What about future generations? Will they just take out loads of money in college and cross their fingers for a bailout? There are no easy answers to these questions other than to say, life isn't fair.

But perhaps the biggest roadblock to Applebaum's plan is that a one-time bailout is a temporary fix to an ongoing problem. What's really needed is a long look at how higher education in the United States is financed. Many would argue the current model is fundamentally broken. Virtually everyone who applies is approved for almost unlimited student loans, regardless of how likely they are to be able to pay them back. But lenders aren't really concerned about that because student loans cannot be discharged in bankruptcy. They know they'll get their money back one way or another. 10

As a result, lenders have no incentive to work with students toward a reasonable repayment plan. And further, colleges have no incentive to keep tuition low — tuition is increasing at a rate double that of inflation — because whether they can afford it or not, students will find a way to pay the bill.

Applebaum's proposal offers a radical and wildly unfeasible solution, both politically and economically, but it's an idea nonetheless. "I'm not saying my solution to the student debt crisis is the very best," he says. "If you disagree with me, what's your solution?"

Topics for Critical Thinking and Writing

1. Why do you suppose Webley prefaces her argument by telling us in paragraph 2 that some of the stories on the Occupy Student Debt site are "heart-wrenching"?

2. What do you think of Webley's final paragraph as a way of ending her essay?

3. Do you have any ideas about forgiving student debts that are not touched on in Webley's essay? If so, what are they? How would you work them into the essay?

"I'm looking for a career that won't be obsolete before my student loan is paid off."

Alfred Edmond Jr.

Alfred Edmond Jr. is senior vice president/multimedia editor-at-large of Black Enterprise, *a media organization that publishes* Black Enterprise *magazine. He appears often on television and on nationally syndicated radio programs.*

Why Asking for a Job Applicant's Facebook Password Is Fair Game

"Should business owners be allowed to ask job applicants for their Facebook passwords?" Many people who watched me on MSNBC's *Your Business* on Sunday were surprised to hear that my answer is "Yes," including the show's host, J. J. Ramberg. This question became a hot news topic last week, especially in business and social media circles, when Congress failed to pass legislation that would have banned the practice of employers asking employees to reveal their Facebook passwords.

Now, if I was asked the same question as a guest on a show called *Your Career*, I would have been hard-pressed to think of a situation where I would share my Facebook password with a potential employer. For me to consider it, I would have to want the job pretty badly, with the amount and type of compensation (including benefits, perks, and even an equity stake in the company) being major considerations. But before doing so, I would see if there were other ways I could address the potential employer's concerns without revealing my password, such as changing my privacy settings to give them the ability to view all of my Facebook content. If they persisted with their request for my password, I would try to negotiate terms to strictly limit both their use of the password and the length of time the potential employer would have access to it before I could change it. I might even consider getting an employment attorney to negotiate an agreement, including terms of confidentiality, to be signed by both me and the potential employer before sharing my password.

Of course, for the vast majority of positions, neither I nor a company looking to hire would deem it worth the time and expense to jump through all of these hoops. Most companies would not care to have password access to an applicant's social media accounts. (For what it's worth, Facebook's terms of rights and responsibilities forbids users from sharing their passwords.) In probably 99 percent of such cases, if a potential employer made such a request, my answer would be, "No, I will not share my password. Are there alternatives you are willing to consider to satisfy your concerns?" I'd accept that I'd risk not being hired as a result. On the other hand, if that was all it took for me not to be hired, I'd question how badly they really wanted me in the first place, as well as whether that was the kind of place I would have been happy working for. But for certain companies and positions, especially if I wanted the job badly enough, I'd consider a request for my Facebook password at least up for negotiation.

That said, my response on *Your Business* was from the perspective of the business owner. And if I'm the owner of certain types of businesses, or trying to fill certain types of positions, I believe I should be able to ask job applicants for access to their Facebook accounts. The applicant may choose not to answer, but I should be able to ask. Depending on the position, knowing everything I possibly can about an applicant is critical to not only making the best hire, but to protecting the interests of my current employees, customers, and partners as well as the financial interests of the company.

On *Your Business*, I pointed to an example where I believe a request 5
for a Facebook password as part of the hiring process is entirely reasonable: the child care industry. If I am running a school or a day care center, the time to find out that a teacher or other worker has a record of inappropriate social media communication with minors, or worse, a history of or predilection for sexual relationships with students, is during the hiring process—as New York City is finding out the hard way, with an epidemic of public school employees being revealed to have had such relationships with students. To me, such a request falls into

the same category of checking the backgrounds of potential employees as the common (also still debated) practice of asking job applicants to agree to a credit check, especially for jobs that will require them to handle money, keep the books, or carry out other fiscal duties on behalf of a company. In these and other cases, safety and security issues, and the legal liability that they create for business owners if they are not adequately addressed during the hiring process, outweigh the job applicant's expectation of privacy when it comes to their social media activities.

Speaking of which, I can still hear people screaming (actually tweeting and retweeting) that an employer asking for your Facebook password is a horrible invasion of privacy. Well, for those of you who still believe in Santa Claus, I strongly recommend that you read *The Filter Bubble: What the Internet Is Hiding from You* by Eli Pariser (Penguin Press). Or you can just take my advice and let go of the illusion of privacy on social media. The courts are conflicted, at best, on whether we as social media users have a right to an expectation of privacy, with many cases being decided against such expectations. The last place you want to share anything that is truly private is on your Facebook page or any other social media platform. Better to think of social media as the ultimate "Front Street." No matter what Facebook's privacy policies are (which they can change at will without your permission) and what privacy tools and settings they offer (which they also change whenever it suits their business models), always assume that posting on Facebook is just the ticking time bomb version of you shouting your private business from the middle of Times Square—on steroids.

To paraphrase a quote shared in *The Filter Bubble*, if you're getting something for free, you're not the customer, you're the product. Social media is designed for the information shared on it to be searched and shared—and mined for profit. The business model is the very antithesis of the expectation of privacy. To ignore that reality is to have blind faith in Facebook, Google, Twitter, etc., operating in your best interests above all else, at all times. (I don't.)

Whether you agree with me or not about whether a potential employer asking you for your Facebook password is fair game, I hope you'll take my advice: When considering what to share via social media, don't think business vs. personal. Think public vs. private. And if something is truly private, do not share it on social media out of a misplaced faith in the expectation of privacy.

This debate is far from over, and efforts to update existing, but woefully outdated, privacy laws—not to mention the hiring practices of companies—to catch up with the realities of social media will definitely continue. I'd like to know where you stand, both as entrepreneurs and business owners, as well as potential job applicants. And I'd especially like to hear from human resources and recruiting experts. How far is too far when it comes to a potential employer investigating the social media activity of a job applicant?

Topics for Critical Thinking and Writing

1. Employers *do* (at least at the time we are writing) have the right to require drug tests and personality tests. Do you think they should also legally be allowed to ask for a password to Facebook, or should Congress pass legislation outlawing the practice? If employers are legally allowed to ask, would you provide the password? Why, or why not?

2. Would Edmond's case be strengthened if he gave one or two additional examples—beyond the "child care industry" that he mentions in paragraph 5—of jobs that, a reader might agree, require a thorough background check? What examples can you think of? Would you say that applicants for these jobs should be willing to reveal their Facebook password to a potential employer?

3. In paragraph 7 Edmond paraphrases: "If you're getting something for free, you're not the customer, you're the product." Paraphrase this passage yourself (on paraphrase, see page 39) so that it would be clear to a reader who tells you that he or she finds it puzzling.

Sherry Turkle

Sherry Turkle, born in Brooklyn, New York, in 1948, is Professor of the Social Studies of Science and Technology at the Massachusetts Institute of Technology. Turkle, the author of numerous books, including Alone Together *(2011), often appears on television as a commentator on media. We reprint an essay that originally appeared in the* New York Times, *April 22, 2012.*

The Flight from Conversation

We live in a technological universe in which we are always communicating. And yet we have sacrificed conversation for mere connection.

At home, families sit together, texting and reading e-mail. At work executives text during board meetings. We text (and shop and go on Facebook) during classes and when we're on dates. My students tell me about an important new skill: It involves maintaining eye contact with someone while you text someone else; it's hard, but it can be done.

Over the past fifteen years, I've studied technologies of mobile connection and talked to hundreds of people of all ages and circumstances about their plugged-in lives. I've learned that the little devices most of us carry around are so powerful that they change not only what we do, but also who we are.

We've become accustomed to a new way of being "alone together." Technology-enabled, we are able to be with one another, and also elsewhere, connected to wherever we want to be. We want to customize our lives. We want to move in and out of where we are because the thing we value most is control over where we focus our attention. We have gotten used to the idea of being in a tribe of one, loyal to our own party.

Our colleagues want to go to that board meeting but pay attention 5 only to what interests them. To some this seems like a good idea, but we can end up hiding from one another, even as we are constantly connected to one another.

A businessman laments that he no longer has colleagues at work. He doesn't stop by to talk; he doesn't call. He says that he doesn't want to interrupt them. He says they're "too busy on their e-mail." But then he pauses and corrects himself. "I'm not telling the truth. I'm the one who doesn't want to be interrupted. I think I should. But I'd rather just do things on my BlackBerry."

A sixteen-year-old boy who relies on texting for almost everything says almost wistfully, "Someday, someday, but certainly not now, I'd like to learn how to have a conversation."

In today's workplace, young people who have grown up fearing conversation show up on the job wearing earphones. Walking through a college library or the campus of a high-tech start-up, one sees the same thing: We are together, but each of us is in our own bubble, furiously connected to keyboards and tiny touch screens. A senior partner at a Boston law firm describes a scene in his office. Young associates lay out their suite of technologies: laptops, iPods, and multiple phones. And then they put their earphones on. "Big ones. Like pilots. They turn their desks into cockpits." With the young lawyers in their cockpits, the office is quiet, a quiet that does not ask to be broken.

In the silence of connection, people are comforted by being in touch with a lot of people—carefully kept at bay. We can't get enough of one another if we can use technology to keep one another at distances we can control: not too close, not too far, just right. I think of it as a Goldilocks effect.

Texting and e-mail and posting let us present the self we want to be. 10 This means we can edit. And if we wish to, we can delete. Or retouch: the voice, the flesh, the face, the body. Not too much, not too little—just right.

Human relationships are rich; they're messy and demanding. We have learned the habit of cleaning them up with technology. And the move from conversation to connection is part of this. But it's a process in which we shortchange ourselves. Worse, it seems that over time we stop caring, we forget that there is a difference.

We are tempted to think that our little "sips" of online connection add up to a big gulp of real conversation. But they don't. E-mail, Twitter, Facebook, all of these have their places—in politics, commerce, romance, and friendship. But no matter how valuable, they do not substitute for conversation.

Connecting in sips may work for gathering discrete bits of information or for saying, "I am thinking about you." Or even for saying, "I love you." But connecting in sips doesn't work as well when it comes to understanding and knowing one another. In conversation we tend to one another. (The word itself is kinetic; it's derived from words that mean to move, together.) We can attend to tone and nuance. In conversation, we are called upon to see things from another's point of view.

Face-to-face conversation unfolds slowly. It teaches patience. When we communicate on our digital devices, we learn different habits. As we ramp up the volume and velocity of online connections, we start to expect faster answers. To get these, we ask one another simpler questions; we dumb down our communications, even on the most important matters. It is as though we have all put ourselves on cable news. Shakespeare might have said, "We are consum'd with that which we were nourish'd by."

And we use conversation with others to learn to converse with our- 15 selves. So our flight from conversation can mean diminished chances to learn skills of self-reflection. These days, social media continually asks us what's "on our mind," but we have little motivation to say something truly self-reflective. Self-reflection in conversation requires trust. It's hard to do anything with 3,000 Facebook friends except connect.

As we get used to being shortchanged on conversation and to getting by with less, we seem almost willing to dispense with people altogether. Serious people muse about the future of computer programs as psychiatrists. A high school sophomore confides to me that he wishes he could talk to an artificial intelligence program instead of his dad about dating; he says the A.I. would have so much more in its database. Indeed, many people tell me they hope that as Siri, the digital assistant on Apple's iPhone, becomes more advanced, "she" will be more and more like a best friend—one who will listen when others won't.

During the years I have spent researching people and their relationships with technology, I have often heard the sentiment "No one is listening to me." I believe this feeling helps explain why it is so appealing to have a Facebook page or a Twitter feed—each provides so many automatic listeners. And it helps explain why—against all reason—so many of us are willing to talk to machines that seem to care about us. Researchers around the world are busy inventing sociable robots, designed to be companions to the elderly, to children, to all of us.

One of the most haunting experiences during my research came when I brought one of these robots, designed in the shape of a baby seal, to an elder-care facility, and an older woman began to talk to it about the loss of her child. The robot seemed to be looking into her eyes. It seemed to be following the conversation. The woman was comforted.

And so many people found this amazing. Like the sophomore who wants advice about dating from artificial intelligence and those who look forward to computer psychiatry, this enthusiasm speaks to how much we have confused conversation with connection and collectively seem to have embraced a new kind of delusion that accepts the simulation of compassion as sufficient unto the day. And why would we want to talk about love and loss with a machine that has no experience of the arc of human life? Have we so lost confidence that we will be there for one another?

We expect more from technology and less from one another and 20 seem increasingly drawn to technologies that provide the illusion of companionship without the demands of relationship. Always-on/always-on-you devices provide three powerful fantasies: that we will always be heard; that we can put our attention wherever we want it to be; and that we never have to be alone. Indeed our new devices have turned being alone into a problem that can be solved.

When people are alone, even for a few moments, they fidget and reach for a device. Here connection works like a symptom, not a cure, and our constant, reflexive impulse to connect shapes a new way of being.

Think of it as "I share, therefore I am." We use technology to define ourselves by sharing our thoughts and feelings as we're having them. We used to think, "I have a feeling; I want to make a call." Now our impulse is, "I want to have a feeling; I need to send a text."

So, in order to feel more, and to feel more like ourselves, we connect. But in our rush to connect, we flee from solitude, our ability to be separate and gather ourselves. Lacking the capacity for solitude, we turn to other people but don't experience them as they are. It is as though we use them, need them as spare parts to support our increasingly fragile selves.

We think constant connection will make us feel less lonely. The opposite is true. If we are unable to be alone, we are far more likely to be lonely. If we don't teach our children to be alone, they will know only how to be lonely.

I am a partisan for conversation. To make room for it, I see some first, deliberate steps. At home, we can create sacred spaces: the kitchen, the dining room. We can make our cars "device-free zones." We can demonstrate the value of conversation to our children. And we can do the same thing at work. There we are so busy communicating that we often don't have time to talk to one another about what really matters. Employees asked for casual Fridays; perhaps managers should introduce conversational Thursdays. Most of all, we need to remember—in between texts and e-mails and Facebook posts—to listen to one another, even to the boring bits, because it is often in unedited moments, moments in which we hesitate and stutter and go silent, that we reveal ourselves to one another.

I spend the summers at a cottage on Cape Cod, and for decades I walked the same dunes that Thoreau once walked. Not too long ago, people walked with their heads up, looking at the water, the sky, the sand, and at one another, talking. Now they often walk with their heads down, typing. Even when they are with friends, partners, children, everyone is on their own devices.

So I say, look up, look at one another, and let's start the conversation.

TOPICS FOR CRITICAL THINKING AND WRITING

1. Imagine a period when the book—or even the handwritten manuscript—was not yet invented. Now look at Turkle's first paragraph. Think of someone saying what Turkle says, but saying it about the invention of writing, and of the manuscript or book.

2. In paragraph 3 Turkle says that the little devices that we carry "change not only what we we do, but also who we are." We might reply that, yes, of course, almost everything that touches us changes what we are. The invention of the movie theater changed us: Instead of conversing with family or friends, and generating our own entertainment, we sat isolated in the dark for several hours. The possession of an automobile changes us, the move to a new address brings us into contact with new people who may change us—we may even marry one of them—and certainly the engendering of children changes us (or it ought to). But

do you agree with Turkle that the recent electronic devices produce changes of an unexpected sort?

3. In paragraph 14 Turkle suggests that when we communicate electronically, as opposed to when we communicate face-to-face or with pen and paper, "we dumb down our communications, even on the most important matters." Is she describing your behavior? Explain.

4. In paragraph 23 Turkle says, "we flee from solitude, our ability to be separate and gather ourselves." Is this passage true for you? Explain. Might a case be made that, far from being lonely, people who use Facebook and comparable sites are often stimulated to participate in civic and political activities? Does your own experience offer any evidence, one way or the other? Explain.

5. Do you think Turkle's final two paragraphs make an effective ending? Explain.

 For additional arguments online, visit the e-Pages at **bedfordstmartins.com/barnetbedau**.

4

Visual Rhetoric:
Images as Arguments

A picture is worth a thousand words.

— PROVERB

"What is the use of a book," thought Alice, "without pictures or conversations?"

— LEWIS CARROLL

SOME USES OF IMAGES

Most visual materials that accompany written arguments serve one of two functions—they appeal to the emotions (e.g., a photograph of a calf in a pen so narrow that the calf cannot turn, in an essay on animal liberation) or they clarify numerical data (e.g., a graph showing five decades of male and female law school enrollments). There are of course additional uses for pictures, for example, cartoons may add a welcome touch of humor or satire, but in this chapter we concentrate on appeals to emotion and briefly on graphs and related images.

APPEALS TO THE EYE

We began the preceding chapter by distinguishing between *argument,* which we said relies on reason (*logos*), and *persuasion,* which we said is a broad term that can include appeals to the emotions (*pathos*)—for example, an appeal to pity. Threats, too, can be persuasive. As Al Capone famously said, "You can get a lot more done with a kind word and a gun than with a kind word alone." Indeed, most of the remarks that we can think of link persuasion not with the power of reason but with the power of emotional appeals, of flattery, of threats, and of appeals to self-interest. We have in mind passages spoken not only by the likes of the racketeer

Al Capone, but by more significant figures. Consider these two remarks, which both use the word *interest* in the sense of "self-interest":

> Would you persuade, speak of Interest, not Reason.
> —Ben Franklin

> There are two levers for moving men—interest and fear.
> —Napoleon Bonaparte

An appeal to self-interest is obviously at the heart of most advertisements: "Buy *X* automobile, and members of the opposite sex will find you irresistible," "Use *Y* instant soup, and your family will love you more," "Try *Z* cereal and enjoy regularity." We will look at advertisements later in this chapter, but first let's talk a bit more about the use and abuse of visual material in persuasion.

When we discussed the appeal to emotion (p. 103), we quoted from Mark Antony's speech to the Roman populace in Shakespeare's *Julius Caesar*. You will recall that Antony stirred the mob by displaying Caesar's blood-stained mantle, that is, by supplementing his words with visual material:

> Look, in this place ran Cassius' dagger through;
> See what a rent the envious Casca made;
> Through this, the well-belovèd Brutus stabbed. . . .

In courtrooms today, trial lawyers and prosecutors still do this sort of thing when

- they exhibit photos of a bloody corpse, or
- they introduce as witnesses small children who sob as they describe the murder of their parents.

The appeal clearly is not to reason but to the jurors' emotions—and yet, can we confidently say that this sort of visual evidence—this attempt to stir anger at the alleged perpetrator of the crime and pity for the victims—is irrelevant? Why shouldn't jurors vicariously experience the assault?

When we think about it—and it takes only a moment of thinking—the appeal in the courtroom to the eye and then to the heart or mind is evident even in smaller things, such as the clothing that the lawyers wear and the clothing that they advise their clients to wear. To take the most obvious, classic example: The mugger who normally wears jeans, a T-shirt, and a leather jacket appears in court in a three-piece suit, dress shirt, and necktie. Lawyers know that in arguing a case, visuals make statements—perhaps not logical arguments but nevertheless meaningful statements that will attract or repel jurors.

Another sort of visual appeal connected with some arguments should be mentioned briefly—the visual appeal of the specific setting in which the argument occurs. Martin Luther King Jr.'s great speech of August 28, 1963, "I Have a Dream," still reads very well on the page, but part of its

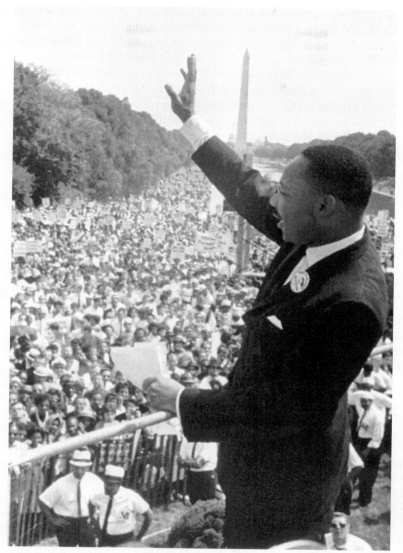

Martin Luther King Jr. delivering his "I Have a Dream" speech on August 28, 1963, from the steps of the Lincoln Memorial. The visual aspects—the setting (the Lincoln Memorial with the Washington Monument and the Capitol in the distance) and King's gestures—are part of the persuasive rhetoric of the speech.

immense appeal when it was first given was due to its setting: King spoke to some 200,000 people in Washington, D.C., as he stood on the steps of the Lincoln Memorial. That setting, rich with associations of slavery and of freedom, was part of King's argument.

Pictures—and here we get to our chief subject—are also sometimes used as parts of arguments because pictures make statements. Some pictures, like Edvard Munch's *The Scream* (below), make obvious statements: The swiftly receding diagonal lines of the fence and the walkway, the wavy sky, and the vibrating vertical lines to the right of the figure all convey the great agitation experienced by the figure in the woodcut.

Some pictures, like the photographs shown to members of Congress during the debate over whether permission should be given to drill in the Arctic National Wildlife Refuge are a bit less obvious:

- *Opponents* of drilling showed beautiful pictures of polar bears frolicking, wildflowers in bloom, and caribou on the move.
- *Proponents* of drilling showed bleak pictures of what they called "barren land" and "a frozen wasteland."

Both sides knew very well that images are powerful persuaders, and they did not hesitate to use images as supplements to words.

We again invite you to think about the appropriateness of using images in arguments. Should argument be entirely a matter of reason, of logic (*logos*), without appeals to the emotions (*pathos*)? Or can images

(Edvard Munch, *The Scream.* © 2007 The Munch Museum/ The Munch-Ellingsen Group/Artists Rights Society [ARS], NY. Digital Image ©/The Museum of Modern Art, NY. Licensed by SCALA/Art Resource. Reproduction, including downloading, of Munch works is prohibited by copyright laws and international conventions without the express written permission of Artists Rights Society [ARS], New York.)

of the sort that we have already mentioned provide visual (and emotional) support for reasons that are offered? The statement that "the Arctic National Wildlife Refuge is a home for abundant wildlife, notably polar bears, caribou, and wildflowers" may not mean much until it is reinforced with breathtaking images. (And, similarly, the statement that "most of the ANWR land is barren" may not mean much until it is corroborated by images of the vast bleakness.)

Images played an important role in the activities of the antislavery movement in the nineteenth century. On the top left is a diagram that shows how human cargo was packed into a slave ship; it was distributed with Thomas Clarkson's *Essay on the Slavery and Commerce of the Human Species* (1804). On the top right is Frederick W. Mercer's photograph (April 2, 1863) of Gordon, a "badly lacerated" runaway slave. Images such as the slave ship and Gordon were used against the claims of slaveowners that slavery was a humane institution—claims that also were supported by illustrations, such as the woodcut at the bottom, titled *Attention Paid to a Poor Sick Negro*, from Josiah Priest's *In Defense of Slavery* (1843).

> **A RULE FOR WRITERS:** If you think that pictures will help you to make the point you are arguing, include them with captions explaining sources and relevance.

ARE SOME IMAGES NOT FIT TO BE SHOWN?

Images of suffering—human or, as animal rights activists have made us see, animal—can be immensely persuasive. In the nineteenth century, for instance, the antislavery movement made extremely effective use of images in its campaign. We reproduce two antislavery images here, as well as a counterimage that sought to assure viewers that slavery is a beneficent system (p. 145). But are there some images not fit to print?

Until recently, many newspapers did not print pictures of lynched African Americans, hanged and burned and maimed. The reasons for not printing such images probably differed in the South and North: Southern papers may have considered the images to be discreditable to whites, while Northern papers may have deemed the images too revolting. Even today, when it is commonplace to see in newspapers and on television

Huynh Cong (Nick) Ut, *The Terror of War: Children on Route 1 near Trang Bang*

Eddie Adams, *Execution of Viet Cong prisoner, Saigon,* 1968

screens pictures of dead victims of war, or famine, or traffic accidents, one rarely sees bodies that are horribly maimed. (For traffic accidents, the body is usually covered, and we see only the smashed car.) The U.S. government has refused to release photographs showing the bodies of American soldiers killed in the war in Iraq, and it has been most reluctant to show pictures of dead Iraqi soldiers and civilians. Only after many Iraqis refused to believe that Saddam Hussein's two sons had been killed did the U.S. government reluctantly release pictures showing the blood-spattered faces of the two men—and some American newspapers and television programs refused to use the images.

There have been notable exceptions to this practice, such as Huynh Cong (Nick) Ut's 1972 photograph of children fleeing a napalm attack in Vietnam (p. 146), which was widely reproduced in the United States and won the photographer a Pulitzer Prize in 1973. The influence of this particular photograph cannot be measured, but it is widely felt to have played a substantial role in increasing public pressure to end the Vietnam War. Another widely reproduced picture of horrifying violence is Eddie Adams's picture (1968, above) of a South Vietnamese chief of police firing a pistol into the head of a Viet Cong prisoner.

The issue remains: Are some images unacceptable? For instance, although capital punishment is legal in parts of the United States—by methods including lethal injection, hanging, shooting, and electrocution—every state in the Union prohibits the publication of pictures showing a criminal being executed. (On this topic, see Wendy Lesser, *Pictures at an Execution* [1993].)

The most famous recent example of an image widely thought to be unprintable concerns the murder of Daniel Pearl, a Jewish reporter for the *Wall Street Journal*. Pearl was captured and murdered in June 2002 by Islamic terrorists in Pakistan. His killers videotaped Pearl reading a statement denouncing American policy and being decapitated. The video also shows a man's arm holding Pearl's head. The video ends with the killers making several demands (such as the release of the Muslim prisoners being held by the United States in Guantánamo Bay, Cuba) and asserting that "if our demands are not met, this scene will be repeated again and again."

The chief arguments against reproducing in newspapers material from this video were that

- the video and even still images from it are unbearably gruesome;
- showing the video would traumatize the Pearl family; and
- the video is propaganda by an enemy.

Those who favored broadcasting the video on television and printing still images from it in newspapers tended to argue that

- the photo will show the world what sort of enemy the United States is fighting;
- newspapers have published pictures of other terrifying sights (notably, people leaping out of windows of New York's twin towers and endless pictures of the space shuttle *Challenger* exploding); and
- no one was worried about protecting the families of these other victims from seeing painful images.

But ask yourself if the comparison of the Daniel Pearl video to the photos of the twin towers and of the *Challenger* is valid. You may respond that the individuals in the twin towers pictures are not specifically identifiable and that the images of the *Challenger*, though horrifying, are not as visually revolting as the picture of a severed head held up for view.

The *Boston Phoenix*, a weekly newspaper, published some images from the Daniel Pearl video and also put a link to the video (with a warning that the footage is "extremely graphic") on its Web site. The editor of the *Phoenix* justified publication on the three grounds we list. Pearl's wife, Mariane Pearl, was quoted in various newspapers as condemning the "heartless decision to air this despicable video," and a spokeswoman for the Pearl family, when asked for comment, referred reporters to a statement issued earlier, which said that broadcasters who show the video

> fall without shame into the terrorists' plan. . . . Danny believed that journalism was a tool to report the truth and foster understanding—not perpetuate propaganda and sensationalize tragedy. We had hoped that no part of this tape would ever see the light of day. . . . We urge all

networks and news outlets to exercise responsibility and not aid the terrorists in spreading their message of hate and murder.[1]

Although some journalists expressed regret that Pearl's family was distressed, they insisted that journalists have a right to reproduce such material and that the images can serve the valuable purpose of shocking viewers into awareness.

Politics and Pictures

Consider, too, the controversy that erupted in 1991, during the Persian Gulf War, when the U.S. government decided that newspapers would not be allowed to photograph coffins returning with the bodies of military personnel killed during the war. In later years the policy was sometimes ignored, but in 2003 the George W. Bush administration decreed that there would be "no arrival ceremony for, or media coverage of, deceased military personnel returning [from Iraq or Afghanistan] . . . to the Dover (Delaware) base." The government enforced the policy strictly.

Members of the news media strongly protested, as did many others, chiefly arguing that

- The administration was trying to sanitize the war, i.e., was depriving the public of important information—images—that showed the real cost of the war.

- Grief for the deaths of military personnel is not a matter only for the families of the deceased. The sacrifices were made for the nation, and the nation should be allowed to grieve. Canada and Britain have no such ban, and when the coffins are transported the public lines the streets to pay honor to the fallen warriors. In fact, in Canada a portion of the highway near the Canadian base has been renamed, "Highway of Heroes."

- The coffins at Dover Air Force base are not identified by name, so there is no issue about intruding on the privacy of grieving families.

The chief arguments in defense of the ban were

- Photographs violate the privacy of the families.

- If the arrival of the coffins at Dover is given publicity, some grieving families will think they should go to Dover to be present when the bodies arrive, and this may cause a financial hardship on the families.

- If the families give their consent, the press is *not* barred from individual graveside ceremonies at hometown burials. The ban extends only to the arrival of the coffins at Dover Air Force Base.

[1]Quoted in the *Hartford Courant,* June 5, 2002, and reproduced on the Internet by the Freedom of Information Center, under the heading "Boston Paper Creates Controversy."

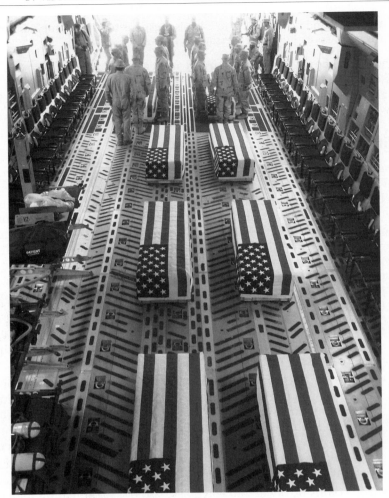

Coffins at Dover Air Force Base, Delaware

In February 2009, President Obama changed the policy and permitted coverage of the transfer of bodily remains. In his Address to the Joint Session of Congress, February 24, 2009, he said, "For seven years we have been a nation at war. No longer will we hide its price." On February 27, Defense Secretary Robert M. Gates announced that the government ban was lifted and that families will decide whether to allow photographs and videos of the "dignified transfer process at Dover."

EXERCISE

In an argumentative essay of about 250 words—perhaps two or three paragraphs—give your view of the issue of permitting photos of military

Alexander Gardner, *Home of a Rebel Sharpshooter*

coffins. In an opening paragraph you may want to explain the issue, and in this same paragraph you may want to summarize the arguments that you reject. The second (and perhaps final) paragraph of a two-paragraph essay may give the reasons you reject those arguments. Additionally, you may want to devote a third paragraph to a more general reflection.

Topic for Critical Thinking and Writing

Marvin Kalb, a distinguished journalist, was quoted as saying that the public has a right to see the tape of Daniel Pearl's murder but that "common sense, decency, [and] humanity would encourage editors . . . to say 'no, it is not necessary to put this out.' There is no urgent demand on the part of the American people to see Daniel Pearl's death." What is your view?

Query   In June 2006 two American soldiers were captured in Iraq. Later their bodies were found, dismembered and beheaded. Should newspapers have shown photographs of the mutilated bodies? Why, or why not? (In July 2006, insurgents in Iraq posted images on the Internet, showing a soldier's severed head beside his body.)

Another issue concerning the appropriateness or inappropriateness of showing images occurred early in 2006. In September 2005 a Danish newspaper, accused of being afraid to show political cartoons that were hostile to Muslim terrorists, responded by publishing twelve cartoons. One cartoon, for instance, showed the Prophet Muhammad wearing a turban that looked like a bomb. The images at first did not arouse much attention, but when in January 2006 they were reprinted in Norway, they attracted worldwide attention and outraged Muslims, most of whom regard any depiction of the Prophet as blasphemous. The upshot is that some Muslims in various Islamic nations burned Danish embassies and engaged in other acts of violence. Most non-Muslims agreed that the images were in bad taste, and apparently in deference to Islamic sensibilities (but possibly also out of fear of reprisals) very few Western newspapers reprinted the cartoons when they covered the news events. Most newspapers (including the *New York Times*) were content merely to describe the images. These papers believed that readers had to be told the news but because the drawings were so offensive to some persons they should be described rather than reprinted. A controversy then arose: Do readers of a newspaper deserve to *see* the evidence for themselves, or can a newspaper adequately fulfill its function by offering only a verbal description?

Persons who argued that the images should be reproduced generally made these points:

- Newspapers should yield neither to the delicate sensibilities of some readers nor to threats of violence.

- Jews for the most part do not believe that God should be depicted (the prohibition against "graven images" is found in Exodus 20.3), but they raise no objections to such Christian images as Michelangelo's painting of God awakening Adam, depicted on the ceiling of the Sistine Chapel. Further, when Andres Serrano (a Christian) in 1989 exhibited a photograph of a small plastic crucifix submerged in urine, it outraged a wider public—several U.S. senators condemned it because the artist had received federal funds—but virtually all newspapers showed the image, and many even printed its title, *Piss Christ*. That is, the subject was judged to be newsworthy, and the fact that some viewers would regard the image as blasphemous was not considered highly relevant.

- We value freedom of speech, and newspapers should not be intimidated. When certain pictures are a matter of news, the pictures should be shown to readers.

On the other hand, opposing voices were heard:

- Newspapers should—must—recognize deep-seated religious beliefs. They should indeed report the news, but there is no reason to *show* images that some people regard as blasphemous. The images can be adequately *described* in words.

- The Jewish response to Christian images of God and even the tolerant Christian's response to Serrano's image of Christ immersed in urine are simply irrelevant to the issue of whether images of the Prophet Muhammad should be represented in a Western newspaper. Virtually all Muslims regard depictions of the Prophet as blasphemous, and that is what counts.

- Despite all the Western talk about freedom of the press, the press does *not* reproduce all images that become matters of news. For instance, news items about the sale of child pornography do not include images of the pornographic photos.

Exercises: Thinking about Images

1. Does the display of the cartoons constitute an argument? If so, what is the conclusion, and what are the premises? If not, then what sort of statement, if any, does publishing these cartoons constitute?

2. Hugh Hewitt, an evangelical Christian, offered a comparison to the cartoon of Muhammad with a bomblike turban. Suppose, he asked, an abortion clinic had been bombed by someone who said he was an Evangelical Christian. Would newspapers publish "a cartoon of Christ's crown of thorns transformed into sticks of TNT?" Do you think they would? If you were the editor of a paper, would you? Why, or why not?

3. One American newspaper, the *Boston Phoenix*, did not publish any of the cartoons "out of fear of retaliation from the international brotherhood of radical and bloodthirsty Islamists who seek to impose their will on those who do not believe as they do. . . . We could not in good conscience place the men and women who work at the *Phoenix* and its related companies in physical jeopardy." Evaluate this position.

READING ADVERTISEMENTS

Advertising is one of the most common forms of visual persuasion we encounter in everyday life. None of us is so unsophisticated these days as to believe everything we see in an ad, yet the influence of advertising in our culture is pervasive and subtle. Consider, for example, a much-reproduced poster sponsored by Gatorade and featuring Michael Jordan. Such an image costs an enormous amount to produce and disseminate, and nothing in it is left to chance. The photograph of Jordan is typical, his attitude simultaneously strained and graceful, his face exultant, as he performs the feat for which he is so well known and about which most of us could only dream. We are aware of a crowd watching him, but the people in this crowd appear tiny, blurred, and indistinct compared to the huge image in the foreground; the photograph, like the crowd, focuses solely on Jordan. He is a legend, an icon of American culture. He is dressed not in his Chicago Bulls uniform but in a USA jersey, connecting his act of gravity-defying athleticism with the entire nation and with our sense of patriotism. The red, white, and blue of the uniform strengthens this impression in the original color photograph of the advertisement.

What do we make of the verbal message boldly written along the left-hand margin of the poster, "Be like Mike"? We are certainly not foolish enough to believe that drinking Gatorade will enable us to perform like Michael Jordan on the basketball court. But who among us wouldn't like to "Be like Mike" in some small way, to enjoy even a glancing association with his athletic grace and power—to say nothing of his fame, wealth, and sex appeal? Though the makers of Gatorade surely know we will not all rush out to buy their drink to improve our game, they are banking on the expectation that the association of their name with Jordan, and our memory of their logo in association with Jordan's picture, will create a positive impression of their product. If Mike drinks Gatorade—well, why shouldn't I give it a try? The good feelings and impressions created by the ad will, the advertisers hope, travel with us the next time we consider buying a sports drink.

As we discuss the power of advertising, it is appropriate to say a few words about the corporate logos that appear everywhere these days—on billboards, in newspapers and magazines, on television, on Web sites, and on T-shirts. It is useful to think of a logo as a sort of advertisement in shorthand. It is a single, usually simple, image that carries with it a world of associations and impressions. (The makers of Gatorade would certainly hope that we will be reminded of Michael Jordan and his slam dunk when we see their product name superimposed over the orange lightning bolt.)

Let's look at two additional advertisements, each of which relies almost entirely on an image rather than on words. The first, an ad for a TV comedy that made its debut in 2009, boldly gives the title of the show and the name of the network, but the most interesting words are in tiny print:

Funny. On so many levels.

These words flatter the readers, thus making the readers highly susceptible to the implicit message, "Look at this program." Why do we say the words are flattering? For three reasons:

- The small size of the type implies that the reader is not someone whose attention can be caught only by headlines.
- The pun on "levels" (physical levels, and levels of humor) is a witty way of telling us that the show offers not only the low comedy of physical actions but also the high comedy of witty talk—talk that, for instance, may involve puns.

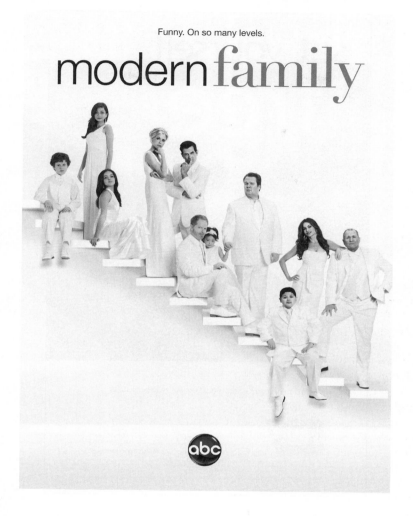

- The two terse incomplete sentences assume that the sophisticated reader does not need to have things explained at length.

The picture itself is attractive, showing what seems to be a wide variety of people (though of course we are not shown any faces or bodies that in real life might cause us some uneasiness) posed in the style of a family portrait. Indeed, these wholesome figures, standing in affectionate poses, are all dressed in white (without any ketchup stains) and are neatly framed (except for the patriarch, at the extreme right) by a pair of seated youngsters whose legs dangle down from the levels. The modern family, we are told, is large and varied (this one includes a gay son and his partner, and their adopted Vietnamese baby), smart and warm. And best of all, it is "Funny. On so many levels."

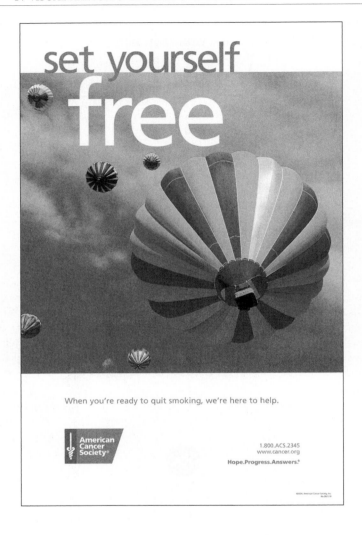

The second ad features two lines of text that are also short and sweet: "Set yourself free" and "When you're ready to quit smoking, we're here to help." The first of these lines—with "free" in large letters—is reinforced by the image of free-floating balloons, which in this context almost seem to be giant lungs. The implication is that once the viewer decides to quit smoking, the air will be purer, lungs will fully distend, and there will be a great sense of freedom; one will no longer be tied down in the way that an addiction to tobacco ties one down or restrains one's freedom. The second sentence, beneath the picture—on ground level, so to speak—assures the reader that when the addict is "ready to quit smoking, we're here to help." Who, after all, wouldn't want to be "set . . . free" (especially into the wonderful world of the floating balloons that soar in

✓ A CHECKLIST FOR ANALYZING IMAGES
(ESPECIALLY ADVERTISEMENTS)

☐ What is the overall effect of the design? Colorful and busy (suggesting activity)? Quiet and understated (for instance, chiefly white and grays, with lots of empty space)? Old-fashioned or cutting edge?

☐ What about the image immediately gets your attention? Size? Position on the page? Beauty of the image? Grotesqueness of the image? Humor?

☐ Who is the audience for the image? Affluent young men? Housewives? Retired persons?

☐ What is the argument?

☐ Does the text make a rational appeal (*logos*) ("Tests at a leading university prove that . . . ," "If you believe X, you should vote 'No' on this referendum")?

☐ Does the image appeal to the emotions, to dearly held values (*pathos*)? Examples: Images of starving children or maltreated animals appeal to our sense of pity; images of military valor may appeal to our patriotism; images of luxury may appeal to our envy; images of sexually attractive people may appeal to our desire to be like them; images of violence or of extraordinary ugliness (as, for instance, in some ads showing a human fetus being destroyed) may seek to shock us.

☐ Does the image make an ethical appeal — that is, does it appeal to our character as a good human being (*ethos*)? Ads by charitable organizations often appeal to our sense of decency, fairness, and pity, but ads that appeal to our sense of prudence (ads for insurance companies or for investment houses) also essentially are making an ethical appeal.

☐ What is the relation of print to image? Does the image do most of the work, or does it serve to attract us and to lead us on to read the text?

the tobacco-free air), and who wouldn't want the assurance that, if the experience is a bit risky, someone is there to help?

TOPICS FOR CRITICAL THINKING AND WRITING

1. Imagine that you work for a business that advertises in a publication such as *Time* or *Newsweek,* for instance, a vacation resort, a manufacturer of clothes, or an automaker. Design an advertisement: Describe the picture and write the text, and then, in an essay of 500 words, explain who

your target audience is (college students? young couples about to buy their first home? retired persons?) and explain why you use the sorts of appeals (for instance, to reason, to the emotions, to a sense of humor) that you do.

2. It is often said that colleges, like businesses, are selling a product. Examine a brochure or catalog that is sent to prospective applicants to a college, and analyze the kinds of appeals that some of the images make.

WRITING ABOUT A POLITICAL CARTOON

Most editorial pages print political cartoons as well as editorials. Like the writers of editorials, cartoonists seek to persuade, but they rarely use words to *argue* a point. True, they may use a few words in speech balloons or in captions, but generally the drawing does most of the work. Because their aim usually is to convince the viewer that some person's action or proposal is ridiculous, cartoonists almost always **caricature** their subjects:

- They exaggerate the subject's distinctive features to the point where
- The subject becomes grotesque and ridiculous—absurd, laughable, contemptible.

True, it is scarcely fair to suggest that because, say, the politician who proposes such-and-such is short, fat, and bald his proposal is ridiculous, but that is the way cartoonists work. Further, cartoonists are concerned with producing a striking image, not with exploring an issue, so they almost always oversimplify, implying that there really is no other sane view.

In the course of saying that (a) the figures in the cartoon are ridiculous and *therefore* their ideas are contemptible, and (b) there is only one side to the issue, cartoonists often use **symbolism**, for instance:

- symbolic figures (Uncle Sam),
- animals (the Democratic donkey and the Republican elephant),
- buildings (the White House stands symbolically for the president of the United States),
- things (a bag with a dollar sign on it usually symbolizes a bribe).

For anyone brought up in our culture, these symbols (like the human figures who are represented) are obvious, and cartoonists assume that viewers will instantly recognize the symbols and figures, will get the joke, and will see the absurdity of whatever it is that the cartoonist is seeking to demolish.

In writing about the argument presented in a cartoon, normally you will discuss the ways in which the cartoon makes its point. Caricature, we have said, usually implies, "This is ridiculous, as you can plainly see by the absurdity of the figures depicted" or "What *X*'s proposal adds up to, despite

---

✓ A CHECKLIST FOR EVALUATING AN ANALYSIS
   OF POLITICAL CARTOONS

☐ Is a lead-in provided?

☐ Is a brief but accurate description of the drawing provided?

☐ Is the source of the cartoon cited (and perhaps commented on)?

☐ Is a brief report of the event or issue that the cartoon is dealing with and an explanation of all of the symbols included?

☐ Is there a statement of the cartoonist's claim (point, thesis)?

☐ Is there an analysis of the evidence, if any, that the image offers in support of the claim?

☐ Is there an analysis of the ways in which the content and style of the drawing help to convey the message?

☐ Is there adequate evaluation of the effectiveness of the drawing?

☐ Is there adequate evaluation of the effectiveness of the text (caption or speech balloons) and of the fairness of the cartoon?

---

its apparent complexity, is nothing more than . . ." As we have already said, this sort of persuasion, chiefly by ridicule, probably is unfair: A funny-looking person *can offer* a thoughtful political proposal, and almost certainly the issue is more complicated than the cartoonist indicates. But this is largely the way cartoons work, by ridicule and by omitting counter-arguments, and we should not reject the possibility that the cartoonist has indeed put his or her finger on the absurdity of the issue.

Probably your essay will include an *evaluation* of the cartoon; indeed, the *thesis* underlying your analytic/argumentative essay may be (for instance) that the cartoon is effective (persuasive) for such-and-such reasons, but it is also unfair for such-and-such reasons.

In analyzing the cartoon—in grasping the attitude of the cartoonist—consider such things as

- the relative size of the figures in the image;
- the quality of the lines—thin and spidery, or thick and seemingly aggressive;
- the amount of empty space in comparison with the amount of heavily inked space (a drawing with lots of inky areas will convey a more oppressive sense than a drawing that is largely open);
- the degree to which text is important, and what the text says—is it witty? Heavy-handed?

Caution: If your instructor lets you choose a cartoon, be sure to choose one with sufficient complexity to make the exercise worthwhile. (See also Idea Prompt 4.1.)

IDEA PROMPT 4.1 ANALYSIS OF A POLITICAL CARTOON

Context	*Who is the artist? Where and when was it published?*	"This cartoon by Walt Handelsman was originally published in *Newsday* on September 12, 2009. Handelsman, a Pulitzer Prize–winning cartoonist, drew this cartoon in response to recent breaches of political decorum."
Description	*What does the cartoon look like?*	"It depicts a group of Washington, D.C., tourists being driven past what the guide calls 'The Museum of Modern American Political Discourse,' a building in the shape of a giant toilet."
Analysis	*How does the cartoon make its point? Is it effective?*	"The toilet as a symbol of the level of political discussion dominates the cartoon, effectively driving home the point that as Americans we are watching our leaders sink to new lows as they debate the future of our nation. Seen on a scale similar to familiar monuments in Washington, Handelsman may be in fact pointing out that today's politicians, rather than being remembered for great achievements like those of George Washington or Abraham Lincoln, will instead be remembered for their rudeness and aggression."

Let's look at an example. Jackson Smith wrote this essay in a composition course at Tufts University.

Jackson Smith

Pledging Nothing?

(Student Essay)

Gary Markstein's cartoon about the Pledge of Allegiance is one of dozens that can be retrieved by a search engine. It happens that every one of the cartoons that I retrieved mocked the courts for ruling that schools cannot require students to recite the Pledge of Allegiance in its present form, which includes the words "under God." I personally object to these words, so the cartoons certainly do not speak for me, but I'll try as impartially as possible to analyze the strength of Markstein's cartoon.

Markstein shows us, in the cartoon, four school children reciting the Pledge. Coming out of all four mouths is a speech balloon with the words, "One nation under nothing in particular." The children are facing a furled American flag, and to the right of the flag is a middle-aged female teacher, whose speech balloon is in the form of a cloud, indicating that she is *thinking* rather than saying the words, "God help us."

Certainly the image grabs us: Little kids lined up reciting the Pledge of Allegiance, an American flag, a maternal-looking teacher, and, in fact, if one examines the cartoon closely, one sees an apple on the teacher's desk. It's almost a Norman Rockwell scene, except, of course, it is a cartoon, so the figures are all a bit grotesque—but, still, they are nice folks. What is *not* nice, Markstein says, is what these kids must recite, "One nation under nothing in particular." In fact the cartoon is far from telling the truth. Children who recite the Pledge without the words "under God" will still be saying that they are pledging allegiance to something quite specific—the United States:

> I pledge allegiance to the flag of the United States of America, and to the Republic for which it stands: one nation indivisible, with Liberty and Justice for all.

That's really quite a lot, very far from Markstein's "under nothing in particular." But no one, I suppose, expects fairness in a political cartoon—and of course this cartoon *is* political, because the issue of the Pledge has become a political football, with liberals on the whole wanting the words "under God" removed and conservatives on the whole wanting the words retained.

Let's now look at some of the subtleties of the cartoon. First, although, as I have said, cartoons present grotesque caricatures, the figures here are all affectionately presented. None of these figures is menacing. The teacher, with her spectacles and her rather dumpy figure, is clearly a benevolent figure, someone who in the eyes of the cartoonist rightly is disturbed about the fate of these little kids who are not allowed to say the words "under God." (Nothing, of course, prevents the children from speaking about God when they are not in the classroom. Those who believe in God can say grace at mealtime, can go to Sunday School, can go to church regularly, can pray before they go to bed, etc.) Markstein suggests that the absence of these words makes the entire Pledge meaningless ("under nothing in particular"), and in a master stroke he has conveyed this idea of impoverishment by showing a tightly furled flag, a flag that is presented as minimally as possible. After all, the flag could have been shown more fully, perhaps hanging from a pole that extended from a wall into the classroom, or the flag could have been displayed extended against a wall. Instead we get the narrowest of flags, something that is not much more than a furled umbrella, identifiable as the American flag by its stripes and a few stars in the upper third. Markstein thus cleverly suggests that with the loss of the words "under God," the flag itself is reduced to almost nothing.

Fair? No. Effective? Yes, and that's the job of a cartoonist. Readers 5 probably give cartoons no more than three or four seconds, and Markstein has made the most of those few seconds. The reader gets his point, and if the reader already holds this view, he or she probably says, "Hey, here's a great cartoon." I don't hold that view, but I am willing to grant that it is a pretty good cartoon, effectively making a point that I think is wrong-headed.

VISUALS AS AIDS TO CLARITY: MAPS, GRAPHS, TABLES, AND PIE CHARTS

Maps were obviously part of the argument in the debate over drilling in the Arctic National Wildlife Refuge.

- Advocates of drilling argued that drilling would take place only in a tiny area. Their map showed Alaska, with an indication (in gray) of the much smaller part of Alaska that was the Refuge, and a further indication (cross-hatched) of what these advocates of drilling emphasized was a minuscule part of the Refuge.

- Opponents, however, showed maps indicating the path of migrating caribou and the roads that would have to be constructed across the refuge to get to the area where the drilling would take place.

Graphs, tables, and pie charts usually present quantitative data in visual form, helping writers clarify mind-numbing statistical assertions. For instance, a line graph may tell us how many immigrants came to the United States in each decade of the last century.

A bar graph (the bars can run either horizontally or vertically) offers similar information; we can see at a glance that, say, the second bar is almost double the length of the first, indicating that the number is almost double.

A pie chart is a circle divided into wedges so that we can see—literally—how a whole is divided into its parts. We can see, for instance, that of the entire pie—which may represent registered voters in a certain state—one-fourth are registered Democrats, one-fifth are registered Republicans, and the remainder do not give a party affiliation.

✓ ## A CHECKLIST FOR CHARTS AND GRAPHS

☐ Is the source authoritative?

☐ Is the source cited?

☐ Will the chart or graph be intelligible to the imagined audience?

☐ Is the caption, if any, clear and helpful?

A NOTE ON USING VISUALS IN YOUR OWN PAPER

Every paper uses some degree of visual persuasion, merely in its appearance: perhaps a title page, certainly margins (ample—but not so wide that they tell the reader that the writer is unable to write a paper of the assigned length), double-spacing for the convenience of the reader, paragraphing

COMING TO AMERICA . . .

Both the percentage and number of foreign-born people in the United States dropped during much of the twentieth century, but after 1970, the tide was turning again.

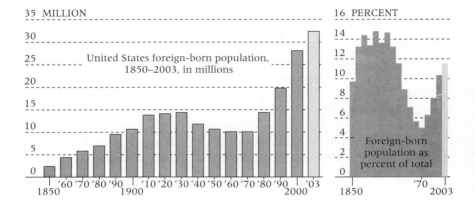

. . . FROM NEAR AND FAR

Central America, Mexico, and Asia contribute most to the foreign-born population.

Foreign-born population by
region of birth, 2002

*Most recent estimate
Source: United States Census Bureau

(again for the convenience of the reader), and so on. But you may also want to use images—for example, pictures, graphs, or pie charts. Keep a few guidelines in mind as you begin to work with images, "writing" visuals into your own argument with at least as much care as you would read them in others':

- Consider the needs and attitudes of your audience, and select the type of visuals—graphs, drawings, photographs—likely to be most persuasive to that audience.

(DILBERT © Scott Adams. Distributed by permission of United Features Syndicate, Inc.)

- Consider the effect of color, composition, and placement within your document. Because images are most effective when they appear near the text that supplements them, do not group all of your images at the end of the paper.

Remember especially that images are almost never self-supporting or self-explanatory. They may be evidence for your argument (Ut's photograph of napalm victims is *very* compelling evidence of suffering), but they are not arguments themselves.

- Be sure to explain each image that you use, integrating it into the verbal text that provides the logic and principal support of your thesis.

- Be sure to cite the source of any image, for instance, a graph or a pie chart, that you paste into your argument.

A NOTE ON FORMATTING YOUR PAPER: DOCUMENT DESIGN

Even if you do not use pictures or graphs or charts, the format you use—the margins, the font, the headings and subheadings, if any, will still give your paper a visual aspect. NoonewantstoreadapaperthatlookslikethisOR LIKETHIS*ORLIKETHIS*ANDCERTAINLYNOT**LIKETHIS**ORLIKETHIS. For academic papers, margins (one inch on each side), spacing (double-spaced), and font and size (Times New Roman, 12 point) are pretty well standardized, and it is usually agreed that the text should be justified at the left rather than centered (to avoid rivers of white down the page), but you are still in charge of some things, notably headings and bulleted or numbered lists—as well as, of course, the lengths of your paragraphs.

Headings in a long paper (more than five pages) are functional, helping to guide the reader from unit to unit, but the extra white space—a decorative element—is also functional, giving the reader's eye a moment of rest. Longish academic papers often use one, two, or even three levels of headings, normally distinguished by type size, position, and highlighting

("highlighting" includes the use of CAPITALS, **boldface**, and *italic*). Here are examples of three levels:

FIRST-LEVEL HEADING

Second-Level Heading

Third-Level Heading

If you use headings, you must be consistent in the form. For instance, if you use a noun phrase such as "the present system" printed in CAPITAL LETTERS for the first of your first-level headings, you must use noun phrases and caps for the rest of your first-level headings, thus:

THE PRESENT SYSTEM
THE NEED TO CHANGE

But you need not use noun phases and you need not use capitals. You may use, for instance, *-ing* headings (gerund phrases), and you may decide to capitalize only the first letter of each word other than prepositions and articles, thus:

Thinking about Immigration

Reviewing the Past

Thinking about the Future

Reconsidering Legislation

And here are headings that use a single word:

Problems

Answers

Strengths

Weaknesses

Finally, headings that consist of questions can be effective:

What Are We Now Doing?

Why Should We Change?

Caution: Although headings can be useful in a paper of moderate or considerable length, they almost never are useful in a paper of five or fewer pages.

ADDITIONAL IMAGES FOR ANALYSIS

In 1936, photographer Dorothea Lange (1895–1965) took a series of pictures, including the two below, of a migrant mother and her children. Widely reprinted in the nation's newspapers, these photographs helped to dramatize for the American public the poverty of displaced workers during the Great Depression.

TOPICS FOR CRITICAL THINKING AND WRITING

1. Lange drew increasingly near to her subject as she took a series of pictures. Make a list of details gained and lost by framing the mother and children more closely. The final shot in the series (above) became the most famous and most widely reprinted. Do you find it more effective than the other? Why, or why not?

2. Note the expression on the mother's face, the position of her body, and the way she interacts with her children. What sorts of relationships are implied? Why is it significant that she does not look at her children or at the camera? How is the effect of the photographs altered based on how much we can see of the children's faces?

3. As we mentioned earlier in this chapter, these photographs constitute a sort of persuasive "speech." Of what, exactly, might the photographer be trying to persuade her viewers? Try to state the purpose of Lange's photographs by completing this sentence, "Lange would like the viewers of her photographs to . . ." Write a brief essay (250 words) making the same case. Compare your written argument to Lange's visual one. Which form of persuasion do you find more effective? Why?

4. Whom do you think Lange had in mind as her original audience? What assumptions does she make about that audience? What sorts of evidence does she use to reach them?

During World War II, the U.S. government produced a series of posters bearing the legend "This is the enemy." These posters depicted racially stereotyped images of both German and Japanese soldiers, generally engaged in acts of savage violence.

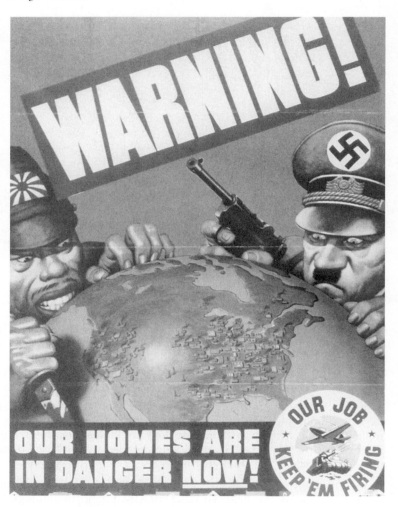

TOPICS FOR CRITICAL THINKING AND WRITING

1. It has been claimed that one role of propaganda is to dehumanize the enemy so that (a) soldiers will feel less remorse about killing opposing soldiers and (b) civilians will continue to support the war effort. What specific features of this poster contribute to this propaganda function?

2. Some would claim that such a racially provocative image of a Japanese soldier should never have been used because of the potential harm to all Asians, including patriotic Asian Americans. (Consisting solely of Japanese American volunteers, the 442nd Regimental Combat Team was by war's end the most decorated unit in U.S. military history for its size and length of service.) Others believe that the ordinary rules do not apply in times of national crisis and that, as the old saying has it, "All's fair in love and war." In an essay of 500 words, argue for one or the other of these propositions. Refer to this poster as one piece of your evidence.

From ancient times until the eighteenth century, when newspapers began to be read widely, public posting was about the only way to reach a large audience. The invention of movable type in the fifteenth century made the dissemination of posted bills and handbills inexpensive, and such bills (along with newspaper

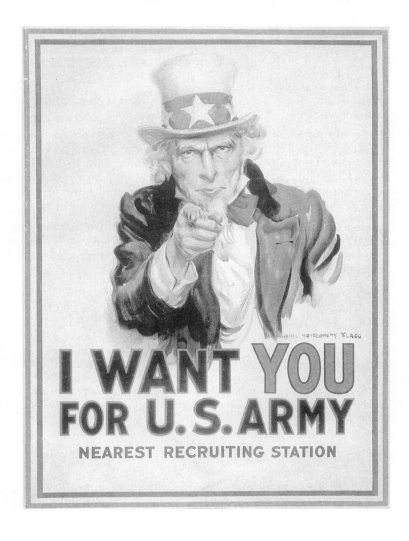

advertisements) were the most common forms of advertising until well into the twentieth century. (Commercial radio broadcasting began only in 1920, and television was not an important medium before 1945.) I Want You *is by James Montgomery Flagg.*

Topics for Critical Thinking and Writing

1. Imagine that this figure of Uncle Sam was in profile, pointing either to the right or left. Would the effect be the same? Why? Imagine the figure as a three-quarter view. Again, would the effect be different? Why? Which of the three versions do you think would be the most effective? Explain your reasons.

2. Approximately what is the date of this poster? What makes you give it this date?

Additional Topics for Critical Thinking and Writing

Gather some of the graphic materials used to promote and reflect your college or university—including a screen shot of its Web site, the college catalog, and the brochures and other materials sent to prospective students.

1. What is the dominant image that your college or university administration seems to be putting forth? Are there different, maybe even competing, images of your school at work? How accurate a story do these materials tell about your campus? Write an essay (250 words) in which you explain to prospective students the ways in which the promotional materials capture, or fail to capture, the true spirit of your campus.

2. Compare the Web site of your institution to one or two from very different institutions—perhaps a community college, a large state university, or an elite private college. How do you account for the similarities and differences among the sites?

Nora Ephron

Nora Ephron, (1941–2012) attended Wellesley College. She worked as a reporter for the New York Post *and as a columnist and senior editor for* Esquire. *Ephron wrote screenplays and directed films, including* Sleepless in Seattle *(1993), and continued to write essays on a wide variety of topics. "The Boston Photographs" is from her collection* Scribble, Scribble: Notes on the Media *(1978).*

The Boston Photographs

"I made all kinds of pictures because I thought it would be a good rescue shot over the ladder . . . never dreamed it would be anything

else. . . . I kept having to move around because of the light set. The sky was bright and they were in deep shadow. I was making pictures with a motor drive and he, the fire fighter, was reaching up and, I don't know, everything started falling. I followed the girl down taking pictures. . . . I made three or four frames. I realized what was going on and I completely turned around, because I didn't want to see her hit."

You probably saw the photographs. In most newspapers, there were three of them. The first showed some people on a fire escape—a fireman, a woman, and a child. The fireman had a nice strong jaw and looked very brave. The woman was holding the child. Smoke was pouring from the building behind them. A rescue ladder was approaching, just a few feet away, and the fireman had one arm around the woman and one arm reaching out toward the ladder. The second picture showed the fire escape slipping off the building. The child had fallen on the escape and seemed about to slide off the edge. The woman was grasping desperately at the legs of the fireman, who had managed to grab the ladder. The third picture showed the woman and child in midair, falling to the ground. Their arms and legs were outstretched, horribly distended. A potted plant was falling too. The caption said that the woman, Diana Bryant, nineteen, died in the fall. The child landed on the woman's body and lived.

The pictures were taken by Stanley Forman, thirty, of the *Boston Herald American*. He used a motor-driven Nikon F set at 1/250, f5.6-S. Because of the motor, the camera can click off three frames a second. More than four hundred newspapers in the United States alone carried the photographs: The tear sheets from overseas are still coming in. The

New York Times ran them on the first page of its second section; a paper in south Georgia gave them nineteen columns; the *Chicago Tribune,* the *Washington Post,* and the *Washington Star* filled almost half their front pages, the *Star* under a somewhat redundant headline that read: SENSATIONAL PHOTOS OF RESCUE ATTEMPT THAT FAILED.

The photographs are indeed sensational. They are pictures of death in action, of that split second when luck runs out, and it is impossible to look at them without feeling their extraordinary impact and remembering, in an almost subconscious way, the morbid fantasy of falling, falling off a building, falling to one's death. Beyond that, the pictures are classics, old-fashioned but perfect examples of photojournalism at its most spectacular. They're throwbacks, really, fire pictures, 1930s tabloid shots; at the same time they're technically superb and thoroughly modern — the sequence could not have been taken at all until the development of the motor-driven camera some sixteen years ago.

Most newspaper editors anticipate some reader reaction to photographs like Forman's; even so, the response around the country was 5 enormous, and almost all of it was negative. I have read hundreds of the letters that were printed in letters-to-the-editor sections, and they repeat the same points. "Invading the privacy of death." "Cheap sensationalism." "I thought I was reading the *National Enquirer.*" "Assigning the agony of a human being in terror of imminent death to the status of a side-show act." "A tawdry way to sell newspapers." The *Seattle Times* received sixty letters and calls; its managing editor even got a couple of them at home. A reader wrote the *Philadelphia Inquirer: "Jaws* and *Towering Inferno* are playing downtown; don't take business away from people who pay good money to advertise in your own paper." Another reader wrote the *Chicago Sun-Times:* "I shall try to hide my disappointment that Miss Bryant wasn't wearing a skirt when she fell to her death. You could have had some award-winning photographs of her underpants as her skirt billowed over her head, you voyeurs." Several newspaper editors wrote columns defending the pictures: Thomas Keevil of the *Costa Mesa* (California) *Daily Pilot* printed a ballot for readers to vote on whether they would have printed the pictures; Marshall L. Stone of Maine's *Bangor Daily News,* which refused to print the famous assassination picture of the Vietcong prisoner in Saigon, claimed that the Boston pictures showed the dangers of fire escapes and raised questions about slumlords. (The burning building was a five-story brick apartment house on Marlborough Street in the Back Bay section of Boston.)

For the last five years, the *Washington Post* has employed various journalists as ombudsmen, whose job is to monitor the paper on behalf of the public. The *Post*'s current ombudsman is Charles Seib, former managing editor of the *Washington Star;* the day the Boston photographs appeared, the paper received over seventy calls in protest. As Seib later wrote in a column about the pictures, it was "the largest reaction to a published item that I have experienced in eight months as the *Post's* ombudsman. . . .

"In the *Post's* newsroom, on the other hand, I found no doubts, no second thoughts . . . the question was not whether they should be printed but how they should be displayed. When I talked to editors . . . they used words like 'interesting' and 'riveting' and 'gripping' to describe them. The pictures told of something about life in the ghetto, they said (although the neighborhood where the tragedy occurred is not a ghetto, I am told). They dramatized the need to check on the safety of fire escapes. They dramatically conveyed something that had happened, and that is the business we're in. They were news. . . .

"Was publication of that [third] picture a bow to the same taste for the morbidly sensational that makes gold mines of disaster movies? Most papers will not print the picture of a dead body except in the most unusual circumstances. Does the fact that the final picture was taken a millisecond before the young woman died make a difference? Most papers will not print a picture of a bare female breast. Is that a more inappropriate subject for display than the picture of a human being's last agonized instant of life?" Seib offered no answers to the questions he raised, but he went on to say that although as an editor he would probably have run the pictures, as a reader he was revolted by them.

In conclusion, Seib wrote: "Any editor who decided to print those pictures without giving at least a moment's thought to what purpose they served and what their effect was likely to be on the reader should ask another question: Have I become so preoccupied with manufacturing a product according to professional traditions and standards that I have forgotten about the consumer, the reader?"

It should be clear that the phone calls and letters and Seib's own reaction were occasioned by one factor alone: the death of the woman. Obviously, had she survived the fall, no one would have protested; the pictures would have had a completely different impact. Equally obviously, had the child died as well — or instead — Seib would undoubtedly have received ten times the phone calls he did. In each case, the pictures would have been exactly the same — only the captions, and thus the responses, would have been different.

But the questions Seib raises are worth discussing — though not exactly for the reasons he mentions. For it may be that the real lesson of the Boston photographs is not the danger that editors will be forgetful of reader reaction, but that they will continue to censor pictures of death precisely because of that reaction. The protests Seib fielded were really a variation on an old theme — and we saw plenty of it during the Nixon-Agnew years — the "Why doesn't the press print the good news?" argument. In this case, of course, the objections were all dressed up and cleverly disguised as righteous indignation about the privacy of death. This is a form of puritanism that is often justifiable; just as often it is merely puritanical.

Resources for Teaching

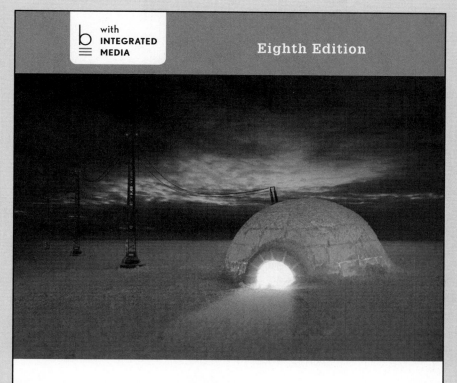

with
INTEGRATED
MEDIA

Eighth Edition

Critical Thinking, Reading, and Writing

A Brief Guide to Argument

Sylvan Barnet
Hugo Bedau

Critical Thinking, Reading, and Writing

A Brief Guide to Argument

Resources for Teaching

Critical Thinking, Reading, and Writing

A Brief Guide to Argument

Eighth Edition

SYLVAN BARNET
Professor of English, Tufts University

HUGO BEDAU
Professor of Philosophy, Tufts University

Bedford/St. Martin's   Boston • New York

Manufactured in the United States of America.

8 7   6 5 4 3
f e   d c b a

For information, write: Bedford/St. Martin's, 75 Arlington Street, Boston, MA 02116
(617-399-4000)

ISBN 978-1-4576-6154-9

Preface

These notes, like the book they accompany, are the work of two people—one a teacher of literature and composition, the other a teacher of philosophy. No single set of notes can fully satisfy all instructors or even be of much use to all instructors, but we hope that our alliance enables us to produce material that has something of interest for almost everyone.

THE SCOPE OF THESE NOTES

If the two of us succeed in being of some use, it is partly because we have different approaches and partly because we do not methodically treat every anthologized essay the same way. We treat all of the essays and literary works, but we treat some briefly, some extensively, some chiefly from a rhetorician's point of view, and some chiefly from a philosopher's point of view. We consistently keep in mind, however, the fact that because teachers of composition courses devote many hours to reading students' papers, they have correspondingly fewer hours to devote to working up the background for unfamiliar essays. We therefore provide fairly extensive background on some topics, notably animal rights and immigration, so that an instructor who happens to be relatively unfamiliar with a topic nevertheless can teach with ease the essays we reprint.

Beyond providing background on specialized topics, in these notes we simply touch on various matters we discuss in our classes. We realize that something is artificial here: What you do in class depends heavily on your students and also on the stage in the course at which you are discussing an essay. Further, what you do in class depends even more heavily on your ideas of what teaching is. Still, we hope you will scan these comments and find at least some of them useful; if the comments seem utterly wrongheaded, they may nevertheless be useful in providing material to react against.

THE SYLLABUS

All instructors have their own ideas about how to use the text in a composition course. Which essays are assigned, and in what sequence and at what pace, depends partly on whether you require a short research paper, several short research papers, or a long research paper. Still, our suggestion (for what it is worth) is to teach the first six chapters (Parts One and Two) in sequence.

Part One: In Chapter 1 we would glance fairly briefly at Jena McGregor's essay and would spend more time on Harlan Coben's "The Undercover Parent." We say we would spend more time on Coben's essay not because it is better written or is more interesting or more important, but simply because Coben's essay is followed by letters of response, and we would ask students to write their own letters, imagining as an audience the readers of Coben's essay. Coben's topic is one that allows students to offer opinions based on experience.

In Chapter 2 we would deal briefly with Susan Jacoby's essay (it is examined at some length in the text) and would spend considerably more time on the three essays that constitute the casebook on free speech. We certainly would discuss, in Chapter 2, the student's essay on the Pledge of Allegiance, and again, we would ask students to evaluate it and to explain why they would give it the grades they do. Such discussion, obviously, will help you to understand what students' ideas are concerning good and bad writing. In Chapter 3, we probably would teach two or three of the eight essays. Notice that Chapter 3 includes an essay on student indebtedness (Webley's) and two essays on Facebook.

To cover Part One (Chapters 1–4) will take about four meetings if, at the beginning of the course, you give only brief writing assignments, or five or six meetings if you require substantial writing to accompany the reading assignments. In our discussions of these chapters in this manual, we offer a few suggestions about essays printed later in the book that go well with the early chapters, but we don't think it is necessary to supplement these first three chapters.

If in teaching Chapter 3 — on syllogisms, evidence, and so on — you wish to inform students about the Toulmin model, you will want to supplement Chapter 3 with Chapter 8, which is devoted to that topic. Also relevant to Chapter 3 is Chapter 9, A Logician's View: Deduction, Induction, Fallacies, a fuller and somewhat more difficult discussion of topics set forth in Chapter 3. Our suggestion is this: If you have strong students and you wish to emphasize the role of logic in persuasive writing, assign Chapter 9. Otherwise, skip Chapter 9.

We also would spend part of a class hour discussing the images in Chapter 4, in particular Dorothea Lange's migrant mother and the anonymous poster entitled "Our Homes Are in Danger Now!" partly because students enjoy discussing them and partly because later in the term, we may ask our students to analyze images in the casebooks.

Part Two: Although Part One includes a discussion of writing (especially concerning annotating and summarizing), our chief discussion of writing is in Part Two (Chapters 5–7): writing an analysis of an argument, writing an argument, and using sources to write a research paper. Each chapter in Part Two can be covered in a meeting, but you probably will want to give two meetings to Chapter 5, Writing an Analysis of an Argument — one to discuss Nicholas Kristof's editorial and the student's analysis of it, and another to discuss the arguments in at least one of the other essays included in the chapter. In connection with these chapters on writing an argument — especially in connection with Chapter 6, where we talk about the audience as a collaborator — you may also want to assign Chapter 10 in Part Three, A Psychologist's View: Rogerian Argument.

Part Three, Further Views on Argument, contains three chapters already mentioned, A Philosopher's View: The Toulmin Model (8), A Logician's View: Deduction, Induction, Fallacies (9), A Psychologist's View: Rogerian Argument (10); it also contains three additional chapters, A Rhetorician's View (11), A Literary Critic's View (12), and A Debater's View (13).

Part Four offers a casebook on the state and the individual: What Is the Ideal Society? This chapter includes some literary material as well as classic arguments from Martin Luther King, Jr., Elizabeth Cady Stanton, and Plato, among others.

EXERCISES

All of the essays and literary selections in the text are followed by exercises, but in these notes, we include some additional topics for discussion and writing.

Contents

Critical Thinking, Reading, and Writing

A Brief Guide to Argument

Part One

CRITICAL THINKING AND READING

1
Critical Thinking (p. 3)

Although the ideas in this introductory chapter are pretty straightforward, many of them will be new to some students, and we have therefore tried to illustrate them with a fairly extended discussion of just one example—the West Virginia law of 1989 that restricts a driver's license to those over eighteen, unless they are still in school, in which case they are eligible for a license at sixteen.

It's extremely instructive to see that sometimes a great deal can be extracted from very little—in this instance, from one statute on a perfectly ordinary matter. We've tried to present in the manageable scope of this humdrum example many of the considerations discussed in greater detail elsewhere in the book. This example gives the student a real taste of what critical thinking, reading, and writing involve, as well as of what lies ahead in the rest of the book.

Bruce Eric Kaplan

He Saves All His Critical Thinking for My Behavior (p. 4)

We reproduce this cartoon because we think it is amusing, and of course what makes it amusing is largely the fact that it sets forth a concept of "critical thinking" that is exactly the opposite of the kind of critical thinking we recommend in the text. The text emphasizes the importance of questioning *one's own* assumptions, but the man in the cartoon clearly does *not* question his assumptions; rather, according to the caption, he questions the behavior (and presumably the assumptions beneath the behavior) of his wife. His stance and his facial expression—especially his down-turned mouth—clearly indicate his self-confidence and his disapproval of the world around him.

The Florida Case (p. 4)

First of all, it may be helpful to remind students that the First Amendment to the U.S. Constitution says, "Congress shall make no law respecting an establishment of religion, or prohibiting the free exercise thereof."

Now for the veil case in Florida. We confess that we don't understand the judge's decision. In our view, it is unreasonable to require a photograph on the license on the grounds that the state has a compelling need for persons to carry an ID. Neither the state nor the federal government requires an ID of all citizens and aliens resident in the United States, and indeed tens of thousands of people in Florida do not carry a photo ID. These people include not only those who do not drive but also those who do legally drive on the basis of a driver's license issued by one of the fourteen states that does not require a photograph on the license.

As our second question (in Topics for Critical Thinking and Writing) implies, we are also uneasy about the logic of saying that although this plantiff is *un*likely to cause harm, she must remove the veil because *other* veiled persons might cause harm.

1

In our draft of the text manuscript, we had a third question along these lines: "Some strict Islamic countries prohibit women from driving. Can it therefore be argued that if Ms. Freeman is a sincere Muslim, she should not seek a driver's license?" We dropped this question because it seemed to us that the rules of certain Islamic countries are not necessarily relevant to the beliefs and actions of a Muslim in this country, but conceivably the question might be raised in class.

According to newspaper reports, American Muslims were divided about the case, and indeed it took the Council on American-Islamic Relations several months before it reached a consensus supporting Freeman, agreement that the state was violating her religious freedom. Among the opinions offered by Muslims were these:

- Islamic law does not oblige women to cover their faces in all circumstances.

- She could have her photo taken by a woman, and if stopped by a male police officer, she could explain the issue and request that he call a female police officer, to whom she would then show the license.

- She could unveil for the picture because she tried her best to follow God's will.

- She could unveil for the picture because Muslims need to support the U.S. national security efforts.

- She is drawing bad publicity for Muslims, and this episode is getting in the way of more important civil liberties where Muslim rights are being attacked.

- She is right to refuse; the court is infringing on religious liberty.

A very different but, in a way, faintly related matter: While we were working on this material, we happened, by sheer chance, to be reading a collection of essays, *The Visual Culture of American Religions* (2001), edited by David Morgan and Sally M. Promey. This book contains an essay by Promey in which she mentions (p. 40) that in 1997, a coalition of Muslim groups wrote a letter to the justices of the U.S. Supreme Court asking them to remove from Adolph Weinman's frieze in the North Courtroom (1931–1932) the face on an image of Muhammad. The image appears with those of other lawgivers, such as Moses, Confucius, and Napoleon. The relevant part of the relief is reproduced on page 41 of Promey's essay.

Islamic art, within a religious context, rarely represents living forms—such representation is thought to be a sacrilegious imitation of the work of Allah—and even more rarely does it represent holy figures. On the rare occasions when Muhammad is shown, his face is veiled, and sometimes his body is represented by a halo of light. One can easily grasp, then, the distress experienced by most Muslims who may see the relatively realistic image in the frieze. Nihad Awad, for instance, director of the Council on American-Islamic Relations, had told the Court that he viewed the image as "sacrilege." At the risk of seeming facetious or blasphemous or both—we are neither; we are in earnest—we might compare the response of a Muslim to the unveiled Muhammad with the response of a devout Christian who might somehow encounter a frontal representation of a nude adult Jesus. The Court replied with a letter from Chief Justice Rehnquist, dated March 11, 1997, saying that the image of Muhammad would not be changed because "it was intended only to recognize him, among many other lawgivers, as an important figure on the history of law . . . [and not] as a form of idol worship." The Court did, however, order a change in the brochure distributed to visitors to the Court. Promey quotes part of the description, but by means of Google we summoned up the whole brochure. (Just type "courtroom friezes north and south walls," and you will get it.) The revised description of Muhammad runs thus:

Muhammad (c. 570–632) The Prophet of Islam. He is depicted holding the Qur'an. The Qur'an provides the primary source of Islamic Law. Prophet Muhammad's teachings explain and implement Qur'anic principles. The figure above is a well-intentioned attempt by the sculptor, Adolph Weinman, to honor Muhammad and it bears no resemblance to Muhammad. Muslims generally have a strong aversion to sculptured or pictured representations of their Prophet.

2

Again, the issue of veiled women is different from the issue of representing the Prophet, but conceivably it may come up in class. You may want to ask your students to write letters representing their views of what the Court's letter should have said.

Speaking of courts and religion, for a comment on question 3 in the text concerning a monument of the Ten Commandments in a courtroom, see p. 6 in this manual.

Drivers' Licenses and Dropouts (p. 9)

An update on the issue of preventing dropouts from holding drivers' licenses before they are eighteen: We have been told that several states have found that confiscating the licenses of dropouts does *not* keep youngsters in school, and taking away the licenses of failing or disruptive youngsters does not spur them to better work or to better behavior. In fact, some teachers say it is counterproductive because it turns the teacher (in the view of these students) into even more of an enemy than is usual.

Steve Jeffries

Play Ball! (student essay) (p. 12)

We briefly discuss this essay in the text, so we need not spend much time here, though we want to add a few points.

First, although our own view about the issue of homeschoolers participating in public school extracurricular activities differs from Jeffries's view, we think this is a very good essay—thoughtful, clear, effectively written. We do, however, have a mixed response to the title. When we first saw the essay, we liked the title—and we continue to think it has merit—but on reflection, we wonder if "Play Ball!" (a term associated with baseball) goes well with an opening paragraph that is devoted to a football player. Does it set up the expectation that we will hear something about baseball and thus disappoint the reader?

To our brief discussion of the opening paragraph, we would add that in our view, the sentences are shapely and interestingly balanced. Notice, for instance, that the longish penultimate sentence (twenty-eight words) in this paragraph is effectively followed by a short decisive sentence (six words).

The second paragraph is devoted to setting forth the opposing views. We cannot think of any significant objection that it ignores, and, given the imposed limitations of space, we believe it does a good job of stating the objections.

Our chief objection to the essay, perhaps oddly, is that Jeffries pretty much limits his discussion to extracurricular sports. We think he might have strengthened it—been more appealing to academic folks like us—if he talked about letting homeschoolers participate in those kinds of activities, *including academic subjects*, that public schools offer but home-schooling usually cannot. For instance, if his argument had said that, yes, homeschool-ers in effect opt out of certain things because their families believe they can cover those things better than the public school can. But there are of course certain kinds of things that homeschooling cannot do as well. For instance, chemistry probably cannot be taught effectively at home, and, similarly, Chinese probably cannot be learned at home unless a parent reads and speaks Chinese or is willing to hire a tutor. That is, we think the essay might have been stronger—might have been more appealing to *us*—if the argument covered academic work as well as extracurricular activities. The overall angle would be that it is in the interest of *society* to let homeschoolers participate in public school activities when homeschooling cannot offer the appropriate facilities. We probably would be more likely to go along with the idea of letting homeschoolers play on the baseball team if we thought they might also take the public school chemistry or Chinese course.

Harlan Coben

The Undercover Parent (p. 21)

In the text itself, we offer our own paragraph-by-paragraph discussion of the rhetoric of Coben's essay, and rhetoric—the art of using language persuasively—is what we think should be the primary subject of the discussion in a composition course rather than the issue that Coben addresses. But yes, we also recognize that the rhetoric is *about* something that is used in the service of arguing a particular cause. The cause Coben advocates is probably unpopular with adults, as his first paragraph indicates. We have never taught this essay: It will be interesting to hear how students respond. Our guess is that many students will think that Coben is making a good point.

You or your students may find that our analysis in the text is defective in one way or another. If so, the class can have a good time pointing out its inadequacies and can thereby learn that not everything they read in print is true. But if you think our analysis is a satisfactory interpretation of the ways in which Coben makes his point, you may want to turn directly to the topics that we offer, or to issues that students raise in class. (Our own favorite pedagogical practice when we teach an op-ed piece is is to ask students to write a response.)

Jena McGregor

Military Women in Combat: Why Making It Official Matters (p. 28)

We address, in sequence, the topics that we set forth in the book.

1. McGregor's tone: We think readers will agree that McGregor appears to be unpretentious, reasonable, fair-minded, a person of goodwill, not a one-sided bullying advocate. Indeed, at least at the beginning, one almost thinks one is reading a news report, a narrative ("Last week, female soldiers began formally moving into jobs in previously all-male battalions") rather than an argument. But of course the piece *is* an argument, and this is indicated at the very outset, in the subtitle: "Why Making It Official Matters."

   The tone throughout is thoughtful and courteous (e.g., "Another way to break down the ceiling would be," "But . . . it's easy to see," "Both changes may be difficult"), and we believe that even readers who ultimately are unconvinced will nevertheless agree that McGregor is, as we have just said, reasonable and fair-minded.

2. The term *brass ceiling* by means of a rhyme, of course, plays on the term *glass ceiling*, the transparent barrier that lets women (in the business world) see the higher echelons but keeps women from reaching them. The barrier in the military is here called *brass* because the insignia of commissioned officers (the admiral's gold stripes, the general's stars) are colloquially called *brass*, as in "the top brass will never approve of this."

3. McGregor does *not* mention one argument that is sometimes offered against putting women into direct combat: A captured female soldier might be raped. You may want to invite your students to discuss the strengths and weaknesses of this argument. When we raised the issue, the general response was that the argument had no weight at all: (a) Captured men, too, can be raped, and (b) captured men and women can be tortured and killed. So given the circumstances, the issue of possible rape is hardly decisive. Still, even if your students raise these responses, we think it is worth discussing whether McGregor should have introduced the argument and then briefly rebutted it.

4. The argument concerning body strength is almost always present in discussions of the issue of women in combat. In comparing such matters as upper-body strength

4

or bone density of men and of women, one of course is speaking in generalities, not about particular individuals. But the gist is (as we say in our fourth topic in the text), some people argue that in some circumstances, women—again, we are speaking in general—are less competent than men are. Usually, in discussions about women in combat, upper-body strength is cited, and the standard examples concern pulling a wounded comrade out of a tank or off a battlefield. The idea is females are OK as, say, tank mechanics behind the lines, but not as members of a tank crew. We assume everyone would agree about the difference in upper-body strength, but we have also encountered the statement that when males enter competition, their testosterone level rises, increasing their hemoglobin and hence (this is getting complicated) their blood's capacity to carry oxygen, thus heightening the brain's sense of confidence and appetite for risk (the so-called *winner effect*). In short, heightened testosterone supposedly heightens courage. We have no idea if any of this business about testosterone = courage = a better fighter on the battlefield is true.

In any case, putting aside the issue of whether women should be allowed on the frontlines, we see the force of McGregor's argument that battlefield experience should not be a requirement for top command. Surely the requirement is a vestige of antiquated macho thoughts about what war is.

5. Presumably, the change in policy—women are now allowed to be in combat—makes women eligible for the top posts; so presumably, (a) the possibility of a military career is more attractive to the best and brightest women, and (b) as McGregor points out, there may indeed be more diversity of thought at the top (the assumption here is that diversity of thought is a good thing because it may lead to wiser decisions).

6. As for whether—if there is a national draft—women should be drafted, well, discuss.

EXERCISE 3 *(p. 32)*

As we mention earlier in this manual in connection with the case of the Muslim woman vs. Florida, a frieze in the Supreme Court depicts Muhammad, along with Moses and other lawgivers, so there is some sort of precedent for introducing religion into the courthouse.

In the wee hours of the morning on July 31, 2001, Chief Justice Roy Moore of the Alabama Supreme Court had a 5,280-pound granite monument that was engraved with the Ten Commandments placed in the lobby of the Alabama Supreme Court. Civil liberties groups sued, arguing that the monument violated the First Amendment, which prohibits the government from supporting religion. Judge Moore insisted that the Ten Commandments are the basis of the secular law of our country. In November 2002, Federal District Court Judge Myron H. Thompson ordered Moore to remove the monument. Thompson noted that the excerpts from Exodus 20:1–17 (and also with slight differences in Deuteronomy 5:6–21) are a Protestant version of the commandments (the translation Moore used is the King James Version). Jewish, Roman Catholic, Lutheran, and Eastern Orthodox scriptures use slightly different versions of the Ten Commandments; so the version in the courthouse seems to endorse one particular faith, though (as we say in the text) the judge and his supporters say that the monument is a symbol of the roots of American law, not an endorsement of one religion.

A very few words about the differences may be useful. The Roman Catholic and Lutheran churches combine (take as one commandment) the passage forbidding the worship of other gods and the passage forbidding the making of images, and they treat as two commandments the prohibition in Exodus 20:17 against coveting a neighbor's wife (the ninth commandment) and house (the tenth). Most Protestants and Eastern Orthodox

Christians take the first commandment to be "You shall have no other gods before me" and the second commandment to be the injunction against the making of images. Modern Jewish usage counts verse 2 as the first commandment and verses 3–6 as the second.

When the federal judge ruled that the monument must be removed, there was considerable public protest. Rev. Patrick Mahoney of the Christian Defense Coalition and Rev. Rob Schenck, president of the National Clergy Council, led supporters to Montgomery, where they kneeled en masse in front of the monument. A round-the-clock operation was begun, with people unfurling bedrolls on the courthouse steps.

Moore is no stranger to controversy. When he was a circuit court judge in Gadsden, he hung a wooden plaque with the commandments in his courtroom. It generated controversy—enough controversy to encourage him to run as "the Ten Commandments judge" in 2000 in his successful campaign for chief justice. When the associate justices unanimously overruled the chief justice, he was temporarily removed from presiding over the court, pending a trial by the Alabama Court of the Judiciary.

The last time that the U.S. Supreme Court ruled on a case concerning government display of the Ten Commandments was in 1980, in *Stone v. Graham*. Stone was one of a group of parents who challenged a Kentucky law that required all public schools to post the Ten Commandments in every classroom. The money for the printed commandments was provided by private sources, and each copy said, at the bottom, "Secular application of the Ten Commandments is clearly seen in its adoption as the fundamental legal code of Western civilization and the Common Law of the United States." The Court, however, rejected (five to four) this argument, holding that just because Kentucky said that its law had a secular purpose did not make it so. And it rejected as irrelevant the fact that private funds were used.

Justice Rehnquist, in a dissenting opinion, wrote:

> The Supreme Court should defer to the State in determining the secular purpose of postings. The State Legislature and State Courts both believe that the postings have a secular purpose, and the Court should respect this; especially given that the secular purpose, the "Ten Commandments have had a significant impact on the development of the legal codes of the Western world," is acknowledged to be true.

Back to Judge Moore: On August 21, 2003, the eight associated justices of the Alabama Supreme Court overruled Moore, their chief justice, and unanimously ordered that the monument be removed from the lobby. Starting the next day, a fine of $5,000 a day was to be imposed if the monument remained in public view. Moore had been told by the federal judge that he could display the monument in his private chambers, if he wished.

Here are two interesting complications concerning the display of the Ten Commandments in or on a courthouse: (1) As we mention in our discussion of the Florida veil case, the image of Muhammad appears on a frieze in the U.S. Supreme Court. The image of Moses also appears there, holding the Ten Commandments as part of a display of lawgivers, including Hammurabi and Confucius. The courts have ruled that this sort of display of the Ten Commandments within a court is acceptable because it is part of a larger historical display; (2) On August 13, 2003, a federal appeals court in Pennsylvania refused to reconsider a ruling that allowed a 1920 plaque with the Ten Commandments to remain on the façade of a courthouse in suburban Philadelphia. The three-judge panel of the Third U.S. Circuit Court of Appeals had ruled in June that the plaque did *not* constitute an official endorsement of religion because the county commissioners who wanted to keep it were moved by an interest in historic preservation, not religion.

It is probably true—at least Gallup Polls suggest this—that most Americans consider the Ten Commandments as valid rules for a good secular life, but few can give a moderately accurate rendition of even half of the commandments. And in any case, the argument that the commandments are a symbol of the roots of American law, not an endorsement of one religion, seems odd when one remembers that the very first commandment concerns monotheism, the second prohibits the making of "graven images" (by the way, how many Americans adhere to this commandment?), the third prohibits taking the Lord's name in vain, and the fourth concerns observing the sabbath. True, the remaining commandments (concerning respect for parents, killing, adultery, stealing, perjury, and covetousness) are more evidently secular, but even these are ultimately rooted in a particular theology.

We will let Judge Moore have the next-to-last word. According to a report in the *Boston Globe*, August 21, 2003, on CBS's *The Early Show* he said:

> This case is not about politics or religion. It's about the acknowledgement of God. . . . We must acknowledge God because our Constitution says our Judicial system is established upon God.

The last word: A special ethics panel (appointed by various legal organizations, the Alabama governor, and the lieutenant governor) on November 13, 2003, unanimously voted to remove Chief Justice Roy Moore from the Alabama Supreme Court. (The panel's vote was binding only if unanimous.) A topic for argument: Should an *un*elected panel have the power to remove an elected judge?

EXERCISE 4 *(p. 32)*

In addition to arguments concerning aesthetics and cost, the chief argument seems to be that a barrier is not effective: People who want to commit suicide will find other sites where they can kill themselves. That is, according to persons who hold this view, the bridge does not cause suicide, it does not tempt people who otherwise would not commit suicide. Further, it has been argued that barriers might actually increase the number of people who jump to their deaths because barriers would drive such people to other locations — let's say a cliff or a tall building — where there is no possibility that they would be talked out of their acts. Apparently, a considerable number — but we don't have the statistics — of potential bridge-jumpers are persuaded not to jump.

7

2
Critical Reading: Getting Started (p. 34)

The major points made in this chapter—that one should read carefully and that making a summary helps one to grasp an argument—are obvious, and perhaps that's why students often ignore them. Our experience suggests that students often fail to grasp the main points of an argument not because it is especially difficult but merely because they do not read it carefully. But if they do read it carefully (aided by writing a summary), they are likely to find ideas arising—differences with the author. Therefore, the process of writing a summary of someone else's ideas can be a way of generating ideas of one's own. Drawing on the assumptions in Chapter 1, it may be useful to ask students to underline any explicit assumptions that the writer makes (these will probably appear in the summary) and then to think about, and to jot down, any assumptions present but *not* stated.

Susan Jacoby

A First Amendment Junkie (p. 47)

With Susan Jacoby's essay, we hope to show that even where the language is informal, the topic is familiar, and the argument is fairly easy, a second or third reading may reveal things not perceived in a quick scanning.

At this stage in the course, we are less intent on exploring the pros and cons of the issue than on teaching how to read, how to summarize, and how to become aware of explicit and implicit assumptions. "How to read" includes developing awareness of persona and tone, and it is worth discussing the title (even though it is the editors', because the original title was simply "Hers," the unvarying title of a weekly column in the *New York Times*), and worth discussing the ways in which Jacoby establishes a persona.

Although in the text we do not discuss the role of a persona until Chapter 5, preliminary discussion in class can help to pave the way for the students' later encounter with the topic. Because a writer's choice of a persona depends partly on the audience, it is appropriate to discuss this essay *as an argument for readers of a specific newspaper.* It's not a bad idea to ask students to read a couple of issues of the *Times*. Students who have been taught to write in a somewhat stiff, impersonal manner may be surprised to learn from Jacoby (and other columnists in the paper) that they can use "I" and that they can even use colloquial diction ("junkie") in some contexts.

Our second question in the text, on Jacoby's next-to-last paragraph, is prompted by our thought that although the essay is always clear, she makes some leaps. The women who favor censorship in paragraph 1 are, on the whole, women who see pornography as one kind of violence against women. Paragraph 5 gets into kiddie porn—a related issue, but not the same issue. Jacoby probably introduces it to dissociate herself from the extreme position of some opponents of censorship. (It is usually a good idea to distance oneself from extremists who share one's views.) But the issue of young people surfaces again in paragraphs 13 and 14. There is, of course, a connection between Jacoby's arguments that parents should protect the young and her argument that adult-oriented pornography, however objectionable, should not be censored. The connection is that it is the job of adults to fulfill their responsibilities, and not to "shift responsibility from individuals to institutions" (para. 13).

Question 3, on the final paragraph, aims at getting students to see that a final paragraph need not begin "Thus we see" and need not summarize all the points argued earlier.

Question 5, about what is or is not permitted under the "absolute interpretation of the First Amendment," is meant to provoke some thought about whether anyone does or should want the free-speech clause to include protection of offensive and possibly harmful acts—when the acts are wholly verbal (as seems tolerated by Justice Black's remark quoted in Jacoby's para. 2). Falsely shouting "Fire!" in a crowded theater may be no more than a speech act, but it was Justice Holmes's famous example of speech *not* protected by the First Amendment because in a context of utterance such as his example provides, these words would cause "a clear and present danger" of *harm* (and not merely annoyance, offense, or other hostile feelings) to the innocent.

For a discussion of constitutional law on the First Amendment, see Archibald Cox, *Freedom of Expression* (1981). An older book, still of great value, is Thomas I. Emerson's *The System of Freedom of Expression* (1970). A somewhat more recent book on the subject is by Anthony Lewis, *Make No Law* (1991).

Note: We discuss in the text, on page 50, Jacoby's essay from the point of view of the Toulmin method.

Zachary Shemtob and David Lat

Executions Should Be Televised (p. 53)

In stating the objections to their view that (to quote the title of the essay) "Executions Should Be Televised," the authors insist (para. 13) that they do not assume (with Sister Helen Prejean and other foes of capital punishment) that visibility would engender revulsion against the practice and thus would stimulate support for opposition to capital punishment. The authors, claiming to be open-minded, say that they advocate making executions public simply because (to quote their final paragraph), "A democracy demands a citizenry as informed as possible about the costs and benefits of society's ultimate punishment."

To our ears, this statement does not quite ring true. We can't understand how seeing a televised image of an execution—whether the criminal dies with a smile or a grimace on his or her face, whether his or her body is contorted or apparently relaxed—gives us as much information "about the costs and benefits of society's ultimate punishment." We somehow cannot escape thinking that Shemtob and Lat oppose capital punishment and think (like Prejean and others whom they name) that if the public could see it put into practice, the public would be so repelled that it would oppose the punishment. That is, we think there is an underlying irony here: The authors argue, with a straight face, that executions should be televised so that the public can be better informed, but the reader—well, the writer of this page in this instructor's handbook—believes that their proposal is so monstrous that its real purpose is to engender opposition to capital punishment. (Yes, we use the word *proposal* because we we wish to evoke thoughts of Swift's "A Modest *Proposal*," which similarly offers a monstrous argument with a straight face.)

Maybe. Or maybe some folks would take pleasure in witnessing a painful death. Here's something to think about. Thomas Macaulay (1800–1859) famously said, "The Puritans hated bear-baiting, not because it gave pain to the bear, but because it gave pleasure to the spectators." Macaulay was being witty, taking a poke at what he assumed were pleasure-hating Puritans. But can't a good case be made that indeed we ought not to take pleasure in certain kinds of things (in Macaulay's comment, setting dogs upon a chained bear)? If this is true, and if we think that some viewers will relish the spectacle offered by executions, well, then, shouldn't such spectacles be banned? Discuss. (We return to this point in our discussion [p. 26 in this manual] of Nora Ephron's essay of photographs of a woman falling to her death.)

Gwen Wilde (student essay)

Why the Pledge of Allegiance Should Be Revised (p. 56)

We begin by saying that we would give this essay an A. We think it is clear, thoughtful, and courteous—on a subject that has engendered plenty of intemperate writing. Admittedly, the title is not especially engaging, but it has the merit of clearly announcing both the topic and the thesis, and for those reasons we think it is not bad.

The first paragraph is informative, probably telling most readers something they did not know (that the original version of the Pledge did not include the words "under God"). The next paragraph advances the necessary information—that the phrase was added in 1954—and the paragraph ends with an explicit statement of the thesis:

> In my view, the addition of the words "under God" is inappropriate, and they are needlessly divisive—an odd revision for a Nation that is said to be "indivisible."

If we had written the sentence, we probably would have used *because* instead of *and* ("because they are needlessly divisive" rather than "and they are needlessly divisive"), but that's a small point. What we like about the student's sentence is the wordplay involved with *divisive* and *indivisible*.

Wilde goes on to question the meaning of President Eisenhower's words—we ourselves find them a bit fuzzy—and she then points out (para. 5) that "in the Pledge patriotism is connected with religious belief." She goes on to give a reason for suggesting that even though a large percentage of Americans believe in God, the words "under God" do not belong in the Pledge ("several million Americans do *not* believe in God").

We find especially interesting her brief discussion (para. 9) of the use of the motto "In God We Trust" on American coinage. Given Wilde's position on the words "under God" in the Pledge, we would have guessed that she would also object to the motto on coins. Presumably, she introduces this issue—effectively, we believe—to show that she is *not* a fanatic who objects to every tiny hint of religion in American public life.

The quotation from Associate Justice David Souter lets the reader know that Wilde has done some homework, and her comment on the quotation shows that she is thinking carefully about the quotation. In her final paragraph, she reiterates her thesis, but she manages not to be merely repetitive. For instance, in this paragraph she introduces the information that "the Founding Fathers . . . never mentioned God in the Constitution." But perhaps what especially animates this final paragraph, in which there is little new information, is the note of urgency, for instance, when Wilde says, "Yes, they [students] can remain silent when others recite these two words, but, again, why should they have to remain silent?"

A week or two after we drafted the material that you have just read, we came across some comments by Ronald Dworkin on this topic (as well as on intelligent design and on gay marriage) in the *New York Review of Books* (September 21, 2006). Dworkin finds the Pledge "coercive," but he adds, "That coercive impact, however, is in fact not very strong and so though the official Pledge is a violation of liberty it is not a practically serious one." Dworkin goes on (as in fact the student did) to introduce a comparison with the pious words on our coinage, but unlike the student, Dworkin thinks the words in the Pledge are as innocuous as the words on money. Dworkin says:

> Just as an atheist can fish in his pocket for a coin that bears a message of trust in God or stand at the opening ceremony of prayer in congressional or court sessions without any sense of self-betrayal, so he can mouth the words of the Pledge, or skip the words he finds objectionable, without loss of integrity. (p. 28)

Our own view, for what it is worth, is that Wilde is right in thinking that a child reciting the Pledge is *not at all* like (to quote Dworkin) "an atheist fish[ing] in his pocket for a coin that bears a message of trust in God." The atheist—unless he or she is dedicated to removing every vestige of religion—probably hardly thinks of the words when fishing for a coin, but a child reciting the Pledge must be thinking of the words, whether he or she recites them or remains silent.

Discuss.

A Note on Hate Speech

The argument about whether hate speech (for example, racial epithets) should be permitted on the campus is not likely to go away, nor is it likely to be answered definitively. Here are the chief arguments that we have encountered.

Arguments in favor of restricting speech on the campus:

1. Speech demeaning a person's color, creed, sex, sexual orientation, or other personal attributes creates a hostile learning environment—a workplace in which work cannot be done—and thus such speech infringes on the rights of others. Sometimes this argument is supported by being compared with sexual harassment: The courts have upheld regulations against sexual harassment in the workplace. Thus, if women have a right to work in a nonthreatening environment, then students have a right to study in an atmosphere free of racial (or other) harassment. But how exact is the comparison?

2. Limitation of such speech is allowable under the "fighting-words" doctrine. A face-to-face insult using four-letter words or other epithets addressed to an individual or a small group is not intended to discover truth or initiate dialogue; rather, it is an attempt to injure and inflame. Such language is not protected by the First Amendment, according to the Supreme Court in *Chaplinsky v. New Hampshire* (1942). (In this case, a man shouted into the face of a police officer that he was a "Goddamned racketeer and a damned fascist.")

3. A college or university fosters unlimited inquiry, *not* unlimited speech. Hate speech does not lead to advances in knowledge.

4. Outlawing hate speech would not mean that there would be limitations on discussions even of heinous ideas in situations that allow for rebuttal or for persons to choose not to attend.

Arguments against restricting speech on campus:

1. Restrictions against remarks about race, creed, and so forth, violate the rights of free speech under the First Amendment. Such remarks do not come under the fighting-words doctrine because it is not clear that they will produce violence, especially if they are comments about groups rather than specific individuals.

2. By tolerating (rather than suppressing) such speech, we are in a better position to diagnose the real problems that give rise to racist speech and can try to face them directly, not indirectly through regulation and prohibition.

3. We all need to develop a thicker skin to merely verbal utterances that offend. If we don't, then either we will foolishly attempt to protect *everyone* from whatever speech offends them, or we will yield the platform and rostrum to whoever is nastiest among us. Either way threatens disaster; the best remedy for bad speech is still better speech, not silence.

4. Exactly which words are to be prohibited? When three students at the University of Wisconsin complained that they had been called *rednecks*, the administration told them that *redneck* is "not a demeaning term." Or consider the word *Negro*, once considered a polite term, used by African Americans both privately and publicly, but now regarded by many as demeaning. Another example: *Queer* used to be, and for many people still is, a demeaning term for a homosexual, but in the last few years, many homosexuals have used the term, as in the group called Queer Nation.

The Supreme Court decided (June 1992) that an ordinance against hate speech enacted by the city of St. Paul was unconstitutional. The ordinance banned any action "which one knows . . . arouses anger, alarm, or resentment in others on the basis of race, color, creed, religion or gender." The case did not concern speech on the campus, but it did concern expression of racial hate—the burning of a cross on the lawn of a black family that had recently moved into a white neighborhood. In *R.A.V. v. St. Paul,* Justice Scalia, writing for the majority of five (Kennedy, Rehnquist, Scalia, Souter, Thomas) held that government may not opt for "silencing speech on the basis of its content."

The majority opinion, holding that the St. Paul ordinance was impermissibly narrow, acknowledged that hate speech directed at race or religion was hurtful but did not concede that there was any difference in kind between a racial epithet and, for instance, an insult directed at union membership or political affiliation. The court made the point that burning a cross on someone's lawn is "reprehensible," but it insisted that "St. Paul has sufficient means [such as trespassing laws] to prevent such behavior without adding the First Amendment to the fire."

The other four justices agreed that the St. Paul ordinance was unconstitutional, but they would have struck it down on the less-sweeping ground that it was written in too broad a manner. The justices who did not sign the majority opinion (Blackmun, O'Connor, Stevens, White) were troubled by the refusal of the majority to see that certain kinds of hate speech are especially evil. Justice White, for instance, said that the city's

> selective regulation reflects the city's judgment that harms based on race, color, creed, religion, or gender are more pressing public concerns than the harms caused by other fighting words. . . . In light of our nation's long and painful experience with discrimination, this determination is plainly reasonable.

Justice Stevens, in a footnote, glancing at the Los Angeles riots earlier in the year, wrote:

> One need look no further than the recent social unrest in the nation's cities to see that race-based threats may cause more harm to society and to individuals than other threats. . . . Until the nation matures beyond that condition, laws such as St. Paul's ordinance will remain reasonable and justifiable.

In short, the justices who refrained from joining the majority valued free speech not as something good in itself but as something instrumental. That is, they valued speech on the ground, that it serves a constructive purpose by helping to create a better informed electorate and therefore a better country. In this view, speech that is harmful need not be protected.

According to a report in the *New York Times* (June 24, 1992), a spokesperson for the American Council on Education said that the consequences of the decision for colleges and universities were unclear. Private institutions faced fewer constitutional restraints, the report said, than did public institutions, but it was thought that those educational institutions with codes would probably modify them. For instance, after a federal court in 1989 declared unconstitutional the code of the University of Michigan in Ann Arbor, the university adopted a provisional code prohibiting

> physical acts or threats or verbal slurs, invectives or epithets referring to an individual's race, ethnicity, religion, sex, sexual orientation, creed, national origin, ancestry, age, or handicap made with the purpose of injuring the person to whom the words or actions are directed and that are not made as part of a discussion or exchange of an idea, ideology, or philosophy.

You might want to ask your students to evaluate the Michigan provisional code.

A CASEBOOK FOR CRITICAL READING: SHOULD SOME KINDS OF SPEECH BE CENSORED? (p. 60)

Preliminary Note: Free Speech in the Age of YouTube

Our heading, "Free Speech in the Age of YouTube," is the title of an article in the *New York Times* by Somini Sengupta (September 23, 2012). We summarize Sengupta's piece here.

Companies are usually accountable only to shareholders, but Internet companies—because they deal in speech—must make decisions about what kind of expression is allowed. In September 2012, a video mocking Mohammad circulated on YouTube (owned by Google) and provoked a storm of protest in the Islamic world. An attack on the American Embassy in Libya resulted in the death of the ambassador and three other Americans.

The question: Should Google allow access to the video in Libya (or in other Muslim countries)? Google in fact then restricted the piece in Libya and in six other countries where it is unlawful to show disrespect for the Prophet.

Two additional points:

• Apple and Google ordinarily obey the laws of countries in which they do business.

• International law does *not* protect speech designed to cause violence.

A CASEBOOK FOR CRITICAL READING: SHOULD SOME KINDS OF SPEECH BE CENSORED? (p. 60)

Susan Brownmiller

Let's Put Pornography Back in the Closet (p. 61)

First, a point made by Wendy Kaminer in an essay in *Take Back the Night*, edited by Laura Lederer (the book in which Susan Brownmiller's essay also appears): In recent years, feminists such as Brownmiller have been arguing that pornography is not merely dirty (obscene) but is, by virtue of images of violence against women, a threat to society. The distinction, Kaminer explains, is important. "Obscenity" is not constitutionally protected, but it is very narrowly defined. According to the Supreme Court ruling in *Miller v. California* (1973), obscene material is material "that the average person, applying community standards . . . would find . . . as a whole, appeals to the prurient interest" and "taken as a whole, lacks serious artistic, political, or scientific value." It is extremely difficult to prove in court that a work is obscene. Moreover, although almost any piece of hard-core pornography probably fits this description, enforcement of obscenity laws is difficult because the government may not prohibit publication of any material before the courts decide it is obscene. Each book or magazine must individually be judged obscene before it may be enjoined. Kaminer points out that a store with one thousand books cannot be closed because of fifty or even five hundred obscenity convictions. The stock that has not been judged obscene can be sold.

The newer view of pornography, developed especially by Catharine MacKinnon and Andrea Dworkin, sees it not merely as obscenity but as material that depicts the subjugation of women. Pornography is said to represent violence against women, thereby impeding their chances of achieving equal opportunity. It should be mentioned, by the way, that although some feminists oppose pornography on the grounds that it is humiliating to women, other feminists argue that (1) modern feminism is itself linked to sexual liberation, and (2) feminists who fear pornography unwittingly reinforce the notion that women are sexually passive.

Brownmiller, claiming that the battle for free speech has on the whole been won, asserts that pornography is not chiefly a matter of free speech; but she, like MacKinnon and Dworkin, politicizes the issue and thereby tends to legitimize pornography. That is, by seeing it as political speech, these writers bring it into a constitutionally protected area. Of course if they can demonstrate that pornography is a threat to society—a "clear and present danger"—then they will have put it in an area not constitutionally protected, but it is very difficult to prove that something is a "clear and present danger" (cf. question 3).

A February 1986 ruling of the Supreme Court is relevant. The Court ruled *un*constitutional an Indianapolis ordinance that forbade pornography on the ground that it is a form of discrimination against women. The ordinance, drafted with the help of MacKinnon and Dworkin, defined pornography as "the graphic sexually explicit subordination of women, whether in pictures or in words," if it showed them enjoying "pain or humiliation" or if they were in "positions of servility or submission or display." Brownmiller is especially concerned about images of these sorts. Although the Supreme Court did not explain why it declared the ordinance unconstitutional, perhaps we can guess the rationale by considering the explanation of Judge Frank Easterbrook, for the court of appeals, when he ruled against the city ordinance. Easterbrook said that the Indianapolis law "discriminates on the grounds of the content of speech" by establishing "an 'approved' view of women." "This is thought control," he said, for this law attempted to silence explicit speech that did not conform to a particular view of women. He also pointed out that the law could be applied to Homer's epics and to Joyce's *Ulysses*.

Now to look, briefly, a little more closely at Brownmiller's essay. She begins by calling free speech "one of the great foundations on which our democracy rests," thus putting herself on the side of virtue, a good strategy when arguing. Brownmiller then goes on to indicate that she would not burn *Ulysses*, *Lady Chatterley's Lover*, and the *Tropic* books. Again she is on the side of virtue, or at least of classic liberal thought. In short, Brownmiller devotes her first seven paragraphs to showing that she is for democracy and the arts. In paragraph 8 she says she is "not opposed to sex and desire," again establishing her credentials as a liberal. In paragraph 9 she briefly explains why feminists *do* object to pornography (it degrades women), and the remainder of the essay (less than half of the total) amplifies the point. In paragraph 14 she raises an important point that we mentioned earlier in this commentary—not all speech is protected. But as we suggested, although the Constitution does not protect a person who falsely shouts "Fire!" in a crowded theater (a "clear and present danger"), there is some question about whether pornography represents such a danger. Still, by mentioning false advertising and the cry of "Fire," paragraph 14 effectively suggests that pornography is not necessarily protected.

Charles R. Lawrence III

On Racist Speech (p. 64)

In recent years, so-called hate speech on campus has provoked anger and dismay among students, faculty, staff, and the public at large. Any attempt to control such speech by official regulation seems likely to be on a collision course with the First Amendment. Or so most academic administrators concluded, after *Doe v. University of Michigan* (1989). In that case, regulations restricting free speech on the Michigan campus, arising out of a desire to resist "a rising tide of racial intolerance and harassment on campus," were permanently enjoined by Judge Avern Cohn. Judge Cohn had no difficulty permitting regulations as to time, place, and manner of speech. His concern was about the way the university's regulations governed *content*. He held that any regulations against the content of "speech" on no stronger ground than that it was "offensive"—even "gravely so [to] large numbers of people"—was unconstitutionally vague and overbroad.

Charles R. Lawrence is himself African American (see his para. 15) (by the way, he's the brother of Sara Lawrence Lightfoot, author of the widely acclaimed *Balm in Gilead: Journey of a Healer* [1988]), and he presents a measured defense of narrowly drawn regulations against hate speech. No enemy of the First Amendment (see paras. 1 and 14–19), he nonetheless doubts whether its defenders really will act on the proposition, touted by the American Civil Liberties Union in its perennial defense of the First Amendment, that the best remedy for bad speech is more and better speech (para. 17).

Lawrence's position (question 2) is clear from the opening sentence of paragraph 8: If regulations of conduct on campus are needed to protect minority students from harassment and personal vilification, then "equal educational opportunity" is the "compelling justification" for them. We would agree; a few students have no right to make campus life intolerable for others by language, gesture, or symbol that interferes with their rightful access to all the campus has to offer.

But we would also urge that before any such regulations are adopted, one needs to reflect carefully on several basic facts. Everyone finds some words or pictures offensive, but what offends one does not always offend others. Not everything that is offensive is seriously harmful (or counts as harassment). Finally, not everything offensive can be prevented. We all need to develop a thick skin to the merely offensive, lest we find ourselves provoked into violent response or timidly cowering before verbal bullies. We all also need to cultivate a civil environment, free of insulting, degrading, and offensive behavior, verbal or otherwise, especially on a college campus.

Part of what makes the whole hate speech issue so controversial and difficult are the uncertainties that surround the key words "assaultive speech," "verbal vilification," and the like (question 4). Lawrence does not attempt to define these terms explicitly, nor does he provide illustrative and convincing examples of verbal conduct that is "assaultive" or "vilifying." (Students could be usefully asked to give such examples—genuine or hypothetical—and then see whether they can give sensible definitions of these terms.) Nor does Lawrence draft a model set of regulations for hate speech that would prevent (or make liable to punishment for) the harm such speech causes and still pass constitutional muster.

We suspect that Lawrence would deny that straight white males are as vulnerable to insulting posters and the like as are certain other classes of students (blacks, women, gays). The reason is that political power and social status have traditionally been the preserve of white males so that as a class they are relatively immune to the power of offensive language to degrade and intimidate. Of course, Lawrence might still argue (as we would) that straight white males ought not to have to endure insults because of their race or sexual orientation and that regulations protecting women or blacks or homosexuals from vilification ought to be extended equally to all classes of students.

Derek Bok

Protecting Freedom of Expression on the Campus (p. 69)

Like Charles R. Lawrence III (see the previous essay in the chapter), Derek Bok is trained as a lawyer, avows his personal allegiance to the First Amendment, and speaks from a position of concern about racially provocative speech and symbols on a private university campus. (This last point is important because the courts seem to agree that *private* colleges and universities are not bound by the First Amendment, as are public institutions. Notice that in paragraph 9, Bok rightly refuses to use this reason for favoring regulations of free speech on the Harvard campus.) But where Lawrence speaks in measured tones on behalf of the victims of "hate speech," Bok seems to speak for the vast majority of bystanders, those who are neither victims nor offenders where hate speech is concerned.

Bok offers three very different reasons for opposing attempts to curtail hate speech. First, unlike Lawrence, he is doubtful whether the class of harmful verbal and graphic symbols can be suitably defined so that they can be regulated without infringing on full freedom of expression (para. 10). Second, even if such regulations could be drafted and enforced, they would not change racist attitudes or bring greater mutual respect and decency to campus life (para. 11). Finally, irrepressible adolescents will gleefully "test the limits" of these regulations, thereby aggravating the nuisance and trying the patience of deans and disciplinary committees (para. 12). From our own experience, we are strongly inclined to agree with Bok on all these points, even if they do not constitute the last word on the subject.

What constructive measures against hate speech does Bok recommend? First, prospective victims ought to learn to "ignore" nasty and hateful speech; second, the rest of the campus community ought to counsel and persuade would-be vilifiers to mend their ways, lest they do grave harm to some of their fellow students (para. 13). Sensible advice, indeed—but perhaps too easily issued by one who himself is neither black, female, gay, or (it would appear) in any other way a member of a group specially vulnerable to verbal assault. Indeed, we can understand how some will judge Bok's counsels to be unimaginative and deeply disappointing.

Notice, too, that although Bok cites several grounds for restricting speech (para. 7), they do not include the ground Lawrence mentioned in the previous essay—namely, ensuring equal educational opportunity to minority students.

Pedagogical Note: One case study that students have enjoyed exploring in relation to Bok's essay is the topic of flag burning.

If some students do see the American flag as sacred, as something that is desecrated when it is burned by angry protestors, do they also see the Confederate flag as sacred, as something that deserves special protection? You might remind them (or inform them) that the Confederate flag (or a variation) has flown over the capitol buildings of some southern states and has evoked strong protests. In the early months of 2000, for instance, the National Association for the Advancement of Colored People (NAACP) organized a boycott of South Carolina because the Confederate battle flag was displayed over the state's capitol. For some citizens, the flag celebrated the "southern heritage"—for instance, the gallantry of Confederate soldiers. For others, most obviously the NAACP, the flag offensively celebrated slavery. Incidentally, a compromise was reached that satisfied almost no one: The flag was removed from the capitol building and was flown elsewhere on the capitol grounds.

16

3
Critical Reading: Getting Deeper into Arguments (p. 74)

This chapter may seem to hold our major discussion of arguing, for in it we talk about definitions, assumptions, induction, deduction, and evidence (and we do think it is essential reading for students), but we think that the upcoming three chapters — Writing an Analysis of an Argument, Developing an Argument of Your Own, and Using Sources — are equally important. Moreover, for especially strong students, Part Three will be valuable. It includes a summary of the Toulmin method for analyzing arguments and then offers further discussion of deduction and induction from a philosophic point of view. It also includes a survey of fallacies (Chapter 9), Carl R. Rogers's "Communication: Its Blocking and Its Facilitation" (Chapter 10), and Max Shulman's entertaining and informative "Love Is a Fallacy" (Chapter 9).

Nothing is particularly difficult in the chapter; most students should have no trouble with it.

Note: In our discussion of *analogy* we give Judith Thomson's example in which (during the course of an argument on abortion) she invites the reader to imagine that he or she wakes up and finds that a violinist whose body has not been functioning adequately has been hooked up to the reader's body. Thomson's essay originally appeared in *Philosophy and Public Affairs* 1.1 (Fall 1971): 47–66, and is reprinted in her book *Rights, Restitution, and Risk* (1986).

George F. Will

Being Green at Ben and Jerry's (p. 107)

We discuss this essay at length in the text, so there is no need for much additional comment here. We do want to say, however, that you may find it useful to discuss not only Will's essay but also our comments on it: We will not be surprised if students (and some instructors) markedly disagree with our observations. We think the piece is engaging, largely because it is so entertaining. In our view, what makes it at least moderately persuasive is not so much the statistics (though these do have some power) but the wit that pervades the essay and (we confess sheepishly) the hint of scatology in those sentences about the mound of manure and the bag of flatulence. As we say in the text, Will's final paragraph says nothing about oil or the Arctic National Wildlife Refuge, and thus it might seem ("'seem?' nay, 'is!'") irrelevant, but it is entertaining and, alas, a bit of humor may outweigh a good deal of earnest logic. Having said this — and we continue to believe that much of Will's effectiveness here is in his wit — we want to say again that he does have other arrows in his quiver, such as statistics.

Apparently the problem of bovine burps and flatulence continues to be serious and will get worse because the production of beef and milk is expected to double in the next thirty years. It turns out that the most damaging aspect of the milk industry (from an environmental point of view) is not the burning of fossil fuels for transportation or packaging, but the emissions of cows — 200–400 pounds of methane a year per cow. (Methane is second only to carbon dioxide as a heat-trapping emission associated with global warming.) The *New York Times* ran an article ("Greening the Herds," June 5, 2009, p. A12) about some dairy farmers who are making an effort to reduce the methane output of cows. These farmers have adjusted the diet of the herds, diminishing the amount of corn and soy and increasing the amount of alfalfa and flaxseed. The results are said to be very encouraging, but the feed now costs more, so there is some uncertainty about whether this practice will be widely imitated.

Stanley Fish

When "Identity Politics" Is Rational (p. 114)

Consider the definition of "identity politics" that Fish offers in his first paragraph. If we follow the guidance we offer in *Current Issues* on the best way to write a definition, we get something slightly at variance with what he offers. Thus, we would say that one engages in identity politics if and only if one votes for or against someone or something because of his or her skin color, ethnicity, religion, gender, sexual orientation, or any other marker that leads one to affirm or deny what someone says independently of that person's reasons, ideas, or politics. A bit of a mouthful, to be sure, but it captures the essential idea of a good definition, namely, that it be neither too broad nor too narrow.

Fish identifies two different forms of identity politics in paragraph 9: The tribal version and the interest version. He argues that the tribal version has little to recommend it (there are, he admits, rare exceptions to this generalization). As for the interest version, he sees no alternative to it. If you can't rely on your considered judgments, on what can you rely? Fish devotes paragraph 10 to a good account of his answer to this implicit rhetorical question.

Gloria Jiménez (student essay)

Against the Odds, and against the Common Good (p. 118)

We think this is a first-rate essay—thoughtful and effectively written. The title has a nice parallel: The first sentence is informative and sensible, and the second sentence, though long, is shapely and easily readable. We think this long sentence is readable partly because it begins with a strong signal at the start (the transitional word *Still*), because it contains a parallel ("bringing a bit of excitement . . . bringing a vast amount of money"), and because it ends with an independent clause ("the states should not be in the business of urging people to gamble"). The second paragraph amplifies the point, again with a clear transition (*and*, plus a word—*urge*—picked up from the previous sentence). The organization of the entire essay also, in our view, contributes to its clarity: The opening states the thesis clearly; arguments in favor of lotteries are then presented lucidly (in fact, they are numbered); and we are told which are the less important arguments (discussed first and relatively briefly) and which are more important (discussed last and relatively fully).

Jiménez's idea of putting some emphasis on the slogans strikes us as especially interesting. Anyone can talk, rather generally, about the pros and cons of the issue, but she has shrewdly presented some highly engaging sentences ("There Is No Such Thing as a Losing Ticket") and then discusses their implications. She has also done a little research so that she can offer effective details rather than mere opinions.

In our first question in the text, we do raise what we think is a significant point. Jiménez neglects to discuss a common argument: If our state doesn't run a lottery, our citizens will just gamble in the lottery of some other state, so we will lose revenue and gain nothing. We don't know what Jiménez's response would be, and we are not sure even of our own, but we are inclined to think along these lines: (1) Although some people—those who live near the border of the state—will gamble in the lottery of another state, many will not; (2) if gambling is wrong, especially because the majority of people who gamble are the ones who can least afford it, the state should not sponsor it in any case, even if adjoining states do sponsor it.

Our second question in the text asks if readers find the essay a bit "too preachy." (This was the response of one of our students when we showed her the essay.) We don't see it that way. Admittedly, the essay is highly schematic and takes the high moral ground, but we think the tone is engaging ("an almost sure-fire way of getting nothing for something," "dreams of an easy buck," "It's against the odds," "an activity that is close to pickpocketing"). Our chief uneasiness—and we want to say again that we think this is a first-rate essay—is with the somewhat solemn introduction of the first person: "I now get to the point in my argument," "I say that this argument is delicate," "Let me end a bit indirectly." On the other hand, we do tell students that there is nothing wrong with using the first person and that obvious evasions ("It has been argued in this paper") usually are not the way to go. Perhaps Jiménez might have reduced the use of the first person slightly—for instance, by saying "This argument is delicate" rather than "I say that this argument is delicate"—but we want to reiterate that we think the essay is excellent.

Anna Lisa Raya (student essay)

It's Hard Enough Being Me (p. 121)

As we weigh in our headnote in the text, Anna Lisa Raya published this essay while she was an undergraduate. Your students may very well find that they can do just as well.

If you have looked at the questions that we pose in the text, you have probably guessed that we think Raya is a bit unclear about *why* she "had to define [herself] according to the broad term 'Latina'" (para. 2). The closest she comes, we think, to offering an explanation is when she says that in "El Sereno, I felt like I was part of a majority, whereas at the College I am a minority" (para. 2).

But even this sentence, we think, doesn't say *why* she "had" to define herself. Pressure from the majority? From the minority? Again, she says (para. 8), "To be fully Latina in college . . . I *must* know Spanish." But (again) *who* demands that she be "fully Latina"? As we read the essay, we are inclined to guess that the demand comes from Latinos and Latinas who emphasize their heritage and want Raya to celebrate it, but we don't think she is explicit on the point. She ends by asserting—briefly, in Spanish and in English—that she will be herself. We think this ending is rhetorically effective since it uses both languages.

There is, however, a further difficulty. Exactly what does it mean to be true to oneself? Of course, we can say that we don't steal (we are not that sort of person) or that we don't cheat (again, we are not that sort of person). But isn't "the self" really constructed out of relationships to others? We are loving (or neglectful) parents or children, we are serious (or frivolous) students, we are serious (or casual) about advancing in a career, and so on. We have many selves (parent, child, student, worker), and it is not always easy to know *which* self we must be true to.

Ronald Takaki

The Harmful Myth of Asian Superiority (p. 123)

In his first paragraph, Ronald Takaki introduces the term *model minority*, a term our fifth question asks students to consider. Takaki couples this term with being financially *successful*, and it's our impression that when Asian Americans are said to be a *model minority*, the term does usually imply financial success, conjuring up images of prosperous merchants, engineers, lawyers, and so on. But it's our impression, too, that the term also implies three other things: academic success (strong undergraduate work and graduate or professional work), family stability, and a low crime rate. Takaki is scarcely concerned with these matters, though in paragraph 7 he mentions "gangs" of Asian Americans (an indirect glance at crime), and in paragraphs 8–10 he touches on Asian American laborers—though it turns out, in paragraph 12, that some Korean greengrocers are highly educated.

Chiefly, Takaki is concerned with disproving the myth of financial success, and he wants to do this for two reasons: The myth is harmful to Asian Americans (because the rest of America mistakenly thinks this minority is doing very well), and it is harmful to African Americans (because the rest of America uses the Asian Americans as a stick to beat the African Americans). To demonstrate that the financial success of the Asian Americans is a myth, Takaki introduces statistics—and indeed it is partly because of his statistics and because of his comments on the possible deceptiveness of some figures that we include Takaki's essay in this chapter. As early as his fourth paragraph, he points out that statistics may be misleading. He doesn't cite specific figures, but he says (convincingly, we think) that it's not enough to point to "figures on the high earnings of Asian Americans relative to Caucasians." Why not? Because, he says, Asian Americans tend to be concentrated in places with a high cost of living (Hawaii, California, New York). This is a telling point. Again, even without giving specific figures, he sets the reader thinking, giving the reader cause to be skeptical about the figures.

The bulk of the essay (paras. 4–14) is devoted to the finances of Asian Americans, but surely Takaki's purpose in demythologizing Asian Americans is twofold: to say something that will help Asian Americans and to say something that will help African Americans. Although African Americans are mentioned in only paragraphs 3 and 15, their appearance is significant, especially because one of the two appearances is in the final paragraph.

This essay makes use of statistics and also calls attention to the misuse of statistics. You may want to invite students to examine Takaki's statistics. We wonder, for instance, exactly how significant it is that "twenty-five percent of the people in New York City's Chinatown lived below the poverty level in 1980" (para. 8). For the figure to be meaningful, one would probably have to know what percentage of the rest of America lived below the poverty level in 1980. And in any case, why cite a figure from 1980 in an essay written in 1990? That's a long time ago; surely there must be a more recent figure.

You may want to invite the class to bring in some statistics on this or another issue, perhaps gathered from an article in *Time* or *Newsweek* or from a textbook, and to discuss their possible limitations.

James Q. Wilson

Just Take Away Their Guns (p. 125)

Our question 1 goes to the heart of this essay: What sentence in James Wilson's essay best expresses his thesis? We suggest the answer is in this sentence in paragraph 4, when Wilson writes: "The most effective way to reduce illegal gun-carrying is to encourage the police to take guns away from people who carry them without a permit." Why do we focus on this sentence? First, it echoes the title of the essay ("Just Take Away Their Guns"). As we suggest elsewhere in the text, a good title will often signal the writer's main thesis. Second, the quoted sentence implies that the *goal* of gun control is to get guns out of the hands of those most likely to use them illegally, and that the *best means to this end* is authorizing the police to stop and frisk. Any careful reader of Wilson's essay will see that it is this second point and its ramifications that get most of Wilson's attention in the rest of the article.

Our second question is intended to get the student to look carefully at the research Wilson cites and to evaluate just what that research implies. One cannot infer that displaying or firing guns in self-defense actually prevented victimization in all, most, or even many of the million cases where guns were used for this purpose. Nor are we told in how many of these million cases the gun user was under a misapprehension (no robbery or other crime was in the offing) or in how many other cases children or others in the household caused accidental deaths or injuries by firearms. So on balance, we do not know anything from this research about the extent to which safety in the home was increased (or decreased) by the availability and use of firearms by ordinary citizens to prevent crimes. The only legitimate use of the statistics Wilson reports here is the very limited use he himself makes of them in the final sentence of his paragraph.

How might a defender of gun control respond to Wilson's barb quoted in our question 3? In his twelfth paragraph, Wilson thinks it is "politically absurd" for a citizen in crime-infested America to seek laws that "forbid or severely restrict the sale of guns." This is the preface to his remark we quote in the question.

Before proceeding with a reply, as the question asks, we draw the reader's attention to the extreme and perhaps misleading generalization in his remark quoted above. Are the restrictions and prohibitions to which he refers here confined only to handguns? Or does he think all restrictions on firearms of whatever sort are "politically absurd"? We do not think it is "politically absurd" for the government to forbid outright all sales of automatic weapons, dumdum bullets, antitank weapons, and the like except to authorized purchasers. Perhaps Wilson would agree. If so, he might have easily made that clear.

More to the point, we think the gun-control advocate might reply to Wilson's challenge along these lines:

First, no government can hope to shield its citizens against all criminal harms, even if, by deterrence and incapacitation, not to mention moral education, government does keep crime from overwhelming us. (Ask the class: How many of you were the victims of crime earlier today? Earlier this week? This month? How many of you were *not* victims only because you used a weapon to frighten off a would-be assailant?) So it is unfair to describe our "government" as "having failed to protect" our persons and property. Its successes vastly outnumber its failures.

Second, society has to weigh *all* the consequences of our current virtually uncontrolled gun ownership practices against the alternative of varying degrees of restriction and prohibition. It is not enough just to look at the ways in which guns in the hands of the citizenry have deterred crime. Those successes have to be measured against the many costs that Wilson nowhere mentions (notably, suicides and other killings and accidents that would not have occurred except for the availability at all hours of loaded handguns).

In our question 5, we ask the reader to confront the racial impact of Wilson's proposal, which he candidly mentions. We agree with his prediction: Widespread use of stop-and-frisk practices aimed at removing guns from those without permits to possess them will in practice do exactly what he says. Is this a fatal objection to his proposal? Yes, if you think that young black males have enough problems already without the added burden of heightened attention from the police, or that stop-and-frisk practices will lead mainly to more shoot-outs with police on the mean streets of urban America. No, if you think that black neighborhoods are far more likely to be victimized by black offenders than are white neighborhoods, that the best way to protect the bulk of the black population is to get illegal guns out of the hands of would-be black offenders, and that the best way to do this is to encourage adoption of Wilson's stop-and-frisk proposal.

Kayla Webley

Is Forgiving Student Loan Debt a Good Idea? (p. 129)

Our first question in the book asks why, in her second paragraph, Webley makes the point that reading some of the stories retold on the Student Debt site is a heartrending experience. The answer, of course—at least from the point of view of someone writing an argument—is that (to get directly to the point) this author will soon reject the views expressed by the authors of those stories; so at the outset, she wants to express her sympathy, to establish an engaging *ethos* lest she later seem coldhearted. And indeed, at the end of her essay, she again expresses sympathy with Robert Applebaum's idea, though she characterizes it as "wildly unfeasible."

In short, she begins and ends by indicating that her heart is in the right place—but the body of the essay severely criticizes Applebaum's idea. First, she quotes Justin Wolfers's devastating critique. Then she goes on to assert that, in fact, most indebted students *can* repay the loans (paras. 6–7), and in paragraph 8 she talks about alternatives for those who cannot repay the loans. In 9 she raises the issue of fairness: Why should taxpayers foot the bill for college graduates?

In short, she sees no merit in Applebaum's idea—except (and here we get to Webley's final paragraph) that it *is* an idea, and ideas are what is wanted. Thus, although she shreds Applebaum in the body of the essay, she expresses sympathy for debtors at the beginning, and at the end she gives credit to Applebaum for at least offering an idea, even if it is "wildly unfeasible."

The essay ends in a time-tested way by putting the ball in the reader's court: "[W]hat's your solution?" We have often heard our colleagues grumpily say that they do not want their students to use formulas, but in fact real writers—Webley writes for *Time* magazine—often *do* use formulas, time-tested patterns and devices. The important point is that within the formulaic structure, they write carefully, thoughtfully, and engagingly.

Alfred Edmond Jr.

Why Asking for a Job Applicant's Facebook Password Is Fair Game (p. 132)

We were astounded to learn that some employers ask job candidates for their passwords to Facebook, and that this request is legal. But, well, lots of things astound us today. (Reminder: It is *not* legal for a potential employer to inquire about age, race or ethnicity, sex [gender], marital status, pregnancy, religion, or disability.)

Given the fact that (in our view) Edmond is taking an outrageous position, we think he does a pretty good job of defending it. First of all, in his second paragraph he indicates that in other circumstances he would take a different position. Then, with a clear transition at the beginning of his fourth paragraph ("That said, my response"), he begins a defense of his earlier position, and we think he gives a good example, in the fifth paragraph, when he cites "the child care industry." The trouble, from our point of view, is that we cannot think of any other example that is equally forceful. Working in a facility with mentally impaired persons might come close.

The problem, as we see it, is that some (many?) people think they are performing a helpful social service when they reveal highly personal information. Thus, they may think they are helping to break down harmful stereotypes, helping to reduce prejudices, when they reveal to certain persons that, for instance, they are gay or deeply depressed or addicted to certain medicines. In our view, Edmond gives sound advice when he says, "Don't think business vs. personal. Think public vs. private. And if something is truly private, do not share it on social media out of a misplaced faith in the expectation of privacy."

These words of Edmond make sense to us, but we continue to doubt that sense can be made out of his title, beyond perhaps the child care industry.

Addendum: Should Colleges Monitor the Posts and Tweets of Athletes?

The issue is different, of course, but a discussion of Edmond's essay can easily get into related issues of what is and what is not acceptable in posts and tweets. Here we want to summarize a discussion that we came across in *Time*, October 22, 2012, pages 56–57.

North Carolina (UNC) defensive tackle Marvin Austin in 2011 posted something about partying that led the National Collegiate Athletic Association (NCAA) to investigate, and it found that he had received cash gifts. Other athletes on the team also had broken rules, and the NCAA ultimately banned UNC's football team from the 2012 postseason and reduced its allotment of football scholarships for the next three years.

Because some colleges receive a great deal of money from their football program, they of course worry that athletes may inflict damage on the program. Therefore some of these colleges prohibit the athletes from using Twitter. Some colleges permit the use of Twitter but require the athletes (in the words of Utah State University) to "grant full remission for the university and other third-party monitors to gain access to the 'friends only,' 'private,' and similarly designated areas." Such a policy even requires a student athlete to sign a waiver: "To the extent that any federal, state, or local law prohibits the Athletic Department from accessing my social networking accounts, I hereby waive any and all such rights and protections." As *Time* puts it, the university thus requires the student to license the university to ignore the law. On the other hand, some states have offered protection to the students. *Time* reports that California has a law forbidding colleges to "require or request" that a student or prospective student "divulge any personal social media information."

Sherry Turkle

The Flight from Conversation (p. 136)

Turkle's essay is one of many essays we have encountered that express alarm at the alleged harmful effects of social media. There are, of course, counterviews, and we want to begin this brief discussion by mentioning Adam Gopnik's entertaining survey of books on the topic, "How the Internet Gets Inside Us," *New Yorker*, February 14, 2011. Gopnik divides the commentaries into three groups:

> Call them the Never-Betters, the Better-Nevers, and the Ever-Wasers. The Never-Betters believe that we're on the brink of a new utopia, where information will be free and democratic, news will be made from the bottom up, love will reign, and cookies will bake themselves. The Better-Nevers think that we would have been better off if the whole thing had never happened, that the world that is coming to an end is superior to the one that is taking its place, and that, at a minimum, books and magazines create private space for minds in ways that twenty-second bursts of information don't. The Ever-Wasers insist that at any moment in modernity something like this is going on, and that a new way of organizing data and connecting users is always thrilling to some and chilling to others—that something like this is going on is exactly what makes it a modern moment.

Gopnik amusingly illustrates his categories thus:

> When the electric toaster was invented, there were, no doubt, books that said that the toaster would open up horizons for breakfast undreamed of in the days of burning bread over an open flame; books that told you that the toaster would bring an end to the days of creative breakfast, since our children, growing up with uniformly sliced bread, made to fit a single opening, would never know what a loaf of their own was like; and books that told you that sometimes the toaster would make breakfast better and sometimes it would make breakfast worse, and that the cost for finding this out would be the price of the book you'd just bought.

Probably most of us sometimes feel one way, sometimes another way, and sometimes a third way—in Gopknik's terms, Never-Better, Better-Never, and Ever-Waser—which is to say that we think there is something important here, and yet . . . . Take Turkle's eighth paragraph, in which she comments on today's young people in a library, together but each in his or her own bubble. Yes, thinks the Ever-Waser, just like when people in olden decades sat in a library reading books, together but each in his or her own bubble.

One other point: When we first read Turkle's essay, we were briefly puzzled by her reference in paragraph 13 to "the word," and we had to reread a few sentences. She is in fact talking about the word *conversation*, ultimately derived from the Latin verb *convertere*, "to turn around." You may want to ask students to offer conjectures about other words with *vers* in them, for instance, *averse, adversary, diverse, obverse, reverse.*

4
Visual Rhetoric: Images as Arguments (p. 141)

Dorothea Lange

Migrant Mother (photographs) (p. 167)

We think most students will agree that the more tightly framed image is more moving. The other is interesting, but the lamp in the lower left, the lean-to, the landscape at the right, and the faces of the two children—especially the appealing face of the child resting her chin on the mother's shoulder—provide distractions. In the famous image, which is more symmetrical than the other and almost surely puts us in mind of traditional paintings of the Madonna and child, the two faceless children have turned to the mother for comfort. Further, the mother's hand touches her chin, somewhat suggesting the pose of Rodin's *The Thinker;* but whereas Rodin's muscular man is an image of strength—mental as well as physical—Lange's migrant mother is an image of powerlessness. We can admire her courage, and we know that her children love her because they turn to her for comfort, but we also know that however hard she thinks, she is not going to solve her problem.

A few further points about the image: In 1958, one Florence Thompson (1903–1983), a woman of Cherokee heritage, revealed that she was the subject of the photograph. In 1936, when the photograph was taken, Thompson was the mother of eight childen, two of whom were illegitimate. (She later had three children by a man to whom she was not married.) Question: What might the effect of the photo be if it showed eight children rather than three? Our own view—purely a conjecture, of course, since Lange did not take such a photograph—is that an image showing an impoverished woman with eight children might provoke some thoughts that she was irresponsible. In any case, we find it hard to imagine that a photograph showing Thompson with eight children could have the dignity and the power that the famous image does have.

Among the useful books on Lange are Linda Gordon's *Dorothea Lange: A Life Beyond Limits* (2009) and Anne Whiston Spirn's *Daring to Look: Dorothea Lange's Photographs and Reports from the Field* (2009).

Anonymous

Our Homes Are in Danger Now! (poster) (p. 168)

We think it is interesting that although Hitler is shown, a specific Japanese person (Emperor Hirohito or General and later Prime Minister Tojo) is not shown. Apparently during World War II, no single Japanese face was sufficiently familiar to American viewers to stand for Japanese aggression. Perhaps behind this failure to identify an individual Japanese is the common Western stereotype that "they all look alike."

Why does Hitler have a gun and the Japanese a knife? There is no need to comment on the gun, but probably the knife suggests the racist idea that Asians are more primitive than Caucasians.

The globe that Hitler and the Japanese are grabbing shows the United States, and the text ("OUR HOMES ARE IN DANGER NOW!") is given visual form by little houses on the map. Speaking of little houses, why is the image of the American response—a bomber and a tank, encircled by the words "*OUR JOB* KEEP 'EM FIRING"—so small? Presumably to emphasize our vulnerability. We Americans are the little kids on the block, menaced by hulking bullies.

James Montgomery Flagg

I Want YOU (poster) (p. 169)

We are concerned here less with the medium than with the message. Our concern with the medium is with body language initiated on Flagg's poster. The assertive pointing scarcely needs explanation, but most students will be less aware of the implication of the full-face view, versus, say, a three-quarter view, or a profile. Facial expression is more conspicuous in a front view than in a profile. A profile tends to be expressionless, immutable (that is why it is commonly used on coins and medals), but a front view can more obviously catch the emotion of a moment. Moreover, a front view confronts the spectator, looks into the spectator's space, and suggests an all-seeing and inescapable presence. Flagg's Uncle Sam unreservedly reveals his emotions, dominates us, stares us down. Although the written message ("I want YOU for U.S. Army") is, when you think about it, directed only to potential recruits, Uncle Sam's assertive finger and his penetrating eyes are directed to every viewer; the effect is to make *all* passersby feel guilty, so that they will make additional efforts on behalf of their country.

Two notes: (1) The origin of Uncle Sam is obscure, but he seems to have come into being during the War of 1812. It is said that the name derives from "Uncle" Sam Wilson, an inspector of army supplies. The initials "U.S." (to indicate government property) were stamped on army barrels and crates, but they apparently were taken to stand for "Uncle Sam." The iconography was fixed by the latter part of the nineteenth century; Uncle Sam was tall and lean with white hair and chin whiskers, tall hat with stars and stripes, swallowtail coat, vest, and striped pants. He can be kindly in a gruff way, but for the most part, despite the clownish costume, he is stern and energetic. (2) Flagg eliminated the usual stripes from the hat, and by eliminating the lower half of the body, with its striped pants, he made the figure less extravagant. He modeled the face on his own but took the composition from a British poster by Alfred Leete, which showed the head of Lord Kitchener, the Recruiting General, and a foreshortened hand emerging from a cuff, above the legend "Your Country Needs YOU." Leete's poster is reproduced in John Barnicoat's *A Concise History of Posters* (1969, p. 226), and in Harold F. Henderson's *The Poster* (1968, p. 75). For German and Italian versions of similarly gesturing figures, see Max Gallo, *The Poster in History* (1974, pp. 166–67). See also Robert Phillipe's *Political Graphics* (1982), not only for the illustrations but also for the valuable text. For anonymous parodies of Flagg's poster, produced to oppose the Vietnam War, as well as for a large, color reproduction of Flagg's poster itself, see *Arms and the Artist* (1977), selected by Denis Thomas: No. 94 shows a bandaged Uncle Sam, not pointing vigorously, but weakly extending a hand as if in need of support, with the legend, in Flagg's lettering, "I Want OUT"; no. 96 reproduces Flagg's format, but with Uncle Sam as a skeleton. We have heard of (but not seen) a more affectionate parody, suitable for hanging in a child's room: Uncle Sam, pointing the usual accusatory finger, stares out above the legend, "I Want YOU to Clean Up Your Room."

A comment toward a suggestion for writing: There is yet another aspect to Flagg's message. How do we know the approximate date? That is, what in the *style* lets us know that this poster is from World War I? After all, the hairstyle and the costume of the figure are not a giveaway, as they would be in most old posters and advertisements, and as they are in Leete's picture of Kitchener. It might be interesting to ask a class what approximate date they would give to Flagg's poster, and why. (The poster was created in 1917. It was used again in World War II, but that is irrelevant.) Perhaps the resulting discussion (or essays) will help students understand something of what instructors mean by "style." Our own feeling is that the lettering, indebted to hand-painted signs of the late nineteenth century, clearly belongs to the early part of the twentieth century, and the realistic drawing is characteristic of posters for World War I rather than for World War II. The posters of World War II tended to show, in a very simple way, the influence of cubism and of abstract art; figures, if they were not photographs or close copies of photographs, tended to be flat and even geometric. A face might be a mere plane with no shading, or it might have a strongly demarked shadow, giving it at most only two planes. Often the designs give the effect of a collage or montage, thus further moving away from the tradition of illusionistic drawing.

Nora Ephron

The Boston Photographs (p. 170)

Many people get agitated when images that they take to be pornographic are published in magazines or are hung on museum walls. Your students know this, but they may not know that until quite recently, many people thought that images of violence should not be shown. Respectable newspapers did not show the blood-spattered corpses of gangland killings. That sort of image was left to the tabloids. The chief exceptions were photographs of persons killed in war, but even these were acceptable only if the dead seemed intact and asleep. Severed limbs, decapitated bodies, and agonized faces were not tolerated. But exactly why were they not tolerated?

"All the news that's fit to print" was and still is the slogan of the *New York Times*. And just as some news stories were judged unprintable—let's say stories about prostitution and abortion—so were some images. Probably the idea behind this informal code was that such stories and images pander to a taste that ought not to be nourished. We are reminded of Thomas Babington Macaulay's comment on bearbaiting: "The Puritan hated bear-baiting not because it gave pain to the bear, but because it gave pleasure to the spectators." An astute remark, not merely a wisecrack at the expense of Puritans. Why, indeed, do we in the United States prohibit cockfighting in all but two states? Surely not merely because a few birds suffer for relatively brief periods—a tiny number, when compared with the enormous numbers of birds that suffer for months until they have grown large enough to be slaughtered for food. Presumably forty-eight states prohibit cockfighting because their citizens think—rightly—that spectators ought not to take pleasure in the sight of birds maiming each other. The idea is as old as Plato: Our base appetites ought not to be nourished.

To get back to certain kinds of pictures of violence, the idea behind censoring them was that these images appeal to impulses that ought to be suppressed, not nourished. It is pretty hard for anyone today to favor censorship, but when you look at the pictures in James Allen et al., *Without Sanctuary: Lynching Photography in America* (2000), and you learn that some of these horrifying images of burned and castrated bodies were printed as picture postcards and inscribed with playful comments (e.g., "This is the barbecue we had last night"), well, one understands what Plato and the Puritans were getting at.

In our text, the most horrifying image is not reproduced in Ephron's essay but is Huynh Cong (Nick) Ut's photograph on page 146, "The Terror of War" (1972). This picture, which was widely printed in newspapers, is said to have played an enormous role in turning American public opinion against the war in Vietnam. (For details, see Denise Chong's *The Girl in the Picture: The Story of Kim Phuc, the Photograph, and the Vietnam War* [2000].) Conceivably, some people take pleasure in the horror it depicts, but surely its publication was justified by its message: "What is going on over there is unbelievably horrifying." On June 8, 1972, American-backed South Vietnamese pilots trying to kill Viet Cong troops dropped napalm canisters near a pagoda where villagers had taken refuge. The girl in the center of the picture had torn off her clothing in an effort to free herself from the searing napalm jelly. A viewer looks with horror at the picture, but—and we say this with much unease—part of our interest in the photograph probably is aesthetic. In its terrifying way, it is a beautiful photograph, admirably composed, the sort of composition that

Henri Cartier-Bresson called "the decisive moment," the moment when the flux of the world suddenly takes shape and seems to say something. The four figures nearest to the camera run forward, but they take us back relentlessly. The boy at the extreme left shows his agony in his wide-open mouth and his slightly contorted posture; the naked girl in the center, vulnerable in her nudity, is by virtue of her outstretched arms in a posture that reminds a viewer of the crucified Jesus; the small boy toward the right (like the smaller boy who is the second figure from the left) is apparently too young to understand the horror, but the girl who holds his hand reveals her terror in her face. And behind them, apparently walking rather than running, apparently a relentless and unemotional force (we can see no expression on their faces) pushing these victims forward, are four soldiers (one is almost totally hidden by the girl at the right). And still further back, behind the soldiers, is a flat backdrop of the smoking village.

Is this photo merely an image of a most regrettable incident—like, say, a fire in Boston that kills a woman who falls from an unstable fire escape? Or does it have meaning? And, if so, what is its meaning? Ephron doesn't talk about this image, but she does make a relevant point in her next-to-last photograph, when she talks about car wrecks and says that newspapers will print images of wrecked cars but not of dead bodies: "But the significance of fatal automobile accidents is not that a great deal of steel is twisted but that people die. Why not show it?" And in her final paragraph she introduces an aesthetic element when she says, of the Boston photographs, "They deserve to be printed because they are great pictures, breathtaking pictures of something that happened. That they disturb readers is exactly as it should be: that's why photojournalism is often more powerful than written journalism."

In short, although doubtless there are some people who enjoy the violence depicted in some images, images of the sort that Ephron is talking about (photos by Stanley Forman) and images like Ut's rivet our attention because—one can hardly dare to say it—the horror is transformed by the artistry. This is *not* to say that the horror is diminished. Far from it; the horror is made memorable, enduring, and perhaps even eternal.

Part Two

CRITICAL WRITING

5
Writing an Analysis of an Argument (p. 179)

Although we offer incidental comments about *writing* in Chapters 2 and 3—with comments on audience, tone, organization, and so on—this chapter and Chapter 6 contain our primary discussions of writing.

In Chapter 10, we reprint Carl R. Rogers's "Communication: Its Blocking and Its Facilitation," an essay that has interested many teachers of rhetoric because of its emphasis on psychological aspects of persuasion. The essay is fairly short and easy, and because it is mainly about a writer's interaction with an audience, it may well be assigned in conjunction with this chapter.

If you want to give a writing assignment *not* based on a reading assignment, this suggestion may be useful:

Write a letter (150–300 words) to the editor of a newspaper, responding to an editorial or to a published letter. Hand in the material you are responding to, along with your essay.

Nicholas D. Kristof

For Environmental Balance, Pick Up a Rifle (p. 186)

The student essay by Betsy Swinton, "Tracking Kristof," provides what we think is a thorough discussion of Kristof's essay. We in turn discuss Swinton's analysis, so we won't rehash the issue any further here.

Jeff Jacoby

Bring Back Flogging (p. 196)

Our society takes pretty much for granted that punishment for crimes will take the form of imprisonment, except for juveniles and first offenders, who may be offered probation instead. But the prison (as distinct from the jail, traditionally used only to detain accused persons prior to trial) is a relatively new invention in England and the United States, dating only from the end of the eighteenth century (see Michel Foucault, *Discipline and Punish: The Birth of the Prison* [1977], and Michael Ignatieff, *A Just Measure of Pain: The Penitentiary in the Industrial Revolution, 1750–1850* [1978]). Corporal punishments—the stocks, flogging, branding, mutilation, and hanging—are as old as recorded history, and some of these modes of punishment remain in use today, for example, in Saudi Arabia. Except for the death penalty, all such practices have been abandoned in the United States, and probably few would survive constitutional challenge were a legislature foolish enough to reintroduce them.

The case of flogging (or whipping) is different. Whipping survived in Delaware until 1952; in 1989, a bill was filed in the Delaware legislature to bring back the whipping post (see *New York Times*, January 29, 1989), but it failed to pass. It may come as a surprise to learn that the U.S. Supreme Court has yet to rule on the constitutionality of this classic mode of punishment. And for reasons Jeff Jacoby offers in his essay—inexpensiveness, brevity of duration, humiliation of offenders, and above all, physical pain—it retains a certain attractiveness in some quarters. Not until 1983, however, in the book *Just and Painful: A Case for the Corporal Punishment of Criminals* by criminologist Graeme Newman, did anyone in recent years seriously defend flogging. (Newman proposed electric shocks, carefully calibrated to suit the crime of the offender, followed by whipping if the offender recidivates, and incarceration only after repeated convictions for violent crimes.)

Our question 3 goes to the heart of the issue, as Jacoby realizes: Is it true that flogging (in whatever form and degree) is more degrading or brutal than imprisonment, and on that ground—entirely apart from any other consideration—ought to be abolished? Jacoby raises the issue and disposes of it with a rhetorical question ("where is it written, . . .?" para. 12). Flogging always brings to mind scenes of merciless beating; but such brutality is not necessary. It also often has overtones of sadistic pleasure aroused by the sight of naked flesh being turned to a bloody pulp; but, again, that is not necessary. Some opponents of flogging as punishment (including the authors of this manual) are repelled by the whole idea and cannot imagine inflicting such punishment on anyone, no matter what the crime, or encouraging others to do it for us. But is this mere sentimentality, or is detesting such a practice a good enough reason for opposing it? Perhaps one can argue that when the abuses of imprisonment that Jacoby rightly reminds us of are compared with the abuses of flogging that Jacoby ignores, it is far from clear whether a reasonable and humane person ought to join him in preferring flogging.

Gerard Jones

Violent Media Is Good for Kids (p. 199)

First, we must confess that Jones's title irritates us: Pedants that we are, we wince when we see or hear *media* (from the Latin plural of *medium*) used as a singular noun. Still, we do understand that this usage is widely accepted, so we will grit our teeth and say only that we think "media is" sounds dreadful.

Jones's essay is not at all the sort of thing that most instructors want their students to write—it is essentially a personal essay—but it is devoted to a topic that has received a good deal of academic attention: the effect of imaginary violence on human beings. Probably the earliest extant major treatment of the issue in Western writing is Plato's denunciation of the poets in *The Republic*. The argument comes down to the idea that tragic and epic poets nourish the passions of their auditors, in other words stimulate human passions and therefore diminish human rationality. An almost comic version of this position appears in Boswell's *Life of Johnson*, where Boswell reports (September 23, 1777) a conversation with Johnson on the topic of the effect of music. Johnson told Boswell that music had little effect on him, and Boswell then reports his own responses to the power of music:

> I told him that [music] affected me to such a degree as often to agitate my nerves painfully, producing in my mind alternate sensations of pathetic dejection so that I was ready to shed tears, and of daring resolution, so that I was inclined to rush into the thickest part of the battle. "Sir," said he, "I should never hear it, if it made me such a fool."

Plenty of people agree that the arts stimulate passion, and that this is a Bad Thing. A common argument against pornography is that it stimulates unwholesome passions, and indeed plenty of sex offenders have said that they got their ideas (e.g., for bizarre forms of assault and murder) from films or books. On the other hand, one of the arguments offered in defense of pornography is that it may serve as a harmless release: The man who might otherwise rape a woman allegedly finds a release in a pornographic DVD.

The most famous defense of the depiction of antisocial emotions in literature is Aristotle's reply to Plato in the *Poetics*. Aristotle is talking about tragic drama in verse, but if what he says is true, it probably applies equally well to prose fiction. He says that when we perceive the artistic presentation of violence, we experience a *catharsis*. The trouble is, there is much argument about the exact meaning of *catharsis*. The basic Greek sense of the term is "purgation," in the medical sense—a laxative that purges the bowels. If something close to this is Aristotle's meaning, the idea is that we get rid of our emotions by experiencing them and discharging them harmlessly in the theater. It apparently is sort of like smashing a dish when one is angry; but do people really do this sort of thing, and if they do, does it work? That is, do the arts offer a sort of laxative for the emotions? We are back to the idea that porno allows the reader/viewer to get rid of unwholesome passions in a harmless way. But many scholars say that "purification" (or "cleansing") rather than "purgation" (or "discharge") is what Aristotle meant. Things get complicated here, but one version of this interpretation holds that by purification, Aristotle means that we see the *proper* objects of such emotions as pity and terror. For instance, when we witness a production of *King Lear*, we see an action that indeed evokes pity and terror, and we thus learn which kinds of actions should be pitied and which kinds of actions are terrifying.

Some decades ago, Bruno Bettelheim, in *The Uses of Enchantment* (1976), argued that fairy tales that are filled with violence serve a wholesome purpose. In the story of "Hansel and Gretel," for example, there is a wicked witch, and the story ends with the children pushing the witch into an oven. Plenty of violence there. But, Bettelheim said, that's not bad. For one thing, he argued, such stories let children know that there are monstrous people in the world. Not everyone is a loving mother or father. Second, Bettelheim claimed, these stories serve to assure children that *their own* savage impulses are not unique, not aberrations, but are part of what all people have. That is, these stories serve the useful purpose of introducing children to the dark side of life. According to Bettelheim, children need to see that there are such impulses and need to learn how to handle them so that they may act maturely.

If you reread Jones's essay, you will hear plenty of Bettelheim. In the first paragraph Jones tells us that his parents insulated him from the real world of violence and that he "suffocated [his] deepest fears and desires under a nice-boy persona." In the fourth paragraph he tells us that he was "freed" by the image of the Hulk, who was an image of his own "stifled rage and buried desire for power." Jones claims to have seen something of his own history repeated in the life of his son. In the eleventh paragraph Jones says:

> Pretending to have superhuman powers helps children conquer the feelings of powerlessness that inevitably come with being so young and small.

We have not taught this essay, but we think that one good way to handle it is to ask students if parts or all of it rings true to their experience. They might then be asked to write an analysis of violence in media (or in one medium), drawing on their own experience but using a rather more academic style than Jones uses.

Justin Cronin

Confessions of a Liberal Gun Owner (p. 203)

We address, in sequence, the topics that we set forth in the book.

1. Cronin's title—rather than our imagined title of "Confessions of a Texas Gun Owner"—offers an engaging surprise. Gun owners in Texas presumably are not a rare species, but liberal gun owners are. In short, Cronin's title contains a hook, something that snares the reader's attention, whereas our invented alternative invites the response of "Ho hum, so what's new?"

2. Why so much autobiography? Because Cronin, in effect, is offering an essay based chiefly on one big—indeed, life-changing—experience, rather than an essay based largely on thinking analytically while sitting at desk, the sort of argumentative essay that would include statements such as "The three principle arguments in

favor of. . . ," and "On the other hand, we can counter the first of these arguments by offering two objections. . . ," and so forth.

3. Our view (based exclusively on our reading of the essay) is that Cronin is a very engaging guy, a good teacher, and a good colleague. He is earnest, clear, respectful of other ideas, and so on.

4. What *arguments* does he offer? Here, alas, we get uneasy. He does a good job of telling us how he came to feel the way he feels—but does he convince his readers that his position is sound? Because he does not much concern himself with setting forth and refuting opposing views, or offering anything in the way of statistics, we think that the skeptical reader probably remains skeptical. And there is a further problem: The life-changing experience that he reports (his decision to arm himself) is based on something that did *not* happen: He assures us (para. 11) that "chaos" would have occurred if the storm had hit Houston. But the storm did not hit Houston, and Cronin therefore cannot point to chaos—and the consequent need for a gun. Doubtless he could have called attention to other cities that have experienced looting, and these instances might have provided support for the argument that law-abiding folks need guns to protect their families—but he does not provide such evidence (e.g., statistics about looting after the flood in New Orleans), and we think this omission weakens his essay.

5. To this question (What would you say to a reader who told you that he or she didn't quite get Cronin's essay?) we offer no response—because, as we have just indicated, we are puzzled by Cronin's strategy of building an argument largely on something that did not happen. We will be interested in the responses of students.

6. Cronin in paragraph 13 sets forth his credentials as a liberal (he favors gun regulation, and he "loathes" the NRA), in effect reaffirming the strategy of his title and of his first paragraph. Still, it would have been interesting (and we think it would have been more convincing) if he had indicated exactly what sort of regulation he favors.

7. The comment that a short paragraph is usually an *underdeveloped* paragraph is true for analytic paragraphs (i.e., for most paragraphs in most argumentative essays) but of course is not true for some other kinds of paragraphs, and certainly not for all paragraphs in an essay that is largely biographical, as here, where Cronin reports the responses of a gun instructor and of his sixteen-year-old daughter. The paragraphs are especially effective partly *because* they are so short; they are packed with dynamite.

Peter Singer

Animal Liberation (p. 207)

This essay is an earlier version of text that became the opening chapter of Peter Singer's remarkably influential *Animal Liberation: A New Ethics for Our Treatment of Animals* (1975). In his book, Singer elaborates on all his basic ideas, and especially "speciesism" (para. 18), to which he devotes a whole chapter.

Speciesism is the arbitrary favorable preference for members of our own species, and its logical consequence is an equally arbitrary but indifferent or hostile attitude toward lower species. Whether the analogy to racism, sexism, and other -*isms* is as instructive as Singer implies is another matter. In any case, he argues (para. 19) that the "case for Animal Liberation" does not depend on the analogy.

What, then, is animal liberation? Singer never says in so many words (see para. 3), but it amounts to, or at least can be stated as, a series of dos and don'ts: Don't kill animals to eat their flesh or to clothe your body, don't experiment on animals to save human lives or to reduce human misery, don't remove animals from their natural habitat. In short, don't treat animals as you would not like to be treated yourself.

Singer's opening paragraph is a model for the use of analogy to gain the high ground right from the start. Each of his readers will be able to identify with one or another of the groups he mentions that has been discriminated against in the past and so is immediately but unwittingly vulnerable to the "expansion of our moral horizons" about to unfold.

Singer worries (para. 12; our question 3) whether having intentions is necessarily, albeit mysteriously, connected with having the capacity to use language. We doubt that it is, and he does, too. Surely anyone who spends time with dogs and cats readily ascribes intentions to them ("He's trying to catch the stick when you throw it," "She's waiting to pounce on the mouse as soon as it moves"), and this use of intentional thinking is no more anthropomorphic than is ascribing intentions to other people. To insist that the latter is intelligible but the former isn't, because other people can speak a language whereas animals can't, pretty obviously begs the question. To insist that no creature can have an intention unless it can state what its intentions are is far too broad a thesis to defend; it would entail insisting that many human creatures do not have intentions, or act intentionally, when we believe they do. And so even if animals can't use language, because they lack the capacity, they may yet have minds enough to warrant a concern about how we intentionally treat them.

On what grounds does Singer base drawing the line where he does to demark the creatures that deserve our concern from those that don't? Why not draw the line elsewhere, particularly at the point that divides the living from the nonliving (not dead but inorganic or inert)? It wouldn't be at all satisfactory for Singer to answer: "Because I talk about creatures that can feel, and I don't about those that can't," although this reading seems to be true. But this can't be his answer because he does not want his argument to turn to who cares about what; he knows that most of us simply do not and will not easily come to care about animal welfare. A better line for him to take would be to refer to the *interests* of creatures and to the *equality* of their interests (para. 6), on the ground that only creatures with a capacity to suffer have interests, the first and foremost of which is to diminish their own suffering, pain, and discomfort. But on closer inspection, is it not still true that *all living* things have interests? Surely, a dogwood tree in the front yard has an interest in air, water, sunlight, and space to grow, even if it feels no pain when it is denied these things or when its leaves are plucked or—heaven forfend!—its branches slashed. To reason in this manner is to tie the concept of having an interest in something to the concept of something being good for a thing (water is surely good for a plant). But this is not what Singer does; rather, he ties a creature's interests to what it can feel. (See how he handles the case of the year-old infant in para. 15.)

When one goes in the other direction, as some have (for example, Christopher Stone, in *Should Trees Have Standing?* [1988]), a whole environmental ethic begins to unfold, but with alarming consequences, for even all but the most scrupulous vegetarian will neglect and even ruthlessly violate the interests of other living entities.

If we enlarge our moral community to include plants as well as animals—because all living entities have interests and because one interest is as good as another "from the point of view of the universe" (the criterion proposed by the utilitarian Henry Sidgwick, which Singer invokes in his *Animal Liberation*)—what will our moral principles permit us to eat? Not much, perhaps only unfruitful food, such as some of the surfeit of seeds and nuts produced by plants, and dead flesh, perhaps including even human flesh (our question 10). Killing to eat may be entirely ruled out, but eating what is dead isn't unless one appeals to some other moral principles besides the utilitarian notions Singer relies on.

This discussion can be put into an argument of this form: Because we have to eat to live, either we eat things that have interests or we don't. If we do, then we violate the equal interests of other creatures and thus act immorally. If we don't, then we can't kill living plants to eat them, any more than we can kill living animals to eat them. Instead, our survival depends on eating dropped fruit and seeds and carrion. Some readers will regard this argument as a reductio ad absurdum of Singer's position. Others will argue that it shows how difficult it is to formulate moral principles that we can really live by consistently and self-consciously.

Although persons who in journals debate with Singer often say that he subscribes to "animal rights," Singer has repeatedly denied that he believes that animals have "rights." Setting forth his disagreement with Tom Regan's *The Case for Animal Rights* (1983), Singer discusses the point at some length in the *New York Review of Books* (January 17, 1985, pp. 46–52). In a letter in the issue of April 25, 1985 (p. 57), he reaffirms his point. Singer explains that his view is utilitarian; he grants that conceivably there would be circumstances in which an experiment on an animal stands to reduce human suffering so much that it would be permissible to carry it out even if it involved some harm to the animal. (This would be true, he says in his letter of April 25, 1985, even if the animal were a human being.) In this letter he explains that, as a utilitarian, he advocates stopping animal experiments because

1. The suffering of an immense number of animals would be spared,
2. "The benefits lost would be uncertain," and
3. "The incentive thus provided for the speedy development of alternative methods of conducting research [would be] the most powerful imaginable."

Singer's essay, as we say in our headnote in the text, was first published in 1973 in the *New York Review of Books.* In the issue of May 15, 2003, Singer published, again in the *New York Review of Books,* "Animal Liberation at Thirty," a review of the state of the argument. His new essay makes special mention of the following books: Roger Scruton, *Animal Rights and Wrongs* (London: Metro, 1998); Paola Cavalieri, *The Animal Question: Why Non-human Animals Deserve Human Rights* (Oxford: Oxford University Press, 2001); David DeGrazia, *Taking Animals Seriously: Mental Life and Moral Status* (Cambridge: Cambridge University Press, 1996); Matthew Scully, *Dominion: The Power of Man, Suffering of Animals, and the Call to Mercy* (New York: St. Martin's, 2002).

We considered using the new piece instead of the first piece, but we finally decided that the first piece is much better for our use (the basic argument is set forward with few distractions), whereas in the recent piece Singer tries to take account of numerous questions and developments. But anyone—teacher or student—doing further work on this topic will want to consult the new essay.

Jonathan Swift

A Modest Proposal (p. 220)

Unlike Brady's essay, where the title in conjunction with the author's name immediately alerts the reader that the essay cannot be taken straight, Swift's essay does not provide an obvious clue right away. In fact, some students don't perceive the irony until it is pointed out to them. Such imperceptiveness is entirely understandable. Swift's language is somewhat remote from twenty-first-century language, and in any case students don't expect satire in a collection of arguments. Moreover, it's hard today to know when a projector (the eighteenth-century name for someone with a bright idea) is kidding. A student who has not understood that "A Modest Proposal" is a satire may be extremely embarrassed upon learning the truth in public. To avoid this possibility, we usually begin the discussion by talking about Swift as a satirist who is known chiefly through *Gulliver's Travels,* and so on.

Most commentators on "A Modest Proposal" have concentrated on the persona of the speaker—his cool use of statistics, his way of regarding human beings as beasts ("a child just dropped from its dam" in para. 4, for example, or his reference to wives as "breeders" in para. 6), and, in short, his unawareness of the monstrosity of his plan to turn the children into "sound, useful members of the commonwealth" (para. 2), a plan that, by destroying children, will supposedly make the proposer "a preserver of the nation" (para. 2). Much of this complacent insensitivity and even craziness is apparent—on rereading—fairly early, as in the odd reference (para. 1) to "three, four, or six children" (what happened to five?), or, for that matter, in the phrases already quoted from paragraph 2. And of course it is true that one object of Swift's attack is the persona, a figure who, despite his profession that he is rational, practical, and compassionate, perhaps can be taken as an emblem of English indifference to Irish humanity. (But the speaker is an Irishman, not an Englishman.) More specifically, the leading object of attack can be said to be political reformers, especially those who heartlessly bring statistics ("I calculate," "I have reckoned," "I have already computed") where humane feelings should rule.

It is less often perceived, however, that the satire is also directed against the Irish themselves, with whom Swift was, by this time, fed up. *Satire* is almost too mild a word for the vehemence of "savage indignation" (Swift's own epitaph refers to his *saeva indignatio*) with which Swift denounces the Irish. Yes, he in effect says, the English treat the Irish abominably, but the Irish take no reasonable steps to help themselves. Even in so small a detail as the proposer's observation that his plan would cause husbands to stop beating pregnant wives (para. 26), we hear criticism not of the English but of the Irish. The chief denunciation of the Irish is evident, however, in the passage beginning with paragraph 29, in which Swift lists the "other expedients" that indeed the Irish themselves could (but do not) undertake to alleviate their plight.

In short, commentators who see Swift's essay simply as a scathing indictment of English hardheartedness are missing much of the point. One can almost go so far as to say that Swift's satire against the projector is directed not only against his impracticality and his unconscious cruelty but also against his folly in trying to help a nation that, out of stupidity and vanity, obstinately refuses to help itself. The projector sees the Irish as mere flesh; Swift at this time apparently saw them as something more exasperating, flesh that is stupid and vain. Swift was, we think, more than half in earnest when he had his crazy projector say, "I desire the reader will observe, that I calculate my remedy for this one individual kingdom of Ireland and for no other that was, is, or, I think ever can be upon earth."

If you wish students to do some research, you can ask them to look at Swift's "Irish Tracts" (*Prose Works*, ed. Herbert Davis, 12: 1–90, especially *Intelligencer* 19: 54–61), where they will find Swift arguing for the "other expedients" that his projector dismisses.

Related points:

1. This essay has ample material to demonstrate the use of the method that Aristotle calls "the ethical proof," that is, the pleader's use of his or her ethical character to persuade an audience. (Of course, here it backfires: We soon see a monster, not a benevolist.) Thus, in paragraph 1, the author shows his moral sensibility in using such expressions as "melancholy object" and "helpless infants." Also relevant is the projector's willingness to listen to other views—which he then of course always complacently rejects. (One might ask students to examine this issue through the eyes of Carl Rogers, who in his essay in Chapter 10 of the text urges writers to regard the views of the opposition sympathetically, not merely as points to be dismissed.)

2. A scattering of anti–Roman Catholic material (for example, references to "papists") indicates that the speaker, for all his insistence on his objectivity, is making a prejudiced appeal to emotions.

3. Instructors interested in satiric techniques will probably want to call attention to Swift's abundant use of diminution, such as people reduced to animals and to statistics.

Additional Topics for Critical Thinking and Writing

1. Drawing only on the first three paragraphs, write a brief characterization (probably three or four sentences) of the speaker—that is, of the persona whom Swift invents. Do not talk about Swift the author; talk only about the anonymous speaker of these three paragraphs. Support your assertions by quoting words or phrases from the paragraphs.

2. In an essay of 150–250 words, characterize the speaker of "A Modest Proposal," and explain how Swift creates this character. You may want to make use of your answer to the previous question, pointing out that at first we think such-and-such, but later, picking up clues that Swift provides, we begin to think thus-and-so. You may wish, also, to devote a few sentences to the last paragraph of Swift's essay.

3. What is the speaker arguing for? What is Swift arguing for?

4. Write a modest proposal of your own, suggesting a solution to some great social problem. Obvious topics include war, crime, and racism, but choose any topic that almost all people agree is a great evil. Do not choose a relatively controversial topic such as gay rights, vivisection, gun control, or right-to-work laws. Your proposed solution should be, like Swift's, outrageous, but your essay should not be silly. In the essay, you should satirize some identifiable way of thinking.

5. Following the same basic assignment as the previous one, this time write an essay on a topic that is controversial and about which you have strong feelings.

6
Developing an Argument of Your Own (p. 228)

In this chapter we try to help students get and develop ideas, chiefly by urging them (1) to ask themselves questions, (2) to write and rewrite, (3) to think of their audience as their collaborator, and (4) to submit drafts to peers for review. We think instructors will agree with us on the value of these practices. The trick is to convince students that even those who are pretty good writers will profit by working along these lines and, similarly, that even those who have difficulty writing *can* write interesting and effective papers if they make use of these suggestions.

All writers have their own methods of writing. Some can write only with a pen, whereas others can write only with a word processor; Balzac believed he needed the smell of rotten apples to stimulate his pen. Still, allowing for individual needs, we think it is honest to tell students that, in general, the sooner they begin an assignment, and the more they think about it and put their thoughts into notes and drafts, the better their essay will be. In an effort to make this point, we give in the text Emily Andrews's preliminary notes and second thoughts, as well as the final version of her essay.

Emily Andrews (student essay)

Why I Don't Spare "Spare Change" (p. 264)

As our comments in the text indicate, we think the essay is an effective piece of writing, but you may disagree, and you may want students to discuss its strengths and weaknesses and perhaps even to write a critical analysis or a response.

7
Using Sources (p. 267)

In our teaching, we try to inculcate the idea that the "research paper" is not a genre found only in the land of Freshman English or even in the larger realm of College Writing but is something that flourishes (under different descriptions, of course) wherever writing is required. That is, we try to help students to see that when, say, one writes a letter to a school newspaper, complaining that a coach has been fired, one first does (or ought to do) a little homework, finding out the won-lost record to strengthen the letter. And of course almost all reports written for businesses require research.

Students are more likely to work enthusiastically on their papers if they understand that using sources is an activity in which all literate people sometimes engage. In fact, students engage in research all the time, for instance, when they consult a book of baseball statistics or a catalog of recordings or when they talk with friends to find out what courses they should take next semester.

To give students some practice in finding materials (and in learning something), you might ask them to produce a bibliography of recent writings on, say, pornography, racist speech, or euthanasia, with summaries of two or three articles.

Part Three

FURTHER VIEWS ON ARGUMENT

8
A Philosopher's View:
The Toulmin Model (p. 337)

Of the many attempts by philosophers in recent decades to explain the logic of ordinary argumentation—and to do so in a manner that the general reader (especially undergraduates and faculty not trained in formal logic) can grasp—none has been as well received as the work of Stephen Toulmin. Toulmin began his career at Cambridge at the end of Ludwig Wittgenstein's tenure there as a professor and for many years was on the philosophy faculty of the University of Southern California.

Why Toulmin's model of argumentation should have proved so popular where others have failed is not entirely clear to us. No doubt his reputation as a philosopher among philosophers has helped; but that is hardly the whole story because few philosophers teach informal logic and fewer still use his book *The Uses of Argument* (1958, 1969) to do it. Surely his desire to avoid forcing every kind of argument into some version of an Aristotelian syllogism is attractive. Perhaps it is mostly that the six-step model he offers with its untechnical nomenclature ("claim," "ground," and so on) is relatively more user-friendly than what the competition has to offer. Whatever the explanation, we think instructors using this book, especially those making their first acquaintance with Toulmin's method here, will find it rewarding to study (if not also to teach).

9
A Logician's View:
Deduction, Induction, Fallacies (p. 349)

The purpose of this chapter is to develop at somewhat greater length the tools of reasoning introduced in Chapter 3. Here, in a few dozen pages, we divide the subject into three natural and familiar parts: deductive reasoning, inductive reasoning, and fallacious reasoning.

To take them in reverse order, we identify and illustrate eighteen fallacies. The list can be extended; for example, in the latest edition of his standard textbook, *With Good Reason,* 6th ed. (2004), S. Morris Engel identifies and discusses a dozen more. Few instructors will want to introduce their students to all the fallacies that we discuss; but we would hope that instructors would find it useful to dwell on a few from time to time. Here, we want to mention a popular fallacy (of the sort that logicians call "formal") that does not appear in our text or in Engel's textbook: the fallacy of *denying the antecedent.*

Consider this argument:

1. If it's raining, then the streets will be wet.

2. It isn't raining.

3. Therefore, the streets aren't wet.

This argument has the obvious form: if p then q; not p; therefore not q. The trouble is that this argument form is invalid; to see why, just consider the example above. Surely, it is possible the streets *are* wet—for example, a catch basin overflowed, the street cleaners flushed down the street—despite no rain at all. This argument is invalid because of its form, and we cannot trust any argument of this form. It has a related invalid argument form that is almost equally popular; its name is *affirming the consequent,* and this is its form: if p, then q; q; therefore, p. We leave it to your imagination to see why this form of argument is also invalid.

A large fraction (we cannot be more precise) of our daily reasoning is inductive, and to the few pages in Chapter 3 devoted to this topic we have added seven or eight more pages in this chapter. In the following pages, our aim is to take a couple of examples (involving fatality, or the risk thereof, caused by smoking) as the skeleton on which to hang our discussion of evidence, observation, inference, probability, confirmation, and related concepts essential to inductive reasoning. Brief though our discussion is, we think that at a minimum it should help instructors make these important concepts more accessible and usable by students and thus add to their available tools for diagnosing and constructing arguments.

Finally, we begin the chapter with a discussion of deduction, amplifying what we offered as a bare-bones introduction in Chapter 3. Here we offer another dozen terms (*dilemma, hypothetical syllogism,* and so on) that are standard vocabulary for the discussion of formal deductive reasoning. Some instructors may find it useful to work their way through our discussion with their students in class (perhaps in conjunction with the parallel material found in Chapter 3). Most instructors, we suspect, will find this material of use mainly for occasional reference. All (at least all instructors) can profit to greater or lesser degree merely by (carefully) reading these pages once over.

Exercise: Fallacies—or Not? (p. 381)

1. Abortion might be said to be a form of prenatal homicide—the killing of an unborn human being—but not murder, since the human embryo and fetus are months away from being a person. The fallacy is using a term (*murder*) that connotes the death of a person when no person is present in a prenatal homicide.

2. We think that it does matter whether the person in question is dying in any case, and whether he or she is suffering pain, especially pain that cannot be controlled by drugs.

3. The fallacy here is arguing for a general rule on the basis of a sample of one.

4. Invoking a right to listen whenever and to whatever you want is silly; the fallacy here is that there is no such right in the first place.

5. The comment suggests that it's better to be selfish and safe than altruistic at some personal risk. But is it really better? Better according to what standard or criterion? We side with the Good Samaritan, not with his selfish critic.

6. The epigram comes from American history out west in the 1870s. The fallacy here is tacitly recommending a violent course of action when dealing with strangers—or foreign nations—that is, assuming without any evidence that you cannot trust whoever knocks on your door.

7. There really isn't any fallacy here; the three generalizations are often invoked because they sum briefly the truth of the matter.

8. No fallacy here, either.

9. The fallacy here is inferring from dozens of suicide leaps off the bridge that there is no other or better way to prevent such acts than by closing the bridge down.

10. The fallacy here, from a practical point of view, is that there is little in common between the Japanese American claim for reparations and the current claim by African Americans for reparations. The Japanese American community in 1942 was well defined and relatively small in number, and calculating its losses was not an insuperable task. In all three respects, the situation with today's African Americans is different.

11. This is controversial, but we think that the statement is essentially correct. True, trees and stones do not bleed, whereas dogs and cats, as well as wild animals, do, and they also can feel pain. For some, following the lead of the great Jeremy Bentham, these feelings—pleasure and pain—are all that matters. One of us thinks otherwise. Human rights take their origin from the way they connect with distinctive capacities that only humans (so far) are known to have, chief among which is a sense of self. (The other of us has kept as many as four dogs at once. He holds a different view.)

12. The fallacy here is treating a mathematical average carried to one decimal point as though it were a whole number, in this case a number of children. For example, suppose there were 15 children whose ages sum to 45. The average age of the children is 45 divided by 15, or 3—a whole number. But suppose the ages of the 15 children sum to 42. Now the average is 2.8—not the number of children in any family.

13. The fallacy here is the same as the one we met in item 3.

14. It is possible to do as the Red Queen does, verdict first and evidence later. But you couldn't run a criminal justice system following this rule. The fallacy here is treating verdict and evidence as though the order or sequence in which they are carried out doesn't matter to the outcome of the trial, when of course it usually does. This rule violates a fundamental rule of criminal law, namely, that the accused has

a right to see the evidence being used against him, except after the trial is over, at which point giving the defendant access to the evidence against him is largely no longer of interest.

15. What counts as an "adequate reason" to believe that the moon has a back side when no such thing could be seen? Notice that the issue here is not whether the moon is spherical. Eclipses surely suggest that it has a circular (even if not spherical) shape. A spherical back side is surely a possibility. Since the issue is not whether you can rule out any particular shape for a back side, it seems reasonable to assume that the moon has some sort of back side, just as every three-dimensional object does.

16. The fallacy here is thinking of alcoholism as a highly likely outcome from steadily increasing the consumption of alcohol. It all depends on the dosage and the frequency. We can easily imagine cases of this sort; they turn on the volume and strength of the alcohol being imbibed. And because volume and frequency of consumption are relevant to the onset of alcoholism, we can equally imagine cases where no such addiction develops, because the dosage is small and the frequency moderate.

17. The big Indian is the mother of the little Indian.

18. This is the notorious gambler's fallacy, also known as the Monte Carlo fallacy. If you toss a coin fifteen times and each time the coin comes up heads, or comes up tails, or alternates heads and tails, you are probably dealing with some kind of unfair coin. If you toss a fair coin, the odds are 50-50 that it will come up heads. Since the heads-or-tails behavior of a fair coin has no effect on the *next* toss, the a priori probability of a coin coming up heads on the next toss is again 50-50, that is, identical to the a priori probability of the coin coming up tails. The fallacy is to think that the outcome of the current toss of a fair coin has some effect on the outcome of the next toss, and so on indefinitely, when it doesn't.

19. Well, in a lighthearted mood, one might agree; perhaps a bit of exercise each Sunday morning would be good for what ails one. But the reply of the loyal churchgoer will be that we have spiritual needs, too, and they cannot be served by walking or jogging. The fallacy, if there is one, is to think that physical needs are more important than spiritual ones, when a reasonable person might seek ways to satisfy both kinds of needs.

20. The fallacy here is ad hominem, acting as though a person's political affiliations govern all the beliefs and behavior of that person. Perhaps they do, but that is highly unlikely.

21. The fallacy here is post hoc, ergo propter hoc ("after this, therefore because of this"). For all we know, the terrorists have backed off, but not because our defense systems are so good. Perhaps they have run out of large sums of cash to buy weapons and finance attacks. Perhaps the supply of suicidal terrorists has declined. Perhaps they are thinking up new attacks that they will unleash in the next few weeks or months. And so on.

22. Well, just how reliable are press releases from the White House these days? Can we trust whatever they tell us? Surely, caution is advised. Pretty clearly, anyone who argues in this manner is committing the fallacy of appeal to authority, and also is arguing in a circle—offering as evidence the very issue that is to be proved. The statement comes down to this: You can trust them because they are trustworthy.

23. True, the theory of evolution so far cannot explain how life began. But perhaps in time it will, or perhaps some entirely new theory will supersede natural selection in the spirit of Darwin. In any case, it is an empirical question just how much Darwinism can explain. There is no reason to think that the failure, so far, of

natural selection to explain the origin of life is a reason for believing that intelligent design is the best or the only other explanation.

24. We are not devotees of Serrano's career, and we think the title he chose, *Piss Christ*, is in the worst possible taste. But there is no fallacy, certainly not any obvious one, on which to hang such a judgment. Given that the image (it is a photograph) exists (or did exist), we can imagine many who would like to see it if only to make a judgment of its worth for themselves. As for public funding, we are not deeply troubled by using a tiny portion of federal tax revenues to support the project; we do, however, find it difficult to see how Serrano's photograph could win out against any serious competition for public support. But let the panel of judges for such competitions decide on the merits.

25. We think the statement is true—but we would go further. Thomas should have expected more evidence before he believed his eyes. To settle the question in his mind—viz., is this man the resurrected Jesus of Nazareth, the Son of God—more evidence than a few scars on the man's body is required. After all, we are talking about one of the greatest miracle stories of western civilization, and it is difficult to overestimate the evidence it is reasonable to require. The fallacy, if any, lies in Thomas's willingness to believe on the strength of the slender evidence before him.

26. One way to read this narrative is to judge the baseball player guilty of the fallacy of post hoc, ergo propter hoc, which we have seen earlier in item 21.

27. This is an old Yankee saying, but it's not much of a dilemma. If it's a small hole, you could fix it in the rain, provided the rain is not too heavy. Better still, you could fix it on a day of good weather, knowing that it will rain sometime in the future, even if not soon, and that it's better to fix the hole than to leave it, even if doing so interrupts something you'd rather do, like working in the garden or watching the Patriots on their way to another Super Bowl victory. The fallacy here is thinking there is a serious dilemma when there isn't.

28. Because there's a better explanation. What we are witnessing is what sailors call a ship hull down on the horizon. The hull disappears from view as the ship moves steadily away from the pier (or shore) and at right angles to the beach (or shore), and so on with ever taller parts of the ship until the entire ship is lost to view. But no sinking is involved—though of course it might be involved. It's just very unlikely.

29. *Proves* in this familiar saying means "tests" (cf. the related noun, *proof*, when we speak of a photographic *proof* or when we say, "The proof of the pudding is in the eating"). Surely testing a rule by looking for exceptions is an important aspect of scientific reasoning. The fallacy lies in misunderstanding what *proves* means in this context.

30. Herbivores eat fruit and vegetable matter. Herbs such as oregano, thyme, rosemary, sage, and the rest do not form the diet of any herbivores, so far as we know. Perhaps the reason is that herbs tend to grow on small plants, whereas your standard herbivores—elephants, hippopotami—feast on large leaves.

31. First, the text of the ad is ambiguous. Does it mean "More doctors smoke Camels than smoke any other cigarette" or does it mean "More doctors smoke Camels than all the doctors who smoke other cigarettes plus all those who abstain from smoking"? The former version is probably what is meant. In any case, there is an appeal to authority implicit in the caption. Who am I to argue with doctors; if they prefer Camels, I should at least try a pack and see how I like them. Besides, if doctors prefer Camels, then surely these cigarettes must be safe to smoke whether or not others are equally safe. (All nonsense.)

32. Killing five to save one is absurd on its face—unless, of course, the five are hardened criminals and the one is a Nobel Prize–winning scientist. The really

tempting alternative is killing one to save five. This version violates the Kantian principle that one should never use a person as a means to serve the ends of other persons—in this case, the desire of the five to survive. Of course, if the one consents to being used by the five for their survival, that's another matter altogether. Morality respects sacrifice; it does not demand it. We cannot lodge a complaint if no one volunteers to be sacrificed. If the right to life means anything at all, it means that the many have no right to take the life of the one, since to do so violates the right to life of the one. There is, of course, much more to be said. Some of that more can be found in the slender volume by Hugo Bedau, *Making Mortal Choices: Three Exercises in Moral Casuistry* (1997).

Max Shulman

Love Is a Fallacy (p. 383)

There are lots of laughs here, but the piece *does* teach effectively; students are more likely to remember Max Shulman's discussion of fallacies than ours. One can also use the story — especially the first paragraph—to talk about style. Read the first sentence aloud in class ("Cool was I and logical") and ask students what sorts of expectations are set up. Most will see that he *must* be kidding. And so on through the paragraph, to "And—think of it!—I was only eighteen."

We urge you to assign this story.

10
A Psychologist's View:
Rogerian Argument (p. 392)

Carl R. Rogers

Communication: Its Blocking and Its Facilitation (p. 394)

An occasional student has told us that Carl R. Rogers is "merely trying to apply psychology" to outwit his opponent, but we believe this interpretation is mistaken. Rogers was much concerned with reducing tension so that issues could be more easily discussed, not with deceiving the parties involved. Still, it is easy to see how students might think that "psychology" is a weapon to be wielded—something akin to bluffing at poker—in order to win. We are reminded of the advice that an old actor gave to a young one: "The most important thing is sincerity. When you can fake *that*, you can do anything."

It's not hard to find comments about argument that come close to the actor's view. Consider, for instance, Samuel Butler's "It is not he who gains the exact point in dispute who scores most in controversy, but he who has shown the most forbearance and the better temper." Or Lord Chesterfield's advice to his son: "If you would convince others, seem open to conviction yourself." But Butler's concern with scoring most and Chesterfield's use of *seem* (as opposed to *be*) set their comments sharply apart from Rogers's. Similarly, consider Ben Franklin: "Those disputing, contradicting, and confuting people are generally unfortunate in their affairs. They get victory, sometimes, but they never get good will, which be of more use to them." Rogers would probably agree, but he would rightly claim that he is not concerned with gaining goodwill so that it will be of "use" to him; he is concerned with helping the world to achieve peace.

Much closer to Rogers than Butler, Chesterfield, or Franklin is Pascal: "When we wish to correct with advantage, and to show another that he errs, we must notice from what side he views the matter, for on that side it is usually true." Close—but still short of Rogers's view, since Rogers recognizes that the other side not only may be right from its own point of view but may indeed be right enough so that we can come to accept at least part of that point of view. Consider these key statements:

> The whole task of psychotherapy is the task of dealing with a failure in communication. (para. 1)

> If you really understand another person in this way, if you are willing to enter his private world and see the way life appears to him, without any attempt to make evaluative judgments, you run the risk of being changed yourself. You might see it his way, you might find yourself influenced in your attitudes or your personality. (para. 11)

We imagine that most people would agree with Rogers in theory, but some opposing voices have been heard. For us, the most telling objection is that Rogers speaks as a white male—that is, as a member of the group that for centuries has done most of the speaking and has done very little listening. His advice—in effect, "Calm down, listen to me, and see things from my point of view"—is good advice for people like Rogers but is less useful (we have heard it said) for women, gays and lesbians, blacks, Hispanics, and other marginalized people. Some members of these groups say that they have listened long enough, and that it is now their turn to speak out and to speak out forcefully. Let straight, white males, they argue, do the listening for a change.

One other point must be made about Rogerian argument. Rogers was talking about *talking,* about people who are actually facing their hearers. But instructors who use our book are for the most part concerned with *writing,* and they may wonder if Rogers's essay is relevant to writers. We offer two short answers: (1) Assign and discuss the essay, and (2) urge students to make use of the checklist in the text (p. 400) when they write their next essays. We think that if students read the essay and pay attention to the checklist, they not only will write better essays but also may become better people.

Edward O. Wilson

Letter to a Southern Baptist Minister (p. 400)

When students read an essay, they are inevitably concerned chiefly with the content of the argument rather than with the essayist's strategies, but here and there in our text we urge students to study an essayist's *ways* of arguing. That is, we urge them to see how the writer is conducting the argument. We give Wilson's essay in this chapter not because we are especially concerned with his views of God or, for that matter, of nature, but because we want students to see how he goes about talking to—well, we can put it bluntly—the opposition. And this will be our concern here.

The opening paragraph in effect offers a warm, hearty handshake. In the very first sentence Wilson says, "I feel I know you well enough to call you friend." In the second sentence he says that "we grew up in the same faith," and in the third he is a bit more specific: "I went under the water." In other words, Wilson, like the pastor whom he addresses, was baptized. (Not all students will understand "I went under the water.") In the fourth sentence he confesses that he no longer is a believer, but in this very sentence he goes on to express confidence that if he and his reader speak of their "deepest beliefs," it will be "in a spirit of mutual respect and good will." After all, he goes on to say, assuring his reader, not only are they both Americans but they are Southerners, people who share a code of "civility and good manners." Wilson has certainly made every effort to ingratiate himself. Only the most churlish reader would refuse to listen to what Wilson has to say.

Paragraph 2: Wilson begins, "I write to you now for your counsel and help." Well, what reader (or listener) would refuse to offer advice and help to this nice man who says he needs our assistance? Wilson then goes on to sketch his reader's central views.

Paragraph 3: Wilson begins, by way of contrast, with a sketch of his own views, which of course differ sharply from his supposed auditor's.

Paragraph 5: Wilson asserts that the "difference in worldview" does not separate the two men in all things, and he goes on to say that both of them value "security, freedom of choice, personal dignity, and a cause to believe in that is larger than ourselves." This last belief is especially important: "A cause . . . that is larger than ourselves" has a vaguely religious sound that is not present in "freedom of choice."

Paragraph 6: The paragraph begins, "Let us see, then, if we can, and you are willing, to meet." Again we hear the earnest expression of a desire to share, to work things out courteously.

Paragraph 7: After "Pastor, we need your help," Wilson says, "The Creation—living Nature—is in deep trouble." Notice—and we think this is very important—that Wilson uses a capital letter for "Creation." We think the use of a capital is important because it is our guess that his auditor might use a capital letter in speaking of "the Creator." That is, Wilson is doing all that he possibly can do to establish common ground, to speak the language of his auditor.

It would be very easy to proceed through the essay in this fashion, but it is unnecessary; so let's jump to paragraph 14, which Wilson begins thus:

To make the point in good Gospel manner, let me tell the story of a young man newly trained for the ministry, and so fixed in his Christian faith that he referred all questions of morality to readings from the Bible.

Again, in his reference to "good Gospel manner," Wilson reminds us that he was brought up as a churchgoer—remember, in his first paragraph he said that he "went under the water"—and he then goes on to offer the surprising information that the young man of the story was Charles Darwin, in 1832. The next paragraph quotes from Darwin in 1859, speaking of "grandeur," and of something "breathed into a few forms or into one." We take it that Darwin's "breathed into" evokes Genesis 2:7, "And the Lord God formed man of the dust of the ground, and breathed into his nostrils the breath of life. And man became a living soul." Darwin was doing his best to imply that his vision had its affinities with the Judeo-Christian vision, and that's what Wilson is also doing, for instance, in his seventeenth paragraph, where he speaks of Darwin's "*reverence* (emphasis ours) for life."

The essay concludes with the assertion that Wilson and his Christian reader "have a common purpose," at least concerning the "life-and-death issue" of the future of the planet. It's all very Rogerian.

11

A Rhetorician's View: Rhetorical Analysis of Nontraditional Texts (p. 404)

Unfortunately, today in ordinary speech, the word *rhetoric* is chiefly used with negative connotations, in such phrases as "empty rhetoric," "mere rhetoric," and "rhetoric, not action." On the other hand, criticism of rhetoric is hardly new: In ancient times, Plato criticized the Sophists for pretty much the same reason that some people today criticize "rhetoric," that is, that it allegedly is divorced from truth and is used chiefly for deceptive purposes.

The high view of rhetoric of course is very different: It is (as we several times say in the text) both (1) an *instrument for discovering truth* and then (2) an instrument for propagating the truth by means of persuasive devices, and thus it is an art or a skill that every responsible citizen should possess. As teachers of argumentative writing, we subscribe to this high view.

Here are two quotations affirming the high value of rhetoric:

Histories make men wise; poets, witty; the mathematics, subtle; natural philosophy, deep, moral, grave; logic and rhetoric, able to contend.

Francis Bacon (1561–1626)

The design of Rhetoric is to remove those Prejudices that lie in the way of Truth; to Reduce the Passions to the Government of Reasons; to place our Subject in a Right Light, and excite our Hearers to a due consideration of it.

Mary Astell (1666–1731)

This chapter is especially concerned with providing students with tools that enable them to analyze twenty-first-century forms of argument, for example, electronic communications.

12
A Literary Critic's View:
Arguing about Literature (p. 420)

Classroom discussion usually centers on the meaning of a work, and almost always some-one raises the question, "Do you really think that's what the author intended?" But ever since the publication of W. K. Wimsatt Jr. and Monroe C. Beardsley's "The Intentional Fallacy," *Sewanee Review* 54 (Summer 1946), conveniently reprinted in W. K. Wimsatt Jr.'s *The Verbal Icon* (1954), it has been impossible (we think) to talk easily about the author's intention.

To begin with, most authors have not in any explicit way set forth their inten-tions: We have, for example, *Hamlet,* but not Shakespeare's comment on his intention in the drama. Nevertheless, students may say that if an author has stated what he or she intended, we should interpret the work accordingly. But we might respectfully point out that the stated intention is not always fulfilled in the work. The author doubtless intended to write a great work—but does this intention mean that the work is great? The author intended to write a serious work—but we may find it absurd. Does the author's intention make the work less absurd? Or, conversely, the writer may have intended only to earn money. A famous instance is Dr. Johnson, hurriedly writing *Rasselas* to pay the costs of his mother's funeral but nevertheless producing a masterpiece. Wimsatt and Beardsley have taught us that the work "means" what the work itself says, not what the author says he or she meant it to mean. In the words of Lillian Hellman, "The writer's intention hasn't anything to do with what he achieves." Or in the words of D. H. Lawrence, "Never trust the artist. Trust the tale."

Although "The Intentional Fallacy" remains the classic text, you may want to suggest that students interested in this topic should read Beardsley's later comments on inten-tion in his *Aesthetics: Problems in the Philosophy of Criticism* (1958) and in his *The Possibility of Criticism* (1970).

The proper question to ask, we believe, is not "What did the author mean?" but, rather, "What does the text say?" We can, of course, try to see what the work meant in its own day—that is, in its historical context. For instance, if we are thinking about *The Merchant of Venice* or about *Othello,* we can try to collect information about Elizabethan atti-tudes toward Jews or toward Moors, respectively, but even with such material, we will not be able to say much about Shakespeare's intention. *The Merchant of Venice* contains at least one extended passage (3.1.55–65) in which Shylock is presented far more sympathetically than any Jew in any other Elizabethan text (Did Shakespeare perhaps find Shylock coming to life, and did he give him better lines than he intended?). As for *Othello,* well, no other Elizabethan drama has a tragic hero who is a Moor. The mere fact that Shakespeare alone made a Moor the central figure in a tragedy—a genre that displayed human greatness— suggests that we will not get much insight into Othello by seeing how other dramatists represented Moors or, for that matter, even by seeing how Shakespeare represented Moors in other plays (*Titus Andronicus* and *The Merchant of Venice*). To read *Othello* is to see a Moor who is incontestably different from the Moors in all other Elizabethan plays (including Shakespeare's other plays), and we do great injustice to the heroic Othello if we push him into the mold of "the Elizabethan Moor," which in effect means the Moor as depicted by people who were not Shakespeare.

Let's take a particular passage in T. S. Eliot's "The Love Song of J. Alfred Prufrock". After the epigraph from Dante, the poem begins thus: "Let us go then, you and I." Who is the "you"? In this manual we suggest that "Prufrock" is an internal monologue in which the timid self ("I") addresses his own amorous self as "you." (We don't say that *every* "you" in the poem is the amorous self.) It happens that a reader asked Eliot (apparently in the mid-1940s, some thirty years after Eliot wrote the poem) who the "you" is, and Eliot replied:

> As for THE LOVE SONG OF J. ALFRED PRUFROCK anything I say now must be somewhat conjectural, as it was written so long ago that my memory may deceive me; but I am pre-pared to assert that the "you" in THE LOVE SONG is merely some friend or companion, presumably of the male sex, whom the speaker is at that moment addressing. . . .

> (Kristian Smidt, *Poetry and Belief in the Work of T. S. Eliot*, 85.)

Several points are worth noting: (1) The statement was made long after the poem was written, and Eliot grants that any such late statement "must be somewhat conjectural"; (2) he nevertheless is "prepared to assert" that the "you" is "some friend or companion"; (3) although he is prepared to make this assertion, the assertion itself is rather imprecise (there is a difference between a "friend" and a "companion") and he immediately goes on to reveal (by saying "presumably of the male sex") that he himself no longer has (if he ever did have) a clear idea of who the "you" is. How helpful, then, is his comment? True, if one wants to say that the author is the decisive authority, presumably one can rule out the view that the "you" in the poem is (for the most part) the amorous self, the self urg-ing the timid self to go forward. But, we suggest, the test is to read the poem to see if the suggestion makes sense.

Eliot himself occasionally commented at some length on the topic of intention. For instance, in "The Social Function of Poetry" (1945) after saying that "a great deal more goes to the making of poetry than the conscious purpose of the poet," he went on to add, "And in recent times, a reason why we have become more cautious in accepting a poet's expressed intention as evidence of what he was really doing, is that we have all become more conscious of the role of the unconscious." And in "The Frontiers of Criticism" (1956) he mentions, of a published interpretation of "Prufrock" that he had recently read, "[The author set forth] an attempt to find out what the poem really meant—whether that was what I had meant it to mean or not. And for that I was grateful." Possibly Eliot's expres-sion of gratitude is spoken with tongue in cheek (though we do not think so), but even if one does think Eliot is being ironic, the case for the authority of the author's interpreta-tion is undermined; the author may (or may not) be speaking ironically, so how much weight can we give to his comments? In any case, in the context of the entire essay, it is clear that Eliot really does believe that a work cannot be reduced to what the author "intended."

One last quotation from Eliot, this one from *The Use of Poetry and the Use of Criticism* (1933, 130):

> A poet can try, of course, to give an honest report of the way in which he himself writes: the result may, if he is a good observer, be illuminating. And in one sense, but a very lim-ited one, he knows better what his poems "mean" than can anyone else; he may know the history of their composition, the material which has gone in and come out in an unrecog-nisable form, and he knows what he was trying to do and what he was meaning to mean. But what a poem means is as much what it means to others as what it means to the author; and indeed, in the course of time a poet may become merely a reader in respect to his own works, forgetting his original meaning.

These sentences make sense, but we also see the force of the commonsense view that a competent author shapes the material so that it embodies his or her meaning. This mean-ing may change during the process of composition—the writer finds his or her intention shifting and therefore revises the work—but, in this view, the creator of a work does know, at the end, what the meaning of the work is. Notice that we say "a competent author." Obviously an incompetent author may compose a work that is inadvertently incoherent or ludicrous and be unaware of the result. But a competent author, in this view, shapes the work—admittedly modifying the original intention as the work proceeds—and at the end has produced a work in which all of the elements cohere and on whose meaning he

49

or she can comment. This, we say, is a commonsense view; the only trouble, again, is that most writers have not commented on their works (for example, Chaucer, Shakespeare), and those writers who have commented (for example, Eliot) have often made inconclusive remarks. Aside from Eliot, none of the poets, story writers, or dramatists represented in this book have commented on the works we reprint.

Robert Frost

Mending Wall (p. 426)

Some critics applaud the neighbor in Robert Frost's "Mending Wall," valuing his respect for barriers. For an extreme version, see Robert Hunting, "Who Needs Mending?" *Western Humanities Review,* 17 (Winter 1963: 88–89). The gist of this faction is that the neighbor wisely realizes—as the speaker does not—that individual identity depends on respect for boundaries. Such a view sees the poem as a Browningesque dramatic monologue like "My Last Duchess," in which the self-satisfied speaker unknowingly gives himself away.

Richard Poirier, in *Robert Frost* (1977), makes the interesting point that it is not the neighbor (who believes that "good fences make good neighbors") who initiates the ritual of mending the wall; rather, it is the speaker: "I let my neighbor know beyond the hill." Poirier suggests that "if fences do not 'make good neighbors,' the making of fences can," for it makes for talk—even though the neighbor is hopelessly taciturn. For a long, judicious discussion of the poem, see John C. Kemp, *Robert Frost: The Poet as Regionalist* (1979, 13–25).

Andrew Marvell

To His Coy Mistress (p. 435)

First, we touch on our final question, the emendation of "glew" to "dew" in line 34. This emendation has found wide acceptance, but the original reading may be right, not in the ordinary sense of glue, of course, but in a sense that H. Grierson suggested, "a shining gum found on some trees."

Probably most of the discussion in class will concentrate on the structure of the poem and the question of whether the poem is offensively sexist. As for the tripartite structure, which we call attention to in a question in the text, we want to make two points here. First, we do not see it as a Hegelian matter of thesis/antithesis/synthesis, although many readers do see it this way. We see it, as we indicate in the text, as a matter of a supposition, a refutation, and a deduction.

The supposition is somewhat comic, with the lover offering to devote two hundred years to the praise of each breast, and it is even somewhat bawdy in his offer to devote "thirty thousand to the rest": After all, what can "the rest" be, after he has praised her forehead, eyes, and breasts? This apparently leisurely state might, at first thought, seem to be ideal for a lover, but when one thinks about it, one perceives its barrenness: "We would sit down, and think which way / To walk, and pass our long love's day" (lines 3–4). Nothing is fulfilled: "An age at least to every part, / And the last age should show your heart" (lines 17–18), which is to say that after centuries of praising this or that part, the last age—an unimaginably long period—would be devoted to praising the countless good qualities of her heart, for instance her generosity, kindness, piety, and whatever else. It all sounds rather barren.

The second unit begins with lines that are among the most famous in English literature: "But at my back I always hear / Time's wingèd chariot hurrying near" (lines 21–22). These lines seem to introduce swiftness and vitality into the poem; but when one comes to think further about this unit, one notices that, at least so far as the man and the woman are concerned, they don't do much here either. In the "deserts of vast eternity," her beauty will *not* be found; his song will *not* be heard; they will not embrace. The chief actors will be the worms, who will "try" her virginity. If in the first unit the speaker spoofs the woman, showing her as a caricature of the disdainful mistress, in the second unit he savagely attacks her verbally, with talk of graves and worms. And here, too, as we have just said, nothing much happens.

In the third unit, there is plenty of (imagined) action, action that they share, unlike the earlier action of the speaker praising the beloved or of her refusing his offers. This joint action, sexual union, is indicated by "we," "us," and "our." But the imagery and the emotion are not what we might have expected. The savagery persists, notably in the images of "fire" and "birds of prey" (rather than the doves of Venus, which we might expect in a love poem) and in the verbs "devour" and "tear." Instead of time devouring the lovers, they devour time, but now we feel that the speaker's assertions lacerate himself as well as the beloved.

This gets us to our main point: We see the poem not so much as primarily a love poem or even as a poem of seduction (which is what disturbs many students), but as primarily a poem about the desperate condition of human beings, as the speaker sees it. To this extent, what interests a reader (we think) is the emotional states through which the speaker moves, from teasing the beloved (the first unit), to twisting the knife (the second unit), to forcing himself to face the facts that he has been thrusting under her eyes (the third unit).

Kate Chopin

The Story of an Hour (p. 438)

The first sentence of Kate Chopin's story, of course, proves to be essential to the end, though during the middle of the story, the initial care to protect Mrs. Mallard from the "sad message" seems almost comic. Students may assume, too easily, that Mrs. Mallard's "storm of grief" is hypocritical. They may not notice that the renewal after the first shock is stimulated by the renewal of life around her ("the tops of trees . . . were all aquiver with the new spring of life") and that before she achieves a new life, Mrs. Mallard first goes through a sort of death and then tries to resist renewal: Her expression "indicated a suspension of intelligent thought," she felt something "creeping out of the sky," and she tried to "beat it back with her will," but she soon finds herself "drinking in a very elixir of life through that open window," and her thoughts turn to "spring days, and summer days."

Implicit in the story is the idea that her life as a wife—which she had thought was happy—was in fact a life of repression or subjugation, and the awareness comes to her only at this late stage. The story has two surprises: The change from grief to joy proves not to be the whole story, for we get the second surprise, the husband's return and Mrs. Mallard's death. The last line ("the doctors . . . said she had died . . . of joy that kills") is doubly ironic: The doctors wrongly assume that she was overjoyed to find that her husband was alive, but they were not wholly wrong in guessing that her last day of life brought her great joy.

In a sense, moreover, the doctors are right (though not in the sense they mean) in saying that she "died of heart disease." That is, if we take the "heart" in a metaphorical sense to refer to love and marriage, we can say that the loss of her new freedom from her marriage is unbearable. This is not to say (though many students do say it) that her marriage was miserable. The text explicitly says "she had loved him—sometimes." The previous paragraph in the story nicely calls attention to certain aspects of love—a satisfying giving of the self—and yet also to a most unpleasant yielding to force: "There would be no one to live for her during those coming years; she would live for herself. There would be no powerful will bending her in that blind persistence with which men and women believe they have a right to impose a private will upon a fellow creature."

A biographical observation: Chopin's husband died in 1882, and her mother died in 1885. In 1894, in an entry in her diary, she connected the two losses with her growth. "If it were possible for my husband and my mother to come back to earth, I feel that I would unhesitatingly give up every thing that has come into my life since they left it and join my existence again with theirs. To do that, I would have to forget the past ten years of my growth—my real growth."

Having said what we have to say about the story, we now offer our own responses to the critical assertions in the text to which we ask students to respond.

1. We don't think the railroad accident is a symbol of the destructiveness of the Industrial Revolution. In our view, something in a text becomes symbolic by virtue of being emphasized, perhaps by being presented at considerable length or perhaps by being repeated at intervals. Nothing in the story connects the train with the Industrial Revolution; it is not, for instance, said to have altered the landscape, changing what was once an agrarian community into an industrial community. On the other hand, we think that in this story the coming of spring is symbolic of new life. Why? For one thing, Chopin explicitly says in the fifth paragraph that the "tops of trees . . . were all aquiver with the new spring life." She goes on to talk of "the delicious breath of rain" and of sparrows twittering. The rain of course is refreshing, and it is a fact that water brings about renewed life. Further, literary tradition (cf. Chaucer's reference to April showers at the start of *The Canterbury Tales*) has given spring showers a symbolic meaning. Sparrows are associated with sexuality (the sparrow is an attribute of Aphrodite), but we don't usually bring this up in class because Chopin mentions the sparrows only briefly and because students are not likely to know of the tradition. (This point seems to us not worth arguing.) A few paragraphs later Chopin tells us that something was coming toward Mrs. Mallard "out of the sky, reaching toward her through the sounds, the scents, the color that filled the air." Surely, therefore, it is reasonable to say that Chopin is emphasizing the season—its sounds, scents, and colors. A few paragraphs later, Chopin tells us that Mrs. Mallard was thinking of "spring days, summer days." In short, *in the story* spring is given an emphasis that the train is not, and so we tend to think that the spring is not just the spring but is something more, something whose implications we should attend to.

2. To say that the story claims that women rejoice in the deaths of their husbands seems to us to be a gross overgeneralization. The story is about one particular woman. True, in reading any work we may find ourselves saying, "Yes, life is sometimes like that," or some such thing. But nothing in the story suggests that it is about "women," and certainly nothing suggests that Mrs. Mallard's response toward the death of her husband is *typical* of "women."

3. The view that her death at the end of the story is a just punishment strikes us as going far beyond the text; we find no evidence that Chopin judges Mrs. Mallard harshly, and we think we can point to contrary evidence—for instance, to the sympathetic way in which her response is set forth.

5. We do not agree that the story is good *because* it has a surprise ending—but we also do not condemn it because of the ending. True, some critics would argue that surprise endings are tricks, that such endings are far less important than plausible characters, and so on. Our own view is that if a story offers virtually nothing but a surprise ending, it is probably a weak story—one can hardly read it a second time with any interest—but a certain amount of surprise surely is desirable. Most, maybe all, realistic prose fiction makes use of foreshadowing; expectations are set up, but they are fulfilled in slightly unexpected ways. We are reminded of a passage in E. M. Forster's *Aspects of the Novel* (1927):

> Shock, followed by the feeling, "Oh, that's all right," is a sign that all is well with plot: characters, to be real, ought to run smoothly, but a plot ought to cause surprise.

Of course one might argue that this view is arbitrary; here is a chance to ask students what values they might establish—what makes them say that a story is good or bad or so-so.

Plato

"The Greater Part of the Stories Current Today We Shall Have to Reject" (p. 443)

This excerpt from Plato's *Republic* is a passage near the end of Book II, in which Socrates undertakes to describe the proper education for that handful of the young intended to become the guardians or rulers of the ideal state. (Throughout the dialogue, we hear nothing about how the rest of the population is to be educated, that presumably being a matter of no interest.) After explaining the importance of "gymnastics," or bodily training, Socrates turns to "music," or training for the soul. To be fair, one must not take Platonic-Socratic admonitions out of context; nevertheless, there is some reason to believe that—unlike Socrates, who relied on the free air of Athens to carry out his ideas about education of the citizenry—Plato, the son of an Athenian nobleman, really did believe that a stricter regimen involving some censorship of the prevailing methods was appropriate.

Plato's argument for discarding the Homeric tales about the gods depends on accepting the principle that whatever is good can be the cause only of good things—hence the gods, being wholly good, cannot cause any of the bad things that the prevailing mythology attributes to them. Plato knows that the gods are wholly good only because that is part of his implicit definition of deity—as though he had said, "I [we?] wouldn't call it divine unless it was (morally) good."

Plato even goes so far as to allege that in his ideal state, it would be "sinful, inexpedient, and inconsistent" to permit the poets to say that "those who were punished were made wretched through god's action." Presumably, he thinks it would be inconsistent to allow this statement (question 3) because it would contradict something that the elder guardian-teachers themselves avow: namely, that (as Plato says at the end of the excerpt) "God is the cause, not of all things, but only of good." Thus when a poet presents a story in which a god is depicted as making a person "wretched" (and we assume that being made wretched is not a "good" thing, but that getting your deserved punishment is), this interpretation contradicts the doctrine above because it makes the god out to be the cause of something not "good."

Some will complain that Plato assumes, on no explicit evidence, that "children cannot distinguish between what is allegory and what isn't," and he shows throughout that he underestimates the capacity of children to distinguish the silly from the serious, the cheap from the dear, and the obscene from the respectful (our question 2). It is, of course, an empirical question—and not an easy one to answer—whether children can make these distinctions. But it is needless to speculate whether they can make them in the abstract or in a wholly nonsocial environment. As we remember our childhood and that of our friends, we testify that we had no great difficulty in making these distinctions and that an unremitting diet of Saturday afternoon B-grade films at the local movie palace or the standard TV fare of the 1950s did not hopelessly muddle our values and our sense of reality. Obviously, we did not feed only on such stuff, any more than children today see nothing except what is on the most violent television shows. Even if we overestimate our own ability as youngsters to sort the wheat from the chaff, we doubt that the best way to develop judgment about what is harmful, tasteless, offensive, and worse is to deny all access to the meretricious, salacious, and blasphemous. Even if this is too serene (or radical) a view to gain favor, one must eventually face the question *quis custodiet custodies,* or "Who shall guard the guardians?" Plato does not need to worry about this problem because he, unlike the rest of us, deals by definition with an ideal state and its appropriately ideal government, one that is incapable of the provinciality of every known board of public censorship.

13
A Debater's View: Individual Oral Presentations and Debate (p. 450)

If you require students to engage in formal debates, you may want to put a few books on reserve in the library. We especially recommend Bill Hill and Richard W. Leeman, *The Art and Practice of Argumentation and Debate* (1997). Also of some use are Jon M. Ericson, James J. Murphy, and Raymond Bud Zeuschner, *The Debater's Guide*, 3rd ed. (2003), and Leslie Phillips, William S. Hicks, and Douglas R. Springer, *Basic Debate*, 4th ed. (1996).

If you don't use formal debates but you do ask students to make oral presentations, we think you may still suggest that students read this chapter, paying special attention to the checklist. And you may want to emphasize these four points:

1. Provide transitions, such as *In the first place, further,* and *finally.*

2. Summarize occasionally, especially as you move from one point to the next.

3. Have a pretty full outline, and don't hesitate to glance at it occasionally while speaking, but do not read your speech.

4. As a listener, be courteous (no eye-rolling).

Part Four

A CASEBOOK ON THE STATE AND THE INDIVIDUAL

14
What Is the Ideal Society? (p. 463)

We at first thought of having a section titled "Utopia," but as we worked on it, the idea seemed needlessly limited, and "Utopia" gave way to the present chapter. Still, several of the readings we give here are utopian. The utopian element in this section allows us here to introduce a comment by Gertrude Himmelfarb, in *Marriage and Morals among the Victorians* (1986):

> "Utopian" is one of the more ambiguous words in our vocabulary. To some it signifies an ideal that is commendable if not entirely realistic, a goal to aspire to, a vision of excellence that leads us, if not to the best, then at least to the better—a benign and altogether innocent image. To others it suggests exactly the opposite, a dangerous illusion which tempts us, in the name of the best, to reject the better and end up with the worse. The yearning for perfection that makes reality seem irredeemably flawed creates so large a discrepancy between the ideal and the reality that nothing less will suffice than a total transformation of reality—of society, the polity, the economy, above all, of human nature.

Thomas More

From *Utopia* (p. 463)

For a sampling of the amazing variety of interpretations of Thomas More's *Utopia*, one has to look at only the essays reprinted in the Norton Critical Edition of *Utopia* (1975), edited by Robert M. Adams. *Utopia* has been seen, for example, as a book advocating Christianity (in particular, Roman Catholicism), communism, or colonialism. It seems fairly clear to us, however, that More is not advocating any of these things, at least not as an end in itself. Rather, in this humanistic work, he is giving his version of an ideal state based on *reason* alone. But he is a Christian speaking to Christians; presumably his sixteenth-century readers were supposed to say to themselves, "If people without revelation can achieve this degree of decency, surely we, with Christ's help, can achieve more. Our society is far inferior to Utopia; let us strive to equal and then to surpass it."

Perhaps the best short essay on *Utopia* is Edward Surtz's introduction to the Yale paper edition, though Father Surtz sees the book as more Christian than do many other commentators. Among Surtz's points are these:

1. The Utopians are typically Renaissance people, balancing Epicureanism with Christianity, having the best of both worlds. They pursue personal pleasure "until it conflicts with social or religious duties, that is, with the just claims of God or fellow citizens" (p. xiv). The term *pleasure* covers many kinds of actions, from scratching an itch to doing virtuous deeds.

2. Utopian communism "is not an end in itself but the best means to the end: pleasure for all the citizens collectively as well as individually" (p. xiv). "The ultimate Utopian ideal of communism is . . . to be of one mind. . . . Sharing material possessions can succeed only if there is first one heart and soul in all" (p. xv).

3. Modern critics too often emphasize More's political, social, and economic innovations and neglect his opinions on education, ethics, philosophy, and religion.

4. More's Utopians are not saints; some are even criminals. More does *not* believe, as some moderns do, that people can be conditioned (brainwashed) to think they are freely cooperating in a society that in fact enslaves them. More's Utopians have some leeway, as in the choice of an occupation and in the use of leisure. Believing in the immutability of the soul, they believe that one's final end is not worship of the state but union with the Absolute.

Most students, when asked for the meaning of *utopian*, will come up with such pejorative words as *unrealistic, impractical, escapist*. They will be surprised, then, to see how realistic More's view of human nature is. He is fully aware, for instance, of such vices as laziness and, especially, pride—not only in nonutopian countries but even in Utopia. Indeed, he seems to feel that most of our ills are due to pride. To restrain pride, almost all Utopians must engage in manual labor and must wear a simple garment, and, again to restrain pride, there is no private property. Notice that More does not put the blame for our wicked actions entirely on private property or on any other economic factors. True, he does say that Europeans greedily seek to attain superfluities because they fear they may some day be in want, but it is evident that even Utopia has wrongdoers. That is, even the utopian system cannot prevent some people from engaging in wicked behavior. More does think, however, that some systems allow our wicked natures to thrive, and so he devises a political, economic, and social system that keeps down pride (the root of the other deadly sins).

But it is not only pride that is kept in check. Utopia is severely regulated in many ways. For instance, Utopians are free to do what they wish during their leisure time— provided that they don't loaf, gamble, or hunt. Similarly, they are free to talk—provided that they don't talk politics, except at special times. Discussion of state affairs, except at the appointed times and places, is punishable by death. George Orwell's Big Brother is present in More's Utopia, but R. W. Chambers is probably right when he argues (in his *Thomas More* [1935]) that Utopia is founded not on terrorism, but on "religious enthusiasm," in particular on faith in God and in the immortality of the soul. Still, even "religious enthusiasm" has, for many readers, something unpleasant about it—something too monastic, too rigid, too disciplined, too cold.

Although one understands and sympathizes with More's condemnation of the pride that engenders social injustice, one can't help but feel that Utopia, with its rational distribution of labor and its evening lectures on edifying topics, is the poorer for lacking the messy vitality of life. (In Utopia, everything seems terribly static: The constitution doesn't change, population is fixed, clothing is uniform, freedom of thought is limited.) On the other hand, we must remember that in the Europe of More's day (and still in much of the world), the masses had to toil from sunrise to sunset to live at a subsistence level. Today's college students (and their professors) find More's Utopia overly restrictive, but they should remember that (1) it is a society of material prosperity for all citizens and a society with a good deal of leisure, and (2) it was freer and more tolerant than any of the European societies of its day.

Additional Topics for Critical Thinking and Writing

1. Can it be said that whatever the merits or weaknesses of More's proposal, he has astutely diagnosed the problems of society?

2. More's spokesman says that European society "is a conspiracy of the rich to advance their own interests under the pretext of organizing society" (para. 41). Can the same be said of our society? Explain.

3. Is More's view of human nature "utopian" in the modern sense of the word; that is, is it uncharacteristically benign? Explain.

Niccolò Machiavelli

From *The Prince* (p. 477)

Harvey Mansfield Jr., in the introduction to his translation of *The Prince* (1985), argues that for Niccolò Machiavelli, the only moral laws are those made by human beings: "The rules or laws that exist are those made by governments or other powers acting under necessity, and they must be obeyed out of the same necessity. Whatever is necessary may be called just or reasonable, but justice is no more reasonable than what a person's prudence tells him he must acquire for himself, or submit to, because men cannot afford justice in any sense that transcends their own preservation" (p. xi).

This reading seems, in a way, much like the work of Karl Marx, who argues that ideology (including ideas of justice) is created by the ruling class, though Marx also seems to believe that because this class achieved power through historical necessity, its ideals—during the period in which it holds power—indeed are true. Witness Marx's praise of the bourgeoisie for redeeming the masses from the "idiocies" of rural life.

Perhaps the heart of the issue is this: Although we may believe that we should be governed by people of honor, Machiavelli (and most utilitarians) would argue that personal goodness and political usefulness are distinct things. A person may be an adulterer, a liar, a sadist, or whatever but may still be an effective guardian of the state. Or, expressed more mildly, a governor may sometimes have to sacrifice personal morality for the safety of the state. Bernard Williams argues, in *Public and Private Morality* (Stuart Hampshire, ed., 1978), that to preserve civilized life, we need politicians who can bring themselves to behave more badly than we ourselves could do. We want them to be as good as possible—and certainly not to be people who act wickedly on a whim or take pleasure in acting wickedly —but to be able to sacrifice personal moral values for political ones. (This idea makes for lively class discussion.)

A related point: If a leader is widely regarded as immoral, he or she loses an important strength: the goodwill of the public. A small example: A senator who is known to have extramarital affairs can probably survive and can be an effective and even an important senator, but a senator who is regarded as a lecher probably cannot.

On the question of whether cruelty may be beneficial to the state: Machiavelli apparently believed that before a state can be justly ruled, there must be a ruler, and to survive, the ruler must be cunning and ruthless. One wonders, of course, if a person with these qualities will also act reasonably, using power for the well-being of the state rather than for purely personal goals. Machiavelli, living in the turmoil of early sixteenth-century Italy, concentrates on the qualities necessary for a leader to survive. Thomas More (see the previous selection in the text), on the other hand, shows us a utopia with almost no political problems, and thus he can concentrate on the morality of the state rather than on the personal characteristics of the governors. Or put it this way: In Machiavelli, it is the ruler against his rivals and his subjects, whereas in More, it is society against the individual's unruly passions.

Additional Topics for Critical Thinking and Writing

1. Imitating Machiavelli's style, notably his use of contrasting historical examples, write an essay of 500 words, presenting an argument on behalf of your own view of some quality necessary in a leader today. You may, for example, want to argue that a leader must be a master of television appearances or must be truthful, compassionate, or versed in history. Your essay will, in a sense, be one chapter in a book called *The Prince Today.*

2. James M. Burns's biography of President Franklin Delano Roosevelt is titled *Roosevelt: The Lion and the Fox* (1956). Judging from your rereading of this selection

from *The Prince,* indicate in a paragraph the characteristics of Roosevelt that the biographer is suggesting by this title. Read Burns's biography and write a thousand-word essay in which you evaluate the aptness of the title, given the facts about Roosevelt's career and Machiavelli's views.

Thomas Jefferson

The Declaration of Independence (p. 486)

In discussing almost any argument (for that matter, in discussing any writing), it is usually helpful to consider the intended or imagined *audience(s)*. With minimal assistance, students can see that the Declaration of Independence has several audiences (question 1). These audiences can perhaps be described thus:

1. The "candid world" (para. 5), addressed out of "a decent respect to the opinions of mankind" (para. 1)

2. The king and his ministers (the grievances are blamed on them)

3. The British people (students who do a research paper on the Declaration will learn that some passages censuring the British people were deleted to maintain good relations)

4. France (the Declaration announces that the "United Colonies" have "full power to levy War, conclude Peace, contract Alliances, establish Commerce, and to do all other Acts and Things which Independent States may of right do." Most historians see in these words a bid for foreign aid—military supplies from France)

5. Those colonists who were not eager for independence

Attention may be given to the *speaker* of the Declaration—that is, to the self-image (question 3) that the colonists present. Jefferson refers to "a decent respect to the opinions of mankind" (para. 1), and he admits that "Governments long established should not be changed for light and transient causes" (para. 4). Notice, too, his assertion that "We Have Petitioned for Redress in the most humble terms" (para. 33). In short, the colonists present themselves not as radicals or firebrands, but as patient, long-suffering people who are willing to put their case before the tribunal of the world. Notice such words as *duty, necessary,* and *necessity.* They are not rebels; rather, they have been "plundered" and "ravaged" and are exerting a right—the right of the people to alter or to abolish a government that fails to fulfill the legitimate purpose of government (para. 4).

Some attention in class can also be profitably given to discussing the *structure* of the work:

1. The first sentence announces the colonists' purpose, explaining "the causes which impel them to the separation."

2. The core of the document is an exposition of the causes, in two sections:

   a. Theoretical and general justification (for example, "self-evident" truths) and

   b. The list of despotic British actions.

3. The Declaration concludes with the response of the colonies (the signers pledge their lives).

Students can also be shown how the explicit assumptions of the Declaration—

1. All men are created equal and are endowed with "unalienable rights,"

2. Governments are instituted to preserve these rights,

3. People have a duty and a right to throw off a despotic government,

— can be cast into this *syllogism:*

1. If a government is despotic, the people have a right to overthrow it and to form a new government.

2. The British government of the American colonies is despotic.

3. Therefore, the people have a right to overthrow it and to form a new government.

The major premise is not argued but is asserted as an "unalienable right." The minor premise is arrived at inductively (instances are cited, and a generalization is drawn from them).

Additional Topics for Critical Thinking and Writing

1. The Declaration is an argument for revolution in a particular society. Investigate conditions in some society (for example, Cuba, China, Iran, El Salvador, Nicaragua), and argue that, on the grounds of the Declaration, people in that society do—or do not—have the right to revolt.

2. Read Chapter 19 of John Locke's *Essay Concerning Civil Government* (first published in 1690) and write a 500-word essay in which you identify all those passages or ideas found in Locke that appear also in the Declaration. Are there any ideas in Locke's chapter that have no parallel in the Declaration but that nevertheless seem to you to be relevant to its purpose and content?

Elizabeth Cady Stanton

Declaration of Sentiments and Resolutions (p. 490)

Elizabeth Cady Stanton's Declaration of 1848 is the historic precursor of the decade-long effort that finally failed in 1982 to enact an Equal Rights Amendment (ERA) to the Constitution. The Fourteenth Amendment, enacted twenty years after the first Woman's Rights Convention at Seneca Falls, New York, did provide that no state "shall . . . deprive any person of life, liberty, or property without due process of law, nor deny any person within its jurisdiction the equal protection of the laws." At face value, that might look like the rejection of gender as a basis for lawful discrimination. Opponents of ERA in the 1970s who professed sympathy with feminist claims for constitutional equality often pointed to the language quoted as if that settled the matter. Not so, however.

The term *male* entered the Constitution in the Fourteenth Amendment itself (see section 2), thereby helping to etch more clearly the implicit and historic male bias of the Constitution and the laws from the beginning and indicating that "due process" and "equal protection" were not to be given a gender-free reading. An Illinois case of 1873 settled this issue for decades. Arguing that she was entitled under the Fourteenth Amendment to be admitted to the bar, Myra Bradwell unsuccessfully fought her case through the state courts to the U.S. Supreme Court. The language of the majority's decision enshrined in constitutional interpretation the worst excesses of male chauvinism (see *Bradwell v. Illinois*, 83 U.S. 130 [1873]). Even the right to vote ("elective franchise") (para. 4) was not incorporated into the Constitution until 1920 (the Nineteenth Amendment). Full equality of the sexes under the laws and the Constitution, whether or not it is a good thing, still does not exist in our society.

Civil death (question 3) is the ultimate extreme to which a person can be reduced: denial by law of all civil rights, privileges, immunities, and liberties. (Not even prisoners on death row, today, suffer civil death.) Stanton elaborates the point (paras. 9–11). It was commonplace among feminists of the nineteenth century to point out that marriage under law was functionally equivalent to civil death.

It was not, however, functionally equivalent to chattel slavery (which was to last another fifteen years after the Seneca Falls Convention; not surprisingly, the women who organized the convention were staunch abolitionists). It might be a useful classroom exercise for students to explore the differences under law in the 1840s between the status of American white women, as the Declaration reports it, and the status of American black slaves. An excellent source for slave law is A. Leon Higginbotham Jr., *In the Matter of Color* (1978).

Martin Luther King Jr.

I Have a Dream (p. 495)

The setting (the steps of the Lincoln Memorial, in Washington, D.C., on the centennial of the Emancipation Proclamation) plays an important part in this speech. By the way, few students know that the Emancipation Proclamation did not in fact free any slaves. In 1862, President Lincoln announced that he would declare free the slaves of any state that did not return to the Union. None of the states that had seceded accepted the invitation to return, and so on January 1, 1863, he announced the Emancipation Proclamation. It did not apply to slaves in states such as Maryland and Kentucky that had chosen to stay in the Union, and of course, it had no force in the Confederacy. Still, the symbolic importance of the Proclamation was and is immense, and it is part of King's speech.

King's association with Lincoln is evident not only in the setting but also in the language. The opening words, "Five score," evoke the "Four score and seven years ago" of the Gettysburg Address, and Lincoln himself was evoking the language of the Bible. King's speech, too, richly evokes the Bible ("dark and desolate valley," "God's children," "cup of bitterness," "trials and tribulations," "storms of persecution," "every hill and mountain shall be made low, the rough places will be made plain and the crooked places will be made straight, and the glory of the Lord shall be revealed, and all flesh shall see it together"—this last from Isaiah 40:4–5).

Another symbol, in addition to Lincoln and to the Bible, is the "American dream" (para. 11, but foreshadowed in the title of the speech), which King, like most other Americans, identifies with the remark in the Declaration of Independence that "All men are created equal." King also identifies his dream (and himself) with "My country, 'tis of thee," and (in the final paragraph) with black spirituals.

The exalted language of the Bible and the Declaration is joined with the humble language of commerce, the "promissory note," the "bad check" of paragraphs 3 and 4, and the whole (because it is a speech) is rich in evocative repetition, especially parallelisms (again a biblical device).

All these devices and allusions are fairly obvious, and that is part of their point. King is emphasizing that speaker and audience share a culture; and though the immediate audience in Washington was predominantly black, King knew that his words would also reach a larger audience of whites—whites who share this culture.

The structure (question 6) is this: The first part gives a historical perspective; the second, an exhortation not to fall into evil; the third, an exposition of the dream, a picture of the better world that the hearers can help to bring about.

Additional Topic for Critical Thinking and Writing

King's speech stresses the twin themes of equality and freedom and does not suggest that the two might be in tension or conflict with each other. Do you agree that there is no tension? Try to state precisely the freedom(s) and equalities for which King pleads. Is our society any closer to achieving these goals today, do you think, than in 1963?

W. H. Auden

The Unknown Citizen (p. 499)

In "The Unknown Citizen," the speaker's voice is obviously not the poet's. The speaker—appropriately unidentified in a poem about a society without individuals—is apparently a bureaucrat. For such a person, a "saint" is not one who is committed to spiritual values but one who causes no trouble.

Additional Topics for Critical Thinking and Writing

1. What is W. H. Auden satirizing in "The Unknown Citizen"? (Students might be cautioned to spend some time thinking about whether Auden is satirizing the speaker, the citizen, conformism, totalitarianism, technology, or what.)

2. Write a prose eulogy of 250 words satirizing contemporary conformity or, if you prefer, contemporary individualism.

3. Was the speaker free? Was he happy? Argue your view.

4. In a paragraph or two, sketch the values of the speaker of the poem, and then sum them up in a sentence or two. Finally, in as much space as you feel you need, judge these values.

Langston Hughes

Let America Be America Again (p. 500)

It is sometimes difficult to remember that poets (or at least some of them) once were regarded as national bards, celebrating the ideals of society. On the whole, today we distrust public oratory, and we are much more comfortable with the idea of the poet as the reporter of private feelings. In short, we prefer the private lyric to such public lyric forms as the ode and the hymn. People who believe that poetry ought to address public themes are likely to complain that poetry has turned inward on itself and has retreated from life. They may point out that although there are all sorts of poetry festivals and public readings, the poetry is likely to be confessional—for instance, the expression of the emotions of an abandoned woman, a gay man, or the child of immigrant Jews or Hispanics. In fact, such poems are deeply rooted in the politics and social practices of our age.

Still, it must be said that poems explicitly about the nation—patriotic poems—are now rare. We can hardly imagine a poet today writing something like "Barbara Frietchie" (the stuff of our school days), "Paul Revere's Ride," or "O Captain, My Captain." Today we seem chiefly to value what Harold Bloom has crankily called "The Poetry of Resentment." Hughes did not by any means write the sort of poetry that Bloom castigates, but the Hughes poems that we value most highly do seem to come directly from the life that he observed closely—for instance, his poems about prostitution and poverty in Harlem. But there is another Hughes, the Hughes who for a while saw himself as an heir to Walt Whitman and especially to Carl Sandburg, and it was in this role that he wrote "Let America Be America Again." Although the influence of Whitman and Sandburg was great, Hughes of course drew also on black sources. In particular, the motif that America has been America (the land of the free) only for some whites was common in black prose, for instance, in the writings of Frederick Douglass. Hughes also drew, very evidently, on radical socialist thought, and doubtless that is why (as we indicate in question 3) *Esquire* published only the first fifty lines. Lines 1–50 offer a strong indictment, but they stop short of preaching revolution. The gist of the idea in these lines is that America today should be true to its original ideals, the ideals of the founding fathers. No one can disapprove of this ideal. But Hughes goes a bit further: Blacks, he says, have not shared in this society ("America never was America to me"), and early in the poem, he links the marginalization of blacks with that of poor whites (line 19) and immigrants (line 45). True enough; almost everyone would grant, "Yes, it's not just that today we have lost some of our ideals; we failed from the start to extend them to all of our people." But beyond line 50 the poem gets more radical, as Hughes specifies additional victims—unemployed people on relief (line 53) and Native Americans (line 65). The suggestion that injustice extended to groups beyond blacks must have sounded menacing enough even to the liberal editors of *Esquire*, but in line 73 we hear (and the editors of *Esquire* must have heard) a still more radical note, a call to revolution: "We must take back our land again" and "We, the people, must redeem / The land, the mines, the plants, the rivers" (lines 82–83). The editors doubtless knew that this talk of the redemptive power of "the people," especially as opposed to the "leeches" of line 72, was the voice of the extreme left wing. Our own view, for what it is worth, is that the shorter poem (lines 1–50, as opposed to 1–86) is the better poem, partly, we confess, because the call to "take back" the land is left unexplained.

Ursula K. Le Guin

The Ones Who Walk Away from Omelas (p. 503)

When Thomas More called his book *Utopia,* he punned on the Greek "good place" (*eu topos*) and on "no place" (*ou topos*). Like all of the rest of us, he knew that the fully happy society is "no place," if only because accidents, disease, and death are part of life. Ursula K. Le Guin's narrator gives us a fairly detailed description of an imagined happy society (para. 1)— Omelas is "bright-towered by the sea," the old celebrants in the festival wear "long stiff robes of mauve and gray," and the boys and girls are "naked in the bright air, with mudstained feet and ankles and long, lithe arms"—but the narrator also is vague about many things that we would dearly like to know. For instance, although the narrator tells us that there is no king and there are no slaves in Omelas, the narrator also makes a confession, "I do not know the rules and laws of their society" (para. 3). The story includes other confessions of ignorance, and at one point, the narrator, aware that the narrative thus far has been unconvincing and fairy-tale-like (for example, those bright towers by the sea), almost gives up and urges the reader to imagine Omelas "as your own fancy bids."

Doubtless Le Guin is vague about important matters because she—like everyone else—cannot depict a convincing utopia that can withstand scrutiny. But she is also vague for a more important reason: She is not earnestly writing a utopian tale like, say, Edward Bellamy's *Looking Backward*. Rather, she is raising a moral problem, or, more exactly, she is amplifying a problem that William James had raised. Omelas need not be a convincing presentation of the perfectly happy life, and indeed the narrator makes Omelas most convincing when he (or she?) prefaces the information about the suffering child with these words: "Do you believe? Do you accept the festival, the city, the joy? No? Then let me describe one more thing" (para. 6). When we learn about the wretched child, Omelas becomes much more believable, for we are all aware that much of our happiness in fact depends on the suffering of others. These others may be the exploited workers whose painful labor allows us to eat and dress well; they may be the sick, whose ills make some physicians prosperous; they may be the aggrieved, whose lawsuits pay the college tuition for the children of lawyers; they may even be the suffering animals whose pain in medical laboratories may help to alleviate our own pain. In short, whoever we are, some of our happiness depends on the misfortunes of other creatures—and at times we are aware of this fact. Le Guin's happy city now becomes easily understandable: It is an image not of an ideal world but of our world.

Where a parable usually evokes a fairly clear moral and leaves us in little doubt about how we ought to act, this story leaves us puzzled. It heightens our awareness of a cruel fact of society, but it does not tell us how we can reform our society. Put another way, where does one go when one walks away from Omelas? Can we really envisage the possibility of a happy life that is not in any way based on suffering and injustice somewhere? Is the story therefore pointless, mere fantasy, mere escapism? Presumably, Le Guin is simply seeking to make us think so that we will learn to act in ways that minimize the suffering of others. It is inconceivable that life will ever be utopian, but it is not inconceivable that injustice and human suffering may be reduced.

Additional Topics for Critical Thinking and Writing

1. How convincing does the narrator think the picture of Omelas is? Why do you suppose that Le Guin does not offer details about the laws of the land? Does Omelas become more convincing when we learn about the child? Support your response with evidence.

2. What is the point of walking away from Omelas? Can the walker go to a better society? If not, is the story pointless? (Put another way, the story is a fantasy, but is it also escapist fiction?)

Helen Prejean

Executions Are Too Costly — Morally (p. 509)

Sister Helen Prejean has proved to be the most influential figure — speaker, lobbyist, film consultant, writer, and spiritual adviser to men on death row — currently opposing the death penalty in the United States. Her humor, warmth, and compassion have been much admired, and she has earned the respect of many whose lives have been ravaged by the murder of a loved one — whether in a crime of homicide or in a legally authorized execution. She has brought to the public debate a down-home human approach noticeably absent from much of the discourse on this subject.

The excerpt we reprint from her popular book *Dead Man Walking* is devoted largely to examining the biblical support for (or opposition to) capital punishment. She neglects to mention what many think is the best single passage in the Bible on this subject, Genesis 4:9–16 — God's response to Cain for murdering his brother, Abel. God punishes Cain in three ways: He is exiled, he is cursed, and he is stigmatized (so that others will recognize him for the murderer he is). Perhaps no other passage in the Bible so personalizes God's punishment meted out to a murderer — not perhaps a perfect paradigm for how today's opponents of the death penalty would have murderers punished, but worthy of their thoughtful reflection.

The Judeo-Christian posture on the death penalty is a long story. A small fraction of it is related in paragraphs 11 through 15. Those who seek more must consult the hefty recent monograph by James J. Megivern, *The Death Penalty: An Historical and Theological Survey* (1997). Professor Megivern explains how the Christian church at the time of the First Crusade (1095) abandoned its early commitment to pacifism in favor of Christian triumphalism with sword in hand, led by Pope Gregory VII (1073–1085), his successor Pope Urban II (1042–1099), and St. Bernard of Clairvaux (1090–1153). Their enemies were infidels (read Jews and Muslims) and soon thereafter Christian heretics. According to Megivern, the epitome of this transformation in the Christian ethic of war and peace, of violence and pacifism, appears in the *Chanson d'Antioche*, "the greatest of the vernacular epics of the First Crusade." Christ is portrayed as hanging on the cross and assuring the good thief to his side that "from over the seas will come a new race which will take *revenge* on the death of the father." Thus, as Megivern notes, was brought to pass a "total reversal of the actual teachings of Jesus."

Seib takes it for granted that the widespread though fairly recent newspaper policy against printing pictures of dead bodies is a sound one; I don't know that it makes any sense at all. I recognize that printing pictures of corpses raises all sorts of problems about taste and titillation and sensationalism; the fact is, however, that people die. Death happens to be one of life's main events. And it is irresponsible—and more than that, inaccurate—for newspapers to fail to show it, or to show it only when an astonishing set of photos comes in over the Associated Press wire. Most papers covering fatal automobile accidents will print pictures of mangled cars. But the significance of fatal automobile accidents is not that a great deal of steel is twisted but that people die. Why not show it? That's what accidents are about. Throughout the Vietnam war, editors were reluctant to print atrocity pictures. Why *not* print them? That's what that was about. Murder victims are almost never photographed; they are granted their privacy. But their relatives are relentlessly pictured on their way in and out of hospitals and morgues and funerals.

I'm not advocating that newspapers print these things in order to teach their readers a lesson. The *Post* editors justified their printing of the Boston pictures with several arguments in that direction; every one of them is irrelevant. The pictures don't show anything about slum life; the incident could have happened anywhere, and it did. It is extremely unlikely that anyone who saw them rushed out and had his fire escape strengthened. And the pictures were not news—at least they were not national news. It is not news in Washington, or New York, or Los Angeles that a woman was killed in a Boston fire. The only newsworthy thing about the pictures is that they were taken. They deserve to be printed because they are great pictures, breathtaking pictures of something that happened. That they disturb readers is exactly as it should be: that's why photojournalism is often more powerful than written journalism.

Topics for Critical Thinking and Writing

1. In paragraph 5 Ephron refers to "the famous assassination picture of the Vietcong prisoner in Saigon" (see p. 147). The photo shows the face of a prisoner who is about to be shot in the head at close range. Jot down the reasons why you would or would not approve of printing this photo in a newspaper. Think, too, about this: If the photo on page 146 were not about a war—if it did not include the soldiers and the burning village in the rear but instead showed children fleeing from an abusive parent or from an abusive sibling—would you approve of printing it in a newspaper?

2. In paragraph 9 Ephron quotes a newspaperman as saying that before printing Forman's pictures of the woman and the child falling from the fire escape, editors should have asked themselves "what purpose they served and what their effect was likely to be on the reader." If you were

an editor, what would your answers be? By the way, the pictures were *not* taken in a poor neighborhood, and they did *not* expose slum conditions.

3. In 50 words or so, write a precise description of what you see in the third of the Boston photographs. Do you think readers of your description would be "revolted" by the picture (para. 8), as were many viewers, the *Washington Post*'s ombudsman among them? Why, or why not?

4. Ephron thinks it would be a good thing if more photographs of death and dying were published by newspapers (paras. 11–13). In an essay of 500 words, state her reasons and your evaluation of them.

 For additional arguments online, visit the e-Pages at **bedfordstmartins.com/barnetbedau**.

PART TWO

CRITICAL WRITING

5

Writing an Analysis of an Argument

This is what we can all do to nourish and strengthen one another: listen to one another very hard, ask questions, too, send one another away to work again, and laugh in all the right places.

—NANCY MAIRS

I don't wait for moods. You accomplish nothing if you do that. Your mind must know it has got to get down to work.

—PEARL S. BUCK

Fear not those who argue but those who dodge.

—MARIE VON EBNER-ESCHENBACH

ANALYZING AN ARGUMENT

Examining the Author's Thesis

Most of your writing in other courses will require you to write an analysis of someone else's writing. In a course in political science you may have to analyze, say, an essay first published in *Foreign Affairs,* perhaps reprinted in your textbook, that argues against raising tariff barriers to foreign trade. Or a course in sociology may require you to analyze a report on the correlation between fatal accidents and drunk drivers under the age of twenty-one. Much of your writing, in short, will set forth reasoned responses to your reading as preparation for making an argument of your own.

Obviously you must understand an essay before you can analyze it thoughtfully. You must read it several times—not just skim it—and (the hard part) you must think critically about it. Again, you'll find that your thinking is stimulated if you take notes and if you ask yourself questions about the material. Are there any Web sites or organizations dedicated to the material you are analyzing? If there are, visit some to see what others are saying about the material you are reviewing. Notes will help you to keep track of the writer's thoughts and also of your own responses to the writer's thesis. The writer probably *does* have a thesis, a claim, a point, and if so, you must try to locate it. Perhaps the thesis is explicitly stated in the title or in a sentence or two near the beginning of the essay or in a concluding paragraph, but perhaps you will have to infer it from the essay as a whole.

Notice that we said the writer *probably* has a thesis. Much of what you read will indeed be primarily an argument; the writer explicitly or implicitly is trying to support some thesis and to convince you to agree with it. But some of what you read will be relatively neutral, with the argument just faintly discernible—or even with no argument at all. A work may, for instance, chiefly be a report: Here are the data, or here is what *X*, *Y*, and *Z* said; make of it what you will. A report might simply state how various ethnic groups voted in an election. In a report of this sort, of course, the writer hopes to persuade readers that the facts are correct, but no thesis is advanced, at least not explicitly or perhaps even consciously; the writer is not evidently arguing a point and trying to change our minds. Such a document differs greatly from an essay by a political analyst who presents similar findings to persuade a candidate to sacrifice the votes of this ethnic bloc and thereby get more votes from other blocs.

Examining the Author's Purpose

While reading an argument, try to form a clear idea of the author's **purpose.** Judging from the essay or the book, was the purpose to persuade, or was it to report? An analysis of a pure report (a work apparently without a thesis or argumentative angle) on ethnic voting will deal chiefly with the accuracy of the report. It will, for example, consider whether the sample poll was representative.

Much material that poses as a report really has a thesis built into it, consciously or unconsciously. The best evidence that the prose you are reading is argumentative is the presence of two kinds of key terms: transitions that imply the drawing of a conclusion and verbs that imply proof (see Idea Prompt 5.1). Keep your eye out for such terms, and scrutinize

IDEA PROMPT 5.1 DRAWING CONCLUSIONS
AND IMPLYING PROOF

Transitions that imply the drawing of a conclusion	*therefore, because, for the reason that, consequently*
Verbs that imply proof	*confirms, verifies, accounts for, implies, proves, disproves, is (in)consistent with, refutes, it follows that*

their precise role whenever they appear. If the essay does not advance a thesis, think of one that it might support or some conventional belief that it might undermine.

Examining the Author's Methods

If the essay advances a thesis, you will want to analyze the strategies or methods of argument that allegedly support the thesis.

- Does the writer quote authorities? Are these authorities competent in this field? Are equally competent authorities who take a different view considered?

- Does the writer use statistics? If so, who compiled them, and are they appropriate to the point being argued? Can they be interpreted differently?

- Does the writer build the argument by using examples or analogies? Are they satisfactory?

- Are the writer's assumptions acceptable?

- Does the writer consider all relevant factors? Has he or she omitted some points that you think should be discussed? For instance, should the author recognize certain opposing positions and perhaps concede something to them?

- Does the writer seek to persuade by means of ridicule? If so, is the ridicule fair: Is it supported also by rational argument?

- Is the argument aimed at a particular audience?

In writing your analysis, you will want to tell your reader something about the author's purpose and something about the author's **methods.** It is usually a good idea at the start of your analysis—if not in the first paragraph, then in the second or third—to let the reader know the purpose (and thesis, if there is one) of the work you are analyzing and then to summarize the work briefly.

Next you will probably find it useful (your reader will certainly find it helpful) to write out *your* thesis (your evaluation or judgment). You might say, for instance, that the essay is impressive but not conclusive, or is undermined by convincing contrary evidence, or relies too much on unsupported generalizations, or is wholly admirable. Remember, because your paper is itself an argument, it needs its own thesis.

And then, of course, comes the job of setting forth your analysis and the support for your thesis. There is no one way of going about this work. If, say, your author gives four arguments (for example, an appeal to common sense, the testimony of authorities, the evidence of comparisons, and an appeal to self-interest), you might want to do one of the following:

- Take up these four arguments in sequence.

- Discuss the simplest of the four and then go on to the more difficult ones.

- Discuss the author's two arguments that you think are sound and then turn to the two that you think are not sound (or perhaps the reverse).

- Take one of these approaches and then clinch your case by constructing a fifth argument that is absent from the work under scrutiny but in your view highly important.

In short, the organization of your analysis may or may not follow the organization of the work you are analyzing.

Examining the Author's Persona

You will probably also want to analyze something a bit more elusive than the author's explicit arguments: the author's self-presentation. Does the author seek to persuade readers partly by presenting himself or herself as conscientious, friendly, self-effacing, authoritative, tentative, or in some other light? Most writers do two things:

- They present evidence.

- They present themselves (or, more precisely, they present the image of themselves that they wish us to behold).

In some persuasive writing this **persona** or **voice** or presentation of the self may be no less important than the presentation of evidence. In other cases, the persona may not much matter, but our point is that you should spend a little time looking at the author's self-presentation to consider if it's significant.

In establishing a persona, writers adopt various rhetorical strategies, ranging from the use of characteristic words to the use of a particular form of organization. For instance,

- The writer who speaks of an opponent's "gimmicks" instead of "strategy" probably is trying to downgrade the opponent and also to convey the self-image of a streetwise person.

- On a larger scale, consider the way in which evidence is presented and the kind of evidence offered. One writer may first bombard the reader with facts and then spend relatively little time drawing conclusions. Another may rely chiefly on generalizations, waiting until the end of the essay to bring the thesis home with a few details. Another may begin with a few facts and spend most of the space reflecting on these. One writer may seem professorial or pedantic, offering examples of an academic sort; another, whose examples are drawn from ordinary life, may seem like a regular guy.

All such devices deserve comment in your analysis.

The writer's persona, then, may color the thesis and help it develop in a distinctive way. If we accept the thesis, it is partly because the writer has won our goodwill by persuading us of his or her good character (*ethos,* in Aristotle's terms). Later we talk more about the appeal to the character of the speaker—the so-called *ethical appeal,* but here we may say that good writers present themselves not as wise-guys, bullies, or pompous asses but as decent people whom the reader would like to invite to dinner.

The author of an essay may, for example, seem fair-minded and open-minded, treating the opposition with great courtesy and expressing interest in hearing other views. Such a tactic is itself a persuasive device. Or take an author who appears to rely on hard evidence such as statistics. This reliance on seemingly objective truths is itself a way of seeking to persuade—a rational way, to be sure, but a mode of persuasion nonetheless.

Especially in analyzing a work in which the author's persona and ideas are blended, you will want to spend some time commenting on the persona. Whether you discuss it near the beginning of your analysis or near the end will depend on your own sense of how you want to construct your essay, and this decision will partly depend on the work you are analyzing. For example, if the author's persona is kept in the background and is thus relatively invisible, you may want to make that point fairly early to get it out of the way and then concentrate on more interesting matters. If, however, the persona is interesting—and perhaps seductive, whether because it seems so scrupulously objective or so engagingly subjective—you may want to hint at this quality early in your essay and then develop the point while you consider the arguments.

In short, the author's self-presentation usually matters. Reorganize its effect, whether positive or negative.

Examining Persona and Intended Audience

A key element in understanding an argument lies in thinking about the intended audience—how the author perceives the audience and what strategies the author uses to connect to it. We have already said something about the creation of the author's persona. An author with a loyal following is, almost by definition, someone who in earlier writings has presented an engaging persona, a persona with a trustworthy *ethos.* A trusted author can sometimes cut corners and can perhaps adopt a colloquial tone that would be unacceptable in the writing of an unknown author.

Authors who want to win the assent of their audiences need to think about how they present information and how they present *themselves.* Think about how you prefer people to talk to you or address you. What sorts of language do you find engaging? Much of course depends on the circumstances, notably the topic, the audience, and the place. A joke may be useful in an argument about whether the government should regulate junk food, but almost surely a joke will be inappropriate—will backfire, will alienate the audience—in an argument about abortion. The *way* an author addresses the reader (through an invented persona) can have a significant impact on the reader's perception of the author, which is to say perception of the author's *views*, the author's *argument*. A slip in tone or an error of fact, however small, may be enough for the audience to dismiss the author's argument. Understanding audience means thinking about all of the possible audiences that may come into contact with your writing or your message, and thinking about the consequences of what you write and where it is published.

You may recall a tweet by Lebron James, who formerly played basketball for the Cleveland Cavaliers but who now plays for the Miami Heat. After James left the Cavaliers (and his home state of Ohio), the Los Angeles Lakers beat the Cavaliers by fifty-five points, and James tweeted: "Crazy. Karma is a b****. Gets you every time. It's not good to wish bad on anybody. God sees everything!" Cleveland fans not surprisingly perceived his tweet as a slap in the face. The broader audience, too, outside of Cleveland, perceived it as uncalled for. Lebron James clearly did not think about his audience(s). To put it in rhetorical terms, Lebron James vastly diminished his *ethos*. Doubtless he wishes he could retract the tweet, but, as the ancient Roman poet Horace said, *"Nescit vox missa reverti"* ("The word once spoken can never be recalled"), or, in plain proverbial English, "Think twice before you speak."

Consider Facebook status updates. Have you ever posted a status update and wished you could take it back only to find out it was too late? People you did not want to see it saw it before you could remove it. Have you ever

---

> ✓ **A CHECKLIST FOR ANALYZING AN AUTHOR'S INTENDED AUDIENCE**
>
> ☐ Where did the piece appear? Who published it? Why, in your view, might someone have found it worth publishing?
>
> ☐ In what technological format does this piece appear? Print journal? Online magazine? Blog? What does the technological format say about the piece or the author?
>
> ☐ Is the writing relatively informal, for instance, a tweet or a Facebook status update? Who is the intended audience? Are there other audiences who may also have an interest but whom the author has failed to consider? Why is this medium good or bad for the message?
>
> ☐ If *you* are the intended audience, what shared values do you have with the author?
>
> ☐ What strategies does the writer use to create a connection with the audience?

tweeted or even texted something you wished you hadn't? When reading and writing more formal essays, it is equally important to think about who wrote what you are reading, and who will read what you are writing.

Summary

In the last few pages we have tried to persuade you that, in writing an analysis of your reading, you must do the following:

- Read and reread thoughtfully. Composing and keeping notes will help you to think about what you are reading.
- Be aware of the purpose of the material to which you are responding.

We have also tried to point out these facts:

- Most of the nonliterary material that you will read is designed to argue, to report, or to do both.
- Most of this material also presents the writer's personality, or voice, and this voice usually merits attention in an analysis. An essay on, say, nuclear war, in a journal devoted to political science may include a voice that moves from an objective tone to a mildly ironic tone to a hortatory tone, and this voice is worth commenting on.

Possibly all this explanation is obvious. There is yet another point, equally obvious but often neglected by students who begin by writing an analysis and end up by writing only a summary, a shortened version of the work they have read: Although your essay is an analysis of someone else's writing, and you may have to include a summary of the work you are writing about, your essay is *your* essay, your analysis, not a mere summary. The thesis, the organization, and the tone are yours.

- Your thesis, for example, may be that, although the author is convinced she has presented a strong case, her case is far from proved because, . . .
- Your organization may be deeply indebted to the work you are analyzing, but it need not be. The author may have begun with specific examples and then gone on to make generalizations and to draw conclusions, but you may begin with the conclusions.
- Your tone, similarly, may resemble your subject's (let's say the voice is courteous academic), but it will nevertheless have its own ring, its own tone of, say, urgency, caution, or coolness.

Most of the essays that we have included thus far are more or less in an academic style, and indeed several are by students and by professors. But argumentative writing is not limited to academicians — if it were, your college would not be requiring you to take a course in the subject. The following essay, in a breezy style, comes from a columnist who writes for the *New York Times*.

✔ A CHECKLIST FOR ANALYZING A TEXT

Have I considered all of the following matters?

☐ Who is the author? What stake might he or she have in writing this piece?

☐ Is the piece aimed at a particular audience? A neutral audience? What is your evidence? Persons who are already sympathetic to the author's point of view? A hostile audience?

☐ What is the author's thesis (argument, main point, claim)?

☐ What assumptions does the author make? Do I share them? If not, why not?

☐ Does the author ever confuse facts with beliefs or opinions?

☐ What appeals does the author make? To reason (*logos*), for instance, with statistics, the testimony of authorities, and personal experience? To the emotions (*pathos*), for instance, by an appeal to "our better nature," or to widely shared values? To our sense that the speaker is trustworthy (*ethos*)?

☐ How convincing is the evidence? Why do you think so?

☐ Are significant objections and counterevidence adequately discussed?

☐ How is the text organized, and is the organization effective? Are the title, the opening paragraphs, and the concluding paragraphs effective? In what ways?

☐ If visual materials such as graphs, pie charts, or pictures are used, how persuasive are they? Do they make a logical appeal? (Charts and graphs presumably make a logical appeal.) Do they make an emotional appeal? An ethical appeal?

☐ What is the author's tone? Is it appropriate?

☐ To what extent has the author convinced me? Why?

AN ARGUMENT, ITS ELEMENTS, AND A STUDENT'S ANALYSIS OF THE ARGUMENT

Nicholas D. Kristof

Nicholas D. Kristof (b. 1959) grew up on a farm in Oregon. After graduating from Harvard, he was awarded a Rhodes scholarship to Oxford, where he studied law. In 1984 he joined the New York Times *as a correspondent, and since 2001 he has written as a columnist. He has won two Pulitzer Prizes.*

For Environmental Balance, Pick Up a Rifle

Here's a quick quiz: Which large American mammal kills the most humans each year?

It's not the bear, which kills about two people a year in North America. Nor is it the wolf, which in modern times hasn't killed anyone in this country. It's not the cougar, which kills one person every year or two.

Rather, it's the deer. Unchecked by predators, deer populations are exploding in a way that is profoundly unnatural and that is destroying the ecosystem in many parts of the country. In a wilderness, there might be ten deer per square mile; in parts of New Jersey, there are up to 200 per square mile.

One result is ticks and Lyme disease, but deer also kill people more directly. A study for the insurance industry estimated that deer kill about 150 people a year in car crashes nationwide and cause $1 billion in damage. Granted, deer aren't stalking us, and they come out worse in these collisions—but it's still true that in a typical year, an American is less likely to be killed by Osama bin Laden than by Bambi.

If the symbol of the environment's being out of whack in the 1960s   5 was the Cuyahoga River in Cleveland catching fire, one such symbol today is deer congregating around what they think of as salad bars and what we think of as suburbs.

So what do we do? Let's bring back hunting.

Now, you've probably just spilled your coffee. These days, among the university-educated crowd in the cities, hunting is viewed as barbaric.

The upshot is that towns in New York and New Jersey are talking about using birth control to keep deer populations down. (Liberals presumably support free condoms, while conservatives back abstinence education.) Deer contraception hasn't been very successful, though.

Meanwhile, the same population bomb has spread to bears. A bear hunt has been scheduled for this week in New Jersey—prompting outrage from some animal rights groups (there's also talk of bear contraception: make love, not cubs).

As for deer, partly because hunting is perceived as brutal and vaguely   10 psychopathic, towns are taking out contracts on deer through discreet private companies. Greenwich, Connecticut, budgeted $47,000 this year to pay a company to shoot eighty deer from raised platforms over four nights—as well as $8,000 for deer birth control.

Look, this is ridiculous.

We have an environmental imbalance caused in part by the decline of hunting. Humans first wiped out certain predators—like wolves and cougars—but then expanded their own role as predators to sustain a rough ecological balance. These days, though, hunters are on the decline.

According to "Families Afield: An Initiative for the Future of Hunting," a report by an alliance of shooting organizations, for every hundred hunters who die or stop hunting, only sixty-nine hunters take their place.

I was raised on *Bambi*—but also, as an Oregon farm boy, on venison and elk meat. But deer are not pets, and dead deer are as natural as live deer. To wring one's hands over them, perhaps after polishing off a hamburger, is soggy sentimentality.

What's the alternative to hunting? Is it preferable that deer die of 15 disease and hunger? Or, as the editor of *Adirondack Explorer* magazine suggested, do we introduce wolves into the burbs?

To their credit, many environmentalists agree that hunting can be green. The New Jersey Audubon Society this year advocated deer hunting as an ecological necessity.

There's another reason to encourage hunting: it connects people with the outdoors and creates a broader constituency for wilderness preservation. At a time when America's wilderness is being gobbled away for logging, mining, or oil drilling, that's a huge boon.

Granted, hunting isn't advisable in suburban backyards, and I don't expect many soccer moms to install gun racks in their minivans. But it's an abdication of environmental responsibility to eliminate other predators and then refuse to assume the job ourselves. In that case, the collisions with humans will simply get worse.

In October, for example, Wayne Goldsberry was sitting in a home in northwestern Arkansas when he heard glass breaking in the next room. It was a home invasion—by a buck.

Mr. Goldsberry, who is six feet one inch and weighs two hundred 20 pounds, wrestled with the intruder for forty minutes. Blood spattered the walls before he managed to break the buck's neck.

So it's time to reestablish a balance in the natural world—by accepting the idea that hunting is as natural as bird-watching.

TOPICS FOR CRITICAL THINKING AND WRITING

1. What is Kristof's chief thesis? (State it in one sentence.)

2. Does Kristof make any assumptions—tacit or explicit—with which you disagree? With which you agree? Write them down.

3. Is the slightly humorous tone of Kristof's essay inappropriate for a discussion of deliberately killing wild animals? Why, or why not?

4. If you are familiar with *Bambi*, does the story make any *argument* against killing deer, or does the story appeal only to our emotions?

5. Do you agree that "hunting is as natural as bird-watching" (para. 21)? In any case, do you think that an appeal to what is "natural" is a good argument for expanding the use of hunting?

6. To whom is Kristof talking? How do you know?

The Essay Analyzed

OK, time's up. Let's examine Kristof's essay with an eye to identifying those elements we mentioned earlier in this chapter (pp. 179–86) that deserve notice when examining *any* argument: the author's *thesis, purpose, methods, persona,* and *audience.* And while we're at it, let's also notice some other features of Kristof's essay that will help us appreciate its effects and evaluate it. We will thus be in a good position to write an evaluation or an argument that confirms, extends, or even rebuts Kristof's argument.

But first, a caution: Kristof's essay appeared in a newspaper where paragraphs are customarily very short, partly to allow for easy reading and partly because the columns are narrow and even short paragraphs may extend for an inch or two. If his essay were to appear in a book, doubtless the author would join many of the paragraphs, making longer units. In analyzing a work, think about where it originally appeared. A blog, a print journal, an online magazine? Does the format in some measure influence the piece?

Title   By combining "Environmental Balance" with "Rifle"—terms that don't seem to go together—Kristof starts off with a bang. He gives a hint of his *topic* (something about the environment) and of his thesis (some sort of way of introducing ecological balance). He also conveys something of his persona by introducing a rifle into the environment. He is, the title suggests, a no-nonsense, hard-hitting guy.

Opening Paragraphs   Kristof immediately grabs hold of us ("Here's a quick quiz") and asks a simple question, but one that we probably have not thought much about: "Which large American mammal kills the most humans each year?" In his second paragraph he tells us it is *not* the bear—the answer most readers probably come up with—nor is it the cougar. Not until the third paragraph does Kristof give us the answer, the deer. But remember, Kristof is writing in a newspaper, where paragraphs customarily are very short. It takes us only a few seconds to get to the third paragraph and the answer.

Thesis   What is the basic thesis Kristof is arguing? Somewhat unusually, Kristof does *not* announce it in its full form until his sixth paragraph ("Let's bring back hunting"), but, again, his paragraphs are very short, and if the essay were published in a book, Kristof's first two paragraphs probably would be combined, as would the third and fourth.

Purpose   Kristof's purpose is clear: He wants to *persuade* readers to adopt his view. This amounts to trying to persuade us that his thesis (stated above) is *true.* Kristof, however, does not show that his essay is argumentative or persuasive by using many of the key terms that normally mark argumentative prose. He doesn't call anything his *conclusion*, none of his statements is labeled *my premises*, and he doesn't connect clauses or sentences with *therefore* or *because.* Almost the only traces of the language of argument are "Granted" (para. 18) and "So" (that is, *therefore*) in his final paragraph.

Despite the lack of argumentative language, the argumentative nature of his essay is clear. He has a thesis—one that will strike many readers as highly unusual—and he wants readers to accept it, so he must go on to *support* it; accordingly, after his introductory paragraphs, in which he calls attention to a problem and offers a solution (his thesis), he must offer evidence, and that is what much of the rest of the essay seeks to do.

Methods   Although Kristof will have to offer evidence, he begins by recognizing the folks on the other side, "the university-educated crowd in the cities, [for whom] hunting is viewed as barbaric" (para. 7). He goes on to spoof this "crowd" when, speaking of methods of keeping the deer population down, he says in paragraph 8, "Liberals presumably support free condoms, while conservatives back abstinence education." Ordinarily it is a bad idea to make fun of persons who hold views other than your own—after all, they just may be on to something, they just might know something you don't know, and, in any case, impartial readers rarely want to align themselves with someone who mocks others. In the essay we are looking at, however, Kristof gets away with this smart-guy tone because he (a) has loyal readers and (b) has written the entire essay in a highly informal or playful manner. Think again about the first paragraph, which begins "Here's a quick quiz." The informality is not only in the contraction (*Here's* versus *Here is*), but in the very idea of beginning by grabbing the readers and thrusting a quiz at them. The playfulness is evident throughout: For instance, immediately after Kristof announces his thesis, "Let's bring back hunting," he begins a new paragraph (7) with, "Now, you've probably just spilled your coffee."

Kristof's methods of presenting evidence include providing **statistics** (paras. 3, 4, 10, and 13), giving **examples** (paras. 10, 19–20), and citing **authorities** (paras. 13 and 16).

Persona   Kristof presents himself as a confident, no-nonsense fellow, a persona that not many writers can get away with, but that probably is acceptable in a journalist who regularly writes a newspaper column. His readers know what to expect, and they read him with pleasure. But it probably would be inadvisable for an unknown writer to adopt this persona, unless perhaps he or she were writing for an audience that could be counted on to be friendly (in this instance, an audience of hunters). If this essay appeared in a hunting magazine, doubtless it would please and entertain its audience. It would not convert anybody, but conversion would not be its point if it were published in a magazine read by hunters. In the *New York Times,* where the essay originally appeared, Kristof could count on a moderately sympathetic audience because he has a large number of faithful readers, but one can guess that many of these readers—chiefly city dwellers—read him for entertainment rather than for information about how they should actually behave.

By the way, when we speak of "faithful readers" we are in effect saying that the author has established good *ethos*, has convinced those readers that he or she is *worth* reading.

Closing Paragraphs   The first two of the last three paragraphs report an episode (the 200-pound buck inside the house) that Kristof presumably thinks is pretty conclusive evidence. The final paragraph begins with "So," strongly implying a logical conclusion to the essay.

Let's now turn to a student's analysis of Kristof's essay and then to our analysis of the student's analysis. (We should say that the analysis of Kristof's essay that you have just read is partly indebted to the student's essay that you are about to read.)

Betsy Swinton

Professor Knowles

English 101B

March 12, 2013

Tracking Kristof

Nicholas D. Kristof's "For Environmental Balance, Pick Up a Rifle" is an engaging piece of writing, but whether it is convincing is something I am not sure about. And I am not sure about it for two reasons: (1) I don't know much about the deer problem, and that's my fault; (2) I don't know much about the deer problem, and that's Kristof's fault. The first point needs no explanation, but let me explain the second.

Kristof is making an argument, offering a thesis: Deer are causing destruction, and the best way to reduce the destruction is to hunt deer. For all that I know, he may be correct both in his comment about what deer are doing and also in his comment about what must be done about deer. My ignorance of the situation is regrettable, but I don't think that I am the only reader from Chicago who doesn't know much about the deer problems in New Jersey, Connecticut, and Arkansas, the states that Kristof specifically mentions in connection with the deer problem. He announces his thesis early enough, in his sixth paragraph, and he is entertaining throughout his essay, but does he make a convincing case? To ask "Does he make a convincing case?" is to ask "Does he offer adequate evidence?" and "Does he show that his solution is better than other possible solutions?"

To take the first question: In a short essay Kristof can hardly give overwhelming evidence, but he does convince me that there is a problem. The most convincing evidence he gives appears in paragraph 16, where he says that the New Jersey Audubon Society "advocated deer hunting as an ecological necessity." I don't really know anything about the New Jersey Audubon Society, but I suppose that they are

Swinton 2

people with a deep interest in nature and in conservation, and if even such a group advocates deer hunting, there must be something to this solution.

I am even willing to accept his argument that, in this nation of meat-eaters, "to wring one's hands over them [dead deer], perhaps after polishing off a hamburger, is soggy sentimentality" (para. 14). According to Kristof, the present alternative to hunting deer is that we leave the deer to "die of disease and hunger" (para. 15). But what I am not convinced of is that there is no way to reduce the deer population other than by hunting. I don't think Kristof adequately explains why some sort of birth control is inadequate. In his eighth paragraph he makes a joke about controlling the birth of deer ("Liberals presumably support free condoms, while conservatives back abstinence education"), and the joke is funny, but it isn't an argument, it's just a joke. Why can't food containing some sort of sterilizing medicine be put out for the starving deer, food that will nourish them and yet make them unreproductive? In short, I don't think he has fairly informed his readers of alternatives to his own positions, and because he fails to look at counterproposals, he weakens his own proposal.

Although Kristof occasionally uses a word or phrase that suggests argument, such as "Granted" (para. 18), "So" (final paragraph), and "There's another reason" (para. 17), he relies chiefly on forceful writing rather than on reasoning. And the second of his two reasons for hunting seems utterly unconvincing to me. His first, as we have seen, is that the deer population (and apparently the bear population) is out of control. His second (para. 17) is that hunting "connects people with the outdoors and creates a broader constituency for wilderness preservation." I am not a hunter and I have never been one. Perhaps that's my misfortune, but I don't think I am missing anything. And when I hear Kristof say, in his final sentence—the climactic place in his essay—that "hunting is as

Swinton 3

natural as bird-watching," I rub my eyes in disbelief. If he had me at least half-convinced by his statistics and his citation of the Audubon Society, he now loses me when he argues that hunting is "natural." One might as well say that war is natural, rape is natural, bribery is natural—all these terrible things occur, but we ought to deplore them and we ought to make every effort to see that they disappear.

In short, I think that Kristof has written an engaging essay, and he may well have an important idea, but I think that in his glib final paragraph, where he tells us that "hunting is as natural as bird-watching," he utterly loses the reader's confidence.

AN ANALYSIS OF THE STUDENT'S ANALYSIS

Swinton's essay seems to us to be excellent, doubtless the product of a good deal of thoughtful revision. She does not cover every possible aspect of Kristof's essay—she concentrates on his reasoning and she says very little about his style—but we think that, given the limits of space (about 500 words), she does a good job. What makes this student's essay effective?

- The essay has a title ("Tracking Kristof") that is of at least a little interest; it picks up Kristof's point about hunting, and it gives a hint of what is to come.

✓ A CHECKLIST FOR WRITING AN ANALYSIS
OF AN ARGUMENT

Have I asked myself the following questions?

☐ Early in my essay have I accurately stated the writer's thesis (claim) and summarized his or her supporting reasons? Have I explained to my reader any disagreement about definitions of important terms?

☐ Have I, again fairly early in my essay, indicated where I will be taking my reader, i.e., have I indicated my general response to the essay I am analyzing?

☐ Have I called attention to the strengths, if any, and the weaknesses, if any, of the essay?

☐ Have I commented not only on the *logos* (logic, reasoning) but also on the *ethos* (character of the writer, as presented in the essay)? For instance, has the author convinced me that he or she is well-informed and is a person of goodwill? Or, on the other hand, does the writer seem to be chiefly concerned with ridiculing those who hold a different view?

☐ If there is an appeal to *pathos* (emotion, originally meaning "pity for suffering," but now interpreted more broadly to include appeals to patriotism, humor, or loyalty to family, for example), is it acceptable? If not, why not?

☐ Have I used occasional brief quotations to let my reader hear the author's tone and to ensure fairness and accuracy?

☐ Is my analysis effectively organized?

☐ Have I taken account of the author's audience(s)?

☐ Does my essay, perhaps in the concluding paragraphs, indicate my agreement or disagreement with the writer but also my view of the essay as a piece of argumentative writing?

☐ Is my tone appropriate?

- The author promptly identifies her subject (she names the writer and the title of his essay) early.

- Early in the essay she gives us a hint of where she will be going (in her first paragraph she tells us that Kristof's essay is "engaging . . . *but* . . .").

- She recognizes Kristof's audience at the start, and she suggests that he may not have given thought to this matter of the audience.

- She uses a few brief quotations, to give us a feel for Kristof's essay and to let us hear the evidence for itself, but she does not pad her essay with long quotations.

- She takes up all of Kristof's main points.

- She gives her essay a reasonable organization, letting us hear Kristof's thesis, letting us know the degree to which she accepts it, and finally letting us know her specific reservations about the essay.

- She concludes without the formality of "in conclusion"; "in short" nicely does the trick.

- Notice, finally, that she sticks closely to Kristof's essay. She does not go off on a tangent about the virtues of vegetarianism or the dreadful politics of the *New York Times,* the newspaper that published Kristof's essay. She was asked to analyze the essay, and she has done so.

EXERCISE

Take one of the essays not yet discussed in class or an essay assigned now by your instructor, and in an essay of 500 words analyze and evaluate it, guided by the checklists and examples we have provided.

ARGUMENTS FOR ANALYSIS

Jeff Jacoby

Jeff Jacoby is a columnist for the Boston Globe, *where this essay was originally published on the op-ed page on February 20, 1997.*

Bring Back Flogging

Boston's Puritan forefathers did not indulge miscreants lightly.

For selling arms and gunpowder to Indians in 1632, Richard Hopkins was sentenced to be "whipt, & branded with a hott iron on one of his cheekes." Joseph Gatchell, convicted of blasphemy in 1684, was ordered "to stand in pillory, have his head and hand put in & have his toung drawne forth out of his mouth, & peirct through with a hott iron." When Hannah Newell pleaded guilty to adultery in 1694, the court ordered "fifteen stripes Severally to be laid on upon her naked back at the Common Whipping post." Her consort, the aptly named Lambert Despair, fared worse: He was sentenced to twenty-five lashes "and that on the next Thursday Immediately after Lecture he stand upon the Pillory for . . . a full hower with Adultery in Capitall letters written upon his brest."

Corporal punishment for criminals did not vanish with the Puritans— Delaware didn't get around to repealing it until 1972—but for all relevant purposes, it has been out of fashion for at least 150 years. The day is long past when the stocks had an honored place on the Boston Common, or when offenders were publicly flogged. Now we practice a more enlightened, more humane way of disciplining wrongdoers: We lock them up in cages.

Imprisonment has become our penalty of choice for almost every offense in the criminal code. Commit murder; go to prison. Sell cocaine; go to prison. Kite checks; go to prison. It is an all-purpose punishment, suitable—or so it would seem—for crimes violent and nonviolent, motivated by hate or by greed, plotted coldly or committed in a fit of passion. If anything, our preference for incarceration is deepening—behold the slew of mandatory minimum sentences for drug crimes and "three-strikes-you're-out" life terms for recidivists. Some 1.6 million Americans are behind bars today. That represents a 250 percent increase since 1980, and the number is climbing.

We cage criminals at a rate unsurpassed in the free world, yet few 5 of us believe that the criminal justice system is a success. Crime is out of control, despite the deluded happy talk by some politicians about how "safe" cities have become. For most wrongdoers, the odds of being arrested, prosecuted, convicted, and incarcerated are reassuringly long. Fifty-eight percent of all murders do *not* result in a prison term. Likewise 98 percent of all burglaries.

Many states have gone on prison-building sprees, yet the penal system is choked to bursting. To ease the pressure, nearly all convicted felons are released early—or not locked up at all. "About three of every four convicted criminals," says John DiIulio, a noted Princeton criminologist, "are on the streets without meaningful probation or parole supervision." And while everyone knows that amateur thugs should be deterred before they become career criminals, it is almost unheard of for judges to send first- or second-time offenders to prison.

Meanwhile, the price of keeping criminals in cages is appalling—a common estimate is $30,000 per inmate per year. (To be sure, the cost to society of turning many inmates loose would be even higher.) For tens of thousands of convicts, prison is a graduate school of criminal studies: They emerge more ruthless and savvy than when they entered. And for many offenders, there is even a certain cachet to doing time—a stint in prison becomes a sign of manhood, a status symbol.

But there would be no cachet in chaining a criminal to an outdoor post and flogging him. If young punks were horsewhipped in public after their first conviction, fewer of them would harden into lifelong felons. A humiliating and painful paddling can be applied to the rear end of a crook for a lot less than $30,000—and prove a lot more educational than ten years' worth of prison meals and lockdowns.

Are we quite certain the Puritans have nothing to teach us about dealing with criminals?

Of course, their crimes are not our crimes: We do not arrest blas- 10 phemers or adulterers, and only gun control fanatics would criminalize the sale of weapons to Indians. (They would criminalize the sale of weapons to anybody.) Nor would the ordeal suffered by poor Joseph Gatchell—the tongue "peirct through" with a hot poker—be regarded today as anything less than torture.

But what is the objection to corporal punishment that doesn't maim or mutilate? Instead of a prison term, why not sentence at least some criminals—say, thieves and drunk drivers—to a public whipping?

"Too degrading," some will say. "Too brutal." But where is it written that being whipped is more degrading than being caged? Why is it more brutal to flog a wrongdoer than to throw him in prison—where the risk of being beaten, raped, or murdered is terrifyingly high?

The *Globe* reported in 1994 that more than two hundred thousand prison inmates are raped each year, usually to the indifference of the guards. "The horrors experienced by many young inmates, particularly those who . . . are convicted of nonviolent offenses," former Supreme Court Justice Harry Blackmun has written, "border on the unimaginable." Are those horrors preferable to the short, sharp shame of corporal punishment?

Perhaps the Puritans were more enlightened than we think, at least on the subject of punishment. Their sanctions were humiliating and painful, but quick and cheap. Maybe we should readopt a few.

Topics for Critical Thinking and Writing

1. When Jacoby says (para. 3) that today we are more "enlightened" than our Puritan forefathers because where they used flogging, "We lock them up in cages," is he being ironic? Explain.

2. Suppose you agree with Jacoby. Explain precisely (a) what you mean by *flogging* (does Jacoby explain what he means?) and (b) how much flogging is appropriate for the crimes of housebreaking, rape, robbery, and murder.

3. In an essay of 250 words, explain why you think that flogging would be more (or less) degrading and brutal than imprisonment.

4. At the end of his essay Jacoby draws to our attention the terrible risk of being raped in prison as an argument in favor of replacing imprisonment

with flogging. Do you think he mentions this point at the end because he believes it is the strongest or most persuasive of all those he mentions? Why, or why not?

5. It is often said that corporal punishment does not have any effect or, if it does, that the effect is the negative one of telling the recipient that violence is an acceptable form of behavior. But suppose it were demonstrated that the infliction of physical pain reduced at least certain kinds of crimes, perhaps shoplifting or unarmed robbery. Should we adopt the practice?

6. Jacoby draws the line (para. 11) at punishment that would "maim or mutilate." Why draw the line here? Some societies punish thieves by amputating a hand. Suppose we knew that this practice really did seriously reduce theft. Should we adopt it? How about adopting castration (surgical or chemical) for rapists? For child molesters?

Gerard Jones

Gerard Jones (b. 1957), author of several works of fiction and nonfiction, has written many comic books for Marvel Comics and other publishers.

Violent Media Is Good for Kids

At thirteen I was alone and afraid. Taught by my well-meaning, progressive, English-teacher parents that violence was wrong, that rage was something to be overcome and cooperation was always better than conflict, I suffocated my deepest fears and desires under a nice-boy persona. Placed in a small, experimental school that was wrong for me, afraid to join my peers in their bumptious rush into adolescent boyhood, I withdrew into passivity and loneliness. My parents, not trusting the violent world of the late 1960s, built a wall between me and the crudest elements of American pop culture.

Then the Incredible Hulk smashed through it.

One of my mother's students convinced her that Marvel Comics, despite their apparent juvenility and violence, were in fact devoted to lofty messages of pacifism and tolerance. My mother borrowed some, thinking they'd be good for me. And so they were. But not because they preached lofty messages of benevolence. They were good for me because they were juvenile. And violent.

The character who caught me, and freed me, was the Hulk: overgendered and undersocialized, half-naked and half-witted, raging against a frightened world that misunderstood and persecuted him. Suddenly I had a fantasy self to carry my stifled rage and buried desire for power. I had a fantasy self who was a self: unafraid of his desires and the world's disapproval, unhesitating and effective in action. "Puny boy follow Hulk!" roared my fantasy self, and I followed.

I followed him to new friends—other sensitive geeks chasing their   5
own inner brutes—and I followed him to the arrogant, self-exposing,
self-assertive, superheroic decision to become a writer. Eventually, I left
him behind, followed more sophisticated heroes, and finally my own lead
along a twisting path to a career and an identity. In my thirties, I found
myself writing action movies and comic books. I wrote some Hulk stories, and met the geek-geniuses who created him. I saw my own creations
turned into action figures, cartoons, and computer games. I talked to the
kids who read my stories. Across generations, genders, and ethnicities I
kept seeing the same story: people pulling themselves out of emotional
traps by immersing themselves in violent stories. People integrating the
scariest, most fervently denied fragments of their psyches into fuller senses
of selfhood through fantasies of superhuman combat and destruction.

A scene from Gerard Jones and Gene Ha's comic
book "Oktane"

I have watched
my son living the same
story — transforming
himself into a blood-
thirsty dinosaur to em-
bolden himself for the
plunge into preschool, a
Power Ranger to muscle
through a social compe-
tition in kindergarten.
In the first grade, his
friends started climbing
a tree at school. But he
was afraid: of falling, of
the centipedes crawling
on the trunk, of sharp
branches, of his friends'
derision. I took my cue
from his own fantasies
and read him old Tarzan
comics, rich in combat
and bright with flashing
knives. For two weeks
he lived in them. Then
he put them aside. And
he climbed the tree.

But all the while,
especially in the wake
of the recent burst of
school shootings, I heard
pop psychologists insist-
ing that violent stories
are harmful to kids, heard

teachers begging parents to keep their kids away from "junk culture," heard a guilt-stricken friend with a son who loved Pokémon lament, "I've turned into the bad mom who lets her kid eat sugary cereal and watch cartoons!"

That's when I started the research.

"Fear, greed, power-hunger, rage: these are aspects of our selves that we try not to experience in our lives but often want, even need, to experience vicariously through stories of others," writes Melanie Moore, Ph.D., a psychologist who works with urban teens. "Children need violent entertainment in order to explore the inescapable feelings that they've been taught to deny, and to reintegrate those feelings into a more whole, more complex, more resilient selfhood."

Moore consults to public schools and local governments, and is also 10 raising a daughter. For the past three years she and I have been studying the ways in which children use violent stories to meet their emotional and developmental needs—and the ways in which adults can help them use those stories healthily. With her help I developed Power Play, a program for helping young people improve their self-knowledge and sense of potency through heroic, combative storytelling.

We've found that every aspect of even the trashiest pop-culture story can have its own developmental function. Pretending to have superhuman powers helps children conquer the feelings of powerlessness that inevitably come with being so young and small. The dual-identity concept at the heart of many superhero stories helps kids negotiate the conflicts between the inner self and the public self as they work through the early stages of socialization. Identification with a rebellious, even destructive, hero helps children learn to push back against a modern culture that cultivates fear and teaches dependency.

At its most fundamental level, what we call "creative violence"—head-bonking cartoons, bloody videogames, playground karate, toy guns—gives children a tool to master their rage. Children will feel rage. Even the sweetest and most civilized of them, even those whose parents read the better class of literary magazines, will feel rage. The world is uncontrollable and incomprehensible; mastering it is a terrifying, enraging task. Rage can be an energizing emotion, a shot of courage to push us to resist greater threats, take more control, than we ever thought we could. But rage is also the emotion our culture distrusts the most. Most of us are taught early on to fear our own. Through immersion in imaginary combat and identification with a violent protagonist, children engage the rage they've stifled, come to fear it less, and become more capable of utilizing it against life's challenges.

I knew one little girl who went around exploding with fantasies so violent that other moms would draw her mother aside to whisper, "I think you should know something about Emily. . . ." Her parents were separating, and she was small, an only child, a tomboy at an age when her classmates were dividing sharply along gender lines. On the

The title character of "Oktane" gets nasty.

playground she acted out *Sailor Moon* fights, and in the classroom she wrote stories about people being stabbed with knives. The more adults tried to control her stories, the more she acted out the roles of her angry heroes: breaking rules, testing limits, roaring threats.

Then her mother and I started helping her tell her stories. She wrote them, performed them, drew them like comics: sometimes bloody, sometimes tender, always blending the images of pop culture with her own most private fantasies. She came out of it just as fiery and strong, but more self-controlled and socially competent: a leader among her peers, the one student in her class who could truly pull boys and girls together.

I worked with an older girl, a middle-class "nice girl," who held   15
herself together through a chaotic family situation and a tumultuous adolescence with gangsta rap. In the mythologized street violence of Ice T, the rage and strutting of his music and lyrics, she found a theater of the mind in which she could be powerful, ruthless, invulnerable. She avoided the heavy drug use that sank many of her peers, and flowered in college as a writer and political activist.

I'm not going to argue that violent entertainment is harmless. I think it has helped inspire some people to real-life violence. I am going to argue that it's helped hundreds of people for every one it's hurt, and that it can help far more if we learn to use it well. I am going to argue that our fear of "youth violence" isn't well-founded on reality, and that the fear can do more harm than the reality. We act as though our highest priority is to prevent our children from growing up into murderous thugs—but modern kids are far more likely to grow up too passive, too distrustful of themselves, too easily manipulated.

We send the message to our children in a hundred ways that their craving for imaginary gun battles and symbolic killings is wrong, or at least dangerous. Even when we don't call for censorship or forbid *Mortal Kombat*, we moan to other parents within our kids' earshot about the "awful violence" in the entertainment they love. We tell our kids that it isn't nice to play-fight, or we steer them from some monstrous action figure to a prosocial doll. Even in the most progressive households, where we make such a point of letting children feel what they feel, we rush to substitute an enlightened discussion for the raw material of rageful fantasy. In the process, we risk confusing them about their natural aggression in the same way the Victorians confused their children about their sexuality. When we try to protect our children from their own feelings and fantasies, we shelter them not against violence but against power and selfhood.

TOPICS FOR CRITICAL THINKING AND WRITING

1. In his final paragraph Jones mentions the Victorian treatment of sexuality. Why does he bring this in? Does his use of this point make for an effective ending? Explain.

2. In an essay of 300 words, explain whether you think Jones has made the case for violence in an effective and persuasive way. If so, what is it about his article that makes it effective and persuasive? If it is not, where do the problems lie?

3. What kinds of violence does Jones advocate?

4. Does violence play as large a part in the life of teenage girls as it does in the life of teenage boys? Why, or why not?

5. How would you characterize the audience Jones is addressing? What is your evidence?

Justin Cronin

Justin Cronin is an award-winning novelist who teaches at Rice University, in Houston, Texas.

Confessions of a Liberal Gun Owner

I am a New England liberal, born and bred. I have lived most of my life in the Northeast—Boston, New York, and Philadelphia—and my politics are devoutly Democratic. In three decades, I have voted for a Republican exactly once, holding my nose, in a mayoral election in which the Democratic candidate seemed mentally unbalanced.

I am also a Texas resident and a gun owner. I have half a dozen pistols in my safe, all semiautomatics, the largest capable of holding twenty rounds. I go to the range at least once a week, have applied for a concealed carry license, and am planning to take a tactical training course in the spring. I'm currently shopping for a shotgun, either a Remington 870 Express Tactical or a Mossberg 500 Flex with a pistol grip and adjustable stock.

Except for shotguns (firing one feels like being punched by a prizefighter), I enjoy shooting. At the range where I practice, most of the staff knows me by sight if not by name. I'm the guy in the metrosexual eyeglasses and Ralph Lauren polo, and I ask a lot of questions: What's the best way to maintain my sight picture with both eyes open? How do I clear a stove-piped round?

There is pleasure to be had in exercising one's rights, learning something new in midlife, and mastering the operation of a complex tool, which is one thing a gun is. But I won't deny the seductive psychological power that firearms possess. I grew up playing shooting games, pretending to be Starsky or Hutch or one of the patrolmen on *Adam-12*, the two most boring TV cops in history.

A prevailing theory holds that boys are simultaneously aware of 5 their own physical powerlessness and society's mandate that they serve as protectors of the innocent. Pretending to shoot a bad guy assuages this anxiety, which never goes away completely. This explanation makes sense to me. Another word for it is catharsis, and you could say that, as a novelist, I've made my living from it.

There are a lot of reasons that a gun feels right in my hand, but I also own firearms to protect my family. I hope I never have to use one for this purpose, and I doubt I ever will. But I am my family's last line of defense. I have chosen to meet this responsibility, in part, by being armed. It wasn't a choice I made lightly. I am aware that, statistically speaking, a gun in the home represents a far greater danger to its inhabitants than to an intruder. But not every choice we make is data-driven. A lot comes from the gut.

Apart from the ones in policemen's holsters, I don't think I saw a working firearm until the year after college, when a friend's girlfriend, after four cosmopolitans, decided to show off the .38 revolver she kept in her purse. (Half the party guests dived for cover, including me.)

It wasn't until my mid-forties that my education in guns began, in the course of writing a novel in which pistols, shotguns, and rifles, but also heavy weaponry like the AR-15 and its military analogue, the M-16, were widely used. I suspected that much of the gunplay I'd witnessed in movies and television was completely wrong (it is) and hired an instructor for a daylong private lesson "to shoot everything in the store." The gentleman who met me at the range was someone whom I would have called "a gun nut." A former New Yorker, he had relocated to Texas because of its lax gun laws and claimed to keep a pistol within arm's reach even when he showered. He was perfect, in other words, for my purpose.

My relationship to firearms might have ended there, if not for a coincidence of weather. Everybody remembers Hurricane Katrina; fewer recall Hurricane Rita, an even more intense storm that headed straight for Houston less than a month later. My wife and I arranged to stay at a friend's house in Austin, packed up the kids and dog, and headed out of town — or tried to. As many as 3.7 million people had the same idea, making Rita one of the largest evacuations in history, with predictable results.

By two in the morning, after six hours on the road, we had made   10
it all of fifty miles. The scene was like a snapshot from the Apocalypse: crowds milling restlessly, gas stations and mini-marts picked clean and heaped with trash, families sleeping by the side of the road. The situation had the hopped-up feel of barely bottled chaos. After Katrina, nobody had any illusions that help was on its way. It also occurred to me that there were probably a lot of guns out there—this was Texas, after all. Here I was with two tiny children, a couple of thousand dollars in cash, a late-model S.U.V. with half a tank of gas and not so much as a heavy book to throw. When my wife wouldn't let me get out of the car so the dog could do his business, that was it for me. We jumped the median, turned around, and were home in under an hour.

As it happened, Rita made a last-minute turn away from Houston. But what if it hadn't? I believe people are basically good, but not all of them and not all the time. Like most citizens of our modern, technological world, I am wholly reliant upon a fragile web of services to meet my most basic needs. What would happen if those services collapsed? Chaos, that's what.

It didn't happen overnight, but before too long my Northeastern liberal sensibilities, while intact on other issues, had shifted on the question of gun ownership. For my first pistol I selected a little Walther .380. I shot it enough to decide it was junk, upgraded to a full-size Springfield 9-millimeter, liked it but wanted something with a thumb safety, found a nice Smith & Wesson subcompact that fit the bill, but along the way got a little bit of a gun-crush on the Beretta M-9—and so on.

Lots of people on both sides of the aisle own firearms, or don't, for reasons that supersede their broader political and cultural affiliations. Let me be clear: my personal armory notwithstanding. I think guns are woefully under-regulated. It's far too easy to buy a gun—I once bought one in a parking lot—and I loathe the National Rifle Association. Some of the Obama administration's proposals strike me as more symbolic than effective, with some 300 million firearms on the loose. But the White House's recommendations seem like a good starting point and nothing that would prevent me from protecting my family in a crisis. The AR-15 is a fascinating weapon, and, frankly, a gas to shoot. So is a tank, and I don't need to own a tank.

Alas, the days of à la carte politics like mine seem over, if they ever even existed. The bigger culprit is the far right and the lunatic pronouncements of those like Rush Limbaugh. But in the weeks since

Newtown, I've watched my Facebook feed, which is dominated by my coastal friends, fill up with antigun dispatches that seemed divorced from reality. I agree it would be nice if the world had exactly zero guns in it. But I don't see that happening, and calling gun owners "a bunch of inbred rednecks" doesn't do much to advance rational discussion.

Thus, my secret life—though I guess it's not such a secret anymore. My wife is afraid of my guns (though she also says she's glad I have them). My sixteen-year-old daughter is a different story. The week before her fall semester exams, we allowed her to skip school for a day, a tradition in our house. The rule is, she gets to do whatever she wants. This time, she asked to take a pistol lesson. She's an NPR listener like me, but she's also grown up in Texas, and the fact that one in five American women is a victim of sexual assault is not lost on her. In the windowless classroom off the range, the instructor ran her through the basics, demonstrating with a Glock 9-millimeter: how to hold it, load it, pull back the slide.

"You'll probably have trouble with that part," he said. "A lot of the women do."

"Oh really?" my daughter replied, and with a cagey smile proceeded to rack her weapon with such authority you could have heard it in the parking lot.

A proud-papa moment? I confess it was.

Topics for Critical Thinking and Writing

1. This essay could with equal accuracy be called "Confessions of a Texas Gun Owner." Why do you suppose Cronin chose the title he did, rather than our imagined title? That is, why is his title better—better for his purposes—than our invented title?

2. Why does Cronin devote so many sentences to autobiographical matters, since, in fact, none of the autobiography actually involves using a gun to protect himself or his family against an intruder?

3. How would you characterize Cronin's persona as he presents it in this essay? Does he try to speak with authority, connect with his audience on a personal level, or employ another strategy to gain his reader's trust? Do you feel that his persona effectively connects with you as a reader? Why, or why not?

4. What *arguments* does Cronin offer on behalf of gun ownership? Do you think his case—his thesis, his point, his Big Idea—might have been strengthened if he had cited statistics or authorities, or do you think that such evidence probably would have been inappropriate in what is essentially a highly personal essay?

5. In paragraph 12 Cronin writes, "It didn't happen overnight, but before too long my Northeastern liberal sensibilities . . . had shifted on the question of gun ownership." Suppose a reader said to you, "I don't

really understand exactly why his attitude shifted. What *happened* that made him shift? I don't get it." What would you say to this questioner?

6. In paragraph 13 Cronin says that he believes "guns are woefully under-regulated," and that he "loathe[s] the National Rifle Association," but he doesn't go into any detail about what sorts of regulations he favors. Do you think his essay might have been more convincing if he had given us details along these lines? Explain.

7. Each of Cronin's last three paragraphs is very short. We have discussed how, in general, a short paragraph is usually an underdeveloped paragraph. Do you think these paragraphs are underdeveloped—or do you think Cronin knows exactly what he is doing? Explain.

Peter Singer

Peter Singer (b. 1946) is the Ira W. DeCamp Professor of Bioethics at Princeton University. A native of Australia, he is a graduate of the University of Melbourne and Oxford University and the author or editor of more than two dozen books, including Animal Liberation *(1975),* Practical Ethics *(1979),* Rethinking Life and Death *(1995), and* One World: The Ethics of Globalization *(2002). He has written on a variety of ethical issues, but he is especially known for caring about the welfare of animals.*

This essay originally appeared in the New York Review of Books *(April 5, 1973), as a review of* Animals, Men and Morals, *edited by Stanley and Roslind Godlovitch and John Harris.*

Animal Liberation

I

We are familiar with Black Liberation, Gay Liberation, and a variety of other movements. With Women's Liberation some thought we had come to the end of the road. Discrimination on the basis of sex, it has been said, is the last form of discrimination that is universally accepted and practiced without pretense, even in those liberal circles which have long prided themselves on their freedom from racial discrimination. But one should always be wary of talking of "the last remaining form of discrimination." If we have learned anything from the liberation movements, we should have learned how difficult it is to be aware of the ways in which we discriminate until they are forcefully pointed out to us. A liberation movement demands an expansion of our moral horizons, so that practices that were previously regarded as natural and inevitable are now seen as intolerable.

Animals, Men and Morals is a manifesto for an Animal Liberation movement. The contributors to the book may not all see the issue this way. They are a varied group. Philosophers, ranging from professors to graduate students, make up the largest contingent. There are five of them, including the three editors, and there is also an extract from the unjustly neglected German philosopher with an English name, Leonard Nelson, who died in 1927. There are essays by two novelist/critics, Brigid Brophy and Maureen Duffy, and another by Muriel the Lady Dowding, widow of Dowding of Battle of Britain fame and the founder of "Beauty without Cruelty," a movement that campaigns against the use of animals for furs and cosmetics. The other pieces are by a psychologist, a botanist, a sociologist, and Ruth Harrison, who is probably best described as a professional campaigner for animal welfare.

Whether or not these people, as individuals, would all agree that they are launching a liberation movement for animals, the book as a whole amounts to no less. It is a demand for a complete change in our attitudes to nonhumans. It is a demand that we cease to regard the exploitation of other species as natural and inevitable, and that, instead, we see it as a continuing moral outrage. Patrick Corbett, Professor of Philosophy at Sussex University, captures the spirit of the book in his closing words:

> We require now to extend the great principles of liberty, equality, and fraternity over the lives of animals. Let animal slavery join human slavery in the graveyard of the past.

The reader is likely to be skeptical. "Animal Liberation" sounds more like a parody of liberation movements than a serious objective. The reader may think: We support the claims of blacks and women for equality because blacks and women really are equal to whites and males—equal in intelligence and in abilities, capacity for leadership, rationality, and so on. Humans and nonhumans obviously are not equal in these respects. Since justice demands only that we treat equals equally, unequal treatment of humans and nonhumans cannot be an injustice.

This is a tempting reply, but a dangerous one. It commits the non- 5 racist and nonsexist to a dogmatic belief that blacks and women really are just as intelligent, able, etc., as whites and males—and no more. Quite possibly this happens to be the case. Certainly attempts to prove that racial or sexual differences in these respects have a genetic origin have not been conclusive. But do we really want to stake our demand for equality on the assumption that there are no genetic differences of this kind between the different races or sexes? Surely the appropriate response to those who claim to have found evidence for such genetic differences is not to stick to the belief that there are no differences, whatever the evidence to the contrary; rather one should be clear that the claim to equality does not depend on IQ. Moral equality is distinct from factual equality. Otherwise it would be nonsense to talk to the equality of human beings, since humans, as individuals, obviously differ in intelligence and almost any ability one cares to name. If possessing greater intelligence does not entitle one human to exploit another, why should it entitle humans to exploit nonhumans?

Jeremy Bentham expressed the essential basis of equality in his famous formula: "Each to count for one and none for more than one."

In other words, the interests of every being that has interests are to be taken into account and treated equally with the like interests of any other being. Other moral philosophers, before and after Bentham, have made the same point in different ways. Our concern for others must not depend on whether they possess certain characteristics, though just what that concern involves may, of course, vary according to such characteristics.

Bentham, incidentally, was well aware that the logic of the demand for racial equality did not stop at the equality of humans. He wrote:

> The day *may* come when the rest of the animal creation may acquire those rights which never could have been withholden from them but by the hand of tyranny. The French have already discovered that the blackness of the skin is no reason why a human being should be abandoned without redress to the caprice of a tormentor. It may one day come to be recognized that the number of the legs, the villosity of the skin, or the termination of the *os sacrum*, are reasons equally insufficient for abandoning a sensitive being to the same fate. What else is it that should trace the insuperable line? Is it the faculty of reason, or perhaps the faculty of discourse? But a full-grown horse or dog is beyond comparison a more rational, as well as a more conversable animal, than an infant of a day, or a week, or even a month, old. But suppose they were otherwise, what would it avail? The question is not, Can they *reason*? nor Can they *talk*? but, Can they *suffer*?[1]

Surely Bentham was right. If a being suffers, there can be no moral justification for refusing to take that suffering into consideration, and, indeed, to count it equally with the like suffering (if rough comparisons can be made) of any other being.

So the only question is: Do animals other than man suffer? Most people agree unhesitatingly that animals like cats and dogs can and do suffer, and this seems also to be assumed by those laws that prohibit wanton cruelty to such animals. Personally, I have no doubt at all about this and find it hard to take seriously the doubts that a few people apparently do have. The editors and contributors of *Animals, Men and Morals* seem to feel the same way, for although the question is raised more than once, doubts are quickly dismissed each time. Nevertheless, because this is such a fundamental point, it is worth asking what grounds we have for attributing suffering to other animals.

It is best to begin by asking what grounds any individual human has for supposing that other humans feel pain. Since pain is a state of consciousness, a "mental event," it can never be directly observed. No observations, whether behavioral signs such as writhing or screaming or physiological or neurological recordings, are observations of pain itself. Pain is something one feels, and one can only infer that others are feeling it from various external indications. The fact that only philosophers

---

[1] *The Principles of Morals and Legislation,* ch. XVII, sec. 1, footnote to paragraph 4. [All notes are the author's unless otherwise specified.]

are ever skeptical about whether other humans feel pain shows that we regard such inference as justifiable in the case of humans.

Is there any reason why the same inference should be unjustifiable 10 for other animals? Nearly all the external signs which lead us to infer pain in other humans can be seen in other species, especially "higher" animals such as mammals and birds. Behavioral signs—writhing, yelping, or other forms of calling, attempts to avoid the source of pain, and many others—are present. We know, too, that these animals are biologically similar in the relevant respects, having nervous systems like ours which can be observed to function as ours do.

So the grounds for inferring that these animals can feel pain are nearly as good as the grounds for inferring other humans do. Only nearly, for there is one behavioral sign that humans have but nonhumans, with the exception of one or two specially raised chimpanzees, do not have. This, of course, is a developed language. As the quotation from Bentham indicates, this has long been regarded as an important distinction between man and other animals. Other animals may communicate with each other, but not in the way we do. Following Chomsky,[2] many people now mark this distinction by saying that only humans communicate in a form that is governed by rules of syntax. (For the purposes of this argument, linguists allow those chimpanzees who have learned a syntactic sign language to rank as honorary humans.) Nevertheless, as Bentham pointed out, this distinction is not relevant to the question of how animals ought to be treated, unless it can be linked to the issue of whether animals suffer.

This link may be attempted in two ways. First, there is a hazy line of philosophical thought, stemming perhaps from some doctrines associated with Wittgenstein, which maintains that we cannot meaningfully attribute states of consciousness to beings without language. I have not seen this argument made explicit in print, though I have come across it in conversation. This position seems to me very implausible, and I doubt that it would be held at all if it were not thought to be a consequence of a broader view of the significance of language. It may be that the use of a public, rule-governed language is a precondition of conceptual thought. It may even be, although personally I doubt it, that we cannot meaningfully speak of a creature having an intention unless that creature can use a language. But states like pain, surely, are more primitive than either of these, and seem to have nothing to do with language.

Indeed, as Jane Goodall points out in her study of chimpanzees, when it comes to the expression of feelings and emotions, humans tend to fall back on nonlinguistic modes of communication which are often found among apes, such as a cheering pat on the back, an exuberant embrace, a clasp of hands, and so on.[3] Michael Peters makes a similar

---

[2]**Chomsky** Noam Chomsky (b. 1928), a professor of linguistics and the author of (among other books) *Language and Mind* (1972). [Editors' note.]
[3]Jane van Lawick-Goodall, *In the Shadow of Man* (Houghton Mifflin, 1971), p. 225.

point in his contribution to *Animals, Men and Morals* when he notes that the basic signals we use to convey pain, fear, sexual arousal, and so on are not specific to our species. So there seems to be no reason at all to believe that a creature without language cannot suffer.

The second, and more easily appreciated way of linking language and the existence of pain is to say that the best evidence that we can have that another creature is in pain is when he tells us that he is. This is a distinct line of argument, for it is not being denied that a non-language-user conceivably could suffer, but only that we could know that he is suffering. Still, this line of argument seems to me to fail, and for reasons similar to those just given. "I am in pain" is not the best possible evidence that the speaker is in pain (he might be lying) and it is certainly not the only possible evidence. Behavioral signs and knowledge of the animal's biological similarity to ourselves together provide adequate evidence that animals do suffer. After all, we would not accept linguistic evidence if it contradicted the rest of the evidence. If a man was severely burned, and behaved as if he were in pain, writhing, groaning, being very careful not to let his burned skin touch anything, and so on, but later said he had not been in pain at all, we would be more likely to conclude that he was lying or suffering from amnesia than that he had not been in pain.

Even if there were stronger grounds for refusing to attribute pain to those who do not have a language, the consequences of this refusal might lead us to examine these grounds unusually critically. Human infants, as well as some adults, are unable to use language. Are we to deny that a year-old infant can suffer? If not, how can language be crucial? Of course, most parents can understand the responses of even very young infants better than they understand the responses of other animals, and sometimes infant responses can be understood in the light of later development. 15

This, however, is just a fact about the relative knowledge we have of our own species and other species, and most of this knowledge is simply derived from closer contact. Those who have studied the behavior of other animals soon learn to understand their responses at least as well as we understand those of an infant. (I am not referring to Jane Goodall's and other well-known studies of apes. Consider, for example, the degree of understanding achieved by Tinbergen from watching herring gulls.[4]) Just as we can understand infant human behavior in the light of adult human behavior, so we can understand the behavior of other species in the light of our own behavior (and sometimes we can understand our own behavior better in the light of the behavior of other species).

The grounds we have for believing that other mammals and birds suffer are, then, closely analogous to the grounds we have for believing that other humans suffer. It remains to consider how far down the evolutionary scale this analogy holds. Obviously it becomes poorer when we get further away from man. To be more precise would require a detailed

---

[4]N. Tinbergen, *The Herring Gull's World* (Basic Books, 1961).

examination of all that we know about other forms of life. With fish, reptiles, and other vertebrates the analogy still seems strong, with molluscs like oysters it is much weaker. Insects are more difficult, and it may be that in our present state of knowledge we must be agnostic about whether they are capable of suffering.

If there is no moral justification for ignoring suffering when it occurs, and it does occur in other species, what are we to say of our attitudes toward these other species? Richard Ryder, one of the contributors to *Animals, Men and Morals,* uses the term "speciesism" to describe the belief that we are entitled to treat members of other species in a way in which it would be wrong to treat members of our own species. The term is not euphonious, but it neatly makes the analogy with racism. The nonracist would do well to bear the analogy in mind when he is inclined to defend human behavior toward nonhumans. "Shouldn't we worry about improving the lot of our own species before we concern ourselves with other species?" he may ask. If we substitute "race" for "species" we shall see that the question is better not asked. "Is a vegetarian diet nutritionally adequate?" resembles the slaveowner's claim that he and the whole economy of the South would be ruined without slave labor. There is even a parallel with skeptical doubts about whether animals suffer, for some defenders of slavery professed to doubt whether blacks really suffer in the way whites do.

I do not want to give the impression, however, that the case for Animal Liberation is based on the analogy with racism and no more. On the contrary, *Animals, Men and Morals* describes the various ways in which humans exploit nonhumans, and several contributors consider the defenses that have been offered, including the defense of meat-eating mentioned in the last paragraph. Sometimes the rebuttals are scornfully dismissive, rather than carefully designed to convince the detached critic. This may be a fault, but it is a fault that is inevitable, given the kind of book this is. The issue is not one on which one can remain detached. As the editors state in their Introduction:

> Once the full force of moral assessment has been made explicit there can be no rational excuse left for killing animals, be they killed for food, science, or sheer personal indulgence. We have not assembled this book to provide the reader with yet another manual on how to make brutalities less brutal. Compromise, in the traditional sense of the term, is simple unthinking weakness when one considers the actual reasons for our crude relationships with the other animals.

The point is that on this issue there are few critics who are genuinely 20 detached. People who eat pieces of slaughtered nonhumans every day find it hard to believe that they are doing wrong; and they also find it hard to imagine what else they could eat. So for those who do not place nonhumans beyond the pale of morality, there comes a stage when further argument seems pointless, a stage at which one can only accuse one's opponent of hypocrisy and reach for the sort of sociological account of our practices and the way we defend them that is attempted by David Wood in his contribution to his book. On the other hand, to those unconvinced by the arguments, and unable to accept that they are merely rationalizing their dietary preferences and their fear of being thought peculiar, such sociological explanations can only seem insultingly arrogant.

II

The logic of speciesism is most apparent in the practice of experimenting on nonhumans in order to benefit humans. This is because the issue is rarely obscured by allegations that nonhumans are so different from humans that we cannot know anything about whether they suffer. The defender of vivisection cannot use this argument because he needs to stress the similarities between man and other animals in order to justify the usefulness to the former of experiments on the latter. The researcher who makes rats choose between starvation and electric shocks to see if they develop ulcers (they do) does so because he knows that the rat has a nervous system very similar to man's, and presumably feels an electric shock in a similar way.

Richard Ryder's restrained account of experiments on animals made me angrier with my fellow men than anything else in this book. Ryder, a clinical psychologist by profession, himself experimented on animals before he came to hold the view he puts forward in his essay. Experimenting on animals is now a large industry, both academic and commercial. In 1969, more than 5 million experiments were performed in Britain, the vast majority without anesthetic (though how many of these involved pain is not known). There are no accurate U.S. figures, since there is no federal law on the subject, and in many cases no state law either. Estimates vary from 20 million to 200 million. Ryder suggests that 80 million may be the best guess. We tend to think that this is all for vital medical research, but of course it is not. Huge numbers of animals are used in university departments from Forestry to Psychology, and even more are used for commercial purposes, to test whether cosmetics can cause skin damage, or shampoos eye damage, or to test food additives or laxatives or sleeping pills or anything else.

A standard test for foodstuffs is the "LD50." The object of this test is to find the dosage level at which 50 percent of the test animals will die. This means that nearly all of them will become very sick before finally succumbing or surviving. When the substance is a harmless one, it may be necessary to force huge doses down the animals, until in some cases sheer volume or concentration causes death.

Ryder gives a selection of experiments, taken from recent scientific journals. I will quote two, not for the sake of indulging in gory details, but in order to give an idea of what normal researchers think they may legitimately do to other species. The point is not that the individual researchers are cruel men, but that they are behaving in a way that is allowed by our speciesist attitudes. As Ryder points out, even if only 1 percent of the experiments involve severe pain, that is 50,000 experiments in Britain each year, or nearly 150 every day (and about fifteen times as many in the United States, if Ryder's guess is right). Here then are two experiments:

> O. S. Ray and R. J. Barrett of Pittsburgh gave electric shocks to the feet of 1,042 mice. They then caused convulsions by giving more intense shocks through cup-shaped electrodes applied to the animals' eyes or through pressure spring clips attached to their ears. Unfortunately some of the mice who "successfully completed Day One training were found sick or dead prior to testing on Day Two." [*Journal of Comparative and Physiological Psychology*, 1969, vol. 67, pp. 110–116]
>
> At the National Institute for Medical Research, Mill Hill, London, W. Feldberg and S. L. Sherwood injected chemicals into the brains of cats—"with a number of widely different substances, recurrent patterns of reaction were obtained. Retching, vomiting, defecation, increased salivation and greatly accelerated respiration leading to panting were common features." . . .
>
> The injection into the brain of a large dose of Tubocuraine caused the cat to jump "from the table to the floor and then straight into its cage, where it started calling more and more noisily whilst moving about restlessly and jerkily . . . finally the cat fell with legs and neck flexed, jerking in rapid clonic movements, the condition being that of a major [epileptic] convulsion . . . within a few seconds the cat got up, ran for a few yards at high speed, and fell in another fit. The whole process was repeated several times within the next ten minutes, during which the cat lost faeces and foamed at the mouth."
>
> This animal finally died thirty-five minutes after the brain injection. [*Journal of Physiology*, 1954, vol. 123, pp. 148–167]

There is nothing secret about these experiments. One has only to 25 open any recent volume of a learned journal, such as the *Journal of Comparative and Physiological Psychology*, to find full descriptions of experiments of this sort, together with the results obtained—results that are frequently trivial and obvious. The experiments are often supported by public funds.

It is a significant indication of the level of acceptability of these practices that, although these experiments are taking place at this moment on university campuses throughout the country, there has, so far as I know, not been the slightest protest from the student movement. Students have been rightly concerned that their universities should not discriminate on grounds of race or sex, and that they should not serve the purposes of the military or big business. Speciesism continues undisturbed, and many students participate in it. There may be a few qualms at first, but since everyone regards it as normal, and it may even be a required part of a course, the student soon becomes hardened and, dismissing his earlier feelings as "mere sentiment," comes to regard animals as statistics rather than sentient beings with interests that warrant consideration.

Argument about vivisection has often missed the point because it has been put in absolutist terms: Would the abolitionist be prepared to let thousands die if they could be saved by experimenting on a single animal? The way to reply to this purely hypothetical question is to pose another: Would the experimenter be prepared to experiment on a human orphan under six months old, if it were the only way to save many lives? (I say "orphan" to avoid the complication of parental feelings, although in doing so I am being overfair to the experimenter, since the nonhuman subjects of experiments are not orphans.) A negative answer to this question indicates that the experimenter's readiness to use nonhumans is simple discrimination, for adult apes, cats, mice, and other mammals are more conscious of what is happening to them, more self-directing, and, so far as we can tell, just as sensitive to pain as a human infant. There is no characteristic that human infants possess that adult mammals do not have to the same or a higher degree.

(It might be possible to hold that what makes it wrong to experiment on a human infant is that the infant will in time develop into more than the nonhuman, but one would then, to be consistent, have to oppose abortion, and perhaps contraception, too, for the fetus and the egg and sperm have the same potential as the infant. Moreover, one would still have no reason for experimenting on a nonhuman rather than a human with brain damage severe enough to make it impossible for him to rise above infant level.)

The experimenter, then, shows a bias for his own species whenever he carries out an experiment on a nonhuman for a purpose that he would not think justified him in using a human being at an equal or lower level of sentience, awareness, ability to be self-directing, etc. No one familiar with the kind of results yielded by these experiments can have the slightest doubt that if this bias were eliminated the number of experiments performed would be zero or very close to it.

III

If it is vivisection that shows the logic of speciesism most clearly, it is 30 the use of other species for food that is at the heart of our attitudes toward them. Most of *Animals, Men and Morals* is an attack on meat eating—an attack which is based solely on concern for nonhumans, without reference to arguments derived from consideration of ecology, macrobiotics, health, or religion.

The idea that nonhumans are utilities, means to our ends, pervades our thought. Even conservationists who are concerned about the slaughter of wildfowl but not about the vastly greater slaughter of chickens for our tables are thinking in this way—they are worried about what we would lose if there were less wildlife. Stanley Godlovitch, pursuing

the Marxist idea that our thinking is formed by the activities we undertake in satisfying our needs, suggests that man's first classification of his
environment was into Edibles and Inedibles. Most animals came into the
first category, and there they have remained.

Man may always have killed other species for food, but he has never
exploited them so ruthlessly as he does today. Farming has succumbed
to business methods, the objective being to get the highest possible ratio
of output (meat, eggs, milk) to input (fodder, labor costs, etc.). Ruth
Harrison's essay "On Factory Farming" gives an account of some aspects
of modern methods, and of the unsuccessful British campaigns for effective controls, a campaign which was sparked off by her *Animal Machines*
(London: Stuart, 1964).

Her article is in no way a substitute for her earlier book. This is a pity
since, as she says, "Farm produce is still associated with mental pictures
of animals browsing in the fields . . . of hens having a last forage before
going to roost. . . ." Yet neither in her article nor elsewhere in *Animals,
Men and Morals* is this false image replaced by a clear idea of the nature
and extent of factory farming. We learn of this only indirectly, when we
hear of the code of reform proposed by an advisory committee set up by
the British government.

Among the proposals, which the government refused to implement
on the grounds that they were too idealistic, were: "*Any animal should at
least have room to turn around freely.*"

Factory farm animals need liberation in the most literal sense. Veal   35
calves are kept in stalls 5 feet by 2 feet. They are usually slaughtered
when about four months old, and have been too big to turn in their stalls
for at least a month. Intensive beef herds, kept in stalls only proportion-
ately larger for much longer periods, account for a growing percentage
of beef production. Sows are often similarly confined when pregnant,
which, because of artificial methods of increasing fertility, can be most of
the time. Animals confined in this way do not waste food by exercising,
nor do they develop unpalatable muscle.

"*A dry bedded area should be provided for all stock.*" Intensively kept
animals usually have to stand and sleep in slatted floors without straw,
because this makes cleaning easier.

"*Palatable roughage must be readily available to all calves after one week
of age.*" In order to produce the pale veal housewives are said to prefer,
calves are fed on an all-liquid diet until slaughter, even though they are
long past the age at which they would normally eat grass. They develop
a craving for roughage, evidenced by attempts to gnaw wood from their
stalls. (For the same reason, their diet is deficient in iron.)

"*Battery cages for poultry should be large enough for a bird to be able to
stretch one wing at a time.*" Under current British practice, a cage for four
or five laying hens has a floor area of 20 inches by 18 inches, scarcely
larger than a double page of the *New York Review of Books*. In this space,

on a sloping wire floor (sloping so the eggs roll down, wire so the dung drips through) the birds live for a year or eighteen months while artificial lighting and temperature conditions combine with drugs in their food to squeeze the maximum number of eggs out of them. Table birds are also sometimes kept in cages. More often they are reared in sheds, no less crowded. Under these conditions all the birds' natural activities are frustrated, and they develop "vices" such as pecking each other to death. To prevent this, beaks are often cut off, and the sheds kept dark.

How many of those who support factory farming by buying its produce know anything about the way it is produced? How many have heard something about it, but are reluctant to check up for fear that it will make them uncomfortable? To nonspeciesists, the typical consumer's mixture of ignorance, reluctance to find out the truth, and vague belief that nothing really bad could be allowed seems analogous to the attitudes of "decent Germans" to the death camps.

There are, of course, some defenders of factory farming. Their arguments are considered, though again rather sketchily, by John Harris. Among the most common: "Since they have never known anything else, they don't suffer." This argument will not be put by anyone who knows anything about animal behavior, since he will know that not all behavior has to be learned. Chickens attempt to stretch wings, walk around, scratch, and even dustbathe or build a nest, even though they have never lived under conditions that allowed these activities. Calves can suffer from maternal deprivation no matter at what age they were taken from their mothers. "We need these intensive methods to provide protein for a growing population." As ecologists and famine relief organizations know, we can produce far more protein per acre if we grow the right vegetable crop, soy beans for instance, than if we use the land to grow crops to be converted into protein by animals who use nearly 90 percent of the protein themselves, even when unable to exercise. 40

There will be many readers of this book who will agree that factory farming involves an unjustifiable degree of exploitation of sentient creatures, and yet will want to say that there is nothing wrong with rearing animals for food, provided it is done "humanely." These people are saying, in effect, that although we should not cause animals to suffer, there is nothing wrong with killing them.

There are two possible replies to this view. One is to attempt to show that this combination of attitudes is absurd. Roslind Godlovitch takes this course in her essay, which is an examination of some common attitudes to animals. She argues that from the combination of "animal suffering is to be avoided" and "there is nothing wrong with killing animals" it follows that all animal life ought to be exterminated (since all sentient creatures will suffer to some degree at some point in their lives). Euthanasia is a contentious issue only because we place some value on living. If we did not, the least amount of suffering would justify it. Accordingly, if we deny that we have a duty to exterminate all animal life, we must concede that we are placing some value on animal life.

This argument seems to me valid, although one could still reply that the value of animal life is to be derived from the pleasures that life can have for them, so that, provided their lives have a balance of pleasure over pain, we are justified in rearing them. But this would imply that we ought to produce animals and let them live as pleasantly as possible, without suffering.

At this point, one can make the second of the two possible replies to the view that rearing and killing animals for food is all right so long as it is done humanely. This second reply is that so long as we think that a nonhuman may be killed simply so that a human can satisfy his taste for meat, we are still thinking of nonhumans as means rather than as ends in themselves. The factory farm is nothing more than the application of technology to this concept. Even traditional methods involve castration, the separation of mothers and their young, the breaking up of herds, branding or earpunching, and of course transportation to the abattoirs and the final moments of terror when the animal smells blood and senses danger. If we were to try rearing animals so that they lived and died without suffering, we should find that to do so on anything like the scale of today's meat industry would be a sheer impossibility. Meat would become the prerogative of the rich.

I have been able to discuss only some of the contributions to this 45 book, saying nothing about, for instance, the essays on killing for furs and for sport. Nor have I considered all the detailed questions that need to be asked once we start thinking about other species in the radically different way presented by this book. What, for instance, are we to do about genuine conflicts of interest like rats biting slum children? I am not sure of the answer, but the essential point is just that we *do* see this as a conflict of interests, that we recognize that rats have interests too. Then we may begin to think about other ways of resolving the conflict—perhaps by leaving out rat baits that sterilize the rats instead of killing them.

I have not discussed such problems because they are side issues compared with the exploitation of other species for food and for experimental purposes. On these central matters, I hope that I have said enough to show that this book, despite its flaws, is a challenge to every human to recognize his attitudes to nonhumans as a form of prejudice no less objectionable than racism or sexism. It is a challenge that demands not just a change of attitudes, but a change in our way of life, for it requires us to become vegetarians.

Can a purely moral demand of this kind succeed? The odds are certainly against it. The book holds out no inducements. It does not tell us that we will become healthier, or enjoy life more, if we cease exploiting animals. Animal Liberation will require greater altruism on the part of mankind than any other liberation movement, since animals are incapable of demanding it for themselves, or of protesting against their exploitation by votes, demonstrations, or bombs. Is man capable of such genuine altruism? Who knows? If this book does have a significant effect, however, it will be a vindication of all those who have believed that man has within himself the potential for more than cruelty and selfishness.

TOPICS FOR CRITICAL THINKING AND WRITING

1. In his fourth paragraph Singer formulates an argument on behalf of the skeptical reader. Examine that argument closely, restate it in your own words, and evaluate it. Which of its premises is most vulnerable to criticism? Why?

2. Singer quotes with approval (para. 7) Bentham's comment, "The question is not, Can they *reason?* nor Can they *talk?* but, Can they *suffer?*" Do you find this argument persuasive? Can you think of any effective challenge to it?

3. Singer allows that, although developed linguistic capacity is not necessary for a creature to have pain, perhaps such a capacity is necessary for "having an intention" (para. 12). Do you think this concession is correct? Have you ever seen animal behavior that you would be willing to describe or explain as evidence that the animal has an intention to do something, despite knowing that the animal cannot talk?

4. Singer thinks that the readiness to experiment on animals argues against believing that animals don't suffer pain (see para. 21). Do you agree with this reasoning?

5. Singer confesses (para. 22) to being made especially angry "with my fellow men" after reading the accounts of animal experimentation. What is it that aroused his anger? Do such feelings, and the acknowledgment that one has them, have any place in a sober discussion about the merits of animal experimentation? Why, or why not?

6. What is "factory farming" (paras. 32–40)? Why is Singer opposed to it?

7. To the claim that there is nothing wrong with "rearing animals for food," provided it is done "humanely" (para. 41), Singer offers two replies (paras. 42–44). In an essay of 250 words summarize them briefly, and then indicate whether either persuades you and why or why not.

8. Suppose someone were to say to Singer: "You claim that capacity to suffer is the relevant factor in deciding whether a creature deserves to be treated as my moral equal. But you're wrong. The relevant factor is whether the creature is *alive.* Being alive is what matters, not being capable of feeling pain." In one or two paragraphs declare what you think would be Singer's reply.

9. Do you think it is worse to kill an animal for its fur than to kill, cook, and eat an animal? Is it worse to kill an animal for sport than to kill it for medical experimentation? What is Singer's view? Explain your view, making use of Singer's if you wish, in an essay of 500 words.

10. Are there any arguments, in your opinion, that show the immorality of eating human flesh (cannibalism) but that do not show a similar objection to eating animal flesh? Write a 500-word essay in which you discuss the issue.

Jonathan Swift

Jonathan Swift (1667–1745) was born in Ireland of English stock. An Anglican clergyman, he became Dean of St. Patrick's in Dublin in 1723, but the post he really wanted, one of high office in England, was never given to him. A prolific pamphleteer on religious and political issues, Swift today is known not as a churchman but as a satirist. His best-known works are Gulliver's Travels *(1726, a serious satire but now popularly thought of as a children's book) and* "A Modest Proposal" *(1729). In "A Modest Proposal," which was published anonymously, Swift addresses the great suffering that the Irish endured under the British.*

A Modest Proposal

For Preventing the Children of Poor People in Ireland from Being a Burden to Their Parents or Country, and for Making Them Beneficial to the Public

It is a melancholy object to those who walk through this great town or travel in the country, when they see the streets, the roads, and cabin doors, crowded with beggars of the female sex, followed by three, four, or six children, all in rags and importuning every passenger for an alms. These mothers, instead of being able to work for their honest livelihood, are forced to employ all their time in strolling to beg sustenance for their helpless infants: who as they grow up either turn thieves for want of work, or leave their dear native country to fight for the Pretender in Spain, or sell themselves to the Barbadoes.

I think it is agreed by all parties that this prodigious number of children in the arms, or on the backs, or at the heels of their mothers, and frequently of their fathers, is in the present deplorable state of the kingdom a very great additional grievance; and, therefore, whoever could find out a fair, cheap, and easy method of making these children sound, useful members of the commonwealth, would deserve so well of the public as to have his statue set up for a preserver of the nation.

But my intention is very far from being confined to provide only for the children of professed beggars; it is of a much greater extent, and shall take in the whole number of infants at a certain age who are born of parents in effect as little able to support them as those who demand our charity in the streets.

As to my own part, having turned my thoughts for many years upon this important subject, and maturely weighed the several schemes of our projectors,[1] I have always found them grossly mistaken in their computation. It is true, a child just dropped from its dam may be supported by her milk for a solar year, with little other nourishment; at most not above the value of 2s.,[2] which the mother may certainly get, or the value in scraps, by her lawful occupation of begging; and it is exactly at one year old that I propose to provide for them in such a manner as instead of being a charge upon their parents or the parish, or wanting food and raiment for the rest of their lives, they shall on the contrary contribute to the feeding, and partly to the clothing, of many thousands.

There is likewise another great advantage in my scheme, that it will   5 prevent those voluntary abortions, and that horrid practice of women murdering their bastard children, alas! too frequent among us! sacrificing the poor innocent babes I doubt more to avoid the expense than the shame, which would move tears and pity in the most savage and inhuman breast.

The number of souls in this kingdom being usually reckoned one million and a half, of these I calculate there may be about 200,000 couple whose wives are breeders; from which number I subtract 30,000 couple who are able to maintain their own children (although I apprehend there cannot be so many, under the present distress of the kingdom); but this being granted, there will remain 170,000 breeders. I again subtract 50,000 for those women who miscarry, or whose children die by accident or disease within the year. There only remain 120,000 children of poor parents annually born. The question therefore is, how this number shall be reared and provided for? which, as I have already said, under the present situation of affairs, is utterly impossible by all the methods hitherto proposed. For we can neither employ them in handicraft or agriculture; we neither build houses (I mean in the country) nor cultivate land; they can very seldom pick up a livelihood by stealing, till they arrive at six years old, except where they are of towardly parts; although I confess they learn the rudiments much earlier; during which time they can, however, be properly looked upon only as probationers; as I have been informed by a principal gentleman in the county of Cavan, who protested to me that he never knew above one or two instances under the age of six, even in a part of the kingdom so renowned for the quickest proficiency in that art.

I am assured by our merchants, that a boy or a girl before twelve years old is no salable commodity; and even when they come to this age they will not yield above 3£. or 3£. 2s. 6d.[3] at most on the exchange; which cannot turn to account either to the parents or kingdom, the charge of nutriment and rags having been at least four times that value.

---

[1]**projectors** Persons who devise plans. [All notes are the editors'.]
[2]**2s** Two shillings.
[3]**£ . . . . d** £ is an abbreviation for "pound sterling" and *d.*, for "pence."

I shall now therefore humbly propose my own thoughts, which I hope will not be liable to the least objection.

I have been assured by a very knowing American of my acquaintance in London, that a young healthy child well nursed is at a year old a most delicious, nourishing, and wholesome food, whether stewed, roasted, baked, or broiled; and I make no doubt that it will equally serve in a fricassee or a ragout.

I do therefore humbly offer it to public consideration that of the 10 120,000 children already computed, 20,000 may be reserved for breed, whereof only one-fourth part to be males; which is more than we allow to sheep, black cattle, or swine; and my reason is, that these children are seldom the fruits of marriage, a circumstance not much regarded by our savages; therefore one male will be sufficient to serve four females. That the remaining 100,000 may, at a year old, be offered in sale to the persons of quality and fortune through the kingdom; always advising the mother to let them suck plentifully in the last month, so as to render them plump and fat for a good table. A child will make two dishes at an entertainment for friends; and when the family dines alone, the fore or hind quarter will make a reasonable dish, and seasoned with a little pepper or salt will be very good boiled on the fourth day, especially in winter.

I have reckoned upon a medium that a child just born will weigh twelve pounds, and in a solar year, if tolerably nursed, will increase to twenty-eight pounds.

I grant this food will be somewhat dear, and therefore very proper for landlords, who, as they have already devoured most of the parents, seem to have the best title to the children.

Infant's flesh will be in season throughout the year, but more plentiful in March, and a little before and after: for we are told by a grave author, an eminent French physician, that fish being a prolific diet, there are more children born in Roman Catholic countries about nine months after Lent than at any other season; therefore, reckoning a year after Lent, the markets will be more glutted than usual, because the number of popish infants is at least three to one in this kingdom: and therefore it will have one other collateral advantage, by lessening the number of papists among us.

I have already computed the charge of nursing a beggar's child (in which list I reckon all cottagers, laborers, and four-fifths of the farmers) to be about 2s. per annum, rags included; and I believe no gentleman would repine to give 10s. for the carcass of a good fat child, which, as I have said, will make four dishes of excellent nutritive meat, when he has only some particular friend or his own family to dine with him. Thus the squire will learn to be a good landlord, and grow popular among the tenants; the mother will have 8s. net profit, and be fit for work till she produces another child.

Those who are more thrifty (as I must confess the times require) 15 may flay the carcass; the skin of which artificially dressed will make admirable gloves for ladies, and summer boots for fine gentlemen.

As to our city of Dublin, shambles[4] may be appointed for this purpose in the most convenient parts of it, and butchers we may be assured will not be wanting: although I rather recommend buying the children alive, and dressing them hot from the knife as we do roasting pigs.

A very worthy person, a true lover of his country, and whose virtues I highly esteem, was lately pleased in discoursing on this matter to offer a refinement upon my scheme. He said that many gentlemen of this kingdom, having of late destroyed their deer, he conceived that the want of venison might be well supplied by the bodies of young lads and maidens, not exceeding fourteen years of age nor under twelve; so great a number of both sexes in every country being now ready to starve for want of work and service; and these to be disposed of by their parents, if alive, or otherwise by their nearest relations. But with due deference to so excellent a friend and so deserving a patriot, I cannot be altogether in his sentiments; for as to the males, my American acquaintance assured me from frequent experience that their flesh was generally tough and lean, like that of our schoolboys by continual exercise, and their taste disagreeable; and to fatten them would not answer the charge. Then as to the females, it would, I think, with humble submission be a loss to the public, because they soon would become breeders themselves: and besides, it is not improbable that some scrupulous people might be apt to censure such a practice (although indeed very unjustly), as a little bordering upon cruelty; which, I confess, has always been with me the strongest objection against any project, how well soever intended.

But in order to justify my friend, he confessed that this expedient was put into his head by the famous Psalmanazar[5] a native of the island Formosa, who came from thence to London about twenty years ago: and in conversation told my friend, that in his country when any young person happened to be put to death, the executioner sold the carcass to persons of quality as a prime dainty; and that in his time the body of a plump girl of fifteen, who was crucified for an attempt to poison the emperor, was sold to his imperial majesty's prime minister of state, and other great mandarins of the court, in joints from the gibbet, at 400 crowns. Neither indeed can I deny, that if the same use were made of several plump young girls in this town, who without one single groat to their fortunes cannot stir abroad without a chair, and appear at the playhouse and assemblies in foreign fineries which they never will pay for, the kingdom would not be the worse.

Some persons of a depending spirit are in great concern about the vast number of poor people, who are aged, diseased, or maimed, and I have been desired to employ my thoughts what course may be taken to

---

[4]**shambles** Slaughterhouses.
[5]**Psalmanazar** George Psalmanazar (c. 1679–1763), a Frenchman who claimed to be from Formosa (now Taiwan); he wrote *An Historical and Geographical Description of Formosa* (1704). The hoax was exposed soon after publication.

ease the nation of so grievous an encumbrance. But I am not in the least pain upon that matter, because it is very well known that they are every day dying and rotting by cold and famine, and filth and vermin, as fast as can be reasonably expected. And as to the young laborers, they are now in as hopeful a condition: They cannot get work, and consequently pine away for want of nourishment, to a degree that if at any time they are accidentally hired to common labor, they have not strength to perform it; and thus the country and themselves are happily delivered from the evils to come.

I have too long digressed, and therefore shall return to my subject. 20 I think the advantages by the proposal which I have made are obvious and many, as well as of the highest importance.

For first, as I have already observed, It would greatly lessen the number of papists, with whom we are yearly overrun, being the principal breeders of the nation as well as our most dangerous enemies; and who stay at home on purpose to deliver the kingdom to the Pretender, hoping to take their advantage by the absence of so many good Protestants, who have chosen rather to leave their country than stay at home and pay tithes against their conscience to an Episcopal curate.

Secondly, The poor tenants will have something valuable of their own, which by law may be made liable to distress and help to pay their landlord's rent, their corn and cattle being already seized, and money a thing unknown.

Thirdly, Whereas the maintenance of 100,000 children from two years old and upward, cannot be computed at less than 10s. apiece per annum, the nation's stock will be thereby increased £50,000 per annum, beside the profit of a new dish introduced to the tables of all gentlemen of fortune in the kingdom who have any refinement in taste. And the money will circulate among ourselves, the goods being entirely of our own growth and manufacture.

Fourthly, The constant breeders beside the gain of 8s. sterling per annum by the sale of their children, will be rid of the charge of maintaining them after the first year.

Fifthly, This food would likewise bring great custom to taverns, 25 where the vintners will certainly be so prudent as to procure the best receipts for dressing it to perfection, and consequently have their houses frequented by all the fine gentlemen, who justly value themselves upon their knowledge in good eating; and a skillful cook who understands how to oblige his guests will contrive to make it as expensive as they please.

Sixthly, This would be a great inducement to marriage, which all wise nations have either encouraged by rewards or enforced by laws and penalties. It would increase the care and tenderness of mothers toward their children, when they were sure of a settlement for life to the poor babes, provided in some sort by the public, to their annual profit instead of expense. We should see an honest emulation among the married women, which of them would bring the fattest child to the market. Men would become as fond of their wives during the time of their pregnancy as they are now of their mares in foal, their cows in calf, their sows when they are ready to farrow; nor offer to beat or kick them (as is too frequent a practice) for fear of a miscarriage.

Many other advantages might be enumerated. For instance, the addition of some thousand carcasses in our exportation of barreled beef, the propagation of swine's flesh, and improvement in the art of making good bacon, so much wanted among us by the great destruction of pigs, too frequent at our table; which are no way comparable in taste or magnificence to a well-grown, fat, yearling child, which roasted whole will make a considerable figure at a lord mayor's feast or any other public entertainment. But this and many others I omit, being studious of brevity.

Supposing that 1,000 families in this city would be constant customers for infants' flesh, besides others who might have it at merry-meetings, particularly at weddings and christenings, I compute that Dublin would take off annually about 20,000 carcasses; and the rest of the kingdom (where probably they will be sold somewhat cheaper) the remaining 80,000.

I can think of no one objection that will possibly be raised against this proposal, unless it should be urged that the number of people will be thereby much lessened in the kingdom. This I freely own, and it was indeed one principal design in offering it to the world. I desire the reader will observe, that I calculate my remedy for this one individual kingdom of Ireland and for no other that ever was, is, or I think ever can be upon earth. Therefore let no man talk to me of other expedients: of taxing our absentees at 5s. a pound; of using neither clothes nor household furniture except what is of our own growth and manufacture; of utterly rejecting the materials and instruments that promote foreign luxury; of curing the expensiveness of pride, vanity, idleness, and gaming in our women; of introducing a vein of parsimony, prudence, and temperance; of learning to love our country, in the want of which we differ even from Laplanders and the inhabitants of Topinamboo; of quitting our animosities and factions, nor acting any longer like the Jews, who were murdering one another at the very moment their city was taken; of being a little cautious not to sell our country and conscience for nothing; of teaching landlords to have at least one degree of mercy toward their tenants; lastly, of putting a spirit of honesty, industry, and skill into our shopkeepers; who, if a resolution could now be taken to buy only our native goods, would immediately unite to cheat and exact upon us in the price the measure, and the goodness, nor could ever yet be brought to make one fair proposal of just dealing, though often and earnestly invited to it.

Therefore I repeat, let no man talk to me of these and the like expe- 30 dients, till he has at least some glimpse of hope that there will be ever some hearty and sincere attempt to put them in practice.

But as to myself, having been wearied out for many years with offering vain, idle, visionary thoughts, and at length utterly despairing of success, I fortunately fell upon this proposal; which, as it is wholly new, so it has something solid and real, of no expense and little trouble, full in our own power, and whereby we can incur no danger in disobliging England. For this kind of commodity will not bear exportation, the flesh being of too tender a consistence to admit a long continuance in salt, although perhaps I could name a country which would be glad to eat up our whole nation without it.

After all, I am not so violently bent upon my own opinion as to reject any offer proposed by wise men, which shall be found equally innocent, cheap, easy, and effectual. But before something of that kind shall be advanced in contradiction to my scheme, and offering a better, I desire the author or authors will be pleased maturely to consider two points. First, as things now stand, how they will be able to find food and raiment for 100,000 useless mouths and backs. And secondly, there being a round million of creatures in human figure throughout this kingdom, whose subsistence put into a common stock would leave them in debt 2,000,000£. sterling, adding those who are beggars by profession to the bulk of farmers, cottagers, and laborers, with the wives and children who are beggars in effect; I desire those politicians who dislike my overture, and may perhaps be so bold as to attempt an answer, that they will first ask the parents of these mortals, whether they would not at this day think it a great happiness to have been sold for food at a year old in the manner I prescribe, and thereby have avoided such a perpetual scene of misfortunes as they have since gone through by the oppression of landlords, the impossibility of paying rent without money or trade, the want of common sustenance, with neither house nor clothes to cover them from the inclemencies of the weather, and the most inevitable prospect of entailing the like or greater miseries upon their breed for ever.

I profess, in the sincerity of my heart, that I have not the least personal interest in endeavoring to promote this necessary work, having no other motive than the public good of my country, by advancing our trade, providing for infants, relieving the poor, and giving some pleasure to the rich. I have no children by which I can propose to get a single penny; the youngest being nine years old, and my wife past childbearing.

TOPICS FOR CRITICAL THINKING AND WRITING

1. In paragraph 4 the speaker of the essay mentions proposals set forth by "projectors"—that is, by advocates of other proposals or projects. On the basis of the first two paragraphs of "A Modest Proposal," how would you characterize *this* projector, the speaker of the essay? Write your characterization in one paragraph. Then, in a second paragraph, characterize the projector as you understand him, having read the entire essay. In your second paragraph, indicate what *he thinks he is* and also what the reader sees he really is.

2. The speaker or persona of "A Modest Proposal" is confident that selling children "for a good table" (para. 10) is a better idea than any of

the then current methods of disposing of unwanted children, including abortion and infanticide. Can you think of any argument that might favor abortion or infanticide for parents in dire straits, rather than the projector's scheme?

3. In paragraph 29 the speaker considers, but dismisses out of hand, several other solutions to the wretched plight of the Irish poor. Write a 500-word essay in which you explain each of these ideas and their combined merits as an alternative to the solution he favors.

4. What does the projector imply are the causes of the Irish poverty he deplores? Are there possible causes he has omitted? If so, what are they?

5. Imagine yourself as one of the poor parents to whom Swift refers, and write a 250-word essay explaining why you prefer not to sell your infant to the local butcher.

6. The modern version of the problem to which the proposal is addressed is called "population policy." How would you describe our nation's current population policy? Do we have a population policy, in fact? If not, what would you propose? If we do have one, would you propose any changes in it? Why, or why not?

7. It is sometimes suggested that just as persons need to get a license to drive a car, to hunt with a gun, or to marry, a husband and wife ought to be required to get a license to have a child. Would you favor this idea, assuming that it applied to you as a possible parent? Would Swift? Explain your answers in an essay of 500 words.

8. Consider the six arguments advanced in paragraphs 21 to 26, and write a 1,000-word essay criticizing all of them. Or if you find that one or more of the arguments are really unanswerable, explain why you find it so compelling.

9. By means of research online or at the library, find out what audience Swift was addressing. How do you think the audience responded?

10. Write your own "modest proposal," ironically suggesting a solution to a problem. Possible topics: health care or schooling for the children of illegal immigrants, overcrowded jails, children who have committed a serious crime, homeless people.

 For additional arguments online, visit the e-Pages at **bedfordstmartins.com/barnetbedau**.

6

Developing an Argument
of Your Own

*The difficult part in an argument is not to defend one's opinion but to
know what it is.*

— ANDRÉ MAUROIS

*Imagine that you enter a parlor. You come late. When you arrive, others
have long preceded you, and they are engaged in a heated discussion,
a discussion too heated for them to pause and tell you exactly what it is
about. In fact, the discussion had already begun long before any of them
got there, so that no one present is qualified to retrace for you all the steps
that had gone before. You listen for a while, until you decide that you
have caught the tenor of the argument; then you put in your oar. Someone
answers; you answer him; another comes to your defense; another aligns
himself against you, to either the embarrassment or gratification of your
opponent, depending upon the quality of your ally's assistance. However,
the discussion is interminable. The hour grows late, you must depart. And
you do depart, with the discussion still vigorously in progress.*

— KENNETH BURKE

*No greater misfortune could happen to anyone than that of developing a
dislike for argument.*

— PLATO

PLANNING, DRAFTING, AND
REVISING AN ARGUMENT

First, hear the wisdom of Mark Twain: "When the Lord finished the world,
He pronounced it good. That is what I said about my first work, too. But
Time, I tell you, Time takes the confidence out of these incautious early
opinions."

All of us, teachers and students, have our moments of confidence, but
for the most part we know that it takes considerable effort to write clear,

thoughtful, seemingly effortless prose. In a conversation we can cover ourselves with such expressions as "Well, I don't know, but I sort of think . . . ," and we can always revise our position ("Oh, well, I didn't mean it that way"), but once we have handed in the final version of our writing, we are helpless. We are (putting it strongly) naked to our enemies.

Getting Ideas: Argument as an Instrument of Inquiry

In Chapter 1 we quoted Robert Frost, "To learn to write is to learn to have ideas," and we offered suggestions about getting ideas, a process traditionally called **invention**. A moment ago we said that we often improve our ideas when we try to explain them to someone else. Partly, of course, we are responding to questions or objections raised by our companion in the conversation. But partly we are responding to ourselves: Almost as soon as we hear what we have to say, we may find that it won't do, and, if we are lucky, we may find a better idea surfacing. One of the best ways of getting ideas is to talk things over.

The process of talking things over usually begins with the text that you are reading: Your notes, your summary, and your queries parenthetically incorporated within your summary are a kind of dialogue between you and the author you are reading. More obviously, when you talk with friends about your topic, you are trying out and developing ideas. You are arguing, but not chiefly to persuade; rather, you are using argument in order to find the truth. Finally, after reading, taking notes, and talking, you may feel that you now have clear ideas and need only put them into writing. And so you take a sheet of blank paper, and perhaps a paralyzing thought suddenly strikes: "I have ideas but just can't put them into words."

Despite what many people believe,

- Writing is not only a matter of putting one's ideas into words.
- Just as talking with others is a way of getting ideas, *writing is a way of getting and developing ideas.* Or, as we have already said, *argument* is an instrument of inquiry as well as of persuasion.

Writing, in short, can be an important part of critical thinking. One big reason we have trouble writing is our fear of putting ourselves on record, but another big reason is our fear that we have no ideas worth putting down. But by writing notes—or even free associations—and by writing a draft, however weak, we can help ourselves to think our way toward good ideas.

Freewriting   Writing for five or six minutes, nonstop, without censoring what you produce is one way of improving your thoughts. Some people who write on a computer find it useful to dim the screen so they won't be tempted to look up and fiddle too soon with what they have just written. Later they illuminate the screen, scroll back, and notice some keywords or passages that can be used later in drafting a paper. If you've kept notes on your blog or in a Google Doc, now is a good time to access them and to copy and paste some of your ideas.

Listing   Writing down keywords, just as you do when you make a shopping list, is another way of getting ideas. When you make a shopping list, you write *ketchup,* and the act of writing it reminds you that you also need hamburger rolls—and *that* in turn reminds you (who knows how or why?) that you also need a can of tuna fish. Similarly, when you prepare a list of ideas for a paper, just writing down one item will often generate another. Of course, when you look over the list, you will probably drop some of these ideas—the dinner menu will change—but you are making progress. If you have a smartphone, use it to write down thoughts. You can even e-mail these notes to yourself so you can access them later.

Diagramming   Sketching some sort of visual representation of an essay is a kind of listing. Three methods of diagramming are especially common:

- **Clustering**   Write, in the middle of a sheet of paper, a word or phrase summarizing your topic (for instance, *health care;* see diagram, below), circle it, and then write down and circle a related word (for example, *gov't-provided*). Perhaps this leads you to write *higher taxes,* and you then circle this phrase and connect it to *gov't-provided.* The next thing that occurs to you is *employer-provided*—and so you write this down and circle it. You will not connect this to *higher taxes,* but you will connect it to *health care* because it is a sort of parallel to *gov't-provided.* The next thing that occurs to you is *unemployed people.* This category does not connect easily with *employer-provided,* so you won't connect these two terms with a line, but you probably will connect *unemployed people* with *health care* and maybe also with *gov't-provided.* Keep going, jotting down ideas and making connections where possible, indicating relationships.

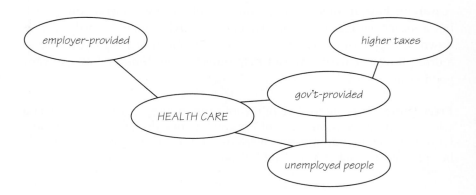

- **Branching**   Some writers find it useful to build a tree, moving from the central topic to the main branches (chief ideas) and then to the twigs (aspects of the chief ideas).

- **Comparing in columns**   Draw a line down the middle of the page, and then set up two columns showing oppositions. For instance, if you are concerned with health care, you might head one column *gov't-provided* and the other *employer-provided*. Under the first column, you might write *covers unemployed,* and under the second column, you might write *omits unemployed.* You might go on to write, under the first column, *higher taxes,* and under the second, *higher prices*—or whatever else relevant comes to mind.

All of these methods can, of course, be executed with pen and paper, but you may also be able to use them on your computer depending on the capabilities of your software.

Whether you are using a computer or a pen, you put down some words and almost immediately see that they need improvement, not simply a little polishing but a substantial overhaul. You write, "Race should be counted in college admissions for two reasons," and as soon as you write these words, a third reason comes to mind. Or perhaps one of those "two reasons" no longer seems very good. As E. M. Forster said, "How can I know what I think till I see what I say?" We have to see what we say, we have to get something down on paper, before we realize that we need to make it better.

Writing, then, is really **rewriting**—that is, **revising**—and a revision is a *re-vision,* a second look. The essay that you submit—whether a hard copy or on Blackboard—should be clear and may even seem effortless to the reader, but in all likelihood the clarity and apparent ease are the result of a struggle with yourself, a struggle during which you greatly improved your first thoughts. You begin by putting down your ideas, such as they are, perhaps even in the random order in which they occurred, but sooner or later comes the job of looking at them critically, developing what is useful in them and removing what is not. If you follow this procedure you will be in the company of Picasso, who said that he "advanced by means of destruction." Those passages that you cut or destroy can be kept in another file in case you want to revisit what you have removed. Sometimes, you end up restoring them.

Whether you advance bit by bit (writing a sentence, revising it, writing the next, and so on) or whether you write an entire first draft and then revise it and revise it again and again is chiefly a matter of temperament. Probably most people combine both approaches, backing up occasionally but trying to get to the end fairly soon so that they can see rather quickly what they know, or think they know, and can then start the real work of thinking, of converting their initial ideas into something substantial.

Asking Questions   Getting ideas, we said when we talked about **topics** and **invention** strategies in Chapter 1 (p. 16) is mostly a matter of asking (and then thinking about) questions. We append questions to the end of each argumentative essay in this book, not to torment you but to help you to think about the arguments—for instance, to turn your attention to especially important matters. If your instructor asks you to write an answer to one of these questions, you are lucky: Examining the question will stimulate your mind to work in a definite direction.

If a topic is not assigned, and you are asked to write an argumentative essay, you will find that some ideas (possibly poor ones, at this stage, but that doesn't matter because you will soon revise) will come to mind if you ask yourself questions. You can begin finding where you stand on an issue (**stasis**) by asking the following five basic questions:

1. What is *X*?
2. What is the value of *X*?
3. What are the causes (or the consequences) of *X*?
4. What should (or ought or must) we do about *X*?
5. What is the evidence for my claims about *X*?

Let's spend a moment looking at each of these questions.

1. **What is *X*?** We can hardly argue about the number of people sentenced to death in the United States in 2000—a glance at the appropriate government report will give the answer—but we can argue about whether capital punishment as administered in the United States is discriminatory. Does the evidence, we can ask, support the view that in the United States the death penalty is unfair? Similarly, we can ask whether a human fetus is a human being (in saying what something is, must we take account of its potentiality?), and, even if we agree that a fetus is a human being, we can further ask about whether it is a person. In *Roe v. Wade* the U.S. Supreme Court ruled that even the "viable" unborn human fetus is not a "person" as that term is used in the Fifth and Fourteenth Amendments. Here the question is this: Is the essential fact about the fetus that it is a person?

An argument of this sort makes a claim—that is, it takes a stand, but notice that it does not also have to argue for an action. Thus, it may argue that the death penalty is administered unfairly—that's a big enough issue—but it need not go on to argue that the death penalty should be abolished. After all, another possibility is that the death penalty should be administered fairly. The writer of the essay may be doing enough if he or she establishes the truth of the claim and leaves to others the possible responses.

2. **What is the value of *X*?** College courses often call for literary judgments. No one can argue with you if you say you prefer the plays of Tennessee Williams to those of Arthur Miller. But academic papers are not mere declarations of preferences. As soon as you say that Williams is a better playwright than Miller, you have based your preference on implicit standards, and it is incumbent on you to support your preference by giving

evidence about the relative skill, insight, and accomplishments of Williams and of Miller. Your argument is an evaluation. The question now at issue is the merits of the two authors and the standards appropriate for such an appraisal.

In short, an essay offering an evaluation normally has two purposes:

- to set forth an assessment, and
- to convince the reader that the assessment is reasonable.

In writing an evaluation, you will have to rely on criteria, and these will vary depending on your topic. For instance, if you are comparing the artistic merit of the plays by Williams and by Miller, you may want to talk about the quality of the characterization, the importance of the theme, and so on. But if the topic is "Which playwright is more suitable to be taught in high school?" other criteria may be appropriate, such as

- the difficulty of the author's language,
- the sexual content of some scenes, and
- the presence of obscene words.

Or consider a nonliterary issue: On balance, are college fraternities and sororities good or bad? If good, how good? If bad, how bad? What criteria can we use in making our evaluation? Probably some or all of the following:

- testimony of authorities (for instance, persons who can offer first-hand testimony about the good or bad effects),
- inductive evidence (we can collect examples of good or bad effects),
- appeals to logic ("it follows, therefore, that . . ."), and
- appeals to emotion (for instance, an appeal to our sense of fairness).

3. **What are the causes (or the consequences) of *X*?** Why did the rate of auto theft increase during a specific period? If we abolish the death penalty, will that cause the rate of murder to increase? Notice, by the way, that such problems may be complex. The phenomena that people usually argue about—say, such things as inflation, war, suicide, crime—have many causes, and it is therefore often a mistake to speak of *the* cause of *X*. A writer in *Time* mentioned that the life expectancy of an average American male is about sixty-seven years, a figure that compares unfavorably with the life expectancy of males in Japan and Israel. The *Time* writer suggested that an important cause of the relatively short life span is "the pressure to perform well in business." Perhaps. But the life expectancy of plumbers is no greater than that of managers and executives. Nutrition authority Jean Mayer, in an article in *Life*, attributed the relatively poor longevity of American males to a diet that is "rich in fat and poor in nutrients." Doubtless other authorities propose other causes, and in all likelihood no one cause accounts for the phenomenon.

Or take a second example of discussions of causality, this one concerning the academic performance of girls in single-sex schools, middle schools, and high schools. It is pretty much agreed (based on statistical evidence) that the graduates of these schools do better, as a group, than girls who graduate from co-educational schools. *Why* do girls in single-sex schools tend, as a group, to do better? What is the *cause*? The administrators of girls' schools usually attribute the success to the fact (we are admittedly putting the matter bluntly) that young women flourish better in an atmosphere free from male intimidation: They allegedly gain confidence and become more expressive when they are not threatened by males. And this may be the answer, but skeptics have attributed the success to two other causes:

- Most single-sex schools require parents to pay tuition and it is a documented fact that the children of well-to-do parents do better, academically, than the children of poor parents.

- Further, most single-sex schools are private schools, and they select their students from a pool of candidates. Admissions officers naturally select those candidates who seem to be academically promising—that is, they select students who have *already done well academically*.[1]

In short, the girls who graduate from single-sex schools may owe their later academic success not to the atmosphere inside the schools but to the fact that even at the time they were admitted to these schools they were academically stronger—we are, again, speaking of a cohort, not of individuals—than the girls who attend co-ed schools.

The lesson? Be cautious in attributing a cause. There may be several causes.

The kinds of support that usually accompany claims of cause include:

- factual data, especially statistics;
- analogies ("The Roman Empire declined because of *X* and *Y*," "Our society exhibits *X* and *Y*, and therefore . . ."); and
- inductive evidence.

4. **What should (or ought or must) we do about *X*?** Must we always obey the law? Should the law allow eighteen-year-olds to drink alcohol? Should eighteen-year-olds be drafted to do one year of social service? Should pornography be censored? Should steroid use by athletes be banned? Ought there to be Good Samaritan laws, making it a

---

[1]Until 2004 federal regulations discouraged public schools from separating boys from girls. As of the time of this comment [2009] there are only ninety-five single-sex public schools, twelve of which are in New York City. An article in the *New York Times*, 11 March 2009, page A20, suggests that there is little evidence that girls do better than boys in these schools. Indeed, in California a much-touted program in which six public middle schools and high schools were turned into single-sex academies has been abandoned.

legal duty for a stranger to intervene to save a person from death or great bodily harm, when one might do so with little or no risk to one-self? These questions involve conduct and policy; how we answer them will reveal our values and principles.

An essay answering questions of this sort usually

- begins by explaining what the issue (the problem) is, then
- states why the reader should care about it, then
- offers the proposed solution, then
- considers alternative solutions, and finally
- reaffirms the merit of the proposed solution, especially in the light of the audience's interests and needs.

You will recall that throughout this book we have spoken about devices that help a writer to get ideas. If in drafting an essay concerned with policy you begin by writing down your thoughts on the five bulleted items we have just given, you will almost surely uncover ideas that you didn't know you had.

Support for claims of policy usually include

- statistics,
- appeals to common sense and to the reader's moral sense, and
- testimony of authorities.

5. **What is the evidence for my claims about X?** In commenting on the four previous topics, we have talked about the kinds of support that are commonly offered, but a few additional points can be made.

Critical reading, writing, and thinking depend essentially on identifying and evaluating the evidence for and against the claims one makes and encounters in the writings of others. It is not enough to have an *opinion* or belief one way or the other; you need to be able to support your opinions—the bare fact of your sincere belief in what you say or write is not itself any *evidence* that what you believe is true.

So what are good reasons for opinions, adequate evidence for one's beliefs? The answer, of course, depends on what kind of belief or opinion, assertion or hypothesis, claim or principle you want to assert. For example, there is good evidence that President John F. Kennedy was assassinated on November 22, 1963, because this is the date for his death reported in standard almanacs. You could further substantiate the date by checking the back issues of the *New York Times*. But a different kind of evidence is needed to support the proposition that the chemical composition of water is H_2O. And you will need still other kinds of evidence to support your beliefs about the likelihood of rain tomorrow, the probability that the Red Sox will win the pennant this year, the twelfth digit in the decimal expansion of pi, the average cumulative grades of the graduating seniors over the past three years in your college, the relative merits of *Hamlet* and *Death of a Salesman,* and the moral dimensions of sexual harassment. None of these issues is merely a matter of opinion; yet about some of them, educated and informed people may disagree over the reasons and the evidence and what they show. Your job as a critical thinker is to be alert to the relevant reasons and evidence and to make the most of them as you present your views.

Again, an argument may answer two or more of these five basic questions. Someone who argues that pornography should (or should not) be censored

- will have to mark out the territory of the discussion by defining pornography (our first question: What is *X*?). The argument probably
- will also need to examine the consequences of adopting the preferred policy (our third question) and
- may even have to argue about its value (our second question). Some people maintain that pornography produces crime, but others maintain that it provides a harmless outlet for impulses that otherwise might vent themselves in criminal behavior.
- Further, someone arguing about the wisdom of censoring pornography might have to face the objection that censorship, however desirable on account of some of its consequences, may be unconstitutional and that, even if censorship were constitutional, it would (or might) have undesirable side effects, such as repressing freedom of political opinion.
- And one will always have to keep asking oneself our fifth question, What is the evidence for my claims?

Thinking about one or more of these questions may get you going. For instance, thinking about the first question, What is *X*?, will require you to produce a definition, and as you work at producing a satisfactory definition, you may find new ideas arising. If a question seems relevant, start writing, even if you write only a fragmentary sentence. You'll probably find that one word leads to another and that ideas begin to appear. Even if these ideas seem weak as you write them, don't be discouraged; you have put something on paper, and returning to these words, perhaps in five minutes or perhaps the next day, you will probably find that some are not at all bad and that others will stimulate you to better ones.

It may be useful to record your ideas in a special notebook or in a private blog or a Google Doc reserved for the purpose. Such a **journal** can be a valuable resource when it comes time to write your paper. Many students find it easier to focus their thoughts on writing if during the period of gestation they have been jotting down relevant ideas on something more substantial than slips of paper or loose sheets. The very act of designating a notebook or blog as your journal for a course can be the first step in focusing your attention on the eventual need to write a paper.

Take advantage of the free tools at your disposal. Use the Internet and free Web tools, including RSS feeds, Google (Drive, sites, and others), Yahoo!, blogs, and wikis to help you organize your initial ideas and to solicit feedback. Talking with others can help, but sometimes we do not have time to chat about our ideas. By using an RSS feed on a Web site that you think will provide good information on your topic (or a topic you are thinking about), you can notify yourself via e-mail if the site has uploaded new material such as news links or op-eds. Posting a blog entry in a public space about your topic can also foster conversations about your topic and help you discover other opinions. Using the Internet to uncover and refine your topic is common, especially in the beginning of the research process.

If what we have just said does not sound convincing, and you know from experience that you often have trouble getting started with your writing, don't despair; first aid is at hand in a sure-fire method that we will now explain.

The Thesis or Main Point

Let's assume that you are writing an argumentative essay—perhaps an evaluation of an argument in this book—and you have what seems to be a pretty good draft or at least a bunch of notes that are the result of hard thinking. You really do have ideas now, and you want to present them effectively. How will you organize your essay? No one formula works best for every essayist and for every essay, but it is usually advisable to formulate a basic **thesis** (a claim, a central point, a chief position) and to state it early. Every essay that is any good, even a book-length one, has a thesis (a main point), which can be stated briefly, usually in a sentence. Remember Coolidge's remark on the preacher's sermon on sin: "He was against it." Don't confuse the **topic** (sin) with the thesis (sin is bad). The thesis is the argumentative theme, the author's primary claim or contention, the proposition that the rest of the essay will explain and defend. Of course, the thesis may sound commonplace, but the book or essay or sermon ought to develop it interestingly and convincingly.

 A CHECKLIST FOR A THESIS STATEMENT

Consider the following questions:

☐ Does the statement make an arguable assertion rather than (a) merely assert an unarguable fact, (b) merely announce a topic, or (c) declare an unarguable opinion or belief?

☐ Is the statement broad enough to cover the entire argument that I will be presenting, and is it narrow enough for me to be able to cover the topic in the space allotted?

Here are some sample theses:

- Smoking should be prohibited in all enclosed public places.
- Smoking should be limited to specific parts of enclosed public places and entirely prohibited in small spaces, such as elevators.
- Proprietors of public places such as restaurants and sports arenas should be free to determine whether they wish to prohibit, limit, or impose no limitations on smokers.

Imagining an Audience

Of course, the questions that you ask yourself to stimulate your thoughts will depend primarily on what you are writing about, but additional questions are always relevant:

- Who are my readers?
- What do they believe?
- What common ground do we share?
- What do I want my readers to believe?
- What do they need to know?
- Why should they care?

These questions require a little comment. The literal answer to the first probably is "my teacher," but (unless you are given instructions to the contrary) you should not write specifically for your teacher. Instead, you should write for an audience that is, generally speaking, like your classmates. In short, your imagined audience is literate, intelligent, and moderately well-informed, but it does not know everything that you know, and it does not know your response to the problem that you are addressing. It needs more information to make an intelligent decision.

The essays in this book are from many different sources, each with its own audience. An essay from the *New York Times* is addressed to the educated general reader; an essay from *Ms.* magazine is addressed to readers sympathetic to feminism. An essay from *Commonweal,* a Roman Catholic publication addressed to the nonspecialist, is likely to differ in point of view or tone from one in *Time,* even though both articles may advance approximately the same position. The writer of the article in *Commonweal* may, for example, effectively cite church fathers and distinguished Roman Catholic writers as authorities, whereas the writer of the *Time* article would probably cite few or even none of these figures because a non-Catholic audience might be unfamiliar with them or, even if familiar, might be unimpressed by their views.

The tone as well as the gist of the argument is in some degree shaped by the audience. For instance, popular journals, such as the *National Review* and *Ms.* magazine, are more likely to use ridicule than are journals chiefly addressed to, say, an academic audience.

The Audience as Collaborator

If you imagine an audience and keep asking yourself what this audience needs to be told and what it doesn't need to be told, you will find that material comes to mind, just as it comes to mind when a friend asks you what a film you saw was about, who was in it, and how you liked it.

Your readers do not have to be told that Thomas Jefferson was an American statesman in the early years of this country's history, but they do have to be told that Elizabeth Cady Stanton was a late-nineteenth-century American feminist. Why? You need to identify Stanton because it's your hunch that your classmates never heard of her, or even if they may have heard the name, they can't quite identify it. But what if your class has been assigned an essay by Stanton? In that case your imagined reader knows Stanton's name and knows at least a little about her, so you don't have to identify Stanton as an American of the nineteenth century. But you do still have to remind your reader about relevant aspects of her essay, and you do have to tell your reader about your responses to them.

After all, even if the instructor has assigned an essay by Stanton, you cannot assume that your classmates know the essay inside out. Obviously, you can't say, "Stanton's third reason is also unconvincing," without reminding the reader, by means of a brief summary, of her third reason. Again,

- Think of your classmates—people like you—as your imagined readers; and
- Be sure that your essay does not make unreasonable demands.

If you ask yourself,

- "What do my readers need to know?" and
- "What do I want them to believe?"

you will find some answers arising, and you will start writing.

We have said that you should imagine your audience as your classmates. But this is not the whole truth. In a sense, your argument is addressed not simply to your classmates but to the world interested in ideas. Even if you can reasonably assume that your classmates have read only one work by Stanton, you will not begin your essay by writing "Stanton's essay is deceptively easy." You will have to name the work; it is possible that a reader has read some other work by Stanton. And by precisely identifying your subject, you help to ease the reader into your essay.

Similarly, you won't begin by writing,

The majority opinion in *Walker v. City of Birmingham* held that . . .

Rather, you'll write something like this:

In *Walker v. City of Birmingham*, the U.S. Supreme Court ruled in 1966 that city authorities acted lawfully when they jailed Martin Luther King

Jr. and other clergymen in 1963 for marching in Birmingham without a permit. Justice Potter Stewart delivered the majority opinion, which held that . . .

By the way, if you think you suffer from a writing block, the mere act of writing out such readily available facts will help you to get started. You will find that writing a few words, perhaps merely copying the essay's title or an interesting quotation from the essay, will stimulate you to write down thoughts that you didn't know you had in you.

Here, again, are the questions about audience. If you write on a computer, consider putting these questions into a file. For each assignment, copy the questions into the file you are currently working on, and then, as a way of generating ideas, *enter your responses, indented, under each question.*

1. Who are my readers?
2. What do they believe?
3. What common ground do we share?
4. What do I want my readers to believe?
5. What do they need to know?
6. Why should they care?

Thinking about your audience can help you to get started; even more important, it can help you to get ideas. Our second and third questions about the audience ("What do they believe?" and "How much common ground do we share?") will usually help you get ideas flowing.

- Presumably your imagined audience does not share your views, or at least does not fully share them. But why?
- How can these readers hold a position that to you seems unreasonable?

If you try to put yourself into your readers' shoes—and in your essay you will almost surely summarize the views that you are going to speak against—and if you think about what your audience knows or thinks it knows, you will find yourself getting ideas. Spend time online reviewing Web sites that are dedicated to your topic. What do they have to say, and why do the authors hold these views?

You do not believe (let's assume) that people should be allowed to smoke in enclosed public places, but you know that some people hold a different view. Why do they hold it? Try to state their view *in a way that would be satisfactory to them.* Having done so, you may come to perceive that your conclusions and theirs differ because they are based on different premises, perhaps different ideas about human rights. Examine the opposition's premises carefully, and explain, first to yourself and ultimately to your readers, why you find some premises unacceptable.

Possibly some facts are in dispute, such as whether nonsmokers may be harmed by exposure to tobacco. The thing to do, then, is to check the facts. If you find that harm to nonsmokers has not been proved, but you nevertheless believe that smoking should be prohibited in enclosed public places, of course you can't premise your argument on the wrongfulness of harming the innocent (in this case, the nonsmokers). You will have to develop arguments that take account of the facts, whatever they are.

Among the relevant facts there surely are some that your audience or your opponent will not dispute. The same is true of the values relevant to the discussion; the two of you are very likely to agree, if you stop to think about it, that you share belief in some of the same values (such as the principle mentioned above, that it is wrong to harm the innocent). These areas of shared agreement are crucial to effective persuasion in argument.

> **A RULE FOR WRITERS:** If you wish to persuade, you'll have to begin by finding premises you can share with your audience.

There are two good reasons why you should identify and isolate the areas of agreement:

- There is no point in disputing facts or values on which you and your readers really agree.
- It usually helps to establish goodwill between you and your opponent when you can point to beliefs, assumptions, facts, and values that the two of you share.

In a few moments we will return to the need to share some of the opposition's ideas.

Recall that in composing college papers it is usually best to write for a general audience, an audience rather like your classmates but without the specific knowledge that they all share as students enrolled in one course. If the topic is smoking in public places, the audience presumably consists of smokers and nonsmokers. Thinking about our fifth question on page 240 — "What do [readers] need to know?" — may prompt you to give statistics about the harmful effects of smoking. Or if you are arguing on behalf of smokers, it may prompt you to cite studies claiming that no evidence conclusively demonstrates that cigarette smoking is harmful to nonsmokers. If indeed you are writing for a general audience and you are not advancing a highly unfamiliar view, our second question ("What does the audience believe?") is less important here, but if the audience is specialized, such as an antismoking group, a group of restaurant owners who fear that antismoking regulations will interfere with their business, or a group of civil libertarians, an effective essay will have to address their special beliefs.

In addressing their beliefs (let's assume that you do not share them or do not share them fully), you must try to establish some common

✓ **A CHECKLIST FOR IMAGINING AN AUDIENCE**

Have I asked myself the following questions?

☐ Who are my readers? How do I know?

☐ How much about the topic do they know?

☐ Have I provided necessary background (including definitions of special terms) if the imagined readers probably are not especially familiar with the topic?

☐ Are these imagined readers likely to be neutral? Sympathetic? Hostile? Have I done enough online research to have something to offer to a hostile audience?

☐ If they are neutral, have I offered good reasons to persuade them? If they are sympathetic, have I done more than merely reaffirm their present beliefs? That is, have I perhaps enriched their views or encouraged them to act? If they are hostile, have I taken account of their positions, recognized their strengths but also called attention to their limitations, and offered a position that may persuade these hostile readers to modify their position?

ground. If you advocate requiring restaurants to provide nonsmoking areas, you should at least recognize the possibility that this arrangement will result in inconvenience for the proprietor. But perhaps (the good news) the restaurant will regain some lost customers or will attract some new customers. This thought should prompt you to think of kinds of evidence, perhaps testimony or statistics.

When you formulate a thesis and ask questions about it, such as who the readers are, what do they believe, what do they know, and what do they need to know, you begin to get ideas about how to organize the material or at least to see that some sort of organization will have to be worked out. The thesis may be clear and simple, but the reasons (the argument) may take many pages. The thesis is the point; the argument sets forth the evidence that is offered to support the thesis.

The Title

It's not a bad idea to announce your thesis in your **title.** If you scan the table of contents of this book, you will notice that a fair number of essayists use the title to let the readers know, at least in a very general way, what position will be advocated. Here are a few examples of titles that take a position:

Gay Marriages: Make Them Legal

"Diversity" Is a Smoke Screen for Discrimination

Why Handguns Must Be Outlawed

True, these titles are not especially engaging, but the reader welcomes them because they give some information about the writer's thesis.

Some titles do not announce the thesis, but they at least announce the topic:

Is All Discrimination Unfair?

On Racist Speech

Why Make Divorce Easy?

Although not clever or witty, these titles are informative.

Some titles seek to attract attention or to stimulate the imagination:

A First Amendment Junkie

A Crime of Compassion

Addicted to Health

All of these are effective, but a word of caution is appropriate here. In your effort to engage your reader's attention, be careful not to sound like a wise guy. You want to engage your readers, not turn them off.

Finally, be prepared to rethink your title *after* you have finished the last draft of your paper. A title somewhat different from your working title may be an improvement because the emphasis of your finished paper may have turned out to be rather different from what you expected when you first thought of a title.

The Opening Paragraphs

Opening paragraphs are difficult to write, so don't worry about writing an effective opening when you are drafting. Just get some words down on paper, and keep going. But when you revise your first draft — really a zero draft — you probably should begin to think seriously about the effect of your opening.

A good introduction arouses the reader's interest and helps prepare the reader for the rest of the paper. How? Opening paragraphs usually do at least one (and often all) of the following:

- attract the reader's interest (often with a bold statement of the thesis or with an interesting relevant statistic, quotation, or anecdote),
- prepare the reader's mind by giving some idea of the topic and often of the thesis,
- give the reader an idea of how the essay is organized, and
- define a key term.

You may not wish to announce your thesis in your title, but if you don't announce it there, you should set it forth early in the argument, in your introductory paragraph or paragraphs. In an essay called "Human Rights and Foreign Policy," Jeanne J. Kirkpatrick merely announces her topic (subject) as opposed to her thesis (point), but she begins to hint at the thesis in her first paragraph, by deprecating President Jimmy Carter's policy:

> In this paper I deal with three broad subjects: first, the content and consequences of the Carter administration's human rights policy; second, the prerequisites of a more adequate theory of human rights; and third, some characteristics of a more successful human rights policy.

Or consider this opening paragraph from Peter Singer's "Animal Liberation" (p. 207):

> We are familiar with Black Liberation, Gay Liberation, and a variety of other movements. With Women's Liberation some thought we had come to the end of the road. Discrimination on the basis of sex, it has been said, is the last form of discrimination that is universally accepted and practiced without pretense, even in those liberal circles which have long prided themselves on their freedom from racial discrimination. But one should always be wary of talking of "the last remaining form of discrimination." If we have learned anything from the liberation movements, we should have learned how difficult it is to be aware of the ways in which we discriminate until they are forcefully pointed out to us. A liberation movement demands an expansion of our moral horizons, so that practices that were previously regarded as natural and inevitable are now seen as intolerable.

Although Singer's introductory paragraph nowhere mentions animal liberation, in conjunction with the essay's title it gives us a good idea of what Singer is up to and where he is going. Singer knows that his audience will be skeptical, so he reminds them that in previous years many were skeptical of reforms now taken for granted. He adopts a strategy used fairly often by writers who advance unconventional theses: Rather than beginning with a bold announcement of a thesis that may turn off some of his readers because it sounds offensive or absurd, Singer warms up his audience, gaining their interest by cautioning them politely that although they may at first be skeptical of animal liberation, if they stay with his essay they may come to feel that they have expanded their horizons.

Notice, too, that Singer begins by establishing common ground with his readers; he assumes, probably correctly, that they share his view that other forms of discrimination (now seen to be unjust) were once widely practiced and were assumed to be acceptable and natural. In this paragraph, then, Singer is not only showing himself to be fair-minded but is also letting readers know that he will advance a daring idea. His opening wins their attention and goodwill. A writer can hardly hope to do more. (In a few pages we will talk a little more about winning the audience.)

In your introductory paragraphs:

- You may have to give some background information that your readers will need to keep in mind if they are to follow your essay.

- You may wish to define some terms that are unfamiliar or that you use in an unusual sense.

- If you are writing for an online publication (where your teacher or audience will encounter your argument on the Web), you might establish a context for your argument by linking to a news video that outlines your topic, or you might offer your thesis and then link to a news story that supports your claim. (Remember that using any videos, images, or links also requires a citation of some kind.) The beauty of publishing the piece in an online environment is that you can often link directly to your sources and use sources more easily than if you were submitting a hard copy.

After announcing the topic, giving the necessary background, and stating your position (and perhaps the opposition's) in as engaging a manner as possible, it is usually a good idea to give the reader an idea of *how* you will proceed—that is, what the organization will be. In other words, use the introduction to set up the organization of your essay. Your teachers may assign four- to six-page mini-research papers or they may assign ten- to fifteen-page research papers; if they assign an online venue, ask them about the approximate word count. Whatever the length, every paper needs to have a clear organization. The introduction is where you can

- hook your reader
- reveal your thesis and topic, and
- explain how you will organize your discussion of the topic—what you will do first, second, third, etc.

Look at Kirkpatrick's opening paragraph (page 244) for an obvious illustration. She tells us she will deal with three subjects, and she names them. Her approach in the paragraph is concise, obvious, and effective.

> **A RULE FOR WRITERS:** In writing or at least in revising these paragraphs, keep in mind this question: What do my readers need to know? Remember, your aim throughout is to write *reader-friendly* prose, and keeping the needs and interests of your audience constantly in mind will help you achieve this goal.

Similarly, you may, for instance, want to announce fairly early that there are four common objections to your thesis and that you will take them up one by one, beginning with the weakest (or most widely held, or whatever) and moving to the strongest (or least familiar), after which you will advance your own view in greater detail. Not every argument begins with refuting the other side, though many arguments do. The point to remember is that you usually ought to tell your readers where you will be taking them and by what route. In effect, you are giving them an outline.

Organizing and Revising the Body of the Essay

We begin with a wise remark by a newspaper columnist, Robert Cromier: "The beautiful part of writing is that you don't have to get it right the first time—unlike, say, a brain surgeon."

In drafting your essay you will of course begin with an organization that seems to you to make sense, but you may well find, in rereading the draft, that some other organization is better. Here, for a start, is an organization that is common in argumentative essays.

1. Statement of the problem or issue
2. Statement of the structure of the essay (its organization)
3. Statement of alternative solutions
4. Arguments in support of the proposed solution
5. Arguments answering possible objections
6. A summary, resolution, or conclusion

Let's look at each of these six steps.

1. **Statement of the problem or issue**   Whether the problem is stated briefly or at length depends on the nature of the problem and the writer's audience. If you haven't already defined unfamiliar terms or terms you use in a special way, probably now is the time to do so. In any case, it is advisable here to state the problem objectively (thereby gaining the trust of the reader) and to indicate why the reader should care about the issue.

2. **Statement of the structure of the essay**   After stating the problem at the appropriate length, the writer often briefly indicates the structure of the rest of the essay. The commonest structure is suggested below, in points 3 and 4.

3. **Statement of alternative (but less adequate) solutions**   In addition to stating the alternatives fairly—let the readers know that you

have done your homework—the writer probably conveys willingness to recognize not only the integrity of the proposals but also the (partial) merit of at least some of the alternative solutions.

The point made in the previous sentence is important and worth amplifying. Because it is important to convey your goodwill—your sense of fairness—to the reader, it is advisable to let your reader see that you are familiar with the opposition and that you recognize the integrity of those who hold that view. This you do by granting its merits as far as you can. (For more about this approach, see the essay by Carl R. Rogers on p. 394.)

The next stage, which constitutes most of the body of the essay, usually is this:

4. **Arguments in support of the proposed solution**   The evidence offered will, of course, depend on the nature of the problem. Relevant statistics, authorities, examples, or analogies may come to mind or be available. This is usually the longest part of the essay.

5. **Arguments answering possible objections**   These arguments may suggest that

   a. The proposal won't work (perhaps it is alleged to be too expensive, to make unrealistic demands on human nature, or to fail to get to the heart of the problem).

   b. The proposed solution will create problems greater than the difficulty to be resolved. (A good example of a proposal that produced dreadful unexpected results is the law mandating a prison term for anyone over eighteen in possession of an illegal drug. Heroin dealers then began to use children as runners, and cocaine importers followed the practice.)

6. **A summary, resolution, or conclusion**   Here the writer may seek to accommodate the views of the opposition as far as possible but clearly suggest that the writer's own position makes good sense. A conclusion—the word comes from the Latin *claudere*, "to shut"—ought to provide a sense of closure, but it can be much more than a restatement of the writer's thesis. It can, for instance, make a quiet emotional appeal by suggesting that the issue is important and that the ball is now in the reader's court.

Of course not every essay will follow this six-step pattern, but let's assume that in the introductory paragraphs you have sketched the topic (and have shown or nicely said, or implied, that the reader doubtless is interested in it) and have fairly and courteously set forth the opposition's view, recognizing its merits ("I grant that," "admittedly," "it is true that") and indicating the degree to which you can share part of that view. You now want to set forth your arguments explaining why you differ on some essentials.

In setting forth your own position, you can begin either with your strongest reasons or your weakest. Each method of organization has advantages and disadvantages.

- If you begin with your strongest reason, the essay may seem to peter out.

- If you begin with your weakest reason, you build to a climax, but your readers may not still be with you because they may have felt at the start that the essay was frivolous.

The solution to this last possibility is to make sure that even your weakest argument is an argument of some strength. You can, moreover, assure your readers that stronger points will soon be offered and you offer this point first only because you want to show that you are aware of it and that, slight though it is, it deserves some attention. The body of the essay, then, is devoted to arguing a position, which means offering not only supporting reasons but also refutations of possible objections to these reasons.

Doubtless you will sometimes be uncertain, as you draft your essay, whether to present a given point before or after another point. When you write, and certainly when you revise, try to put yourself into your reader's shoes: Which point do you think the reader needs to know first? Which point *leads to* which further point? Your argument should not be a mere list of points, of course; rather, it should clearly integrate one point with another in order to develop an idea. But in all likelihood you won't have a strong sense of the best organization until you have written a draft and have reread it.

> **A RULE FOR WRITERS:** When you revise, make sure that your organization is clear to your readers.

Checking Paragraphs   When you revise your draft, watch out also for short paragraphs. Although a paragraph of only two or three sentences (like some in this chapter) may occasionally be helpful as a transition between complicated points, most short paragraphs are undeveloped paragraphs. Newspaper editors favor very short paragraphs because they can be read rapidly when printed in the narrow columns typical of newspapers. Many of the essays reprinted in this book originally were published in newspapers, hence they consist of very short paragraphs, but they should *not* be regarded as models for your own writing. A second note about paragraphs: Writers for online venues often "chunk" (that is, they provide extra space for paragraph breaks) rather than write a continuous flow. These writers chunk their text for several reasons, but chiefly because breaking up paragraphs and adding space between them makes some types of writing "scannable": The screen is easier to navigate because it is not packed with text in a 12-pt font. The breaks in paragraphs also allow the reader to see a complete paragraph without having to scroll.

Checking Transitions   Make sure, too, in revising, that the reader can move easily from the beginning of a paragraph to the end and from one paragraph to the next. Transitions help the reader to perceive the connections between the units of the argument. For example ("For example" is a transition, of course, indicating that an illustration will follow), they may illustrate, establish a sequence, connect logically, amplify, compare, contrast, summarize, or concede (see Idea Prompt 6.1). Transitions serve as guideposts that enable your reader to move easily through your essay.

When writers revise an early draft, they chiefly

- **unify** the essay by eliminating irrelevancies;
- **organize** the essay by keeping in mind an imagined audience;
- **clarify** the essay by fleshing out thin paragraphs, by making certain that the transitions are adequate and by making certain that generalizations are adequately supported by concrete details and examples.

We are not talking about polish or elegance; we are talking about fundamental matters. Be especially careful not to abuse the logical connectives (*thus, as a result,* and so on). If you write several sentences followed by *therefore* or a similar word or phrase, be sure that what you write after the *therefore* really *does follow* from what has gone before. Logical connectives are not mere transitional devices used to link disconnected bits of prose. They are supposed to mark a real movement of thought — the essence of an argument.

The Ending

What about concluding paragraphs, in which you try to summarize the main points and reaffirm your position?

If you can look back over your essay and add something that enriches it and at the same time wraps it up, fine, but don't feel compelled to say, "Thus, in conclusion, I have argued *X, Y,* and *Z,* and I have refuted Jones." After all, *conclusion* can have two meanings: (1) ending, or finish, as the ending of a joke or a novel; or (2) judgment or decision reached after deliberation. Your essay should finish effectively (the first sense), but it need not announce a judgment (the second).

If the essay is fairly short, so that a reader can more or less keep the whole thing in mind, you may not need to restate your view. Just make sure that you have covered the ground and that your last sentence is a good one. Notice that the student essay printed later in this chapter (p. 264) does not end with a formal conclusion, though it ends conclusively, with a note of finality.

By a note of finality we do *not* mean a triumphant crowing. It's usually far better to end with the suggestion that you hope you have by now indicated why those who hold a different view may want to modify it and accept yours.

IDEA PROMPT 6.1 USING TRANSITIONS IN ARGUMENT

Illustrate	*for example, for instance, consider this case*	"Many television crime dramas contain scenes of graphic violence. For example, in the episode of *Law and Order* titled ..."
Establish a sequence	*a more important objection, a stronger example, the best reason*	"A stronger example of the ways that TV violence is susceptible to being mimicked is ..."
Connect logically	*thus, as a result, therefore, so, it follows*	"Therefore, the Federal Communications Commission ought to consider more carefully regulating what types of violence they allow on the air."
Amplify	*further, in addition to, moreover*	"Further, fines for networks that violate these regulations should be steeper because ..."
Compare	*similarly, in a like manner, just as, analogously*	"Just as the FCC regulates language and sexuality on broadcast TV ..."
Contrast	*on the other hand, in contrast, however, but*	"On the other hand, studies have shown that violent television ..."
Summarize	*in short, briefly*	"In short, the basic premise of his argument is ..."
Concede	*admittedly, granted, to be sure*	"Admittedly, there are many points on which the author is correct."

If you study the essays in this book, or, for that matter, the editorials and op-ed pieces in a newspaper, you will notice that writers often provide a sense of closure by using one of the following devices:

- a return to something in the introduction,
- a glance at the wider implications of the issue (for example, if smoking is restricted, other liberties are threatened),
- an anecdote that engagingly illustrates the thesis,
- a suggestion that the reader can take some specific action, i.e., that the ball is now in the reader's court, or

- a brief summary (but this sort of ending may seem unnecessary and even tedious, especially if the paper is short and if the summary merely repeats what has already been said).

> **A RULE FOR WRITERS:** Emulate John Kenneth Galbraith, a distinguished writer on economics. Galbraith said that in his fifth draft he introduced the note of spontaneity for which his writing was famous.

Two Uses of an Outline

The Outline as a Preliminary Guide   Some writers find it useful to sketch an **outline** as soon as they think they know what they want to say, even before they write a first draft. This procedure can be helpful in planning a tentative organization, but remember that in revising a draft new ideas will arise, and the outline may have to be modified. A preliminary outline is chiefly useful as a means of getting going, not as a guide to the final essay.

The Outline as a Way of Checking a Draft   Whether or not you use a preliminary outline, we strongly suggest that after you have written what you hope is your last draft, you make an outline of it; there is no better way of finding out whether the essay is well organized.

Go through the draft and write down the chief points in the order in which you make them. That is, prepare a table of contents—perhaps a phrase for each paragraph. Next, examine your notes to see what kind of sequence they reveal in your paper:

- Is the sequence reasonable? Can it be improved?
- Are any passages irrelevant?
- Does something important seem to be missing?

If no coherent structure or reasonable sequence clearly appears in the outline, then the full prose version of your argument probably doesn't have any either. Therefore, produce another draft, moving things around, adding or subtracting paragraphs—cutting and pasting into a new sequence, with transitions as needed—and then make another outline to see if the sequence now is satisfactory.

You are probably familiar with the structure known as a **formal outline.** Major points are indicated by I, II, III; points within major points are indicated by A, B, C; divisions within A, B, C are indicated by 1, 2, 3; and so on. Thus,

I. Arguments for opening all Olympic sports to professionals
    A. Fairness
        1. Some Olympic sports are already open to professionals.
        2. Some athletes who really are not professionals are classified as professionals.
    B. Quality (achievements would be higher)

You may want to outline your draft according to this principle, or it may be enough if you simply write a phrase for each paragraph and indent the subdivisions. But keep these points in mind:

- It is not enough for the parts to be ordered reasonably.
- The order must be made clear to the reader, probably by means of transitions such as *for instance, on the other hand, we can now turn to an opposing view,* and so on.

Here is another way of thinking about an outline. For each paragraph, write

- what the paragraph *says,* and
- what the paragraph *does.*

An opening paragraph might be outlined thus:

- What the paragraph *says* is that the words "under God" in the Pledge of Allegiance should be omitted.
- What the paragraph *does* is, first, it informs the reader of the thesis, and second, it *provides some necessary background,* for instance, that the words were not in the original wording of the Pledge.

A dual outline of this sort will help you to see whether you have a final draft or a draft that needs refinement.

A Last Word about Outlines

Outlines may seem rigid to many writers, especially to writers who customarily compose online, where we are accustomed to cutting, copying, moving, and deleting as we draft. However, as we said earlier, an outline—whether you write it before you draft a single word or use it to evaluate the organization of something you have already written—is meant to be a guide rather than a straitjacket that confines you. Many writers who compose electronically find that the ability to keep banging out words—typing is so much easier than pushing a pen or pencil—and to cut and paste without actually reaching for scissors makes it easy to produce an essay that readers may find difficult to follow. (There is much truth in the proverb, "Easy writing makes hard reading.") If you compose electronically, and especially if you find yourself continually adding, deleting, and moving text around without a clear organizational goal in mind, be sure to read and outline your draft, and then examine the outline to see if indeed there is a reasonable organization.

Outlines are especially helpful for long essays, but even short ones benefit from a bit of advanced planning, a list of a few topics (drawn from notes already taken) that help to keep the writer moving in an orderly way. A longer work such as an honors or a master's thesis typically requires careful planning. An outline will be a great help in assuring that you will produce something that a reader can easily follow—but of course you may find, as you write, that the outline needs to be altered.

✔ A CHECKLIST FOR ORGANIZING AN ARGUMENT

☐ Does the introduction let the readers know where the author is taking them?

☐ Does the introduction state the problem or issue?

  ☐ Does it state the claim (the thesis)?

  ☐ Does it suggest the organization of the essay, thereby helping the reader to follow the argument?

☐ Do subsequent paragraphs support the claim?

  ☐ Do they offer evidence?

  ☐ Do they face objections to the claim and offer reasonable responses?

  ☐ Do they indicate why the author's claim is preferable?

  ☐ Do transitions (signposts such as "Furthermore," "On the other hand,"and "Consider as an example") guide the reader through the argument?

☐ Does the essay end effectively, with a paragraph (or at most two paragraphs) bringing a note of closure, for instance, by indicating that the proposed solution is relatively simple? By admitting that, although the proposed solution will be difficult to implement, it is certainly feasible? By reminding the reader of the urgency of the problem?

When readers finish reading, they should feel that the writer has brought them to a decisive point and now is not just abruptly and unexpectedly stopping.

Tone and the Writer's Persona

Although this book is chiefly about argument in the sense of rational discourse—the presentation of reasons in support of a thesis or conclusion—the appeal to reason is only one form of persuasion. Another form is the appeal to emotion—to pity, for example. Aristotle saw, in addition to the appeal to reason and the appeal to emotion, a third form of persuasion, the appeal to the character of the speaker. He called it the **ethical appeal** (the Greek word for this kind of appeal is **ethos,** "character"). The idea is that effective speakers convey the suggestion that they are

- informed,
- intelligent,
- fair-minded (persons of goodwill), and
- honest.

Because they are perceived as trustworthy, their words inspire confidence in their listeners. It is, of course, a fact that when we read an argument we are often aware of the *person* or *voice* behind the words, and our assent to the argument depends partly on the extent to which we can share the speaker's assumptions, look at the matter from the speaker's point of view—in short, *identify* with this speaker.

How can a writer inspire the confidence that lets readers identify themselves with him or her? To begin with, the writer should possess the virtues Aristotle specified: intelligence or good sense, honesty, and benevolence or goodwill. As the Roman proverb puts it, "No one gives what he does not have." Still, possession of these qualities is not a guarantee that you will convey them in your writing. Like all other writers, you will have to revise your drafts so that these qualities become apparent, or, stated more moderately, you will have to revise so that nothing in the essay causes a reader to doubt your intelligence, honesty, and goodwill. A blunder in logic, a misleading quotation, a snide remark, even an error in spelling—all such slips can cause readers to withdraw their sympathy from the writer.

But of course all good argumentative essays do not sound exactly alike; they do not all reveal the same speaker. Each writer develops his or her own voice or (as literary critics and teachers call it) **persona.** In fact, one writer will have several voices or personae, depending on the topic and the audience. The president of the United States delivering an address on the State of the Union has one persona; chatting with a reporter at his summer home he has another. This change is not a matter of hypocrisy. Different circumstances call for different language. As a French writer put it, there is a time to speak of "Paris" and a time to speak of "the capital of the nation." When Lincoln spoke at Gettysburg, he didn't say "Eighty-seven years ago," but "Four score and seven years ago." We might say that just as some occasions required him to be the folksy Honest Abe, the occasion of the dedication of hallowed ground required him to be formal and solemn, and so the president of the United States appropriately used biblical language. The election campaigns called for one persona, and the dedication of a military cemetery—a different rhetorical situation—called for a different persona. For examples on how to vary tone, see Idea Prompt 6.2.

> **A RULE FOR WRITERS:** Present yourself so that your readers see you as knowledgeable, honest, open-minded, and interested in helping them to think about an issue of significance.

When we talk about a writer's persona, we mean the way in which the writer presents his or her attitudes

IDEA PROMPT 6.2 VARYING TONE

Abraham Lincoln	*Four score and seven years ago our fathers brought forth on this continent a new nation, conceived in liberty, and dedicated to the proposition that all men are created equal.*	Invokes Biblical rhetoric ("Four score and seven years ago") in an appeal to national unity
More academic tone	*In 1776, America's Founding Fathers drafted and signed the Declaration of Independence, at the heart of which were the Enlightenment ideals of equality and individual liberty.*	Incorporates specific factual information and connects to overarching ideas
More informal tone	*Nearly a hundred years ago, the United States was founded in order to provide greater freedom and equality to its citizens.*	Is accurate but simplified, forgoing much detail
Too informal for most academic writing	*The US was created way back then so that everyone would be free.*	Mischaracterizes or oversimplifies the thought process

- toward *the self,*
- toward *the audience,* and
- toward *the subject.*

Thus, if a writer says,

> I have thought long and hard about this subject, and I can say with assurance that . . .

we may feel that we are listening to a self-satisfied ass who probably is simply mouthing other people's opinions. Certainly he is mouthing clichés: "long and hard," "say with assurance."

Let's look at a slightly subtler example of an utterance that reveals an attitude. When we read that

> President Nixon was hounded out of office by journalists,

we hear a respectful attitude toward Nixon ("President Nixon") and a hostile attitude toward the press (they are beasts, curs who "hounded" our elected leader). If the writer's attitudes were reversed, she might have said something like this:

> The press turned the searchlight on Tricky Dick's criminal shenanigans.

"Tricky Dick" and "criminal" are obvious enough, but notice that "shenanigans" also implies the writer's contempt for Nixon, and of course, "turned the searchlight" suggests that the press is a source of illumination, a source of truth. The original version and the opposite version both say that the press was responsible for Nixon's resignation, but the original version ("President Nixon was hounded") conveys indignation toward journalists, whereas the revision conveys contempt for Nixon.

These two versions suggest two speakers who differ not only in their view of Nixon but also in their manner, including the seriousness with which they take themselves. Although the passage is very short, it seems to us that the first speaker conveys righteous indignation ("hounded"), whereas the second conveys amused contempt ("shenanigans"). To our ears the tone, as well as the point, differs in the two versions.

We are talking about **loaded words,** words that convey the writer's attitude and that by their connotations are meant to win the reader to the writer's side. Compare the words in the left-hand column with those in the right:

freedom fighter	terrorist
pro-choice	pro-abortion
pro-life	antichoice
economic refugee	illegal alien
terrorist surveillance	domestic spying

The words in the left-hand column sound like good things; speakers who use these words are seeking to establish themselves as virtuous people who are supporting worthy causes. The **connotations** (associations, overtones) of these pairs of words differ, even though the **denotations** (explicit meanings, dictionary definitions) are the same, just as the connotations of *mother* and *female parent* differ, although the denotations are the same. Similarly, although Lincoln's "four score and seven" and "eighty-seven" both denote "thirteen less than one hundred," they differ in connotation.

Tone is not only a matter of connotations (*hounded out of office* versus, let's say, *compelled to resign,* or *pro-choice* versus *pro-abortion*); it is also a matter of such things as the selection and type of examples. A writer who offers many examples, especially ones drawn from ordinary life, conveys a persona different from that of a writer who offers no examples or only an occasional invented instance. The first of these probably is, one might say, friendlier, more down-to-earth.

Last Words on Tone　On the whole, when writing an argument, it is advisable to be courteous and respectful of your topic, of your audience, and of people who hold views you are arguing against. It is rarely good for one's own intellectual development to regard as villains or fools persons who hold views different from one's own, especially if some of them are in the audience. Keep in mind the story of the two strangers on a train who, striking up a conversation, found that both were clergymen, though of different faiths. Then one said to the other, "Well, why shouldn't we be friends? After all, we both serve God, you in your way and I in His."

Complacency is all right when telling a joke but not when offering an argument:

- Recognize opposing views.
- Assume they are held in good faith.
- State them fairly (if you don't, you do a disservice not only to the opposition but also to your own position because the perceptive reader will not take you seriously).
- Be temperate in arguing your own position: "If I understand their view correctly . . ."; "It seems reasonable to conclude that . . ."; "Perhaps, then, we can agree that . . ."
- Write calmly: If you become overly emotional your readers may interpret you as biased or unreasonable — even a bit nutty — and they may lose their confidence in you.

One way to practice thinking about tone and persona is in your professional e-mails. As a student you probably send many e-mails to your classmates and to your instructors or other offices on campus (the financial aid office, the parking/traffic office, your instructors, your advisor, etc.). As teachers, we are often surprised at how flippant and inattentive students are when e-mailing.

We, One, or I?

The use of *we* in the last sentence brings us to another point: May the first-person pronouns *I* and *we* be used? In this book, because two of us are writing, we often use *we* to mean the two authors. And we sometimes use *we* to mean the authors and the readers. This shifting use of one word can be troublesome, but we hope (clearly the *we* here refers only to the authors) that we have avoided any ambiguity. But can, or should, or must an individual use *we* instead of *I*? The short answer is no.

If you are simply speaking for yourself, use *I*. Attempts to avoid the first-person singular by saying things like "This writer thinks . . . ," and "It is thought that . . . ," and "One thinks that . . . ," are far more irritating (and wordy) than the use of *I*. The so-called editorial *we* is as odd-sounding in a student's argument as is the royal *we*. Mark Twain said that the only ones who can appropriately say *we* are kings, editors, and people with a tapeworm. And because one *one* leads to another, making the sentence sound (James Thurber's words) "like a trombone solo," it's best to admit that you are the author, and to use *I*. But there is no need to preface every sentence with "I think." The reader knows that the essay is yours; just write it, using *I* when you must, but not needlessly.

Often you will see *I* in journalistic writing and of course in autobiographical writing—and you will see it in some argumentative writing, too—but in most argumentative writing it is best to state the facts and (when drawing reasonable conclusions from them) to keep yourself in the background. Why? The more you use *I* in an essay, the more your readers will attach *you* directly to the argument and may regard your position as personal rather than as relevant to themselves.

✔ A CHECKLIST FOR ATTENDING TO THE NEEDS OF THE AUDIENCE

- ☐ Do I have a sense of what the audience probably knows about the issue?
- ☐ Do I have a sense of what the audience probably thinks about the issue?
- ☐ Have I stated the thesis clearly and sufficiently early in the essay?
- ☐ How much common ground do we probably share?
- ☐ Have I, in the paper, tried to establish common ground and then moved on to advance my position?
- ☐ Have I supported my arguments with sufficient details?
- ☐ Have I used the appropriate language (for instance, defined terms that are likely to be unfamiliar)?
- ☐ Have I indicated why my readers should care about the issue and should accept or at least take seriously my views?
- ☐ Is the organization clear?
- ☐ Have I used transitions where they are needed?
- ☐ If visual material (charts, graphs, pictures) will enhance my arguments, have I used them?
- ☐ Have I presented myself as a person who is (a) fair, (b) informed, and (c) worth listening to? In short, have I conveyed a strong *ethos*?

Avoiding Sexist Language

Courtesy as well as common sense requires that you respect the feelings of your readers. Many people today find offensive the implicit sexism in the use of male pronouns to denote not only men but also women ("As the reader follows the argument, he will find . . ."). And sometimes the use of the male pronoun to denote all people is ridiculous: "An individual, no matter what his sex, . . ."

In most contexts there is no need to use gender-specific nouns or pronouns. One way to avoid using *he* when you mean any person is to use *he or she* (or *she or he*) instead of *he,* but the result is sometimes a bit cumbersome—although it is superior to the overly conspicuous *he/she* and to *s/he.*

Here are two simple ways to solve the problem:

- *Use the plural* ("As readers follow the argument, they will find . . ."), or

- *Recast the sentence* so that no pronoun is required ("Readers following the argument will find . . .").

Because *man* and *mankind* strike many readers as sexist when used in such expressions as "Man is a rational animal" and "Mankind has not yet solved this problem," consider using such words as *human being, person, people, humanity,* and *we.* (*Examples:* "Human beings are rational animals"; "We have not yet solved this problem.")

PEER REVIEW

Your instructor may suggest—or may even require—that you submit an early draft of your essay to a fellow student or small group of students for comment. Such a procedure benefits both author and readers: You get the responses of a reader and the student-reader gets experience in thinking about the problems of developing an argument, especially in thinking about such matters as the degree of detail that a writer needs to offer to a reader and the importance of keeping the organization evident to a reader.

Oral peer reviews allow for the give and take of discussion, but probably most students and most instructors find written peer reviews more helpful because reviewers think more carefully about their responses to the draft, and they help essayists to get beyond a knee-jerk response to criticism. Online reviews on a class Web site or through e-mail are especially helpful precisely because they are not face to face; the peer reviewer gets practice *writing,* and the essayist is not directly challenged. Sharing documents via Google Doc works well for peer review. You can copy and paste your essay into a Google Doc (if you did not compose it there) and then share it with a classmate who is sitting next to you.

✓ A PEER REVIEW CHECKLIST FOR A DRAFT
OF AN ARGUMENT

Read the draft through quickly. Then read it again, with the following questions in mind. Remember: You are reading a draft, a work in progress. You are expected to offer suggestions, and it is also expected that you will offer them courteously.

☐ In a sentence, indicate the degree to which the draft shows promise of fulfilling the assignment.

☐ Is the writer's tone appropriate? Who is the audience?

☐ Looking at the essay as a whole, what thesis (main idea) is advanced?

☐ Are the needs of the audience kept in mind? For instance, do some words need to be defined? Is the evidence (for instance, the examples and the testimony of authorities) clear and effective?

☐ Can I accept the assumptions? If not, why not?

☐ Is any obvious evidence (or counterevidence) overlooked?

☐ Is the writer proposing a solution? If so,

  ☐ Are other equally attractive solutions adequately examined?

  ☐ Has the writer overlooked some unattractive effects of the proposed solution?

☐ Looking at each paragraph separately,

  ☐ What is the basic point?

  ☐ How does each paragraph relate to the essay's main idea or to the previous paragraph?

  ☐ Should some paragraphs be deleted? Be divided into two or more paragraphs? Be combined? Be put elsewhere? (If you outline the essay by writing down the gist of each paragraph, you will get help in answering these questions.)

  ☐ Is each sentence clearly related to the sentence that precedes and to the sentence that follows? If not, in a sentence or two indicate examples of good and bad transitions.

  ☐ Is each paragraph adequately developed? Are there sufficient details, perhaps brief supporting quotations from the text?

  ☐ Are the introductory and concluding paragraphs effective?

☐ What are the paper's chief strengths?

☐ Make at least two specific suggestions that you think will assist the author to improve the paper.

A STUDENT'S ESSAY, FROM
ROUGH NOTES TO FINAL VERSION

While we were revising this textbook, we asked the students in one of our classes to write a short essay (500–750 words) on some ethical problem that concerned them. Because this assignment was the first writing assignment in the course, we explained that a good way to get ideas is to ask oneself some questions, write down responses, question those responses, and write freely for ten minutes or so, not worrying about contradictions. We invited our students to hand in their initial notes along with the finished essay, so that we could get a sense of how they proceeded as writers. Not all of them chose to hand in their notes, but we were greatly encouraged by those who did. What was encouraging was the confirmation of an old belief, the belief—we call it a fact—that students will hand in a thoughtful essay if before they prepare a final version they nag themselves, ask themselves *why* they think this or that, write down their responses, and are not afraid to change their minds as they proceed.

Here are the first notes of a student, Emily Andrews, who elected to write about whether to give money to street beggars. She simply put down ideas, one after the other.

Help the poor? Why do I (sometimes) do it?

I feel guilty, and think I should help them: poor, cold, hungry (but also some of them are thirsty for liquor, and will spend the money on liquor, not on food).

I also feel annoyed by them—most of them.

Where does the expression "the deserving poor" come from?

And "poor but honest"? Actually, that sounds a bit odd. Wouldn't "rich but honest" make more sense?

Why don't they work? Fellow with red beard, always by bus stop in front of florist's shop, always wants a handout. He is a regular, there all day every day, so I guess he is in a way "reliable," so why doesn't he put the same time in on a job?

Or why don't they get help? Don't they know they need it? They *must* know they need it.

Maybe that guy with the beard is just a con artist. Maybe he makes more money by panhandling than he would by working, and it's a lot easier!

Kinds of poor — how to classify??
> drunks, druggies, etc.
> mentally ill (maybe drunks belong here, too)
> decent people who have had terrible luck

Why private charity?

Doesn't it make sense to say we (fortunate individuals) should give something — an occasional handout — to people who have had terrible luck? (I suppose some people might say that there is no need for any of us to give anything — the government takes care of the truly needy — but I *do* believe in giving charity. A month ago a friend of the family passed away, and the woman's children suggested that people might want to make a donation in her name, to a shelter for battered women. I know my parents made a donation.)

BUT how can I tell who is who, which are which? Which of these people asking for "spare change" really need (deserve???) help, and which are phonies? Impossible to tell.

Possibilities:
> Give to no one
> Give to no one but make an annual donation, maybe to United Way
> Give a dollar to each person who asks. This would probably not cost me even a dollar a day
> Occasionally do without something — maybe a CD — or a meal in a restaurant — and give the money I save to people who seem worthy.

WORTHY? What am I saying? How can I, or anyone, tell? The neat-looking guy who says he just lost his job may be a phony, and the dirty bum — probably a drunk — may desperately need food. (OK, so what if he spends the money on liquor instead of food? At least he'll get a little pleasure in life. No! It's not all right if he spends it on drink.)

Other possibilities:
> Do some volunteer work?
> To tell the truth, I don't want to put in the time. I don't feel *that* guilty.

So what's the problem?

Is it, How I can help the very poor (handouts, or through an organization)? or

How I can feel less guilty about being lucky enough to be able to go to college, and to have a supportive family?

I can't quite bring myself to believe I should help every beggar who approaches, but I also can't bring myself to believe that I should do nothing, on the grounds that:

    a. it's probably their fault

    b. if they are deserving, they can get gov't help. No, I just can't believe that. Maybe some are too proud to look for government help, or don't know that they are entitled to it.

What to do?

On balance, it seems best to

    a. give to United Way

    b. maybe also give to an occasional individual, if I happen to be moved, without worrying about whether he or she is "deserving" (since it's probably impossible to know).

A day after making these notes Emily reviewed them, added a few points, and then made a very brief selection from them to serve as an outline for her first draft:

Opening para.: "poor but honest"? Deserve "spare change"?

Charity: private or through organizations?

    pros and cons

    guy at bus

    it wouldn't cost me much, but . . . better to give through organizations

Concluding para.: still feel guilty?

    maybe mention guy at bus again?

After writing and revising a draft, Emily Andrews submitted her essay to a fellow student for peer review. She then revised her work in light of the suggestions she received and in light of her own further thinking.

On the next page we give the final essay. If after reading the final version you reread the early notes, you will notice that some of the notes never made it into the final version. But without the notes, the essay probably could not have been as interesting as it is. When the writer made the notes, she was not so much putting down her ideas as *finding* ideas by the process of writing.

Emily Andrews

Professor Barnet

English 102

January 15, 2010

Why I Don't Spare "Spare Change"

"Poor but honest." "The deserving poor." I don't know the origin of these quotations, but they always come to mind when I think of "the poor." But I also think of people who, perhaps through alcohol or drugs, have ruined not only their own lives but also the lives of others in order to indulge in their own pleasure. Perhaps alcoholism and drug addiction really are "diseases," as many people say, but my own feeling — based, of course, not on any serious study — is that most alcoholics and drug addicts can be classified with the "undeserving poor." And that is largely why I don't distribute spare change to panhandlers.

But surely among the street people there are also some who can rightly be called "deserving." Deserving what? My spare change? Or simply the government's assistance? It happens that I have been brought up to believe that it is appropriate to make contributions to charity — let's say a shelter for battered women — but if I give some change to a panhandler, am I making a contribution to charity and thereby helping someone, or, on the contrary, am I perhaps simply encouraging someone not to get help? Or maybe even worse, am I supporting a con artist?

If one believes in the value of private charity, one can give either to needy individuals or to charitable organizations. In giving to a panhandler one may indeed be helping a person who badly needs help, but one cannot be certain that one is giving to a needy individual. In giving to an organization such as the United Way, on the other hand, one can feel that one's money is likely to be used wisely. True, confronted by a beggar one may feel that *this* particular

unfortunate individual needs help at *this* moment — a cup of coffee
or a sandwich — and the need will not be met unless I put my hand
in my pocket right now. But I have come to think that the beggars
whom I encounter can get along without my spare change, and indeed
perhaps they are actually better off for not having money to buy
liquor or drugs.

It happens that in my neighborhood I encounter few
panhandlers. There is one fellow who is always by the bus stop where
I catch the bus to the college, and I never give him anything precisely
because he is always there. He is such a regular that, I think, he
ought to be able to hold a regular job. Putting him aside, I probably
don't encounter more than three or four beggars in a week. (I'm not
counting street musicians. These people seem quite able to work for a
living. If they see their "work" as playing or singing, let persons who
enjoy their performances pay them. I do not consider myself among
their audience.) The truth of the matter is that, since I meet so few
beggars, I could give each one a dollar and hardly feel the loss. At
most, I might go without seeing a movie some week. But I know
nothing about these people, and it's my impression — admittedly based
on almost no evidence — that they simply prefer begging to working. I
am not generalizing about street people, and certainly I am not talking
about street people in the big urban centers. I am talking only about
the people whom I actually encounter.

That's why I usually do not give "spare change," and I don't
think I will in the future. These people will get along without me.
Someone else will come up with money for their coffee or their liquor, or,
at worst, they will just have to do without. I will continue to contribute
occasionally to a charitable organization, not simply (I hope) to salve
my conscience but because I believe that these organizations actually do
good work. But I will not attempt to be a mini-charitable organization,
distributing (probably to the unworthy) spare change.

THE ESSAY ANALYZED

Finally, here are a few comments about the essay:

The title is informative, alerting the reader to the topic and the author's position. (By the way, the student told us that in her next-to-last draft the title was "Is It Right to Spare 'Spare Change'?" This title, like the revision, introduces the topic but not the author's position.)

The opening paragraph holds a reader's interest, partly by alluding to the familiar phrase "the deserving poor" and partly by introducing the *un*familiar phrase "the *un*deserving poor." Notice, too, that this opening paragraph ends by clearly asserting the author's thesis. Writers need not always announce their thesis early, but it is usually advisable to do so.

Paragraph two begins by voicing what probably is the reader's somewhat uneasy—perhaps even negative—response to the first paragraph. That is, *the writer has a sense of her audience;* she knows how her reader feels, and she takes account of the feeling.

Paragraph three clearly sets forth the alternatives. A reader may disagree with the writer's attitude, but the alternatives seem to be stated fairly.

Paragraphs four and five are more personal than the earlier paragraphs. The writer, more or less having stated what she takes to be the facts, now is entitled to offer a highly personal response to them.

The final paragraph nicely wraps things up by means of the words "spare change," which go back to the title and to the end of the first paragraph. The reader thus experiences a sensation of completeness. The essayist, of course, has not solved the problem for all of us for all time, but she presents a thoughtful argument and ends the essay effectively.

EXERCISE

In a brief essay, state a claim and support it with evidence. Choose an issue in which you are genuinely interested and about which you already know something. You may want to interview a few experts and do some reading, but don't try to write a highly researched paper. Sample topics:

1. Students in laboratory courses should not be required to participate in the dissection of animals.
2. Washington, D.C., should be granted statehood.
3. Women should, in wartime, be exempted from serving in combat.
4. The annual Miss America contest is an insult to women.
5. The government should not offer financial support to the arts.
6. The chief fault of the curriculum in high school was . . .
7. No specific courses should be required in colleges or universities.

 For additional arguments online, visit the e-Pages at **bedfordstmartins.com/barnetbedau**.

Using Sources

Research is formalized curiosity. It is poking and prying with a purpose.

—ZORA NEALE HURSTON

There is no way of exchanging information that does not involve an act of judgment.

—JACOB BRONOWSKI

For God's sake, stop researching for a while and begin to think.

—WALTER HAMILTON MOBERLY

A problem adequately stated is a problem on its way to being solved.

—R. BUCKMINSTER FULLER

I have yet to see any problem, however complicated, which, when you looked at it in the right way, did not become still more complicated.

—POUL ANDERSON

WHY USE SOURCES?

We have pointed out that one gets ideas by writing. In the exercise of writing a draft, ideas begin to form, and these ideas stimulate further ideas, especially when one questions—when one *thinks* about—what one has written. But of course in writing about complex, serious questions, nobody is expected to invent all the answers. On the contrary, a writer is expected to be familiar with the chief answers already produced by others and to make use of them through selective incorporation and criticism. In short, writers are not expected to reinvent the wheel; rather, they are expected to make good use of it and perhaps round it off a bit or replace a defective spoke. In order to think out your own views in writing, you are expected to do some preliminary research into the views of others.

When you are trying to understand an issue, high-quality sources will inform you of the various approaches others have taken and will help you establish what the facts are. Once you are informed enough to take a position, the sources you present to your readers will inform and persuade them, just as expert witnesses are sometimes brought in to inform and persuade a jury.

Research isn't limited to the world of professors and scientists. In one way or another, everyone does research at some point. If you want to persuade your city council to increase the number of bicycle lanes on city streets, you could bolster your argument with statistics on how much money the city could save if more people rode their bikes to work. If you decide to open your own business, you would do plenty of market research to persuade your bank that you could repay a loan. Sources (whether published information or data you gather yourself through interviews, surveys, or observation) are not only useful for background information; well-chosen and carefully analyzed sources are evidence for your readers that you know what you're talking about and that your interpretation is sound.

In Chapters 5 and 6 we discussed *ethos* as an appeal that establishes credibility with readers. When you do competent research and thereby let your audience see that you have done your homework, it increases your *ethos*; your audience will trust you because they see that you are well-informed, offering them not just your opinions but also an awareness of other opinions and of the relevant facts. Conducting thorough research not only helps you to develop your argument but it also shows respect for your audience.

Research is often misconstrued as the practice of transcribing information. In fact, it's a process of asking questions and gathering information that helps you come to conclusions about an issue. By using the information you find as evidence, you can develop an effective argument. But don't spend too much time searching and then waiting until the last minute to start writing. As you begin your search, write down observations and questions. When you find a useful source, take notes on what you think it means in your own words. This way, you won't find yourself with a pile of printouts and books and no idea what to say about them. What you have to say will flow naturally out of the prewriting you've already done—and that prewriting will help guide your search.

The process of research isn't always straightforward and neat. It involves scanning what other people have said about a topic and seeing what kinds of questions have been raised. As you poke and pry, you will learn more about the issue, and that, in turn, will help you develop a question to focus your efforts. Once you have a central idea—a thesis— you can sharpen your search to seek out the evidence that will make your readers sit up and take notice.

Consider arguments about whether athletes should be permitted to take anabolic steroids, drugs that supposedly build up muscle, restore energy, and enhance aggressiveness. A thoughtful argument on this subject will have to take account of information that the writer can gather only by doing some research.

- Do steroids really have the effects commonly attributed to them?
- Are they dangerous?
- If they are dangerous, how dangerous are they?

After all, competitive sports are inherently dangerous, some of them highly so. Many boxers, mixed martial arts fighters, jockeys, and football players have suffered severe injury, even death, from competing. Does anyone believe that anabolic steroids are more dangerous than the contests themselves? Obviously, again, a respectable argument about steroids will have to show awareness of what is known about them.

Or take this question:

> Why did President Truman order that atomic bombs be dropped on Hiroshima and Nagasaki?

The most obvious answer is to end the war, but some historians believe he had a very different purpose. In their view, Japan's defeat was ensured before the bombs were dropped, and the Japanese were ready to surrender; the bombs were dropped not to save American (or Japanese) lives but to show Russia that the United States would not be pushed around. Scholars who hold this view, such as Gar Alperovitz in *Atomic Diplomacy* (1965), argue that Japanese civilians in Hiroshima and Nagasaki were incinerated not to save the lives of American soldiers who otherwise would have died in an invasion of Japan but to teach Stalin a lesson. Dropping the bombs, it is argued, marked not the end of the Pacific War but the beginning of the cold war.

One must ask: What evidence supports this argument or claim or thesis, which assumes that Truman could not have thought the bomb was needed to defeat the Japanese because the Japanese knew they were defeated and would soon surrender without a hard-fought defense that would cost hundreds of thousands of lives? What about the momentum that had built up to use the bomb? After all, years of effort and $2 billion had been expended to produce a weapon with the intention of using it to end the war against Germany. But Germany had been defeated without the use of the bomb. Meanwhile, the war in the Pacific continued unabated. If the argument we are considering is correct, all this background counted for little or nothing in Truman's decision, a decision purely diplomatic and coolly indifferent to human life. The task for the writer is to evaluate the evidence available and then to argue for or against the view that Truman's purpose in dropping the bomb was to impress the Soviet government.

A student writing on the topic will certainly want to consult the chief books on the subject (Alperovitz's, cited above, Martin Sherwin's *A World Destroyed* [1975], and John Toland's *The Rising Sun* [1970]) and perhaps reviews of them, especially the reviews in journals devoted to political science. (Reading a searching review of a serious scholarly book is a good way to identify quickly some of the book's main contributions and controversial claims.) Truman's letters and statements and books and articles about Truman are also clearly relevant, and doubtless important articles are to be found in recent issues of scholarly journals and electronic sources. In fact, even an essay on such a topic as whether Truman was morally justified in using the atomic bomb for *any* purpose will be a stronger essay if it is well-informed about such matters as the estimated loss of life that an invasion would have cost, the international rules governing weapons, and Truman's own statements about the issue.

How does one go about finding the material needed to write a well-informed argument? We will provide help, but first we want to offer a few words about choosing a topic.

CHOOSING A TOPIC

We will be brief. If a topic is not assigned, choose one that

- interests you and
- can be researched with reasonable thoroughness in the allotted time.

Topics such as censorship, the environment, and sexual harassment obviously impinge on our lives, and it may well be that one such topic is of especial interest to you. But the scope of these topics makes researching them potentially overwhelming. Type the word *censorship* into an **Internet** search engine, and you will be referred to millions of information sources.

This brings us to our second point—a manageable topic. Any of the previous topics would need to be narrowed substantially before you could begin searching in earnest. Similarly, a topic such as the causes of World War II can hardly be mastered in a few weeks or argued in a ten-page paper. It is simply too big.

You can, however, write a solid paper analyzing, evaluating, and arguing for or against General Eisenhower's views on atomic warfare. What were they, and when did he hold them? (In his books of 1948 and 1963 Eisenhower says that he opposed the use of the bomb before Hiroshima and that he argued with Secretary of War Henry Stimson against dropping it, but what evidence supports these claims? Was Eisenhower attempting to rewrite history in his books?) Eisenhower's own writings and books and other information sources on Eisenhower will, of course, be the major sources for a paper on this topic, but you will also want to look at books and articles about Stimson and at publications that contain information about the views of other generals, so that, for instance, you can compare Eisenhower's view with Marshall's or MacArthur's.

Spend a little time exploring a topic to see if it will be interesting and manageable by taking one or more of these approaches.

- Do a Web search on the topic. Though you may not use any of the sites that turn up, you can quickly put your finger on the pulse of popular approaches to the issue by scanning the first page or two of results to see what issues are getting the most attention.

- Plug the topic into one of the library's article databases. Again, just by scanning titles you can get a sense of what questions are being raised.

- Browse the library shelves where books on the topic are kept. A quick check of the tables of contents of recently published books may give you ideas of how to narrow the topic.

- Ask a librarian to show you where specialized reference books on your topic are found. Instead of general encyclopedias, try sources like these:
  CQ Researcher
  Encyclopedia of Applied Ethics
  Encyclopedia of Bioethics
  Encyclopedia of Crime and Justice
  Encyclopedia of Science, Technology, and Ethics

- Talk to an expert. Members of the faculty who specialize in the area of your topic might be able to spell out some of the most significant controversies around a topic and may point you toward key sources.

FINDING MATERIAL

What strategy you use for finding good sources will depend on your topic. Researching a current issue in politics or popular culture may involve reading recent newspaper articles, scanning information on government Web sites, and locating current statistics. Other topics may be best tackled by seeking out books and scholarly journal articles that are less timely but more in-depth and analytical. You may want to supplement library and Web sources with your own fieldwork by conducting surveys or interviews.

Critical thinking is crucial to every step of the research process. Whatever strategy you use, remember that you will want to find material that is authoritative, represents a balanced approach to the issues, and is persuasive. As you choose your sources, bear in mind they will be serving as your "expert witnesses" as you make a case to your audience. Their quality and credibility are crucial to your argument.

If you find what seems to be an excellent source, look at some of the sources that this author repeatedly cites.

Finding Quality Information on the Web

The Web is a valuable source of information for many topics and less helpful for others. In general, if you're looking for information on public policy, popular culture, current events, legal affairs, or for any subject of interest to agencies of the federal or state government, the Web is likely to have useful material. If you're looking for literary criticism or scholarly analysis of historical or social issues, you will be better off using library databases, described later in this chapter.

To make good use of the Web, try these strategies.

- Use the most specific terms possible when using a general search engine; put phrases in quotes.

- Use the advanced search option to limit a search to a domain (e.g., *.gov* for government sites) or by date (such as Web sites updated in the past week or month).

- If you're not sure which sites might be good ones for research, try starting with one of the selective directories listed below instead of a general search engine.

- Consider which government agencies and organizations might be interested in your topic and go directly to their Web sites.

- Follow "about" links to see who is behind a Web site and why they put the information on the Web. If there is no "about" link, delete everything after the first slash in the URL to go to the parent site to see if it provides information.

- Use clues in URLs to see where sites originate. For example, URLs containing *.k12* are hosted at elementary and secondary schools, so may be intended for a young audience; those ending in *.gov* are government agencies, so they tend to provide official information.

- Always bear in mind that the sources you choose must be persuasive to your audience. Avoid sites that may be dismissed as unreliable or biased.

Some useful Web sites include the following:

Selective Web Site Directories
  Infomine <http://infomine.ucr.edu/>
  ipl2 <http://www.ipl.org>
  Open Directory Project <http://www.dmoz.org>

Current News Sources
  Google News <http://news.google.com>
  Kidon Media-Link <http://www.kidon.com/media-link/index.php>

Digital Primary Sources
  American Memory <http://memory.loc.gov>
  American Rhetoric <http://www.americanrhetoric.com>
  Avalon Project <http://avalon.law.yale.edu/default.asp>

Government Information
  GPO Access <http://www.gpoaccess.gov>
  Thomas (federal legislation) <http://thomas.loc.gov>
  University of Michigan Documents Center <http://www.lib.umich.edu/govdocs/>

Scholarly or Scientific Information
  Google Scholar <http://scholar.google.com>
  Scirus <http://www.scirus.com/>

Statistical Information
  American FactFinder <http://factfinder2.census.gov>
  Fedstats <http://www.fedstats.gov>
  Pew Global Attitudes Project <http://pewglobal.org>
  U.S. Census Bureau <http://www.census.gov>

A WORD ABOUT WIKIPEDIA

Links to Wikipedia (http://www.wikipedia.org) often rise to the top of Web search results. This vast and decentralized site provides over a million articles on a wide variety of topics. However, anyone can contribute to the online encyclopedia, so the accuracy of articles varies, and in some cases, the coverage of a controversial issue is one-sided or disputed. Even when the articles are accurate, they provide only basic information. Wikipedia's founder, Jimmy Wales, cautions students against using it as a source, except for obtaining general background knowledge: "You're in college; don't cite the encyclopedia."[1] Still, Wikipedia often provides valuable bibliographies that will help you to get going.

Finding Articles Using Library Databases

Your library has a wide range of general and specialized databases available through its Web site. Some databases provide references to articles (and perhaps abstracts or summaries) or may provide direct links to the entire text of articles. General and interdisciplinary databases include Academic Search Premier (produced by the EBSCOhost company) and Expanded Academic Index (from InfoTrac).

More specialized databases include PsycINFO (for psychology research) and ERIC (focused on topics in education). Others, such as JSTOR, are full-text digital archives of scholarly journals. You will likely have access to newspaper articles through LexisNexis or Proquest Newsstand, particularly useful for articles that are not available for free on the Web. Look at your library's Web site to see what your options are, or stop by the reference desk for a quick personalized tutorial.

---

[1] "Wikipedia Founder Discourages Academic Use of His Creation," *Chronicle of Higher Education: The Wired Campus,* 12 June 2006, 16 Nov. 2006. http://chronicle.com/wiredcampus/ article/ 1328/wikipedia-founder-discourages-academic-use-of-his-creation

FIGURE 7.1   AN ADVANCED WEB SEARCH

When using databases, first think through your topic using the listing and diagramming techniques described on pages 230–31. List synonyms for your key search terms. As you search, look at words used in titles and descriptors for alternative ideas and make use of the "advanced search" option so that you can easily combine multiple terms. Rarely will you find exactly what you're looking for right away. Try different search terms and different ways to narrow your topic.

Most databases have an advanced search option that offers forms for combining multiple terms. In Figure 7.1, a search on "anabolic steroids" retrieved far too many articles. In this advanced search, three concepts are being combined in a search: anabolic steroids, legal aspects of their use, and use of them by athletes. Related terms are combined with the word "or": *law* or *legal*. The last letters of a word have been replaced with an asterisk so that any ending will be included in the search. *Athlet** will search for *athlete, athletes,* or *athletics.* Options on both sides of the list of articles retrieved offer opportunities to refine a search by date of publication or to restrict the results to only academic journals, magazines, or newspapers.

As with a Web search, you'll need to make critical choices about which articles are worth pursuing. In this example, the first article may not be useful because it concerns German law. The second and third look fairly current and potentially useful. Only the third has a full text link, but the others may be available in another database. Many libraries have a program that will check other databases for you at the push of a button; in this case it's indicated by the "Find full text" button.

As you choose sources, keep track of them by selecting them. Then you can print off, save, or e-mail yourself the references you have selected. You may also have an option to export references to a citation management program such as RefWorks or EndNote. These programs allow you to create your own personal database of sources in which you can store your references and take notes. Later, when you're ready to create a bibliography, these programs will automatically format your references in MLA, APA, or another style. Ask a librarian if one of these programs is available to students on your campus.

Locating Books

The books that your library owns can be found through its online catalog. Typically, you can search by author or title or, if you don't have a specific book in mind, by keyword or subject. As with databases, think about different search terms to use, keeping an eye out for subject headings used for books that appear relevant. Take advantage of an "advanced search" option. You may, for example, be able to limit a search to books on a particular topic in English published within recent years. In addition to books, the catalog will also list DVDs, sound recordings, and other formats.

Unlike articles, books tend to cover broad topics, so be prepared to broaden your search terms. It may be that a book has a chapter or ten pages that are precisely what you need, but the catalog typically doesn't index the contents of books in detail. Think instead of what kind of book might contain the information you need.

Once you've found some promising books in the catalog, note down the call numbers, find them on the shelves, and then browse. Since books on the same topic are shelved together, you can quickly see what additional books are available by scanning the shelves. As you browse, be sure to look for books that have been published recently enough for your purposes. You do not have to read a book cover-to-cover to use it in your research. Instead, skim the introduction to see if it will be useful, then use its table of contents and index to pinpoint the sections of the book that are the most relevant.

If you have a very specific name or phrase you are searching for, you might try typing it into Google Book Search (http://books.google.com), which searches the contents of over 7 million scanned books. Though it tends to retrieve too many results for most topics, and you may only be able to see a snippet of context, it can help you locate a particular quote or identify which books might include an unusual name or phrase. There is a "find in a library" link that will help you determine whether the books are available in your library.

INTERVIEWING PEERS AND LOCAL AUTHORITIES

You ought to try to consult experts—for instance, members of the faculty or other local authorities on art, business, law, and so forth. You can also consult interested laypersons. Remember, however, that experts have their biases and that "ordinary" people may have knowledge that experts lack. When interviewing experts, keep in mind Picasso's comment: "You mustn't always believe what I say. Questions tempt you to tell lies, particularly when there is no answer."

If you are interviewing your peers, you will probably want to make an effort to get a representative sample. Of course, even within a group not all members share a single view—many African Americans favor affirmative action but not all do, and many gays favor legalizing gay marriage but, again, some don't. Make an effort to talk to a range of people who might be expected to offer varied opinions. You may learn some unexpected things.

Here we will concentrate, however, on interviews with experts.

1. **Finding subjects for interviews**   If you are looking for expert opinions, you may want to start with a faculty member on your campus. You may already know the instructor, or you may have to scan the catalog to see who teaches courses relevant to your topic. Department secretaries and college Web sites are good sources of information about the special interests of the faculty and also about lecturers who will be visiting the campus.

2. **Doing preliminary homework**   (a) In requesting the interview, make evident your interest in the topic and in the person. (If you know something about the person, you will be able to indicate why you are asking him or her.) (b) Request the interview, preferably in writing, a week in advance, and ask for ample time—probably half an hour to an hour. Indicate whether the material will be confidential, and (if you want to use a recorder) ask if you may record the interview. (c) If the person accepts the invitation, ask if he or she recommends any preliminary reading, and establish a time and a suitable place, preferably not the cafeteria during lunchtime.

3. **Preparing thoroughly**   (a) If your interviewee recommended any reading or has written on the topic, read the material. (b) Tentatively formulate some questions, keeping in mind that (unless you are simply gathering material for a survey of opinions) you want more than yes or no answers. Questions beginning with *Why* and *How* will usually require the interviewee to go beyond yes and no.

Even if your subject has consented to let you bring a recorder, be prepared to take notes on points that strike you as especially significant; without written notes, you will have nothing if the recorder has malfunctioned. Further, by taking occasional notes you will give the interviewee some time to think and perhaps to rephrase or to amplify a remark.

4. **Conducting the interview**   (a) Begin by engaging in brief conversation, without taking notes. If the interviewee has agreed to let you use a recorder, settle on the place where you will put it. (b) Come prepared with an opening question or two, but as the interview proceeds,

don't hesitate to ask questions that you had not anticipated asking. (c) Near the end (you and your subject have probably agreed on the length of the interview) ask the subject if he or she wishes to add anything, perhaps by way of clarifying some earlier comment. (d) Conclude by thanking the interviewee and by offering to provide a copy of the final version of your paper.

5. **Writing up the interview**   (a) As soon as possible — certainly within twenty-four hours after the interview — review your notes and clarify them. At this stage, you can still remember the meaning of your abbreviated notes and shorthand devices (maybe you have been using *n* to stand for *nurses* in clinics where abortions are performed), but if you wait even a whole day you may be puzzled by your own notes. If you have recorded the interview, you may want to transcribe all of it — the laboriousness of this task is one good reason why many interviewers do not use recorders — and you may then want to scan the whole and mark the parts that now strike you as especially significant. If you have taken notes by hand, type them up, along with your own observations, for example, "Jones was very tentative on this matter, but she said she was inclined to believe that. . . ." (b) Be especially careful to indicate which words are direct quotations. If in doubt, check with the interviewee.

EVALUATING YOUR SOURCES

Each step of the way, you will be making choices about your sources. As your research proceeds, from selecting promising items in a database search to browsing the book collection, you will want to use the techniques for previewing and skimming detailed on pages 34–35 in order to make your first selection. Ask yourself some basic questions.

- Is this source relevant?
- Is it current enough?
- Does the title and/or abstract suggest it will address an important aspect of my topic?
- Am I choosing sources that represent a range of ideas, not simply ones that support my opinion?
- Do I have a reason to believe that these sources are trustworthy?

Once you have collected a number of likely sources, you will want to do further filtering. Examine each one with these questions in mind.

- *Is this source credible? Does it include information about the author and his or her credentials that can help me decide whether to rely on it?* In the case of books, you might check a database for book reviews for a second opinion. In the case of Web sites, find out where the site came from and why it has been posted on the Web. Don't use a Web source if you can't determine its authorship or purpose.

- *Will my audience find this source credible and persuasive?* Some publishers are more selective about which books they publish than others. University presses, for instance, have several experts read and comment on manuscripts before they decide which to publish. A story about U.S. politics from the *Washington Post*, whose writers conduct firsthand reporting in the nation's capital, carries more clout than a story from a small-circulation newspaper that is drawing its information from a wire service. A scholarly source may be more impressive than a magazine article.

- *Am I using the best evidence available?* Quoting directly from a government report may be more effective than quoting a news story that summarizes the report. Finding evidence that supports your claims in a president's speeches or letters is more persuasive than drawing your conclusions from a page or two of a history textbook.

- *Am I being fair to all sides?* Make sure you are prepared to address alternate perspectives, even if you ultimately take a position. Avoid sources that clearly promote an agenda in favor of ones that your audience will consider balanced and reliable.

- *Can I corroborate my key claims in more than one source?* Compare your sources to ensure that you aren't relying on facts that can't be confirmed. If you're having trouble confirming a source, check with a librarian.

- *Do I really need this source?* It's tempting to use all the books and articles you have found, but if two sources say essentially the same thing, choose the one that is likely to carry the most weight with your audience.

The information you will look for as you evaluate a Web source is often the same as what you need to record in a citation. You can streamline the process of creating a list of works cited by identifying these elements as you evaluate a source.

In Figure 7.2, the URL includes the ending *.gov*—meaning it is a government Web site, an official document that has been vetted. There is an "about" link that will explain the government agency's mission. The date is found at the bottom of the page: "revised 2006." This appears to be a high-quality source of basic information on the issue.

The information you need to cite this report is also on the page; make sure you keep track of where you found the source and when, since Web sites can change. One way to do this is by creating an account

FIGURE 7.2   A HOMEPAGE FROM A GOVERNMENT WEB SITE

1   URL—Site has a .gov domain.

2   Sponsor

3   Author

4   Link will explain that this institute is a government agency.

5   Corporate author

6   Web site name

7   Title of page

8   Table of contents

9   Scanning list will give an idea of whether source is reliable and useful.

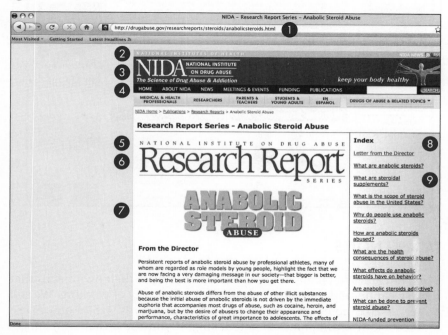

at a social bookmarking site such as Delicious (http://delicious.com) or Diigo (http://diigo.com) where you can store and annotate Web sites.

Figure 7.3 shows how the information on a Web page might lead you to reject it as a source. Clearly, though this site purports to provide educational information, its primary purpose is to sell products. The graphics emphasize the supposed benefits of these performance-enhancing drugs, a visual incentive to promote their use. The disclaimers about legal liability and age requirements send up a red flag.

FIGURE 7.3   A HOMEPAGE FROM A COMMERCIAL WEB SITE

This is a .com (commercial) site.

Table of contents looks useful, but . . .

Disclaimers seem defensive.

Images seem to promote steriod use.

Steroids are for sale.

TAKING NOTES

When it comes to taking notes, all researchers have their own habits that they swear by, and they can't imagine any other way of working. We still prefer to take notes on four-by-six-inch index cards, while others use a notebook or a computer for note taking. If you use a citation management program, such as RefWorks or EndNote, you can store your personal notes and commentary with the citations you have saved. Using the program's search function, you can easily pull together related notes and citations, or you can create project folders for your references so that you can easily review what you've collected.

Whatever method you use, the following techniques should help you maintain consistency and keep organized during the research process:

1. If you use a notebook or cards, write in ink (pencil gets smudgy), and write on only one side of the card or paper. (Notes on the backs of cards tend to get lost, and writing on the back of paper will prevent you from later cutting up and rearranging your notes.) Con-

✔ A CHECKLIST FOR EVALUATING PRINT SOURCES

For Books:

☐ Is the book recent? If not, is the information I will be using from it likely or unlikely to change over time?

☐ What are the author's credentials?

☐ Is the book titled toward entertainment, or is it in-depth and even-handed?

☐ Is the book broad enough in its focus and written in a style I can understand?

☐ Does the book relate directly to my tentative thesis, or is it of only tangential interest?

☐ Do the arguments in the book seem sound, based on what I have learned about skillful critical reading and writing?

For Articles from Periodicals:

☐ Is the periodical recent?

☐ Is the author's name given? Does he or she seem a credible source?

☐ Does the article treat the topic superficially or in-depth? Does it take sides, or does it offer enough context so that you can make up your own mind?

☐ How directly does the article speak to my topic and tentative thesis?

☐ If the article is from a scholarly journal, am I sure I understand it?

sider using an online tool to keep up with your notes and ideas, for instance, a Google Doc, private blog, or wiki.

2. Summarize, for the most part, rather than quote at length.

3. Quote only passages in which the writing is especially effective or passages that are in some way crucial. These will be easy to access and use if kept in an online venue.

4. Make sure that all quotations are exact. Enclose quoted words within quotation marks, indicate omissions by ellipses (three spaced periods: . . .), and enclose within square brackets ([]) any insertions or other additions you make.

5. *Never* copy a passage, changing an occasional word. *Either* copy it word for word, with punctuation intact, and enclose it within quotation marks, *or* summarize it drastically. If you copy a passage but change a word here and there, you may later make the mistake of using your note verbatim in your essay, and you will be guilty of plagiarism.

6. Give the page number of your source, whether you summarize or quote. If a quotation you have copied runs in the original from the bottom of page 210 to the top of page 211, in your notes put

✓ A CHECKLIST FOR EVALUATING ELECTRONIC SOURCES

An enormous amount of valuable material is available on the World Wide Web—but so is an enormous amount of junk. True, there is also plenty of junk in books and journals, but most printed material has been subjected to a review process: Book publishers and editors of journals send manuscripts to specialized readers who evaluate them and recommend whether the material should or should not be published. Publishing on the Web is quite different. Anyone can publish on the Web with no review process: All that is needed is sufficient access to the Internet. Ask yourself:

☐ What person or organization produced the site (a commercial entity, a nonprofit entity, a student, an expert)? Check the electronic address to get a clue about the authorship. If there is a link to the author's homepage, check it out to learn about the author. Does the author have an affiliation with a respectable institution?

☐ What is the purpose of the site? Is the site in effect an infomercial, or is it an attempt to contribute to a thoughtful discussion?

☐ Are the sources of information indicated and verifiable? If possible, check the sources.

☐ Is the site authoritative enough to use? (If it seems to contain review materials or class handouts, you probably don't want to take it too seriously.)

☐ When was the page made available? Is it out of date?

a diagonal line (/) after the last word on page 210, so that later, if in your paper you quote only the material from page 210, you will know that you must cite 210 and not 210–11.

7. Indicate the source. The author's last name is enough if you have consulted only one work by the author; but if you consult more than one work by an author, you need further identification, such as both the author's name and a short title.

8. Add your own comments about the substance of what you are recording. Such comments as "but contrast with Sherwin" or "seems illogical" or "evidence?" will ensure that you are thinking as well as writing and will be of value when you come to transform your notes into a draft. Be sure, however, to enclose such notes within double diagonals (//), or to mark them in some other way, so that later you will know they are yours and not your source's. If you use a computer for note taking, you may wish to write your comments in italics or in a different font.

9. In a separate computer file or notebook page or on separate index cards, write a bibliographic entry for each source. The information in each entry will vary, depending on whether the source is a book,

a periodical, an electronic document, and so forth. The kind of information (for example, author and title) needed for each type of source can be found in the sections on MLA Format: The List of Works Cited (p. 301) or APA Format: The List of References (p. 314).

A NOTE ON PLAGIARIZING, PARAPHRASING, AND USING COMMON KNOWLEDGE

Plagiarism is the unacknowledged use of someone else's work. The word comes from a Latin word for "kidnapping," and plagiarism is indeed the stealing of something engendered by someone else. We won't deliver a sermon on the dishonesty (and folly) of plagiarism; we intend only to help you understand exactly what plagiarism is. The first thing to say is that plagiarism is not limited to the unacknowledged quotation of words.

A *paraphrase* is a sort of word-by-word or phrase-by-phrase translation of the author's language into your own language. Unlike a summary, then, a paraphrase is approximately as long as the original. Why would anyone paraphrase something? There are two good reasons:

- You may, as a reader, want to paraphrase a passage in order to make certain that you are thinking carefully about each word in the original;
- You may, as a writer, want to paraphrase a difficult passage in order to help your reader.

Paraphrase thus has its uses, but it is often unnecessarily used, and students who overuse it may find themselves crossing the border into plagiarism. True, if you paraphrase you are using your own words, but

- you are also using someone else's ideas, and, equally important,
- you are using this other person's sequence of thoughts.

Even if you change every third word in your source, you are plagiarizing. Here is an example of this sort of plagiarism, based on the previous sentence:

Even if you alter every second or third word that your source gives, you still are plagiarizing.

Further, even if the writer of this paraphrase had cited a source after the paraphrase, he or she would still have been guilty of plagiarism. How, you may ask, can a writer who cites a source be guilty of plagiarism? Easy. Readers assume that only the gist of the idea is the source's and that the development of the idea—the way it is set forth—is the present writer's work. A paraphrase that runs to several sentences is in no significant way the writer's work: The writer is borrowing not only the idea but the shape of the presentation, the sentence structure. What the writer needs to do is to write something like this:

> Changing an occasional word does not free the writer from the obligation to cite a source.

And the source would still need to be cited, if the central idea were not a commonplace one.

The point that even if you cite a source for your paraphrase you are nevertheless plagiarizing—unless you clearly indicate that the entire passage is a paraphrase of the source—cannot be overemphasized.

You are plagiarizing if, without giving credit, you use someone else's ideas—even if you put these ideas entirely into your own words. When you use another's ideas, you must indicate your indebtedness by saying something like "Alperovitz points out that . . ." or "Secretary of War Stimson, as Martin Sherwin notes, never expressed himself on this point." Alperovitz and Sherwin pointed out something that you had not thought of, and so you must give them credit if you want to use their findings.

Again, even if after a paraphrase you cite your source, you are plagiarizing. How, you may wonder, can you be guilty of plagiarism if you cite a source? Easy. A reader assumes that the citation refers to information or an opinion, *not* to the presentation or development of the idea; and of course, in a paraphrase you are not presenting or developing the material in your own way.

Now consider this question: *Why* paraphrase? Often there is no good answer. Since a paraphrase is as long as the original, you may as well quote the original, if you think that a passage of that length is worth quoting. Probably it is *not* worth quoting in full; probably you should *not* paraphrase but rather should drastically *summarize* most of it, and perhaps quote a particularly effective phrase or two. As we explained on pages 39–45, the chief reason to paraphrase a passage is to clarify it—that is, to make certain that you and your readers understand a passage that—perhaps because it is badly written—is obscure.

Generally, what you should do is

- Take the idea and put it entirely into your own words, perhaps reducing a paragraph of a hundred words to a sentence of ten words, but you must still give credit for the idea.

- If you believe that the original hundred words are so perfectly put that they cannot be transformed without great loss, you'll have to quote them in full and cite your source. You may in this case want to tell the reader *why* you are quoting at such great length.

In short, chiefly you will quote or you will summarize, and only rarely will you paraphrase, but in all cases you will cite your source. There is no point in paraphrasing an author's hundred words into a hundred of your own. Either quote or summarize, but cite the source.

> ✓ A CHECKLIST FOR AVOIDING PLAGIARISM
>
> ☐ In my notes did I *always* put quoted material within quotation marks?
>
> ☐ In my notes did I summarize *in my own words* and give credit to the source for the idea?
>
> ☐ In my notes did I avoid paraphrasing, that is, did I avoid copying, keeping the structure of the source's sentences but using some of my own words? (Paraphrases of this sort, even with a footnote citing the source, are *not* acceptable, since the reader incorrectly assumes that the writing is essentially yours.)
>
> ☐ If in my paper I set forth a borrowed idea, do I give credit, even though the words and the shape of the sentences are entirely my own?
>
> ☐ If in my paper I quote directly, do I put the words within quotation marks and cite the source?
>
> ☐ Do I *not* cite material that can be considered common knowledge (material that can be found in numerous reference works, such as the date of a public figure's birth or the population of San Francisco or the fact that *Hamlet* is regarded as a great tragedy)?
>
> ☐ If I have the slightest doubt about whether I should or should not cite a source, have I taken the safe course and cited the source?

Keep in mind, too, that almost all generalizations about human nature, no matter how common and familiar (for instance, "males are innately more aggressive than females") are not indisputable facts; they are at best hypotheses on which people differ and therefore should either not be asserted at all or should be supported by some cited source or authority. Similarly, because nearly all statistics (whether on the intelligence of criminals or the accuracy of lie detectors) are the result of some particular research and may well have been superseded or challenged by other investigators, it is advisable to cite a source for any statistics you use unless you are convinced they are indisputable, such as the number of registered voters in Memphis in 1988.

On the other hand, there is something called **common knowledge,** and the sources for such information need not be cited. The term does not, however, mean exactly what it seems to. It is common knowledge, of course, that Ronald Reagan was an American president (so you don't cite a source when you make that statement), and under the conventional interpretation of this doctrine, it is also common knowledge that he was born in 1911. In fact, of course, few people other than Reagan's wife and children know this date. Still, information that can be found in many places and that is indisputable belongs to all of us; therefore, a writer need not cite her source when she says that Reagan was born in 1911. Probably she checked a dictionary or an encyclopedia for the date, but the source doesn't matter. Dozens of sources will give exactly the same information, and in fact, no reader wants to be bothered with a citation on such a point.

Some students have a little trouble developing a sense of what is and what is not common knowledge. Although, as we have just said, readers don't want to hear about the sources for information that is indisputable and can be documented in many places, if you are in doubt about whether to cite a source, cite it. Better risk boring the reader a bit than risk being accused of plagiarism.

Your college probably has issued a statement concerning plagiarism. If there is such a statement, be sure to read it carefully.

COMPILING AN ANNOTATED BIBLIOGRAPHY

When several sources have been identified and gathered, many researchers prepare an annotated bibliography. This is a list providing all relevant bibliographic information (just as it will appear in your Works Cited list or References list) as well as a brief descriptive and evaluative summary of each source—perhaps one to three sentences. Your instructor may ask you to provide an annotated bibliography for your research project.

An annotated bibliography serves four main purposes:

- First, constructing such a document helps you to master the material contained in any given source. To find the heart of the argument presented in an article or book, phrase it briefly, and comment on it, you must understand it fully.

- Second, creating an annotated bibliography helps you to think about how each portion of your research fits into the whole of your project, how you will use it, and how it relates to your topic and thesis.

- Third, an annotated bibliography helps your readers: They can quickly see which items may be especially helpful in their own research.

- Fourth, in constructing an annotated bibliography at this early stage, you will get some hands-on practice at bibliographic format, thereby easing the job of creating your final bibliography (the Works Cited list or References list for your paper).

Following are two examples of entries for an annotated bibliography in MLA (Modern Language Association) format for a project on the effect of violence in the media. The first is for a book, the second for an article from a periodical. Notice that each

- begins with a bibliographic entry—author (last name first), title, and so forth—and then

- provides information about the content of the work under consideration, suggesting how each may be of use to the final research paper.

Clover, Carol J. *Men, Women, and Chain Saws: Gender in the Modern Horror Film*. Princeton: Princeton UP, 1992. The author focuses on Hollywood horror movies of the 1970s and 1980s. She studies representations of women and girls in these movies and the responses of male viewers to female characters, suggesting that this relationship is more complex and less exploitative than the common wisdom claims.

Winerip, Michael. "Looking for an Eleven O'Clock Fix." *New York Times Magazine* 11 Jan. 1998: 30-40. The article focuses on the rising levels of violence on local television news and highlights a station in Orlando, Florida, that tried to reduce its depictions of violence and lost viewers as a result. Winerip suggests that people only claim to be against media violence, while their actions prove otherwise.

As you construct your annotated bibliography, consider posting your Word document in Google Drive for easy access and sharing.

A Rule for Writers: Citation Generators

There are many citation generators available online. These generators allow you to enter the information about your source, and, with a click, they will create Works Cited entries in APA or MLA format. But just as you cannot trust spell- and grammar-checkers in Microsoft Word, you cannot trust these generators. You can use them to cite works, but if you do, be sure to double-check what they produce before submitting your essay. Always remember that responsible writers take care to cite their sources properly and that failure to do so puts you at risk for accusations of plagiarism.

WRITING THE PAPER

Organizing Your Notes

If you have read thoughtfully, taken careful (and, again, thoughtful) notes on your reading, and then (yet again) thought about these notes, you are well on the way to writing a good paper. You have, in fact, already written some of it, in your notes. By now you should clearly have in mind the thesis you intend to argue. But you still have to organize the material, and, doubtless, even as you set about organizing it, you will find points that will require you to do some additional research and much additional thinking.

Divide your notes into clusters, each devoted to one theme or point (for instance, one cluster on the extent of use of steroids, another on evidence that steroids are harmful, yet another on arguments that even if harmful they should be permitted). If your notes are in a computer file, rearrange the notes into appropriate clusters. If you use index cards, simply sort them into packets. If you take notes in a notebook, either mark each note with a number or name indicating the cluster to which it belongs, or cut the notes apart and arrange them as you would cards. Put aside all notes that—however interesting—you now see are irrelevant to your paper.

Next, arrange the clusters or packets into a tentative sequence. In effect, you are preparing a **working outline.** At its simplest, say, you will give three arguments on behalf of X and then three counterarguments. (Or you might decide that it is better to alternate material from the two sets of three clusters each, following each argument with an objection. At this stage, you can't be sure of the organization you will finally use, but you can make a tentative decision.)

The First Draft

Draft the essay, without worrying much about an elegant opening paragraph. Just write some sort of adequate opening that states the topic and your thesis. When you revise the whole later, you can put some effort into developing an effective opening. (Most experienced writers find that the opening paragraph in the final version is almost the last thing they write.)

If your notes are on cards or notebook paper, carefully copy into the draft all quotations that you plan to use. If your notes are in a computer, you may simply cut and paste them from one file to another. Do keep in mind, however, that rewriting or retyping quotations will make you think carefully about them and may result in a more focused and thoughtful paper. (In the next section of this chapter we will talk briefly about leading into quotations and about the form of quotations.) Be sure to include citations in your drafts so that if you must check a reference later it will be easy to do so.

Later Drafts

Give the draft, and yourself, a rest—perhaps for a day or two—and then go back to it. Read it over, make necessary revisions, and then **outline** it. That is, on a sheet of paper chart the organization and development, perhaps by jotting down a sentence summarizing each paragraph or each group of closely related paragraphs. Your outline or map may now show you that the paper obviously suffers from poor organization. For instance, it may reveal that you neglected to respond to one argument or that one point is needlessly treated in two places. It may also help you to see that if you gave three arguments and then three counterarguments, you probably should instead have followed each argument with its rebuttal. On the other hand, if you alternated arguments and objections, it may now seem better to use two main groups, all the arguments and then all the criticisms.

No one formula is always right. Much will depend on the complexity of the material. If the arguments are highly complex, it is better to respond to them one by one than to expect a reader to hold three complex arguments in mind before you get around to responding. If, however, the arguments can be stated briefly and clearly, it is effective to state all three and then to go on to the responses. If you write on a computer, you will find it easy, even fun, to move passages of text around. Even so, you will probably want to print out a hard copy from time to time to review the structure of your paper. Allow enough time to produce several drafts.

A Few More Words about Organization

There is a difference between

- a paper that *has* an organization and
- a paper that helpfully lets the reader know what the organization is.

Write papers of the second sort, but (there is always a "but") take care not to belabor the obvious. Inexperienced writers sometimes either hide the organization so thoroughly that a reader cannot find it or they so ploddingly lay out the structure ("Eighth, I will show . . .") that the reader becomes impatient. Yet it is better to be overly explicit than to be obscure.

The ideal, of course, is the middle route. Make the overall strategy of your organization evident by occasional explicit signs at the beginning of a paragraph ("We have seen . . . ," "It is time to consider the objections . . . ," "By far the most important . . ."); elsewhere make certain that the implicit structure is evident to the reader. When you reread your draft, if you try to imagine that you are one of your classmates, you will probably be able to sense exactly where explicit signs are needed and where they are not needed. Better still, exchange drafts with a classmate in order to exchange (tactful) advice.

Choosing a Tentative Title

By now a couple of tentative titles for your essay should have crossed your mind. If possible, choose a title that is both interesting and informative. Consider these three titles:

Are Steroids Harmful?

The Fuss over Steroids

Steroids: A Dangerous Game

"Are Steroids Harmful?" is faintly interesting, and it lets the reader know the gist of the subject, but it gives no clue about the writer's thesis, the writer's contention or argument. "The Fuss over Steroids" is somewhat better, for it gives information about the writer's position. "Steroids: A Dangerous Game" is still better; it announces the subject ("steroids") and the thesis ("dangerous"), and it also displays a touch of wit because "game" glances at the world of athletics.

Don't try too hard, however; better a simple, direct, informative title than a strained, puzzling, or overly cute one. And remember to make sure that everything in your essay is relevant to your title. In fact, your title should help you to organize the essay and to delete irrelevant material.

The Final Draft

When at last you have a draft that is for the most part satisfactory, check to make sure that **transitions** from sentence to sentence and from paragraph to paragraph are clear ("Further evidence," "On the other hand," "A weakness, however, is apparent"), and then worry about your opening and your closing paragraphs. Your **opening paragraph** should be clear, interesting, and focused; if neither the title nor the first paragraph announces your thesis, the second paragraph probably should do so.

The **final paragraph** need not say, "In conclusion, I have shown that. . . ." It should effectively end the essay, but it need not summarize your conclusions. We have already offered a few words about final paragraphs (p. 249), but the best way to learn how to write such paragraphs is to study the endings of some of the essays in this book and to adopt the strategies that appeal to you.

Be sure that all indebtedness is properly acknowledged. We have talked about plagiarism; now we will turn to the business of introducing quotations effectively.

QUOTING FROM SOURCES

Incorporating Your Reading into Your Thinking: The Art and Science of Synthesis

At the beginning of Chapter 6 we quoted a passage by Kenneth Burke (1887–1993), a college dropout who became one of America's most important twentieth-century students of rhetoric. It is worth repeating:

> Imagine that you enter a parlor. You come late. When you arrive, others have long preceded you, and they are engaged in a heated discussion, a discussion too heated for them to pause and tell you exactly what it is about. In fact, the discussion had already begun long before any of them got there, so that no one present is qualified to retrace for you all the steps that had gone before. You listen for a while, until you decide that you have caught the tenor of the argument; then you put in your oar. Someone answers; you answer him; another comes to your defense; another aligns himself against you, to either the embarrassment

or gratification of your opponent, depending upon the quality of your ally's assistance. However, the discussion is interminable. The hour grows late, you must depart. And you do depart, with the discussion still vigorously in progress.

—*The Philosophy of Literary Form* (Baton Rouge: Louisiana State University Press, 1941), 110–11.

Why do we quote this passage? Because it is your turn to join the unending conversation.

During the process of reading, and afterward, you will want to listen, think, say to yourself something like

- "No, no, I see things very differently; it seems to me that . . . " or
- "Yes, of course, but on one large issue I think I differ," or
- "Yes, sure, I agree, but I would go further and add . . ." or
- "Yes, I agree with your conclusion, but I hold this conclusion for reasons very different from the ones that you offer."

During your composition courses, at least (and we think during your entire life), you will be reading or listening and will sometimes want to put in your oar—you will sometimes want to respond in writing, for example in the form of a Letter to the Editor or in a memo at your place of employment. In the course of your response you almost surely will have to summarize very briefly the idea or ideas you are responding to, so that your readers will understand the context of your remarks. These ideas may not come from a single source; you may be responding to several sources. For instance, you may be responding to a report and also to some comments that the report evoked. In any case, you will state these ideas briefly and fairly and will then set forth your thoughtful responses, thereby giving the reader a statement that you hope represents an advance in the argument, even if only a tiny one. That is, you will **synthesize** sources, combining existing material into something new, drawing nourishment from what has already been said (giving credit, of course), and converting it into something new—a view that you think is worth considering.

Let's pause for a moment and consider this word **synthesis.** You probably are familiar with *photosynthesis*, the chemical process in green plants that produces carbohydrates from carbon dioxide and hydrogen. Synthesis, again, combines pre-existing elements and produces something new. In our use of the word *synthesis*, even a view that you utterly reject becomes a part of your new creation *because it helped to stimulate you to formulate your view;* without the idea that you reject, you might not have developed the view that you now hold. Consider the words of Francis Bacon, Shakespeare's contemporary:

Some books are to be tasted, others to be swallowed, and some few to be chewed and digested.

Your instructor will expect you to digest your sources—this does not mean you need to accept them but only that you need to read them thoughtfully—and that, so to speak, you make them your own thoughts by refining them. Your readers will expect you to tell them *what you make out of your sources*, which means that you will go beyond writing a summary and will synthesize the material into your own contribution. *Your* view is what is wanted, and readers expect this view to be thoughtful—not mere summary and not mere tweeting.

> **A RULE FOR WRITERS:** In your final draft *you must give credit to all of your sources.* Let your reader know whether you are quoting (in this case, you will use quotation marks around all material directly quoted), or whether you are summarizing (you will explicitly say so), or whether you are paraphrasing (again, you will explicitly say so).

The Use and Abuse of Quotations

When is it necessary, or appropriate, to quote? Sometimes the reader must see the exact words of your source; the gist won't do. If you are arguing that Z's definition of *rights* is too inclusive, your readers have to know exactly how Z defined *rights*. Your brief summary of the definition may be unfair to Z; in fact, you want to convince your readers that you are being fair, and so you quote Z's definition, word for word. Moreover, if the passage is only a sentence or two long, or even if it runs to a paragraph, it may be so compactly stated that it defies summary. And to attempt to paraphrase it—substituting *natural* for *inalienable*, and so forth—saves no space and only introduces imprecision. There is nothing to do but to quote it, word for word.

Second, you may want to quote a passage that could be summarized but that is so effectively stated that you want your readers to have the pleasure of reading the original. Of course, readers will not give you credit for writing these words, but they will give you credit for your taste and for your effort to make especially pleasant the business of reading your paper.

In short, use (but don't overuse) quotations. Speaking roughly, quotations

- should occupy no more than 10 to 15 percent of your paper, and
- they may occupy much less.

Most of your paper should set forth your ideas, not other people's ideas.

How to Quote

Long and Short Quotations   **Long quotations** (more than four lines of typed prose or three or more lines of poetry) are set off from your text. To set off material, start on a new line, indent one inch from the left margin, and type the quotation double-spaced. Do not enclose quotations within quotation marks if you are setting them off.

Short quotations are treated differently. They are embedded within the text; they are enclosed within quotation marks, but otherwise they do not stand out.

All quotations, whether set off or embedded, must be exact. If you omit any words, you must indicate the ellipsis by substituting three spaced periods for the omission; if you insert any words or punctuation, you must indicate the addition by enclosing it within square brackets, not to be confused with parentheses.

Leading into a Quotation   Now for a less mechanical matter, the way in which a quotation is introduced. To say that it is "introduced" implies that one leads into it, though on rare occasions a quotation appears without an introduction, perhaps immediately after the title. Normally one leads into a quotation by giving

- the *name of the author* and (no less important)
- *clues signaling the content of the quotation and the purpose* it serves in the present essay. For example:

> William James provides a clear answer to Huxley when he says that ". . ."

The writer has been writing about Huxley and now is signaling readers that they will be getting James's reply. The writer is also signaling (in "a clear answer") that the reply is satisfactory. If the writer believed that James's answer was not really acceptable, the lead-in might have run thus:

> William James attempts to answer Huxley, but his response does not really meet the difficulty Huxley calls attention to. James writes, ". . ."

or thus:

> William James provided what he took to be an answer to Huxley when he said that ". . ."

In this last example, clearly the words "what he took to be an answer" imply that the essayist will show, after the quotation from James, that the answer is in some degree inadequate. Or the essayist may wish to suggest the inadequacy even more strongly:

> William James provided what he took to be an answer to Huxley, but he used the word *religion* in a way that Huxley would not have allowed. James argues that ". . ."

IDEA PROMPT 7.1 SIGNAL PHRASES

Think of your writing as a conversation between you and your sources. As in conversation, you want to be able to move smoothly between different, sometimes contrary, points of view. You also want to be able to set your thoughts apart from those of your sources. Signal phrases make it easy for your readers to know where your information came from and why it's trustworthy by including key facts about the source.

According to psychologist Stephen Ceci . . .

A report published by the U.S. Bureau of Justice Statistics concludes . . .

Feminist philosopher Sandra Harding argues . . .

To avoid repetitiveness, vary your sentence structure.

. . . claims Stephen Ceci.

. . . according to a report published by the U.S. Bureau of Statistics.

Useful verbs to introduce sources:

acknowledges	contends	points out
argues	denies	recommends
believes	disputes	reports
claims	observes	suggests

Note that papers written using MLA style refer to sources in the present tense. Papers written in APA style use the past tense (acknowledged, argued, believed).

 A CHECKLIST FOR USING QUOTATIONS RATHER THAN SUMMARIES

Ask yourself the following questions. If you cannot answer yes to at least one of the questions, consider *summarizing* the material rather than quoting it in full.

☐ Is the quotation given because it is necessary for the reader to see the exact wording of the original?

☐ Is the quotation given because the language is especially engaging?

☐ Is the quotation given because the author is a respected authority and the passage lends weight to my argument?

If after reading something by Huxley the writer had merely given us "William James says . . . ," we wouldn't know whether we were getting confirmation, refutation, or something else. The essayist would have put a needless burden on the readers. Generally speaking, the more difficult the quotation, the more important is the introductory or explanatory lead-in, but even the simplest quotation profits from some sort of brief lead-in, such as "James reaffirms this point when he says . . ."

> **A RULE FOR WRITERS:** In introducing a quotation, it is usually advisable to signal the reader *why* you are using the quotation by means of a lead-in consisting of a verb or a verb and adverb, such as *claims*, or *convincingly shows*, or *admits*.

DOCUMENTATION

In the course of your essay, you will probably quote or summarize material derived from a source. You must give credit, and although there is no one form of documentation to which all scholarly fields subscribe, you will probably be asked to use one of two. One, established by the Modern Language Association (MLA), is used chiefly in the humanities; the other, established by the American Psychological Association (APA), is used chiefly in the social sciences.

We include two papers that use sources. "An Argument for Corporate Responsibility" (p. 319) uses the MLA format. "The Role of Spirituality and Religion in Mental Health" (p. 327) follows the APA format. (You may notice that various styles are illustrated in other selections we have included.)

In some online venues you can link directly to your sources. If your assignment is to write a blog or other online text, linking helps the reader to look at a note or citation or the direct source quickly and easily. For example, if you are describing or referencing a scene in a movie, you can link to reviews of the movie, or to a YouTube of the trailer, or to the exact scene that you are writing about. These kinds of links can help your audience get a clearer sense of your point. When formatting such a link in your text, make sure the link opens in a new window so that readers will not lose their place in the text they are reading. In a blog, linking to your sources usually is easy and helpful.

A Note on Footnotes (and Endnotes)

Before we discuss these two formats, a few words about footnotes are in order. Before the MLA and the APA developed their rules of style, citations commonly were given in footnotes. Although today footnotes are not so frequently used to give citations, they still may be useful for another purpose. (The MLA suggests endnotes rather than footnotes, but most readers seem to think that, in fact, footnotes are preferable to endnotes. After all, who wants to keep shifting from a page of text to a page of notes at the rear?) If you want to include some material that may seem intrusive in the body of the paper, you may relegate it to a footnote. For example, in a footnote you might translate a quotation given in a foreign language, or you might demote from text to footnote a paragraph explaining why you are not taking account of such-and-such a point. By putting the matter in a footnote you are signaling the reader that it is dispensable; it is something relevant but not essential, something extra that you are, so to speak, tossing in. Don't make a habit of writing this sort of note, but there are times when it is appropriate.

MLA Format: Citations within the Text

Brief citations within the body of the essay give credit, in a highly abbreviated way, to the sources for material you quote, summarize, or make use of in any other way. These *in-text citations* are made clear by a list of sources, titled Works Cited, appended to the essay. Thus, in your essay you may say something like this:

> Commenting on the relative costs of capital punishment and life imprisonment, Ernest van den Haag says that he doubts "that capital punishment really is more expensive" (33).

The **citation,** the number 33 in parentheses, means that the quoted words come from page 33 of a source (listed in the Works Cited) written by van den Haag. Without a Works Cited, a reader would have no way of knowing that you are quoting from page 33 of an article that appeared in the February 8, 1985, issue of the *National Review.*

Usually the parenthetic citation appears at the end of a sentence, as in the example just given, but it can appear elsewhere; its position will depend chiefly on your ear, your eye, and the context. You might, for example, write the sentence thus:

> Ernest van den Haag doubts that "capital punishment really is more expensive" than life imprisonment (33), but other writers have presented figures that contradict him.

Five points must be made about these examples:

1. **Quotation marks**   The closing quotation mark appears after the last word of the quotation, *not* after the parenthetic citation. Since the citation is not part of the quotation, the citation is not included within the quotation marks.

2. **Omission of words (ellipsis)**   If you are quoting a complete sentence or only a phrase, as in the examples given, you do not need to indicate (by three spaced periods) that you are omitting material before or after the quotation. But if for some reason you want to omit an interior part of the quotation, you must indicate the omission by inserting an *ellipsis,* the three spaced dots. To take a simple example, if you omit the word "really" from van den Haag's phrase, you must alert the reader to the omission:

> Ernest van den Haag doubts that "capital punishment . . . is more expensive" than life imprisonment (33).

Suppose you are quoting a sentence but wish to omit material from the end of the sentence. Suppose, also, that the quotation forms the end of your sentence. Write a lead-in phrase, quote what you need from your source, then type the bracketed ellipses for the omission, close the quotation, give the parenthetic citation, and finally type a fourth period to indicate the end of your sentence.

Here's an example. Suppose you want to quote the first part of a sentence that runs, "We could insist that the cost of capital punishment be reduced so as to diminish the differences." Your sentence would incorporate the desired extract as follows:

> Van den Haag says, "We could insist that the cost of capital punishment be reduced . . ." (33).

3. **Punctuation with parenthetic citations**   In the preceding examples, the punctuation (a period or a comma in the examples) *follows* the citation. If, however, the quotation ends with a question mark, include the question mark *within* the quotation, since it is part of the quotation, and put a period *after* the citation:

> Van den Haag asks, "Isn't it better — more just and more useful — that criminals, if they do not have the certainty of punishment, at least run the risk of suffering it?" (33).

But if the question mark is your own and not in the source, put it after the citation, thus:

> What answer can be given to van den Haag's doubt that "capital punishment really is more expensive" (33)?

4. **Two or more works by an author**   If your list of Works Cited includes two or more works by an author, you cannot, in your essay, simply cite a page number because the reader will not know which of

the works you are referring to. You must give additional information. You can give it in your lead-in, thus:

> In "New Arguments against Capital Punishment," van den Haag expresses doubt "that capital punishment really is more expensive" than life imprisonment (33).

Or you can give the title, in a shortened form, within the citation:

> Van den Haag expresses doubt that "capital punishment really is more expensive" than life imprisonment ("New Arguments" 33).

5. **Citing even when you do not quote**   Even if you don't quote a source directly, but use its point in a paraphrase or a summary, you will give a citation:

> Van den Haag thinks that life imprisonment costs more than capital punishment (33).

Note that in all of the previous examples, the author's name is given in the text (rather than within the parenthetic citation). But there are several other ways of giving the citation, and we shall look at them now. (We have already seen, in the example given under paragraph 4, that the title and the page number can be given within the citation.)

AUTHOR AND PAGE NUMBER IN PARENTHESES

> It has been argued that life imprisonment is more costly than capital punishment (van den Haag 33).

AUTHOR, TITLE, AND PAGE NUMBER IN PARENTHESES

We have seen that if the Works Cited list includes two or more works by an author, you will have to give the title of the work on which you are drawing, either in your lead-in phrase or within the parenthetic citation. Similarly, if you are citing someone who is listed more than once in the Works Cited, and for some reason you do not mention the name of the author or the work in your lead-in, you must add the information in your citation:

> Doubt has been expressed that capital punishment is as costly as life imprisonment (van den Haag, "New Arguments" 33).

A GOVERNMENT DOCUMENT OR A WORK
OF CORPORATE AUTHORSHIP

Treat the issuing body as the author. Thus, you will write something like this:

The Commission on Food Control, in *Food Resources Today,* concludes that there is no danger (37-38).

A WORK BY TWO OR MORE AUTHORS

If a work is by *two or three authors,* give the names of all authors, either in the parenthetic citation (the first example below) or in a lead-in (the second example below):

There is not a single example of the phenomenon (Smith, Dale, and Jones 182-83).

Smith, Dale, and Jones insist there is not a single example of the phenomenon (182-83).

If there are *more than three authors,* give the last name of the first author, followed by *et al.* (an abbreviation for *et alii,* Latin for "and others"), thus:

Gittleman et al. argue (43) that . . .

or

On average, the cost is even higher (Gittleman et al. 43).

PARENTHETIC CITATION OF AN INDIRECT SOURCE (CITATION OF MATERIAL THAT ITSELF WAS QUOTED OR SUMMARIZED IN YOUR SOURCE)

Suppose you are reading a book by Jones in which she quotes Smith and you wish to use Smith's material. Your citation must refer the reader to Jones—the source you are using—but of course, you cannot attribute the words to Jones. You will have to make it clear that you are quoting Smith, and so after a lead-in phrase like "Smith says," followed by the quotation, you will give a parenthetic citation along these lines:

(qtd. in Jones 324-25).

PARENTHETIC CITATION OF TWO OR MORE WORKS

The costs are simply too high (Smith 301; Jones 28).

Notice that a semicolon, followed by a space, separates the two sources.

A WORK IN MORE THAN ONE VOLUME

This is a bit tricky. If you have used only one volume, in the Works Cited you will specify the volume, and so in the parenthetic in-text citation you will not need to specify the volume. All that you need to include in the citation is a page number, as illustrated by most of the examples that we have given.

If you have used more than one volume, your parenthetic citation will have to specify the volume as well as the page, thus:

> Jackson points out that fewer than one hundred fifty people fit this description (2: 351).

The reference is to page 351 in volume 2 of a work by Jackson.

If, however, you are citing not a page but an entire volume—let's say volume 2—your parenthetic citation will look like this:

> Jackson exhaustively studies this problem (vol. 2).

or

> Jackson (vol. 2) exhaustively studies this problem.

Notice the following points:

- In citing a volume and page, the volume number, like the page number, is given in arabic (not roman) numerals, even if the original used roman numerals to indicate the volume number.
- The volume number is followed by a colon, then a space, then the page number.
- If you cite a volume number without a page number, as in the last example quoted, the abbreviation is *vol.* Otherwise do *not* use such abbreviations as *vol.* and *p.* and *pg.*

AN ANONYMOUS WORK

For an anonymous work, give the title in your lead-in, or give it in a shortened form in your parenthetic citation:

> *A Prisoner's View of Killing* includes a poll taken of the inmates on death row (32).

or

> A poll is available (*Prisoner's View* 32).

AN INTERVIEW

Probably you won't need a parenthetic citation because you'll say something like

> Vivian Berger, in an interview, said . . .

or

According to Vivian Berger, in an interview . . .

and when your reader turns to the Works Cited, he or she will see that Berger is listed, along with the date of the interview. But if you do not mention the source's name in the lead-in, you will have to give it in the parentheses, thus:

Contrary to popular belief, the death penalty is not reserved for serial killers and depraved murderers (Berger).

AN ELECTRONIC SOURCE

Electronic sources, such as those found on the Internet, are generally not divided into pages. Therefore, the in-text citation for such sources cites only the author's name (or, if a work is anonymous, the title):

According to the World Wide Web site for the American Civil Liberties Union . . .

If the source does use pages or breaks down further into paragraphs or screens, insert the appropriate identifier or abbreviation (*p.* or *pp.* for page or pages; *par.* or *pars.* for paragraph or paragraphs; *screen* or *screens*) before the relevant number:

The growth of day care has been called "a crime against posterity" by a spokesman for the Institute for the American Family (Terwilliger, screens 1-2).

MLA Format: The List of Works Cited

As the previous pages explain, parenthetic documentation consists of references that become clear when the reader consults the list titled Works Cited given at the end of an essay.

The list of Works Cited continues the pagination of the essay; if the last page of text is 10, then the Works Cited begins on its own page, in this case page 11. Type the page number in the upper right corner, a half inch from the top of the sheet and flush with the right margin. Next, type the heading Works Cited (*not* enclosed within quotation marks and not italic), centered, one inch from the top, and then double-space and type the first entry.

An Overview   Here are some general guidelines.

FORM ON THE PAGE

- Begin each entry flush with the left margin, but if an entry runs to more than one line, indent a half inch for each succeeding line of the entry. This is known as a hanging indent, and most word processing programs can achieve this effect easily.

- Double-space each entry, and double-space between entries.
- Italicize titles of works published independently—for instance, books, pamphlets, and journals. Enclose within quotation marks a work not published independently—for instance, an article in a journal or a short story.
- If you are citing a book that includes the title of another book, italicize the main title, but do *not* italicize the title mentioned. Example:

    A Study of Mill's On Liberty

- In the sample entries below, pay attention to the use of commas, colons, and the space after punctuation.

ALPHABETICAL ORDER

- Arrange the list alphabetically by author, with the author's last name first.
- For information about anonymous works, works with more than one author, and two or more works by one author, see below.

A Closer Look   Here is more detailed advice.

THE AUTHOR'S NAME

Notice that the last name is given first, but otherwise the name is given as on the title page. Do not substitute initials for names written out on the title page.

If your list includes two or more works by an author, do not repeat the author's name for the second title but represent it by three hyphens followed by a period. The sequence of the works is determined by the alphabetical order of the titles. Thus, Smith's book titled *Poverty* would be listed ahead of her book *Welfare.* See the example on page 303, listing two works by Roger Brown.

Anonymous works are listed under the first word of the title or the second word if the first is *A, An,* or *The* or a foreign equivalent. We discuss books by more than one author, government documents, and works of corporate authorship on pages 304 and 304–305.

THE TITLE

After the period following the author's name, allow one space and then give the title. Take the title from the title page, not from the cover or the spine, but disregard any unusual typography such as the use of all capital letters or the use of the ampersand (&) for *and.* Italicize the title and subtitle (separate them by a colon), but do not italicize the period that concludes this part of the entry.

- Capitalize the first word and the last word.
- Capitalize all nouns, pronouns, verbs, adjectives, adverbs, and sub-ordinating conjunctions (for example, *although, if, because*).
- Do not capitalize (unless it's the first or last word of the title or the first word of the subtitle) articles (*a, an, the*), prepositions (for instance, *in, on, toward, under*), coordinating conjunctions (for instance, *and, but, or, for*), or the *to* in infinitives.

Examples:

The Death Penalty: A New View

On the Death Penalty: Toward a New View

On the Penalty of Death in a Democracy

PLACE OF PUBLICATION, PUBLISHER, DATE, AND MEDIUM OF PUBLICATION

For the place of publication, provide the name of the city; you can usually find it either on the title page or on the reverse of the title page. If a number of cities are listed, provide only the first. If the city is not likely to be known, or if it may be confused with another city of the same name (as is Oxford, Mississippi, with Oxford, England), add the name of the state, abbreviated using the two-letter postal code.

The name of the publisher is abbreviated. Usually the first word is enough (*Random House* becomes *Random*), but if the first word is a first name, such as in *Alfred A. Knopf*, the surname (*Knopf*) is used instead. University presses are abbreviated thus: *Yale UP, U of Chicago P, State U of New York P*.

The date of publication of a book is given when known; if no date appears on the book, write *n.d.* to indicate "no date."

Because you may find your sources in any number of places, each entry should end by indicating the medium of publication for each source ("Print" for books or periodicals, "Web," for sources found on the Internet, and so on).

SAMPLE ENTRIES   Here are some examples illustrating the points we have covered thus far:

Brown, Roger. *Social Psychology*. New York: Free, 1965. Print.

- - - . *Words and Things*. Glencoe, IL: Free, 1958. Print.

Douglas, Ann. *The Feminization of American Culture*. New York: Knopf, 1977. Print.

Hartman, Chester. *The Transformation of San Francisco*. Totowa, NJ: Rowman, 1984. Print.

> Kellerman, Barbara. *The Political Presidency: Practice of Leadership from*
> *Kennedy through Reagan*. New York: Oxford UP, 1984. Print.

Notice that a period follows the author's name and another period follows the title. If a subtitle is given, as it is for Kellerman's book, it is separated from the title by a colon and a space. A colon follows the place of publication, a comma follows the publisher, and a period follows the date.

A BOOK BY MORE THAN ONE AUTHOR

The book is alphabetized under the last name of the first author named on the title page. If there are *two or three authors,* the names of these are given (after the first author's name) in the normal order, *first name first:*

> Gilbert, Sandra M., and Susan Gubar. *The Madwoman in the Attic: The*
> *Woman Writer and the Nineteenth-Century Literary Imagination*. New
> Haven: Yale UP, 1979. Print.

Notice, again, that although the first author's name is given *last name first,* the second author's name is given in the normal order, first name first. Notice, too, that a comma is put after the first name of the first author, separating the authors.

If there are *more than three authors,* give the name only of the first and then add (but *not* enclosed within quotation marks and not italic) *et al.* (Latin for "and others").

> Altshuler, Alan, et al. *The Future of the Automobile*. Cambridge: MIT P,
> 1984. Print.

GOVERNMENT DOCUMENTS

If the writer is not known, treat the government and the agency as the author. Most federal documents are issued by the Government Printing Office (abbreviated to *GPO*) in Washington, D.C.

> United States. Office of Technology Assessment. *Computerized Manufacturing*
> *Automation: Employment, Education, and the Workplace*. Washington:
> GPO, 1984. Print.

WORKS OF CORPORATE AUTHORSHIP

Begin the citation with the corporate author, even if the same body is also the publisher, as in the first example:

> American Psychiatric Association. *Psychiatric Glossary*. Washington: American
> Psychiatric Association, 1984. Print.

Carnegie Council on Policy Studies in Higher Education. *Giving Youth a Better Chance: Options for Education, Work, and Service*. San Francisco: Jossey, 1980. Print.

A REPRINT (FOR INSTANCE, A PAPERBACK VERSION OF AN OLDER CLOTHBOUND BOOK)

After the title, give the date of original publication (it can usually be found on the reverse of the title page of the reprint you are using), then a period, and then the place, publisher, and date of the edition you are using. The example indicates that Gray's book was originally published in 1970 and that the student is using the Vintage reprint of 1971.

Gray, Francine du Plessix. *Divine Disobedience: Profiles in Catholic Radicalism*. 1970. New York: Vintage, 1971. Print.

A BOOK IN SEVERAL VOLUMES

If you have used more than one volume, in a citation within your essay you will (as explained on p. 299) indicate a reference to, say, page 250 of volume 3 thus: (3: 250).

If, however, you have used only one volume of the set—let's say volume 3—in your entry in the Works Cited, specify which volume you used, as in the next example:

Friedel, Frank. *Franklin D. Roosevelt*. Vol. 3. Boston: Little, 1973. Print. 4 vols.

With such an entry in the Works Cited, the parenthetic citation within your essay would be to the page only, not to the volume and page, because a reader who consults the Works Cited will understand that you used only volume 3. In the Works Cited, you may specify volume 3 and not give the total number of volumes, or you may add the total number of volumes, as in the preceding example.

ONE BOOK WITH A SEPARATE TITLE IN A SET OF VOLUMES

Sometimes a set with a title makes use also of a separate title for each book in the set. If you are listing such a book, use the following form:

Churchill, Winston. *The Age of Revolution*. New York: Dodd, 1957. Vol. 3 of *History of the English-Speaking Peoples*. Print. 4 vols. 1956-58.

A BOOK WITH AN AUTHOR AND AN EDITOR

Churchill, Winston, and Franklin D. Roosevelt. *The Complete Correspondence*. Ed. Warren F. Kimball. 3 vols. Princeton: Princeton UP, 1985. Print.

Kant, Immanuel. *The Philosophy of Kant: Immanuel Kant's Moral and Political Writings*. Ed. Carl J. Friedrich. New York: Modern, 1949. Print.

If you are making use of the editor's introduction or other editorial material rather than of the author's work, list the book under the name of the editor rather than of the author, as shown below under An Introduction, Foreword, or Afterword.

A REVISED EDITION OF A BOOK

Arendt, Hannah. *Eichmann in Jerusalem*. Rev. and enlarged ed. New York:
    Viking, 1965. Print.

Honour, Hugh, and John Fleming. *The Visual Arts: A History*. 5th ed.
    Englewood Cliffs, NJ: Prentice, 1999. Print.

A TRANSLATED BOOK

Franqui, Carlos. *Family Portrait with Fidel: A Memoir*. Trans. Alfred MacAdam.
    New York: Random, 1984. Print.

AN INTRODUCTION, FOREWORD, OR AFTERWORD

Goldberg, Arthur J. Foreword. *An Eye for an Eye? The Morality of Punishing by
    Death*. By Stephen Nathanson. Totowa, NJ: Rowman, 1987. v-vi. Print.

Usually an introduction or comparable material is listed under the name of the author of the book (here Nathanson) rather than under the name of the writer of the foreword (here Goldberg), but if you are referring to the apparatus rather than to the book itself, use the form just given. The words *Introduction, Preface, Foreword,* and *Afterword* are neither enclosed within quotation marks nor italicized.

A BOOK WITH AN EDITOR BUT NO AUTHOR

Let's assume that you have used a book of essays written by various people but collected by an editor (or editors), whose name(s) appears on the collection.

LaValley, Albert J., ed. *Focus on Hitchcock*. Englewood Cliffs, NJ: Prentice,
    1972. Print.

If the book has one editor, the abbreviation is *ed.;* if two or more editors, *eds.*

A WORK WITHIN A VOLUME OF WORKS BY ONE AUTHOR

The following entry indicates that a short work by Susan Sontag, an essay called "The Aesthetics of Silence," appears in a book by Sontag titled *Styles of Radical Will*. Notice that the inclusive page numbers of the short work are cited, not merely page numbers that you may happen to refer to but the page numbers of the entire piece.

Sontag, Susan. "The Aesthetics of Silence." *Styles of Radical Will.* New
York: Farrar, 1969. 3-34. Print.

A BOOK REVIEW

Here is an example, citing Gerstein's review of Walker's book. Gerstein's
review was published in a journal called *Ethics.*

Gerstein, Robert S. Rev. of *Punishment, Danger and Stigma: The Morality
of Criminal Justice*, by Nigel Walker. *Ethics* 93 (1983): 408-10. Print.

If the review has a title, give the title between the period following the
reviewer's name and *Rev.*

If a review is anonymous, list it under the first word of the title,
or under the second word if the first is *A, An,* or *The.* If an anonymous
review has no title, begin the entry with *Rev. of ,* and then give the title
of the work reviewed; alphabetize the entry under the title of the work
reviewed.

AN ARTICLE OR ESSAY (NOT A REPRINT) IN A COLLECTION

A book may consist of a collection (edited by one or more persons)
of new essays by several authors. Here is a reference to one essay in such
a book. (The essay by Balmforth occupies pages 19 to 35 in a collection
edited by Bevan.)

Balmforth, Henry. "Science and Religion." *Steps to Christian Understanding.*
Ed. R. J. W. Bevan. London: Oxford UP, 1958. 19-35. Print.

AN ARTICLE OR ESSAY REPRINTED IN A COLLECTION

The previous example (Balmforth's essay in Bevan's collection) was
for an essay written for a collection. But some collections reprint earlier material, such as essays from journals or chapters from books. The
following example cites an essay that was originally printed in a book
called *The Cinema of Alfred Hitchcock.* This essay has been reprinted in a
later collection of essays on Hitchcock, edited by Albert J. LaValley, and it
was LaValley's collection that the student used.

Bogdanovich, Peter. "Interviews with Alfred Hitchcock." *The Cinema of Alfred Hitchcock.* New York: Museum of Modern Art, 1963. 15-18. Rpt.
in *Focus on Hitchcock.* Ed. Albert J. LaValley. Englewood Cliffs, NJ:
Prentice, 1972. 28-31. Print.

The student has read Bogdanovich's essay or chapter, but not in
Bogdanovich's book, where it occupied pages 15 to 18. The material was
actually read on pages 28 to 31 in a collection of writings on Hitchcock

edited by LaValley. Details of the original publication—title, date, page numbers, and so forth—were found in LaValley's collection. Almost all editors will include this information, either on the copyright page or at the foot of the reprinted essay, but sometimes they do not give the original page numbers. In such a case, you need not include the original numbers in your entry.

Notice that the entry begins with the author and the title of the work you are citing (here, Bogdanovich's interviews), not with the name of the editor of the collection or the title of the collection.

AN ENCYCLOPEDIA OR OTHER ALPHABETICALLY ARRANGED REFERENCE WORK

The publisher, place of publication, volume number, and page number do *not* have to be given. For such works, list only the edition (if it is given) and the date.

For a *signed* article, begin with the author's last name. (If the article is signed with initials, check elsewhere in the volume for a list of abbreviations, which will inform you who the initials stand for, and use the following form.)

> Williams, Donald C. "Free Will and Determinism." *Encyclopedia Americana.*
> 1987 ed. Print.

For an *unsigned article,* begin with the title of the article:

> "Automation." *The Business Reference Book.* 1977 ed. Print.

> "Tobacco." *Encyclopaedia Britannica: Macropaedia.* 1988 ed. Print.

A TELEVISION OR RADIO PROGRAM

Be sure to include the title of the episode or segment (in quotation marks), the title of the show (italicized), the network, the call letters and city of the station, and the date of broadcast. Other information, such as performers, narrator, and so forth, may be included if pertinent.

> "Back to My Lai." *60 Minutes.* Narr. Mike Wallace. CBS. 29 Mar. 1998.
> Television.

> "Juvenile Justice." *Talk of the Nation.* Narr. Ray Suarez. Natl. Public Radio.
> WBUR, Boston. 15 Apr. 1998. Radio.

AN ARTICLE IN A SCHOLARLY JOURNAL   The title of the article is enclosed within quotation marks, and the title of the journal is italicized.

Some journals are paginated consecutively; the pagination of the second issue begins where the first issue leaves off. Other journals begin each issue with page 1.

A JOURNAL THAT IS PAGINATED CONSECUTIVELY

Vilas, Carlos M. "Popular Insurgency and Social Revolution in Central
America." *Latin American Perspectives* 15.1 (1988): 55-77. Print.

Vilas's article occupies pages 55 to 77 in volume 15, which was published in 1988. (Notice that the volume number is followed by a space, then by the year in parentheses, and then by a colon, a space, and the page numbers of the entire article.) When available, give the issue number.

A JOURNAL THAT BEGINS EACH ISSUE WITH PAGE 1

If the journal is, for instance, a quarterly, there will be four page 1's each year, so the issue number must be given. After the volume number, type a period and (without hitting the space bar) the issue number, as in the next example:

Greenberg, Jack. "Civil Rights Enforcement Activity of the Department of
Justice." *Black Law Journal* 8.1 (1983): 60-67. Print.

Greenberg's article appeared in the first issue of volume 8 of the *Black Law Journal.*

AN ARTICLE IN A WEEKLY, BIWEEKLY, MONTHLY, OR BIMONTHLY PUBLICATION

Do not include volume or issue numbers, even if given.

Lamar, Jacob V. "The Immigration Mess." *Time* 27 Feb. 1989: 14-15. Print.

Markowitz, Laura. "A Different Kind of Queer Marriage." *Utne Reader*
Sept.-Oct. 2000: 24-26. Print.

AN ARTICLE IN A NEWSPAPER

Because a newspaper usually consists of several sections, a section number or a capital letter may precede the page number. The example indicates that an article begins on page 1 of section 2 and is continued on a later page.

Chu, Harry. "Art Thief Defends Action." *New York Times* 8 Feb. 1989, sec.
2: 1+. Print.

AN UNSIGNED EDITORIAL

"The Religious Tyranny Amendment." Editorial. *New York Times* 15 Mar.
   1998, sec. 4: 16. Print.

A LETTER TO THE EDITOR

Lasken, Douglas. Letter. *New York Times* 15 Mar. 1998, sec. 4: 16. Print.

A PUBLISHED OR BROADCAST INTERVIEW

Give the name of the interview subject and the interviewer, followed by
the relevant publication or broadcast information, in the following format:

Green, Al. Interview with Terry Gross. *Fresh Air*. Natl. Public Radio. WFCR,
   Amherst, MA. 16 Oct. 2000. Radio.

AN INTERVIEW YOU CONDUCT

Jevgrafovs, Alexandre L. Personal [or Telephone] interview. 14 Dec. 2003.

PERSONAL CORRESPONDENCE

Add "TS" for a typed letter, "MS" for a handwritten letter, or "E-mail"
to the end of the citation.

Paso, Robert. Letter [or Message, in the case of E-mail] to the author.
   6 Jan. 2004. TS.

CD-ROM

Books on CD-ROMs are cited very much like their printed counterparts. Add the medium (*CD-ROM*) after the publication information. For
articles, to the usual print citation information, add (1) the title of the
database, italicized; (2) the medium (*CD-ROM*); (3) the vendor's name;
and (4) the date of electronic publication.

Louisberg, Margaret. *Charlie Brown Meets Godzilla: What Are Our Children
   Watching?* Urbana: ERIC Clearinghouse on Elementary and Early
   Childhood Education, 1990. CD-ROM.

"Pornography." *The Oxford English Dictionary*. 2nd ed. CD-ROM. Oxford:
   Oxford UP, 1992.

A PERSONAL OR PROFESSIONAL WEB SITE

Include the following elements, separated by periods: the name of
the person who created the site (omit if not given, as in Figure 7.4), site

FIGURE 7.4 CITING A BLOG

1. Include the URL only if your Instructor requires it.
2. Sponsor of Web site
3. No author given; start citation with the title
4. Title of Web page
5. Publication date
6. Include the medium (Web) and the date you retrieved it.

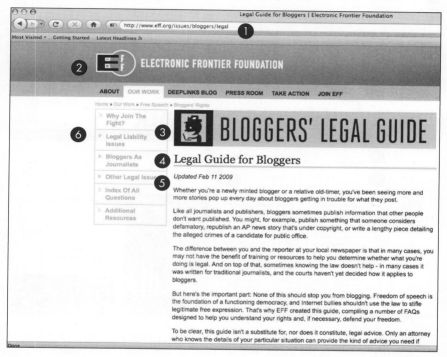

title (italicized), name of any sponsoring institution or organization; date of electronic publication or of the latest update (if given), the medium (*Web*), and the date of access.

> *Legal Guide for Bloggers.* Electronic Frontier Foundation. 11 Feb. 2009.
> Web. 30 May 2009.

AN ARTICLE IN AN ONLINE PERIODICAL

Give the same information as you would for a print article, plus the medium (*Web*) and the date of access. (See Figure 7.5.)

FIGURE 7.5   CITING AN ONLINE MAGAZINE

① Include the URL only if your Instructor requires it.

② Title of periodical

③ Title of article

④ Subtitle of article

⑤ Author

⑥ Publication date

⑦ Include the medium (Web) and the date you retrieved it.

> Acocella, Joan. "In the Blood: Why Do Vampires Still Thrill?" *New Yorker*.
> 16 March 2009. Web. 30 May 2009.

AN ONLINE POSTING

The citation includes the author's name, subject line of posting, description *Online posting* if the posting has no title, name of the forum, date material was posted, the medium (*Web*), and date of access.

> Ricci, Paul. "Global Warming." Global Electronic Science Conference, 10
> June. 1996. Web. 22 Sept. 1997.

A DATABASE SOURCE

Treat material obtained from a computer service, such as Biblio-graphic Retrieval Service (BRS), like other printed material, but at the end of the entry add (if available) the title of the database (italicized), publication medium (*Web*), name of the computer service if known, and date of access.

> Jackson, Morton. "A Look at Profits." *Harvard Business Review* 40 (1962):
> 106-13. *BRS*. Web. 23 Dec. 2006.

Caution: Although we have covered the most usual kinds of sources, it is entirely possible that you will come across a source that does not fit any of the categories that we have discussed. For approximately two hundred pages of explanations of these matters, covering the proper way to cite all sorts of troublesome and unbelievable (but real) sources, see *MLA Handbook for Writers of Research Papers,* Seventh Edition (New York: Modern Language Association of America, 2009).

APA Format: Citations within the Text

Your paper will conclude with a separate page headed References, on which you list all of your sources. If the last page of your essay is numbered 10, number the first page of the References 11.

The APA style emphasizes the date of publication; the date appears not only in the list of references at the end of the paper but also in the paper itself, when you give a brief parenthetic citation of a source that you have quoted or summarized or in any other way used. Here is an example:

> Statistics are readily available (Smith, 1989, p. 20).

The title of Smith's book or article will be given at the end of your paper in the list titled References. We discuss the form of the material listed in the References after we look at some typical citations within the text of a student's essay.

A SUMMARY OF AN ENTIRE WORK

> Smith (1988) holds the same view.

or

> Similar views are held widely (Smith, 1988; Jones & Metz, 1990).

A REFERENCE TO A PAGE OR TO PAGES

> Smith (1988) argues that "the death penalty is a lottery, and blacks usually are the losers" (p. 17).

A REFERENCE TO AN AUTHOR WHO HAS MORE THAN
ONE WORK IN THE LIST OF REFERENCES

If in the References you list two or more works that an author published in the same year, the works are listed in alphabetical order, by the first letter of the title. The first work is labeled *a,* the second *b,* and so on. Here is a reference to the second work that Smith published in 1989:

> Florida presents "a fair example" of how the death penalty is administered
> (Smith, 1989b, p. 18).

APA Format: The List of References

Your brief parenthetic citations are made clear when the reader consults the list you give in the References. Type this list on a separate page, continuing the pagination of your essay.

An Overview   Here are some general guidelines.

FORM ON THE PAGE

- Begin each entry flush with the left margin, but if an entry runs to more than one line, indent five spaces for each succeeding line of the entry.
- Double-space each entry, and double-space between entries.

ALPHABETICAL ORDER

- Arrange the list alphabetically by author.
- Give the author's last name first and then the initial of the first name and of the middle name (if any).
- If there is more than one author, name all of the authors up to seven, again inverting the name (last name first) and giving only initials for first and middle names. (But do not invert the editor's name when the entry begins with the name of an author who has written an article in an edited book.) When there are two or more authors, use an ampersand (&) before the name of the last author. Example (here, of an article in the tenth volume of a journal called *Developmental Psychology*):

> Drabman, R. S., & Thomas, M. H. (1974). Does media violence increase
> children's tolerance of real-life aggression? *Developmental Psychology,*
> *10,* 418-421.

- For eight or more authors, list the first six followed by three ellipses dots and then the last author. If you list more than one work by an author, do so in the order of publication, the earliest first. If two works by an author were published in the same year, give them in alphabetical order by the first letter of the title, disregarding *A, An,* or *The,* and their foreign equivalent. Designate the first work as *a,* the second as *b.* Repeat the author's name at the start of each entry.

Donnerstein, E. (1980a). Aggressive erotica and violence against women. *Journal of Personality and Social Psychology, 39,* 269-277.

Donnerstein, E. (1980b). Pornography and violence against women. *Annals of the New York Academy of Sciences, 347,* 227-288.

Donnerstein, E. (1983). Erotica and human aggression. In R. Green & E. Donnerstein (Eds.), *Aggression: Theoretical and empirical reviews* (pp. 87-103). New York, NY: Academic Press.

FORM OF TITLE

- In references to books, capitalize only the first letter of the first word of the title (and of the subtitle, if any) and capitalize proper nouns. Italicize the complete title (but not the period at the end).

- In references to articles in periodicals or in edited books, capitalize only the first letter of the first word of the article's title (and subtitle, if any) and all proper nouns. Do not put the title within quotation marks or italicize it. Type a period after the title of the article. For the title of the journal and the volume and page numbers, see the next instruction.

- In references to periodicals, give the volume number in arabic numerals, and italicize it. Do *not* use *vol.* before the number, and do not use *p.* or *pg.* before the page numbers.

Sample References   Here are some samples to follow.

A BOOK BY ONE AUTHOR

Pavlov, I. P. (1927). *Conditioned reflexes* (G. V. Anrep, Trans.). London, England: Oxford University Press.

A BOOK BY MORE THAN ONE AUTHOR

Belenky, M. F., Clinchy, B. M., Goldberger, N. R., & Torule, J. M. (1986). *Women's ways of knowing: The development of self, voice, and mind.* New York, NY: Basic Books.

A COLLECTION OF ESSAYS

Christ, C. P., & Plaskow, J. (Eds.). (1979). *Woman-spirit rising: A feminist reader in religion*. New York, NY: Harper & Row.

A WORK IN A COLLECTION OF ESSAYS

Fiorenza, E. (1979). Women in the early Christian movement. In C. P. Christ & J. Plaskow (Eds.), *Woman-spirit rising: A feminist reader in religion* (pp. 84-92). New York, NY: Harper & Row.

GOVERNMENT DOCUMENTS

If the writer is not known, treat the government and the agency as the author. Most federal documents are issued by the U.S. Government Printing Office in Washington, D.C. If a document number has been assigned, insert that number in parentheses between the title and the following period.

United States Congress. Office of Technology Assessment. (1984). *Computerized manufacturing automation: Employment, education, and the workplace*. Washington, DC: U.S. Government Printing Office.

AN ARTICLE IN A JOURNAL WITH CONTINUOUS PAGINATION

Tversky, A., & Kahneman, D. (1981). The framing of decisions and the psychology of choice. *Science, 211*, 453-458.

AN ARTICLE IN A JOURNAL THAT PAGINATES EACH ISSUE SEPARATELY

Foot, R. J. (1988-89). Nuclear coercion and the ending of the Korean conflict. *International Security, 13*(4), 92-112.

The reference informs us that the article appeared in issue number 4 of volume 13.

AN ARTICLE FROM A MONTHLY OR WEEKLY MAGAZINE

Greenwald, J. (1989, February 27). Gimme shelter. *Time, 133,* 50-51.

Maran, S. P. (1988, April). In our backyard, a star explodes. *Smithsonian, 19,* 46-57.

AN ARTICLE IN A NEWSPAPER

Connell, R. (1989, February 6). Career concerns at heart of 1980s campus protests. *Los Angeles Times*, pp. 1, 3.

✓ A CHECKLIST FOR PAPERS USING SOURCES

Ask yourself the following questions:

☐ Are all borrowed words and ideas credited, including those from Internet sources?

☐ Are all summaries and paraphrases acknowledged as such?

☐ Are quotations and summaries not too long?

☐ Are quotations accurate? Are omissions of words indicated by three spaced periods? Are additions of words enclosed within square brackets?

☐ Are quotations provided with helpful lead-ins?

☐ Is documentation in proper form?

And of course, you will also ask yourself the questions that you would ask of a paper that did not use sources, such as:

☐ Is the topic sufficiently narrowed?

☐ Is the thesis (to be advanced or refuted) stated early and clearly, perhaps even in the title?

☐ Is the audience kept in mind? Are opposing views stated fairly and as sympathetically as possible? Are controversial terms defined?

☐ Are assumptions likely to be shared by readers? If not, are they argued rather than merely asserted?

☐ Is the focus clear (evaluation, recommendation of policy)?

☐ Is evidence (examples, testimony, statistics) adequate and sound?

☐ Are inferences valid?

☐ Is the organization clear (effective opening, coherent sequence of arguments, unpretentious ending)?

☐ Is all worthy opposition faced?

☐ Is the tone appropriate?

☐ Has the paper been carefully proofread?

☐ Is the title effective?

☐ Is the introduction effective?

☐ Is the structure reader-friendly?

☐ Is the ending effective?

(*Note:* If no author is given, simply begin with the title followed by the date in parentheses.)

A BOOK REVIEW

Daniels, N. (1984). Understanding physician power [Review of the book *The social transformation of American medicine*]. *Philosophy and Public Affairs, 13,* 347-356.

Daniels is the reviewer, not the author of the book. The book under review is called *The Social Transformation of American Medicine,* but the review, published in volume 13 of *Philosophy and Public Affairs,* had its own title, "Understanding Physician Power."

If the review does not have a title, retain the square brackets, and use the material within as the title. Proceed as in the example just given.

A WEB SITE

American Psychological Association. (1995). Lesbian and gay parenting.
    Retrieved June 12, 2000, from http://www.apa.org/pi/parent.html

AN ARTICLE IN AN ONLINE PERIODICAL

Carpenter, S. (2000, October). Biology and social environments jointly in-
    fluence gender development. *Monitor on Psychology 31*(9). Retrieved
    from http://www.apa.org/monitor/

For a full account of the APA method of dealing with all sorts of unusual citations, see the sixth edition (2010) of the APA manual, *Publication Manual of the American Psychological Association.*

AN ANNOTATED STUDENT RESEARCH PAPER IN MLA FORMAT

The following argument makes good use of sources. Early in the semester the students were asked to choose one topic from a list of ten and to write a documented argument of 750 to 1,250 words (three to five pages of double-spaced typing). The completed paper was due two weeks after the topics were distributed. The assignment, a prelude to working on a research paper of 2,500 to 3,000 words, was in part designed to give students practice in finding and in using sources. Citations are given in the MLA form.

Timmerman 1

Lesley Timmerman

Professor Jennifer Wilson

English 102

15 August 2012

An Argument for Corporate Responsibility

Opponents of corporate social responsibility (CSR) argue that a company's sole duty is to generate profits. According to them, by acting for the public good, corporations are neglecting their primary obligation to make money. However, as people are becoming more and more conscious of corporate impacts on society and the environment, separating profits from company practices and ethics does not make sense. Employees want to work for institutions that share their values, and consumers want to buy products from companies that are making an impact and improving people's lives. Furthermore, businesses exist in an interdependent world where the health of the environment and the well-being of society really do matter. For these reasons, corporations have to take responsibility for their actions, beyond making money for shareholders. For their own benefit as well as the public's, companies must strive to be socially responsible.

In his article "The Case against Corporate Responsibility," *Wall Street Journal* writer Aneel Karnani argues that CSR will never be able to solve the world's problems. Thinking it can, Karnani says, is a dangerous illusion. He recommends that instead of expecting corporate managers to act in the public interest, we should rely on philanthropy and government regulation. Karnani maintains that "Managers who sacrifice profit for the common good [. . .] are in effect imposing a tax on their shareholders and arbitrarily deciding how that money should be spent." In other words, according to Karnani, corporations should not be determining what constitutes

Title is focused and announces the thesis.

Double-space between the title and first paragraph—and throughout the essay.

Brief statement of one side of the issue.

Summary of the opposing view.

Lead-in to quotation.

1" margin on each side and at bottom.

Timmerman 2

socially responsible behavior; individual donors and the government
should. Certainly, individuals should continue to make charitable gifts,
and governments should maintain laws and regulations to protect the
public interest. However, Karnani's reasoning for why corporations
should be exempt from social responsibility is flawed. With very few
exceptions, corporations' socially responsible actions are not arbitrary
and do not sacrifice long-term profits.

In fact, corporations have already proven that they can
contribute profitably and meaningfully to solving significant global
problems by integrating CSR into their standard practices and
long-term visions. Rather than focusing on shareholders' short-term
profits, many companies have begun measuring their success by
"profit, planet and people" — what is known as the "triple bottom
line." Businesses operating under this principle consider their
environmental and social impacts, as well as their financial impacts,
and make responsible and compassionate decisions. For example, such
businesses use resources efficiently, create healthy products, choose
suppliers who share their ethics, and improve economic opportunities
for people in the communities they serve. By doing so, companies
often save money. They also contribute to the sustainability of life
on earth and ensure the sustainability of their own businesses. In
their book *The Triple Bottom Line: How Today's Best-Run Companies
Are Achieving Economic, Social, and Environmental Success*, coauthors
Savitz and Weber demonstrate that corporations need to become
sustainable, in all ways. They argue that "the only way to succeed in
today's interdependent world is to embrace sustainability" (xi). The
authors go on to show that, for the vast majority of companies, a
broad commitment to sustainability enhances profitability (Savitz and
Weber 39).

For example, PepsiCo has been able to meet the financial
expectations of its shareholders while demonstrating its commitment

Essayist's
response to
the quota-
tion.

Author
concisely
states her
position.

Transitions
("For exam-
ple," "also")
alert readers
to where the
writer is tak-
ing them.

to the triple bottom line. In addition to donating over $16 million to help victims of natural disasters, Pepsi has woven concerns for people and for the planet into its company practices and culture (Bejou 4). For instance, because of a recent water shortage in an area of India where Pepsi runs a plant, the company began a project to build community wells (Savitz and Weber 160). Though Pepsi did not cause the water shortage nor was its manufacturing threatened by it, "Pepsi realizes that the well-being of the community is part of the company's responsibility" (Savitz and Weber 161). Ultimately, Pepsi chose to look beyond the goal of maximizing short-term profits. By doing so, the company improved its relationship with this Indian community, improved people's daily lives and opportunities, and improved its own reputation. In other words, Pepsi embraced CSR and ensured a more sustainable future for everyone involved.

Another example of a wide-reaching company that is working toward greater sustainability on all fronts is Walmart. The corporation has issued a CSR policy that includes three ambitious goals: "to be fully supplied by renewable energy, to create zero waste and to sell products that sustain people and the environment" ("From Fringe to Mainstream"). As Dr. Doug Guthrie, dean of George Washington University's School of Business, noted in a recent lecture, if a company as powerful as Walmart were to succeed in these goals, the impact would be huge. To illustrate Walmart's potential influence, Dr. Guthrie pointed out that the corporation's exports from China to the United States are equal to Mexico's total exports to the United States. In committing to CSR, the company's leaders are acknowledging how much their power depends on the earth's natural resources, as well as the communities who produce, distribute, sell, and purchase Walmart's products. The company is also well aware that achieving its goals will "ultimately save the company a great deal of money" ("From Fringe to Mainstream"). For good reason, Walmart, like other companies around the world, is choosing to act in *everyone's* best interest.

> Author now introduces statistical evidence that, if introduced earlier, might have turned the reader off.

Recent research on employees' and consumers' social consciousness offers companies further reason to take corporate responsibility seriously. For example, studies show that workers care about making a difference (Meister). In many cases, workers would even take a pay cut to work for a more responsible, sustainable company. In fact, 45 percent of workers said they would take a 15 percent reduction in pay "for a job that makes a social or environmental impact" (Meister). Even more said they would take a 15 percent cut in pay to work for a company with values that match their own (Meister). The numbers are most significant amongst Millennials (those born between, approximately, 1980 and the early 2000s). Eighty percent of Millennials said they "wanted to work for a company that cares about how it impacts and contributes to society," and over half said they would not work for an "irresponsible company" (Meister). Given this more socially conscious generation, companies are going to find it harder and harder to ignore CSR. To recruit and retain employees, employers will need to earn the admiration, respect, and loyalty of their workers by becoming "good corporate citizen[s]" (qtd. in "From Fringe to Mainstream").

Similarly, studies clearly show that CSR matters to today's consumers. According to an independent report, 80 percent of Americans say they would switch brands to support a social cause (Cone Communications 6). Eighty-eight percent say they approve of companies' using social or environmental issues in their marketing (Cone Communications 5). And 83 percent say they "wish more of the products, services and retailers would support causes" (Cone Communications 5). Other independent surveys corroborate these results, confirming that today's customers, especially Millennials, care about more than just price ("From Fringe to Mainstream").

Furthermore, plenty of companies have seen what happens when they assume that consumers do not care about CSR. For example, in 1997, when Nike customers discovered that their shoes were manufactured by child laborers in Indonesia, the company took a huge financial hit (Guthrie). Today, Information-Age customers are even more likely to educate themselves about companies' labor practices and environmental records. Smart corporations will listen to consumer preferences, provide transparency, and commit to integrating CSR into their long-term business plans.

> Author argues that it is to the *companies'* interest to be socially responsible.

In this increasingly interdependent world, the case against CSR is becoming more and more difficult to defend. Exempting corporations and relying on government to be the world's conscience does not make good social, environmental, or economic sense. Contributors to a recent article in the online journal *Knowledge@Wharton,* published by the Wharton School of Business, agree. Professor Eric Orts maintains that "it is an outmoded view to say that one must rely only on the government and regulation to police business responsibilities. What we need is re-conception of what the purpose of business is" (qtd. in "From Fringe to Mainstream"). The question is, what should the purpose of a business be in today's world? Professor of Business Administration David Bejou of Elizabeth City State University has a thoughtful and sensible answer to that question. He writes,

> Author's lead-in to the quotation guides the reader's response to the quotation.

> . . . it is clear that the sole purpose of a business is not merely that of generating profits for its owners. Instead, because compassion provides the necessary equilibrium between a company's purpose and the needs of its communities, it should be the new philosophy of business. (Bejou 1)

As Bejou implies, the days of allowing corporations to act in their own financial self-interest with little or no regard for their effects on others are over. None of us can afford such a narrow view of business. The world is far too interconnected. A seemingly small corporate decision — to buy coffee beans directly from local growers or to install solar panels — can affect the lives and livelihoods of many people and determine the environmental health of whole regions. A business, just like a government or an individual, therefore has an ethical responsibility to act with compassion for the public good.

Upbeat
ending.

       Fortunately, corporations have many incentives to act responsibly. Customer loyalty, employee satisfaction, overall cost-saving, and long-term viability are just some of the advantages businesses can expect to gain by embracing comprehensive CSR policies. Meanwhile, companies have very little to lose by embracing a socially conscious view. These days, compassion is profitable. Corporations would be wise to recognize the enormous power, opportunity, and responsibility they have to effect positive change.

Timmerman 7

Works Cited

Bejou, David. "Compassion as the New Philosophy of Business." *Journal of Relationship Marketing* 10.1 (2011): 1-6. *Business Source Complete*. Web. 15 Aug. 2012.

Cone Communications. *2010 Cone Cause Evolution Study*. Cone, Inc., 2010. Web. 15 Aug. 2012.

"From Fringe to Mainstream: Companies Integrate CSR Initiatives into Everyday Business." *Knowledge@Wharton*. The Wharton School of the University of Pennsylvania, 23 May 2012. Web. 14 Aug. 2012.

Guthrie, Doug. Keynote address. *Promoting a Comprehensive Approach to Corporate Social Responsibility (CSR)*. *YouTube*. YouTube, 22 May 2012. Web. 11 Aug. 2012.

Karnani, Aneel. "The Case against Corporate Social Responsibility." *The Wall Street Journal*. Dow Jones & Co., Inc., 14 June 2012. Web. 12 Aug. 2012.

Meister, Jeanne. "Corporate Social Responsibility: A Lever for Employee Attraction & Engagement." *Forbes*. Forbes.com, 7 June 2012. Web. 12 Aug. 2012.

Savitz, Andrew W., with Karl Weber. *The Triple Bottom Line: How Today's Best-Run Companies Are Achieving Economic, Social, and Environmental Success*. San Francisco: Jossey-Bass, 2006. Print.

Alphabetical by author's last name.

Hanging indent ½".

An article on a blog without a known author.

A clip from YouTube.

AN ANNOTATED STUDENT
RESEARCH PAPER IN APA FORMAT

The following paper is an example of a student paper that uses APA format.

The Role of Spirituality and Religion

in Mental Health

Laura DeVeau

English 102

Professor Gardner

April 12, 2010

The APA-style cover page gives title, author, and course information.

Short form of title and page number as running head.

The Role of Spirituality and Religion
in Mental Health

It has been called "a vestige of the childhood of mankind," "the feeling of something true, total and absolute," "an otherworldly answer as regards the meaning of life" (Jones, 1991, p. 1; Amaro, 1998; Kristeva, 1987, p. 27). It has been compared to medicine, described as a psychological cure for mental illness, and also referred to as the cause of a dangerous fanaticism. With so many differing opinions on the impact of religion in people's lives, where would one begin a search for the truth? Who has the answer: Christians, humanists, objectivists, atheists, psychoanalysts, Buddhists, philosophers, cults? This was my dilemma at the advent of my research into how religion and spirituality affect the mental health of society as a whole.

Citation of multiple works from references.

In this paper, I explore the claims, widely accepted by professionals in the field of psychology, that religious and spiritual practices have a negative impact on mental health. In addition, though, I cannot help but reflect on how this exploration has changed my beliefs as well. Religion is such a personal experience that one cannot be dispassionate in reporting it. One can, however, subject the evidence provided by those who have studied the issue to critical scrutiny. Having done so, I find myself in disagreement with those who claim religious feelings are incompatible with sound mental health. There is a nearly limitless number of beliefs regarding spirituality. Some are organized and involve rituals like mass or worship. Many are centered around the existence of a higher being, while others focus on the self. I have attempted to uncover the perfect set of values that lead to a better lifestyle, but my research has pointed me in an entirely different direction, where no single belief seems to be adequate but where spiritual belief in general should be valued more highly than it is currently in mental health circles.

Acknowledgment of opposing viewpoints.

Thesis explicitly introduced.

I grew up in a moderately devout Catholic family. Like many young people raised in a household where one religion is practiced by both parents, it never occurred to me to question those beliefs. I went through a spiritual cycle, which I believe much of Western society also experiences. I attended religious services because I had to. I possessed a blind, unquestioning acceptance of what I was being taught because the adults I trusted said it was so. Like many adolescents and young adults, though, I stopped going to church when I was old enough to decide because I thought I had better things to do. At this stage, we reach a point when we begin searching for a meaning to our existence. For some, this search is brought on by a major crisis or a feeling of emptiness in their daily lives, while for others it is simply a part of growing up. This is where we begin to make personal choices, but with the barrage of options, where do we turn?

Beginning with the holistic health movement in the eighties, there has been a mass shift from traditional religions to less structured spiritual practices such as meditation, yoga, the Cabala, and mysticism (Beyerman, 1989). They venture beyond the realm of conventional dogmatism and into the new wave of spirituality. Many of these practices are based on the notion that health of the mind and spirit equals health of the body. Associated with this movement is a proliferation of retreats offering a chance to get in touch with the beauty and silence of nature and seminars where we can take "a break from our everyday environment where our brains are bustling and our bodies are exhausting themselves" ("Psychological benefits," 1999). A major concept of the spiritual new wave is that it focuses inward toward the individual psyche, rather than outward toward another being like a god. Practitioners do not deny the existence of this being, but they believe that to fully love another, we must first understand ourselves. Many find this a preferable alternative to

Author and date cited for summary or paraphrase.

Anonymous source cited by title and date.

religions where the individual is seen as a walking dispenser of sin who is very fortunate to have a forgiving creator. It is also a relief from the scare tactics like damnation used by traditional religions to make people behave. Many, therefore, praise the potential psychological benefits of such spirituality.

While I believe strongly in the benefits of the new wave, I am not willing to do away with structured religion, for I find that it also has its benefits. Without the existence of churches and temples, it would be harder to expose the public to values beneficial to mental stability. It is much more difficult to hand a child a copy of the Cabala and say "Read this, and then get back to me on it" than it is to bring a child to a service where the ideas are represented with concrete examples. My religious upbringing presented me with a set of useful morals and values, and it does the same for millions of others who are brought up in this manner. Many people, including some followers of the new wave, are bitter toward Christianity because of events in history like the Crusades, the Inquisition, the Salem witch trials, and countless other horrific acts supposedly committed in the name of God. But these events were based not on biblical teachings but on pure human greed and lust for power. We should not reject the benevolent possibilities of organized religion on the basis of historical atrocities any more than we should abandon public education because a few teachers are known to mistreat children.

Another factor contributing to the reluctance concerning religion is the existence of cults that seduce people into following their extreme teachings. The victims are often at vulnerable times in their lives, and the leaders are usually very charming, charismatic, and sometimes also psychotic or otherwise mentally unstable. Many argue that if we acknowledge these groups as dangerous cults, then we must do the same for traditional religions such as Christianity and Islam, which are likewise founded on the teachings of charismatic leaders.

Clear transition refers to previous paragraph.

RELIGION IN MENTAL HEALTH   5

Again, though, critics are too quick to conflate all religious and spiritual practice; we must distinguish between those who pray and attend
services and those who commit group suicide because they think that
aliens are coming to take over the world. Cults have provided many
psychologists, who are eager to discount religion as a factor in
improving mental health, with an easy target. Ellis (1993), the
founder of rational-emotive therapy, cites many extreme examples of
religious commitment, such as cults and antiabortion killings, to show
that commitment is hazardous to one's sanity. Anomalies like these
should not be used to speak of religion as a whole, though. Religion is
clearly the least of these people's mental problems.

When the author's name appears in text, only the date is cited in parentheses.

Besides Ellis, there are many others in the field of psychology
who do not recognize religion as a potential aid for improving the
condition of the psyche. Actually, fewer than 45 percent of the members of the American Psychiatric Association even believe in God. The
general American public has more than twice that percentage of religious devotees (Larson, 1998). Going back to the days of Freud, many
psychologists have held atheist views. The father of psychoanalysis
himself called religion a "universal obsessional neurosis." Psychologists have long rejected research that demonstrates the benefits of
spirituality by saying that this research is biased. They claim that
such studies are out to prove that religion helps because the conduc-
tors are religious people who need to justify their beliefs.

While this may be true in some instances, there is also some
quite empirical research available to support the claims of those who
promote religion and spirituality. The *Journal for the Scientific Study of
Religion* has conducted many studies examining the effects of religion
on individuals and groups. In one example, the relationship between
religious coping methods and positive recovery after major stressful
events was observed. The results indicated not only that spirituality
was not harmful to the mind but that "the positive religious coping

RELIGION IN MENTAL HEALTH   6

pattern was tied to benevolent outcomes, including fewer symptoms

Bracketed word in quotation not in original source.

of psychological distress, [and] reports of psychological and spiritual growth as a result of the stressor" (Pargament et al., 1998, p. 721). Clearly, the benefits of piety can, in fact, be examined empirically,

Author, date, and page number are cited for a direct quotation.

and in some cases the results point to a positive correlation between religion and mental health.

But let us get away from statistics and studies. If religion is both useless and dangerous, as so many psychologists claim, we must ask why has it remained so vital a part of humanity for so long. Even if it can be reduced to a mere coping method that humans use to justify their existence and explain incomprehensible events, is it futile? I would suggest that this alone represents a clear benefit to society. Should religion, if it cannot be proven as "true," be eliminated and life based on scientific fact alone? Surely many would find this a pointless existence. With all the conflicting knowledge I have gained about spirituality during my personal journey and my research, one idea is clear. It is not the depth of devotion, the time of life when one turns to religion, or even the particular combination of beliefs

Conclusion restates and strengthens thesis.

one chooses to adopt that will improve the quality of life. There is no right or wrong answer when it comes to self-fulfillment. It is whatever works for the individual, even if that means holding no religious or spiritual beliefs at all. But clearly there *are* benefits to be gained, at least for some individuals, and mental health professionals need to begin acknowledging this fact in their daily practice.

References

Amaro, J. (1998). Psychology, psychoanalysis and religious faith. *Nielsen's psychology of religion pages*. Retrieved from http://www.psywww.com/psyrelig/amaro.html

Beyerman A. K. (1989). *The holistic health movement*. Tuscaloosa, AL: Alabama University Press.

Ellis, A. (1993). Dogmatic devotion doesn't help, it hurts. In B. Slife (Ed.), *Taking sides: Clashing views on controversial psychological issues* (pp. 297-301). New York, NY: Scribner.

Jones, J. W. (1991). *Contemporary psychoanalysis and religion: Transference and transcendence*. New Haven, CT: Yale University Press.

Kristeva, J. (1987). *In the beginning was love: Psychoanalysis and faith*. New York, NY: Columbia University Press.

Larson, D. (1998). Does religious commitment improve mental health? In B. Slife (Ed.), *Taking sides: Clashing views on controversial psychological issues* (pp. 292-296). New York, NY: Scribner.

Pargament, K. I., Smith, B. W., Koening, H. G., & Perez, L. (1998). Patterns of positive and negative religious coping with major life stressors. *Journal for the Scientific Study of Religion, 37*, 710-724.

"Psychological benefits." (1999). *Walking the labyrinth*. Retrieved April 3, 2000, from http://www.labyrinthway.com/html/benefits.html

References begin on a new page.

An online source.

A book.

An article or a chapter in a book.

An article in a journal.

Anonymous source alphabetized by title.

PART THREE

FURTHER VIEWS
on ARGUMENT

8

A Philosopher's View: The Toulmin Model

All my ideas hold together, but I cannot elaborate them all at once.
— JEAN-JACQUES ROUSSEAU

Clarity has been said to be not enough. But perhaps it will be time to go into that when we are within measurable distance of achieving clarity on some matter.
— J. L. AUSTIN

[Philosophy is] a peculiarly stubborn effort to think clearly.
— WILLIAM JAMES

Philosophy is like trying to open a safe with a combination lock: Each little adjustment of the dials seems to achieve nothing, only when everything is in place does the door open.
— LUDWIG WITTGENSTEIN

In Chapter 3, we explained the contrast between making *deductive* and *inductive* arguments, the two main methods people use to reason. Either:

- we make explicit something concealed in what we already accept (**deduction**), or
- we use what we have observed as a basis for asserting or proposing something new (**induction**).

These two types of reasoning share some structural features, as we also noticed. Both deductive and inductive reasoning seek to establish a **thesis** (or conclusion) by offering **reasons** for accepting the conclusion. Thus every argument contains both a thesis and one or more supportive reasons.

After a little scrutiny, we can in fact point to several features shared by all arguments, whether deductive or inductive, good or bad. We use the vocabulary popularized by Stephen Toulmin, Richard Rieke, and

Allan Janik in their book *An Introduction to Reasoning* (1979; second edition 1984) to explore the various elements of argument. Once these elements are understood, it is possible to analyze an argument using their approach and their vocabulary in what has come to be known as "The Toulmin Method."

THE CLAIM

Every argument has a purpose, goal, or aim—namely, to establish a **claim** (*conclusion* or *thesis*). Suppose you are arguing in favor of equal rights for women. You might state your thesis or claim as follows:

> Men and women ought to have equal rights.

A more precise formulation of the claim might be

> Men and women ought to have equal legal rights.

A still more precise formulation might be

> Equal legal rights for men and women ought to be protected by our Constitution.

The third version of this claim states what the controversy in the 1970s over the Equal Rights Amendment was all about. (Both houses of Congress passed it in 1972, but the number of state legislatures that needed to ratify it before the Amendment could be added to the Constitution failed to do so before Congress's mandated deadline of June 30, 1982.)

In other words, the *claim* being made in an argument is the whole point of making the argument in the first place. Consequently, when you read or analyze someone else's argument, the first questions you should ask are these:

- What is the argument intended to prove or establish?
- *What claim is it making?*
- Has this claim been clearly and precisely formulated, so that it unambiguously asserts what its advocate wants it to assert?

GROUNDS

Once we have the argument's purpose or point clearly in mind and thus know what the arguer is aiming to establish, then we can look for the evidence, reasons, support—in short, for the **grounds**—on which that claim is based. In a *deductive* argument, these grounds are the premises from which the claim is deduced; in an *inductive* argument, the grounds are the evidence—which could be based on a sample, an observation, or an experiment—that makes the claim plausible or probable.

Not every kind of claim can be supported by every kind of ground, and, conversely, not every kind of ground gives equally good support for every kind of claim. Suppose, for instance, that I claim half the students in the classroom are women. I can establish the *ground* for this claim in any of several ways. For example:

1. I can count all the women and all the men. Suppose the total equals fifty. If the number of women is twenty-five and the number of men is twenty-five, I have vindicated my claim.
2. I can count a sample of ten students—perhaps the first ten to walk into the classroom—and find that in the sample five of the students are women. I thus have inductive—plausible but not conclusive—grounds for my claim.
3. I can point out that the students in the college divide equally into men and women and then claim that this class is a representative sample of the whole college.

Clearly, ground 1 is stronger than ground 2, and 2 is much stronger than 3.

Up to this point, we have merely restated points about premises and conclusions that were covered in Chapter 3. We want now to consider four additional features of arguments.

WARRANTS

Once we have the claim or the point of an argument fixed in mind and have isolated the evidence or reasons offered in its support, the next question you need to ask is this:

> Exactly how do the reasons offered in support of the conclusion work? In other words, what kind of guarantee—**warrant**—is provided to demonstrate that the reasons proffered actually do support the claim or lead to the conclusion? (A *warrant* in this context is like the *warranty* you get when you buy something.)

In ordinary and straightforward *deductive* arguments, warrants take different forms. In the simplest cases, we can point to the way in which the *meanings* of the key terms are really equivalent. Thus, if John is taller than Bill, then Bill must be shorter than John. We know this because we know what "is shorter than" and "is taller than" mean. If A is taller than B, it must be the case that B is shorter than A; those are the meanings of the phrases being used here. Of course everyone involved does have to know the language well enough to understand the relationship between "is taller than" and "is shorter than." The *warrant* in this case is the common understanding of what those two phrases mean.

In other cases, we may need to be more resourceful. A reliable tactic is to think up a simple *parallel argument*, an argument exactly parallel in form and structure to the argument we are trying to defend. If the two arguments really do have the same form and structure, and we are ready to accept the simpler one, then we can point out that the more complex argument must be accepted—because the two arguments have exactly the same structure. For example, if we want to argue that it is reasonable for FedEx to charge more for their delivery services than the U.S. Postal Service (USPS) does, we could point out that, since it seems entirely reasonable to pay higher costs for special services from the USPS such as overnight delivery promised by a certain time (depending on factors such as location), then it is reasonable to pay even higher fees for similar overnight delivery by FedEx because that service includes sending someone to pick up what you want delivered.

In simple *inductive* arguments, we are likely to point to the way in which observations or sets of data constitute a *representative sample* of a whole population, even if not every member of the sample is strictly in evidence. For instance, when scattered information is plotted on a graph, the trend line does not have to touch each (or even any) of the data points as long as they are scattered above and below the line in roughly equal numbers in pairs that are roughly equidistant from the trend line. We can defend this projection on the grounds that it takes all of the points into account in the least complicated way. In such a case, the warrant is this combination of *inclusiveness* and *simplicity*.

Establishing the warrants for our reasoning—that is, explaining why our grounds really do support our claims—can quickly become a highly technical and exacting procedure that goes far beyond the aims of this book. Even so, developing a "feel" for why reasons or grounds are or are not relevant to what they are alleged to support is important. "That's just my view" is *not* a convincing warrant for any argument. Even without formal training, however, one can sense that something is wrong with many bad arguments. Here is one example: British professor C. E. M. Joad found himself standing on a station platform, annoyed because he had just missed his train. Then another train, making an unscheduled stop, pulled up to the platform in front of him. Joad decided to jump aboard, only to hear the conductor say, "I'm afraid you'll have to get off, Sir. This train doesn't stop here." "In that case," replied the professor, "don't worry. I'm not on it."

BACKING

A really solid argument may need even further support, especially if what is being argued is complicated. *Warrants*, remember, explain the way our *grounds* support our *claims*. The next task, however, is to be able to show that we can back up what we have claimed by showing that the reasons we have given for a claim are good reasons. To establish that kind of further support for an argument is to provide **backing.**

What is appropriate backing for one kind of argument might be quite inappropriate for another kind of argument. For example, the kinds of reasons relevant to support an amendment to the Constitution are completely different from the kinds appropriate to settle the question of what caused the defeat of Napoleon's invasion of Russia. Arguments for the amendment might be rooted in an appeal to fairness, whereas arguments about the military defeat might be rooted in letters and other documents in French and Russian archives. The *canons* (established conventions) of good argument in two such dramatically different cases have to do with the means that scholarly communities in law and history, respectively, have developed over the years to support, defend, challenge, and undermine a given kind of argument.

Another way of stating this point is to recognize that once you have given reasons for a claim, you are then likely to be challenged to explain why your reasons are good reasons—why, that is, anyone should believe your reasons rather than regard them skeptically. They have to be the right kinds of reasons, given the field you are arguing about. Why (to give a simple example) should we accept the testimony of Dr. *X* when Dr. *Y*, equally renowned, supports the opposite side? What more do we need to know before "expert testimony" is appropriately invoked? For a different kind of case: When and why is it safe to rest a prediction on a small though admittedly carefully selected sample? And still another: Why is it legitimate to argue that (1) if I dream I am the King of France, then I must exist, whereas it is illegitimate to argue that (2) if I dream I am the King of France, then the King of France must exist?

To answer challenges of these sorts is to back up one's reasons, to give them legitimate *backing*. No argument is any better than its backing.

MODAL QUALIFIERS

As we have seen, all arguments are made up of assertions or propositions that can be sorted into four categories:

- the *claim* (conclusion, thesis to be established),
- the *grounds* (explicit reasons advanced),
- the *warrant* (guarantee, evidence, or principle that legitimates the ground by connecting it to the claim), and
- the *backing* (relevant support, implicit assumptions).

All of the kinds of propositions that emerge when we assert something in an argument have what philosophers call a **modality**. This means that propositions generally indicate—explicitly or tacitly—the *character* and *scope* of what is believed to be their likely truth.

Character has to do with the nature of the claim being made, the extent of an argument's presumed reach. Both making and evaluating arguments require being clear about whether they are *necessary*, *probable, plausible,* or *possible.* Consider, for example, a claim that it is to the advantage of a college to have a racially diverse student body. Is that *necessarily* or only *probably* true? What about an argument that a runner who easily wins a 100-meter race should also be able to win at 200 meters? Is this *plausible*—or only *possible*? Indicating the *character* with which an assertion is advanced is crucial to any argument for or against it. Furthermore, if there is more than one reason for making a claim, and all of those reasons are *good*, it is still possible that one of those good reasons may be *better* than the others. If so, the better reason should be stressed.

Indicating the *scope* of an assertion is equally crucial to how an argument plays out. *Scope* entails such considerations as whether the proposition is thought to be true *always* or just *sometimes.* Further, is the claim being made supposed to apply in *all* instances or just in *some?* Assertions are usually clearer, as well as more likely to be true, if they are explicitly *quantified* and *qualified.* Suppose, for example, that you are arguing against smoking, and the ground for your claim is this:

Heavy smokers cut short their life span.

In this case, there are three obvious alternative quantifications to choose among: *all* smokers cut short their life span, *most* do, or only *some* do. Until the assertion is quantified in one of these ways, we really do not know what is being asserted—and so we do not know what degree and kind of evidence or counterevidence is relevant. Other quantifiers include *few, rarely, often, sometimes, perhaps, usually, more or less, regularly, occasionally.*

Scope also has to do with the fact that empirical generalizations are typically *contingent* on various factors. Indicating such contingencies clearly is an important way to protect a generalization against obvious counterexamples. Thus, consider this empirical generalization:

Students do best on final examinations if they study hard for them.

Are we really to believe that students who cram ("study hard" in that concentrated sense) for an exam will do better than those who do the work diligently throughout the whole course ("study hard" in that broader sense) and therefore do not need to cram for the final? Probably not; what is really meant is that *all other things being equal* (in Latin, *ceteris paribus*), concentrated study just before an exam will yield good results. Alluding in this way to the contingencies—the things that might derail the argument—shows that the writer is aware of possible exceptions and is conceding them from the start.

In sum, sensitivity to both character and (especially) scope—paying attention to the role played by quantifiers, qualifiers, and contingencies and making sure you use appropriate ones for each of your assertions—will strengthen your arguments enormously. Not least of the benefits is that you will reduce the peculiar vulnerabilities of an argument that is undermined by exaggeration and other misguided generalizations.

REBUTTALS

Very few arguments of any interest are beyond dispute, conclusively knockdown affairs. Only very rarely is the claim of an argument so rigidly tied to its grounds, warrants, and backing—and with its quantifiers and qualifiers argued in so precise a manner—that it proves its conclusion beyond any possibility of doubt. On the contrary, most arguments have many counterarguments, and sometimes one of these counterarguments is more convincing than the original argument.

Suppose someone has taken a sample that appears to be random: An interviewer on your campus accosts the first ten students she encounters, and seven of them are fraternity or sorority members. She is now ready to argue that seven-tenths of enrolled students belong to Greek organizations.

You believe, however, that the Greeks are in the minority and point out that she happens to have conducted her interview around the corner from the Panhellenic Society's office just off Sorority Row. Her random sample is anything but. The ball is now back in her court as you await her response to your rebuttal.

As this example illustrates, it is safe to say that we do not understand our own arguments very well until we have tried to get a grip on the places in which they are vulnerable to criticism, counterattack, or refutation. We have already, in Chapter 3, quoted Edmund Burke—but the passage is worth repeating: "He that wrestles with us strengthens our nerves, and sharpens our skill. Our antagonist is our helper."

To be sure, in everyday conversation we may not enjoy being in the company of people who interrupt to ask what are our grounds, warrants, backing, and so forth. The poet T. S. Eliot amusingly characterized himself as such a person:

How Unpleasant to Meet Mr. Eliot!

How unpleasant to meet Mr. Eliot!
With his features of clerical cut.
And his brow so grim
And his mouth so prim
And his conversation, so nicely
Restricted to What Precisely

And If and Perhaps and But . . .
How unpleasant to meet Mr. Eliot!
(Whether his mouth be open or shut.)

Still, if we wish to make serious progress in thinking and arguing about significant issues, cultivating alertness to possible weak spots in arguments—our own arguments as well as the arguments of others— and incorporating thoughtful responses to anticipated criticisms will always be helpful.

IDEA PROMPT 8.1 CONSTRUCTING A TOULMIN ARGUMENT

Claim	*What is your argument?*	"Driving while texting should be made illegal."
Grounds	*What is your evidence?*	"A 2011 study shows an increase in accidents due to drivers who drive and text."
Warrant	*What reasoning connects your evidence to your argument?*	"We should pass laws that promote safer roads."
Backing	*Why should the reader agree with your grounds?*	"We all use the roads, and we have a duty to make our shared roads as safe as possible."
Rebuttal	*What are the objections to this argument?*	"Many people would ignore this law just as they ignore laws about seatbelts, thereby making it ineffective, so why pass it in the first place?"
Qualifier	*What are the limits of your argument?*	"A ban on texting and driving might save some lives, even if it doesn't fix the whole problem."
One possible Toulmin argument	"In light of a 2011 study that shows that texting while driving has contributed to an increase in deadly automobile accidents, texting while driving should be banned. As a community, we have a responsibility to address such serious threats to our safety. Although many people would continue to text while driving, creating penalties for texting while driving may deter some drivers from engaging in such unsafe behavior."	

PUTTING THE TOULMIN METHOD TO WORK:
Responding to an Argument

Let's take a look at another argument—it happens to be on why buying directly from farmers near you won't save the planet—and see how the Toulmin method can be applied. The checklist on page 346 can help you focus your thoughts as you read.

James E. McWilliams

James E. McWilliams, the author of Just Food, *is an associate professor of history at Texas State University. This piece first appeared in* Forbes Magazine *on August 3, 2009.*

The Locavore Myth: Why Buying from Nearby Farmers Won't Save the Planet

Buy local, shrink the distance food travels, save the planet. The locavore movement has captured a lot of fans. To their credit, they are highlighting the problems with industrialized food. But a lot of them are making a big mistake. By focusing on transportation, they overlook other energy-hogging factors in food production.

Take lamb. A 2006 academic study (funded by the New Zealand government) discovered that it made more environmental sense for a Londoner to buy lamb shipped from New Zealand than to buy lamb raised in the U.K. This finding is counterintuitive—if you're only counting food miles. But New Zealand lamb is raised on pastures with a small carbon footprint, whereas most English lamb is produced under intensive factory-like conditions with a big carbon footprint. This disparity overwhelms domestic lamb's advantage in transportation energy.

New Zealand lamb is not exceptional. Take a close look at water usage, fertilizer types, processing methods, and packaging techniques and you discover that factors other than shipping far outweigh the energy it takes to transport food. One analysis, by Rich Pirog of the Leopold Center for Sustainable Agriculture, showed that transportation accounts for only 11 percent of food's carbon footprint. A fourth of the energy required to produce food is expended in the consumer's kitchen. Still more energy is consumed per meal in a restaurant, since restaurants throw away most of their leftovers.

Locavores argue that buying local food supports an area's farmers and, in turn, strengthens the community. Fair enough. Left unacknowledged, however, is the fact that it also hurts farmers in other parts of the world. The U.K. buys most of its green beans from Kenya. While it's true that the beans almost always arrive in airplanes—the form of transportation that consumes the most energy—it's also true that a campaign to shame English consumers with small airplane stickers affixed to flown-in produce threatens the livelihood of 1.5 million sub-Saharan farmers.

Another chink in the locavores' armor involves the way food miles are calculated. To choose a locally grown apple over an apple trucked in from across the country might seem easy. But this decision ignores economies of scale. To take an extreme example, a shipper sending a truck with 2,000 apples over 2,000 miles would consume the same amount of fuel per apple as a local farmer who takes a pickup 50 miles to sell 50 apples at his stall at the green market. The critical measure here is not food miles but apples per gallon.

The one big problem with thinking beyond food miles is that it's hard to get the information you need. Ethically concerned consumers know very little about processing practices, water availability, packaging waste, and fertilizer application. This is an opportunity for watchdog groups. They should make life-cycle carbon counts available to shoppers.

Until our food system becomes more transparent, there is one thing you can do to shrink the carbon footprint of your dinner: Take the meat off your plate. No matter how you slice it, it takes more energy to bring meat, as opposed to plants, to the table. It takes 6 pounds of grain to make a pound of chicken and 10 to 16 pounds to make a pound of beef. That difference translates into big differences in inputs. It requires 2,400 liters of water to make a burger and only 13 liters to grow a tomato. A majority of the water in the American West goes toward the production of pigs, chickens, and cattle.

The average American eats 273 pounds of meat a year. Give up red meat once a week and you'll save as much energy as if the only food miles in your diet were the distance to the nearest truck farmer.

If you want to make a statement, ride your bike to the farmer's market. If you want to reduce greenhouse gases, become a vegetarian.

✓ A CHECKLIST FOR USING THE TOULMIN METHOD

Have I asked the following questions?
- [ ] What claim does the argument make?
- [ ] What grounds are offered for the claim?
- [ ] What warrants the inferences from the grounds to the claim?
- [ ] What backing supports the claim?
- [ ] With what modalities are the claim and grounds asserted?
- [ ] To what rebuttals are the claim, grounds, and backing vulnerable?

See the companion Web site
bedfordstmartins.com/barnetbedau
for links related to the Toulmin model.

THINKING WITH TOULMIN'S METHOD

Remember to make use of the checklist above as you work to find the claim(s), grounds, and warrant(s) that McWilliams puts forward in this short essay.

- First and foremost, what is the **claim** being made by the author? Is it in his title? The opening sentence? Or is it buried in the first paragraph?

McWilliams really gives away his game in his title, even though he opens the essay itself in a way that might make the reader think he is about to launch into a defense of the locavore movement. He even goes out of his way to praise its members ("To their credit . . ."). The signal that his claim really appears already in the title and that he is *not* going to defend the locavore movement is the way he begins the fourth sentence. Notice that, although you may have been told that starting a sentence with *But* is not the best way to write, McWilliams here does so to good effect. Not only does he dramatically counter what he said just prior to that; he also sets up the final sentence of the paragraph, which turns out to be crucial. In this way, he draws sharp attention to his *claim*. How would you state his claim?

- Second, what are the **grounds,** the evidence or reasons, that the author advances in support of his claim?

As it turns out, McWilliams spells out only one example as evidence for his claim. What is it? Is it convincing? Should he have provided more evidence or reasons at this point? It turns out that he does have other grounds to offer—but he mentions them only later. What are those other pieces of evidence?

- Third, what **warrants** does McWilliams offer to show why we should accept his grounds? What authority does he cite? How effective and convincing is this way of trying to get us to accept the grounds he offered in support of his claim?

The essence of the Toulmin method lies in these three elements: the claim(s), the grounds, and the warrant(s). If you have extracted these from McWilliams's essay, you are well on the way to being able to identify the argument he is putting forward. So far, so good. Further probing, however—looking for the other three elements of the Toulmin method (the backing, the modal qualifiers and quantifiers, and the rebuttal)—is essential before you are in a position to actually evaluate the argument. So let's go on.

- Fourth, what **backing** does McWilliams provide? What reasons does he give that might persuade us to accept his argument? Look for what he claimed came out of the analysis that was his basic warrant. He certainly seems to be using factual information—but what if you challenged him? Has he provided adequate reasons for us to believe him? What could he (or would he have to) be able to tell us if we challenged him with questions like "How do you know . . . ?" or "Why do you believe . . . ?" In other words, has he provided adequate backing? Or does he want us to just accept his statement of the facts?

- Fifth, does McWilliams use **modal qualifiers**? Can you find phrases like "in most cases" or "generally it is true that . . . "? Or does he write so boldly—with little in the way of qualifiers or quantifiers—that one is left uncertain about whether to accept his position? Where might he have effectively used qualifiers?

- Finally, does McWilliams use **rebuttals**, the reasons given in anticipation of someone rejecting the author's claim, or conceding the claim but rejecting the grounds? Does McWilliams anticipate rejections and prepare rebuttals? Does he offer anything to forestall criticisms? If so, what is it that he does? If not, what could or should he have done?

Just how good an argument has McWilliams made? Is he convincing? If you identified weak points in his argument, what are they? Can you help strengthen the argument?

9

A Logician's View: Deduction, Induction, Fallacies

Logic is the anatomy of thought.

— JOHN LOCKE

Logic takes care of itself; all we have to do is to look and see how it does it.

— LUDWIG WITTGENSTEIN

In Chapter 3 we introduced the terms *deduction, induction,* and *fallacy*. Here we discuss them in greater detail.

DEDUCTION

The basic aim of deductive reasoning is to start with some assumption or premise and extract from it a conclusion — a logical consequence — that is concealed but implicit in it. Thus, taking the simplest case, if I assert as a premise

    1a. Nuclear power poses more risks of harm to the environment than fossil fuels.

then it is a matter of simple deduction to infer the conclusion that

    1b. Fossil fuels pose fewer risks of harm to the environment than nuclear power.

Anyone who understands English would grant that 1b follows 1a — or equivalently, that 1b can be validly deduced from 1a — because whatever two objects, *A* and *B*, you choose, if *A* does *more things than B*, then *B* must do *fewer things than A*.

    Thus, in this and all other cases of valid deductive reasoning, we can say not only that we are entitled to *infer* the conclusion from the premise — in this case, infer 1b from 1a—but that the premise *implies* the conclusion. Remember, too, the conclusion (1b) that fossil fuels pose fewer risks than nuclear power—inferred or deduced from the statement (1a) that nuclear power poses more risks—does not depend on the truth of the statement that nuclear power poses more risks. If the speaker (falsely) asserts that nuclear power poses more risks, then the hearer validly (that is to say, logically) concludes that fossil fuels pose fewer risks. Thus, 1b follows from 1a whether or not 1a is true; consequently, if 1a is true, then so is 1b; but if 1a is false, then 1b must be false also.

Let's take another example—more interesting but comparably simple:

2a. President Truman was underrated by his critics.

Given 2a, a claim amply verified by events of the 1950s, one is entitled to infer

2b. His critics underrated President Truman.

On what basis can we argue that 2a implies 2b? The two propositions are equivalent because a rule of English grammar assures us that we can convert the position of subject and predicate phrases in a sentence by shifting from the passive to the active voice (or vice versa) without any change in the conditions that make the proposition true (or false).

Both pairs of examples illustrate that in deductive reasoning, our aim is to transform, reformulate, or restate in our conclusion some (or, as in the two examples above, all) of the information contained in our premises.

Remember, even though a proposition or statement follows from a previous proposition or statement, the statements need not be true. We can see why if we consider another example. Suppose someone asserts or claims that

3a. The Gettysburg Address is longer than the Declaration of Independence.

As every student of American history knows, 3a is false. But false or not, we can validly deduce from it that

3b. The Declaration of Independence is shorter than the Gettysburg Address.

This inference is valid (even though the conclusion is untrue) because the conclusion follows logically (more precisely, deductively) from 3a: In English, as we know, the meaning of "*A* is shorter than *B*," which appears in 3b, is simply the converse of "*B* is longer than *A*," which appears in 3a.

The deductive relation between 3a and 3b reminds us again that the idea of validity, which is so crucial to deduction, is not the same as the idea of truth. False propositions have implications—logical consequences—too, just as true propositions do.

In the three pairs of examples so far, what can we point to as the warrant for our claims? Well, look at the reasoning in each case; the arguments rely on rules of ordinary English, on the accepted meanings of words like *on*, *under*, and *underrated*.

In many cases, of course, the deductive inference or pattern of reasoning is much more complex than that which we have seen in the examples so far. When we introduced the idea of deduction in Chapter 3, we gave as our primary example the *syllogism*. Here is another example:

4. Texas is larger than California; California is larger than Arizona; therefore, Texas is larger than Arizona.

The conclusion in this syllogism is derivable from the two premises; that is, anyone who asserts the two premises is committed to accepting the conclusion as well, whether or not one thinks of it.

Notice again that the *truth* of the conclusion is not established merely by validity of the inference. The conclusion in this syllogism happens to be true. And the premises of this syllogism imply the conclusion. But the argument establishes the conclusion only because both of the premises on which the conclusion depends are true. Even a Californian admits that Texas is larger than California, which in turn is larger than Arizona. In other words, argument 4 is a *sound* argument because (as we explained in Chapter 3) it is valid and all its premises are true. All—and only—arguments that *prove* their conclusions have these two traits.

How might we present the warrant for the argument in 4? Short of a crash course in formal logic, either of two strategies might suffice. One is to argue from the fact that the validity of the inference depends on the meaning of a key concept, *being larger than*. This concept has the property of *transitivity*, a property that many concepts share (for example, *is equal to, is to the right of, is smarter than*—all are transitive concepts). Consequently, whatever *A*, *B*, and *C* are, if *A* is larger than *B*, and *B* is larger than *C*, then *A* will be larger than *C*. The final step is to substitute "Texas," "California," and "Arizona" for *A*, *B*, and *C*, respectively.

A second strategy, less abstract and more graphic, is to think of representing Texas, California, and Arizona by nested circles. Thus, the first premise in argument 4 would look like this:

The second premise would look like this:

The conclusion would look like this:

We can see that this conclusion follows from the premises because it amounts to nothing more than what one gets by superimposing the two premises on each other. Thus, the whole argument can be represented like this:

$$\left(\text{TX}\,\text{CA}\right) + \left(\text{CA}\,\text{AZ}\right) = \left(\text{TX}\,\text{AZ}\right)$$

The so-called middle term in the argument—California—disappears from the conclusion; its role is confined to be the link between the other two terms, Texas and Arizona, in the premises. (This is an adaptation of the technique used in elementary formal logic known as Venn diagrams.) In this manner one can give graphic display to the important fact that the conclusion follows from the premises because one can literally *see* the conclusion represented by nothing more than a representation of the premises.

Both of these strategies bring out the fact that validity of deductive inference is a purely *formal* property of argument. Each strategy abstracts the form from the content of the propositions involved to show how the concepts in the premises are related to the concepts in the conclusion.

For the sake of illustration, here is another syllogistic argument with the same logical features as argument 4. (A nice exercise is to restate argument 5 using diagrams in the manner of argument 4.)

> 5. African American slaves were treated worse than white indentured servants. Indentured white servants were treated worse than free white labor. Therefore, African American slaves were treated worse than free white labor.

Not all deductive reasoning occurs in syllogisms, however, or at least not in syllogisms like the ones in 4 and 5. (The term *syllogism* is sometimes used to refer to any deductive argument of whatever form, provided only that it has two premises.) In fact, syllogisms such as 4 are not the commonest form of our deductive reasoning at all. Nor are they the simplest (and of course, not the most complex). For an argument that is even simpler, consider this:

> 6. If a youth is an African American slave, he is probably treated worse than a youth in indentured service. This youth is an African American slave. Therefore, he is probably treated worse than if he had been an indentured servant.

Here the pattern of reasoning has the form: If *A*, then *B; A;* there-fore, *B.* Notice that the content of the assertions represented by *A* and *B* do not matter; any set of expressions having the same form or structure will do equally well, including assertions built out of meaningless terms, as in this example:

7. If the slithy toves, then the gyres gimble. The slithy toves. There-fore, the gyres gimble.

Argument 7 has the form: If *A*, then *B; A;* therefore *B.* As a piece of deduc-tive inference it is every bit as good as argument 6. Unlike 6, however, 7 is of no interest to us because none of its assertions make any sense (unless you are a reader of Lewis Carroll's "Jabberwocky," and even then the sense of 7 is doubtful). You cannot, in short, use a valid deductive argument to prove anything unless the premises and the conclusion are *true,* but they can't be true unless they *mean* something in the first place.

This parallel between arguments 6 and 7 shows once again that deductive validity in an argument rests on the *form* or structure of the argument, and not on its content or meaning. If all one can say about an argument is that it is valid—that is, its conclusion follows from the premises—one has not given a sufficient reason for accepting the argu-ment's conclusion. It has been said that the Devil can quote Scripture; similarly, an argument can be deductively valid and of no further interest or value whatever because valid (but false) conclusions can be drawn from false or even meaningless assumptions. For example,

8. New York's Metropolitan Museum of Art has the finest collection of abstract impressionist painting in the world. The finest collec-tion of abstract impressionist paintings includes dozens of can-vases by Winslow Homer. Therefore, the Metropolitan Museum of Art has dozens of paintings by Winslow Homer.

Here, the conclusion follows validly from the premises, even though all three propositions are false. Nevertheless, although validity by itself is not enough, it is a necessary condition of any deductive argument that purports to establish its conclusion.

Now let us consider another argument with the same form as 8, only more interesting.

9. If President Truman knew the Japanese were about to surrender, then it was immoral of him to order that atom bombs be dropped on Hiroshima and Nagasaki. Truman knew the Japanese were about to surrender. Therefore, it was immoral of him to order dropping those bombs.

As in the two previous examples, anyone who assents to the premises in argument 9 must assent to the conclusion; the form of arguments 8 and 9 is identical. But do the premises of argument 9 *prove* the conclu-sion? That depends on whether both premises are true. Well, are they?

This turns on a number of considerations, and it is worthwhile pausing to examine this argument closely to illustrate the kinds of things that are involved in answering this question.

Let us begin by examining the second (minor) premise. Its truth is controversial even to this day. Autobiography, memoranda, other documentary evidence—all are needed to assemble the evidence to back up the grounds for the thesis or claim made in the conclusion of this valid argument. Evaluating this material effectively will probably involve not only further deductions but inductive reasoning as well.

Now consider the first (major) premise in argument 9. Its truth doesn't depend on what history shows but on the moral principles one accepts. The major premise has the form of a hypothetical proposition ("if . . . then . . .") and asserts a connection between two very different kinds of things. The antecedent of the hypothetical (the clause following "if") mentions facts about Truman's *knowledge,* and the consequent of the hypothetical (the clause following "then") mentions facts about the *morality* of his conduct in light of such knowledge. The major premise as a whole can thus be seen as expressing *a principle of moral responsibility.*

Such principles can, of course, be controversial. In this case, for instance, is the principle peculiarly relevant to the knowledge and conduct of a president of the United States? Probably not; it is far more likely that this principle is merely a special case of a more general proposition about anyone's moral responsibility. (After all, we know a great deal more about the conditions of our own moral responsibility than we do about those of high government officials.) We might express this more general principle in this way: If we have knowledge that would make our violent conduct unnecessary, then we are immoral if we deliberately act violently anyway. Thus, accepting this general principle can serve as a basis for defending the major premise of argument 9.

We have examined this argument in some detail because it illustrates the kinds of considerations needed to test whether a given argument is not only valid but whether its premises are true—that is, whether its premises really prove the conclusion.

The great value of the form of argument known as hypothetical syllogism, exemplified by arguments 6 and 7, is that the structure of the argument is so simple and so universally applicable in reasoning that it is often both easy and worthwhile to formulate one's claims so that they can be grounded by an argument of this sort.

Before leaving the subject of deductive inference, consider three other forms of argument, each of which can be found in actual use elsewhere in the readings in this volume. The simplest of these is **disjunctive syllogism,** so called because its major premise is a **disjunction.** For example,

> 10. Either censorship of television shows is overdue, or our society
>   is indifferent to the education of its youth. Our society is not

indifferent to the education of its youth. Therefore, censorship of television is overdue.

Notice, by the way, that the validity of an argument, as in this case, does not turn on pedantic repetition of every word or phrase as the argument moves along; nonessential elements can be dropped, or equivalent expressions substituted for variety without adverse effect on the reasoning. Thus, in conversation or in writing, the argument in 10 might actually be presented like this:

11. Either censorship of television is overdue, or our society is indifferent to the education of its youth. But, of course, we aren't indifferent; it's censorship that's overdue.

The key feature of disjunctive syllogism, as example 11 suggests, is that the conclusion is whichever of the disjuncts is left over after the others have been negated in the minor premise. Thus, we could easily have a very complex disjunctive syllogism, with a dozen disjuncts in the major premise, and seven of them denied in the minor premise, leaving a conclusion of the remaining five. Usually, however, a disjunctive argument is formulated in this manner: Assert a disjunction with two or more disjuncts in the major premise; then *deny all but one* in the minor premise; and infer validly the remaining disjunct as the conclusion. That was the form of argument 11.

Another type of argument, especially favored by orators and rhetoricians, is the **dilemma.** Ordinarily we use the term *dilemma* in the sense of an awkward predicament, as when we say, "His dilemma was that he didn't have enough money to pay the waiter." But when logicians refer to a dilemma, they mean a forced choice between two or more equally unattractive alternatives. For example, the predicament of the U.S. government during the mid-1980s as it faced the crisis brought on by terrorist attacks on American civilian targets, which were believed, during that time, to be inspired and supported by the Libyan government, can be formulated in a dilemma:

12. If the United States bombs targets in Libya, innocent people will be killed, and the Arab world will be angered. If the United States doesn't bomb Libyan targets, then terrorists will go unpunished, and the United States will lose respect among other governments. Either the United States bombs Libyan targets, or it doesn't. Therefore, in either case unattractive consequences will follow: The innocent will be killed, or terrorists will go unpunished.

Notice first the structure of the argument: two conditional propositions asserted as premises, followed by another premise that states a **necessary truth.** (The premise, "Either we bomb the Libyans, or we don't," is a disjunction; since its two alternatives are exhaustive, one of the two alternatives must be true. Such a statement is often called analytically true, or a *tautology*.) No doubt the conclusion of this dilemma follows from its premises.

But does the argument prove, as it purports to do, that whatever the U.S. government does, it will suffer "unattractive consequences"? It is customary to speak of "the horns of the dilemma," as though the challenge posed by the dilemma were like a bull ready to gore you whichever direction you turn. But if the two conditional premises failed to exhaust the possibilities, then one can escape from the dilemma by going "between the horns," that is, by finding a third alternative. If (as in this case) that is not possible, one can still ask whether both of the main premises are true. (In this argument, it should be clear that neither of these main premises spells out all or even most of the consequences that could be foreseen.) Even so, in cases where both these conditional premises are true, it may be that the consequences of one alternative are nowhere nearly so bad as those of the other. If that is true, but our reasoning stops before evaluating that fact, we may be guilty of failing to distinguish between the greater and the lesser of two admitted evils. The logic of the dilemma itself cannot decide this choice for us. Instead, we must bring to bear empirical inquiry and imagination to the evaluation of the grounds of the dilemma itself.

Writers commonly use the term *dilemma* without explicitly formulating the dilemma to which they refer, leaving it for the readers to do. And sometimes, what is called a dilemma really isn't one. (Remember the dog's tail? Calling it a leg doesn't make it a leg.) As an example, consider the plight of Sophie in William Styron's novel, *Sophie's Choice*. The scene is Birkenau, the main Nazi extermination camp during World War II. Among the thousands arriving at the prison gates are Sophie and her two children, Jan and Eva. On the train platform they are confronted by a Nazi SS medical officer. He will decide which are the lucky ones; they will live to work in the camp. The rest will go to their death in the gas chambers. When Sophie insists she is Polish but not Jewish, the officer says she may choose one of her children to be saved. Which of the two ought to be saved? On what basis ought Sophie resolve her dilemma? It looks as if she has only two alternatives, each of which presents her with an agonizing outcome. Or is there a third way out?

Finally, one of the most powerful and dramatic forms of argument is **reductio ad absurdum** (from the Latin, meaning "reduction to absurdity"). The idea of a reductio argument is to disprove a proposition by showing the absurdity of its inevitable conclusion. It is used, of course, to refute your opponent's position and prove your own. For example, in Plato's *Republic*, Socrates asks an old gentleman, Cephalus, to define what right conduct is. Cephalus says that it consists of paying your debts and keeping your word. Socrates rejects this answer by showing that it leads to a contradiction. He argues that Cephalus cannot have given the correct answer because if we believe that he did, we will be quickly led into contradictions; in some cases when you keep your word you will nonetheless be doing the wrong thing. For suppose, says Socrates, that you borrowed a weapon from a man, promising to return it when he asks for it. One day he comes to your door, demanding his weapon and swearing angrily that he intends to murder a neighbor. Keeping your word under those circumstances is absurd, Socrates implies, and the reader of the dialogue is left to infer that Cephalus's definition, which led to this result, is refuted.

Let's take a closer look at another example. Suppose you are opposed to any form of gun control, whereas I am in favor of gun control. I might try to refute your position by attacking it with a reductio argument. To do that, I start out by assuming the very opposite of what I believe or favor and try to establish a contradiction that results from following out the consequences of this initial assumption. My argument might look like this:

13. Let's assume your position—namely, that there ought to be no legal restrictions whatever on the sale and ownership of guns. That means that you'd permit having every neighborhood hardware store sell pistols and rifles to whoever walks in the door. But that's not all. You apparently also would permit selling machine guns to children, antitank weapons to lunatics, small-bore cannons to the nearsighted, as well as guns and the ammunition to go with them to anyone with a criminal record. But this is utterly preposterous. No one could favor such a dangerous policy. So the only question worth debating is what kind of gun control is necessary.

Now in this example, my reductio of your position on gun control is not based on claiming to show that you have strictly contradicted yourself, for there is no purely logical contradiction in opposing all forms of gun control. Instead, what I have tried to do is to show that there is a contradiction between what you profess—no gun controls whatever—and what you probably really believe, if only you will stop to think about it—no lunatic should be allowed to buy a loaded machine gun.

My refutation of your position rests on whether I succeed in establishing an inconsistency among your own beliefs. If it turns out that you really believe lunatics should be free to purchase guns and ammunition, then my attempted refutation fails.

In explaining reductio ad absurdum, we have had to rely on another idea fundamental to logic, that of **contradiction,** or inconsistency. (We used this idea, remember, to define validity in Chapter 3. A deductive argument is valid if and only if affirming the premises and denying the conclusion results in a contradiction.) The opposite of contradiction is **consistency,** a notion of hardly less importance to good reasoning than validity. These concepts deserve a few words of further explanation and illustration. Consider this pair of assertions:

14. Abortion is homicide.
15. Racism is unfair.

No one would plausibly claim that we can infer or deduce 15 from 14, or, for that matter, 14 from 15. This almost goes without saying because there is no evident connection between these two assertions. They are unrelated assertions; logically speaking, they are *independent* of each other. In such cases the two assertions are mutually *consistent*; that is, both could be true — or both could be false. But now consider another proposition:

16. Euthanasia is not murder.

Could a person assert 14 (*Abortion is homicide*) and also assert 16 (*Euthanasia is not murder*) and be consistent? This question is equivalent to asking whether one could assert the **conjunction** of these two propositions — namely,

17. Abortion is homicide, and euthanasia is not murder.

It is not so easy to say whether 17 is consistent or inconsistent. The kinds of moral scruples that might lead a person to assert one of these conjuncts (that is, one of the two initial propositions, *Abortion is homicide* and *Euthanasia is not murder*) might lead to the belief that the other one must be false and thus to the conclusion that 17 is inconsistent. (Notice that if 14 were the assertion that *Abortion is murder,* instead of *Abortion is homicide,* the problem of asserting consistently both 14 and 16 would be more acute.) Yet if we think again, we might imagine someone being convinced that there is no inconsistency in asserting that *Abortion is homicide,* say, and that *Euthanasia is not murder,* or even the reverse. (For instance, suppose you believed that the unborn deserve a chance to live and that putting elderly persons to death in a painless manner and with their consent confers a benefit on them.)

Let us generalize: We can say of any set of propositions that they are *consistent* if and only if *all could be true together.* (Notice that it follows from this definition that propositions mutually imply each other, as do *Seabiscuit was America's fastest racehorse* and *America's fastest racehorse was Seabiscuit.*) Remember that, once again, the truth of the assertions in question does not matter. Two propositions can be consistent or not, quite apart from whether they are true. Not so with falsehood: It follows from our definition of consistency that an *inconsistent* proposition must be *false.* (We have relied on this idea in explaining how a reductio ad absurdum works.)

Assertions or claims that are not consistent can take either of two forms. Suppose you assert proposition 14, that abortion is homicide, early in an essay you are writing, but later you assert that

18. Abortion is harmless.

You have now asserted a position on abortion that is strictly contrary to the one with which you began; contrary in the sense that both assertions 14 and 18 cannot be true. It is simply not true that, if an abortion involves killing a human being (which is what *homicide* strictly means), then it causes no one any harm (killing a person always causes harm—even if it is excusable, justifiable, not wrong, the best thing to do in the circumstances, and so on). Notice that although 14 and 18 cannot both be true, they can both be false. In fact, many people who are perplexed about the morality of abortion believe precisely this. They concede that abortion does harm the fetus, so 18 must be false; but they also believe that abortion doesn't kill a person, so 14 must also be false.

Or consider another, simpler case. If you describe the glass as half empty and I describe it as half full, both of us can be right; the two assertions are consistent, even though they sound vaguely incompatible. (This is the reason that disputing over whether the glass is half full or half empty has become the popular paradigm of a futile, purely *verbal disagreement*.) But if I describe the glass as half empty whereas you insist that it is two-thirds empty, then we have a real disagreement; your description and mine are strictly contrary, in that both cannot be true—although both can be false. (Both are false if the glass is only one-quarter full.)

This, by the way, enables us to define the difference between a pair of **contradictory** propositions and a pair of **contrary** propositions. Two propositions are contrary if and only if both cannot be true (though both can be false); two propositions are contradictory if and only if they are such that if one is true the other must be false, and vice versa. Thus, if Jack says that Alice Walker's *The Color Purple* is a better novel than Mark Twain's *Huckleberry Finn*, and Jill says, "No, *Huckleberry Finn* is better than *The Color Purple*," she is contradicting Jack. If what either one of them says is true, then what the other says must be false.

A more subtle case of contradiction arises when two or more of one's own beliefs implicitly contradict each other. We may find ourselves saying "Travel is broadening," and saying an hour later, "People don't really change." Just beneath the surface of these two beliefs lies a self-contradiction: How can travel broaden us unless it influences—and changes—our beliefs, values, and outlook? But if we can't really change ourselves, then traveling to new places won't change us, either. (Indeed, there is a Roman saying to the effect that travelers change the skies above them, not their hearts.) "Travel is broadening" and "People don't change" collide with each other; something has to give.

Our point, of course, is not that you must never say today something that contradicts something you said yesterday. Far from it; if you think you were mistaken yesterday, of course you will take a different position today. But what you want to avoid is what George Orwell called *doublethink* in his novel *1984*: "*Doublethink* means the power of holding two contradictory beliefs in one's mind simultaneously, and accepting them both."

Genuine contradiction, and not merely contrary assertion, is the situation we should expect to find in some disputes. Someone advances a thesis—such as the assertion in 14, *Abortion is homicide*—and someone else flatly contradicts it by the simple expedient of negating it, thus:

19. Abortion is not homicide.

If we can trust public opinion polls, many of us are not sure whether to agree with 14 or with 19. But we should agree that whichever is true, *both* cannot be true, and *both* cannot be false. The two assertions, between them, exclude all other possibilities; they pose a forced choice for our belief. (Again, we have met this idea, too, in a reductio ad absurdum.)

Now it is one thing for Jack and Jill in a dispute or argument to contradict each other. It is quite another matter for Jack to contradict himself. One wants (or should want) to avoid self-contradiction because of the embarrassing position in which one then finds oneself. Once I have contradicted myself, what are others to believe I really believe? What, indeed, *do* I believe, for that matter?

It may be, as Emerson observed, that a "foolish consistency is the hobgoblin of little minds"—that is, it may be shortsighted to purchase a consistency in one's beliefs at the expense of flying in the face of common sense. But making an effort to avoid a foolish inconsistency is the hallmark of serious thinking.

While we are speaking of inconsistency, we should spend a moment on **paradox.** The word refers to two different things:

- an assertion that is essentially self-contradictory and therefore cannot be true and
- a seemingly contradictory assertion that nevertheless may be true.

An example of the first might be, "Evaluations concerning quality in literature are all a matter of personal judgment, but Shakespeare is the world's greatest writer." It is hard to make any sense out of this assertion. Contrast it with a paradox of the second sort, a *seeming* contradiction that may make sense, such as "The longest way round is the shortest way home," or "Work is more fun than fun," or "The best way to find happiness is not to look for it." Here we have assertions that are striking because as soon as we hear them we realize that, although they seem inconsistent and self-defeating, they contain (or may contain) profound truths. Paradoxes of this second sort are especially common in religious texts, where they may imply a mysterious reality concealed by a world of contradictory appearances. Examples are "Some who are last shall be first, and some who are first shall be last" (Jesus, quoted in Luke 13:30), and "Death, thou shalt die" (the poet John Donne, alluding to the idea that the person who has faith in Jesus dies to this world but lives eternally). If you use the word *paradox* in your own writing—for instance, to characterize an argument that you are reading—be sure that your reader will understand in which sense you are using the word. (And, of course, you will not want to write paradoxes of the first, self-contradictory sort.)

INDUCTION

Deduction involves logical thinking that applies to any assertion or claim whatever—because every possible statement, true or false, has its deductive logical consequences. Induction is relevant to one kind of assertion only; namely, to **empirical** or *factual* claims. Other kinds of assertions (such as definitions, mathematical equations, and moral or legal norms) simply are not the product of inductive reasoning and cannot serve as a basis for further inductive thinking.

And so, in studying the methods of induction, we are exploring tactics and strategies useful in gathering and then using **evidence**—empirical, observational, experimental—in support of a belief as its ground. Modern scientific knowledge is the product of these methods, and they differ somewhat from one science to another because they depend on the theories and technology appropriate to each of the sciences. Here, all we can do is discuss generally the more abstract features common to inductive inquiry generally. For fuller details, you must eventually consult your local physicist, chemist, geologist, or their colleagues and counterparts in other scientific fields.

Observation and Inference

Let us begin with a simple example. Suppose we have evidence (actually we don't, but that will not matter for our purposes) in support of the claim that

1. In a sample of 500 smokers, 230 persons observed have cardiovascular disease.

The basis for asserting 1—the evidence or ground—would be, presumably, straightforward physical examination of the 500 persons in the sample, one by one.

With this claim in hand, we can think of the purpose and methods of induction as being pointed in both of two opposite directions: toward establishing the basis or ground of the very empirical proposition with which we start (in this example, the observation stated in 1) or toward understanding what that observation indicates or suggests as a more general, inclusive, or fundamental fact of nature.

In each case, we start from something we *do* know (or take for granted and treat as a sound starting point)—some fact of nature, perhaps a striking or commonplace event that we have observed and recorded—and then go on to something we do *not* fully know and perhaps cannot directly observe. In example 1, only the second of these two orientations is of any interest, and so let us concentrate exclusively on it. Let us also generously treat as a *method* of induction any regular pattern or style of nondeductive reasoning that we could use to support a claim such as that in 1.

Anyone truly interested in the observed fact that *230 of 500 smokers have cardiovascular disease* is likely to start speculating about, and thus be interested in finding out, whether any or all of several other propositions are also true. For example, one might wonder whether

> 2. *All* smokers have cardiovascular disease or will develop it during their lifetimes.

This claim is a straightforward generalization of the original observation as reported in claim 1. When we think inductively about the linkage between 1 and 2, we are reasoning from an observed sample (some smokers—that is, 230 of the 500 *observed*) to the entire membership of a more inclusive class (*all* smokers, whether observed or not). The fundamental question raised by reasoning from the narrower claim 1 to the broader claim 2 is whether we have any ground for believing that what is true of *some* members of a class is true of them *all*. So the difference between 1 and 2 is that of *quantity* or scope.

We can also think inductively about the *relation* between the factors mentioned in 1. Having observed data as reported in 1, we may be tempted to assert a different and profounder kind of claim:

> 3. Smoking *causes* cardiovascular disease.

Here our interest is not merely in generalizing from a sample to a whole class; it is the far more important one of *explaining* the observation with which we began in claim 1. Certainly the preferred, even if not the only, mode of explanation for a natural phenomenon is a *causal* explanation. In proposition 3, we propose to explain the presence of one phenomenon (cardiovascular disease) by the prior occurrence of an independent phenomenon (smoking). The observation reported in 1 is now being used as evidence or support for this new conjecture stated in 3.

Our original claim in 1 asserted no causal relation between anything and anything else; whatever the cause of cardiovascular disease may be, that cause is not observed, mentioned, or assumed in assertion 1. Similarly, the observation asserted in claim 1 is consistent with many explanations. For example, the explanation of 1 might not be 3, but some other, undetected, carcinogenic factor unrelated to smoking—for instance, exposure to high levels of radon. The question one now faces is what can be added to 1, or teased out of it, to produce an adequate ground for claiming 3. (We shall return to this example for closer scrutiny.)

But there is a third way to go beyond 1. Instead of a straightforward generalization, as we had in 2, or a pronouncement on the cause of a phenomenon, as in 3, we might have a somewhat more complex and cautious further claim in mind, such as this:

4. Smoking is a factor in the causation of cardiovascular disease in some persons.

This proposition, like 3, advances a claim about causation. But 4 is obviously a weaker claim than 3. That is, other observations, theories, or evidence that would require us to reject 3 might be consistent with 4; evidence that would support 4 could easily fail to be enough to support 3. Consequently, it is even possible that 4 is true although 3 is false, because 4 allows for other (unmentioned) factors in the causation of cardiovascular disease (genetic or dietary factors, for example) that may not be found in all smokers.

Propositions 2, 3, and 4 differ from proposition 1 in an important respect. We began by assuming that 1 states an empirical fact based on direct observation, whereas these others do not. Instead, they state empirical *hypotheses* or conjectures—tentative generalizations not fully confirmed—each of which goes beyond the observed facts asserted in 1. Each of 2, 3, and 4 can be regarded as an *inductive inference* from 1. We can also say that 2, 3, and 4 are hypotheses relative to 1, even if relative to some other starting point (such as all the information that scientists today really have about smoking and cardiovascular disease) they are not.

Probability

Another way of formulating the last point is to say that whereas proposition 1, a statement of observed fact (*230 out of 500 smokers have cardiovascular disease*), has a **probability** of 1.0—that is, it is absolutely certain—the probability of each of the hypotheses stated in 2, 3, and 4, *relative* to 1 is smaller than 1.0. (We need not worry here about how much smaller than 1.0 the probabilities are, nor about how to calculate these probabilities precisely.) Relative to some starting point other than 1, however, the probability of these same three hypotheses might be quite different. Of course, it still would not be 1.0, absolute certainty. But it takes only a moment's reflection to realize that, whatever may be the probability of 2 or 3 or 4 relative to 1, those probabilities in each case will be quite different relative to different information, such as this:

5. Ten persons observed in a sample of 500 smokers have cardiovascular disease.

The idea that a *given proposition can have different probabilities* relative to different bases is fundamental to all inductive reasoning. It can be convincingly illustrated by the following example. Suppose we want to consider the probability of this proposition being true:

6. Susanne Smith will live to be eighty.

Taken as an abstract question of fact, we cannot even guess what the probability is with any assurance. But we can do better than guess; we can in fact even calculate the answer, if we are given some further information. Thus, suppose we are told that

7. Susanne Smith is seventy-nine.

Our original question then becomes one of determining the probability that 6 is true given 7; that is, relative to the evidence contained in proposition 7. No doubt, if Susanne Smith really is seventy-nine, then the probability that she will live to be eighty is greater than if we know only that

8. Susanne Smith is more than nine years old.

Obviously, a lot can happen to Susanne in the seventy years between nine and seventy-nine that is not very likely to happen to her in the one year between seventy-nine and eighty. And so, proposition 6 is more probable relative to proposition 7 than it is relative to proposition 8.

Let us suppose for the sake of the argument that the following is true:

9. Ninety percent of the women alive at seventy-nine live to be eighty.

Given this additional information, and the information that Susanne is seventy-nine, we now have a basis for answering our original question about proposition 6 with some precision. But suppose, in addition to 8, we are also told that

10. Susanne Smith is suffering from inoperable cancer.

and also that

11. The survival rate for women suffering from inoperable cancer is 0.6 years (that is, the average life span for women after a diagnosis of inoperable cancer is about seven months).

With this new information, the probability that 6 will be true has dropped significantly, all because we can now estimate the probability in relation to a new body of evidence.

The probability of an event, thus, is not a fixed number but one that varies because it is always relative to some evidence—and given different evidence, one and the same event can have different probabilities. In other words, the probability of any event is always relative to how much is known (assumed, believed), and because different persons may know different things about a given event, or the same person may know different things at different times, one and the same event can have two or more probabilities. This conclusion is not a paradox but a logical consequence of the concept of what it is for an event to have (that is, to be assigned) a probability.

If we shift to the *calculation* of probabilities, we find that generally we have two ways to calculate them. One way to proceed is by the method of **a priori** or **equal probabilities**—that is, by reference to the relevant possibilities taken abstractly and apart from any other information. Thus, in an election contest with only two candidates, Smith and Jones, each of the candidates has a fifty-fifty chance of winning (whereas in a three-candidate race, each candidate would have one chance in three of winning). Therefore, the probability that Smith will win is 0.5, and the probability that Jones will win is also 0.5. (The sum of the probabilities of all possible independent outcomes must always equal 1.0, which is obvious enough if you think about it.)

But in politics the probabilities are not reasonably calculated so abstractly. We know that many empirical factors affect the outcome of an election and that a calculation of probabilities in ignorance of those factors is likely to be drastically misleading. In our example of the two-candidate election, suppose Smith has strong party support and is the incumbent, whereas Jones represents a party long out of power and is further handicapped by being relatively unknown. No one who knows anything about electoral politics would give Jones the same chance of winning as Smith. The two events are not equiprobable in relation to all the information available.

Not only that, a given event can have more than one probability. This happens whenever we calculate a probability by relying on different bodies of data that report how often the event in question has been observed to happen. Probabilities calculated in this way are **relative frequencies.** Our earlier hypothetical example of Susanne Smith provides an illustration. If she is a smoker and we have observed that 100 out of a random set of 500 smokers are observed to have cardiovascular disease, we have a basis for claiming that she has a probability of 100 in 500, or 0.2 (one-fifth), of having this disease. However, if we had other data showing that 250 out of 500 women smokers ages eighty or older have cardiovascular disease, we have a basis for believing that there is a probability of 250 in 500, or 0.5 (one-half), that she has this disease. Notice, of course, that in both calculations we assume that Susanne Smith is not among the persons we have examined. In both cases we infer the probability with which she has this disease from observing its frequency in populations that exclude her.

Both methods of calculating probabilities are legitimate; in each case the calculation is relative to observed circumstances. But as the examples show, it is most reasonable to have recourse to the method of equiprobabilities only when few or no other factors affecting possible outcomes are known.

Mill's Methods

Let us return to our earlier discussion of smoking and cardiovascular disease and consider in greater detail the question of a causal connection between the two phenomena. We began thus:

1. In a sample of 500 smokers, 230 persons observed have cardiovascular disease.

We regarded 1 as an observed fact, though in truth, of course, it is mere supposition. Our question now is, how might we augment this information so as to strengthen our confidence that

3. Smoking *causes* cardiovascular disease.

or at least

4. Smoking is a factor in the causation of cardiovascular disease in some persons.

Suppose further examination showed that

12. In the sample of 230 smokers with cardiovascular disease, no other suspected factor (such as genetic predisposition, lack of physical exercise, age over fifty) was also observed.

Such an observation would encourage us to believe 3 or 4 is true. Why? We are encouraged to believe it because we are inclined to believe also that whatever the cause of a phenomenon is, it must *always* be present when its effect is present. Thus, the inference from 1 to 3 or 4 is supported by 12, using **Mill's Method of Agreement,** named after the British philosopher, John Stuart Mill (1806–1873), who first formulated it. It is called a method of agreement because of the way in which the inference relies on *agreement* among the observed phenomena where a presumed cause is thought to be *present.*

Let us now suppose that in our search for evidence to support 3 or 4 we conduct additional research and discover that

13. In a sample of 500 nonsmokers, selected to be representative of both sexes, different ages, dietary habits, exercise patterns, and so on, none is observed to have cardiovascular disease.

This observation would further encourage us to believe that we had obtained significant additional confirmation of 3 or 4. Why? Because we now know that factors present (such as male sex, lack of exercise, family history of cardiovascular disease) in cases where the effect is absent (no cardiovascular disease observed) cannot be the cause. This is an example of **Mill's Method of Difference,** so called because the cause or causal factor of an effect must be *different* from whatever the factors are that are present when the effect is *absent.*

Suppose now that, increasingly confident we have found the cause of cardiovascular disease, we study our first sample of 230 smokers ill with the disease, and discover this:

14. Those who smoke two or more packs of cigarettes daily for ten or more years have cardiovascular disease either much younger or much more severely than those who smoke less.

This is an application of **Mill's Method of Concomitant Variation,** perhaps the most convincing of the three methods. Here we deal not merely with the presence of the conjectured cause (smoking) or the absence of the effect we are studying (cardiovascular disease), as we were previously, but with the more interesting and subtler matter of the *degree and regularity of the correlation* of the supposed cause and effect. According to the observations reported in 14, it strongly appears that the more we have of the "cause" (smoking), the sooner or the more intense the onset of the "effect" (cardiovascular disease).

Notice, however, what happens to our confirmation of 3 and 4 if, instead of the observation reported in 14, we had observed

15. In a representative sample of 500 nonsmokers, cardiovascular disease was observed in 34 cases.

(Let us not pause here to explain what makes a sample more or less representative of a population, although the representativeness of samples is vital to all statistical reasoning.) Such an observation would lead us almost immediately to suspect some other or additional causal factor: Smoking might indeed be *a* factor in causing cardiovascular disease, but it can hardly be *the* cause because (using Mill's Method of Difference) we cannot have the effect, as we do in the observed sample reported in 15, unless we also have the cause.

An observation such as the one in 15, however, is likely to lead us to think our hypothesis that *smoking causes cardiovascular disease* has been disconfirmed. But we have a fallback position ready; we can still defend a weaker hypothesis, namely 4, *Smoking is a factor in the causation of cardiovascular disease in some persons.* Even if 3 stumbles over the evidence in 15, 4 does not. It is still quite possible that smoking is a factor in causing this disease, even if it is not the *only* factor—and if it is, then 4 is true.

Confirmation, Mechanism, and Theory

Notice that in the discussion so far, we have spoken of the *confirmation* of a hypothesis, such as our causal claim in 4, but not of its *verification*. (Similarly, we have imagined very different evidence, such as that stated in 15, leading us to speak of the *dis*confirmation of 3, though not of its *falsi*fication.) Confirmation (getting some evidence for) is weaker than verification (getting sufficient evidence to regard as true), and our (imaginary) evidence so far in favor of 4 falls well short of conclusive support. Further research—the study of more representative or much larger samples, for example—might yield very different observations. It might lead us to conclude that although initial research had confirmed our hypothesis about smoking as the cause of cardiovascular disease, the additional information obtained subsequently disconfirmed the hypothesis. For most interesting hypotheses, both in detective stories and in modern science, there is both confirming and disconfirming evidence simultaneously. The challenge is to evaluate the hypothesis by considering such conflicting evidence.

As long as we confine our observations to *correlations* of the sort reported in our several (imaginary) observations, such as proposition 1, *230 smokers in a group of 500 have cardiovascular disease,* or 12, *230 smokers with the disease share no other suspected factors,* such as lack of exercise, any defense of a *causal* hypothesis such as claim 3, *Smoking causes cardiovascular disease,* or claim 4, *Smoking is a factor in causing the disease,* is not likely to convince the skeptic or lead those with beliefs alternative to 3 and 4 to abandon them and agree with us. Why is that? It is because a causal hypothesis without any account of the *underlying mechanism* by means of which the (alleged) cause produces the effect will seem superficial. Only when we can specify in detail *how* the (alleged) cause produces the effect will the causal hypothesis be convincing.

In other cases, in which no mechanism can be found, we seek instead to embed the causal hypothesis in a larger *theory,* one that rules out as incompatible any causal hypothesis except the favored one. (That is, we appeal to the test of consistency and thereby bring deductive reasoning to bear on our problem.) Thus, perhaps we cannot specify any mechanism—any underlying structure that generates a regular sequence of events, one of which is the effect we are studying—to explain why, for example, the gravitational mass of a body causes it to attract other bodies. But we can embed this claim in a larger body of physical theory that rules out as inconsistent any alternative causal explanation. To do that convincingly in regard to any given causal hypothesis, as this example suggests, requires detailed knowledge of the current state of the relevant body of scientific theory, something far beyond our aim or need to consider in further detail here.

FALLACIES

The straight road on which sound reasoning proceeds gives little latitude for cruising about. Irrationality, carelessness, passionate attachment to one's unexamined beliefs, and the sheer complexity of some issues occasionally spoil the reasoning of even the best of us. Although in this book we reprint many varied voices and arguments, we hope we have reprinted no readings that exhibit the most flagrant errors or commit the graver abuses against the canons of good reasoning. Nevertheless, an inventory of those abuses and their close examination can be an instructive (as well as an amusing) exercise—instructive because the diagnosis and repair of error helps to fix more clearly the principles of sound reasoning on which such remedial labors depend; amusing because we are so constituted that our perception of the nonsense of others can stimulate our mind, warm our heart, and give us comforting feelings of superiority.

The discussion that follows, then, is a quick tour through the twisting lanes, mudflats, forests, and quicksands of the faults that one sometimes encounters in reading arguments that stray from the highway of clear thinking.

Fallacies of Ambiguity

Ambiguity   Near the center of the town of Concord, Massachusetts, is an empty field with a sign reading "Old Calf Pasture." Hmm. A pasture in former times in which calves grazed? A pasture now in use for old calves? An erstwhile pasture for old calves? These alternative readings arise because of **ambiguity;** brevity in the sign has produced a group of words that give rise to more than one possible interpretation, confusing the reader and (presumably) frustrating the sign writer's intentions.

Consider a more complex example. Suppose someone asserts *People have equal rights* and also *Everyone has a right to property.* Many people believe both these claims, but their combination involves an ambiguity. According to one interpretation, the two claims entail that everyone has an *equal right* to property. (That is, you and I each have an equal right to whatever property we have.) But the two claims can also be interpreted to mean that everyone has a *right to equal property.* (That is, whatever property you have a right to, I have a right to the same, or at least equivalent, property.) The latter interpretation is revolutionary, whereas the former is not. Arguments over equal rights often involve this ambiguity.

Division   In the Bible, we are told that the apostles of Jesus were twelve and that Matthew was an apostle. Does it follow that Matthew was twelve? No. To argue in this way from a property of a group to a property of a member of that group is to commit the **fallacy of division.** The example of the apostles may not be a very tempting instance of this error; here is a classic version that is a bit more interesting. If it is true that the average American family has 1.8 children, does it follow that your brother and sister-in-law are likely to have 1.8 children? If you think it does, you have committed the fallacy of division.

Composition   Could an all-star team of professional basketball players beat the Boston Celtics in their heyday—say, the team of 1985 to 1986? Perhaps in one game or two, but probably not in seven out of a dozen games in a row. As students of the game know, teamwork is an indispensable part of outstanding performance, and the 1985 to 1986 Celtics were famous for their self-sacrificing style of play.

The **fallacy of composition** can be convincingly illustrated, therefore, in this argument: *A team of five NBA all-stars is the best team in basketball if each of the five players is the best at his position.* The fallacy is called composition because the reasoning commits the error of arguing from the true premise that each member of a group has a certain property to the not necessarily true conclusion that the group (the composition) itself has the property. (That is, because *A* is the best player at forward, *B* is the best center, and so on, therefore, the team of *A, B, . . .* is the best team.)

Equivocation   In a delightful passage in Lewis Carroll's *Through the Looking-Glass,* the king asks his messenger, "Who did you pass on the road?" and the messenger replies, "Nobody." This prompts the king to observe, "Of course, Nobody walks slower than you," provoking the messenger's sullen response: "I do my best. I'm sure nobody walks much faster than I do." At this the king remarks with surprise, "He can't do that or else he'd have been here first!" (This, by the way, is the classic predecessor of the famous comic dialogue "Who's on First?" between the comedians Bud Abbott and Lou Costello.) The king and the messenger are equivocating on the term *nobody.* The messenger uses it in the normal way as an indefinite pronoun equivalent to "not anyone." But the king uses the word as though it were a proper noun, *Nobody,* the rather odd name of some person. No wonder the king and the messenger talk right past each other.

Equivocation (from the Latin for "equal voice"— that is, giving utterance to two meanings at the same time in one word or phrase) can ruin otherwise good reasoning, as in this example: *Euthanasia is a good death; one dies a good death when one dies peacefully in old age; therefore, euthanasia is dying peacefully in old age.* The etymology of *euthanasia* is literally "a good death," and so the first premise is true. And the second premise is certainly plausible. But the conclusion of this syllogism is false. Euthanasia cannot be defined as a peaceful death in one's old age, for two reasons. First, euthanasia requires the intervention of another person who kills someone (or lets the person die); second, even a very young person can be euthanized. The problem arises because "a good death" is used in the second premise in a manner that does not apply to euthanasia. Both meanings of "a good death" are legitimate, but when used together, they constitute an equivocation that spoils the argument.

The fallacy of equivocation takes us from the discussion of confusions in individual claims or grounds to the more troublesome fallacies that infect the linkages between the claims we make and the grounds (or reasons) for them. These are the fallacies that occur in statements that, following the vocabulary of the Toulmin method, are called the *warrant* of reasoning. Each fallacy is an example of reasoning that involves a **non sequitur** (Latin for "It does not follow"). That is, the *claim* (the conclusion) does not follow from the *grounds* (the premises).

For a start, here is an obvious non sequitur: "He went to the movies on three consecutive nights, so he must love movies." Why doesn't the claim ("He must love movies") follow from the grounds ("He went to the movies on three consecutive nights")? Perhaps the person was just fulfilling an assignment in a film course (maybe he even hated movies so much that he had postponed three assignments to see films and now had to see them all in quick succession), or maybe he went with a girlfriend who was a movie buff, or maybe . . .—well, one can think of any number of other possible reasons.

Fallacies of Presumption

Distorting the Facts   Facts can be distorted either intentionally (to deceive or mislead) or unintentionally, and in either case usually (but not invariably) to the benefit of whoever is doing the distortion. Consider this not entirely hypothetical case. A pharmaceutical company spends millions of dollars to develop a new drug that will help pregnant women avoid spontaneous abortion. The company reports its findings, but it does not also report that it has learned from its researchers of a serious downside for this drug in many cases, resulting in deformed limbs in the neonate. Had the company informed the public of this fact, the drug would not have been certified for use.

Here is another case. Half a century ago the surgeon general reported that smoking cigarettes increased the likelihood that smokers would eventually suffer from lung cancer. The cigarette manufacturers vigorously protested that the surgeon general relied on inconclusive research and was badly misleading the public about the health risks of smoking. It later turned out that the tobacco companies knew that smoking increased the risk of lung cancer—a fact established by the company's own laboratories but concealed from the public. Today, thanks to public access to all the facts, it is commonplace knowledge that inhaled smoke—including secondhand smoke—is a risk factor for many illnesses.

Post Hoc, Ergo Propter Hoc   One of the most tempting errors in reasoning is to ground a claim about causation on an observed temporal sequence; that is, to argue "after this, therefore because of this" (which is what the phrase ***post hoc, ergo propter hoc*** means in Latin). Nearly forty years ago, when the medical community first announced that smoking tobacco caused lung cancer, advocates for the tobacco industry replied that doctors were guilty of this fallacy.

These industry advocates argued that medical researchers had merely noticed that in some people, lung cancer developed *after* considerable smoking, indeed, years after; but (they insisted) this correlation was not at all the same as a causal relation between smoking and lung cancer. True enough. The claim that *A causes B* is not the same as the claim that *B* comes after *A*. After all, it was possible that smokers as a group had some other common trait and that this factor was the true cause of their cancer.

As the long controversy over the truth about the causation of lung cancer shows, to avoid the appearance of fallacious *post hoc* reasoning one needs to find some way to link the observed phenomena (the correlation of smoking and the onset of lung cancer). This step requires some further theory and preferably some experimental evidence for the exact sequence or physical mechanism, in full detail, of how ingestion of tobacco smoke is a crucial factor—and is not merely an accidental or happenstance prior event—in the subsequent development of the cancer.

Many Questions   The old saw, "When did you stop beating your wife?" illustrates the **fallacy of many questions.** This question, as one can readily see, is unanswerable unless all three of its implicit presuppositions are true. The questioner presupposes that (1) the addressee has or had a wife, (2) he has beaten her, and (3) he has stopped beating her. If any of these presuppositions is false, then the question is pointless; it cannot be answered strictly and simply with a date.

Hasty Generalization   From a logical point of view, **hasty generalization** is the precipitous move from true assertions about *one* or a *few* instances to dubious or even false assertions about *all*. For example, while it may be true, based on your personal experience, that the only native Hungarians you personally know do not speak English very well, that is no basis for asserting that all Hungarians do not speak English very well. Or if the clothes you recently ordered online turn out not to fit very well, it doesn't follow that *all* online clothes turn out to be too large or too small. A hasty generalization usually lies behind a **stereotype**—that is, a person or event treated as typical of a whole class. Thus, in 1914, after the German invasion of Belgium, during which some atrocities were committed by the invaders, the German troops were quickly stereotyped by the Allies as brutal savages who skewered helpless babies on their bayonets.

The Slippery Slope   One of the most familiar arguments against any type of government regulation is that if it is allowed, then it will be just the first step down the path that leads to ruinous interference, overregulation, and totalitarian control. Fairly often we encounter this mode of argument in the public debates over handgun control, the censorship of pornography, and physician-assisted suicide. The argument is called the **slippery slope argument** (or the **wedge argument,** from the way we use the thin end of a wedge to split solid things apart; it is also called, rather colorfully, "letting the camel's nose under the tent"). The fallacy here is in implying that the first step necessarily leads to the second, and so on down the slope to disaster, when in fact there is no necessary slide from the first step to the second. (Would handgun registration lead to a police state? Well, it hasn't in Switzerland.) Sometimes the argument takes the form of claiming that a seemingly innocent or even attractive principle that is being applied in a given case (censorship of pornography, to avoid promoting sexual violence) requires one for the sake of consistency to apply the same principle in other cases, only with absurd and catastrophic results (censorship of everything in print, to avoid hurting anyone's feelings).

Here's an extreme example of this fallacy in action:

> Automobiles cause more deaths than handguns do. If you oppose handguns on the ground that doing so would save lives of the innocent, you'll soon find yourself wanting to outlaw the automobile.

Does opposition to handguns have this consequence? Not necessarily. Most people accept without dispute the right of society to regulate the operation of motor vehicles by requiring drivers to have a license, a greater restriction than many states impose on gun ownership. Besides, a gun is a lethal weapon designed to kill, whereas an automobile or truck is a vehicle designed for transportation. Private ownership and use in both cases entail risks of death to the innocent. But there is no inconsistency in a society's refusal to tolerate this risk in the case of guns and its willingness to do so in the case of automobiles.

Closely related to the slippery slope is what lawyers call a **parade of horrors,** an array of examples of terrible consequences that will or might follow if we travel down a certain path. A good example appears in Justice William Brennan's opinion for the Supreme Court in *Texas v. Johnson* (1989), concerned with a Texas law against burning the American flag in political protest. If this law is allowed to stand, Brennan suggests, we may next find laws against burning the presidential seal, state flags, and the Constitution.

False Analogy   Argument by analogy, as we point out in Chapter 3 and as many of the selections in this book show, is a familiar and even indispensable mode of argument. But it can be treacherous because it runs the risk of the **fallacy of false analogy.** Unfortunately, we have no simple or foolproof way of distinguishing between the useful, legitimate analogies and the others. The key question to ask yourself is this: Do the two things put into analogy differ in any essential and relevant respect, or are they different only in unimportant and irrelevant aspects?

In a famous example from his discussion in support of suicide, philosopher David Hume rhetorically asked: "It would be no crime in me to divert the Nile or Danube from its course, were I able to effect such purposes. Where then is the crime of turning a few ounces of blood from their natural channel?" This is a striking analogy, except that it rests on a false assumption. No one has the right to divert the Nile or the Danube or any other major international watercourse; it would be a catastrophic crime to do so without the full consent of people living in the region, their government, and so forth. Therefore, arguing by analogy, one might well say that no one has the right to take his or her own life, either. Thus, Hume's own analogy can be used to argue against his thesis that suicide is no crime. But let us ignore the way in which his example can be turned against him. The analogy is a terrible one in any case. Isn't it obvious that the Nile, whatever its exact course, would continue to nourish Egypt and the Sudan, whereas the blood flowing out of someone's veins will soon leave that person dead? The fact that the blood is the same blood, whether in one's body or in a pool on the floor (just as the water of the Nile is the same body of water whatever path it follows to the sea) is, of course, irrelevant to the question of whether one has the right to commit suicide.

Let us look at a more complex example. During the 1960s, when the United States was convulsed over the purpose and scope of its military involvement in Southeast Asia, advocates of more vigorous U.S. military participation appealed to the so-called domino effect, supposedly inspired by a passing remark from President Eisenhower in the 1950s. The analogy refers to the way in which a row of standing dominoes will collapse, one after the other, if the first one is pushed. If Vietnam turns Communist, according to this analogy, so too will its neighbors, Laos and Cambodia, followed by Thailand and then Burma, until the whole region is as communist as China to the north. The domino analogy (or metaphor) provided, no doubt, a vivid illustration and effectively portrayed the worry of many anti-Communists. But did it really shed any light on the likely pattern of political and military developments in the region? The history of events there during the 1970s and 1980s did not bear out the domino analogy.

Straw Man   It is often tempting to reframe or report your opponent's thesis to make it easier to attack and perhaps refute it. If you do this in the course of an argument, you are creating a straw man, a thing of no substance and easily blown away. The straw man you've constructed is usually a radically conservative or extremely liberal thesis, which few if any would want to defend. That is why it is easier to refute than the view your opponent actually holds. "So you defend the death penalty—and all the horrible things done in its name. No one in his right mind would hold such a view." It's highly unlikely that your friend supports *everything* that has been done in the name of capital punishment—crucifixion and beheading, for example, or execution of the children of the guilty offender.

Special Pleading   We all have our favorites—relatives, friends, and neighbors—and we are all too likely to show that favoritism in unacceptable ways. How about this: "Yes, I know Billy hit Sally first, but he's my son. He's a good boy, and I know he must have had a good reason." Or this: "True, she's late for work again—the third time this week!—but her uncle's my friend, and it will be embarrassing to me if she is fired, so we'll just ignore it." Special pleading inevitably leads to unmerited advantages, as illustrated above.

Begging the Question   The argument over whether the death penalty is a deterrent illustrates another fallacy. From the fact that you live in a death-penalty state and were not murdered yesterday, we cannot infer that the death penalty was a deterrent. Yet it is tempting to make this inference, perhaps because—all unawares—we are relying on the **fallacy of begging the question.** If someone tacitly assumes from the start that the death penalty is an effective deterrent, then the fact that you weren't murdered yesterday certainly looks like evidence for the truth of that assumption. But it isn't, so long as there are competing but unexamined alternative explanations, as in this case. (The fallacy is called "begging the question," *petitio principii* in Latin, because the conclusion of the argument is hidden among its assumptions—and so the conclusion, not surprisingly, follows from the premises.)

Of course, the fact that you weren't murdered is *consistent* with the claim that the death penalty is an effective deterrent, just as someone else's being murdered is also consistent with that claim (for an effective deterrent need not be a *perfect* deterrent). In general, from the fact that two propositions are consistent with each other, we cannot infer that either is evidence for the other.

Note: The term "begging the question" is often wrongly used to mean "raises the question," as in "His action of burning the flag begs the question, What drove him to do such a thing?"

False Dichotomy   Sometimes oversimplification takes a more complex form, in which contrary possibilities are wrongly presented as though they were exhaustive and exclusive. "Either we get tough with drug users, or we must surrender and legalize all drugs." Really? What about doing neither and instead offering education and counseling, detoxification programs, and incentives to "Say no"? A favorite of debaters, **either/or** reasoning always runs the risk of ignoring a third (or fourth) possibility. Some disjunctions are indeed exhaustive: "Either we get tough with drug users, or we do not." This proposition, though vague (what does "get tough" really mean?), is a tautology; it cannot be false, and there is no third alternative. But most disjunctions do not express a pair of *contradictory* alternatives: They offer only a pair of *contrary* alternatives, and mere contraries do not exhaust the possibilities (recall our discussion of contraries versus contradictories on p. 359).

An example of **false dichotomy** can be found in the essay by Jeff Jacoby on flogging (p. 196). His entire discussion is built on the relative superiority of whipping over imprisonment, as though there was no alternative punishment worth considering. But of course, there is, notably community service (especially for white-collar offenders, juveniles, and many first offenders).

Oversimplification   "Poverty causes crime," "Taxation is unfair," "Truth is stranger than fiction"—these are examples of generalizations that exaggerate and therefore oversimplify the truth. Poverty as such can't be the sole cause of crime because many poor people do not break the law.

Some taxes may be unfairly high, others unfairly low—but there is no reason to believe that *every* tax is unfair to all those who have to pay it. Some true stories do amaze us as much or more than some fictional stories, but the reverse is true, too. (In the language of the Toulmin method, **oversimplification** is the result of a failure to use suitable modal qualifiers in formulating one's claims or grounds or backing.)

Red Herring The fallacy of **red herring,** less colorfully named irrelevant thesis, occurs when one tries to distract one's audience by invoking a consideration that is irrelevant to the topic under discussion. (This fallacy probably gets its name from the fact that a rotten herring, or a cured herring, which is reddish, will throw pursuing hounds off the right track.) Consider this case. Some critics, seeking to defend our government's refusal to sign the Kyoto accords to reduce global warming, argue that signing is supported mainly by left-leaning scientists. This argument supposedly shows that global warming—if there is such a thing—is not a serious, urgent issue. But claiming that the supporters of these accords are left-inclined is a red herring, an irrelevant thesis. By raising doubts about the political views of the advocates of signing, it distracts attention from the scientific question (Is there global warming?) and also from the separate political question (Ought the United States sign these accords?). The refusal of a government to sign these accords does not show there is no such thing as global warming. And even if all of the advocates of signing were left-leaning (they aren't), this fact (if it were a fact, but it isn't) would not show that worries about global warming are exaggerated.

Fallacies of Relevance

Tu Quoque The Romans had a word for it: *Tu quoque* means "you, too." Consider this: "You're a fine one, trying to persuade me to give up smoking when you indulge yourself with a pipe and a cigar from time to time. Maybe I should quit, but then so should you. As things stand now, however, it's hypocritical of you to complain about my smoking when you persist in the same habit." The fallacy is this: The merit of a person's argument has nothing to do with the person's character or behavior. Here, the assertion that smoking is bad for one's health is *not* weakened by the fact that a smoker offers the argument.

The Genetic Fallacy A member of the family of fallacies that includes poisoning the well and ad hominem is the **genetic fallacy.** Here the error takes the form of arguing against some claim by pointing out that its origin (genesis) is tainted or that it was invented by someone deserving our contempt. Thus, one might attack the ideas of the Declaration of Independence by pointing out that its principal author, Thomas Jefferson, was a slaveholder. Assuming that it is not anachronistic and inappropriate to criticize a public figure of two centuries ago for practicing slavery, and conceding that slavery is morally outrageous, it is nonetheless fallacious to attack the ideas or even the sincerity of the Declaration by attempting to impeach the credentials of its author. Jefferson's moral faults do not by themselves falsify, make improbable, or constitute counterevidence to the truth or other merits of the claims made in his writings. At most, one's faults cast doubt on one's integrity or sincerity if one makes claims at odds with one's practice.

The genetic fallacy can take other forms less closely allied to ad hominem argument. For example, an opponent of the death penalty might argue,

> Capital punishment arose in barbarous times; but we claim to be civilized; therefore, we should discard this relic of the past.

Such reasoning shouldn't be persuasive because the question of the death penalty for our society must be decided by the degree to which it serves our purposes—justice and defense against crime, presumably—to which its historic origins are irrelevant. The practices of beer- and wine-making are as old as human civilization, but their origin in antiquity is no reason to outlaw them in our time. The curious circumstances in which something originates usually play no role whatever in its validity. Anyone who would argue that nothing good could possibly come from molds and fungi is refuted by Sir Alexander Fleming's discovery of penicillin in 1928.

Poisoning the Well   During the 1970s some critics of the Equal Rights Amendment (ERA) argued against it by pointing out that Marx and Engels, in their *Communist Manifesto,* favored equality of women and men—and therefore the ERA was immoral, undesirable, and perhaps even a Communist plot. This kind of reasoning is an attempt to **poison the well;** that is, an attempt to shift attention from the merits of the argument—the validity of the reasoning, the truth of the claims—to the source or origin of the argument. Such criticism deflects attention from the real issue; namely, whether the view in question is true and what the quality of evidence is in its support. The mere fact that Marx (or Hitler, for that matter) believed something does not show that the belief is false or immoral; just because some scoundrel believes the world is round, that is no reason for you to believe it is flat.

Appeal to Ignorance   In the controversy over the death penalty, the issues of deterrence and executing the innocent are bound to be raised. Because no one knows how many innocent persons have been convicted for murder and wrongfully executed, it is tempting for abolitionists to argue that the death penalty is too risky. It is equally tempting for the proponent of the death penalty to argue that since no one knows how many people have been deterred from murder by the threat of execution, we abolish it at our peril.

Each of these arguments suffers from the same flaw: the **fallacy of appeal to ignorance.** Each argument invites the audience to draw an inference from a premise that is unquestionably true—but what is that premise? It asserts that there is something "we don't know." But what we *don't* know cannot be *evidence* for (or against) anything. Our ignorance is no reason for believing anything, except perhaps that we ought to try to undertake an appropriate investigation in order to reduce our ignorance and replace it with reliable information.

Ad Hominem   Closely allied to poisoning the well is another fallacy, **ad hominem** argument (from the Latin for "against the person"). A critic can easily yield to the temptation to attack an argument or theory by trying to impeach or undercut the credentials of its advocates.

Example: Jones is arguing that prayer should not be permitted in public schools, and Smith responds by pointing out that Jones has twice been convicted of assaulting members of the clergy. Jones's behavior doubtless is reprehensible, but the issue is not Jones, it is prayer in school, and what must be scrutinized is Jones's argument, not his police record or his character.

Appeal to Authority   The example of Jefferson given to illustrate the genetic fallacy can be turned around to illustrate another fallacy. One might easily imagine someone from the South in 1860 defending the slave-owning society of that day by appealing to the fact that no less a person than Jefferson—a brilliant public figure, thinker, and leader by any measure—owned slaves. Or today one might defend capital punishment on the ground that Abraham Lincoln, surely one of the nation's greatest presidents, signed many death warrants during the Civil War, authorizing the execution of Union soldiers. No doubt the esteem in which such figures as Jefferson and Lincoln are deservedly held amounts to impressive endorsement for whatever acts and practices, policies and institutions, they supported. But the **authority** of these figures in itself is not evidence for the truth of their views, and so their authority cannot be a reason for anyone to agree with them. Obviously, Jefferson and Lincoln themselves could not support their beliefs by pointing to the fact that they held them. Because their own authority is no reason for them to believe what they believe, it is no reason for anyone else, either.

Sometimes the appeal to authority is fallacious because the authoritative person is not an expert on the issue in dispute. The fact that a high-energy physicist has won the Nobel Prize is no reason for attaching any special weight to her views on the causes of cancer, the reduction of traffic accidents, or the legalization of marijuana. On the other hand, one would be well advised to attend to her views on the advisability of ballistic missile-defense systems, for there may be a connection between the kind of research for which she received the prize and the defense research projects.

All of us depend heavily on the knowledge of various experts and authorities, and so we tend not to ignore their views. Conversely, we should resist the temptation to accord their views on diverse subjects the same respect that we grant them in the area of their expertise.

Appeal to Fear   The Romans called this fallacy *ad baculum*, "resorting to violence" (*baculum* means "stick," or "club"). Trying to persuade people to agree with you by threatening them with painful consequences is obviously an appeal that no rational person would contemplate. The violence need not be physical; if you threaten someone with the loss of a job, for instance, you are still using a stick. Violence or the threat of harmful consequences in the course of an argument is beyond reason and always shows the haste or impatience of those who appeal to it. It is also an indication that the argument on its merits would be unpersuasive, inconclusive, or worse. President Teddy Roosevelt's epigrammatic doctrine for the kind of foreign policy he favored — "Speak softly but carry a big stick" — illustrates an attempt to have it both ways, an appeal to reason for starters but a recourse to coercion, or the threat of coercion, as a backup if needed.

Finally, we add two fallacies, not easily embraced by Engel's three categories that have served us well thus far (ambiguity, erroneous presumption, and irrelevance): death by a thousand qualifications and protecting the hypothesis.

Death by a Thousand Qualifications   In a letter of recommendation sent in support of an applicant for a job on your newspaper, you find this sentence: "Young Smith was the best student I've ever taught in an English course." Pretty strong endorsement, you think, except that you do not know, because you have not been told, the letter writer is a very junior faculty member, has been teaching for only two years, is an instructor in the history department, taught a section of freshman English as a courtesy for a sick colleague, and had only eight students enrolled in the course. Thanks to these implicit qualifications, the letter writer did not lie or exaggerate in his praise; but the effect of his sentence on you, the unwitting reader, is quite misleading. The explicit claim in the letter, and its impact on you, is quite different from the tacitly qualified claim in the mind of the writer.

Death by a thousand qualifications gets its name from the ancient torture of death by a thousand small cuts. Thus, a bold assertion can be virtually killed, its true content reduced to nothing, bit by bit, as all the appropriate or necessary qualifications are added to it. Consider another example. Suppose you hear a politician describing another country (let's call it Ruritania so as not to offend anyone) as a "democracy" — except it turns out that Ruritania doesn't have regular elections, lacks a written constitution, has no independent judiciary, prohibits religious worship except of the state-designated deity, and so forth. So what is left of the original claim that Ruritania is a democracy is little or nothing. The qualifications have taken all the content out of the original description.

Protecting the Hypothesis   In Chapter 3, we contrasted *reasoning* and *rationalization* (or the finding of bad reasons for what one intends to believe anyway). Rationalization can take subtle forms, as the following example indicates. Suppose you're standing with a friend on the shore or on a pier, and you watch as a ship heads out to sea. As it reaches the horizon, it slowly disappears—first the hull, then the upper decks, and finally the tip of the mast. Because the ship (you both assume) isn't sinking, it occurs to you that you have in this sequence of observations convincing evidence that the earth's surface is curved. Nonsense, says your companion. Light waves sag, or bend down, over distances of a few miles, and so a flat surface (such as the ocean) can intercept them. Hence the ship, which appears to be going "over" the horizon, really isn't: It's just moving steadily farther and farther away in a straight line. Your friend, you discover to your amazement, is a card-carrying member of the Flat Earth Society (yes, there really is such an organization). Now most of us would regard the idea that light rays bend down in the manner required by the Flat Earther's argument as a rationalization whose sole purpose is to protect the flat-earth doctrine against counterevidence. We would be convinced it was a rationalization, and not a very good one at that, if the Flat Earther held to it despite a patient and thorough explanation from a physicist that showed modern optical theory to be quite incompatible with the view that light waves sag.

✓   A CHECKLIST FOR EVALUATING AN ARGUMENT
     FROM A LOGICAL POINT OF VIEW

☐ Is the argument purely deductive, purely inductive, or a mixture of the two?

☐ If it is deductive, is it valid?

☐ If it is valid, are all its premises and assumptions true?

☐ If it is not valid, what fallacy does it commit?

☐ If it is not valid, are the claims at least consistent with each other?

☐ If it is not valid, can you think of additional plausible assumptions that would make it valid?

☐ If the argument is inductive, on what observations is it based?

☐ If the argument is deductive, how probable are its premises and its conclusion?

☐ In any case, can you think of evidence that would further confirm the conclusion? Disconfirm the conclusion?

This example illustrates two important points about the *backing* of arguments. First, it is always possible to protect a hypothesis by abandoning adjacent or connected hypotheses; this is the tactic our Flat Earth friend has used. This maneuver is possible, however, only because—and this is the second point—whenever we test a hypothesis, we do so by taking for granted (usually quite unconsciously) many other hypotheses as well. So the evidence for the hypothesis we think we are confirming is impossible to separate entirely from the adequacy of the connected hypotheses. As long as we have no reason to doubt that light rays travel in straight lines (at least over distances of a few miles), our Flat Earth friend's argument is unconvincing. But once that hypothesis is itself put in doubt, the idea that looked at first to be a pathetic rationalization takes on an even more troublesome character.

There are, then, not one but two fallacies exposed by this example. The first and perhaps graver is in rigging your hypothesis so that *no matter what* observations are brought against it, you will count nothing as falsifying it. The second and subtler is in thinking that as you test one hypothesis, all of your other background beliefs are left safely to one side, immaculate and uninvolved. On the contrary, our beliefs form a corporate structure, intertwined and connected to each other with great complexity, and no one of them can ever be singled out for unique and isolated application, confirmation, or disconfirmation, to the world around us.

Exercise: Fallacies — or Not?

Here, for diversion and practice, are some fallacies in action. Some of these statements, however, are not fallacies. Can you tell which is which? Can you detect *what* has gone wrong in the cases where something has gone wrong? Please explain your reasoning.

1. Abortion is murder—and it doesn't matter whether we're talking about killing a human embryo or a human fetus.
2. Euthanasia is not a good thing, it's murder—and it doesn't matter how painful one's dying may be.
3. Never loan a tool to a friend. I did once and never got it back.
4. If the neighbors don't like our loud music, that's just too bad. After all, we have a right to listen to the music we like when and where we want to play it.
5. The Good Samaritan in the Bible was pretty foolish; he was taking grave risks with no benefits for him in sight.
6. "Shoot first and ask questions afterward" is a good epigram for the kind of foreign policy we need.
7. "You can fool some of the people all of the time, and you can fool all the people some of the time, but you can't fool all the people all of the time." That's what Abraham Lincoln said, and he was right.
8. It doesn't matter whether Shakespeare wrote the plays attributed to him. What matters is whether the plays are any good.

9. The Golden Gate Bridge in San Francisco ought to be closed down. After all, just look at all the suicides that have occurred there.

10. Reparations for African Americans are way overdue; it's just another version of the reparations eventually paid to the Japanese Americans who were wrongly interned in 1942 during World War II.

11. Animals don't have rights any more than do trees or stones. They don't have desires, either. What they have are feelings and needs.

12. The average American family is said to have 2.1 children. This is absurd—did you ever meet 2.1 children?

13. My marriage was a failure, which just proves my point: Don't ever get married in the first place.

14. The Red Queen in *Alice in Wonderland* was right: Verdict first, evidence later.

15. Not until astronauts sailed through space around the moon and could see its back side for themselves did we have adequate reason to believe that the moon even had a back side.

16. If you start out with a bottle of beer a day and then go on to a glass or two of wine on the weekends, you're well on your way to becoming a hopeless drunk.

17. Two Indians are sitting on a fence. The small Indian is the son of the big Indian, but the big Indian is not the small Indian's father. How is that possible?

18. If you toss a coin five times and each time it come up heads, is it more likely than not that on the sixth throw you'll come up heads again—or is it more likely that you'll come up tails? Or is neither more likely?

19. Going to church on a regular basis is bad for your health. Instead of sitting in a pew for an hour each Sunday you'd be better off taking an hour's brisk walk.

20. You can't trust anything he says. When he was young he was an avid Communist.

21. Since 9/11 we've tried and convicted few terrorists, so our defense systems must be working.

22. We can trust the White House in its press releases because it's a reliable source of information.

23. Intelligent design must be true because the theory of evolution can't explain how life began.

24. Andreas Serrano's notorious photograph called *Piss Christ* (1989), showing a small plastic crucifix submerged in a glass of urine, never should have been put on public display, let alone financed by public funds.

25. Doubting Thomas was right—you need more than somebody's say-so to support a claim of resurrection.

26. You are a professional baseball player and you have a good-luck charm. When you wear it the team wins. When you don't wear it the team loses. What do you infer?

27. Resolve the following dilemma: When it rains you can't fix the hole in the roof. When it's not raining there is no need to mend the roof. Conclusion: Leave the roof as it is.

28. You are at the beach and you watch a ship steaming toward the horizon. Bit by bit it disappears from view—first the masts, then the upper deck, then the main deck, then the stern, and then it's gone. Why would it be wrong to infer that the ship is sinking?

29. How can it be true that "it's the exception that proves the rule"? If anything, isn't it the exception that *dis*proves the rule?
30. How come herbivores don't eat herbs?
31. In the 1930s it was commonplace to see ads announcing "More Doctors
Smoke Camels." What do you make of such an ad?
32. Suppose the only way you could save five innocent people was by killing
one of them. Would you do it? Suppose the only way you could save one
innocent person was by killing five others. Would you do it?

Max Shulman

*Having read about proper and improper arguments, you are now well equipped
to read a short story on the topic.*

*Max Shulman (1919–1988) began his career as a writer when he was a jour-
nalism student at the University of Minnesota. Later he wrote humorous novels,
stories, and plays. One of his novels,* Barefoot Boy with Cheek *(1943), was made
into a musical, and another,* Rally Round the Flag, Boys! *(1957), was made into
a film starring Paul Newman and Joanne Woodward.* The Tender Trap *(1954),
a play he wrote with Robert Paul Smith, still retains its popularity with theater
groups.*

*"Love Is a Fallacy" was first published in 1951, when demeaning stereotypes
about women and minorities were widely accepted in the marketplace as well as
the home. Thus, jokes about domineering mothers-in-law or about dumb blondes
routinely met with no objection.*

Love Is a Fallacy

Cool was I and logical. Keen, calculating, perspicacious, acute, and
astute—I was all of these. My brain was as powerful as a dynamo, as precise as a chemist's scales, as penetrating as a scalpel. And—think of it!—I
was only eighteen.

It is not often that one so young has such a giant intellect. Take, for
example, Petey Bellows, my roommate at the university. Same age, same
background, but dumb as an ox. A nice enough fellow, you understand,
but nothing upstairs. Emotional type. Unstable. Impressionable. Worst of
all, a faddist. Fads, I submit, are the very negation of reason. To be swept
up in every new craze that comes along, to surrender yourself to idiocy
just because everybody else is doing it—this, to me, is the acme of mind-
lessness. Not, however, to Petey.

One afternoon I found Petey lying on his bed with an expression of
such distress on his face that I immediately diagnosed appendicitis. "Don't
move," I said. "Don't take a laxative. I'll call a doctor."

"Raccoon," he mumbled thickly.

"Raccoon?" I said, pausing in my flight.

"I want a raccoon coat," he wailed.

I perceived that his trouble was not physical, but mental. "Why do
you want a raccoon coat?"

5

"I should have known it," he cried, pounding his temples. "I should have known they'd come back when the Charleston came back. Like a fool I spent all my money for textbooks, and now I can't get a raccoon coat."

"Can you mean," I said incredulously, "that people are actually wearing raccoon coats again?"

"All the Big Men on Campus are wearing them. Where've you been?"   10

"In the library," I said, naming a place not frequented by Big Men on Campus.

He leaped from the bed and paced the room. "I've got to have a raccoon coat," he said passionately. "I've got to!"

"Petey, why? Look at it rationally. Raccoon coats are unsanitary. They shed. They smell bad. They weigh too much. They're unsightly. They——"

"You don't understand," he interrupted impatiently. "It's the thing to do. Don't you want to be in the swim?"

"No," I said truthfully.   15

"Well, I do," he declared. "I'd give anything for a raccoon coat. Anything!"

My brain, that precision instrument, slipped into high gear. "Anything?" I asked, looking at him narrowly.

"Anything," he affirmed in ringing tones.

I stroked my chin thoughtfully. It so happened that I knew where to get my hands on a raccoon coat. My father had had one in his undergraduate days; it lay now in a trunk in the attic back home. It also happened that Petey had something I wanted. He didn't *have* it exactly, but at least he had first rights on it. I refer to his girl, Polly Espy.

I had long coveted Polly Espy. Let me emphasize that my desire for   20 this young woman was not emotional in nature. She was, to be sure, a girl who excited the emotions, but I was not one to let my heart rule my head. I wanted Polly for a shrewdly calculated, entirely cerebral reason.

I was a freshman in law school. In a few years I would be out in practice. I was well aware of the importance of the right kind of wife in furthering a lawyer's career. The successful lawyers I had observed were, almost without exception, married to beautiful, gracious, intelligent women. With one omission, Polly fitted these specifications perfectly.

Beautiful she was. She was not yet of pin-up proportions, but I felt sure that time would supply the lack. She already had the makings.

Gracious she was. By gracious I mean full of graces. She had an erectness of carriage, an ease of bearing, a poise that clearly indicated the best of breeding. At table her manners were exquisite. I had seen her at the Kozy Kampus Korner eating the specialty of the house—a sandwich that contained scraps of pot roast, gravy, chopped nuts, and a dipper of sauerkraut—without even getting her fingers moist.

Intelligent she was not. In fact, she veered in the opposite direction. But I believed that under my guidance she would smarten up. At any rate, it was worth a try. It is, after all, easier to make a beautiful dumb girl smart than to make an ugly smart girl beautiful.

"Petey," I said, "are you in love with Polly Espy?" 25

"I think she's a keen kid," he replied, "but I don't know if you'd call it love. Why?"

"Do you," I asked, "have any kind of formal arrangement with her? I mean are you going steady or anything like that?"

"No. We see each other quite a bit, but we both have other dates. Why?"

"Is there," I asked, "any other man for whom she has a particular fondness?"

"Not that I know of. Why?" 30

I nodded with satisfaction. "In other words, if you were out of the picture, the field would be open. Is that right?"

"I guess so. What are you getting at?"

"Nothing, nothing," I said innocently, and took my suitcase out of the closet.

"Where you going?" asked Petey.

"Home for the week end." I threw a few things into the bag. 35

"Listen," he said, clutching my arm eagerly, "while you're home, you couldn't get some money from your old man, could you, and lend it to me so I can buy a raccoon coat?"

"I may do better than that," I said with a mysterious wink and closed my bag and left.

"Look," I said to Petey when I got back Monday morning. I threw open the suitcase and revealed the huge, hairy, gamy object that my father had worn in his Stutz Bearcat in 1925.

"Holy Toledo!" said Petey reverently. He plunged his hands into the raccoon coat and then his face. "Holy Toledo!" he repeated fifteen or twenty times.

"Would you like it?" I asked. 40

"Oh yes!" he cried, clutching the greasy pelt to him. Then a canny look came into his eyes. "What do you want for it?"

"Your girl," I said, mincing no words.

"Polly?" he said in a horrified whisper. "You want Polly?"

"That's right."

He flung the coat from him. "Never," he said stoutly. 45

I shrugged. "Okay. If you don't want to be in the swim, I guess it's your business."

I sat down in a chair and pretended to read a book, but out of the corner of my eye I kept watching Petey. He was a torn man. First he looked at the coat with the expression of a waif at a bakery window. Then he turned away and set his jaw resolutely. Then he looked back at the coat, with even more longing in his face. Then he turned away, but with not so much resolution this time. Back and forth his head swiveled, desire waxing, resolution waning. Finally he didn't turn away at all; he just stood and stared with mad lust at the coat.

"It isn't as though I was in love with Polly," he said thickly. "Or going steady or anything like that."

"That's right," I murmured.

"What's Polly to me, or me to Polly?"   50

"Not a thing," said I.

"It's just been a casual kick—just a few laughs, that's all."

"Try on the coat," said I.

He complied. The coat bunched high over his ears and dropped all the way down to his shoe tops. He looked like a mound of dead raccoons. "Fits fine," he said happily.

I rose from my chair. "Is it a deal?" I asked, extending my hand.   55

He swallowed. "It's a deal," he said and shook my hand.

I had my first date with Polly the following evening. This was in the nature of a survey; I wanted to find out just how much work I had to do to get her mind up to the standard I required. I took her first to dinner. "Gee, that was a delish dinner," she said as we left the restaurant. Then I took her to a movie. "Gee, that was a marvy movie," she said as we left the theater. And then I took her home. "Gee, I had a sensaysh time," she said as she bade me good night.

I went back to my room with a heavy heart. I had gravely underestimated the size of my task. This girl's lack of information was terrifying. Nor would it be enough merely to supply her with information. First she had to be taught to *think*. This loomed as a project of no small dimensions, and at first I was tempted to give her back to Petey. But then I got to thinking about her abundant physical charms and about the way she entered a room and the way she handled a knife and fork, and I decided to make an effort.

I went about it, as in all things, systematically. I gave her a course in logic. It happened that I, as a law student, was taking a course in logic myself, so I had all the facts at my fingertips. "Polly," I said to her when I picked her up on our next date, "tonight we are going over to the Knoll and talk."

"Oo, terrif," she replied. One thing I will say for this girl: You would   60
go far to find another so agreeable.

We went to the Knoll, the campus trysting place, and we sat down under an old oak, and she looked at me expectantly: "What are we going to talk about?" she asked.

"Logic."

She thought this over for a minute and decided she liked it. "Magnif," she said.

"Logic," I said, clearing my throat, "is the science of thinking. Before we can think correctly, we must first learn to recognize the common fallacies of logic. These we will take up tonight."

"Wow-dow!" she cried, clapping her hands delightedly.   65

I winced, but went bravely on. "First let us examine the fallacy called Dicto Simpliciter."

"By all means," she urged, batting her lashes eagerly.

"Dicto Simpliciter means an argument based on an unqualified generalization. For example: Exercise is good. Therefore everybody should exercise."

"I agree," said Polly earnestly. "I mean exercise is wonderful. I mean it builds the body and everything."

"Polly," I said gently, "the argument is a fallacy. *Exercise is good* is an unqualified generalization. For instance, if you have heart disease, exercise is bad, not good. Many people are ordered by their doctors *not* to exercise. You must *qualify* the generalization. You must say exercise is *usually* good, or exercise is good *for most people*. Otherwise you have committed a Dicto Simpliciter. Do you see?" 70

"No," she confessed. "But this is marvy. Do more! Do more!"

"It will be better if you stop tugging at my sleeve," I told her, and when she desisted, I continued. "Next we take up a fallacy called Hasty Generalization. Listen carefully: You can't speak French. I can't speak French. Petey Bellows can't speak French. I must therefore conclude that nobody at the University of Minnesota can speak French."

"Really?" said Polly, amazed. "*Nobody?*"

I hid my exasperation. "Polly, it's a fallacy. The generalization is reached too hastily. There are too few instances to support such a conclusion."

"Know any more fallacies?" she asked breathlessly. "This is more fun than dancing even." 75

I fought off a wave of despair. I was getting nowhere with this girl, absolutely nowhere. Still, I am nothing if not persistent. I continued. "Next comes Post Hoc. Listen to this: Let's not take Bill on our picnic. Every time we take him out with us, it rains."

"I know somebody just like that," she exclaimed. "A girl back home—Eula Becker, her name is. It never fails. Every single time we take her on a picnic——"

"Polly," I said sharply, "it's a fallacy. Eula Becker doesn't *cause* the rain. She has no connection with the rain. You are guilty of Post Hoc if you blame Eula Becker."

"I'll never do it again," she promised contritely. "Are you mad at me?"

I sighed. "No, Polly, I'm not mad." 80

"Then tell me some more fallacies."

"All right. Let's try Contradictory Premises."

"Yes, let's," she chirped, blinking her eyes happily.

I frowned, but plunged ahead. "Here's an example of Contradictory Premises: If God can do anything, can He make a stone so heavy that He won't be able to lift it?"

"Of course," she replied promptly. 85

"But if He can do anything, He can lift the stone," I pointed out.

"Yeah," she said thoughtfully. "Well, then I guess He can't make the stone."

"But He can do anything," I reminded her.

She scratched her pretty, empty head. "I'm all confused," she admitted.

"Of course you are. Because when the premises of an argument con-   90
tradict each other, there can be no argument. If there is an irresistible
force, there can be no immovable object. If there is an immovable object,
there can be no irresistible force. Get it?"

"Tell me some more of this keen stuff," she said eagerly.

I consulted my watch. "I think we'd better call it a night. I'll take you
home now, and you go over all the things you've learned. We'll have another session tomorrow night."

I deposited her at the girls' dormitory, where she assured me that
she had had a perfectly terrif evening, and I went glumly home to my
room. Petey lay snoring in his bed, the raccoon coat huddled like a great
hairy beast at his feet. For a moment I considered waking him and telling
him that he could have his girl back. It seemed clear that my project was
doomed to failure. The girl simply had a logic-proof head.

But then I reconsidered. I had wasted one evening; I might as well
waste another. Who knew? Maybe somewhere in the extinct crater of
her mind a few embers still smoldered. Maybe somehow I could fan them
into flame. Admittedly it was not a prospect fraught with hope, but I decided to give it one more try.

Seated under the oak the next evening I said, "Our first fallacy to-   95
night is called Ad Misericordiam."

She quivered with delight.

"Listen closely," I said. "A man applies for a job. When the boss asks
him what his qualifications are, he replies that he has a wife and six children at home, the wife is a helpless cripple, the children have nothing to
eat, no clothes to wear, no shoes on their feet, there are no beds in the
house, no coal in the cellar, and winter is coming."

A tear rolled down each of Polly's pink cheeks. "Oh, this is awful,
awful," she sobbed.

"Yes, it's awful," I agreed, "but it's no argument. The man never answered the boss's question about his qualifications. Instead he appealed to
the boss's sympathy. He committed the fallacy of Ad Misericordiam. Do
you understand?"

"Have you got a handkerchief?" she blubbered.   100

I handed her a handkerchief and tried to keep from screaming while
she wiped her eyes. "Next," I said in a carefully controlled tone, "we will
discuss False Analogy. Here is an example: Students should be allowed
to look at their textbooks during examinations. After all, surgeons have
X rays to guide them during an operation, lawyers have briefs to guide
them during a trial, carpenters have blueprints to guide them when they
are building a house. Why, then, shouldn't students be allowed to look at
their textbooks during an examination?"

"There now," she said enthusiastically, "is the most marvy idea I've
heard in years."

"Polly," I said testily, "the argument is all wrong. Doctors, lawyers,
and carpenters aren't taking a test to see how much they have learned,

but students are. The situations are altogether different, and you can't make an analogy between them."

"I still think it's a good idea," said Polly.

"Nuts," I muttered. Doggedly I pressed on. "Next we'll try Hypothesis 105 Contrary to Fact."

"Sounds yummy," was Polly's reaction.

"Listen: If Madame Curie had not happened to leave a photographic plate in a drawer with a chunk of pitchblende, the world today would not know about radium."

"True, true," said Polly, nodding her head. "Did you see the movie? Oh, it just knocked me out. That Walter Pidgeon is so dreamy. I mean he fractures me."

"If you can forget Mr. Pidgeon for a moment," I said coldly, "I would like to point out that the statement is a fallacy. Maybe Madame Curie would have discovered radium at some later date. Maybe somebody else would have discovered it. Maybe any number of things would have happened. You can't start with a hypothesis that is not true and then draw any supportable conclusions from it."

"They ought to put Walter Pidgeon in more pictures," said Polly. "I 110 hardly ever see him any more."

One more chance, I decided. But just one more. There is a limit to what flesh and blood can bear. "The next fallacy is called Poisoning the Well."

"How cute!" she gurgled.

"Two men are having a debate. The first one gets up and says, 'My opponent is a notorious liar. You can't believe a word that he is going to say.' . . . Now, Polly, think. Think hard. What's wrong?"

I watched her closely as she knit her creamy brow in concentration. Suddenly a glimmer of intelligence—the first I had seen—came into her eyes. "It's not fair," she said with indignation. "It's not a bit fair. What chance has the second man got if the first man calls him a liar before he even begins talking?"

"Right!" I cried exultantly. "One hundred percent right. It's not fair. 115 The first man has *poisoned the well* before anybody could drink from it. He has hamstrung his opponent before he could even start. . . . Polly, I'm proud of you."

"Pshaw," she murmured, blushing with pleasure.

"You see, my dear, these things aren't so hard. All you have to do is concentrate. Think—examine—evaluate. Come now, let's review everything we have learned."

"Fire away," she said with an airy wave of her hand.

Heartened by the knowledge that Polly was not altogether a cretin, I began a long, patient review of all I had told her. Over and over and over again I cited instances, pointed out flaws, kept hammering away without letup. It was like digging a tunnel. At first everything was work, sweat, and darkness. I had no idea when I would reach the light, or even *if* I would. But I persisted. I pounded and clawed and scraped, and finally I was rewarded. I saw a chink of light. And then the chink got bigger and the sun came pouring in and all was bright.

Five grueling nights this took, but it was worth it. I had made a logi-   120
cian out of Polly; I had taught her to think. My job was done. She was worthy of me at last. She was a fit wife for me, a proper hostess for my many mansions, a suitable mother for my well-heeled children.

It must not be thought that I was without love for this girl. Quite the contrary. Just as Pygmalion loved the perfect woman he had fashioned, so I loved mine. I decided to acquaint her with my feelings at our very next meeting. The time had come to change our relationship from academic to romantic.

"Polly," I said when next we sat beneath our oak, "tonight we will not discuss fallacies."

"Aw, gee," she said, disappointed.

"My dear," I said, favoring her with a smile, "we have now spent five evenings together. We have gotten along splendidly. It is clear that we are well matched."

"Hasty Generalization," said Polly brightly.   125

"I beg your pardon," said I.

"Hasty Generalization," she repeated. "How can you say that we are well matched on the basis of only five dates?"

I chuckled with amusement. The dear child had learned her lessons well. "My dear," I said, patting her hand in a tolerant manner, "five dates is plenty. After all, you don't have to eat a whole cake to know that it's good."

"False Analogy," said Polly promptly. "I'm not a cake. I'm a girl."

I chuckled with somewhat less amusement. The dear child had   130
learned her lesson perhaps too well. I decided to change tactics. Obviously the best approach was a simple, strong, direct declaration of love. I paused for a moment while my massive brain chose the proper words. Then I began:

"Polly, I love you. You are the whole world to me, and the moon and the stars and the constellations of outer space. Please, my darling, say that you will go steady with me, for if you will not, life will be meaningless. I will languish. I will refuse my meals. I will wander the face of the earth, a shambling, hollow-eyed hulk."

There, I thought, folding my arms, that ought to do it.

"Ad Misericordiam," said Polly.

I ground my teeth. I was not Pygmalion; I was Frankenstein, and my monster had me by the throat. Frantically I fought back the tide of panic surging through me. At all costs I had to keep cool.

"Well, Polly," I said, forcing a smile, "you certainly have learned your   135
fallacies."

"You're darn right," she said with a vigorous nod.

"And who taught them to you, Polly?"

"You did."

"That's right. So you do owe me something, don't you, my dear? If I hadn't come along you never would have learned about fallacies."

"Hypothesis Contrary to Fact," she said instantly.   140

I dashed perspiration from my brow. "Polly," I croaked, "you mustn't take all these things so literally. I mean this is just classroom stuff. You know that the things you learn in school don't have anything to do with life."

"Dicto Simpliciter," she said, wagging her finger at me playfully.

That did it. I leaped to my feet, bellowing like a bull. "Will you or will you not go steady with me?"

"I will not," she replied.

"Why not?" I demanded.   145

"Because this afternoon I promised Petey Bellows that I would go steady with him."

I reeled back, overcome with the infamy of it. After he promised, after he made a deal, after he shook my hand! "That rat!" I shrieked, kicking up great chunks of turf. "You can't go with him, Polly. He's a liar. He's a cheat. He's a rat."

"Poisoning the Well," said Polly, "and stop shouting. I think shouting must be a fallacy too."

With an immense effort of will, I modulated my voice. "All right," I said. "You're a logician. Let's look at this thing logically. How could you choose Petey Bellows over me? Look at me—a brilliant student, a tremendous intellectual, a man with an assured future. Look at Petey—a knothead, a jitterbug, a guy who'll never know where his next meal is coming from. Can you give me one logical reason why you should go steady with Petey Bellows?"

"I certainly can," declared Polly. "He's got a raccoon coat."   150

Topic for Critical Thinking and Writing

After you have finished reading "Love Is a Fallacy," you may want to write an argumentative essay of 500 to 750 words on one of the following topics: (1) the story, rightly understood, is not antiwoman; (2) if the story is antiwoman, it is equally antiman; (3) the story is antiwoman but nevertheless belongs in this book; or (4) the story is antiwoman and does not belong in the book.

See the companion Web site
bedfordstmartins.com/barnetbedau
for a series of brain teasers and links related to
the logical point of view in argument.

10

A Psychologist's View:
Rogerian Argument

Real communication occurs . . . when we listen with understanding.
—CARL ROGERS

The first duty of a wise advocate is to convince his opponents that he understands their arguments, and sympathizes with their just feelings.
—SAMUEL TAYLOR COLERIDGE

ROGERIAN ARGUMENT: AN INTRODUCTION

Carl R. Rogers (1902–1987), perhaps best known for his book entitled *On Becoming a Person* (1961), was a psychotherapist, not a teacher of writing. This short essay by Rogers has, however, exerted much influence on instructors who teach argument. Written in the 1950s, this essay reflects the political climate of the cold war between the United States and the Soviet Union, which dominated headlines for more than forty years (1947–1989). Several of Rogers's examples of bias and frustrated communication allude to the tensions of that era.

On the surface, many arguments seem to show *A* arguing with *B*, presumably seeking to change *B*'s mind; but *A*'s argument is really directed not to *B* but to *C*. This attempt to persuade a nonparticipant is evident in the courtroom, where neither the prosecutor (*A*) nor the defense lawyer (*B*) is really trying to convince the opponent. Rather, both are trying to convince a third party, the jury (*C*). Prosecutors do not care whether they convince defense lawyers; they don't even mind infuriating defense lawyers because their only real goal is to convince the jury. Similarly, the writer of a letter to a newspaper, taking issue with an editorial, does not expect to change the paper's policy. Rather, the writer hopes to convince a third party, the reader of the newspaper.

But suppose *A* really does want to bring *B* around to *A*'s point of view. Suppose Mary really wants to persuade the teacher to allow her little lamb to stay in the classroom. Rogers points out that when we engage in an argument, if we feel our integrity or our identity is threatened, we will stiffen our position. (The teacher may feel that his or her dignity is compromised by the presence of the lamb and will scarcely attend to Mary's argument.) The sense of threat may be so great that we are unable to consider the alternative views being offered, and we therefore remain unpersuaded. Threatened, we may defend ourselves rather than our argument, and little communication takes place. Of course, a third party might say that we or our opponent presented the more convincing case, but we, and perhaps the opponent, have scarcely listened to each other, and so the two of us remain apart.

Rogers suggests, therefore, that a writer who wishes to communicate with someone (as opposed to convincing a third party) needs to reduce the threat. In a sense, the participants in the argument need to become partners rather than adversaries. Rogers writes, "Mutual communication tends to be pointed toward solving a problem rather than toward attacking a person or group." Thus, an essay on whether schools should test students for use of drugs, need not—and probably should not—see the issue as black or white, *either/or.* Such an essay might indicate that testing is undesirable because it may have bad effects, *but in some circumstances* it may be acceptable. This qualification does not mean that one must compromise. Thus, the essayist might argue that the potential danger to liberty is so great that no circumstances justify testing students for drugs. But even such an essayist should recognize the merit (however limited) of the opposition and should grant that the position being advanced itself entails great difficulties and dangers.

A writer who wishes to reduce the psychological threat to the opposition and thus facilitate the partnership in the study of some issue can do several things:

- one can show sympathetic understanding of the opposing argument,
- one can recognize what is valid in it, and
- one can recognize and demonstrate that those who take the other side are nonetheless persons of goodwill.

Advocates of Rogerian argument are likely to contrast it with Aristotelian argument, saying that the style of argument associated with Aristotle (384–322 B.C., Greek philosopher and rhetorician)

- is adversarial, seeking to refute other views; and
- sees the listener as wrong, someone who now must be overwhelmed by evidence.

In contrast to the confrontational Aristotelian style, which allegedly seeks to present an airtight case that compels belief, Rogerian argument (it is said)

- is nonconfrontational, collegial, and friendly;
- respects other views and allows for plural truths; and
- seeks to achieve some degree of assent rather than convince utterly.

Thus a writer who takes Rogers seriously will, usually, in the first part of an argumentative essay

1. state the problem,
2. give the opponent's position, and
3. grant whatever validity the writer finds in that position—for instance, will recognize the circumstances in which the position would indeed be acceptable.

Next, the writer will, if possible,

4. attempt to show how the opposing position will be improved if the writer's own position is accepted.

Sometimes, of course, the differing positions may be so far apart that no reconciliation can be proposed, in which case the writer will probably seek to show how the problem can best be solved by adopting the writer's own position. We have discussed these matters in Chapter 6, but not from the point of view of a psychotherapist, and so we reprint Rogers's essay here.

Carl R. Rogers

Communication: Its Blocking and Its Facilitation

It may seem curious that a person whose whole professional effort is devoted to psychotherapy should be interested in problems of communication. What relationship is there between providing therapeutic help to individuals with emotional maladjustments and the concern of this conference with obstacles to communication? Actually the relationship is very close indeed. The whole task of psychotherapy is the task of dealing with a failure in communication. The emotionally maladjusted person, the "neurotic," is in difficulty first because communication within himself has broken down, and second because as a result of this his communication with others has been damaged. If this sounds somewhat strange, then let me put it in other terms. In the "neurotic" individual, parts of himself which have been termed unconscious, or repressed, or denied to awareness, become blocked off so that they no longer communicate themselves to the conscious or managing part of himself. As long as this is true, there are distortions in the way he communicates himself to others, and so he suffers both within himself, and in his interpersonal relations. The task of psychotherapy is to help the person achieve, through a special relationship with a therapist, good communication within himself. Once this is achieved he can communicate more freely and more effectively with others. We may say then that psychotherapy is good communication, within and between men. We may also turn that statement around and it will still be true. Good communication, free communication, within or between men, is always therapeutic.

It is, then, from a background of experience with communication in counseling and psychotherapy that I want to present here two ideas. I wish to state what I believe is one of the major factors in blocking or impeding communication, and then I wish to present what in our experience has proven to be a very important way to improving or facilitating communication.

I would like to propose, as an hypothesis for consideration, that the major barrier to mutual interpersonal communication is our very natural tendency to judge, to evaluate, to approve or disapprove, the statement of the person, or the other group. Let me illustrate my meaning with some very simple examples. As you leave the meeting tonight, one of the statements you are likely to hear is, "I didn't like that man's talk." Now what do you respond? Almost invariably your reply will be either approval or disapproval of the attitude expressed. Either you respond, "I didn't either. I thought it was terrible," or else you tend to reply, "Oh, I thought it was really good." In other words, your primary reaction is to evaluate what has just been said to you, to evaluate it from *your* point of view, your own frame of reference.

Or take another example. Suppose I say with some feeling, "I think the Republicans are behaving in ways that show a lot of good sound sense these days," what is the response that arises in your mind as you listen? The overwhelming likelihood is that it will be evaluative. You will find yourself agreeing, or disagreeing, or making some judgment about me such as "He must be a conservative," or "He seems solid in his thinking." Or let us take an illustration from the international scene. Russia says vehemently, "The treaty with Japan is a war plot on the part of the United States." We rise as one person to say "That's a lie!"

This last illustration brings in another element connected with my hypothesis. Although the tendency to make evaluations is common in almost all interchange of language, it is very much heightened in those situations where feelings and emotions are deeply involved. So the stronger our feelings, the more likely it is that there will be no mutual element in the communication. There will be just two ideas, two feelings, two judgments, missing each other in psychological space. I'm sure you recognize this from your own experience. When you have not been emotionally involved yourself, and have listened to a heated discussion, you often go away thinking, "Well, they actually weren't talking about the same thing." And they were not. Each was making a judgment, an evaluation, from his own frame of reference. There was really nothing which could be called communication in any genuine sense. This tendency to react to any emotionally meaningful statement by forming an evaluation of it from our own point of view, is, I repeat, the major barrier to interpersonal communication.

But is there any way of solving this problem, of avoiding this barrier? I feel that we are making exciting progress toward this goal and I would like to present it as simply as I can. Real communication occurs, and this evaluative tendency is avoided, when we listen with understanding. What does that mean? It means *to see the expressed idea and attitude from the other person's point of view, to sense how it feels to him, to achieve his frame of reference in regard to the thing he is talking about.*

Stated so briefly, this may sound absurdly simple, but it is not. It is an approach which we have found extremely potent in the field of psychotherapy. It is the most effective agent we know for altering the basic personality structure of an individual, and improving his relationships and his communications with others. If I can listen to what he can tell me, if I can understand how it seems to him, if I can see its personal meaning for him, if I can sense the emotional flavor which it has for him, then I will be releasing potent forces of change in him. If I can really understand how he hates his father, or hates the university, or hates communists—if I can catch the flavor of his fear of insanity, or his fear of atom bombs, or of Russia—it will be of the greatest help to him in altering those very hatreds and fears, and in establishing realistic and harmonious relationships with the very people and situations toward which he has felt hatred and fear. We know from our research that such empathic understanding—understanding *with* a person, not *about* him—is such an effective approach that it can bring about major changes in personality.

Some of you may be feeling that you listen well to people, and that you have never seen such results. The chances are very great indeed that your listening has not been of the type I have described. Fortunately I can suggest a little laboratory experiment which you can try to test the quality of your understanding. The next time you get into an argument with your wife, or your friend, or with a small group of friends, just stop the discussion for a moment and for an experiment, institute this rule. "Each person can speak up for himself only *after* he has first restated the ideas and feelings of the previous speaker accurately, and to that speaker's satisfaction." You see what this would mean. It would simply mean that before presenting your own point of view, it would be necessary for you to really achieve the other speaker's frame of reference—to understand his thoughts and feelings so well that you could summarize them for him. Sounds simple, doesn't it? But if you try it you will discover it one of the most difficult things you have ever tried to do. However, once you have been able to see the other's point of view, your own comments will have to be drastically revised. You will also find the emotion going out of the discussion, the differences being reduced, and those differences which remain being of a rational and understandable sort.

Can you imagine what this kind of an approach would mean if it were projected into larger areas? What would happen to a labor-management dispute if it was conducted in such a way that labor, without necessarily agreeing, could accurately state management's point of view in a way that management could accept; and management, without approving labor's stand, could state labor's case in a way that labor agreed was accurate? It would mean that real communication was established, and one could practically guarantee that some reasonable solution would be reached.

If then this way of approach is an effective avenue to good commu- 10 nication and good relationships, as I am quite sure you will agree if you try the experiment I have mentioned, why is it not more widely tried and used? I will try to list the difficulties which keep it from being utilized.

In the first place it takes courage, a quality which is not too widespread. I am indebted to Dr. S. I. Hayakawa, the semanticist, for pointing out that to carry on psychotherapy in this fashion is to take a very real risk, and that courage is required. If you really understand another person in this way, if you are willing to enter his private world and see the way life appears to him, without any attempt to make evaluative judgments, you run the risk of being changed yourself. You might see it his way, you might find yourself influenced in your attitudes or your personality. This risk of being changed is one of the most frightening prospects most of us can face. If I enter, as fully as I am able, into the private world of a neurotic or psychotic individual, isn't there a risk that I might become lost in that world? Most of us are afraid to take that risk. Or if we had a Russian communist speaker here tonight, or Senator Joe McCarthy, how many of us would dare to try to see the world from each of these points of view? The great majority of us could not *listen;* we would find ourselves compelled to *evaluate,* because listening would seem too dangerous. So the first requirement is courage, and we do not always have it.

But there is a second obstacle. It is just when emotions are strongest that it is most difficult to achieve the frame of reference of the other person or group. Yet it is the time the attitude is most needed, if communication is to be established. We have not found this to be an insuperable obstacle in our experience in psychotherapy. A third party, who is able to lay aside his own feelings and evaluations, can assist greatly by listening with understanding to each person or group and clarifying the views and attitudes each holds. We have found this very effective in small groups in which contradictory or antagonistic attitudes exist. When the parties to a dispute realize that they are being understood, that someone sees how the situation seems to them, the statements grow less exaggerated and less defensive, and it is no longer necessary to maintain the attitude, "I am 100 percent right and you are 100 percent wrong." The influence of such an understanding catalyst in the group permits the members to come closer and closer to the objective truth involved in the relationship. In this way mutual communication is established and some type of agreement becomes much more possible. So we may say that though heightened emotions make it much more difficult to understand *with* an opponent, our experience makes it clear that a neutral, understanding, catalyst type of leader or therapist can overcome this obstacle in a small group.

This last phrase, however, suggests another obstacle to utilizing the approach I have described. Thus far all our experience has been with small face-to-face groups—groups exhibiting industrial tensions, religious tensions, racial tensions, and therapy groups in which many personal tensions are present. In these small groups our experience, confirmed by a limited amount of research, shows that this basic approach leads to improved communication, to greater acceptance of others and by others, and to attitudes which are more positive and more problem-solving in nature. There is a decrease in defensiveness, in exaggerated statements, in evaluative and critical behavior. But these findings are from small groups. What about trying to achieve understanding between larger groups that are geographically remote? Or between face-to-face groups who are not speaking for themselves, but simply as representatives of others, like the delegates at Kaesong?[1] Frankly we do not know the answers to these questions. I believe the situation might be put this way. As social scientists we have a tentative test-tube solution of the problem of breakdown in communication. But to confirm the validity of this test-tube solution, and to adapt it to the enormous problems of communication breakdown between classes, groups, and nations, would involve additional funds, much more research, and creative thinking of a high order.

Even with our present limited knowledge we can see some steps which might be taken, even in large groups, to increase the amount of listening *with*, and to decrease the amount of evaluation *about*. To be imaginative for a moment, let us suppose that a therapeutically oriented international group went to the Russian leaders and said, "We want to achieve a genuine understanding of your views and even more important, of your attitudes and feelings, toward the United States. We will summarize and resummarize the views and feelings if necessary, until you agree that our description represents the situation as it seems to you." Then suppose they did the same thing with the leaders in our own country. If they then gave the widest possible distribution to these two views, with the feelings clearly described but not expressed in name-calling, might not the effect be very great? It would not guarantee the type of understanding I have been describing, but it would make it much more possible. We can understand the feelings of a person who hates us much more readily when his attitudes are accurately described to us by a neutral third party, than we can when he is shaking his fist at us.

But even to describe such a first step is to suggest another obstacle to this approach of understanding. Our civilization does not yet have enough faith in the social sciences to utilize their findings. The opposite is true of the physical sciences. During the war[2] when a test-tube solution was

15

---

[1] **the delegates at Kaesong** Representatives of North and South Korea met at the border town of Kaesong to arrange terms for an armistice to hostilities during the Korean War (1950–1953). [All notes are the editors'.]
[2] **the war** World War II.

found to the problem of synthetic rubber, millions of dollars and an army of talent was turned loose on the problem of using that finding. If synthetic rubber could be made in milligrams, it could and would be made in the thousands of tons. And it was. But in the social science realm, if a way is found of facilitating communication and mutual understanding in small groups, there is no guarantee that the finding will be utilized. It may be a generation or more before the money and the brains will be turned loose to exploit that finding.

In closing, I would like to summarize this small-scale solution to the problem of barriers in communication, and to point out certain of its characteristics.

I have said that our research and experience to date would make it appear that breakdowns in communication, and the evaluative tendency which is the major barrier to communication, can be avoided. The solution is provided by creating a situation in which each of the different parties come to understand the other from the *other's* point of view. This has been achieved, in practice, even when feelings run high, by the influence of a person who is willing to understand each point of view empathically, and who thus acts as a catalyst to precipitate further understanding.

This procedure has important characteristics. It can be initiated by one party, without waiting for the other to be ready. It can even be initiated by a neutral third person, providing he can gain a minimum of cooperation from one of the parties.

This procedure can deal with the insincerities, the defensive exaggerations, the lies, the "false fronts" which characterize almost every failure in communication. These defensive distortions drop away with astonishing speed as people find that the only intent is to understand, not judge.

This approach leads steadily and rapidly toward the discovery of the truth, toward a realistic appraisal of the objective barriers to communication. The dropping of some defensiveness by one party leads to further dropping of defensiveness by the other party, and truth is thus approached.

This procedure gradually achieves mutual communication. Mutual communication tends to be pointed toward solving a problem rather than toward attacking a person or group. It leads to a situation in which I see how the problem appears to you, as well as to me, and you see how it appears to me, as well as to you. Thus accurately and realistically defined, the problem is almost certain to yield to intelligent attack, or if it is in part insoluble, it will be comfortably accepted as such.

This then appears to be a test-tube solution to the breakdown of communication as it occurs in small groups. Can we take this small-scale answer, investigate it further, refine it; develop it and apply it to the tragic and well-nigh fatal failures of communication which threaten the very existence of our modern world? It seems to me that this is a possibility and a challenge which we should explore.

✓ A CHECKLIST FOR ANALYZING ROGERIAN ARGUMENT

☐ Have I stated the problem and indicated that a dialogue is possible?

☐ Have I stated at least one other point of view in a way that would satisfy its proponents?

☐ Have I been courteous to those who hold views other than mine?

☐ Have I enlarged my own understanding to the extent that I can grant validity, at least in some circumstances, to at least some aspects of other positions?

☐ Have I stated my position and indicated the contexts in which I believe it is valid?

☐ Have I pointed out the ground that we share?

☐ Have I shown how other positions will be strengthened by accepting some aspects of my position?

See the companion Web site **bedfordstmartins.com /barnetbedau** for links related to Rogerian argument.

Edward O. Wilson

Edward O. Wilson, born in in Birmingham, Alabama, in 1929, is an emeritus professor of evolutionary biology at Harvard University. A distinguished writer as well as a researcher and teacher, Wilson has twice won the Pulitzer Prize for General Non-Fiction. We reprint a piece first published in 2006.

Letter to a Southern Baptist Minister

Dear Pastor:

We have not met, yet I feel I know you well enough to call you friend. First of all, we grew up in the same faith. As a boy I too answered the altar call; I went under the water. Although I no longer belong to that faith, I am confident that if we met and spoke privately of our deepest beliefs, it would be in a spirit of mutual respect and good will. I know we share many precepts of moral behavior. Perhaps it also matters that we are both Americans and, insofar as it might still affect civility and good manners, we are both Southerners.

I write to you now for your counsel and help. Of course, in doing so, I see no way to avoid the fundamental differences in our respective worldviews. You are a literalist interpreter of Christian Holy Scripture. You reject the conclusion of science that mankind evolved from lower forms. You believe that each person's soul is immortal, making this planet a way station to a second, eternal life. Salvation is assured those who are redeemed in Christ.

I am a secular humanist. I think existence is what we make of it as individuals. There is no guarantee of life after death, and heaven and hell are what we create for ourselves, on this planet. There is no other home. Humanity originated here by evolution from lower forms over millions of years. And yes, I will speak plain, our ancestors were apelike animals. The human species has adapted physically and mentally to life on Earth and no place else. Ethics is the code of behavior we share on the basis of reason, law, honor, and an inborn sense of decency, even as some ascribe it to God's will.

For you, the glory of an unseen divinity; for me, the glory of the universe revealed at last. For you, the belief in God made flesh to save mankind; for me, the belief in Promethean fire seized to set men free. You have found your final truth; I am still searching. I may be wrong, you may be wrong. We may both be partly right.

Does this difference in worldview separate us in all things? It does not. 5 You and I and every other human being strive for the same imperatives of security, freedom of choice, personal dignity, and a cause to believe in that is larger than ourselves.

Let us see, then, if we can, and you are willing, to meet on the near side of metaphysics in order to deal with the real world we share. I put it this way because you have the power to help solve a great problem about which I care deeply. I hope you have the same concern. I suggest that we set aside our differences in order to save the Creation. The defense of living Nature is a universal value. It doesn't rise from, nor does it promote, any religious or ideological dogma. Rather, it serves without discrimination the interests of all humanity.

Pastor, we need your help. The Creation—living Nature—is in deep trouble. Scientists estimate that if habitat conversion and other destructive human activities continue at their present rates, half the species of plants and animals on Earth could be either gone or at least fated for early extinction by the end of the century. A full quarter will drop to this level during the next half century as a result of climate change alone. The ongoing extinction rate is calculated in the most conservative estimates to be about a hundred times above that prevailing before humans appeared on Earth, and it is expected to rise to at least a thousand times greater or more in the next few decades. If this rise continues unabated, the cost to humanity, in wealth, environmental security, and quality of life, will be catastrophic.

Surely we can agree that each species, however inconspicuous and humble it may seem to us at this moment, is a masterpiece of biology, and well worth saving. Each species possesses a unique combination of genetic traits that fits it more or less precisely to a particular part of the environment. Prudence alone dictates that we act quickly to prevent the extinction of species and, with it, the pauperization of Earth's ecosystems—hence of the Creation.

You may well ask at this point, Why me? Because religion and science are the two most powerful forces in the world today, including especially the United States. If religion and science could be united on the common ground of biological conservation, the problem would soon be solved. If there is any moral precept shared by people of all beliefs, it is that we owe ourselves and future generations a beautiful, rich, and healthful environment.

I am puzzled that so many religious leaders, who spiritually repre- 10 sent a large majority of people around the world, have hesitated to make protection of the Creation an important part of their magisterium. Do they believe that human-centered ethics and preparation for the afterlife are the only things that matter? Even more perplexing is the widespread conviction among Christians that the Second Coming is imminent, and that therefore the condition of the planet is of little consequence. Sixty percent of Americans, according to a 2004 poll, believe that the prophecies of the book of Revelation are accurate. Many of these, numbering in the millions, think the End of Time will occur within the life span of those now living. Jesus will return to Earth, and those redeemed by Christian faith will be transported bodily to heaven, while those left behind will struggle through severe hard times and, when they die, suffer eternal damnation. The condemned will remain in hell, like those already consigned in the generations before them, for a trillion trillion years, enough for the universe to expand to its own, entropic death, time enough for countless universes like it afterward to be born, expand, and likewise die away. And that is just the beginning of how long condemned souls will suffer in hell—all for a mistake they made in choice of religion during the infinitesimally small time they inhabited Earth.

For those who believe this form of Christianity, the fate of 10 million other life forms indeed does not matter. This and other similar doctrines are not gospels of hope and compassion. They are gospels of cruelty and despair. They were not born of the heart of Christianity. Pastor, tell me I am wrong!

However you will respond, let me here venture an alternative ethic. The great challenge of the twenty-first century is to raise people everywhere to a decent standard of living while preserving as much of the rest of life as possible. Science has provided this part of the argument for the ethic: the more we learn about the biosphere, the more complex and beautiful it turns out to be. Knowledge of it is a magic well: the more you draw from it, the more there is to draw. Earth, and especially the razor-thin film of life enveloping it, is our home, our wellspring, our physical and much of our spiritual sustenance.

I know that science and environmentalism are linked in the minds of many with evolution, Darwin, and secularism. Let me postpone disentangling all this (I will come back to it later) and stress again: to protect the beauty of Earth and of its prodigious variety of life forms should be a common goal, regardless of differences in our metaphysical beliefs.

To make the point in good Gospel manner, let me tell the story of a young man, newly trained for the ministry, and so fixed in his Christian faith that he referred all questions of morality to readings from the Bible. When he visited the cathedral-like Atlantic rainforest of Brazil, he saw the manifest hand of God and in his notebook wrote, "It is not possible to give an adequate idea of the higher feelings of wonder, admiration, and devotion which fill and elevate the mind."

That was Charles Darwin in 1832, early into the voyage of HMS *Bea-*   15 *gle*, before he had given any thought to evolution.

And here is Darwin, concluding *On the Origin of Species* in 1859, having first abandoned Christian dogma and then, with his newfound intellectual freedom, formulated the theory of evolution by natural selection: "There is grandeur in this view of life, with its several powers, having been originally breathed into a few forms or into one; and that, whilst this planet has gone cycling on according to the fixed law of gravity, from so simple a beginning endless forms most beautiful and most wonderful have been, and are being, evolved."

Darwin's reverence for life remained the same as he crossed the seismic divide that divided his spiritual life. And so it can be for the divide that today separates scientific humanism from mainstream religion. And separates you and me.

You are well prepared to present the theological and moral arguments for saving the Creation. I am heartened by the movement growing within Christian denominations to support global conservation. The stream of thought has arisen from many sources, from evangelical to unitarian. Today it is but a rivulet. Tomorrow it will be a flood.

I already know much of the religious argument on behalf of the Creation, and would like to learn more. I will now lay before you and others who may wish to hear it the scientific argument. You will not agree with all that I say about the origins of life—science and religion do not easily mix in such matters—but I like to think that in this one life-and-death issue we have a common purpose.

TOPICS FOR CRITICAL THINKING AND WRITING

1. Wilson claims to be a "secular humanist" (para. 3). How would you define that term? Are you a secular humanist? Why, or why not?

2. What does Wilson mean by "metaphysics" (para. 6)? Which if any of his views qualify as metaphysical?

3. Wilson obviously seeks to present his views in a fashion that makes them as palatable as possible. Do you think he succeeds in this endeavor? Write an essay of 500 words arguing for or against his achievement in this regard.

A Rhetorician's View: Rhetorical Analysis of Nontraditional Texts[1]

The media work us over completely. They are so pervasive in their personal, political, economic, aesthetic, psychological, moral, ethical, and social consequences that they leave no part of us untouched, unaffected, unaltered. The medium is the massage.

—MARSHALL MCLUHAN

We not only interpret the character of events . . . we may also interpret our interpretations.

—KENNETH BURKE

A twenty-first-century rhetorician must now consider not only print and traditional texts but also the kinds and types of technologies used to compose and design those texts. Chapters 4, 5, and 6 discussed both reading and analyzing arguments as well as making them, partly in the light of Aristotle's ideas of *ethos* (the character of the speaker or writer), *pathos* (appeals to the emotions), and *logos* (appeals to reason, notably the use of induction and deduction, but also the testimony of authorities and the display of evidence). Aristotle (384–322 B.C.E.), writing almost two thousand years before Gutenberg's invention of movable type and the printing press, was talking chiefly about *oral* arguments, though the Greeks did have written arguments also, in the form of words handwritten on scrolls. Relatively soon after the introduction of movable type and the printing press in the mid-fifteenth century, *written* arguments—books—largely displaced oral arguments, though oral arguments of course remain important even today, notably in courts and classrooms. Nor should we forget political oratory, in Congress and other

[1]This section was contributed by Anthony Atkins, associate professor of English and composition coordinator at the University of North Carolina Wilmington.

political arenas, including televised debates between the candidates for the presidency of the United States.

Compared with Aristotle's chiefly oral world, or even compared with the print world of our parents, today we work with a much more diverse range of texts—for instance, Web sites, Twitter, Facebook, and memes. Nevertheless, we can engage rhetorically with these new texts just as we would with oral texts and with traditional print texts. Furthermore, we engage with these technologic texts for the same reasons that the ancients engaged with their texts. In the world of classical Greece, teachers of rhetoric (at least the best of them) hoped that their teaching would create ethical citizens—effective speakers promoting good causes. Today, rhetoric is an established discipline of study that seeks both to record how people communicate and to teach students how to clearly and responsibly connect their messages with society at large.

> **A RULE FOR WRITERS:** Although the word *rhetoric* today is frequently used with unfavorable connotations, as in *empty rhetoric* and *mere rhetoric*, the traditional meaning of rhetoric (and the meaning in this essay) is the study of language in use, language in real-life situations.

While we still use the Aristotelian strategies of traditional rhetoric, we must acknowledge that even Aristotle, wise though he was, did not envision the rise of the Internet and social and mass media, and the impact those modes of communication would have on our day-to-day communications. Instead of witnessing live speeches in the town square, today we witness and experience Tweets, status updates, online journals and magazines, blogs, and interactive news and sports and entertainment Web sites. Today's town squares exist online, and they are highly interactive; we can instantly respond in detail to most of what we encounter on the Internet, whereas persons listening in the actual physical presence of the speaker cannot do much more than mutter, or, at most boo, hiss, or applaud. The new ways in which we communicate, share ideas, and conduct our private and work lives depend on using digital technologies. Because digital technologies are becoming the backbone of information exchange, rhetoricians have to develop new modes of studying writing and receiving (i.e., interpreting) arguments in a digital age. The New London Group, an association of ten scholars in media, rhetoric, and communication, says:

> [P]rivate lives are being made more public as everything becomes a potential subject of media discussion, resulting in what we refer to as a "conversationalization" of public language. Discourses that were once the domain of the private—the intricacies of the sexual lives of public

figures, discussion of repressed memories of child abuse—are now made unashamedly public.

About the ways in which our work lives are changing, the group says:

> With a new worklife comes a new language. A good deal of this change is the result of new technologies, such as the iconographic, text, and screen-based modes of interacting with automated machinery; "user-friendly" interfaces operate with more subtle levels of cultural embed-dedness than interfaces based on abstract commands. But much of the change is also the result of the new social relationships of work.

Along with these massive but sometimes subtle changes, rhetoric shifts its focus from the traditional concern with writer, message, and audience to a concern with the context surrounding publication or distri-bution, which requires us to ask three additional questions:

- Who is publishing the message?
- In what medium (e.g., print, blog, television) is it published?
- How has the message been adapted to suit the medium in which it is published?

You may be familiar with the sentence, "The medium is the mes-sage," coined by Marshall McLuhan in 1964. McLuhan's point was that the *medium*—a book versus television, for instance—itself is a message. The idea that each medium is in itself a unique kind of stimulus under-lies a pun McLuhan also made, "The medium is the massage."

For a simple example of how technology shapes the message, con-sider a presidential debate. Ordinarily the candidates stand at podiums several yards apart; viewers in the auditorium look chiefly at which-ever person is speaking and pay little attention to the silent candidate. But television directors now commonly use a split screen, bringing the two figures next to each other, and viewers inevitably see not only the speaker but also the immediate reactions of the silent opponent—the raised eyebrows, the frowns, the rolling eyes. In short, the viewers at home, watching the debate on television, experience—because of the medium—a debate that is somewhat different from the debate witnessed by persons in the auditorium, and the home viewer also experiences a debate that is very different from the printed text of the debate a reader encounters in a newspaper.

The three bulleted questions ("Who," "In what medium," "How") influence not only how we read and analyze arguments, but also how we create them. Suppose, for example, you want to make an argument about an aspect of reality TV (as Michelle Dean does on page 415). You may feel that print is not sufficient for your argument; you may decide that you can make a stronger argument by using a blog that allows you to embed clips from the show or links to additional reading.

HOW RHETORICIANS ANALYZE ARGUMENTS

When we interact with texts, we automatically make judgments about them. We come out of a movie theater grumbling that the movie wasn't worth the cost of the ticket, or, on the other hand, perhaps we tell our companion that we are going to recommend this film to our parents. Or we see an ad on TV, and we admire or hate it. Such responses are often the root of rhetorical analysis. When we begin by considering *why* we dislike or like something, we are then in a position to go on — first explaining to ourselves and then to others what the *reasons* are for our judgments. The most important thing for you to do in your role as a rhetorician is to use evidence from your text — whatever the medium — to support your judgments. Nontraditional texts — that is, nonprint texts — can be slightly more difficult to analyze, but you can get a good start by thinking about what evidence from the text you can use to support your opinion. Exactly which aspects of the movie make it not worth the cost of the ticket? What aspect of that television show makes it "the best show on TV"? Why does that commercial make you feel as if you can't live another day without the product it is promoting? When you review the text for evidence, you are clarifying your own initial thoughts; you are searching for truth, and when you think you have found it, you will then try to communicate it to your audience.

You are familiar with analyzing an argument on the basis of its authorship, content, purpose, and audience, and you are familiar with applying the principles of *ethos*, *pathos*, and *logos*. Although you almost surely will consider these traditional principles when analyzing arguments put forward in emerging media, digital texts may call for additional points of analysis. New technologies require that we continue to rethink what counts as an argument. For example, would you consider a Twitter post an argument? Suppose a politician running for office has used Twitter to criticize an opponent's stance on taxing the wealthy. You could analyze the substance of the tweet and decide that this candidate is arguing that we should raise taxes on people who make above a certain amount each year, and you may be correct. But your analysis shouldn't stop there, because you haven't yet considered how the politician has adapted his argument so that it is uniquely suitable to Twitter, which takes advantage of social media tools that traditional texts cannot. Suppose the politician had tagged the tweet with the hashtag #payyour-share. Adding a hashtag would share that tweet with anyone following that tag rather than sharing the tweet only with people who follow the politician. Your analysis would require you to consider how the politician chose a tag that might connect with a new, perhaps sympathetic, audience because a hashtag, while it may seem like a simple tool, is also a critical part of the text.

Blogs, text messages, tweets, and Facebook status updates are significant texts and may well contain genuine arguments. They deserve the same close analysis that we give to traditional print essays, images, and videos. The increasing presence of visual communication in our lives also forces us to contend with and consider just what effect the visual can have on the meaning of a message. For better, or worse, we live in a world where technology increasingly blurs the line between what counts as print and what counts as visual.

Facebook, for example, requires that we post and share our private lives with the public. Facebook users connect, share, and interact with each other by posting, forwarding, liking, and commenting. Facebook contains elements common to print and to visual media, but it is also interactive in a way traditional print and visual media are not. If you have a Facebook account, but you aren't posting or sharing, are you really using Facebook? One way we might think about rhetoric in the twenty-first century, then, is to think about Facebook, Twitter, and most other free Web applications as new categories of media. The application is carrying information to you or from you, and it therefore becomes the vehicle with which you interact with others, with which you convey and receive information.

PRODUCTION, DISTRIBUTION, AND CONSUMPTION: PERFORMING A RHETORICAL ANALYSIS

When you analyze a traditional print argument, you focus much of your analysis on the author's words. Nontraditional texts, however, have proven that arguments do not necessarily rely on words. On a daily basis, you probably interact with complex texts that mix written, visual, and aural elements far more frequently than you do with traditional print. These texts require more than an analysis of their words. If you want to analyze a music video, for example, and you focus your analysis on only the song's lyrics, your analysis is notably incomplete; you have ignored the music and the visuals.

One way to analyze a text, whether print or other, involves thinking about it not as a solitary piece but as part of a social process, that is, considering its function in society and how it incorporates social rules as part of its argument. You might at first think, for example, that a music video is not an argument, but if you consider that a music video is likely to communicate a point of view about what good music is or what it means to be young, then you begin to see a music video in a new light. In order to analyze a cultural artifact, you must consider who produces the text, where it is distributed, and who consumes that text (and how). Put it this way: You want to

- investigate who is making/developing/creating/producing the text you are analyzing;

- explore where that text is displayed/shown/viewed/distributed; and

- think critically about how you/we consume/think about that text.

In the scheme that we describe below, we explain the key words and concepts needed to perform the analysis; we also explain production, distribution, and consumption.

When you analyze the **producer** of a text, consider what cultural values are present in the text, whether they are stated explicitly or implicitly. These values can be examined in the form of **cultural codes,** that is, as statements of an ideal, such as "The ideal X should (be/do/have) Y." Cultural codes are perhaps easiest to see in advertisements. For example, when you watch a commercial for running shoes, the producer of the commercial may seek to entice you to buy these shoes by including footage of athletic people. In this case, the text is telling you, "The ideal healthy body should be sculpted and lean."

When you have decided what text you will be analyzing, brainstorm as many cultural codes (i.e., intended effects) as you can from it. Remember to phrase them in the form of codes: "The ideal X should (be/do/have) Y." The more codes you can generate, the easier it will be to find the most important ones and critique them on the basis of your own experience. Here are some examples of cultural codes:

Gender: Women should be glamorous. (*Sex in the City*)

Gender: Men should be rugged. (an ad for Eddie Bauer)

Ethnicity: Beautiful people have exotic features. (*Elle*)

Economic class: The American dream is to be famous and live a raucous lifestyle. (*US Weekly*)

Age: The elderly are active and vital. (*Betty White's Off Their Rockers*)

As you can see, cultural codes construct *ideal* images (the ideal X should be/do/have Y), and they are adapted to particular media/ideologies.

In the preceding examples, cultural codes are arranged according to cultural categories (gender, ethnicity, class, political and national identity, age, etc.) as represented in assorted media/ideologies. When you analyze a text, ask yourself whether it endorses one or more of these cultural codes. What evidence from the text can you point to that illustrates the ideal?

Distribution is where (the location) the audience encounters the produced effects (the cultural codes). For example, you are likely to encounter codes related to ideals of beauty in magazines such as *Vogue*. Thus distribution refers to the point of intersection between those who produce cultural artifacts (and the cultural codes associated with them) and those who consume and interact with these artifacts and codes.

Today, the spread of technology has assured that points of distribution are more diverse than ever. Cultural codes are conveyed in different ways through different media. Every medium of distribution—from TV shows like *Snapped* and *TMZ* to magazines like *Sports Illustrated* to radio shock jocks like Howard Stern to Web sites like the *Huffington Post*—has a different feel to it, a different *technology* and a different *ideology*. The twenty-first-century rhetorician has to pay careful attention to the particular medium of distribution. Is the artifact distributed via a blog or some other online tool or application? What impact will its distribution have on how the message is promoted and on how it is consumed? Consider, for example, that the *New York Times* is published both in print and in an iPad edition. You may read the print edition from front to back, or skim each page, but if you are an iPad subscriber, the app may recommend stories to you based on what topics have interested you in the past, or those stories may include videos or interactive graphics that change the way you interact with an article. The method of distribution matters, then, in how the *New York Times* reaches different consumers and attracts different audiences.

When we think about **consumption**, we consider the impact cultural codes have on us as *consumers,* people who come into contact with the cultural codes produced by certain artifacts and texts through the media that distribute these artifacts. As consumers (whether readers, viewers, or hearers), we often *accommodate* (passively accept) the cultural codes promoted in the media. For example, in our earlier example concerning the commercial for running shoes, you might accept the producer's communicated ideal that "The ideal healthy body is sculpted and lean." When we accommodate cultural codes without understanding them critically, we allow the media that perpetuate these codes to interpret our worlds for us. That is, we accept their interpretations without questioning the social and cultural values implicit in their assumptions, many of which may run counter to our own social and cultural values.

Suppose, for instance, you have just watched a viral video that promotes environmentalism by showing someone driving a Hummer that is spewing toxic fumes into the air. You could say that this argument relies on the code, "The ideal environmentalist does not drive a Hummer." You could react to this code in one of three ways:

- If you agree that Hummers are terrible for the environment, you are **accommodating** the idea of the video.
- If you deny that global warming is an established scientific fact, or even if you grant that it is a scientific fact but you deny that science has proven that global warming results from combustion of carbon-based fuels, and you further deny that decreased use of these fuels will stop global warming—and therefore you see nothing wrong with buying a Hummer (except maybe the high price)—you are **resisting** the video.

- If you think there is indeed something sound in the anti-Hummer advertisement but you have a wife and four children and two dogs, and, further, you spend a lot of time working "off-road," you might carefully analyze the fuel-consumption of competing vehicles before you make your purchase, in which case you are **negotiating** the anti-Hummer video.

Negotiation, the most useful mode of consumption, involves a process of revision, a process of changing the conditions that give rise to negative aspects of cultural codes. Negotiation also necessitates practical intervention into the processes that construct oppressive social formations, for without intervention, there can be no revision, no positive social or cultural change. We *negotiate* cultural codes when

- we understand their underlying messages and accept the general cultural implications of these codes
- but we acknowledge that there are specific circumstances to which the general codes do not apply.

Using this scheme will help you analyze diverse kinds of texts as well as develop more nuanced arguments about the messages these texts send. In the next section, we'll walk through the analysis of a public service announcement about bullying.

A SAMPLE ANALYSIS: PUBLIC SERVICE ANNOUNCEMENT

Consider the following public service announcement (PSA) on bullying. Public service announcements are usually intended to advise or warn the general public or to facilitate proper civic engagement or participation within a community.

Production

Let's begin our analysis by thinking about the intended audience and cultural codes the PSA produces. We immediately know who the ideal audience is: parents. How do we know this? The evidence is in the artifact/text: "Teach your kids how to be more than a bystander." This is a PSA from StopBullying.gov, a government Web site. What codes can we generate from this simple message?

Class: Ideal parents have access to technologies that distribute PSA announcements.

Class: Ideal parents regardless of class should "teach" their kids how to handle bullying.

Age: Ideal parents are out of high school.

Everybody hates you.

You don't see bullying like this every day.

Your kids do.

Teach your kids how to **be more than a bystander.**

Learn how at StopBullying.gov

Political Orientation: Ideal parents should have jobs and occupations.
Ideal parents should recognize the government as a resource for parenting help.
Ideal parents should trust the government.
Ideal parents believe that bullying can be controlled or stopped.
Ideal parents should be involved with their kids' school.

Along with the cultural codes that we have generated, we want to think about what else we know about the text's production, distribution, and consumption. We also know that this text can be found both online and in print. There is a link on the text, so if we take this piece seriously we ought to visit the site to get more information.

This text is produced by the federal government. Evidence from the text tells us that this announcement is from StopBullying.gov. The fact that we know this helps us understand the context and the nature of the text. When we visit this site, we find out very quickly that October is Bullying Prevention Month. Furthermore, we learn that calling October "Bullying Prevention Month" is not new. In fact, it started in 2006, when it was initiated by PACER's (Parent Advocacy Coalition for Education Rights) National Bullying Prevention Center. Every October, this site presents activities and resources on bullying. We also learn something by looking at who is partnering with StopBullying.gov: The National Education Association, National PTA, American Federation for Teachers, and the National Coalition for Parent Involvement. We also find out that October 10 is designated as Unity Day, a day when people across the country are encouraged to wear orange as a show of support for students who have been bullied. The goal at StopBullying.gov is to help prevent bullying. It aims to send a message around the world to prevent the bullying of students. Given the partners involved, we can infer that much of the interest in this cause comes from parents and teachers.

At this point, you may be wondering why you are being told all this stuff about the background. Well, now that we have done a little research on this text and what it stands for, we are in a better position to think about two of the arguments the text might be making:

- what role the government should play in not only helping to stop bullying but in providing parents and teachers with resources to work to that end and

- what the producers of the text consider to be an ideal family.

For example, the Web site and the PSA are directly targeted to parents who are out of high school. Together, the PSA and the Web site also tell us that parents should trust the government, be involved with their kids' school, and have jobs or occupations. When the text says, "You don't see bullying like this every day. Your kids do," this assertion rests on an assumption that parents do not see bullying because they are not in school or not at school. Presumably, parents have jobs and other grown-up things to do, so would not notice, witness, or see the kinds of bullying that their kids do. Based on the number and kinds of organizations that partner with StopBullying.gov, we also know that the main source of concern is from parents and teachers and presupposes that most bullying occurs at school.

Distribution

This PSA, designed to appear in a magazine, is a *print text*, but PSAs are typically distributed as widely as possible. We may see them on television, hear them on the radio, or read them on billboards at the side of the road; nowadays, we also see them online as we surf various Web sites. Thinking about the distribution for PSAs matters: particular consumers may not come into contact with billboards (lack of car), may not hear radio announcements (no radio), may not see ads on television (no television), or may not find banners online (no Internet access). In thinking about the distribution of this PSA, we have to acknowledge that economic class plays a significant role in the distribution and accessibility of information in multiple venues. And, in fact, if you visit StopBullying.gov, you will see that this PSA is accompanied by additional ones designed for distribution to different media. How do those vary from this one?

Consumption

As we think more about the PSA on bullying, our minds are bound to turn to the question of how we consume the message. If we *accommodate* it, we could focus our argument on what a good job the government is doing to help protect kids from bullying. We might say, for example, that the government is helping parents, schools, teachers, and students have a better educational experience, free from bullying. The large headline "Everybody hates you" grabs the attention of anyone who sees the announcement. We could also argue that it is a good use of tax dollars because the PSA is an effort on the part of the government to protect its citizens—in particular, America's children.

If we *resist* this PSA, we could argue that the government is not responsible for helping parents raise their kids or even that government help of this sort is another example of the government meddling in the lives of citizens. We might also argue that bullying cannot be stopped because the psychological makeup of some students makes bullying inevitable. Some kids just are more aggressive than others, and they always have been. The PSA does not consider what medical or psychological issues might cause bullying. We might continue by arguing that the government should focus its energies and finances on other more serious causes where there was more reason to expect success.

If we decide to *negotiate* the PSA, we might argue that, yes, the PSA does consider a number of reasons for why someone bullies another but the announcement also serves as a reminder that grown-ups, parents, and teachers should pay closer attention to behaviors in the classroom, that we should do a better job of helping kids and students get along and become productive citizens of the community. The PSA, targeted at parents and teachers, also speaks to those without children when it pleads for the reader or viewer of the announcement not to be a "bystander." Although we may not think the government is the best resource for helping to raise our children, we recognize the efforts being made to

---

✓ A CHECKLIST FOR CULTURAL ANALYSIS

☐ What sort of text are you analyzing? A Web site (what kind of Web site?), a printed text, an image, an advertisement, a song or an album, an artifact (for instance a toy, a grocery item, a magazine), a Twitter feed? The kind of text you are analyzing will determine your approach.

☐ Have you thought about the cultural codes of your text: The ideal *X* should be/do/have *Y*?

☐ Have you described the codes and—*using evidence from the text*—have you explained how you reached your conclusion?

☐ Have you thought about where your text is distributed and where people come into contact with your text? Is it online, on television, in a newspaper, a film, etc.?

☐ Have you thought about whether you accommodate, resist, or negotiate the cultural codes illustrated by the text? Do you explain *why* you feel the way you do?

☐ Who is the main audience for the text you are analyzing? How can you tell? Who might be the main audience for the essay or project that you are composing?

☐ What should readers or viewers of your essay or project take away about the text you have analyzed, and what value can others get from it?

---

keep kids as safe and protected as possible. In short, we would recognize in our argument the ways that the PSA is productive and helpful to its audience, but we would also point out its weaknesses.

A SAMPLE CULTURAL ANALYSIS

Michelle Dean

The following essay, a rhetorical analysis of the reality TV phenomenon Here Comes Honey Boo Boo, *was originally published online at* Slate *on August 24, 2012. It was written by Michelle Dean, a lawyer who now writes about class, gender, and television. As you read the essay, think about how Dean constructs an analysis that considers audience, production, distribution, and consumption.*

Here Comes the Hillbilly, Again

Somehow America always goes a little off the rails in the allegedly slow month of August, and this year's party is as wild as any. Republicans can't figure out how babies are made; cutting-and-pasting an article from *The New Yorker* into your *Time* column is no longer a fireable offense; and all the way down in McIntyre, Ga., there is a mother who feeds her child a Mountain Dew-and-Red Bull concoction before the six-year-old gets onstage at beauty pageants. June Shannon, who stars with her daughter Alana "Honey Boo Boo Child" Thompson in TLC's controversial hit *Here Comes Honey Boo Boo*, would have provoked a firestorm even if what she calls "go-go juice" were the only sin she was broadcasting all over Christendom. All that caffeine, pop-culture commentators everywhere clucked, and all that sugar.

Lost in the outrage is just how squarely "go-go juice" fits into America's long tradition of "white trash" entertainment, which for decades has elevated characters like Honey Boo Boo into the nation's objects of fun. The Pepsi Co. borrowed the Mountain Dew brand-name from slang for moonshine; in the 1960s, it was explicitly advertised as a "hillbilly" drink. The campaign's entertaining TV ads, which you can watch on YouTube, were scored by twangy banjos and errant buckshot and plotted around a "stone-hearted gal" who will open her heart to you if you only take a swig. Watching these old videos after an episode or two of *Honey Boo Boo* makes at least one thing clear: The hillbilly has regained the spotlight in American culture.

As Anthony Harkins observes in *Hillbilly: A Cultural History of an American Icon*, one of the hillbilly's signature moves is to peak, popularity-wise, just when Americans sense that things in general are headed south. Its first true zenith came in the depressed 1930s, a handmaiden to the birth of commercial country music. Another arrived in the turbulent 1960s, when *The Beverly Hillbillies* and *Green Acres* and *Hee Haw* were in their prime. (Those are hardly the only examples, of course: It also popped up in the Ma and Pa Kettle films of the 1940s and 1950s and Paul Webb's 1930s *Esquire* cartoons about "The Mountain Boys," among other places.)

Though the term first referred to mountaineers in the Appalachians and the Ozarks, the hillbilly trope spread to cover pretty much all non-urban territory in America, joined by its cousins in cultural iconography, the "redneck" and "white trash." Today, people even apply that last term to residents of certain New Jersey beachfronts, for instance. Yet, as Harkins points out, no matter where an alleged country bumpkin comes from, he will be derided for his crass behavior. And such ridicule has always been politically coded: The hillbilly figure allows middle-class white people to offload the venality and sin of the nation onto some other constituency, people who live somewhere—anywhere—else. The hillbilly's backwardness highlights the progress more upstanding

Americans in the cities or the suburbs have made. These fools haven't crawled out of the muck, the story goes, because they don't want to.

This idea that the hillbilly's poverty is a choice allows more upscale 5 Americans to feel comfortable while laughing at the antics before them. It also pushes some people to embrace the stereotype as a badge of honor. "Guitars, Cadillacs, hillbilly music / It's the only thing that keeps me hangin' on," Dwight Yoakam once sang. For more contemporary examples of reappropriation, you can attend any number of Tea Party rallies. The classist term "redneck," originally coined to indicate those who worked so hard and so long in the sun that they sported sunburns in the designated anatomical location, likewise has been adopted in the name of all that's good and holy. What's more American than a hard day's work?

June Shannon is a reappropriator par excellence. One of her signature phrases on *Here Comes Honey Boo Boo* is a call to, as she puts it, "redneck-ognize." And yet all the cultural chatter that's attended *Honey Boo Boo* has been less than affectionate. The word of the day across the media is "apocalypse"—that is, the show is a sign of it. It's not just the caffeine highs, either. It's a family of six chopping up a roadkill deer for dinner, belly-flopping in the mud, and—those with delicate constitutions may want to avert their eyes for this next part—farting in public. Even critics who enjoy the show do so from a crouched, defensive posture. People seem to think this has all gone a little too far. Even the *Today Show* is starting to wonder if reality television just might be "exploitative."

I'm not a *Toddlers & Tiaras* fan, so I missed out on Alana's big splash on that show earlier this year. Beauty pageants in general are foreign and noxious to me: I can barely muster the energy to put on lip gloss and mascara. But I watched *Honey Boo Boo* out of curiosity about the fuss, and found myself, somewhat surprisingly, relating to Alana and her milieu. I have fond memories of that Dwight Yoakam song playing softly on my parents' radio as we drove home through the dark from a visit to my grandparents' house in rural Quebec. My family isn't from the South—we're not even from the United States—but I know enough of the land Honey Boo Boo lives in to be dubious of simple accusations of bad parenting and worse morals.

The practices are different, of course, and no, I'm not wild about the caffeine and sugar thing, either. Alana's little-girl grandiosity must become exhausting when experienced in more than thirty-minute increments. But the people raising her are clearly aware of your disdain. Shannon can be delightfully funny when she self-consciously plays with her hillbilly image, warning the audience that she's about to "scratch her bugs," or speaking of her beauty routine: "Granted, I ain't the most beautimous out the box, but a little paint on this barn, shine it back to its original condition. 'Cause it shines up like it's brand new."

That's not to say the humor is always comfortable or even funny. Alana's trademark phrases and mannerisms—"a dollar makes me holler," a particular head swivel she does—are informed by racist stereotypes of black women. This ambiguous borrowing from black culture has always been part of the hillbilly trope as well. Early commercial country music borrowed liberally from black folk music. (Hank Williams learned to play guitar, he said, from a black street performer.) And this borrowing often turned into racist mimicry: The Grand Ole Opry included minstrelsy shows in the 1920s and 1930s. Interestingly, the term "white trash" may have been coined by black slaves in the early nineteenth century to describe poor white people in the South; American attitudes toward poor white people have long been tangled up with "the race problem."

And hillbilly stereotypes have always made it easier for middle-class 10 whites to presume that racism is the exclusive province of "that kind" of person. As Ta-Nehisi Coates has written, "It is comforting to think of racism as species of misanthropy, or akin to child molestation, thus exonerating all those who bear no real hatred in their heart. It's much more troubling to think of it as it's always been—a means of political organization and power distribution."

As that distribution of power becomes more and more unequal, it's no surprise to see the hillbilly here again—on *Here Comes Honey Boo Boo*, on *Jersey Shore*, on MTV's *16 & Pregnant* and *Teen Mom* franchises. These shows reassure us that our struggle is worth it, all economic evidence to the contrary—if only because we would never belly-flop into the mud on cable television. *Here Comes Honey Boo Boo* casts this socioeconomic divide in especially sharp relief, since the show is rooted partly in beauty pageant culture, which, in its own idiosyncratic way, indulges the American belief that you can work and spend your way to greatness. If you can afford the entry fees, the glitter, the makeup, the coach, and the stylists, you will be the Ultimate Supreme, as they say in the business. You'll have the sash to prove it.

But tiny, six-year-old Alana is too crass and happy to get it. She is a terrible pageant queen. Her wigs are always askew, her daisy-dukes ill-fitting, and sometimes she grinds her fake teeth. Those rhinestone-studded bootstraps simply can't pull her up the way she needs them to.

Topics for Critical Thinking and Writing

1. What would you say was Dean's main argument? Support your reasoning with examples.

2. What cultural codes does Dean see as present both in *Here Comes Honey Boo Boo* and in the ensuing criticism of it?

3. *Here Comes Honey Boo Boo* is a reality TV show. How does Dean characterize this medium of distribution?

4. Visit slate.com, where Dean's essay was originally published. With respect to distribution, how would you characterize the technology and

ideology of *Slate*? Is it the kind of site where you would expect to find an essay defending *Here Comes Honey Boo Boo*? Why, or why not?

5. Would you say that Dean's essay accommodates, resists, or negotiates the codes imposed by *Here Comes Honey Boo Boo*?

6. Write an essay (about 500 words) in which you analyze a nontraditional text—perhaps a popular cultural artifact (such as a magazine, toy, or product), a Web site, a smartphone application, a commercial, television show, or anything else, preferably a text with which you have regular contact and to which you have easy access. Get a copy of the text you plan to analyze (you will submit a copy of it when you turn in your final critical essay). Your essay should follow the general structure discussed in this chapter (production, distribution, consumption); you may wish to use Dean's essay as a model. Your essay should have a strong introduction, in which you introduce your text and lay out your basic points of analysis, and a strong conclusion. Within the body of your analysis, make sure you do the following: Discuss who the audience for your text is, what codes the text produces, how the codes are distributed and whether this distribution is effective, and how this text targets you as a consumer, including whether you accommodate, resist, or negotiate the cultural codes you have found within the text. Make certain to use evidence from the text to support your claims.

12

A Literary Critic's View: Arguing about Literature

Literary criticism [is] a reasoned account of the feeling produced upon the critic by the book he is reading.

—D. H. LAWRENCE

A writer is someone for whom writing is more difficult than it is for other people.

—THOMAS MANN

You can never draw the line between aesthetic criticism and social criticism. . . . You start with literary criticism, and however rigorous an aesthete you may be, you are over the frontier into something else sooner or later. The best you can do is to accept these conditions and know what you are doing when you are doing it.

—T. S. ELIOT

Nothing is as easy as it looks.

—MURPHY'S LAW #23

Everything is what it is and not another thing.

—BISHOP JOSEPH BUTLER

You might think that literature—fiction, poetry (including songs), drama— is meant only to be enjoyed, not to be argued about. Yet literature is constantly the subject of argumentative writing—not all of it by teachers of English. For instance, if you glance at the current issue of *Time* or the *New Yorker*, you probably will find a review of a play suggesting that the play is worth seeing or is not worth seeing. Or in the same magazine you may find an article reporting that a senator or member of Congress argued that the National Endowment for the Humanities wasted its grant money by funding research on such-and-such an author or that the National Endowment for the Arts insulted taxpayers by making an award to a writer who defamed the American family.

Probably most writing about literature, whether done by college students, their professors, journalists, members of Congress, or whomever, is devoted to interpreting, judging (evaluating), and theorizing. Let's look at each of these, drawing our examples chiefly from comments about Shakespeare's *Macbeth*.

INTERPRETING

Interpreting is a matter of setting forth the *meaning* or the meanings of a work. For some readers, a work has *a* meaning, the one intended by the writer, which we may or may not perceive. For most critics today, however, a work has *many* meanings—for instance, the meaning it had for the writer, the meanings it has accumulated over time, and the meanings it has for each of today's readers. Take *Macbeth*, a play about a Scottish king, written soon after a Scot—James VI of Scotland—had been installed as James I, King of England. The play must have meant something special to the king—we know that it was presented at court—and something a little different to the ordinary English citizen. And surely it means something different to us. For instance, few if any people today believe in the divine right of kings, although James I certainly did; and few if any people today believe in malignant witches, although witches play an important role in the tragedy. What *we* see in the play must be rather different from what Shakespeare's audience saw in it.

Many interpretations of *Macbeth* have been offered. Let's take two fairly simple and clearly opposed views:

1. Macbeth is a villain who, by murdering his lawful king, offends God's rule, so he is overthrown by God's earthly instruments, Malcolm and Macduff. Macbeth is justly punished; the reader or spectator rejoices in his defeat.

One can offer a good deal of evidence—and if one is taking this position in an essay, of course one must *argue* it—by giving supporting reasons rather than merely asserting the position.

2. Macbeth is a hero-villain, a man who commits terrible crimes but who never completely loses the reader's sympathy; although he is justly punished, the reader believes that with the death of Macbeth the world has become a smaller place.

Again, one *must* offer evidence in an essay that presents this thesis or indeed presents any interpretation. For instance, one might offer as evidence the fact that the survivors, especially Macduff and Malcolm, have not interested us nearly as much as Macbeth has. One might argue, too, that although Macbeth's villainy is undeniable, his conscience never deserts him—here one would point to specific passages and would offer some brief quotations. Macbeth's pained awareness of what he has done, it can be argued, enables the reader to sympathize with him continually.

Or consider an interpretation of Lady Macbeth. Is she simply evil through and through, or are there mitigating reasons for her actions? Might one argue, perhaps in a feminist interpretation, that despite her intelligence and courage she had no outlet for expression except through her husband? To make this argument, the writer might want to go beyond the text of the play, offering as evidence Elizabethan comments about the proper role of women.

JUDGING (OR EVALUATING)

Literary criticism is also concerned with such questions as these: Is *Macbeth* a great tragedy? Is *Macbeth* a greater tragedy than *Romeo and Juliet*? The writer offers an opinion about the worth of the literary work, but the opinion must be supported by an argument, expressed in sentences that offer supporting evidence.

Let's pause for a moment to think about evaluation in general. When we say "This is a great play," are we in effect saying only "I like this play"? That is, are we merely *expressing* our taste rather than *asserting* anything about something out there—something independent of our tastes and feelings? (The next few paragraphs will not answer this question, but they may start you thinking about your own answer.) Consider these three sentences:

1. It's raining outside.
2. I like vanilla.
3. This is a really good book.

If you are indoors and you say that it is raining outside, a hearer may ask for verification. Why do you say what you say? "Because," you reply, "I'm looking out the window." Or "Because Jane just came in, and she is drenched." Or "Because I just heard a weather report." If, on the other hand, you say that you like vanilla, it's almost unthinkable that anyone would ask you why. No one expects you to justify—to support, to give a reason for—an expression of taste.

Now consider the third statement, "This is a really good book." It is entirely reasonable, we think, for someone to ask you *why* you say that. And you reply, "Well, the characters are realistic, and the plot held my interest," or "It really gave me an insight into what life among the rich [or the poor] must be like," or some such thing.

That is, statement 3 at least seems to be stating a fact, and it seems to be something we can discuss, even argue about, in a way that we cannot argue about a personal preference for vanilla. Almost everyone would agree that when we offer an aesthetic judgment we ought to be able to give reasons for it. At the very least, we might say, we hope to show *why* we evaluate the work as we do and to suggest that if our readers try to see it from our point of view they may then accept our evaluation.

Evaluations are always based on assumptions, although these assumptions may be unstated, and in fact the writer may even be unaware of them. Some of these assumptions play the role of criteria; they control the sort of evidence the writer believes is relevant to the evaluation. What sorts of assumptions may underlie value judgments? We will mention a few, merely as examples. Other assumptions are possible, and all of these assumptions can themselves become topics of dispute:

1. A good work of art, although fictional, says something about real life.
2. A good work of art is complex yet unified.
3. A good work of art sets forth a wholesome view of life.
4. A good work of art is original.
5. A good work of art deals with an important subject.

Let's look briefly at these views, one by one.

1. *A good work of art, although fictional, says something about real life.* If you hold the view that literature is connected to life and believe that human beings behave in fairly consistent ways—that is, that each of us has an enduring "character"—you probably will judge as inferior a work in which the figures behave inconsistently or seem not to be adequately motivated. (The point must be made, however, that different literary forms or genres are governed by different rules. For instance, consistency of character is usually expected in tragedy but not in melodrama or in comedy, where last-minute reformations may be welcome and greeted with applause. The novelist Henry James said, "You will not write a good novel unless you possess the sense of reality." He is probably right—but does his view hold for the writer of farces?) In the case of *Macbeth* you might well find that the characters are consistent: Although the play begins by showing Macbeth as a loyal defender of King Duncan, Macbeth's later treachery is understandable, given the temptation and the pressure. Similarly, Lady Macbeth's descent into madness, although it may come as a surprise, may strike you as entirely plausible: At the beginning of the play she is confident that she can become an accomplice to a murder, but she has overestimated herself (or, we might say, she has underestimated her own humanity, the power of her guilty conscience, which drives her to insanity).

2. *A good work of art is complex yet unified.* If Macbeth is only a "tyrant" (Macduff's word) or a "butcher" (Malcolm's word), he is a unified character but he may be too simple and too uninteresting a character to be the subject of a great play. But, one argument holds, Macbeth in fact is a complex character, not simply a villain but a hero-villain, and the play as a whole is complex. *Macbeth* is a good work of art, one might argue, partly because it shows us so many aspects of life (courage, fear, loyalty, treachery, for a start) through a richly varied language (the diction

ranges from a grand passage in which Macbeth says that his bloody hands will "incarnadine," or make red, "the multitudinous seas" to colloquial passages such as the drunken porter's "Knock, knock"). The play shows us the heroic Macbeth tragically destroying his own life, and it shows us the comic porter making coarse jokes about deceit and damnation, jokes that (although the porter doesn't know it) connect with Macbeth's crimes.

3. *A good work of art sets forth a wholesome view of life.* The idea that a work should be judged partly or largely on the moral view that it contains is widely held by the general public. (It has also been held by esteemed philosophers, notably Plato.) Thus, a story that demeans women—perhaps one that takes a casual view of rape—would be given a low rating and so would a play that treats a mass murderer as a hero.

Implicit in this approach is what is called an *instrumentalist* view—the idea that a work of art is an instrument, a means, to some higher value. Thus, many people hold that reading great works of literature makes us better—or at least does not make us worse. In this view, a work that is pornographic or in some other way thought to be immoral will be given a low value. At the time we are writing this chapter, a law requires the National Endowment for the Arts to take into account standards of decency when making awards.

Moral judgments, it should be noted, do not come only from the conservative right; the liberal left has been quick to detect political incorrectness. In fact, except for those people who subscribe to the now unfashionable view that a work of art is an independent aesthetic object with little or no connection to the real world—something like a pretty floral arrangement or a wordless melody—most people judge works of literature largely by their content, by what the works seem to say about life.

- Marxist critics, for instance, have customarily held that literature should make the reader aware of the political realities of life.

- Feminist critics are likely to hold that literature should make us aware of gender relationships—for example, aware of patriarchal power and of female accomplishments.

4. *A good work of art is original.* This assumption puts special value on new techniques and new subject matter. Thus, the *first* playwright who introduces a new subject (say, AIDS) gets extra credit, so to speak. Or to return to Shakespeare, one sign of his genius, it is held, is that he was so highly varied; none of his tragedies seems merely to duplicate another, each is a world of its own, a new kind of achievement. Compare, for instance, *Romeo and Juliet*, with its two youthful and innocent heroes, with *Macbeth*, with its deeply guilty hero. Both plays are tragedies, but we can hardly imagine two more different plays—even if a reader perversely argues that the young lovers are guilty of impetuosity and of disobeying appropriate authorities.

5. *A good work of art deals with an important subject.* Here we are concerned with theme: Great works, in this view, must deal with great themes. Love, death, patriotism, and God, say, are great themes; a work that deals with these may achieve a height, an excellence, that, say, a work describing a dog scratching for fleas may not achieve. (Of course, if the reader feels that the dog is a symbol of humanity plagued by invisible enemies, then the poem about the dog may reach the heights, but then, too, it is *not* a poem about a dog and fleas: It is really a poem about humanity and the invisible.)

The point: In writing an evaluation you must let your reader know *why* you value the work as you do. Obviously, it is not enough just to keep saying that *this* work is great whereas *that* work is not so great; the reader wants to know *why* you offer the judgments that you do, which means that you

- must set forth your criteria and then
- offer evidence that is in accord with them.

THEORIZING

Some literary criticism is concerned with such theoretical questions as these:

> What is tragedy? Can the hero be a villain? How does tragedy differ from melodrama?

✔ A CHECKLIST FOR AN ARGUMENT ABOUT LITERATURE

☐ Is my imagined reader like a typical classmate of mine, someone who is not a specialist in literature but who is open-minded and interested in hearing my point of view about a work?

☐ Is the essay supported with evidence, usually from the text itself but conceivably from other sources (such as a statement by the author, a statement by a person regarded as an authority, or perhaps the evidence of comparable works)?

☐ Is the essay inclusive? Does it take into account all relevant details (which is not to say that it includes everything the writer knows about the work—for instance, that it was made into a film or that the author died poor)?

☐ Is the essay focused? Does the thesis stay steadily before the reader?

☐ Does the essay use quotations, but as evidence, not as padding? Whenever possible, does it abridge or summarize long quotations?

☐ Are all sources fully acknowledged? (For the form of documentation, see Chapter 7.)

Why do tragedies—works showing good or at least interesting people destroyed—give us pleasure?

Does a work of art—a play or a novel, say, a made-up world with imagined characters—offer anything that can be called "truth"? Does an experience of a work of art affect our character?

Does a work of art have meaning in itself, or is the meaning simply whatever anyone wishes to say it is? Does *Macbeth* tell us anything about life, or is it just an invented story?

And, yet again, one hopes that anyone asserting a thesis concerned with any of these topics will offer evidence—will, indeed, *argue* rather than merely assert.

EXAMPLES:
Two Students Interpret Robert Frost's "Mending Wall"

Let's consider two competing interpretations of a poem, Robert Frost's "Mending Wall." We say "competing" because these interpretations clash head-on. Differing interpretations need not be incompatible, of course. For instance, a historical interpretation of *Macbeth*, arguing that an understanding of the context of English-Scottish politics around 1605 helps us to appreciate the play, need not be incompatible with a psychoanalytic interpretation that tells us that Macbeth's murder of King Duncan is rooted in an Oedipus complex, the king being a father figure. Different approaches thus can illuminate different aspects of the work, just as they can emphasize or subordinate different elements in the plot or characters portrayed. But, again, in the next few pages we will deal with mutually incompatible interpretations of the meaning of Frost's poem—of what Frost's poem is about.

After reading the poem and the two interpretations written by students, spend a few minutes thinking about the questions that we raise after the second interpretation.

Robert Frost

Robert Frost (1874–1963) studied for part of one term at Dartmouth College in New Hampshire, then did odd jobs (including teaching), and from 1897 to 1899 was enrolled as a special student at Harvard. He then farmed in New Hampshire, published a few poems in newspapers, did some more teaching, and in 1912 left for England, where he hoped to achieve success as a writer. By 1915 he was known in England, and he returned to the United States. By the time of his death he was the nation's unofficial poet laureate. "Mending Wall" was first published in 1914.

Mending Wall

Something there is that doesn't love a wall,
That sends the frozen-ground-swell under it,
And spills the upper boulders in the sun;
And makes gaps even two can pass abreast.
The work of hunters is another thing: 5
I have come after them and made repair
Where they have left not one stone on a stone,
But they would have the rabbit out of hiding,
To please the yelping dogs. The gaps I mean,
No one has seen them made or heard them made,   10
But at spring mending-time we find them there.
I let my neighbor know beyond the hill;
And on a day we meet to walk the line
And set the wall between us once again.
We keep the wall between us as we go.   15
To each the boulders that have fallen to each.
And some are loaves and some so nearly balls
We have to use a spell to make them balance:
"Stay where you are until our backs are turned!"
We wear our fingers rough with handling them.   20
Oh, just another kind of outdoor game,
One on a side. It comes to little more:
There where it is we do not need the wall:
He is all pine and I am apple orchard.
My apple trees will never get across   25
And eat the cones under his pines, I tell him.
He only says, "Good fences make good neighbors."
Spring is the mischief in me, and I wonder
If I could put a notion in his head:
"*Why* do they make good neighbors? Isn't it   30
Where there are cows? But here there are no cows.
Before I built a wall I'd ask to know
What I was walling in or walling out,
And to whom I was like to give offense.
Something there is that doesn't love a wall,   35
That wants it down." I could say "Elves" to him,
But it's not elves exactly, and I'd rather
He said it for himself. I see him there

Bringing a stone grasped firmly by the top
In each hand, like an old-stone savage armed.   40
He moves in darkness as it seems to me,
Not of woods only and the shade of trees.
He will not go behind his father's saying,
And he likes having thought of it so well
He says again, "Good fences make good neighbors."   45

Jonathan Deutsch

Professor Walton

English 102

5 March 2009

The Deluded Speaker in Frost's "Mending Wall"

Our discussions of "Mending Wall" in high school showed that most people think Frost is saying that walls between people are a bad thing and that we should not try to separate ourselves from each other unnecessarily. Perhaps the wall, in this view, is a symbol for race prejudice or religious differences, and Frost is suggesting that these differences are minor and that they should not keep us apart. In this common view, the neighbor's words, "Good fences make good neighbors" (lines 27 and 45) show that the neighbor is shortsighted. I disagree with this view, but first I want to present the evidence that might be offered for it, so that we can then see whether it really is substantial.

First of all, someone might claim that in lines 23 to 26 Frost offers a good argument against walls:

There where it is we do not need the wall:

He is all pine and I am apple orchard.

My apple trees will never get across

And eat the cones under his pines, I tell him.

The neighbor does not offer a valid reply to this argument; in fact, he doesn't offer any argument at all but simply says, "Good fences make good neighbors."

Another piece of evidence supposedly showing that the neighbor is wrong, it is said, is found in Frost's description of him as "an old-stone savage" and someone who "moves in darkness" (40, 41). And a third piece of evidence is said to be that the neighbor "will not go behind his father's saying" (43), but he merely repeats the saying.

Deutsch 2

There is, however, another way of looking at the poem. As I see it, the speaker is a very snide and condescending person. He is confident that he knows it all and that his neighbor is an ignorant savage; he is even willing to tease his supposedly ignorant neighbor. For instance, the speaker admits to "the mischief in me" (28), and he is confident that he could tell the truth to the neighbor but arrogantly thinks that it would be a more effective form of teaching if the neighbor "said it for himself" (38).

The speaker is not only unpleasantly mischievous and condescending toward his neighbor, but he is also shallow, for he does not see the great wisdom that there is in proverbs. The *American Heritage Dictionary of the English Language,* Third Edition, defines a proverb as "A short, pithy saying in frequent and widespread use that expresses a basic truth." Frost, or at least the man who speaks this poem, does not seem to realize that proverbs express truths. He just dismisses them, and he thinks the neighbor is wrong not to "go behind his father's saying" (43). But there is a great deal of wisdom in the sayings of our fathers. For instance, in the Bible (in the Old Testament) there is a whole book of proverbs, filled with wise sayings such as "Reprove not a scorner, lest he hate thee: rebuke a wise man, and he will love thee" (9:8); "He that trusteth in his riches shall fall" (11:28); "The way of a fool is right in his own eyes" (12:15; this might be said of the speaker of "Mending Wall"); "A soft answer turneth away wrath" (15:1); and (to cut short what could be a list many pages long), "Whoso diggeth a pit shall fall therein" (26:27).

The speaker is confident that walls are unnecessary and probably bad, but he doesn't realize that even where there are no cattle, walls serve the valuable purpose of clearly marking out our territory. They help us to preserve our independence and our individuality. Walls — man-made structures — are a sign of civilization. A wall more or less says, "*This* is mine, but I respect *that* as yours."

Frost's speaker is so confident of his shallow view that he makes fun
of his neighbor for repeating that "Good fences make good neighbors"
(27, 45). But he himself repeats his own saying, "Something there
is that doesn't love a wall" (1, 35). And at least the neighbor has age-
old tradition on his side, since the proverb is the saying of his father.
On the other hand, the speaker has only his own opinion, and he can't
even say what the "something" is.

It may be that Frost meant for us to laugh at the neighbor and
to take the side of the speaker, but I think it is much more likely that
he meant for us to see that the speaker is mean-spirited (or at least
given to unpleasant teasing), too self-confident, foolishly dismissing
the wisdom of the old times, and entirely unaware that he has these
unpleasant characteristics.

Felicia Alonso

Professor Walton

English 102

5 March 2009

The Debate in Robert Frost's "Mending Wall"

I think the first thing to say about Frost's "Mending Wall" is this: The poem is not about a debate over whether good fences do or do not make good neighbors. It is about two debaters: One of the debaters is on the side of vitality, and the other is on the side of an unchanging, fixed — dead, we might say — tradition.

How can we characterize the speaker? For one thing, he is neighborly. Interestingly, it is *he,* and not the neighbor, who initiates the repairing of the wall: "I let my neighbor know beyond the hill" (line 12). This seems strange, since the speaker doesn't see any point in this wall, whereas the neighbor is all in favor of walls. Can we explain this apparent contradiction? Yes; the speaker is a good neighbor, willing to do his share of the work and willing (perhaps in order not to upset his neighbor) to maintain an old tradition even though he doesn't see its importance. It may not be important, he thinks, but it is really rather pleasant, "another kind of outdoor game" (21). In fact, sometimes he even repairs fences on his own, after hunters have destroyed them.

Second, we can say that the speaker is on the side of nature. "Something there is that doesn't love a wall," he says (1, 35), and of course, the "something" is nature itself. Nature "sends the frozen-ground-swell" under the wall and "spills the upper boulders in the sun; / And makes gaps even two can pass abreast" (2–4). Notice that nature itself makes the gaps and that "two can pass abreast" — that is, people can walk together in a companionable way. It is hard to imagine the neighbor walking side by side with anyone.

Third, we can say that the speaker has a sense of humor. When he thinks of trying to get his neighbor interested in the issue, he admits that "the mischief" is in him (28), and he amusingly attributes his playfulness to a natural force, the spring. He playfully toys with the obviously preposterous idea of suggesting to his neighbor that elves caused the stones to fall, but he stops short of making this amusing suggestion to his very serious neighbor. Still, the mere thought assures us that he has a playful, genial nature, and the idea also again implies that not only the speaker but also some sort of mysterious natural force dislikes walls.

Finally, though, of course, he thinks he is right and that his neighbor is mistaken, he at least is cautious in his view. He does not call his neighbor "an old-stone savage" (40); rather, he uses a simile ("like") and then adds that this is only his opinion, so the opinion is softened quite a bit. Here is the description of the neighbor, with italics added to clarify my point. The neighbor is . . .

> *like* an old-stone savage armed. / He moves
>
> in darkness *as it seems to me* . . . (40–41)

Of course, the only things we know about the neighbor are those things that the speaker chooses to tell us, so it is not surprising that the speaker comes out ahead. He comes out ahead not because he is right about walls (real or symbolic) and his neighbor is wrong—that's an issue that is not settled in the poem. He comes out ahead because he is a more interesting figure, someone who is neighborly, thoughtful, playful. Yes, maybe he seems to us to feel superior to his neighbor, but we can be certain that he doesn't cause his neighbor any embarrassment. Take the very end of the poem. The speaker tells us that the neighbor

> . . . will not go behind his father's saying,
>
> And he likes having thought of it so well
>
> He says again, "Good fences make good neighbors."

The speaker is telling *us* that the neighbor is utterly unoriginal and that the neighbor confuses *remembering* something with *thinking*. But the speaker doesn't get into an argument; he doesn't rudely challenge his neighbor and demand reasons, which might force the neighbor to see that he can't think for himself. And in fact we probably like the neighbor just as he is, and we don't want him to change his mind. The words that ring in our ears are not the speaker's but the neighbor's: "Good fences make good neighbors." The speaker of the poem is a good neighbor. After all, one can hardly be more neighborly than to let the neighbor have the last word.

Topics for Critical Thinking and Writing

1. State the thesis of each essay. Do you believe the theses are sufficiently clear and appear sufficiently early in the essays?

2. Consider the evidence that each essay offers by way of supporting its thesis. Do you find some of the evidence unconvincing? Explain.

3. Putting aside the question of which interpretation you prefer, comment on the organization of each essay. Is the organization clear? Do you want to propose some other pattern that you think might be more effective?

4. Consult the Checklist for Peer Review on page 260, and offer comments on one of the two essays. Or: If you were the instructor in the course in which these two essays were submitted, what might be your final comments on each of them? Or: Write an analysis (250–500 words) of the strengths and weaknesses of either essay.

EXERCISES: READING A POEM AND A STORY

Andrew Marvell

Andrew Marvell (1621–1678), born in Hull, England, and educated at Trinity College, Cambridge, was traveling in Europe when the civil war between the Royalists and the Puritans broke out in England in 1642. The Puritans were victorious and established the Commonwealth (the monarchy was restored later, in 1660), and Marvell became a tutor to the daughter of the victorious Lord-General. In 1657 he became an assistant to the blind poet John Milton, who held the title of Latin Secretary (Latin was the language of international diplomacy). In 1659 Marvell was elected to represent Hull in Parliament. As a man of letters, during his lifetime he was known chiefly for some satiric prose and poetry; most of the writings for which he is now esteemed were published posthumously. The following poem was first published in 1681.

To His Coy Mistress°

Had we but world enough, and time,
This coyness,° Lady, were no crime.
We would sit down, and think which way
To walk, and pass our long love's day.
Thou by the Indian Ganges' side   5
Shouldst rubies find; I by the tide
Of Humber° would complain. I would
Love you ten years before the Flood,
And you should, if you please, refuse

Mistress Beloved woman.
coyness Reluctance.
Humber An estuary at Hull, Marvell's birthplace.

Till the Conversion of the Jews.°   10
My vegetable° love should grow
Vaster than empires and more slow;
An hundred years should go to praise
Thine eyes, and on thy forehead gaze;
Two hundred to adore each breast,   15
But thirty thousand to the rest;
An age at least to every part,
And the last age should show your heart.
For, Lady, you deserve this state,°
Nor would I love at lower rate.   20
    But at my back I always hear
Time's wingèd chariot hurrying near;
And yonder all before us lie
Deserts of vast eternity.
Thy beauty shall no more be found,   25
Nor, in thy marble vault, shall sound
My echoing song; then worms shall try°
That long-preserved virginity,
And your quaint° honour turn to dust,
And into ashes all my lust: 30
The grave's a fine and private place,
But none, I think, do there embrace.
    Now therefore, while the youthful hue
Sits on thy skin like morning dew,
And while thy willing soul transpires   35
At every pore with instant fires,
Now let us sport us while we may,
And now, like amorous birds of prey,
Rather at once our time devour
Than languish in his slow-chapt° power.   40
Let us roll all our strength and all
Our sweetness up into one ball,
And tear our pleasures with rough strife
Thorough° the iron gates of life:
Thus, though we cannot make our sun   45
Stand still,° yet we will make him run.

Conversion of the Jews Something that would take place in the remote future, at the
end of history.
vegetable Vegetative or growing.
state Ceremonious treatment.
try Test.
quaint Fastidious or finicky, with a pun on a coarse word defined in an Elizabethan dictionary as "a woman's privities."
slow-chapt Slow-jawed.
Thorough Through.
make our sun stand still An allusion to Joshua, the ancient Hebrew who, according to
the Book of Joshua (10.12–13), made the sun stand still.

TOPICS FOR CRITICAL THINKING AND WRITING

1. The motif that life is short and that we should seize the day (Latin: *Vita brevis carpe diem*) is old. Marvell's poem, in fact, probably has its ultimate source in a classical text called *The Greek Anthology*, a collection of about six thousand short Greek poems composed between the first century B.C. and the tenth century A.D. One poem goes thus, in a fairly literal translation:

   > You spare your maidenhead, and to what profit? For when you come to Hades you will not find your lover, girl. Among the living are the delights of Venus, but, maiden, we shall lie in the underworld mere bones and dust.

   If you find Marvell's poem more impressive, offer reasons for your belief.

2. A student, working from the translation just given, produced this rhyming version:

   > You keep your virginity, but to what end?
   > Below, in Hades, you won't find your friend.
   > On earth we enjoy Venus' sighs and moans;
   > Buried below, we are senseless bones.

   What do you think of this version? Why? Prepare your own version—your instructor may divide the class into groups of four, and each group can come up with a collaborative version—and then compare it with other versions, giving reasons for your preferences.

3. Marvell's poem takes the form of a syllogism (see pp. 85–90). It can be divided into three parts:

   a. "Had we" (that is, "If we had") (line 1), a supposition, or suppositional premise;
   b. "But at my back" (line 21), a refutation;
   c. "Now therefore" (line 33), a deduction.

   Look closely at the poem and develop the argument using these three parts, devoting a few sentences to each part.

4. A student wrote of this poem:

   > As a Christian I can't accept the lover's statement that "yonder all before us lie / Deserts of vast eternity" (lines 23–24). The poem may contain beautiful lines, and it may offer clever reasoning, but the reasoning is based on what my religion tells me is wrong. I not only cannot accept the idea of the poem, but I also cannot enjoy the poem, since it presents a false view of reality.

   What assumptions is this student making about a reader's response to a work of literature? Do you agree or disagree? Why?

5. Here are three additional comments by students. For each, list the writer's assumptions, and then evaluate each comment. You may agree or disagree, in whole or in part, with any comment, but give your reasons.

   a. The poem is definitely clever, and that is part of what is wrong with it. It is a blatant attempt at seduction. The man seems to think he is smarter than the woman he is speaking to, and he "proves" that she should go to bed with him. Since we don't hear her side of the argument, Marvell implies that she has nothing to say and that his argument is sound. What the poet doesn't seem to understand is that there is such a thing as virtue, and a woman need not sacrifice virtue just because death is inevitable.

b. On the surface, "To His Coy Mistress" is an attempt to persuade a woman to go to bed with the speaker, but the poem is really less about sex than it is about the terrifying shortness of life.

c. This is not a love poem. The speaker admits that his impulse is "lust" (line 30), and he makes fun of the girl's conception of honor and virginity. If we enjoy this poem at all, our enjoyment must be in the hope that this would-be date-rapist is unsuccessful.

6. Read the poem several times slowly, perhaps even aloud. Do certain lines seem especially moving, especially memorable? If so, which ones? Give reasons for your belief.

7. In *On Deconstruction* (1982), a study of contemporary literary theory, Jonathan Culler remarks that feminist criticism has often stressed "reading as a woman." This concept, Culler says, affirms the "continuity between women's experience of social and familial structures and their experiences as readers." Do you agree with his suggestion that men and women often interpret literary works differently? Consider Marvell's poem in particular: Identify and discuss phrases and images in it to which men and women readers might (or might not) respond very differently.

8. A small point, but perhaps one of some interest. In the original text, line 34 ends with *glew*, not with *dew*. Most editors assume that the printer made an error, and—looking for a word to rhyme with *hue*—they replace *glew* with *dew*. Another possible emendation is *lew*, an archaic word meaning "warmth." But the original reading has been defended, as a variant of the word *glow*. Your preference? Your reasons?

Kate Chopin

Kate Chopin (1851–1904) was born in St. Louis and named Katherine O'Flaherty. At the age of nineteen she married a cotton broker in New Orleans, Oscar Chopin (the name is pronounced something like "show pan"), who was descended from the early French settlers in Louisiana. After her husband's death in 1883, Kate Chopin turned to writing fiction. The following story was first published in 1894.

The Story of an Hour

Knowing that Mrs. Mallard was afflicted with a heart trouble, great care was taken to break to her as gently as possible the news of her husband's death.

It was her sister Josephine who told her, in broken sentences, veiled hints that revealed in half concealing. Her husband's friend Richards was there, too, near her. It was he who had been in the newspaper office when intelligence of the railroad disaster was received, with

Brently Mallard's name leading the list of "killed." He had only taken the time to assure himself of its truth by a second telegram, and had hastened to forestall any less careful, less tender friend in bearing the sad message.

She did not hear the story as many women have heard the same, with a paralyzed inability to accept its significance. She wept at once, with sudden, wild abandonment, in her sister's arms. When the storm of grief had spent itself she went away to her room alone. She would have no one follow her.

There stood, facing the open window, a comfortable, roomy armchair. Into this she sank, pressed down by a physical exhaustion that haunted her body and seemed to reach into her soul.

She could see in the open square before her house the tops of trees   5 that were all aquiver with the new spring life. The delicious breath of rain was in the air. In the street below a peddler was crying his wares. The notes of a distant song which some one was singing reached her faintly, and countless sparrows were twittering in the eaves.

There were patches of blue sky showing here and there through the clouds that had met and piled one above the other in the west facing her window.

She sat with her head thrown back upon the cushion of the chair, quite motionless, except when a sob came up into her throat and shook her, as a child who has cried itself to sleep continues to sob in its dreams.

She was young, with a fair, calm face, whose lines bespoke repression and even a certain strength. But now there was a dull stare in her eyes, whose gaze was fixed away off yonder on one of those patches of blue sky. It was not a glance of reflection, but rather indicated a suspension of intelligent thought.

There was something coming to her and she was waiting for it, fearfully. What was it? She did not know; it was too subtle and elusive to name. But she felt it, creeping out of the sky, reaching toward her through the sounds, the scents, the color that filled the air.

Now her bosom rose and fell tumultuously. She was beginning to rec-   10 ognize this thing that was approaching to possess her, and she was striving to beat it back with her will—as powerless as her two white slender hands would have been.

When she abandoned herself a little whispered word escaped her slightly parted lips. She said it over and over under her breath: "Free, free, free!" The vacant stare and the look of terror that had followed it went from her eyes. They stayed keen and bright. Her pulses beat fast, and the coursing blood warmed and relaxed every inch of her body.

She did not stop to ask if it were not a monstrous joy that held her. A clear and exalted perception enabled her to dismiss the suggestion as trivial.

She knew that she would weep again when she saw the kind, tender hands folded in death; the face that had never looked save with love upon her, fixed and gray and dead. But she saw beyond that bitter moment a long procession of years to come that would belong to her absolutely. And she opened and spread her arms out to them in welcome.

There would be no one to live for her during those coming years; she would live for herself. There would be no powerful will bending her in that blind persistence with which men and women believe they have a right to impose a private will upon a fellow creature. A kind intention or a cruel intention made the act seem no less a crime as she looked upon it in that brief moment of illumination.

And yet she had loved him—sometimes. Often she had not. What did it matter! What could love, the unsolved mystery, count for in face of this possession of self-assertion which she suddenly recognized as the strongest impulse of her being.   15

"Free! Body and soul free!" she kept whispering.

Josephine was kneeling before the closed door with her lips to the keyhole, imploring for admission. "Louise, open the door! I beg; open the door—you will make yourself ill. What are you doing, Louise? For heaven's sake open the door."

"Go away. I am not making myself ill." No; she was drinking in a very elixir of life through that open window.

Her fancy was running riot along those days ahead of her. Spring days, and summer days, and all sorts of days that would be her own. She breathed a quick prayer that life might be long. It was only yesterday she had thought with a shudder that life might be long.

She arose at length and opened the door to her sister's importuni-   20
ties. There was a feverish triumph in her eyes, and she carried herself unwittingly like a goddess of Victory. She clasped her sister's waist, and together they descended the stairs. Richards stood waiting for them at the bottom.

Some one was opening the front door with a latchkey. It was Brently Mallard who entered, a little travel-stained, composedly carrying his grip-sack and umbrella. He had been far from the scene of accident, and did not even know there had been one. He stood amazed at Josephine's piercing cry; at Richards' quick motion to screen him from the view of his wife.

But Richards was too late.

When the doctors came they said she had died of heart disease—of joy that kills.

TOPICS FOR CRITICAL THINKING AND WRITING

Read the following assertions, and consider whether you agree or disagree, and why. For each assertion, draft a paragraph with your arguments.

1. The railroad accident is a symbol of the destructiveness of the industrial revolution.

2. The story claims that women rejoice in the deaths of their husbands.

3. Mrs. Mallard's death at the end is a just punishment for the joy she takes in her husband's death.

4. The story is rich in irony. Some examples: (1) The other characters think she is grieving, but she is rejoicing; (2) she prays for a long life, but she dies almost immediately; (3) the doctors say she died of "the joy that kills," but they think her joy was seeing her husband alive.

5. The story is excellent because it has a surprise ending.

THINKING ABOUT THE EFFECTS OF LITERATURE

Works of art are artifacts—things constructed, made up, fashioned, just like chairs and houses and automobiles. In analyzing works of literature it is therefore customary to keep one's eye on the complex, constructed object and not simply tell the reader how one feels about it. Instead of reporting their feelings, critics usually analyze the relationships between the parts and the relationship of the parts to the whole.

For instance, in talking about literature we can examine the relationship of plot to character, of one character to another, or of one stanza in a poem to the next. Still, although we may try to engage in this sort of analysis as dispassionately as possible, we all know that inevitably

- we are not only examining something out there,
- but are also examining our own responses.

Why? Because literature has an effect on us. Indeed, it probably has several kinds of effects, ranging from short-range emotional responses ("I really enjoyed this," "I burst out laughing," "It revolted me") to long-range effects ("I have always tried to live up to a line in *Hamlet*, 'This above all, to thine own self be true'"). Let's first look at, very briefly, immediate emotional responses.

Analysis usually begins with a response: "This is marvelous," or "What a bore," and we then go on to try to account for our response. A friend mentions a book or a film to us, and we say, "I couldn't stay with it for five minutes." The friend expresses surprise, and we then go on to explain, giving reasons (to the friend and also to ourselves) why we couldn't stay with it. Perhaps the book seemed too remote from life, or perhaps, on the other hand, it seemed to be nothing more than a transcript of the boring talk that we can overhear on a bus or in an elevator.

In such discussions, when we draw on our responses, as we must, the work may disappear; we find ourselves talking about ourselves. Let's take two extreme examples: "I can't abide *Huckleberry Finn*. How am I expected to enjoy a so-called masterpiece that has a character in it called 'Nigger Jim?'" Or: "T. S. Eliot's anti-Semitism is too much for me to take. Don't talk to me about Eliot's skill with meter, when he has such lines as 'Rachel, *née* Rabinovitch / Tears at the grapes with murderous paws.'"

Although everyone agrees that literature can evoke this sort of strong emotional response, not everyone agrees on how much value we should put on our personal experience. Several of the Topics for Critical Thinking and Writing below invite you to reflect on this issue.

What about the *consequences of the effects* of literature? Does literature shape our character and therefore influence our behavior? It is generally believed that it does have an effect. One hears, for example, that literature (like travel) is broadening, that it makes us aware of, and tolerant of, kinds of behavior that differ from our own and from what we see around us. One of the chief arguments against pornography, for instance, is that it desensitizes us, makes us too tolerant of abusive relationships, relationships in which people (usually men) use other people (usually women) as mere things or instruments for pleasure. (A contrary view should be mentioned: Some people argue that pornography provides a relatively harmless outlet for fantasies that otherwise might be given release in the real world. In this view, pornography acts as a sort of safety valve.)

Discussions of the effects of literature that get into the popular press almost always involve pornography, but other topics are also the subjects of controversy. For instance, in recent decades parents and educators have been much concerned with fairy tales. Does the violence in some fairy tales ("Little Red Riding Hood," "The Three Little Pigs") have a bad effect on children? Do some of the stories teach the wrong lessons, implying that women should be passive, men active ("Sleeping Beauty," for instance, in which the sleeping woman is brought to life by the action of the handsome prince)? The Greek philosopher Plato (427–347 B.C.) strongly believed that the literature we hear or read shapes our later behavior, and since most of the ancient Greek traditional stories (notably Homer's *Odyssey* and *Iliad*) celebrate acts of love and war rather than of justice, he prohibited the reading of such material in his ideal society. (We reprint a relevant passage from Plato on page 443.)

TOPICS FOR CRITICAL THINKING AND WRITING

1. If you have responded strongly (favorably or unfavorably) to some aspect of the social content of a literary work—for instance, its depiction of women or of a particular minority group—in an essay of 250 to 500 words analyze the response, and try to determine whether you are talking chiefly about yourself or the work. (Two works widely regarded as literary masterpieces but nonetheless often banned from classrooms are Shakespeare's *The Merchant of Venice* and Mark Twain's *Huckleberry Finn*. If you have read either of these, you may want to write about it and your response.) Can we really see literary value—*really* see it—in a work that deeply offends us?

2. Most people believe that literature influences life—that in some perhaps mysterious way it helps to shape character. Certainly anyone who
believes that some works should be censored, or at least should be made
unavailable to minors, assumes that they can have a bad influence, so
why not assume that other works can have a good influence?

   Read the following brief claims about literature; then choose one
and write a 250-word essay offering support or taking issue with it.

The pen is mightier than the sword.—EDWARD BULWER LYTTON

The writer isn't made in a vacuum. Writers are witnesses. The reason
we need writers is because we need witnesses to this terrifying century.
—E. L. DOCTOROW

When we read of human beings behaving in certain ways, with the
approval of the author, who gives his benedictions to this behavior by his
attitude towards the result of the behavior arranged by himself, we can
be influenced towards behaving in the same way.—T. S. ELIOT

Poetry makes nothing happen.—W. H. AUDEN

Literature is *without proofs*. By which it must be understood that it cannot
prove, not only *what* it says, but even that it is worth the trouble of saying it.—ROLAND BARTHES

Of course the illusion of art is to make one believe that great literature is
very close to life, but exactly the opposite is true. Life is amorphous, literature is formal. —FRANÇOISE SAGAN

3. At least since the time of Plato (see the piece directly following)
some thoughtful people have wanted to ban certain works of literature because they allegedly stimulate the wrong sorts of pleasure or
cause us to take pleasure in the wrong sorts of things. Consider, by way
of comparison, bullfighting and cockfighting. Of course, they cause pain
to the animals, but branding animals also causes pain and is not banned.
Bullfighting and cockfighting probably are banned in the United States
largely because most of us believe that people should not take pleasure
in these activities. Now to return to literature: Should some kinds of
writing be prohibited because they offer the wrong sorts of pleasure?

Plato

*Plato (427–347 B.C.), an Athenian aristocrat by birth, was the student of one great
philosopher (Socrates) and the teacher of another (Aristotle). His legacy of more
than two dozen dialogues—imaginary discussions between Socrates and one or
more other speakers, usually young Athenians—has been of such influence that
the whole of Western philosophy can be characterized, A. N. Whitehead wrote,
as "a series of footnotes to Plato." Plato's interests encompassed the full range of
topics in philosophy: ethics, politics, logic, metaphysics, epistemology, aesthetics,
psychology, and education.*

   This selection from Plato's Republic, *one of his best-known and longest dialogues, is about the education suitable for the rulers of an ideal society.*

The Republic *begins, typically, with an investigation into the nature of justice. Socrates (who speaks for Plato) convincingly explains to Glaucon that we cannot reasonably expect to achieve a just society unless we devote careful attention to the moral education of the young men who are scheduled in later life to become the rulers. (Here as elsewhere, Plato's elitism and aristocratic bias shows itself; as readers of* The Republic *soon learn, Plato is no admirer of democracy or of a classless society.) Plato cares as much about what the educational curriculum should exclude as what it should include. His special target was the common practice in his day of using for pedagogy the Homeric tales and other stories about the gods. He readily embraces the principle of censorship, as the excerpt explains, because he thinks it is a necessary means to achieve the ideal society.*

"The Greater Part of the Stories Current Today We Shall Have to Reject"

"What kind of education shall we give them then? We shall find it difficult to improve on the time-honored distinction between the physical training we give to the body and the education we give to the mind and character."

"True."

"And we shall begin by educating mind and character, shall we not?"

"Of course."

"In this education you would include stories, would you not?"   5

"Yes."

"These are of two kinds, true stories and fiction.[1] Our education must use both, and start with fiction."

"I don't know what you mean."

"But you know that we begin by telling children stories. These are, in general, fiction, though they contain some truth. And we tell children stories before we start them on physical training."

"That is so."   10

"That is what I meant by saying that we must start to educate the mind before training the body."

"You are right," he said.

"And the first step, as you know, is always what matters most, particularly when we are dealing with those who are young and tender. That is the time when they are easily molded and when any impression we choose to make leaves a permanent mark."

"That is certainly true."

---

[1]The Greek word *pseudos* and its corresponding verb meant not only "fiction" — stories, tales — but also "what is not true" and so, in suitable contexts, "lies": and this ambiguity should be borne in mind. [Editors' note: All footnotes are by the translator, but some have been omitted.]

"Shall we therefore readily allow our children to listen to any sto-   15
ries made up by anyone, and to form opinions that are for the most
part the opposite of those we think they should have when they
grow up?"

"We certainly shall not."

"Then it seems that our first business is to supervise the production of
stories, and choose only those we think suitable, and reject the rest. We
shall persuade mothers and nurses to tell our chosen stories to their children, and by means of them to mold their minds and characters which are
more important than their bodies. The greater part of the stories current
today we shall have to reject."

"Which are you thinking of?"

"We can take some of the major legends as typical. For all, whether
major or minor, should be cast in the same mold and have the same
effect. Do you agree?"

"Yes: but I'm not sure which you refer to as major."   20

"The stories in Homer and Hesiod and the poets. For it is the poets
who have always made up fictions and stories to tell to men."

"What sort of stories do you mean and what fault do you find in
them?"

"The worst fault possible," I replied, "especially if the fiction is an ugly
one."

"And what is that?"

"Misrepresenting the nature of gods and heroes, like a portrait painter   25
whose portraits bear no resemblance to their originals."

"That is a fault which certainly deserves censure. But give me more
details."

"Well, on the most important of subjects, there is first and foremost the foul story about Ouranos[2] and the things Hesiod says he did, and
the revenge Cronos took on him. While the story of what Cronos did,
and what he suffered at the hands of his son, is not fit as it is to be lightly
repeated to the young and foolish, even if it were true; it would be best to
say nothing about it, or if it must be told, tell it to a select few under oath
of secrecy, at a rite which required, to restrict it still further, the sacrifice
not of a mere pig but of something large and difficult to get."

"These certainly are awkward stories."

"And they shall not be repeated in our state, Adeimantus," I said. "Nor
shall any young audience be told that anyone who commits horrible crimes,
or punishes his father unmercifully, is doing nothing out of the ordinary
but merely what the first and greatest of the gods have done before."

"I entirely agree," said Adeimantus, "that these stories are unsuitable."   30

---

[2]**Ouranos** The sky, the original supreme god. Ouranos was castrated by his son Cronos to
separate him from Gaia (mother earth). Cronos was in turn deposed by Zeus in a struggle
in which Zeus was helped by the Titans.

"Nor can we permit stories of wars and plots and battles among the gods; they are quite untrue, and if we want our prospective guardians to believe that quarrelsomeness is one of the worst of evils, we must certainly not let them be told the story of the Battle of the Giants or embroider it on robes, or tell them other tales about many and various quarrels between gods and heroes and their friends and relations. On the contrary, if we are to persuade them that no citizen has ever quarreled with any other, because it is sinful, our old men and women must tell children stories with this end in view from the first, and we must compel our poets to tell them similar stories when they grow up. But we can admit to our state no stories about Hera being tied up by her son, or Hephaestus being flung out of Heaven by his father for trying to help his mother when she was getting a beating, nor any of Homer's Battles of the Gods, whether their intention is allegorical or not. Children cannot distinguish between what is allegory and what isn't, and opinions formed at that age are usually difficult to eradicate or change; we should therefore surely regard it as of the utmost importance that the first stories they hear shall aim at encouraging the highest excellence of character."

"Your case is a good one," he agreed, "but if someone wanted details, and asked what stories we were thinking of, what should we say?"

To which I replied, "My dear Adeimantus, you and I are not engaged on writing stories but on founding a state. And the founders of a state, though they must know the type of story the poet must produce, and reject any that do not conform to that type, need not write them themselves."

"True: but what are the lines on which our poets must work when they deal with the gods?"

"Roughly as follows," I said. "God must surely always be represented   35
as he really is, whether the poet is writing epic, lyric, or tragedy."

"He must."

"And in reality of course god is good, and he must be so described."

"Certainly."

"But nothing good is harmful, is it?"[3]

"I think not."   40

"Then can anything that is not harmful do harm?"

"No."

"And can what does no harm do evil?"

"No again."

"And can what does no evil be the cause of any evil?"   45

---

[3]The reader of the following passage should bear the following ambiguities in mind: (1) the Greek word for good (*agathos*) can mean (a) morally good, (b) beneficial or advantageous; (2) the Greek word for evil (*kakos*) can also mean harm or injury; (3) the adverb of *agathos* (*eu*—the well) can imply either morally right or prosperous. The word translated "cause of" could equally well be rendered "responsible for."

"How could it?"

"Well then; is the good beneficial?"

"Yes."

"So it must be the cause of well-being."

"Yes."

"So the good is not the cause of everything, but only of states of well-being and not of evil."

"Most certainly," he agreed.

"Then god, being good, cannot be responsible for everything, as is commonly said, but only for a small part of human life, for the greater part of which he has no responsibility. For we have a far smaller share of good than of evil, and while god must be held to be the sole cause of good, we must look for some factors other than god as cause of the evil."

"I think that's very true," he said.

"So we cannot allow Homer or any other poet to make such a stupid mistake about the gods, as when he says that

Zeus has two jars standing on the floor of his palace, full of fates, good in one and evil in the other

and that the man to whom Zeus allots a mixture of both has 'varying fortunes sometimes good and sometimes bad,' while the man to whom he allots unmixed evil is 'chased by ravening despair over the face of the earth.'[4] Nor can we allow references to Zeus as 'dispenser of good and evil.' And we cannot approve if it is said that Athene and Zeus prompted the breach of solemn treaty and oath by Pandarus, or that the strife and contentions of the gods were due to Themis and Zeus. Nor again can we let our children hear from Aeschylus that

God implants a fault in man, when he wishes to destroy a house utterly.

No: We must forbid anyone who writes a play about the sufferings of Niobe (the subject of the play from which these last lines are quoted), or the house of Pelops, or the Trojan war, or any similar topic, to say they are acts of god; or if he does he must produce the sort of interpretation we are now demanding, and say that god's acts were good and just, and that the sufferers were benefited by being punished. What the poet must not be allowed to say is that those who were punished were made wretched through god's action. He may refer to the wicked as wretched because they needed punishment, provided he makes it clear that in punishing them god did them good. But if a state is to be run on the right lines, every possible step must be taken to prevent anyone, young or old, either saying or being told, whether in poetry or prose, that god,

---

[4]Quotations from Homer are generally taken from the translations by Dr. Rieu in the Penguin series. At times (as here) the version quoted by Plato differs slightly from the accepted text.

being good, can cause harm or evil to any man. To say so would be sinful, inexpedient, and inconsistent."

"I should approve of a law for this purpose and you have my vote for it," he said.

"Then of our laws laying down the principles which those who write or speak about the gods must follow, one would be this: *God is the cause, not of all things, but only of good.*"

"I am quite content with that," he said.

TOPICS FOR CRITICAL THINKING AND WRITING

1. In the beginning of the dialogue Plato says that adults recite fictions to very young children and that these fictions help to mold character. Think of some stories that you heard or read when young, such as "Snow White and the Seven Dwarfs" or "Ali Baba and the Forty Thieves." Try to think of a story that, in the final analysis, is not in accord with what you consider to be proper morality, such as a story in which a person triumphs through trickery or a story in which evil actions—perhaps murders—are set forth without unfavorable comment. (Was it naughty of Jack to kill the giant?) On reflection, do you think children should not be told such stories? Why, or why not? Or think of the early film westerns, in which, on the whole, the Indians (except for an occasional Uncle Tonto) are depicted as bad guys and the whites (except for an occasional coward or rustler) are depicted as good guys. Many people who now have gray hair enjoyed such films in their childhood. Are you prepared to say that such films are not damaging? Or on the other hand, are you prepared to say they are damaging and should be prohibited?

2. It is often objected that censorship of reading matter and of television programs available to children underrates their ability to think for themselves and to discount the dangerous, obscene, and tawdry. Do you agree with this objection? Does Plato?

3. Plato says that allowing poets to say what they please about the gods in his ideal state would be "inconsistent." Explain what he means by this criticism, and then explain why you agree or disagree with it.

4. Do you believe that parents should censor the "fiction" their children encounter (literature, films, pictures, music) but that the community should not censor the "fiction" of adults? Write an essay of 500 words on one of these topics: "Censorship and Rock Lyrics"; "X-Rated Films"; "Ethnic Jokes." (These topics are broadly worded; you can narrow one and offer whatever thesis you wish.)

5. Were you taught that any of the founding fathers ever acted disreputably or that any American hero had any serious moral flaw? Or that America ever acted immorally in its dealings with other nations? Do you think it appropriate for children to hear such things?

THINKING ABOUT GOVERNMENT FUNDING FOR THE ARTS

Our government supports the arts, including writers, by giving grants to numerous institutions. On the other hand, the amount that the government contributes is extremely small when compared to the amounts given to the arts by most European governments. Consider the following questions.

1. Should taxpayers' dollars be used to support the arts? Why, or why not?
2. What possible public benefit can come from supporting the arts? Can one argue that we should support the arts for the same reasons that we support the public schools, that is, to have a civilized society?
3. If dollars are given to the arts, should the political content of the works be taken into account, or only the aesthetic merit? Can we separate content from aesthetic merit? (The best way to approach this issue probably is to begin by thinking of a strongly political work.)
4. Is it censorship not to award public funds to writers whose work is not approved of, or is it simply a matter of refusing to reward them with taxpayers' dollars?
5. Should decisions about grants to writers be made chiefly by government officials or chiefly by experts in the field? Why?

13

A Debater's View: Individual Oral Presentations and Debate

He who knows only his own side of the case knows little of that.

——JOHN STUART MILL

A philosopher who is not taking part in discussions is like a boxer who never goes into the ring.

——LUDWIG WITTGENSTEIN

Freedom is hammered out on the anvil of dissension, dissent, and debate.

——HUBERT HUMPHREY

INDIVIDUAL ORAL PRESENTATIONS

Forensic comes from a Latin word *foris,* meaning "out of doors," which also produced the word *forum,* an open space in front of a public building. In the language of rhetoricians, the place where one delivers a speech to an audience is the forum—whether it is a classroom, a court of law, or the steps of the Lincoln Memorial.

Your instructor may ask you to make an oral presentation (in this case the forum is the classroom), and if your instructor doesn't make such a demand, later life almost certainly will: You will find that at a job interview you will be expected to talk persuasively about what good qualities or experience you can bring to the place of employment. When you have a job you will sometimes have to summarize a report orally or orally argue a case—for instance, that your colleagues should do something they may be hesitant to do.

The goal of your classroom talk is to persuade the audience to share your view, or, if you can't get them to agree completely, to get them to see that at least there is something to be said for this view—that it is a position a reasonable person can hold.

Elsewhere in this book we have said that the subjects of persuasive writing are usually

- matters of fact (for instance, statistics show that the death penalty does — or does not — deter crime), or
- matters of value (abortion is — or is not — immoral), or
- matters of policy (government should — or should not — give money to faith-based institutions).

> **TWO RULES FOR SPEAKERS:**
> - *In preparing your oral presentation, keep your thesis in mind.* You may be giving counterarguments, examples, definitions, and so forth, but make sure that your thesis is always evident to your audience.
> - *Keep your audience in mind.* Inevitably you will have to make assumptions about what the audience does and does not know about your topic. Do not overestimate their knowledge, and do not underestimate their intelligence.

Whatever your subject, when you draft and revise your talk, make certain that a thesis statement underlies the whole (for instance, "Proposition 2 is a bad idea because. . . .")

The text of an oral presentation ought not to be identical with the text of a written presentation. Both must have a clear **organization,** but oral presentations usually require that the organization be made a bit more obvious, with abundant **signposts** such as "Before I talk about *X,*" "When I discussed *Y,* I didn't mention such-and-such because I wanted to concentrate on a single instance, but now is the time to consider *Y,*" and so on. You will also have to repeat a bit more than you would in a written presentation. After all, a reader can turn back to check a sentence or a statistic but an auditor cannot, so rather than saying (as one might in a printed text), "When we think further about Smith's comment, we realize. . . ," you will repeat what Smith said before you go on to analyze the statement.

You will want to think carefully about the organization of your talk. We've already stressed the need to develop essays with clear thesis statements and logical supporting points. Oral presentations are no different, but remember that when you are speaking in public, a clear organization will always help alleviate anxiety and reassure you. Thus, you can deliver a powerful message without getting tripped up yourself. We suggest you try the following:

- Outline your draft in advance in order to make sure that it has clear organization.

- Inform your audience at the start what the organization of your presentation will be. Early in the talk you probably should say something along these lines, though not in so abbreviated a form:

  > "In talking about *A*, I'll have to define a few terms, *B* and *C*, and I will also have to talk about two positions that differ from mine, *D* and *E*. I'll then try to show why *A* is the best policy to pursue, clearly better than *D* and *E*."

- So that your listeners can easily follow you, be sure to use transitions such as "Furthermore," "Therefore," "Although it is often said," and "It may be objected that," so that your listeners can easily follow your train of thought. Sometimes you may even remind the listeners what the previous stages were, with such a comment as "We have now seen three approaches to the problem of . . . ."

Methods of Delivery

After thinking about helping your audience to follow your speech, you might want to consider how much help you'll need delivering it. Depending on your comfort level with the topic and your argument, you might decide to

- deliver a memorized talk without notes,
- read the talk from a text, or
- speak from an outline, perhaps with quotations and statistics written down.

Each of these methods has its strengths and its weaknesses. A memorized talk allows for plenty of eye contact with the audience but unless you are a superb actor it is almost surely going to seem a bit mechanical. A talk that you read from a text will indeed let you say to an audience exactly what you want to say (with the best possible wording), but reading a text inevitably establishes some distance between you and the audience, even if you occasionally glance up from your pages. If you talk from a mere outline, almost surely some of your sentences will turn out to be a bit awkward—though a tiny bit of awkwardness may help to convey sincerity and may therefore be a plus.

Whatever the form of delivery, try to convey the impression that you are conversing with your audience, not talking down to them—even though if you are on a platform you will be literally talking down.

You may want to use **audiovisual aids** in your presentation. These can range from such low-tech materials as handouts, blackboards, and whiteboards to high-tech PowerPoint presentations. Each has its advantages and its disadvantages. For instance, if you distribute handouts when the talk begins, the audience may start thumbing through them even while you are making your opening comments. And although PowerPoint can be a highly useful aid, some speakers make too much use of it simply because it is available. It happens that the day before writing this discussion the author witnessed a PowerPoint presentation, which began with the speaker projecting on the screen the date, the speaker's name, and the name of the university at which the talk was being delivered. Well, most of us knew the date, and we all knew the speaker's name and the name of the university where we were. It seemed like overkill. The truth is, the talk simply did not need any images at all, and we ended up wondering why the speaker bothered with PowerPoint.

For a delightful parody of this sort of talk, consider "The Gettysburg Powerpoint Presentation" (http://norvig.com/Gettysburg/). It begins thus:

And now please welcome President Abraham Lincoln.
Good morning. Just a second while I get this connection to work. Do I press this button here? Function-F7? No, that's not right. Hmmm. Maybe I'll have to reboot. Hold on a minute. Um, my name is Abe Lincoln and I'm your president. While we're waiting, I want to thank Judge David Wills, chairman of the committee supervising the dedication of the Gettysburg cemetery. It's great to be here, Dave, and you and the committee are doing a great job. Gee, sometimes this new **technology** does have glitches, but **we couldn't live without it, could we?** Oh—is it ready? OK, here we go.

The lesson? Yes, use audiovisual material if it will help you to present your material, but do not use it if it adds nothing or if you have not mastered the technology.

✓ A CHECKLIST FOR AN ORAL PRESENTATION

Keep the following in mind, whether you are evaluating someone else's talk or preparing your own.

Delivery

☐ Voice loud enough but not too loud.

☐ Appropriate degree of speed — neither hurried nor drawn out.

☐ Dress and attitude toward audience appropriate.

☐ Gestures and eye contact appropriate.

☐ Language clear, e.g., technical words adequately explained.

☐ Visual aids, if any, appropriate and effectively used.

Content

☐ Thesis clear, and kept in view.

☐ Argument steadily advanced, with helpful transitions.

☐ Thesis supported by evidence.

☐ Lightweight material, e.g., bits of humor, relevant and genuinely engaging.

One final point: If you do use visual material, *make certain that any words on the images are large enough to be legible to your audience:* A graph with tiny words will not impress your audience, even if you read the words aloud.

THE AUDIENCE

It is not merely because topics are complicated that we cannot agree that one side is reasonable and right and the other side irrational and wrong. The truth is, we are swayed not only by reason (*logos*) but also by appeals to the emotions (*pathos*) and by the character of the speaker (*ethos*). We can combine these last two things and put it this way: Sometimes we are inclined to agree with *X* rather than with *Y* because *X* strikes us as a more appealing person (perhaps more open-minded, more intelligent, better informed, more humane, and less cold). *X* is the sort of person we want to have as a friend. We disagree with *Y*—or at least we are unwilling to associate ourselves with *Y*—because *Y* is, well, *Y* just isn't the sort of person we want to agree with. *Y*'s statistics don't sound right, or *Y* seems like a bully; for some reason, we just don't have confidence in *Y*. Confidence is easily lost: Alas, even a mispronunciation will diminish the audience's confidence in *Y*. As Peter de Vries said, "You can't be happy with someone who pronounces both *d*'s in Wednesday."

Earlier in the book we talked about the importance of **tone** and of the writer's **persona.** And we have made the point that the writer's tone will depend partly on the audience. A person who is writing for a conservative journal whose readership is almost entirely conservatives can adopt a highly satiric manner in talking about liberals and will meet with much approval. But if this conservative writer is writing in a liberal journal and hopes to get at least a sympathetic hearing, he or she will have to avoid satire and wisecracks and will have to present himself or herself as a person of goodwill who is open-minded and eager to address the issue seriously.

The **language** that you use—the degree to which it is formal as opposed to colloquial, and the degree to which it is technical as opposed to general—will also depend on the audience. Speaking a bit broadly, in oral argument speak politely but not formally. You do *not* want to be one of those people who "talk like a book." But you also don't want to be overly colloquial. Choose a middle course, probably a notch below the style you would use if you were handing in a written paper. For instance, in an oral presentation you might say, "We'll consider this point in a minute or two," whereas in a written paper you probably will write "We will consider this point shortly."

Technical language is entirely appropriate *if* your audience is familiar with it. If you are arguing before members of Amnesty International about the use of torture, you can assume certain kinds of specialized knowledge. You can, for instance, breezily speak of the DRC and of KPCS, and your listeners will know what you are talking about because Amnesty International has been active with issues concerning the Democratic Republic of Congo and the Kimberley Process Certification Scheme. On the other hand, if you are arguing the same case before a general public, you will have to explain these abbreviations, and you may even have to explain what Amnesty International is.

If you are arguing before your classmates, you probably have a pretty good idea of what you can assume they know and what you can assume they do not know.

DELIVERY

Your audience will in some measure determine not only your tone but also the way you appear when you give the speech. Part of the delivery is the speaker's **appearance.** The medium is part of the message. The president can appear in jeans when he chats about his reelection plans, but he wears a suit and a tie when he delivers the State of the Union address. Just as we wear one kind of **clothing** when we play tennis, another when we attend classes, and yet another when we go for a job interview, an effective speaker dresses appropriately. A lawyer arguing before the Supreme Court wears a dark suit or dress, and if the lawyer is male he wears a necktie. The same lawyer, arguing at a local meeting, speaking as a community resident who objects to a proposal to allow a porno store to open near a school, may well dress informally, maybe in jeans, to show that he or she is not at all stuffy but still feels that a porno store goes too far.

Your appearance when you speak is not merely a matter of your clothing; it includes your **facial expressions,** your **posture,** your **gestures,** your general demeanor. All that we can say here is that you should avoid those bodily motions—swaying, thumping the table, putting on and taking off eyeglasses, craning your neck, smirking—that are so distracting that they cause the audience to concentrate on the distraction rather than on the argument. ("That's the third time he straightened his necktie. I wonder how many more times he will—oops, that's the fourth!"). Most of us are not aware of our annoying habits; if you are lucky, a friend, when urged, will tell you about them. You may lose a friend, but you will gain some good advice.

You probably can't do much about your **voice**—it may be high-pitched, or it may be gravelly—but you can make sure that you speak loudly enough for the audience to hear you, slowly enough for it to understand you, and clearly enough for it to understand you.

We have some advice about **quotations.** First, if possible, use an effective quotation or two, partly because—we will be frank—the quotations probably are more impressively worded than anything you can come up with on your own. A quotation may be the chief thing that your audience comes away with: "Hey, yes, I liked that: 'War is too important to be left to the generals'" or "When it comes down to it, I agree with that Frenchman who said 'If we are to abolish the death penalty, I should like to see the first step taken by the murderers'" or "You know, I think it was all summed up in that line by Margaret Mead, something like, 'No one would remember the Good Samaritan if he'd had only good intentions. He had money as well.' Yes, that's pretty convincing. Morality isn't enough. You need money." You didn't invent the words that you quote, but you did bring them to the attention of your listeners, and your listeners will be grateful to you.

A second bit of advice about quotations: When you quote, do *not* begin by saying "quote," and do not end by saying "end quote" (or as we once heard a speaker endlessly say, quotation after quotation, "unquote") and do not hook the air with your fingers. How do you make it clear that you are quoting, and how do you make it clear that you have finished quoting? Begin with a clear lead-in ("In *Major Barbara* George Bernard Shaw touches on this issue, when Barbara says, . . ."), slightly pause, and then slightly change (for instance, elevate) your voice. When you have finished quoting—again a slight pause and a return to your normal voice—be sure to use words that clearly indicate the quotation is finished, such as "Shaw here says what everyone thinks," or "Shaw's comment is witty but short-sighted," or "Barbara's point, then, is. . . ."

Our third and last piece of advice concerning quotations is this: If the quotation is only a phrase or a brief sentence, you can memorize it and be confident that you will remember it, but if it is longer than a sentence, write it on a sheet in your notes or on a four-by-six-inch card in print large enough for you to read easily. You have chosen these words because they are effectively put, so you don't want to misquote them or even hesitate in delivering them.

THE TALK

As for the talk itself, well, we have been touching on it in our discussion of such matters as the speaker's relation to the audience, the speaker's need to provide signposts, and the use of quotations. All of our comments in earlier chapters about developing a written argument are relevant also to oral arguments, but here we should merely emphasize that because the talk is oral and the audience cannot look back to an earlier page to remind itself of some point, the speaker may have to repeat and summarize a bit more than is usual in a written essay.

Remember, too, that a reader can *see* when the essay ends—there is blank space at the end of the page—but a listener depends on aural cues. Nothing is more embarrassing—and less effective as argument—than a speaker who seems (to the audience) to suddenly stop and sit down. In short, give your hearers ample clues that you are ending (post such signs as "Finally" or "Last" or "Let me end by saying"), and be sure to end with a strong sentence. It probably won't be as good as the end of the Gettysburg address ("government of the people, by the people, for the people, shall not perish from the earth"), nor will it be as good as the end of Martin Luther King's "I Have a Dream" speech ("Free at last! Free at last! Thank God Almighty, we are free at last!"), but those are the models to emulate.

FORMAL DEBATES

It would be nice if all arguments ended with everyone, participants and spectators, agreeing that the facts are clear, that one presentation is more reasonable than the other, and therefore that one side is right and the other side is wrong. But in life, most issues are complicated. High school students may earnestly debate—this is a real topic in a national debate—

Resolved: That education has failed its mission in the United States,

but it takes only a moment of reflection to see that neither the affirmative nor the negative can be true. Yes, education has failed its mission in many ways, but, No, it has succeeded in many ways. Its job now is (in the words of Samuel Beckett) to try again: "Fail. Fail again. Fail better."

Debates of this sort, conducted before a judge and guided by strict rules concerning "Constructive Speeches," "Rebuttal Speeches," and "Cross-Examinations" are not attempts to get at the truth; like lawsuits, they are attempts to win a case. Each speaker seeks not to persuade the opponent but only to convince the judge. Although most of this section is devoted not to forensics in the strictest sense but more generally to the presentation of oral arguments, we begin with the standard format.

Standard Debate Format

Formal debates occur within a structure that governs the number of speeches, the order of the speeches, and the maximum time for each speech. The format may vary from place to place, but there is always a structure. In most debates, a formal resolution states the reason for the debate ("Resolved: That capital punishment be abolished in juvenile cases"). The affirmative team supports the resolution; the negative team denies its legitimacy. The basic structure has three parts:

- *The constructive phase,* in which the debaters construct their cases and develop their arguments (usually for ten minutes);
- *The rebuttal,* in which debaters present their responses and also present their final summary (usually for five minutes); and
- *The preparation,* in which the debater prepares for presenting the next speech. (During the preparation—a sort of time-out—the

debater is not addressing the opponent or audience. The total time allotted to a team is usually six or eight minutes, which the individual debaters divide as they wish.)

We give, very briefly, the usual structure of each part, though it should be mentioned that another common format calls for a cross-examination of the First Affirmative Construction by the Second Negative, a cross-examination of the First Negative Construction by the First Affirmative, a cross-examination of the Second Affirmative by the First Negative, and a cross-examination of the Second Negative by the Second Affirmative:

First Affirmative Constructive Speech: Serves as introduction, giving summary overview, definitions, criteria for resolution, major claims and evidence, statement, and intention to support the resolution.

First Negative Constructive Speech: Responds by introducing the basic position, challenges the definitions and criteria, suggests the line of attack, emphasizes that the burden of proof lies with the affirmative, rejects the resolution as unnecessary or dangerous, and supports the status quo.

Second Affirmative Constructive: Rebuilds the affirmative case; refutes chief attacks, especially concerning definitions, criteria, and rationale (philosophic framework); and further develops the affirmative case.

Second Negative Constructive: Completes the negative case, if possible advances it by rebuilding portions of the first negative construction, and contrasts the entire negative case with the entire affirmative case.

✔ A CHECKLIST FOR PREPARING FOR A DEBATE

☐ Have I done adequate preparation in research?

☐ Are my notes legible, with accurate quotations and impressive sources?

☐ Am I prepared to take good notes during the debate?

☐ Is my proposition clearly stated?

☐ Do I have adequate evidence to support the thesis (main point)?

☐ Do I have backup points in mind?

☐ Have I given thought to issues opponents may raise?

☐ Does the opening properly address the instructor, the audience, the opponents? (Remember, you are addressing an audience, not merely the opponents.)

☐ Are my visual aids focused on major points?

☐ Is my demeanor professional, and is my dress appropriate?

First Negative Rebuttal: Attacks the opponents' arguments and defends the negative constructive arguments (but a rebuttal may *not* introduce new constructive arguments).

First Affirmative Rebuttal: Usually responds first to the second negative construction and then to the first negative rebuttal.

Second Negative Rebuttal: Constitutes final speech for the negative, summarizing the case and explaining to the judge why the negative should be declared the winner.

Second Affirmative Rebuttal: Summarizes the debate, responds to issues pressed by the second negative rebuttal, and suggests to the judge that the affirmative team should win.

PART FOUR

A CASEBOOK on the STATE and the INDIVIDUAL

14

What Is the Ideal Society?

Thomas More

The son of a prominent London lawyer, More (1478–1535) served as a page in the household of the Archbishop of Canterbury, went to Oxford University, and then studied law in London. More's charm, brilliance, and gentle manner caused Erasmus, the great Dutch humanist who became his friend during a visit to London, to write to a friend: "Did nature ever create anything kinder, sweeter, or more harmonious than the character of Thomas More?"

More served in Parliament, became a diplomat, and after holding several important positions in the government of Henry VIII, rose to become lord chancellor. But when Henry married Anne Boleyn, broke from the Church of Rome, and established himself as head of the Church of England, More refused to subscribe to the Act of Succession and Supremacy. Condemned to death as a traitor, he was executed in 1535, nominally for treason but really because he would not recognize the king rather than the pope as the head of his church. A moment before the ax fell, More displayed a bit of the whimsy for which he was known: When he put his head on the block, he brushed his beard aside, commenting that his beard had done no offense to the king. In 1886 the Roman Catholic Church beatified More, and in 1935, the four-hundredth anniversary of his death, it canonized him as St. Thomas More.

More wrote Utopia *(1514–15) in Latin, the international language of the day. The book's name, however, is Greek for "no place" (ou topos), with a pun on "good place" (eu topos). Utopia owes something to Plato's* Republic *and something to then-popular accounts of voyagers such as Amerigo Vespucci.* Utopia *purports to record an account given by a traveler named Hytholodaeus (Greek for "learned in nonsense"), who allegedly visited Utopia. The work is playful, but it is also serious. In truth, it is hard to know exactly where it is serious and how serious it is. One inevitably wonders, for example, if More the devoted Roman Catholic could really have advocated euthanasia. And could More the persecutor of heretics really have approved of the religious tolerance practiced in Utopia? Is he perhaps in effect saying, "Let's see what reason, unaided by Christian revelation, can tell us about an ideal society"? But if so, is he nevertheless also saying, very strongly, that Christian countries, though blessed with the revelation of Christ's teachings, are far behind these unenlightened pagans?* Utopia *has been widely praised by all sorts of readers—from Roman Catholics to communists—but for all sorts of reasons. The selection presented here is about one-twelfth of the book (in a translation by Paul Turner).*

From *Utopia*

[A DAY IN UTOPIA]

And now for their working conditions. Well, there's one job they all do, irrespective of sex, and that's farming. It's part of every child's education. They learn the principles of agriculture at school, and they're taken for regular outings into the fields near the town, where they not only watch farm work being done, but also do some themselves, as a form of exercise.

Besides farming which, as I say, is everybody's job, each person is taught a special trade of his own. He may be trained to process wool or flax, or he may become a stonemason, a blacksmith, or a carpenter. Those are the only trades that employ any considerable quantity of labor. They have no tailors or dressmakers, since everyone on the island wears the same sort of clothes—except that they vary slightly according to sex and marital status—and the fashion never changes. These clothes are quite pleasant to look at, they allow free movement of the limbs, they're equally suitable for hot and cold weather—and the great thing is, they're all home-made. So everybody learns one of the other trades I mentioned, and by everybody I mean the women as well as the men—though the weaker sex are given the lighter jobs, like spinning and weaving, while the men do the heavier ones.

Most children are brought up to do the same work as their parents, since they tend to have a natural feeling for it. But if a child fancies some other trade, he's adopted into a family that practices it. Of course, great care is taken, not only by the father, but also by the local authorities, to see that the foster father is a decent, respectable type. When you've learned one trade properly, you can, if you like, get permission to learn another—and when you're an expert in both, you can practice whichever you prefer, unless the other one is more essential to the public.

The chief business of the Stywards[1]—in fact, practically their only business—is to see that nobody sits around doing nothing, but that everyone gets on with his job. They don't wear people out, though, by keeping them hard at work from early morning till late at night, like cart horses. That's just slavery—and yet that's what life is like for the working classes nearly everywhere else in the world. In Utopia they have a six-hour working day—three hours in the morning, then lunch—then a two-hour break—then three more hours in the afternoon, followed by supper. They go to bed at 8 P.M., and sleep for eight hours. All the rest of the twenty-four they're free to do what they like—not to waste their

---

[1]**Stywards** In Utopia, each group of thirty households elects a styward; each town has two hundred stywards, who elect the mayor. [All notes are the editors'.]

time in idleness or self-indulgence, but to make good use of it in some congenial activity. Most people spend these free periods on further education, for there are public lectures first thing every morning. Attendance is quite voluntary, except for those picked out for academic training, but men and women of all classes go crowding in to hear them—I mean, different people go to different lectures, just as the spirit moves them. However, there's nothing to stop you from spending this extra time on your trade, if you want to. Lots of people do, if they haven't the capacity for intellectual work, and are much admired for such public-spirited behavior.

After supper they have an hour's recreation, either in the gardens or in the communal dining-halls, according to the time of year. Some people practice music, others just talk. They've never heard of anything so silly and demoralizing as dice, but they have two games rather like chess. The first is a sort of arithmetical contest, in which certain numbers "take" others. The second is a pitched battle between virtues and vices, which illustrates most ingeniously how vices tend to conflict with one another, but to combine against virtues. It also shows which vices are opposed to which virtues, how much strength vices can muster for a direct assault, what indirect tactics they employ, what help virtues need to overcome vices, what are the best methods of evading their attacks, and what ultimately determines the victory of one side or the other.

But here's a point that requires special attention, or you're liable to get the wrong idea. Since they only work a six-hour day, you may think there must be a shortage of essential goods. On the contrary, those six hours are enough, and more than enough to produce plenty of everything that's needed for a comfortable life. And you'll understand why it is, if you reckon up how large a proportion of the population in other countries is totally unemployed. First you have practically all the women—that gives you nearly 50 percent for a start. And in countries where the women *do* work, the men tend to lounge about instead. Then there are all the priests, and members of so-called religious orders—how much work do they do? Add all the rich, especially the landowners, popularly known as nobles and gentlemen. Include their domestic staffs—I mean those gangs of armed ruffians that I mentioned before. Finally, throw in all the beggars who are perfectly hale and hearty, but pretend to be ill as an excuse for being lazy. When you've counted them up, you'll be surprised to find how few people actually produce what the human race consumes.

And now just think how few of these few people are doing essential work—for where money is the only standard of value, there are bound to be dozens of unnecessary trades carried on, which merely supply luxury goods or entertainment. Why, even if the existing labor force were distributed among the few trades really needed to make life reasonably comfortable, there'd be so much overproduction that prices would fall too low for the workers to earn a living. Whereas, if you took all those engaged in nonessential trades, and all who are too lazy to work—each of whom consumes twice as much of the products of other people's labor as any of the producers themselves—if you put the whole lot of them on to something useful, you'd soon see how few hours' work a day would be amply sufficient to supply all the necessities and comforts of life—to which you might add all real and natural forms of pleasure.

[THE HOUSEHOLD]

But let's get back to their social organization. Each household, as I said, comes under the authority of the oldest male. Wives are subordinate to their husbands, children to their parents, and younger people generally to their elders. Every town is divided into four districts of equal size, each with its own shopping center in the middle of it. There the products of every household are collected in warehouses, and then distributed according to type among various shops. When the head of a household needs anything for himself or his family, he just goes to one of these shops and asks for it. And whatever he asks for, he's allowed to take away without any sort of payment, either in money or in kind. After all, why shouldn't he? There's more than enough of everything to go round, so there's no risk of his asking for more than he needs—for why should anyone want to start hoarding, when he knows he'll never have to go short of anything? No living creature is naturally greedy, except from fear of want—or in the case of human beings, from vanity, the notion that you're better than people if you can display more superfluous property than they can. But there's no scope for that sort of thing in Utopia.

[UTOPIAN BELIEFS]

The Utopians fail to understand why anyone should be so fascinated by the dull gleam of a tiny bit of stone, when he has all the stars in the sky to look at—or how anyone can be silly enough to think himself better than other people, because his clothes are made of finer woollen thread than theirs. After all, those fine clothes were once worn by a sheep, and they never turned it into anything better than a sheep.

Nor can they understand why a totally useless substance like gold   10 should now, all over the world, be considered far more important than human beings, who gave it such value as it has, purely for their own convenience. The result is that a man with about as much mental agility as a lump of lead or a block of wood, a man whose utter stupidity is paralleled only by his immorality, can have lots of good, intelligent people at his beck and call, just because he happens to possess a large pile of gold coins. And if by some freak of fortune or trick of the law—two equally effective methods of turning things upside down—the said coins were suddenly transferred to the most worthless member of his domestic staff, you'd soon see the present owner trotting after his money, like an extra piece of currency, and becoming his own servant's servant. But what puzzles and disgusts the Utopians even more is the idiotic way some people have of practically worshipping a rich man, not because they owe him money or are otherwise in his power, but simply because he's rich — although they know perfectly well that he's far too mean to let a single penny come their way, so long as he's alive to stop it.

They get these ideas partly from being brought up under a social system which is directly opposed to that type of nonsense, and partly from their reading and education. Admittedly, no one's allowed to become a full-time student, except for the very few in each town who appear as children to possess unusual gifts, outstanding intelligence, and a special aptitude for academic research. But every child receives a primary education, and most men and women go on educating themselves all their lives during those free periods that I told you about. . . .

In ethics they discuss the same problems as we do. Having distinguished between three types of "good," psychological, physiological, and environmental, they proceed to ask whether the term is strictly applicable to all of them, or only to the first. They also argue about such things as virtue and pleasure. But their chief subject of dispute is the nature of human happiness — on what factor or factors does it depend? Here they seem rather too much inclined to take a hedonistic view, for according to them human happiness consists largely or wholly in pleasure. Surprisingly enough, they defend this self-indulgent doctrine by arguments drawn from religion — a thing normally associated with a more serious view of life, if not with gloomy asceticism. You see, in all their discussions of happiness they invoke certain religious principles to supplement the operations of reason, which they think otherwise ill-equipped to identify true happiness.

The first principle is that every soul is immortal, and was created by a kind God, Who meant it to be happy. The second is that we shall be rewarded or punished in the next world for our good or bad behavior in this one. Although these are religious principles, the Utopians find rational grounds for accepting them. For suppose you didn't accept them? In that case, they say, any fool could tell you what you ought to do. You should go all out for your own pleasure, irrespective of right and wrong. You'd merely have to make sure that minor pleasures didn't interfere with major ones, and avoid the type of pleasure that has painful aftereffects. For what's the sense of struggling to be virtuous, denying yourself the pleasant things of life, and deliberately making yourself uncomfortable, if there's nothing you hope to gain by it? And what *can* you hope to gain by it, if you receive no compensation after death for a thoroughly unpleasant, that is, a thoroughly miserable life?

Not that they identify happiness with every type of pleasure — only with the higher ones. Nor do they identify it with virtue — unless they belong to a quite different school of thought. According to the normal view, happiness is the *summmum bonum*[2] toward which we're naturally impelled by virtue—which in their definition means following one's natural impulses, as God meant us to do. But this includes obeying the instinct to be reasonable in our likes and dislikes. And reason also teaches us, first to love and reverence Almighty God, to Whom we owe our existence and our potentiality for happiness, and secondly to get through life as comfortably and cheerfully as we can, and help all other members of our species to do so too.

The fact is, even the sternest ascetic tends to be slightly inconsistent 15 in his condemnation of pleasure. He may sentence *you* to a life of hard labor, inadequate sleep, and general discomfort, but he'll also tell you to do your best to ease the pains and privations of others. He'll regard all such attempts to improve the human situation as laudable acts of humanity—for obviously nothing could be more humane, or more natural for a human being, than to relieve other people's sufferings, put an end to their miseries, and restore their *joie de vivre*, that is, their capacity for pleasure. So why shouldn't it be equally natural to do the same thing for oneself?

Either it's a bad thing to enjoy life, in other words, to experience pleasure—in which case you shouldn't help anyone to do it, but should try to save the whole human race from such a frightful fate—or else, if it's good for other people, and you're not only allowed, but positively obliged to make it possible for them, why shouldn't charity begin at home? After all, you've a duty to yourself as well as to your neighbor, and, if Nature says you must be kind to others, she can't turn round the next moment and say you must be cruel to yourself. The Utopians therefore regard the enjoyment of life—that is, pleasure—as the natural object of all human efforts, and natural, as they define it, is synonymous with virtuous. However, Nature also wants us to help one another to enjoy life, for the very good reason that no human being has a monopoly of her affections. She's equally anxious for the welfare of every member of the species. So of course she tells us to make quite sure that we don't pursue our own interests at the expense of other people's.

On this principle they think it right to keep one's promises in private life, and also to obey public laws for regulating the distribution of "goods"—by which I mean the raw materials of pleasure—provided such laws have been properly made by a wise ruler, or passed by common consent of a whole population, which has not been subjected to any form of violence or deception. Within these limits they say it's sensible to consult one's own interests, and a moral duty to consult those of the community as well. It's wrong to deprive someone else of a pleasure so that you can enjoy one yourself, but to deprive yourself of a pleasure so that you can add to someone else's enjoyment is an act of humanity

[2]*summmum bonum* Latin for "the highest good."

by which you always gain more than you lose. For one thing, such benefits are usually repaid in kind. For another, the mere sense of having
done somebody a kindness, and so earned his affection and goodwill,
produces a spiritual satisfaction which far outweighs the loss of a physical one. And lastly—a belief that comes easily to a religious mind—God
will reward us for such small sacrifices of momentary pleasure, by giving
us an eternity of perfect joy. Thus they argue that, in the final analysis,
pleasure is the ultimate happiness which all human beings have in view,
even when they're acting most virtuously.

Pleasure they define as any state or activity, physical or mental, which
is naturally enjoyable. The operative word is *naturally.* According to them,
we're impelled by reason as well as an instinct to enjoy ourselves in any
natural way which doesn't hurt other people, interfere with greater pleasures, or cause unpleasant aftereffects. But human beings have entered
into an idiotic conspiracy to call some things enjoyable which are naturally nothing of the kind—as though facts were as easily changed as
definitions. Now the Utopians believe that, so far from contributing to
happiness, this type of thing makes happiness impossible—because, once
you get used to it, you lose all capacity for real pleasure, and are merely
obsessed by illusory forms of it. Very often these have nothing pleasant
about them at all—in fact, most of them are thoroughly disagreeable. But
they appeal so strongly to perverted tastes that they come to be reckoned
not only among the major pleasures of life, but even among the chief reasons for living.

In the category of illusory pleasure addicts they include the kind of
person I mentioned before, who thinks himself better than other people
because he's better dressed than they are. Actually he's just as wrong
about his clothes as he is about himself. From a practical point of view,
why is it better to be dressed in fine woollen thread than in coarse? But
he's got it into his head that fine thread is naturally superior, and that
wearing it somehow increases his own value. So he feels entitled to far
more respect than he'd ever dare to hope for, if he were less expensively
dressed, and is most indignant if he fails to get it.

Talking of respect, isn't it equally idiotic to attach such importance to 20
a lot of empty gestures which do nobody any good? For what real pleasure can you get out of the sight of a bared head or a bent knee? Will
it cure the rheumatism in your own knee, or make you any less weak
in the head? Of course, the great believers in this type of artificial pleasure are those who pride themselves on their "nobility." Nowadays that
merely means that they happen to belong to a family which has been
rich for several generations, preferably in landed property. And yet they
feel every bit as "noble" even if they've failed to inherit any of the said
property, or if they have inherited it and then frittered it all away.

Then there's another type of person I mentioned before, who has a
passion for jewels, and feels practically superhuman if he manages to get
hold of a rare one, especially if it's a kind that's considered particularly

precious in his country and period—for the value of such things varies according to where and when you live. But he's so terrified of being
taken in by appearances that he refuses to buy any jewel until he's
stripped off all the gold and inspected it in the nude. And even then he
won't buy it without a solemn assurance and a written guarantee from
the jeweler that the stone is genuine. But my dear sir, why shouldn't a
fake give you just as much pleasure, if you can't, with your own eyes,
distinguish it from a real one? It makes no difference to you whether it's
genuine or not—any more than it would to a blind man!

And now, what about those people who accumulate superfluous
wealth, for no better purpose than to enjoy looking at it? Is their pleasure a real one, or merely a form of delusion? The opposite type of psy-
chopath buries his gold, so that he'll never be able to use it, and may
never even see it again. In fact, he deliberately loses it in his anxiety
not to lose it—for what can you call it but lost, when it's put back into
the earth, where it's no good to him, or probably to anyone else? And
yet he's tremendously happy when he's got it stowed away. Now, apparently, he can stop worrying. But suppose the money is stolen, and ten
years later he dies without ever knowing it has gone. Then for a whole
ten years he has managed to survive his loss, and during that period
what difference has it made to him whether the money was there or
not? It was just as little use to him either way.

Among stupid pleasures they include not only gambling—a form of
idiocy that they've heard about but never practiced—but also hunting
and hawking. What on earth is the fun, they ask, of throwing dice onto
a table? Besides, you've done it so often that, even if there was some fun
in it at first, you must surely be sick of it by now. How can you possibly
enjoy listening to anything so disagreeable as the barking and howling of
dogs? And why is it more amusing to watch a dog chasing a hare than
to watch one dog chasing another? In each case the essential activity is
running—if running is what amuses you. But if it's really the thought
of being in at the death, and seeing an animal torn to pieces before your
eyes, wouldn't pity be a more appropriate reaction to the sight of a weak,
timid, harmless little creature like a hare being devoured by something
so much stronger and fiercer?

So the Utopians consider hunting below the dignity of free men,
and leave it entirely to butchers, who are, as I told you, slaves. In their
view hunting is the vilest department of butchery, compared with which
all the others are relatively useful and honorable. An ordinary butcher
slaughters livestock far more sparingly, and only because he has to,
whereas a hunter kills and mutilates poor little creatures purely for his
own amusement. They say you won't find that type of blood lust even
among animals, unless they're particularly savage by nature, or have
become so by constantly being used for this cruel sport.

There are hundreds of things like that, which are generally regarded 25
as pleasures, but everyone in Utopia is quite convinced that they've

got nothing to do with real pleasure, because there's nothing naturally enjoyable about them. Nor is this conviction at all shaken by the argument that most people do actually enjoy them, which would seem to indicate an appreciable pleasure content. They say this is a purely subjective reaction caused by bad habits, which can make a person prefer unpleasant things to pleasant ones, just as pregnant women sometimes lose their sense of taste, and find suet or turpentine more delicious than honey. But however much one's judgment may be impaired by habit or ill health, the nature of pleasure, as of everything else, remains unchanged.

Real pleasures they divide into two categories, mental and physical. Mental pleasures include the satisfaction that one gets from understanding something, or from contemplating truth. They also include the memory of a well-spent life, and the confident expectation of good things to come. Physical pleasures are subdivided into two types. First there are those which fill the whole organism with a conscious sense of enjoyment. This may be the result of replacing physical substances which have been burnt up by the natural heat of the body, as when we eat or drink. Or else it may be caused by the discharge of some excess, as in excretion, sexual intercourse, or any relief of irritation by rubbing or scratching. However, there are also pleasures which satisfy no organic need, and relieve no previous discomfort. They merely act, in a mysterious but quite unmistakable way, directly on our senses, and monopolize their reactions. Such is the pleasure of music.

Their second type of physical pleasure arises from the calm and regular functioning of the body—that is, from a state of health undisturbed by any minor ailments. In the absence of mental discomfort, this gives one a good feeling, even without the help of external pleasures. Of course, it's less ostentatious, and forces itself less violently on one's attention than the cruder delights of eating and drinking, but even so it's often considered the greatest pleasure in life. Practically everyone in Utopia would agree that it's a very important one, because it's the basis of all the others. It's enough by itself to make you enjoy life, and unless you have it, no other pleasure is possible. However, mere freedom from pain, without positive health, they would call not pleasure but anesthesia.

Some thinkers used to maintain that a uniformly tranquil state of health couldn't properly be termed a pleasure since its presence could only be detected by contrast with its opposite—oh yes, they went very thoroughly into the whole question. But that theory was exploded long ago, and nowadays nearly everybody subscribes to the view that health is most definitely a pleasure. The argument goes like this—illness involves pain, which is the direct opposite of pleasure, and illness is the direct opposite of health, therefore health involves pleasure. They don't think it matters whether you say that illness *is* or merely *involves* pain. Either way it comes to the same thing. Similarly, whether health *is* a pleasure, or merely *produces* pleasure as inevitably as fire produces heat, it's equally logical to assume that where you have an uninterrupted state of health you cannot fail to have pleasure.

Besides, they say, when we eat something, what really happens is this. Our failing health starts fighting off the attacks of hunger, using the food as an ally. Gradually it begins to prevail, and, in this very process of winning back its normal strength, experiences the sense of enjoyment which we find so refreshing. Now, if health enjoys the actual battle, why shouldn't it also enjoy the victory? Or are we to suppose that when it has finally managed to regain its former vigor—the one thing that it has been fighting for all this time—it promptly falls into a coma, and fails to notice or take advantage of its success? As for the idea that one isn't conscious of health except through its opposite, they say that's quite untrue. Everyone's perfectly aware of feeling well, unless he's asleep or actually feeling ill. Even the most insensitive and apathetic sort of person will admit that it's delightful to be healthy—and what is delight, but a synonym for pleasure?

They're particularly fond of mental pleasures, which they consider 30 of primary importance, and attribute mostly to good behavior and a clear conscience. Their favorite physical pleasure is health. Of course, they believe in enjoying food, drink, and so forth, but purely in the interests of health, for they don't regard such things as very pleasant in themselves—only as methods of resisting the stealthy onset of disease. A sensible person, they say, prefers keeping well to taking medicine, and would rather feel cheerful than have people trying to comfort him. On the same principle it's better not to need this type of pleasure than to become addicted to it. For, if you think that sort of thing will make you happy, you'll have to admit that your idea of perfect felicity would be a life consisting entirely of hunger, thirst, itching, eating, drinking, rubbing, and scratching—which would obviously be most unpleasant as well as quite disgusting. Undoubtedly these pleasures should come right at the bottom of the list, because they're so impure. For instance, the pleasure of eating is invariably diluted with the pain of hunger, and not in equal proportions either—for the pain is both more intense and more prolonged. It starts before the pleasure, and doesn't stop until the pleasure has stopped too.

So they don't think much of pleasures like that, except insofar as they're necessary. But they enjoy them all the same, and feel most grateful to Mother Nature for encouraging her children to do things that have to be done so often, by making them so attractive. For just think how dreary life would be, if those chronic ailments, hunger and thirst, could only be cured by foul-tasting medicines, like the rarer types of disease!

They attach great value to special natural gifts such as beauty, strength, and agility. They're also keen on the pleasures of sight, hearing, and smell, which are peculiar to human beings—for no other species admires the beauty of the world, enjoys any sort of scent, except as a method of locating food, or can tell the difference between a harmony and a discord. They say these things give a sort of relish to life.

However, in all such matters they observe the rule that minor pleasures mustn't interfere with major ones, and that pleasure mustn't cause pain—which they think is bound to happen, if the pleasure is immoral. But they'd never dream of despising their own beauty, overtaxing their strength, converting their agility into inertia, ruining their physique by going without food, damaging their health, or spurning any other of Nature's gifts, unless they were doing it for the benefit of other people or of society, in the hope of receiving some greater pleasure from God in return. For they think it's quite absurd to torment oneself in the name of an unreal virtue, which does nobody any good, or in order to steel oneself against disasters which may never occur. They say such behavior is merely self-destructive, and shows a most ungrateful attitude toward Nature—as if one refused all her favors, because one couldn't bear the thought of being indebted to her for anything.

Well, that's their ethical theory, and short of some divine revelation, they doubt if the human mind is capable of devising a better one. We've no time to discuss whether it's right or wrong—nor is it really necessary, for all I undertook was to describe their way of life, not to defend it.

[TREATMENT OF THE DYING]

As I told you, when people are ill, they're looked after most sympathetically, and given everything in the way of medicine or special food that could possibly assist their recovery. In the case of permanent invalids, the nurses try to make them feel better by sitting and talking to them, and do all they can to relieve their symptoms. But if, besides being incurable, the disease also causes constant excruciating pain, some priests and government officials visit the person concerned, and say something like this:

"Let's face it, you'll never be able to live a normal life. You're just a nuisance to other people and a burden to yourself—in fact you're really leading a sort of posthumous existence. So why go on feeding germs? Since your life's a misery to you, why hesitate to die? You're imprisoned in a torture chamber—why don't you break out and escape to a better world? Or say the word, and we'll arrange for your release. It's only common sense to cut your losses. It's also an act of piety to take the advice of a priest, because he speaks for God."

If the patient finds these arguments convincing, he either starves himself to death, or is given a soporific and put painlessly out of his misery. But this is strictly voluntary, and, if he prefers to stay alive, everyone will go on treating him as kindly as ever.

[THE SUMMING UP]

Well, that's the most accurate account I can give you of the Utopian Republic. To my mind, it's not only the best country in the world, but the only one that has any right to call itself a republic. Elsewhere, people are always talking about the public interest, but all they really care about is private property. In Utopia, where's there's no private property, people take their duty to the public seriously. And both attitudes are perfectly reasonable. In other "republics" practically everyone knows that, if he doesn't look out for himself, he'll starve to death, however prosperous his country may be. He's therefore compelled to give his own interests priority over those of the public; that is, of other people. But in Utopia, where everything's under public ownership, no one has any fear of going short, as long as the public storehouses are full. Everyone gets a fair share, so there are never any poor men or beggars. Nobody owns anything, but everyone is rich—for what greater wealth can there be than cheerfulness, peace of mind, and freedom from anxiety? Instead of being worried about his food supply, upset by the plaintive demands of his wife, afraid of poverty for his son, and baffled by the problem of finding a dowry for his daughter, the Utopian can feel absolutely sure that he, his wife, his children, his grandchildren, his great-grandchildren, his great-great-grandchildren, and as long a line of descendants as the proudest peer could wish to look forward to, will always have enough to eat and enough to make them happy. There's also the further point that those who are too old to work are just as well provided for as those who are still working.

Now, will anyone venture to compare these fair arrangements in Utopia with the so-called justice of other countries?—in which I'm damned if I can see the slightest trace of justice or fairness. For what sort of justice do you call this? People like aristocrats, goldsmiths, or moneylenders, who either do no work at all, or do work that's really not essential, are rewarded for their laziness or their unnecessary activities by a splendid life of luxury. But laborers, coachmen, carpenters, and farmhands, who never stop working like cart horses, at jobs so essential that, if they *did* stop working, they'd bring any country to a standstill within twelve months—what happens to them? They get so little to eat, and have such a wretched time, that they'd be almost better off if they *were* cart horses. Then at least, they wouldn't work quite such long hours, their food wouldn't be very much worse, they'd enjoy it more, and they'd have no fears for the future. As it is, they're not only ground down by unrewarding toil in the present, but also worried to death by the prospect of a poverty-stricken old age—since their daily wages aren't enough to support them for one day, let alone leave anything over to be saved up when they're old.

Can you see any fairness or gratitude in a social system which lav- 40 ishes such great rewards on so-called noblemen, goldsmiths, and people like that, who are either totally unproductive or merely employed in producing luxury goods or entertainment, but makes no such kind provision for farmhands, coal heavers, laborers, carters, or carpenters, without whom society couldn't exist at all? And the climax of ingratitude comes when they're old and ill and completely destitute. Having taken advantage of them throughout the best years of their lives, society now forgets all the sleepless hours they've spent in its service, and repays them for all the vital work they've done, by letting them die in misery. What's more, the wretched earnings of the poor are daily whittled away by the rich, not only through private dishonesty, but through public legislation. As if it weren't unjust enough already that the man who contributes most to society should get the least in return, they make it even worse, and then arrange for injustice to be legally described as justice.

In fact, when I consider any social system that prevails in the modern world, I can't, so help me God, see it as anything but a conspiracy of the rich to advance their own interests under the pretext of organizing society. They think up all sorts of tricks and dodges, first for keeping safe their ill-gotten gains, and then for exploiting the poor by buying their labor as cheaply as possible. Once the rich have decided that these tricks and dodges shall be officially recognized by society—which includes the poor as well as the rich—they acquire the force of law. Thus an unscrupulous minority is led by its insatiable greed to monopolize what would have been enough to supply the needs of the whole population. And yet how much happier even these people would be in Utopia! There, with the simultaneous abolition of money and the passion for money, how many other social problems have been solved, how many crimes eradicated! For obviously the end of money means the end of all those types of criminal behavior which daily punishments are powerless to check: fraud, theft, burglary, brawls, riots, disputes, rebellion, murder, treason, and black magic. And the moment money goes, you can also say goodbye to fear, tension, anxiety, overwork, and sleepless nights. Why, even poverty itself, the one problem that has always seemed to need money for its solution, would promptly disappear if money ceased to exist.

Let me try to make this point clearer. Just think back to one of the years when the harvest was bad, and thousands of people died of starvation. Well, I bet if you'd inspected every rich man's barn at the end of that lean period you'd have found enough corn to have saved all the lives that were lost through malnutrition and disease, and prevented anyone from suffering any ill effects whatever from the meanness of the weather and the soil. Everyone could so easily get enough to eat, if it weren't for that blessed nuisance, money. There you have a brilliant invention which was designed to make food more readily available. Actually it's the only thing that makes it unobtainable.

I'm sure that even the rich are well aware of all this, and realize how much better it would be to have everything one needed, than lots of things one didn't need—to be evacuated altogether from the danger area, than to dig oneself in behind a barricade of enormous wealth. And I've no doubt that either self-interest, or the authority of our Savior Christ—Who was far too wise not to know what was best for us, and far too kind to recommend anything else—would have led the whole world to adopt the Utopian system long ago, if it weren't for that beastly root of all evils, pride. For pride's criterion of prosperity is not what you've got yourself, but what other people haven't got. Pride would refuse to set foot in paradise, if she thought there'd be no underprivileged classes there to gloat over and order about—nobody whose misery could serve as a foil to her own happiness, or whose poverty she could make harder to bear, by flaunting her own riches. Pride, like a hellish serpent gliding through human hearts—or shall we say, like a sucking-fish that clings to the ship of state?—is always dragging us back, and obstructing our progress toward a better way of life.

But as this fault is too deeply ingrained in human nature to be easily eradicated, I'm glad that at least one country has managed to develop a system which I'd like to see universally adopted. The Utopian way of life provides not only the happiest basis for a civilized community, but also one which, in all human probability, will last forever. They've eliminated the root causes of ambition, political conflict, and everything like that. There's therefore no danger of internal dissension, the one thing that has destroyed so many impregnable towns. And as long as there's unity and sound administration at home, no matter how envious neighboring kings may feel, they'll never be able to shake, let alone to shatter, the power of Utopia. They've tried to do so often enough in the past, but have always been beaten back.

Topics for Critical Thinking and Writing

1. More, writing early in the sixteenth century, was living in a primarily agricultural society. Laborers were needed on farms, but might More have had any other reason for insisting (para. 1) that all people should do some farming and that farming should be "part of every child's education"? Do you think everyone should put in some time as a farmer? Why, or why not?

2. More indicates that in the England of his day many people loafed or engaged in unnecessary work (producing luxury goods, for one thing), putting an enormous burden on those who engaged in useful work. Is this condition, or any part of it, true of our society? Explain.

3. The Utopians cannot understand why the people of other nations value gems, gold, and fine clothes. If you value any of these, can you offer an explanation?

4. What arguments can you offer against the Utopians' treatment of persons who are incurably ill and in pain?

5. Take three or four paragraphs to summarize More's report of the Utopians' idea of pleasure.

6. More's Utopians cannot understand why anyone takes pleasure in gambling or in hunting. If either activity gives you pleasure, in an essay of 500 words explain why, and offer an argument on behalf of your view.

7. As More makes clear in the part we entitle "The Summing Up," in Utopia there is no private property. In a sentence or two summarize the reasons he gives for this principle, and then in a paragraph evaluate them.

Niccolò Machiavelli

Niccolò Machiavelli (1469–1527) was born in Florence at a time when Italy was divided into five major states: Venice, Milan, Florence, the Papal States, and Naples. Although these states often had belligerent relations with one another as well as with lesser Italian states, under the Medici family in Florence they achieved a precarious balance of power. In 1494, however, Lorenzo de' Medici, who had ruled from 1469 to 1492, died, and two years later Lorenzo's successor was exiled when the French army arrived in Florence. Italy became a field where Spain, France, and Germany competed for power. From 1498 to 1512 Machiavelli held a high post in the diplomatic service of the Florentine Republic, but when the French army reappeared and the Florentines in desperation recalled the Medici, Machiavelli lost his post, was imprisoned, tortured, and then exiled. Banished from Florence, he nevertheless lived in comfort on a small estate nearby, writing his major works and hoping to obtain an office from the Medici. In later years he was employed in a few minor diplomatic missions, but even after the collapse and expulsion of the Medici in 1527 and the restoration of the republic, he did not regain his old position of importance. He died shortly after the restoration.

Our selection comes from The Prince, *which Machiavelli wrote in 1513 during his banishment, hoping that it would interest the Medici and thus restore him to favor; but the book was not published until 1532, five years after his death. In this book of twenty-six short chapters, Machiavelli begins by examining different kinds of states, but the work's enduring power resides in the discussions (in Chapters 15–18, reprinted here) of qualities necessary to a prince — that is, a head of state. Any such examination obviously is based in part on assumptions about the nature of the citizens of the realm.*

This selection was taken from a translation edited by Peter Bondanella and Mark Musa.

From *The Prince*

ON THOSE THINGS FOR WHICH MEN, AND PARTICULARLY PRINCES, ARE PRAISED OR BLAMED

Now there remains to be examined what should be the methods and procedures of a prince in dealing with his subjects and friends. And because I know that many have written about this, I am afraid that by writing about it again I shall be thought of as presumptuous, since in discussing this material I depart radically from the procedures of others. But since my intention is to write something useful for anyone who understands it, it seemed more suitable to me to search after the effectual truth of the matter rather than its imagined one. And many writers have imagined for themselves republics and principalities that have never been seen nor known to exist in reality; for there is such a gap between how one lives and how one ought to live that anyone who abandons what is done for what ought to be done learns his ruin rather than his preservation: for a man who wishes to make a vocation of being good at all times will come to ruin among so many who are not good. Hence it is necessary for a prince who wishes to maintain his position to learn how not to be good, and to use this knowledge or not to use it according to necessity.

Leaving aside, therefore, the imagined things concerning a prince, and taking into account those that are true, I say that all men, when they are spoken of, and particularly princes, since they are placed on a higher level, are judged by some of these qualities which bring them either blame or praise. And this is why one is considered generous, another miserly (to use a Tuscan word, since "avaricious" in our language is still used to mean one who wishes to acquire by means of theft; we call "miserly" one who excessively avoids using what he has); one is considered a giver, the other rapacious; one cruel, another merciful; one treacherous, another faithful; one effeminate and cowardly, another bold and courageous; one humane, another haughty; one lascivious, another chaste; one trustworthy, another cunning; one harsh, another lenient; one serious, another frivolous; one religious, another unbelieving; and the like. And I know that everyone will admit that it would be a very praiseworthy thing to find in a prince, of the qualities mentioned above, those that are held to be good; but since it is neither possible to have them nor to observe them all completely, because human nature does not permit it, a prince must be prudent enough to know how to escape the bad reputation of those vices that would lose the state for him, and must protect himself from those that will not lose it for him, if this is possible; but if he cannot, he need not concern himself unduly if he ignores these less serious vices. And, moreover, he need not worry about incurring the bad reputation of those vices without which it would be difficult to hold his state; since, carefully taking everything into account, one will discover that something which appears to be a virtue, if pursued, will end in his destruction; while some other thing which seems to be a vice, if pursued, will result in his safety and his well-being.

ON GENEROSITY AND MISERLINESS

Beginning, therefore, with the first of the above-mentioned qualities, I say that it would be good to be considered generous; nevertheless, generosity used in such a manner as to give you a reputation for it will harm you; because if it is employed virtuously and as one should employ it, it will not be recognized and you will not avoid the reproach of its opposite. And so, if a prince wants to maintain his reputation for generosity among men, it is necessary for him not to neglect any possible means of lavish display; in so doing such a prince will always use up all his resources and he will be obliged, eventually, if he wishes to maintain his reputation for generosity, to burden the people with excessive taxes and to do everything possible to raise funds. This will begin to make him hateful to his subjects, and, becoming impoverished, he will not be much esteemed by anyone; so that, as a consequence of his generosity, having offended many and rewarded few, he will feel the effects of any slight unrest and will be ruined at the first sign of danger; recognizing this and wishing to alter his policies, he immediately runs the risk of being reproached as a miser.

A prince, therefore, unable to use this virtue of generosity in a manner which will not harm himself if he is known for it, should, if he is wise, not worry about being called a miser; for with time he will come to be considered more generous once it is evident that, as a result of his parsimony, his income is sufficient, he can defend himself from anyone who makes war against him, and he can undertake enterprises without overburdening his people, so that he comes to be generous with all those from whom he takes nothing, who are countless, and miserly with all those to whom he gives nothing, who are few. In our times we have not seen great deeds accomplished except by those who were considered miserly; all others were done away with. Pope Julius II, although he made use of his reputation for generosity in order to gain the papacy, then decided not to maintain it in order to be able to wage war; the present King of France has waged many wars without imposing extra taxes on his subjects, only because his habitual parsimony has provided for the additional expenditures; the present King of Spain, if he had been considered generous, would not have engaged in nor won so many campaigns.

Therefore, in order not to have to rob his subjects, to be able to ⁵ defend himself, not to become poor and contemptible, and not to be forced to become rapacious, a prince must consider it of little importance if he incurs the name of miser, for this is one of those vices that permits him to rule. And if someone were to say: Caesar with his generosity came to rule the empire, and many others, because they were generous and known to be so, achieved very high positions; I reply: You are either already a prince or you are on the way to becoming one; in the first instance such generosity is damaging; in the second it is very necessary to be thought generous. And Caesar was one of those who wanted to gain the principality of Rome; but if, after obtaining this, he had lived and had not moderated his expenditures, he would have destroyed that empire. And if someone were to reply: There have existed many princes who have accomplished great deeds with their armies who have been reputed to be generous; I answer you: A prince either spends his own money and that of his subjects or that of others; in the first case he must be economical; in the second he must not restrain any part of his generosity. And for that prince who goes out with his soldiers and lives by looting, sacking, and ransoms, who controls the property of others, such generosity is necessary; otherwise he would not be followed by his troops. And with what does not belong to you or to your subjects you can be a more liberal giver, as were Cyrus, Caesar, and Alexander; for spending the wealth of others does not lessen your reputation but adds to it; only the spending of your own is what harms you. And there is nothing that uses itself up faster than generosity, for as you employ it you lose the means of employing it, and you become either poor or despised or, in order to escape poverty, rapacious and hated. And above all other things a prince must guard himself against being despised and hated; and generosity leads you to both one and the other. So it is wiser to live with the reputation of a miser, which produces reproach without hatred, than to be forced to incur the reputation of rapacity, which produces reproach along with hatred, because you want to be considered as generous.

ON CRUELTY AND MERCY AND WHETHER IT IS BETTER TO BE LOVED THAN TO BE FEARED OR THE CONTRARY

Proceeding to the other qualities mentioned above, I say that every prince must desire to be considered merciful and not cruel; nevertheless, he must take care not to misuse this mercy. Cesare Borgia[1] was considered cruel; nonetheless, his cruelty had brought order to Romagna, united it, restored it to peace and obedience. If we examine this carefully, we shall see that he was more merciful than the Florentine people, who, in order to avoid being considered cruel, allowed the destruction of Pistoia.[2] Therefore, a prince must not worry about the reproach of cruelty when it is a matter of keeping his subjects united and loyal; for with a very few examples of cruelty he will be more compassionate than those who, out of excessive mercy, permit disorders to continue, from which arise murders and plundering; for these usually harm the community at large, while the executions that come from the prince harm one individual in particular. And the new prince, above all other princes,

---

[1]**Cesare Borgia** The son of Pope Alexander VI, Cesare Borgia (1476–1507) was ruthlessly opportunistic. Encouraged by his father, in 1499 and 1500 he subdued the cities of Romagna, the region including Ferrara and Ravenna. [All notes are the editors' unless otherwise specified.]

[2]**Pistoia** A town near Florence; Machiavelli suggests that the Florentines failed to treat dissenting leaders with sufficient severity.

cannot escape the reputation of being called cruel, since new states are full of dangers. And Virgil, through Dido, states: "My difficult condition and the newness of my rule make me act in such a manner, and to set guards over my land on all sides."[3]

Nevertheless, a prince must be cautious in believing and in acting, nor should he be afraid of his own shadow; and he should proceed in such a manner, tempered by prudence and humanity, so that too much trust may not render him imprudent nor too much distrust render him intolerable.

From this arises an argument: whether it is better to be loved than to be feared, or the contrary. I reply that one should like to be both one and the other; but since it is difficult to join them together, it is much safer to be feared than to be loved when one of the two must be lacking. For one can generally say this about men: that they are ungrateful, fickle, simulators and deceivers, avoiders of danger, greedy for gain; and while you work for their good they are completely yours, offering you their blood, their property, their lives, and their sons, as I said earlier, when danger is far away; but when it comes nearer to you they turn away. And that prince who bases his power entirely in their words, finding himself stripped of other preparations, comes to ruin; for friendships that are acquired by a price and not by greatness and nobility of character are purchased but are not owned, and at the proper moment they cannot be spent. And men are less hesitant about harming someone who makes himself loved than one who makes himself feared because love is held together by a chain of obligation which, since men are a sorry lot, is broken on every occasion in which their own self-interest is concerned; but fear is held together by a dread of punishment which will never abandon you.

A prince must nevertheless make himself feared in such a manner that he will avoid hatred, even if he does not acquire love; since to be feared and not to be hated can very well be combined; and this will always be so when he keeps his hands off the property and the women of his citizens and his subjects. And if he must take someone's life, he should do so when there is proper justification and manifest cause; but, above all, he should avoid the property of others; for men forget more quickly the death of their father than the loss of their patrimony. Moreover, the reasons for seizing their property are never lacking; and he who begins to live by stealing always finds a reason for taking what belongs to others; on the contrary, reasons for taking a life are rarer and disappear sooner.

But when the prince is with his armies and has under his command 10 a multitude of troops, then it is absolutely necessary that he not worry about being considered cruel; for without that reputation he will never

---

[3]In *Aeneid* I, 563–64, **Virgil** (70–19 B.C.) puts this line into the mouth of **Dido**, the queen of Carthage.

keep an army united or prepared for any combat. Among the praise-worthy deeds of Hannibal[4] is counted this: that, having a very large army, made up of all kinds of men, which he commanded in foreign lands, there never arose the slightest dissension, neither among themselves nor against their prince, both during his good and his bad fortune. This could not have arisen from anything other than his inhuman cruelty, which, along with his many other abilities, made him always respected and ter-rifying in the eyes of his soldiers; and without that, to attain the same effect, his other abilities would not have sufficed. And the writers of his-tory, having considered this matter very little, on the one hand admire these deeds of his and on the other condemn the main cause of them.

And that it be true that his other abilities would not have been suf-ficient can be seen from the example of Scipio,[5] a most extraordinary man not only in his time but in all recorded history, whose armies in Spain rebelled against him; this came about from nothing other than his excessive compassion, which gave to his soldiers more liberty than military discipline allowed. For this he was censured in the senate by Fabius Maximus, who called him the corruptor of the Roman militia. The Locrians, having been ruined by one of Scipio's officers, were not avenged by him, nor was the arrogance of that officer corrected, all because of his tolerant nature; so that someone in the senate who tried to apologize for him said that there were many men who knew how not to err better than they knew how to correct errors. Such a nature would have, in time, damaged Scipio's fame and glory if he had maintained it during the empire; but, living under the control of the senate, this harm-ful characteristic of his not only concealed itself but brought him fame.

I conclude, therefore, returning to the problem of being feared and loved, that since men love at their own pleasure and fear at the pleasure of the prince, a wise prince should build his foundation upon that which belongs to him, not upon that which belongs to others: He must strive only to avoid hatred, as has been said.

HOW A PRINCE SHOULD KEEP HIS WORD

How praiseworthy it is for a prince to keep his word and to live by integrity and not by deceit everyone knows; nevertheless, one sees from the experience of our times that the princes who have accomplished great deeds are those who have cared little for keeping their promises and who have known how to manipulate the minds of men by shrewd-ness; and in the end they have surpassed those who laid their founda-tions upon honesty.

---

[4]**Hannibal** The Carthaginian general (247–183 B.C.) whose crossing of the Alps with ele-phants and full baggage train is one of the great feats of military history.
[5]**Scipio** Publius Cornelius Scipio Africanus the Elder (235–183 B.C.), the conqueror of Hannibal in the Punic Wars. The mutiny of which Machiavelli speaks took place in 206 B.C.

You must, therefore, know that there are two means of fighting: one according to the laws, the other with force; the first way is proper to man, the second to beasts; but because the first, in many cases, is not sufficient, it becomes necessary to have recourse to the second. Therefore, a prince must know how to use wisely the natures of the beast and the man. This policy was taught to princes allegorically by the ancient writers, who described how Achilles and many other ancient princes were given to Chiron[6] the Centaur to be raised and taught under his discipline. This can only mean that, having a half-beast and half-man as a teacher, a prince must know how to employ the nature of the one and the other; and the one without the other cannot endure.

Since, then, a prince must know how to make good use of the nature 15 of the beast, he should choose from among the beasts the fox and the lion; for the lion cannot defend itself from traps and the fox cannot protect itself from wolves. It is therefore necessary to be a fox in order to recognize the traps and a lion in order to frighten the wolves. Those who play only the part of the lion do not understand matters. A wise ruler, therefore, cannot and should not keep his word when such an observance of faith would be to his disadvantage and when the reasons which made him promise are removed. And if men were all good, this rule would not be good; but since men are a sorry lot and will not keep their promises to you, you likewise need not keep yours to them. A prince never lacks legitimate reasons to break his promises. Of this one could cite an endless number of modern examples to show how many pacts, how many promises have been made null and void because of the infidelity of princes; and he who has known best how to use the fox has come to a better end. But it is necessary to know how to disguise this nature well and to be a great hypocrite and a liar: and men are so simpleminded and so controlled by their present necessities that one who deceives will always find another who will allow himself to be deceived.

I do not wish to remain silent about one of these recent instances. Alexander VI[7] did nothing else, he thought about nothing else, except to deceive men, and he always found the occasion to do this. And there never was a man who had more forcefulness in his oaths, who affirmed a thing with more promises, and who honored his word less; nevertheless, his tricks always succeeded perfectly since he was well acquainted with this aspect of the world.

Therefore, it is not necessary for a prince to have all of the above-mentioned qualities, but it is very necessary for him to appear to have them. Furthermore, I shall be so bold as to assert this; that having them and practicing them at all times is harmful; and appearing to have them

---

[6]**Chiron** (Kī'ron) A centaur (half man, half horse) who was said in classical mythology to have been the teacher not only of Achilles but also of Theseus, Jason, Hercules, and other heroes.

[7]**Alexander VI** Pope from 1492 to 1503; father of Cesare Borgia.

useful; for instance, to seem merciful, faithful, humane, forthright, religious, and to be so; but his mind should be disposed in such a way that should it become necessary not to be so, he will be able and know how to change to the contrary. And it is essential to understand this: that a prince, and especially a new prince, cannot observe all those things by which men are considered good, for in order to maintain the state he is often obliged to act against his promise, against charity, against humanity, and against religion. And therefore, it is necessary that he have a mind ready to turn itself according to the way the winds of Fortune and the changeability of affairs require him; and, as I said above, as long as it is possible, he should not stray from the good, but he should know how to enter into evil when necessity commands.

A prince, therefore, must be very careful never to let anything slip from his lips which is not full of the five qualities mentioned above: He should appear, upon seeing and hearing him, to be all mercy, all faithfulness, all integrity, all kindness, all religion. And there is nothing more necessary than to seem to possess this last quality. And men in general judge more by their eyes than their hands; for everyone can see but few can feel. Everyone sees what you seem to be, few perceive what you are, and those few do not dare to contradict the opinion of the many who have the majesty of the state to defend them; and in the actions of all men, and especially of princes, where there is no impartial arbiter, one must consider the final result.[8] Let a prince therefore act to seize and to maintain the state; his methods will always be judged honorable and will be praised by all; for ordinary people are always deceived by appearances and by the outcome of a thing; and in the world there is nothing but ordinary people; and there is no room for the few, while the many have a place to lean on. A certain prince of the present day, whom I shall refrain from naming, preaches nothing but peace and faith, and to both one and the other he is entirely opposed; and both, if he had put them into practice, would have cost him many times over either his reputation or his state.

Topics for Critical Thinking and Writing

1. In the opening paragraph, Machiavelli claims that a ruler who wishes to keep in power must "learn how not to be good"—that is, must know where and when to ignore the demands of conventional morality. In the rest of the excerpt, does he give any convincing evidence to support this claim? Can you think of any recent political event in which a political leader violated the requirements of morality, as Machiavelli advises?

[8]The Italian original, *si guarda al fine*, has often been mistranslated as "the ends justify the means," something Machiavelli never wrote. [Translators' note.]

2. Machiavelli says in paragraph 1 that "a man who wishes to make a vocation of being good at all times will come to ruin among so many who are not good." (By the way, the passage is ambiguous. "At all times" is, in the original, a squinting modifier. It may look backward to "being good" or forward to "will come to ruin," but Machiavelli probably means, "A man who at all times wishes to make a vocation of being good will come to ruin among so many who are not good.") Is this view realistic or cynical? (What is the difference between these two?) Assume for the moment that the view is realistic. Does it follow that society requires a ruler who must act according to the principles Machiavelli sets forth?

3. In his second paragraph Machiavelli claims that it is impossible for a ruler to exhibit *all* the conventional virtues (trustworthiness, liberality, and so on). Why does he make this claim? Do you agree with it?

4. In paragraph 4 Machiavelli cites as examples Pope Julius II, the king of France, the king of Spain, and other rulers. Is he using these examples to illustrate his generalizations or to provide evidence for them? If you think he is using them to provide evidence, how convincing do you find the evidence? (Consider: Could Machiavelli be arguing from a biased sample?)

5. In paragraphs 6 to 10 Machiavelli argues that it is sometimes necessary for a ruler to be cruel, and so he praises Cesare Borgia and Hannibal. What in human nature, according to Machiavelli, explains this need to have recourse to cruelty? (By the way, how do you think *cruelty* should be defined here?)

6. Machiavelli says that Cesare Borgia's cruelty brought peace to Romagna and that, on the other hand, the Florentines who sought to avoid being cruel in fact brought pain to Pistoia. Can you think of recent episodes supporting the view that cruelty can be beneficial to society? If so, restate Machiavelli's position, using these examples from recent history. Then go on to write two paragraphs, arguing on behalf of your two examples. Or if you believe that Machiavelli's point here is fundamentally wrong, explain why, again using current examples.

7. In *The Prince*, Machiavelli is writing about how to be a successful ruler. He explicitly says he is dealing with things as they are, not things as they should be. Do you think that in fact one can write usefully about statecraft without considering ethics? Explain. Or you may want to think about it in this way: The study of politics is often called *political science*. Machiavelli can be seen as a sort of scientist, objectively analyzing the nature of governing—without offering any moral judgments. In an essay of 500 words, argue for or against the view that the study of politics is rightly called *political science*.

8. In the final paragraph, Machiavelli declares that "one must consider the final result." Taking account of the context, do you think the meaning is that (a) any end, goal, or purpose of anyone justifies using any means to reach it or (b) the end of governing the state, nation, or country justifies using any means to achieve it? Or do you think Machiavelli means both? Something else entirely?

9. In 500 words, argue that an important contemporary political figure does or does not act according to Machiavelli's principles.

10. If you have read the selection from Thomas More's *Utopia*, write an essay of 500 words on one of these two topics: (a) why More's book is or is not wiser than Machiavelli's or (b) why one of the books is more interesting than the other.

11. More and Machiavelli wrote their books at almost exactly the same time. Write a dialogue of two or three double-spaced typed pages in which the two men argue about the nature of the state. (During the argument, they will have to reveal their assumptions about the nature of human beings and the role of government.)

Thomas Jefferson

Thomas Jefferson (1743–1826) was a congressman, the governor of Virginia, the first secretary of state, and the president of the United States, but he said he wished to be remembered for only three things: drafting the Declaration of Independence, writing the Virginia Statute for Religious Freedom, and founding the University of Virginia. All three were efforts to promote freedom.

Jefferson was born in Virginia and educated at William and Mary College in Williamsburg, Virginia. After graduating he studied law, was admitted to the bar, and in 1769 was elected to the Virginia House of Burgesses, his first political office. In 1776 he went to Philadelphia as a delegate to the second Continental Congress, where he was elected to a committee of five to write the Declaration of Independence. Jefferson drafted the document, which was then subjected to some changes by the other members of the committee and by the Congress. Although he was unhappy with the changes (especially with the deletion of a passage against slavery), his claim to have written the Declaration is just.

The Declaration of Independence

When in the course of human events, it becomes necessary for one people to dissolve the political bands which have connected them with another, and to assume among the Powers of the earth, the separate and equal station to which the Laws of Nature and of Nature's God entitle them, a decent respect to the opinions of mankind requires that they should declare the causes which impel them to the separation.

We hold these truths to be self-evident, that all men are created equal, that they are endowed by their Creator with certain unalienable Rights, that among these are Life, Liberty and the pursuit of Happiness.

That to secure these rights, Governments are instituted among Men, deriving their just powers from the consent of the governed.

That whenever any Form of Government becomes destructive of these ends, it is the Right of the People to alter or to abolish it, and to institute a new Government, laying its foundation on such principles and organizing its powers in such form, as to them shall seem most likely to effect their Safety and Happiness. Prudence, indeed, will dictate that Governments long established should not be changed for light and transient causes; and accordingly all experience hath shown that mankind are more disposed to suffer, while evils are sufferable, than to right themselves by abolishing the forms to which they are accustomed. But when a long train of abuses and usurpations pursuing invariably the same Object evinces a design to reduce them under absolute Despotism, it is their right, it is their duty, to throw off such government, and to provide new Guards for their future security.

Such has been the patient sufferance of these Colonies; and such is 5 now the necessity which constrains them to alter their former Systems of Government. The history of the present King of Great Britain is a history of repeated injuries and usurpations, all having in direct object the establishment of an absolute Tyranny over these States. To prove this, let Facts be submitted to a candid world.

He has refused his Assent to Laws, the most wholesome and necessary for the public good.

He has forbidden his Governors to pass Laws of immediate and pressing importance, unless suspended in their operation till his Assent should be obtained; and when so suspended, he has utterly neglected to attend to them.

He has refused to pass over Laws for the accommodation of large districts of people, unless those people would relinquish the right of Representation in the Legislature, a right inestimable to them and formidable to tyrants only.

He has called together legislative bodies at places unusual, uncomfortable, and distant from the depository of their Public Records, for the sole purpose of fatiguing them into compliance with his measures.

He has dissolved Representative Houses repeatedly, for opposing 10 with manly firmness his invasions on the rights of the people.

He has refused for a long time, after such dissolutions, to cause others to be elected; whereby the Legislative Powers, incapable of Annihilation, have returned to the People at large for their exercise; the State remaining in the mean time exposed to all the dangers of invasion from without, and convulsions within.

He has endeavored to prevent the population of these States, for that purpose obstructing the Laws of Naturalization of Foreigners; refusing to pass others to encourage their migration hither, and raising the conditions of new Appropriations of Lands.

He has obstructed the Administration of Justice, by refusing his Assent to Laws for establishing Judiciary Powers.

He has made Judges dependent on his Will alone, for the tenure of their offices, and the amount and payment of their salaries.

He has erected a multitude of New Offices, and sent hither swarms 15 of Officers to harass our People, and eat out their substance.

He has kept among us, in time of peace, Standing Armies without the consent of our Legislature.

He has affected to render the Military independent of and superior to the Civil Power.

He has combined with others to subject us to jurisdictions foreign to our constitution, and unacknowledged by our laws; giving his Assent to their acts of pretended Legislation:

For quartering large bodies of armed troops among us:

For protecting them, by a mock Trial, from Punishment for any Mur- 20 ders which they should commit on the Inhabitants of these States:

For cutting off our Trade with all parts of the world:

For imposing Taxes on us without our Consent:

For depriving us in many cases, of the benefits of Trial by Jury:

For transporting us beyond Seas to be tried for pretended offenses:

For abolishing the free System of English Laws in a Neighbouring 25 Province, establishing therein an Arbitrary government, and enlarging its boundaries so as to render it at once an example and fit instrument for introducing the same absolute rule into these Colonies:

For taking away our Charters, abolishing our most valuable Laws, and altering fundamentally the Forms of our Governments.

For suspending our own Legislatures, and declaring themselves invested with Power to legislate for us in all cases whatsoever.

He has abdicated Government here, by declaring us out of his Protection and waging War against us.

He has plundered our seas, ravaged our Coasts, burnt our towns and destroyed the Lives of our people.

He is at this time transporting large Armies of foreign Mercenaries 30 to compleat the works of death, desolation and tyranny, already begun with circumstances of Cruelty & perfidy scarcely paralleled in the most barbarous ages, and totally unworthy the Head of a civilized nation.

He has constrained our fellow Citizens taken Captive on the high Seas to bear Arms against their Country, to become the executioners of their friends and Brethren, or to fall themselves by their Hands.

He has excited domestic insurrections amongst us, and has endeavored to bring on the inhabitants of our frontiers, the merciless Indian Savages, whose known rule of warfare is an undistinguished destruction of all ages, sexes and conditions.

In every stage of these Oppressions We Have Petitioned for Redress in the most humble terms: Our repeated petitions have been answered only by repeated injury. A Prince, whose character is thus marked by every act which may define a Tyrant, is unfit to be the ruler of a free People.

Nor have We been wanting in attention to our British brethren. We have warned them from time to time of attempts by their legislature to extend an unwarrantable jurisdiction over us. We have reminded them of the circumstances of our emigration and settlement here. We have appealed to their native justice and magnanimity and we have conjured them by the ties of our common kindred to disavow these usurpations, which would inevitably interrupt our connections and correspondence. They too have been deaf to the voice of justice and of consanguinity. We must, therefore, acquiesce in the necessity, which denounces our Separation, and hold them, as we hold the rest of mankind, Enemies in War, in Peace Friends.

We, therefore, the Representatives of the United States of America, 35 in General Congress, Assembled, appealing to the Supreme Judge of the world of the rectitude of our intentions, do, in the Name, and by Authority of the good People of these Colonies, solemnly publish and declare, That these United Colonies are, and of Right ought to be, Free and Independent States; that they are Absolved from all Allegiance to the British Crown, and that all political connection between them and the State of Great Britain, is and ought to be totally dissolved; and that as Free and Independent States, they have full power to levy War, conclude Peace, contract Alliances, establish Commerce, and so all the other Acts and Things which Independent States may of right do. And for the support of this Declaration, with a firm reliance on the protection of Divine Providence, we mutually pledge to each other our lives, our Fortunes and our sacred Honor.

TOPICS FOR CRITICAL THINKING AND WRITING

1. According to the first paragraph, for what audience was the Declaration written? What other audiences do you think the document was (in one way or another) addressed to?

2. The Declaration states that it is intended to "prove" that the acts of the government of George III had as their "direct object the establishment of an absolute Tyranny" in the American colonies (para. 5). Write an essay of 500 to 750 words showing whether the evidence offered in the Declaration "proves" this claim to your satisfaction. (You will, of course, want to define *absolute tyranny*.) If you think further evidence is needed to "prove" the colonists' point, indicate what this evidence might be.

3. Paying special attention to the paragraphs beginning "That whenever any Form of Government" (para. 4), "In every stage" (para. 33), and "Nor have We been wanting" (para. 34), in a sentence or two set forth the image of themselves that the colonists seek to convey.

4. In the Declaration of Independence it is argued that the colonists are entitled to certain things and that under certain conditions they may behave in a certain way. Make explicit the syllogism that Jefferson is arguing.

5. What evidence does Jefferson offer to support his major premise? His minor premise?

6. In paragraph 2 the Declaration cites "certain unalienable Rights" and mentions three: "Life, Liberty and the pursuit of Happiness." What is an unalienable right? If someone has an unalienable (or inalienable) right, does that imply that he or she also has certain duties? If so, what are these duties? John Locke, a century earlier (1690), asserted that all men have a natural right to "life, liberty, and property." Do you think the decision to drop "property" and substitute "pursuit of Happiness" improved Locke's claim? Explain.

7. The Declaration ends thus: "We mutually pledge to each other our lives, our Fortunes and our sacred Honor." Is it surprising that honor is put in the final, climactic position? Is this a better ending than "our Fortunes, our sacred Honor, and our lives," or than "our sacred Honor, our lives, and our Fortunes?" Why?

8. King George III has asked you to reply, on his behalf, to the colonists, in 500 to 750 words. Write his reply. (Caution: A good reply will probably require you to do some reading about the period.)

9. Write a declaration of your own, setting forth in 500 to 750 words why some group is entitled to independence. You may want to argue that adolescents should not be compelled to attend school, that animals should not be confined in zoos, or that persons who use drugs should be able to buy them legally. Begin with a premise, then set forth facts illustrating the unfairness of the present condition, and conclude by stating what the new condition will mean to society.

Elizabeth Cady Stanton

Elizabeth Cady Stanton (1815–1902), a lawyer's daughter and journalist's wife, proposed in 1848 a convention to address the "social, civil, and religious condition and rights of women." Responding to Stanton's call, women and men from all over the Northeast traveled to the Woman's Rights Convention held in the village of Seneca Falls, New York. Her Declaration, adopted by the Convention—but only after vigorous debate and some amendments by others—became the platform for the women's rights movement in this country.

Declaration of Sentiments and Resolutions

When, in the course of human events, it becomes necessary for one portion of the family of man to assume among the people of the earth a position different from that which they have hitherto occupied, but one to which the laws of nature and of nature's God entitle them, a decent respect to the opinions of mankind requires that they should declare the causes that impel them to such a course.

We hold these truths to be self-evident: that all men and women are created equal; that they are endowed by their Creator with certain inalienable rights; that among these are life, liberty and the pursuit of happiness; that to secure these rights governments are instituted, deriving their just powers from the consent of the governed. Whenever any form of government becomes destructive of these ends, it is the right of those who suffer from it to refuse allegiance to it, and to insist upon the institution of a new government, laying its foundation on such principles, and organizing its powers in such form, as to them shall seem most likely to effect their safety and happiness. Prudence, indeed, will dictate that governments long established should not be changed for light and transient causes; and accordingly all experience hath shown that mankind are more disposed to suffer, while evils are sufferable, than to right themselves by abolishing the forms to which they were accustomed. But when a long train of abuses and usurpations, pursuing invariably the same object, evinces a design to reduce them under absolute despotism, it is their duty to throw off such government, and to provide new guards for their future security. Such has been the patient sufferance of the women under this government, and such is now the necessity which constrains them to demand the equal station to which they are entitled.

The history of mankind is a history of repeated injuries and usurpations on the part of man toward woman, having in direct object the establishment of an absolute tyranny over her. To prove this, let facts be submitted to a candid world.

He has never permitted her to exercise her inalienable right to the elective franchise.

He has compelled her to submit to laws, in the formation of which   5
she had no voice.

He has withheld from her rights which are given to the most ignorant and degraded men—both natives and foreigners.

Having deprived her of this first right of a citizen, the elective franchise, thereby leaving her without representation in the halls of legislation, he has oppressed her on all sides.

He has made her, if married, in the eye of the law, civilly dead.

He has taken from her all right in property, even to the wages she earns.

He has made her, morally, an irresponsible being, as she can commit   10
many crimes with impunity, provided they be done in the presence of her husband. In the covenant of marriage, she is compelled to promise obedience to her husband, he becoming to all intents and purposes, her master—the law giving him power to deprive her of her liberty, and to administer chastisement.

He has so framed the laws of divorce, as to what shall be the proper causes, and in case of separation, to whom the guardianship of the children shall be given, as to be wholly regardless of the happiness of women—the law, in all cases, going upon a false supposition of the supremacy of man, and giving all power into his hands.

After depriving her of all rights as a married woman, if single, and the owner of property, he has taxed her to support a government which recognizes her only when her property can be made profitable to it.

He has monopolized nearly all the profitable employments, and from those she is permitted to follow, she receives but a scanty remuneration. He closes against her all the avenues to wealth and distinction which he considers most honorable to himself. As a teacher of theology, medicine, or law, she is not known.

He has denied her the facilities for obtaining a thorough education, all colleges being closed against her.

He allows her in Church, as well as State, but a subordinate position, 15 claiming Apostolic authority for her exclusion from the ministry, and, with some exceptions, from any public participation in the affairs of the Church.

He has created a false public sentiment by giving to the world a different code of morals for men and women, by which moral delinquencies which exclude women from society, are not only tolerated, but deemed of little account in man.

He has usurped the prerogative of Jehovah himself, claiming it as his right to assign for her a sphere of action, when that belongs to her conscience and to her God.

He has endeavored, in every way that he could, to destroy her confidence in her own powers, to lessen her self-respect, and to make her willing to lead a dependent and abject life.

Now, in view of this entire disfranchisement of one-half the people of this country, their social and religious degradation—in view of the unjust laws above mentioned, and because women do feel themselves aggrieved, oppressed, and fraudulently deprived of their most sacred rights, we insist that they have immediate admission to all the rights and privileges which belong to them as citizens of the United States.

In entering upon the great work before us, we anticipate no small 20 amount of misconception, misrepresentation, and ridicule; but we shall use every instrumentality within our power to effect our object. We shall employ agents, circulate tracts, petition the State and National legislatures, and endeavor to enlist the pulpit and the press in our behalf. We hope this Convention will be followed by a series of Conventions embracing every part of the country.

[The following resolutions were discussed by Lucretia Mott, Thomas and Mary Ann McClintock, Amy Post, Catharine A. F. Stebbins, and others, and were adopted:]

Whereas, The great precept of nature is conceded to be, that "man shall pursue his own true and substantial happiness." Blackstone in his Commentaries remarks, that this law of Nature being coeval with mankind, and dictated by God himself, is of course superior in obligation to any other. It is binding over all the globe, in all countries, and at all times; no human laws are of any validity if contrary to this, and such of them as are valid, derive all their force, and all their validity, and all their authority, mediately and immediately, from this original; therefore,

Resolved, That such laws as conflict, in any way, with the true and substantial happiness of woman, are contrary to the great precept of nature and of no validity, for this is "superior in obligation to any other."

Resolved, That all laws which prevent woman from occupying such a station in society as her conscience shall dictate, or which place her in a position inferior to that of man, are contrary to the great precept of nature, and therefore of no force or authority.

Resolved, That woman is man's equal—was intended to be so by the Creator, and the highest good of the race demands that she should be recognized as such.

Resolved, That the women of this country ought to be enlightened in   25 regard to the laws under which they live, that they may no longer publish their degradation by declaring themselves satisfied with their present position, nor their ignorance, by asserting that they have all the rights they want.

Resolved, That inasmuch as man, while claiming for himself intellectual superiority, does accord to woman moral superiority, it is preeminently his duty to encourage her to speak and teach, as she has an opportunity, in all religious assemblies.

Resolved, That the same amount of virtue, delicacy, and refinement of behavior that is required of woman in the social state, should also be required of man, and the same transgressions should be visited with equal severity on both man and woman.

Resolved, That the objection of indelicacy and impropriety, which is so often brought against woman when she addresses a public audience, comes with a very ill-grace from those who encourage, by their attendance, her appearance on the stage, in the concert, or in feats of the circus.

Resolved, That woman has too long rested satisfied in the circumscribed limits which corrupt customs and a perverted application of the Scriptures have marked out for her, and that it is time she should move in the enlarged sphere which her great Creator has assigned her.

Resolved, That it is the duty of the women of this country to secure to   30 themselves their sacred right to the elective franchise.

Resolved, That the equality of human rights results necessarily from the fact of the identity of the race in capabilities and responsibilities.

Resolved, therefore, That, being invested by the Creator with the same capabilities, and the same consciousness of responsibility for their exercise, it is demonstrably the right and duty of woman, equally with man, to promote every righteous cause by every righteous means; and especially in regard to the great subjects of morals and religion, it is self-evidently her right to participate with her brother in teaching them, both in private and in public, by writing and by speaking, by any instrumentalities proper to be used, and in any assemblies proper to be held; and this being a self-evident truth growing out of the divinely implanted principles of human nature, any custom or authority adverse to it, whether modern or wearing the hoary sanction of antiquity, is to be regarded as a self-evident falsehood, and at war with mankind.

[At the last session Lucretia Mott offered and spoke to the following resolution:]

Resolved, That the speedy success of our cause depends upon the zealous and untiring efforts of both men and women, for the overthrow of the monopoly of the pulpit, and for the securing to woman an equal participation with men in the various trades, professions, and commerce.

TOPICS FOR CRITICAL THINKING AND WRITING

1. Stanton echoes the Declaration of Independence because she wishes to associate her ideas and the movement she supports with a document and a movement that her readers esteem. And she must have believed that if readers esteem the Declaration of Independence, they must grant the justice of her goals. Does her strategy work, or does it backfire by making her essay seem strained?

2. When Stanton insists that women have an "inalienable right to the elective franchise" (para. 4), what does she mean by "inalienable"?

3. Stanton complains that men have made married women, "in the eye of the law, civilly dead" (para. 8). What does she mean by "civilly dead"? How is it possible for a person to be biologically alive and yet civilly dead?

4. Stanton objects that women are "not known" as teachers of "theology, medicine, or law" (para. 13). Is this still true today? Do some research in your library, and then write three 100-word biographical sketches, one each on well-known woman professors of theology, medicine, and law.

5. How might you go about proving (rather than merely asserting) that, as paragraph 24 says, "woman is man's equal—was intended to be so by the Creator"?

6. The Declaration claims that women have "the same capabilities" as men (para. 32). Yet in 1848 Stanton and the others at Seneca Falls knew, or should have known, that history recorded no example of a woman philosopher comparable to Plato or Kant, a composer comparable to Beethoven or Chopin, a scientist comparable to Galileo or Newton, or a mathematician comparable to Euclid or Descartes. Do these facts contradict the Declaration's claim? If not, why not? How else but by different intellectual capabilities do you think such facts can be explained?

7. Stanton's Declaration is over 165 years old. Have all of the issues she raised been satisfactorily resolved? If not, which ones remain?

8. In our society, children have very few rights. For instance, a child cannot decide to drop out of elementary school or high school, and a child cannot decide to leave his or her parents to reside with some other

family that he or she finds more compatible. Whatever your view of children's rights, compose the best Declaration of the Rights of Children that you can.

Martin Luther King Jr.

Martin Luther King Jr. (1929–1968) was born in Atlanta and educated at Morehouse College, Crozer Theological Seminary, and Boston University. In 1954 he was called to serve as a Baptist minister in Montgomery, Alabama. During the next two years he achieved national fame when, using a policy of nonviolent resistance, he successfully led the boycott against segregated bus lines in Montgomery. He then organized the Southern Christian Leadership Conference, which furthered civil rights, first in the South and then nationwide. In 1964 he was awarded the Nobel Peace Prize. Four years later he was assassinated in Memphis, Tennessee, while supporting striking garbage workers.

The speech presented here was delivered from the steps of the Lincoln Memorial, in Washington, D.C., in 1963, the hundredth anniversary of the Emancipation Proclamation. King's immediate audience consisted of more than two hundred thousand people who had come to demonstrate for civil rights.

I Have a Dream

I am happy to join with you today in what will go down in history as the greatest demonstration for freedom in the history of our nation.

Five score years ago, a great American, in whose symbolic shadow we stand today, signed the Emancipation Proclamation. This momentous decree came as a great beacon light of hope to millions of Negro slaves who had been seared in the flames of withering injustice. It came as a joyous daybreak to end the long night of their captivity. But one hundred years later, the Negro still is not free. One hundred years later, the life of the Negro is still sadly crippled by the manacles of segregation and the chains of discrimination. One hundred years later, the Negro lives on a lonely island of poverty in the midst of a vast ocean of material prosperity. One hundred years later, the Negro is still anguished in the corners of American society and finds himself in exile in his own land. And so we have come here today to dramatize a shameful condition.

In a sense we have come to our nation's capital to cash a check. When the architects of our republic wrote the magnificent words of the Constitution and the Declaration of Independence, they were signing a promissory note to which every American was to fall heir. This note was the promise that all men—yes, black men as well as white men—would be guaranteed the inalienable rights of life, liberty, and the pursuit of happiness.

It is obvious today that America has defaulted on this promissory note insofar as her citizens of color are concerned. Instead of honoring this sacred obligation, America has given the Negro people a bad check, a check which has come back marked "insufficient funds." But we refuse to believe that the bank of justice is bankrupt. We refuse to believe that there are insufficient funds in the great vaults of opportunity of this nation; and so we have come to cash this check, a check that will give us upon demand the riches of freedom and the security of justice.

We have also come to this hallowed spot to remind America of the 5 fierce urgency of *now*. This is no time to engage in the luxury of cooling off or to take the tranquilizing drug of gradualism. *Now* is the time to make real promises of democracy. *Now* is the time to rise from the dark and desolate valley of segregation to the sunlit path of racial justice. *Now* is the time to lift our nation from the quicksands of racial injustice to the solid rock of brotherhood. *Now* is the time to make justice a reality for all of God's children.

It would be fatal for the nation to overlook the urgency of the moment. This sweltering summer of the Negro's legitimate discontent will not pass until there is an invigorating autumn of freedom and equality. Nineteen sixty-three is not an end, but a beginning. And those who hope that the Negro needed to blow off steam and will now be content will have a rude awakening if the nation returns to business as usual. There will be neither rest nor tranquility in America until the Negro is granted his citizenship rights. The whirlwinds of revolt will continue to shake the foundations of our nation until the bright day of justice emerges.

But there is something that I must say to my people who stand on the warm threshold which leads into the palace of justice. In the process of gaining our rightful place, we must not be guilty of wrongful deeds. Let us not seek to satisfy our thirst for freedom by drinking from the cup of bitterness and hatred. We must forever conduct our struggle on the high plane of dignity and discipline. We must not allow our creative protest to degenerate into physical violence. Again and again we must rise to the majestic heights of meeting physical force with soul force. And the marvelous new militancy which has engulfed the Negro community must not lead us to a distrust of all white people; for many of our white brothers, as evidenced by their presence here today, have come to realize that their destiny is tied up with our destiny, and they have come to realize that their freedom is inextricably bound to our freedom.

We cannot walk alone. And as we walk we must make the pledge that we shall always march ahead. We cannot turn back. There are those who are asking the devotees of civil rights, "When will you be satisfied?" We can never be satisfied as long as the Negro is the victim of the unspeakable horrors of police brutality. We can never be satisfied as long as our bodies, heavy with the fatigue of travel, cannot gain lodging in the motels of the highways and the hotels of the cities. We cannot be satisfied as long as the Negro's basic mobility is from a smaller ghetto to a larger one. We can never be satisfied as long as our children are stripped of their selfhood and robbed of their dignity by signs stating "For Whites Only." We cannot be satisfied as long as the Negro in Mississippi cannot vote and a Negro in New York believes he has nothing for which to vote. No, no, we are not satisfied, and we will not be satisfied until justice rolls down like waters and righteousness like a mighty stream.[1]

I am not unmindful that some of you have come here out of great trials and tribulations. Some of you have come fresh from narrow jail cells. Some of you have come from areas where your quest for freedom left you battered by the storms of persecution and staggered by the winds of police brutality. You have been the veterans of creative suffering. Continue to work with the faith that unearned suffering is redemptive.

Go back to Mississippi, and go back to Alabama. Go back to South 10 Carolina. Go back to Georgia. Go back to Louisiana. Go back to the slums and ghettos of our Northern cities, knowing that somehow this situation can and will be changed. Let us not wallow in the valley of despair.

I say to you today, my friends, even though we face the difficulties of today and tomorrow, I still have a dream. It is a dream deeply rooted in the American dream. I have a dream that one day this nation will rise up and live out the true meaning of its creed: "We hold these truths to be self-evident, that all men are created equal." I have a dream that one day, on the red hills of Georgia, sons of former slaves and the sons of former slave owners will be able to sit down together at the table of brotherhood. I have a dream that one day even the state of Mississippi, a state sweltering with the heat of injustice, sweltering with the heat of oppression, will be transformed into an oasis of freedom and justice. I have a dream that my four little children will one day live in a nation where they will not be judged by the color of their skin, but by the content of their character.

I have a dream today. I have a dream that one day down in Alabama—with its vicious racists, with its governor's lips dripping with the words of interposition and nullification—one day right there in Alabama, little black boys and black girls will be able to join hands with little white boys and white girls as sisters and brothers.

I have a dream today. I have a dream that one day every valley shall be exalted and every hill and mountain shall be made low, the rough places will be made plain and the crooked places will be made straight, and the glory of the Lord shall be revealed, and all flesh shall see it together.[2]

This is our hope. This is the faith that I go back to the South with. And with this faith we will be able to hew out of the mountain of despair a stone of hope. With this faith we will be able to transform the jangling discords of our nation into a beautiful symphony of brotherhood. With

---

[1]**justice . . . stream** A quotation from the Hebrew Bible: Amos 5:24. [All notes are the editors'.]

[2]**every valley . . . see it together** Another quotation from the Hebrew Bible: Isaiah 40:4–5.

this faith we will be able to work together, to play together, to struggle together, to go to jail together, to stand up for freedom together, knowing that we will be free one day.

And this will be the day—this will be the day when all of God's chil-   15
dren will be able to sing with new meaning:

> My country, 'tis of thee,
> Sweet land of liberty,
>   Of thee I sing;
> Land where my fathers died,
> Land of the Pilgrim's pride,
> From every mountainside
>   Let freedom ring.

And if America is to be a great nation, this must become true.

And so let freedom ring from the prodigious hilltops of New Hampshire. Let freedom ring from the mighty mountains of New York. Let freedom ring from the heightening Alleghenies of Pennsylvania. Let freedom ring from the snow-capped Rockies of Colorado. Let freedom ring from the curvaceous slopes of California.

But not only that. Let freedom ring from Stone Mountain of Georgia. Let freedom ring from Lookout Mountain of Tennessee. Let freedom ring from every hill and molehill of Mississippi. "From every mountainside let freedom ring."

And when this happens—when we allow freedom to ring, when we let it ring from every village and every hamlet, from every state and every city—we will be able to speed up that day when all of God's children, Black men and white men, Jews and Gentiles, Protestants and Catholics, will be able to join hands and sing in the words of the old Negro spiritual: "Free at last! Free at last! Thank God Almighty. We are free at last!"

TOPICS FOR CRITICAL THINKING AND WRITING

1. Analyze the rhetoric—the oratorical art—of the second paragraph. What, for instance, is gained by saying "five score years ago" instead of "a hundred years ago"? By metaphorically calling the Emancipation Proclamation "a great beacon light of hope"? By saying that "Negro slaves . . . had been seared in the flames of withering injustice"? And what of the metaphors "daybreak" and "the long night of . . . captivity"?

2. Do the first two paragraphs make an effective opening? Why?

3. In the third and fourth paragraphs King uses the metaphor of a bad check. Rewrite the third paragraph *without* using any of King's metaphors, and then in a paragraph evaluate the differences between King's version and yours.

4. King's highly metaphoric speech appeals to emotions. But it also offers *reasons*. What reasons, for instance, does King give to support his belief

that African Americans should not resort to physical violence in their struggle against segregation and discrimination?

5. When King delivered the speech, his audience at the Lincoln Memorial was primarily African American. Do you think that the speech is also addressed to other Americans? Explain.

6. The speech can be divided into three parts: paragraphs 1 through 6; paragraphs 7 ("But there is") through 10; and paragraph 11 ("I say to you today, my friends") to the end. Summarize each of these three parts in a sentence or two so that the basic organization is evident.

7. King says (para. 11) that his dream is "deeply rooted in the American dream." First, what is the American dream, as King seems to understand it? Second, how does King establish his point—that is, what evidence does he use to convince us—that his dream is the American dream? (On this second issue, one might start by pointing out that in the second paragraph King refers to the Emancipation Proclamation. What other relevant documents does he refer to?)

8. King delivered his speech in 1963, more than fifty years ago. In an essay of 500 words, argue that the speech still is—or is not—relevant. Or write an essay of 500 words in which you state what you take to be the "American dream," and argue that it now is or is not readily available to African Americans.

W. H. Auden

Wystan Hugh Auden (1907–1973) was born in York, England, and educated at Oxford University. In the 1930s his witty left-wing poetry earned him wide acclaim as the leading poet of his generation. In 1939 he came to the United States, becoming a citizen in 1946 but returning to England for his last years. Much of Auden's poetry is characterized by a combination of colloquial diction and technical dexterity. The poem reprinted here was originally published in 1940.

The Unknown Citizen

(To JS/07/M/378
This Marble Monument
Is Erected by the State)

He was found by the Bureau of Statistics to be
One against whom there was no official complaint,
And all the reports on his conduct agree
That, in the modern sense of an old-fashioned word, he was a saint,
For in everything he did he served the Greater Community.   5
Except for the War till the day he retired
He worked in a factory and never got fired,
But satisfied his employers, Fudge Motors Inc.
Yet he wasn't a scab or odd in his views,

For his Union reports that he paid his dues,   10
(Our report on his Union shows it was sound)
And our Social Psychology workers found
That he was popular with his mates and liked a drink.
The Press are convinced that he bought a paper every day
And that his reactions to advertisements were normal in every way.   15
Policies taken out in his name prove that he was fully insured,
And his Health-card shows he was once in hospital but left it cured.
Both Producers Research and High-Grade Living declare
He was fully sensible to the advantages of the Installment Plan
And had everything necessary to the Modern Man,   20
A phonograph, radio, a car and a frigidaire.
Our researches into Public Opinion are content
That he held the proper opinions for the time of year;
When there was peace, he was for peace; when there was war, he went.
He was married and added five children to the population,   25
Which our Eugenist says was the right number for a parent of his
    generation,
And our teachers report that he never interfered with their education.
Was he free? Was he happy? The question is absurd:
Had anything been wrong, we should certainly have heard.

Topics for Critical Thinking and Writing

1. Who is the narrator in Auden's poem, and on what sort of occasion is he speaking? How do you know?

2. France, Great Britain, and the United States all have monuments to "The Unknown" (formerly "The Unknown Soldier"). How is Auden's proposed monument like and unlike these war memorials?

3. The poem ends by asking "Was he free? Was he happy?" and the questions are dismissed summarily. Is that because the answers are so obvious? What answers (obvious or subtle) do you think the poem offers to these questions?

4. Evaluate the poem, making clear the reasons behind your evaluation.

5. If you have read the selection from Thomas More's *Utopia*, write an essay of 500 to 750 words—in More's voice—setting forth More's response to Auden's poem.

Langston Hughes

Langston Hughes (1902–1967), an African American writer, was born in Joplin, Missouri, but after his parents divorced, he lived with his grandmother in Lawrence, Kansas, then in Cleveland, and then for fifteen months in Mexico with his father. He returned to the United States in 1921 and spent a year at Columbia University, served as a merchant seaman, and worked in a Paris nightclub, where he showed some of his poems to Dr. Alain Locke, a strong advocate of African American literature. Encouraged by Locke, when Hughes returned to the United States, he studied at the University of Pennsylvania and Lincoln University, where he earned a bachelor's degree. He continued to write, publishing fiction, plays, essays, and biographies; he also founded theaters, gave public readings, and was, in short, a highly visible presence. Esquire *magazine first published an abridged version of "Let America Be America Again" in 1936.*

Let America Be America Again

Let America be America again.
Let it be the dream it used to be.
Let it be the pioneer on the plain
Seeking a home where he himself is free.

(America never was America to me.)   5

Let America be the dream the dreamers dreamed—
Let it be that great strong land of love
Where never kings connive nor tyrants scheme
That any man be crushed by one above.

(It never was America to me.)   10

O, let my land be a land where Liberty
Is crowned with no false patriotic wreath,
But opportunity is real, and life is free,
Equality is in the air we breathe.

(There's never been equality for me,   15
Nor freedom in this "homeland of the free.")

Say, who are you that mumbles in the dark?
And who are you that draws your veil across the stars?

I am the poor white, fooled and pushed apart,
I am the Negro bearing slavery's scars.
I am the red man driven from the land,   20
I am the immigrant clutching the hope I seek—
And finding only the same old stupid plan
Of dog eat dog, of mighty crush the weak.

I am the young man, full of strength and hope,   25
Tangled in that ancient endless chain
Of profit, power, gain, of grab the land!
Of grab the gold! Of grab the ways of satisfying need!
Of work the men! Of take the pay!
Of owning everything for one's own greed!   30

I am the farmer, bondsman to the soil.
I am the worker sold to the machine.

I am the Negro, servant to you all.
I am the people, humble, hungry, mean —
Hungry yet today despite the dream.   35
Beaten yet today — O, Pioneers!
I am the man who never got ahead,
The poorest worker bartered through the years.

Yet I'm the one who dreamt our basic dream
In that Old World while still a serf of kings,   40
Who dreamt a dream so strong, so brave, so true,
That even yet its mighty daring sings
In every brick and stone, in every furrow turned
That's made America the land it has become.
O, I'm the man who sailed those early seas   45
In search of what I meant to be my home —
For I'm the one who left dark Ireland's shore,
And Poland's plain, and England's grassy lea,
And torn from Black Africa's strand I came
To build a "homeland of the free."   50

The free?

Who said the free? Not me?
Surely not me? The millions on relief today?
The millions shot down when we strike?
The millions who have nothing for our pay?   55
For all the dreams we've dreamed
And all the songs we've sung
And all the hopes we've held
And all the flags we've hung,
The millions who have nothing for our pay —   60
Except the dream that's almost dead today.

O, let America be America again —
The land that never has been yet —
And yet must be — the land where *every* man is free.
The land that's mine — the poor man's, Indian's, Negro's, ME —   65
Who made America,
Whose sweat and blood, whose faith and pain,
Whose hand at the foundry, whose plow in the rain,
Must bring back our mighty dream again.

Sure, call me any ugly name you choose —   70
The steel of freedom does not stain.
From those who live like leeches on the people's lives,
We must take back our land again,
America!

O, yes,   75
I say it plain,
America never was America to me,

And yet I swear this oath—
America will be!

Out of the rack and ruin of our gangster death,   80
The rape and rot of graft, and stealth, and lies,
We, the people, must redeem
The land, the mines, the plants, the rivers.
The mountains and the endless plain—
All, all the stretch of these great green states—   85
And make America again!

Topics for Critical Thinking and Writing

1. Hughes says in line 1, "Let America be America again," but do you suppose that America ever was what he seems to assume that it once was? For instance, might not his "pioneer" (line 3) have been sexist and racist? Or is it evident that contemporary society is morally inferior to early American society?

2. In line 24 Hughes speaks of a system "of dog eat dog," where the "mighty crush the weak," and in line 27 he speaks of a system of "profit, power, gain, of grab the land." Do you believe that this charge can be lodged today against our system of capitalism? Explain.

3. When *Esquire* magazine bought the poem, it bought only the first fifty lines. Why do you suppose the magazine declined to publish the remainder? Because the latter part is less good as poetry? Because it is too radical? In an essay of 500 words compare the two versions (lines 1–50 and 1–86), and indicate which version you would publish if you were an editor today and why.

Ursula K. Le Guin

Ursula K. Le Guin was born in 1929 in Berkeley, California, the daughter of a distinguished mother (Theodora Kroeber, a folklorist) and father (Alfred L. Kroeber, an anthropologist). After graduating from Radcliffe College, she earned a master's degree at Columbia University; in 1952 she held a Fulbright Fellowship for study in Paris, where she met and married Charles Le Guin, a historian. She began writing in earnest while bringing up three children. Although her work is most widely known to buffs of science fiction, because it usually has larger moral or political dimensions, it interests many other readers who normally do not care for sci-fi.

Le Guin has said that she was prompted to write the following story by a remark she encountered in William James's "The Moral Philosopher and the Moral Life." James suggests there that if millions of people could be "kept permanently happy on the one simple condition that a certain lost soul on the far-off edge of things should lead a life of lonely torment," our moral sense "would make us immediately feel" it would be "hideous" to accept such a bargain. This story first appeared in New Dimensions 3 *(1973).*

The Ones Who Walk Away from Omelas

With a clamor of bells that set the swallows soaring, the Festival of Summer came to the city Omelas, bright-towered by the sea. The rigging of the boats in harbor sparkled with flags. In the streets between houses with red roofs and painted walls, between old moss-grown gardens and under avenues of trees, past great parks and public buildings, processions moved. Some were decorous: old people in long stiff robes of mauve and gray, grave master workmen, quiet, merry women carrying their babies and chatting as they walked. In other streets the music beat faster, a shimmering of gong and tambourine, and the people went dancing, the procession was a dance. Children dodged in and out, their high calls rising like the swallows' crossing flights over the music and the singing. All the processions wound towards the north side of the city, where on the great water-meadow called the Green Fields boys and girls, naked in the bright air, with mudstained feet and ankles and long, lithe arms, exercised their restive horses before the race. The horses wore no gear at all but a halter without bit. Their manes were braided with streamers of silver, gold, and green. They flared their nostrils and pranced and boasted to one another; they were vastly excited, the horse being the only animal who has adopted our ceremonies as his own. Far off to the north and west the mountains stood up half encircling Omelas on her bay. The air of morning was so clear that the snow still crowning the Eighteen Peaks burned with white-gold fire across the miles of sunlit air, under the dark blue of the sky. There was just enough wind to make the banners that marked the racecourse snap and flutter now and then. In the silence of the broad green meadows one could hear the music winding through the city streets, farther and nearer and ever approaching, a cheerful faint sweetness of the air that from time to time trembled and gathered together and broke out into the great joyous clanging of the bells.

Joyous! How is one to tell about joy? How describe the citizens of Omelas?

They were not simple folk, you see, though they were happy. But we do not say the words of cheer much any more. All smiles have become archaic. Given a description such as this one tends to make certain assumptions. Given a description such as this one tends to look next for the King, mounted on a splendid stallion and surrounded by his noble knights, or perhaps in a golden litter borne by great-muscled slaves. But there was no king. They did not use swords, or keep slaves. They were not barbarians. I do not know the rules and laws of their society, but I suspect that they were singularly few. As they did without monarchy and slavery, so they also got on without the stock exchange, the advertisement, the secret police, and the bomb. Yet I repeat that these were not simple folk, not dulcet shepherds, noble savages, bland utopians. They were not less complex than us. The trouble is that we have a bad habit, encouraged by pedants and sophisticates, of considering happiness as something rather stupid. Only pain is intellectual, only evil interesting. This is the treason of the artist: a refusal to admit the banality of evil and the terrible boredom of pain. If you can't lick 'em, join 'em. If it hurts, repeat it. But to praise despair is to condemn delight, to embrace violence is to lose hold of everything else. We have almost lost hold, we can no longer describe a happy man, nor make any celebration of joy. How can I tell you about the people of Omelas? They were not naïve and happy children—though their children were, in fact, happy. They were mature, intelligent, passionate adults whose lives were not wretched. O miracle! But I wish I could describe it better. I wish I could convince you. Omelas sounds in my words like a city in a fairy tale, long ago and far away, once upon a time. Perhaps it would be best if you imagined it as your own fancy bids, assuming it will rise to the occasion, for certainly I cannot suit you all. For instance, how about technology? I think that there would be no cars or helicopters in and above the streets; this follows from the fact that the people of Omelas are happy people. Happiness is based on a just discrimination of what is necessary, what is neither necessary nor destructive, and what is destructive. In the middle category, however—that of the unnecessary but undestructive, that of comfort, luxury, exuberance, etc.—they could perfectly well have central heating, subway trains, washing machines, and all kinds of marvelous devices not yet invented here, floating light-sources, fuelless power, a cure for the common cold. Or they could have none of that: it doesn't matter. As you like it. I incline to think that people from towns up and down the coast have been coming in to Omelas during the last days before the Festival on very fast little trains and double-decked trams, and that the train station of Omelas is actually the handsomest building in town, though plainer than the magnificent Farmers' Market. But even granted trains, I fear that Omelas so far strikes some of you as goody-goody. Smiles, bells, parades, horses, bleh. If so, please add an orgy. If an orgy would help, don't hesitate. Let us not, however, have temples from which issue beautiful nude priests and priestesses already half in ecstasy and ready to copulate with any man or woman, lover or stranger, who desires union with the deep godhead of the blood, although that was my first idea. But really it would be better not to have any temples in Omelas—at least, not manned temples. Religion yes, clergy no. Surely the beautiful nudes can just wander about, offering themselves like divine soufflés to the hunger of the needy and the rapture of the flesh. Let them join the processions. Let tambourines be struck above the copulations, and the glory of desire be proclaimed upon the gongs, and (a not unimportant point) let the offspring of these delightful rituals be beloved and looked after by all. One thing I know there is none of in Omelas is guilt. But what else should there be? I thought that first there were no drugs, but that is puritanical. For those who like it, the faint insistent sweetness of *drooz* may perfume the ways of the city, *drooz* which first brings a great lightness and brilliance to the mind and limbs, and then after some hours a dreamy languor, and wonderful visions at last of the very arcana and inmost secrets of the Universe, as well as exciting the pleasure of sex beyond all belief; and it is not habit-forming. For more modest tastes I think there ought to be beer. What else, what else belongs in the joyous city? The sense of victory, surely, the celebration of courage. But as we did without clergy, let us do without soldiers. The joy built upon successful slaughter is not the right kind of joy; it will not do; it is fearful and it is trivial. A boundless and generous contentment, a magnanimous triumph felt not against some outer enemy but in communion with the finest and fairest in the souls of all men everywhere and the splendor of the world's summer: this is what swells the hearts of the people of Omelas, and the victory they celebrate is that of life. I really don't think many of them need to take *drooz*.

Most of the processions have reached the Green Fields by now. A marvelous smell of cooking goes forth from the red and blue tents of the provisioners. The faces of small children are amiably sticky; in the benign grey beard of a man a couple of crumbs of rich pastry are entangled. The youths and girls have mounted their horses and are beginning to group around the starting line of the course. An old woman, small, fat, and laughing, is passing out flowers from a basket, and tall young men wear her flowers in their shining hair. A child of nine or ten sits at the edge of the crowd, alone, playing on a wooden flute. People pause to listen, and they smile, but they do not speak to him, for he never ceases playing and never sees them, his dark eyes wholly rapt in the sweet, thin magic of the tune.

He finishes, and slowly lowers his hands holding the wooden flute.   5

As if that little private silence were the signal, all at once a trumpet sounds from the pavilion near the starting line: imperious, melancholy, piercing. The horses rear on their slender legs, and some of them neigh in answer. Sober-faced, the young riders stroke the horses' necks and soothe them, whispering, "Quiet, quiet, there my beauty, my hope. . . ." They begin to form in rank along the starting line. The crowds along the racecourse are like a field of grass and flowers in the wind. The Festival of Summer has begun.

Do you believe? Do you accept the festival, the city, the joy? No? Then let me describe one more thing.

In a basement under one of the beautiful public buildings of Omelas, or perhaps in the cellar of one of its spacious private homes, there is a room. It has one locked door, and no window. A little light seeps in dustily between cracks in the boards, secondhand from a cobwebbed window somewhere across the cellar. In one corner of the little room a couple of mops, with stiff, clotted, foul-smelling heads, stand near a rusty bucket. The floor is dirt, a little damp to the touch, as cellar dirt usually is. The room is about three paces long and two wide: a mere broom closet or disused tool room. In the room a child is sitting. It could be a boy or a girl. It looks about six, but actually is nearly ten. It is feeble-minded. Perhaps it was born defective, or perhaps it has become imbecile through fear, malnutrition, and neglect. It picks its nose and occasionally fumbles vaguely with its toes or genitals, as it sits hunched in the corner farthest from the bucket and the two mops. It is afraid of the mops. It finds them horrible. It shuts its eyes, but it knows the mops are still standing there; and the door is locked; and nobody will come. The door is always locked; and nobody ever comes, except that sometimes—the child has no understanding of time or interval—sometimes the door rattles terribly and opens, and a person, or several people, are there. One of them may come in and kick the child to make it stand up. The others never come close, but peer in at it with frightened, disgusted eyes. The food bowl and the water jug are hastily filled, the door is locked, the eyes disappear. The people at the door never say anything, but the child, who has not always lived in the tool room, and can remember sunlight and its mother's voice, sometimes speaks. "I will be good," it says. "Please let me out. I will be good!" They never answer. The child used to scream for help at night, and cry a good deal, but now it only makes a kind of whining, "eh-haa, eh-haa," and it speaks less and less often. It is so thin there are no calves to its legs; its belly protrudes; it lives on a half-bowl of corn meal and grease a day. It is naked. Its buttocks and thighs are a mass of festered sores, as it sits in its own excrement continually.

They all know it is there, all the people of Omelas. Some of them have come to see it, others are content merely to know it is there. They all know that it has to be there. Some of them understand why, and some do not, but they all understand that their happiness, the beauty of their city, the tenderness of their friendships, the health of their children, the wisdom of their scholars, the skill of their makers, even the abundance of their harvest and the kindly weathers of their skies, depend wholly on this child's abominable misery.

This is usually explained to children when they are between eight 10 and twelve, whenever they seem capable of understanding; and most of those who come to see the child are young people, though often enough an adult comes, or comes back, to see the child. No matter how well the matter has been explained to them, these young spectators are always shocked and sickened at the sight. They feel disgust, which they had thought themselves superior to. They feel anger, outrage, impotence, despite all the explanations. They would like to do something for the child. But there is nothing they can do. If the child were brought up into the sunlight out of that vile place, if it were cleaned and fed and comforted, that would be a good thing, indeed; but if it were done, in that day and hour all the prosperity and beauty and delight of Omelas would wither and be destroyed. Those are the terms. To exchange all the goodness and grace of every life in Omelas for that single, small improvement: to throw away the happiness of thousands for the chance of the happiness of one: that would be to let guilt within the walls indeed.

The terms are strict and absolute; there may not even be a kind word spoken to the child.

Often the young people go home in tears, or in a tearless rage, when they have seen the child and faced this terrible paradox. They may brood over it for weeks or years. But as time goes on they begin to realize that even if the child could be released, it would not get much good of its freedom: a little vague pleasure of warmth and food, no doubt, but little more. It is too degraded and imbecile to know any real joy. It has been afraid too long ever to be free of fear. Its habits are too uncouth for it to respond to humane treatment. Indeed, after so long it would probably be wretched without walls about it to protect it, and darkness for its eyes, and its own excrement to sit in. Their tears at the bitter injustice dry when they begin to perceive the terrible justice of reality, and to accept it. Yet it is their tears and anger, the trying of their generosity and the acceptance of their helplessness, which are perhaps the true source of the splendor of their lives. Theirs is no vapid, irresponsible happiness. They know that they, like the child, are not free. They know compassion. It is the existence of the child, and their knowledge of its existence, that makes possible the nobility of their architecture, the poignancy of their music, the profundity of their science. It is because of the child that they are so gentle with children. They know that if the wretched one were not there snivelling in the dark, the other one, the flute-player, could make no joyful music as the young riders line up in their beauty for the race in the sunlight of the first morning of summer.

Now do you believe in them? Are they not more credible? But there is one more thing to tell, and this is quite incredible.

At times one of the adolescent girls or boys who go to see the child does not go home to weep or rage, does not, in fact, go home at all. Sometimes also a man or woman much older falls silent for a day or two, and then leaves home. These people go out into the street, and walk down the street alone. They keep walking, and walk straight out of the city of Omelas, through the beautiful gates. They keep walking across the farmlands of Omelas. Each one goes alone, youth or girl, man or woman. Night falls; the traveler must pass down village streets, between the houses with yellow-lit windows, and on out into the darkness of the fields. Each alone, they go west or north, towards the mountains. They go on. They leave Omelas, they walk ahead into the darkness, and they do not come back. The place they go towards is a place even less imaginable to most of us than the city of happiness. I cannot describe it at all. It is possible that it does not exist. But they seem to know where they are going, the ones who walk away from Omelas.

Topics for Critical Thinking and Writing

1. Summarize the point of the story—not the plot but what the story adds up to, what the author is getting at. Next, set forth what you would probably do (and why) if you were born in Omelas.

2. Consider the narrator's assertion that happiness "is based on a just discrimination of what is necessary" (para. 3).

3. Do you think the story implies a criticism of contemporary American society? Explain.

Helen Prejean

Sister Helen Prejean, born in Baton Rouge in 1939, has been a member of the Order of the Sisters of St. Joseph of Medaille since 1957. In 1993, she achieved international fame with her book Dead Man Walking: An Eyewitness Account of the Death Penalty in the United States, *based on her experiences counseling prisoners on death row in Louisiana prisons. An excerpt is printed here. A film with the same title, starring Susan Sarandon (as Sister Helen) and Sean Penn, was released in 1995. When confronted with the argument that the death penalty is appropriate revenge for society to take on a murderer, Sister Helen said, "I would not want my death avenged—especially by government, which can't be trusted to control its own bureaucrats or collect taxes equitably or fill a pothole, much less decide which of its citizens to kill." The title is the editors'.*

Executions Are Too Costly—Morally

I think of the running debate I engage in with "church" people about the death penalty. "Proof texts" from the Bible usually punctuate these discussions without regard for the cultural context or literary genre of the passages invoked. (Will D. Campbell, a Southern Baptist minister and writer, calls this use of scriptural quotations "biblical quarterbacking.")

It is abundantly clear that the Bible depicts murder as a crime for which death is considered the appropriate punishment, and one is hard-pressed to find a biblical "proof text" in either the Hebrew Testament or the New Testament which unequivocally refutes this. Even Jesus' admonition "Let him without sin cast the first stone," when he was asked the appropriate punishment for an adulteress (John 8:7)—the Mosaic law prescribed death—should be read in its proper context. This passage is an "entrapment" story, which sought to show Jesus' wisdom in besting his adversaries. It is not an ethical pronouncement about capital punishment.

Similarly, the "eye for eye" passage from Exodus, which pro-death penalty advocates are fond of quoting, is rarely cited in its original context, in which it is clearly meant to limit revenge.

The passage, including verse 22, which sets the context reads:

> If, when men come to blows, they hurt a woman who is pregnant and she suffers a miscarriage, though she does not die of it, the man responsible must pay the compensation demanded of him by the woman's master; he shall hand it over after arbitration. But should she die, you shall give life for life, eye for eye, tooth for tooth, hand for hand, foot for foot, burn for burn, wound for wound, stroke for stroke. (Exodus 21:22–25)

In the example given (patently patriarchal: the woman is considered ₅ the negotiable property of her male master), it is clear that punishment is to be measured out according to the seriousness of the offense. If the child is lost but not the mother, the punishment is less grave than if both mother and child are lost. *Only* an eye for an eye, *only* a life for a life is the intent of the passage. Restraint was badly needed. It was not uncommon for an offended family or clan to slaughter entire communities in retaliation for an offense against one of their members.

Even granting the call for restraint in this passage, it is nonetheless clear—here and in numerous other instances throughout the Hebrew Bible—that the punishment for murder was death.

But we must remember that such prescriptions of the Mosaic Law were promulgated in a seminomadic culture in which the preservation of a fragile society—without benefit of prisons and other institutions—demanded quick, effective, harsh punishment of offenders. And we should note the numerous other crimes for which the Bible prescribes death as punishment:

> contempt of parents (Exodus 21:15, 17; Leviticus 24:17);
>
> trespass upon sacred ground (Exodus 19:12-13; Numbers 1:51; 18:7);
>
> sorcery (Exodus 22:18; Leviticus 20:27);
>
> bestiality (Exodus 22:19; Leviticus 20:15–16);
>
> sacrifice to foreign gods (Exodus 22:20; Deuteronomy 13:1–9);
>
> profaning the sabbath (Exodus 31:14);
>
> adultery (Leviticus 20:10; Deuteronomy 22:22–24);
>
> incest (Leviticus 20:11–13);
>
> homosexuality (Leviticus 20:13);
>
> and prostitution (Leviticus 21:19; Deuteronomy 22:13–21).

And this is by no means a complete list.

But no person with common sense would dream of appropriating such a moral code today, and it is curious that those who so readily invoke the "eye for an eye, life for life" passage are quick to shun other biblical prescriptions which also call for death, arguing that modern societies have evolved over the three thousand or so years since biblical times and no longer consider such exaggerated and archaic punishments appropriate.

Such nuances are lost, of course, in "biblical quarterbacking," and ₁₀ more and more I find myself steering away from such futile discussions. Instead, I try to articulate what I personally believe about Jesus and the ethical thrust he gave to humankind: an impetus toward compassion, a preference for disarming enemies without humiliating and destroying them, and a solidarity with poor and suffering people.

So, what happened to the impetus of love and compassion Jesus set blazing into history?

The first Christians adhered closely to the way of life Jesus had taught. They died in amphitheaters rather than offer homage to worldly emperors. They refused to fight in emperors' wars. But then a tragic diversion happened, which Elaine Pagels has deftly explored in her book *Adam, Eve, and the Serpent:* in 313 c.e. (Common Era) the Emperor Constantine entered the Christian church.

Pagels says, "Christian bishops, once targets for arrest, torture, and execution, now received tax exemptions, gifts from the imperial treasury, prestige, and even influence at court; the churches gained new wealth, power and prominence."

Unfortunately, the exercise of power practiced by Christians in alliance with the Roman Empire — with its unabashed allegiance to the sword — soon bore no resemblance to the purely moral persuasion that Jesus had taught.

In the fifth century, Pagels points out, Augustine provided the theo- 15 logical rationale the church needed to justify the use of violence by church and state governments. Augustine persuaded church authorities that "original sin" so damaged every person's ability to make moral choices that external control by church and state authorities over people's lives was necessary and justified. The "wicked" might be "coerced by the sword" to "protect the innocent," Augustine taught. And thus was legitimated for Christians the authority of secular government to "control" its subjects by coercive and violent means — even punishment by death.

In the latter part of the twentieth century, however, two flares of hope — Mohandas K. Gandhi and Martin Luther King — have demonstrated that Jesus' counsel to practice compassion and tolerance even toward one's enemies can effect social change. Susan Jacoby, analyzing the moral power that Gandhi and King unleashed in their campaigns for social justice, finds a unique form of aggression:

"'If everyone took an eye for an eye,' Gandhi said, 'the whole world would be blind.' But Gandhi did not want to take anyone's eye; he wanted to force the British out of India. . . .''

> Nonviolence and nonaggression are generally regarded as interchangeable concepts — King and Gandhi frequently used them that way — but nonviolence, as employed by Gandhi in India and by King in the American South, might reasonably be viewed as a highly disciplined form of aggression. If one defines aggression in the primary dictionary sense of "attack," nonviolent resistance proved to be the most powerful attack imaginable on the powers King and Gandhi were trying to overturn. The writings of both men are filled with references to love as a powerful force against oppression, and while the two leaders were not using the term "force" in the military sense, they certainly regarded nonviolence as a tactical weapon as well as an expression of high moral principle. The root meaning of Gandhi's concept of *satyagraha* . . . is "holding on to truth" . . . Gandhi also called *satyagraha* the "love force" or "soul force" and explained that he had discovered "in the earliest stages that pursuit of truth did not permit violence being inflicted on

one's opponent, but that he must be weaned from error by patience and sympathy. . . . And patience means self-suffering." So the doctrine came to mean vindication of truth, not by the infliction of suffering on the opponent, but on one's self.

King was even more explicit on this point: the purpose of civil disobedience, he explained many times, was to force the defenders of segregation to commit brutal acts in public and thus arouse the conscience of the world on behalf of those wronged by racism. King and Gandhi did not succeed because they changed the hearts and minds of southern sheriffs and British colonial administrators (although they did, in fact, change some minds) but because they *made the price of maintaining control too high for their opponents* [emphasis mine].

That, I believe, is what it's going to take to abolish the death penalty in this country: we must persuade the American people that government killings are too costly for us, not only financially, but—more important—morally.

The death penalty costs too much. Allowing our government to kill citizens compromises the deepest moral values upon which this country was conceived: the inviolable dignity of human persons.

I have no doubt that we will one day abolish the death penalty in America. It will come sooner if people like me who know the truth about executions do our work well and educate the public. It will come slowly if we do not. Because, finally, I know that it is not a question of malice or ill will or meanness of spirit that prompts our citizens to support executions. It is, quite simply, that people don't know the truth of what is going on. That is not by accident. The secrecy surrounding executions makes it possible for executions to continue. I am convinced that if executions were made public, the torture and violence would be unmasked, and we would be shamed into abolishing executions. We would be embarrassed at the brutalization of the crowds that would gather to watch a man or woman be killed. And we would be humiliated to know that visitors from other countries—Japan, Russia, Latin America, Europe—were watching us kill our own citizens—we, who take pride in being the flagship of democracy in the world.

Topics for Critical Thinking and Writing

1. Suppose you interpret the "eye for eye" passage from Exodus (paras. 3–6) not as a "call for restraint" but as support for the death penalty. Does that mean no exceptions whatsoever—that everyone who kills another must be sentenced to death and executed? Would that require abandoning the distinction between murder and manslaughter or between first- and second-degree murder?

2. Prejean lists ten different crimes for which the Bible prescribes death as the punishment (para. 7) and says "no person with common sense

would dream of appropriating [them] today" (para. 9). Do you agree? In an essay of 500 words, defend or criticize the proposition that the death penalty ought to be confined to the crime of first-degree murder.

3. Do you think that someone who endorses the biblical doctrine of "life for life, eye for eye" (para. 4) is also required by consistency to endorse the death penalty for some or all of the ten nonhomicidal crimes Prejean mentions (para. 7)? Explain.

4. In deciding whether to impose the death penalty for serious crimes, what guidance do you think a secular society, such as ours, ought to accept from the Bible? In an essay of 500 words, defend or criticize this thesis: "Biblical teachings ought to play a central role in deciding how we use the death penalty."

5. Prejean does not propose any alternative to the death penalty. Presumably she would favor some form of imprisonment for crimes involving death. She claims that the death penalty is inconsistent with "the inviolable dignity of human persons" (para. 19). Does consistency require her also to reject flogging? Solitary confinement in prison? Life imprisonment without the possibility of parole? Write a 500-word essay on this theme: "Severe Punishment and the Inviolable Dignity of Human Persons."

6. Prejean thinks that if executions were made public, Americans would soon decide to oppose the death penalty (para. 20). Do you agree? Write a 500-word essay for or against the following proposition: "Executions held in public would soon lead to public rejection of the death penalty."

e-Pages Credits

Art Credits

Index of Authors and Titles

Index of Terms

Inside the e-Pages for *Critical Thinking, Reading, and Writing*

Additional Readings

Oxfam, The Truth about Women and Chocolate [advertisement]

Aurora Meneghello and Serge Bakalian, Trailer for *Default: The Student Loan Movie* [film trailer]

Josh Harkinson/*Mother Jones*, How Industrial Pot Growers Ravage the Land: A Google Earth Tour [news article and video]

United States Agency for International Development, "How to Feed the Future" and "Mobile Phones Tackling Poverty" [infographics]

Barack Obama, President Obama on the Death of Osama bin Laden [speech]

Casey Neistat, Calorie Detective [investigative report]

The White House, 1 Is 2 Many [public service announcement]

Additional Views on Argument

A Moralist's View: Ways of Thinking Ethically

A Lawyer's View: Steps toward Civic Literacy